PRIMO MOBILE XXXXVIIII 49

FROM THE "CARTE DI BALDINI" DESCRIBED IN VOL. I P. 66.

PHOTOGRAVURE J. LEITCH & Co LONDON

A DESCRIPTIVE CATALOGUE OF

PLAYING AND OTHER CARDS

IN THE BRITISH MUSEUM

ACCOMPANIED BY

A CONCISE GENERAL HISTORY OF THE SUBJECT AND

REMARKS ON CARDS OF DIVINATION AND

OF A POLITICO-HISTORICAL

CHARACTER

By WILLIAM HUGHES WILLSHIRE, M.D. Edin.

B M

DEPARTMENT
OF PRINTS AND
DRAWINGS 1977

THIS EDITION PUBLISHED

by

BRITISH MUSEUM PUBLICATIONS LIMITED

1975

First published 1876

This edition 1975

Published in Europe, Japan, the United States, and South America
by S. Emmering, Amsterdam, The Netherlands
Published in the United Kingdom and elsewhere
by British Museum Publications Limited
ISBN 0 7141 0747 6
Printed in The Netherlands

PREFACE TO THE EDITION OF 1975

The year 1976 marks the centenary of the publication of William Hughes Willshire's catalogue of the collection of playing-cards residing in the then Print Room of the British Museum. Recently it has become one of the rarest and most sought after items of card literature: it is a great pleasure to know that once again its contents will be more easily available to the serious collector and historian alike.

The word "serious" is perhaps the keynote. The work has some flaws, mostly concerning concepts long held but later exposed because of an advance in knowledge about cards during the past century: but the aura of the work is that of a serious scholar with an extremely wide knowledge of prints and printing bringing his resources to bear in illuminating many aspects of what was then, and still remains, a very specialised subject. Perhaps most valuable are his detailed descriptive accounts of the early French and English engraved packs, providing a wealth of background information.

Willshire, however, speaks more eloquently for himself than the present writer could ever do. All I can do is congratulate with enthusiasm the enterprise of Mr. Emmering in making this book once more avaible.

SYLVIA MANN

PREFACE.

THE following Descriptive Catalogue of Playing and other Cards comprises several series which are deposited in different departments of the British Museum. It has been deemed advisable to treat the collections as a whole, for the purpose of systematic arrangement, and in order that they might thereby be made more readily available for the purposes of study and reference.

The subject of what are technically called Playing Cards is one not familiar, in its historic and literary aspects, except to the skilled archæologist. In order, therefore, to show the special interest which attaches to these objects, apart from their character as materials for amusement, the purely descriptive portion of the catalogue has been accompanied by succinct explanatory remarks on the several series or divisions, which show the wide range of inquiry and discussion necessary for the proper treatment of the subject.

The task of arrangement, and of the compilation of the present volume, including the introduction, has been executed by Dr. W. Hughes Willshire, under the supervision of the Keeper of the Prints and Drawings.

GEORGE WILLIAM REID.

April 12th, 1876.

TABLE OF CONTENTS.

PART I.

PART II.

APPENDIX.

N.B.—The contraction Bibl., within parenthesis, followed by a number, _e.g._ (Bibl. 9, p. 20) has reference to a work recorded in the " Bibliography," page 343.

A capital letter within parenthesis, followed by a number, _e.g._ (S. 20), has reference to a series of cards or other objects described in the systematic or second portion of the volume.

LIST OF PLATES AND THEIR SUBJECTS IN THE SUPPLEMENTARY VOLUME.

PART I.

A GENERAL HISTORY OF
PLAYING-CARDS.

GENERAL HISTORY OF PLAYING-CARDS.

SECTION I.

INTRODUCTORY.

HOUGH five hundred years have not passed since what may be termed the *positive* history of playing-cards began, we now find these objects spread all over the world, and forming one of the more seductive allurements of all classes of society. The hold thus widely and strongly secured depends, no doubt, on the varied and ready ways in which cards may be made to minister both to the lawful amusement of men, and to that which is condemned as the excitement, or vice, of gambling. The latter, based on the vicissitudes of chance, has ever had a forcible hold on humanity. We have records of very early periods in the world's history, telling that men did then, in some form or other, gamble. No doubt the mode of doing so varied, and the purposes, the value of the stakes, and the results for which the dictates of hazard have been appealed to, have altered, both in place and time. From the beginning, however, and associated with circumstances the most opposite in character, men have sought the determinations of a blind fatuity in preference to the suggestions of a rational guide. From evocation simply of the one in suspense and anxiety, pleasure of the keenest form has been experienced, while from following the other, half the interest has often seemed to vanish. Nor has it happened that under all circumstances this trust in the unforeseen and unknown was necessarily to be reprobated. The commands of the Most High have dictated its pursuance : " And the Lord spake unto Moses . . .

Aaron shall cast lots on the two goats. . . . But the goat on which the lot fell to be the scape-goat." (Levit. xvi.)   Again : " And Joshua cast lots for them in Shiloh before the Lord . . . And the lot of the tribe of the children of Benjamin came up according to their families." (Joshua xviii.)   Nevertheless, it must be remembered that not any trace is to be found in this remote antiquity among the Hebrews of any of the ordinary games of skill or hazard which were afterwards, and are now, so numerous in the western world.   It was not until after the Exile that a great change made itself felt in the manners and customs of the Hebrew people, when Grecian games were introduced by the Herodian princes.

In reference to the Egyptians, however, Sir Gardner Wilkinson observes :—

" It is remarkable that a game still so common" [mora, micare digito, ludere par et impar] " among the lower orders of Italians, should be found to have existed in Egypt from the earliest period of which their paintings remain, even in the reign of the first Osirtasen." (" Ancient Egyptians," vol. ii. p. 415.)

Mora and draughts are represented (vol. i. p. 40) as being played on the sculptures of Beni Hassan in grottoes on the east bank of the Nile, near the Speos Artemidos.   This would be 1740 years B.C., or coeval with Joseph and the first Osirtasen.

" It is, however, evident that dice were already used by the Egyptians in the reign of Rhampsinitus, that monarch, according to Herodotus, being reported to have played with the goddess Ceres, for the allegorical meaning of the story in no way militates against the fact of such a game having been known at the period in question, and the Egyptians, his informants, were necessarily persuaded that it dated at least as early as his era." (Vol. i. p. 126.)

" Plutarch would lead us to believe that dice were a very early invention in Egypt, and acknowledged to be so by the Egyptians themselves, since they were introduced into one of their oldest mythological fables, Mercury being represented playing at dice with the Moon previous to the birth of Osiris, and winning from her the five days of the epact which were added to complete the 365 days of the year." (Wilkinson, op. cit.)

In Case 44 of the Room of Egyptian Antiquities (British Museum), and under the head of " Musical Instruments and Toys," marked 6413-6429, are some Egyptian dice, of the Roman period, along with many latrunculi, or draughtsmen.

" I do not suppose," remarks Sir G. Wilkinson, " that the dice discovered at Thebes and other places are of very remote epoch ; they may not be even of a Pharaonic period, but the simplicity of their form and mode of notation may lead us to suppose them similar to those of the earliest age."

From the time alluded to until now various modes of amusement and gambling have been common, but not any appeals to chance and the excitement of hazard have been so generally popular as those which may be effected through the medium of playing-cards. Nor is this to be wondered at, seeing how convenient the latter are for use, that they appeal to a class of combinations and calculations quite beyond the range of dice, *par et impar,* and similar agents, and that they can be made to afford, in a simplicity of use, amusement and excitement to very illiterate people, as well as by a more complicated application of their powers, a pastime and the pleasure of intense suspense to cultivated intellects. Unfortunately, not any pleasure can be exercised and enjoyed by man without its becoming abused or perverted, and often into a grievous sin. Thus has it been with cards. Scarcely known, in Europe at least, they were made the vehicle for gambling of the most vicious kind, and as such have continued until the present day. Time and money are often recklessly squandered over them, and though the latter which is wasted may be often comparatively but of slight amount, the time which is lost through the fascinations of card-playing is constantly to be deplored.

" How," asks M. Merlin, " is this rapid propagation of cards to be explained ? Is it due to the cupidity of men, or to the tendency of their imagination always to surrender itself to the dreams of illusion, and, consequently, to the chances of hazard ? Or rather, should we not attribute it to these causes in combination with that desire for emotion and excitement, which seems to replace the love of the marvellous so natural to nations which are still young, and so general in Europe during the middle ages ? " (Bibl. 6, p. 2.) " Let us be just, however. Cards have not created the passion of play ; it has been a moral flaw from the highest antiquity ; but they have developed this passion by offering it at once a more manageable and attractive instrument." (*Op. cit.*)

Before the second half of the fifteenth century was completed St. Bernardin, of Sienna, preached against their employment, and his denunciations were succeeded at intervals by those of other moralists, as well as by numerous edicts and laws prohibiting their use. " Gambling," says the old French proverb, " is the child of avarice and the father of despair." Yet not anywhere have there been more affectionate offspring than in the country which gave the saying birth.

It is not generally known, we suspect, that in this country playing at cards on Sunday is still prohibited by law. In the Queen's proclamation against vice, profaneness, and immorality, read every session and assize, is the following passage :—

" And we do hereby strictly enjoin and prohibit all our loving subjects of what degree or quality soever from playing on the Lord's Day at Dice, Cards, or any other game whatsoever, either in public or private houses, or other places whatsoever." (See " Notes and Queries," 1872, vol. x. pp. 311-377.)

A prohibition to play at cards enters, or did enter until lately, among the particulars of apprentices' indentures. Its first appearance occurs in the form of an indenture for an apprentice, according to Dr. Rimbault, in " A Book of Precedents," printed *circa* 1566, and compiled by Thomas Phayer, who describes himself as " Solicitour to the King's and Queen's Majesties." (" Notes and Queries," vol. ii. for 1852, and vol. v. p. 346.)

Notwithstanding the abuses to which playing-cards have been put, there have been always persons, even of the highest moral excellence, who have conscientiously admitted that such a fair and honest use of them might be practised as to render an occasional and festive resort to them quite compatible with strict rules of morality. Archdeacon Butler, *e. g.*, in his sermon on " Christian Liberty," preached before the Duke of Gloucester and the University of Cambridge, on the installation of his Royal Highness as Chancellor in June, 1811, makes reference to the " harmless mirth and innocent amusements of society ; " and quotes a remarkable passage from Jeremy Taylor, who writes, "That cards are themselves lawful I do not know any reason to doubt. He can never be suspected in any criminal sense to tempt the Divine Providence who by contingent things recreates his labour. As for the evil appendages they are all separable from these games, and they may be separated by these advices." " Such," continues the archdeacon, " are the sentiments of one of the most truly pious and most profoundly learned prelates that ever adorned any age or country, nor do I think that the most rigid of our disciplinarians can produce the authority of a wiser or a better man."

There continue many of Jeremy Taylor's and Archdeacon Butler's way of thinking, and who, particularly at Christmas, and following the good old times, introduce, as a matter of course, cards among their amusements, without having any view of seducing parents to rear their sons as gamblers or blacklegs, and their daughters to

> " A youth of frolics, an old age of cards."
> (Hone's "Every Day Book," vol. i. p. 98.)

There is another aspect under which cards may be viewed as having taken a marked hold on certain classes of society. This is their application to the purposes of divination and fortune-telling. According to some authorities, as will be hereafter shown, this particular use of the Tarots cards long preceded the combination with them of a numeral series, and the appliance of the two to the purposes of gambling. These cards of emblematic and mystic character, the Tarots, were born, say they, long since in the East, from whence they were brought by the Gipsies in their knapsacks for thaumaturgic purposes. Thus entering Europe, the nations which received them afterwards added to them the numeral series by which they might obtain the excitement of gambling, and gradually discarded · the emblematic sequence as an incumbrance only. Be this as it may, the question may be passed by for the present, it being observed simply, that whatever hypothetic and presumptive value this theory may possess, there is not any *certainty* about it. The *positive* history of playing-cards, as far as our present knowledge extends, certainly does not commence before the second half of the fourteenth century.

Section II.

ORIGIN OF CARDS.

INCE the year 1704, when the Père Menestrier in his " Bibliothèque Curieuse" (t. 2, p. 174) occupied himself with the history of playing-cards, several learned and interesting works have appeared on the subject. Of these the treatises of Daniel (1720), Bullet (1757), l'Abbè Rive (1780), Breitkopf (1784), Singer (1816), Cicognara (1831), Duchesne aîné (1837), Leber (1842), Chatto (1848), Boiteau d'Ambly (1854), and of Merlin (1869) are by far the most important. Before the time of Menestrier (1704), however, allusions to cards and various games, along with remonstrances against recourse to them, occur in many works, or cards are separately treated of. The first distinct mention of their origin is in " Das Guldin Spil," of Ingold, printed in 1472 by G. Zainer. But such allusions and notices, as likewise the earlier records of them extending back to 1397, are not of that systematic character which is to be met with in the work of Menestrier. Notwithstanding the great amount of research and ingenuity evinced by the writers mentioned, it will be found that we are still uncertain where cards originated, and of the exact time when they made their first appearance in Europe. There has not been any want, it is true, of theories and assertions on these topics, but the honest enquirer, after going through the evidence they offer, must return, we think, the Scotch verdict in respect to all, " not proven."

A general survey of the history and character of playing-cards, as elicited by the researches of investigators since Menestrier, will here be given, in order to render the descriptive catalogue of the numerous examples of cards in the National Collection of greater practical interest and service to those desirous of inquiring into a not unimportant and rather curious subject.

Three chief opinions have been held respecting the country in which cards originated.

Firstly : It has been maintained that they had their birth in the East, and thence were propagated in Europe.

Secondly : That although there appears to be sufficient evidence for believing that cards are of very ancient origin in India and China, yet their presence in Europe is due to an original invention in the latter, and not to their importation from the East.

Thirdly : That not any satisfactory evidence exists showing that playing-cards were ever anything else than of European origin.

In reference to the first opinion, it may be observed that one school of archæologists asserts that cards sprang up in the East among the Arabs, Saracens, or Moors, who introduced them into Europe by way of Spain. This is a very old notion, since it was prevalent in Italy at the end of the fifteenth century. Covelluzzo, who then wrote, observes: " Anno 1379. fu recato in Viterbo el gioco delle carti, che venne de Seracenia e chiamasi tra loro Naib " (Bussi, " Istoria della città di Viterbo.") The locality in the East favoured by others is India, from whence cards are supposed to have made their way into Europe by means of the Gipsies, who carried them about their persons or in their wallets for the purposes of divination and fortune-telling, the Moors, who introduced them into Spain, having obtained them from the Gipsies. Other writers have regarded Egypt as their source, recognising in the cards known as pure Tarots, the pages of a hieroglyphic book containing the principles of the mystic philosophy of that antique land, in a series of symbols and emblematic figures. Nor has China been forgotten, it having been maintained that cards were invented there in the year 1120 of the Christian era.

The theory of the Oriental origin of cards is based chiefly on the following grounds. First: On the statement of Covelluzzo before mentioned. Secondly : On the supposed analogy and relations existing between cards and chess, which latter is undoubtedly of Eastern, if not of Hindustani origin. Thirdly : On the analogies present in certain Indian cards and the games played with them, and European cards, particularly, as may be seen, *e.g.*, in the game of cards known as *Ghengdifeh*, played by the Muhamedans of India. The marks of the suits in these cards, and likewise the rules of the game, have incontestable analogies with those of the Spanish game of *Hombre* and the *Minchiate* of Florence. Fourthly: On the apparent analogy of the word *naïbi*, the name of the primitive European cards, and that of *naypes* (which term is applied to cards in Spain at the present day), to the Hebrew and Arabic words, *nabí, naba, nabaa,* which convey with them the idea of prophecy. On the analogy between the word *Tuchim,* early applied in Provence to the valet or knave, and the Arabic *tu'chan,* signifying darkness, obscurity. On the continued use in connection with the earliest type of cards of certain words apparently of Oriental origin, as, *e.g., tarots, mat, pagad* (see " French Cards of Divination," *postea*), these verbal relations being supposed to fortify the opinion, also, that cards were originally invented for purposes of divination and sortilege rather than those to which European nations have adapted them. Fifthly : On the fondness for and trust that many Eastern people had in divinatory procedures and magic, and the apparent adaptation to such purposes offered by the older European cards now known as *Tarots,* the series of which seems based on combinations of the number 7, the sacred number of the East. On the ability to translate, as it were, the designs of these tarots into the principles of certain Oriental systems of philosophy and mysticism.

The theory of the Oriental origin of cards may be opposed on the following grounds. Firstly : While admitting Covelluzzo's statement as satisfactory, as regards the introduction of cards into Viterbo in the year 1379, it cannot be allowed that his assertion that they were of Saracenic origin has any value beyond that of a personal opinion, or at farthest of an opinion prevalent in Viterbo *when he wrote.* In other words, Covelluzzo was not contemporaneous with the time mentioned, for his chronicle terminates in 1480, one hundred years after the date he deals with. Moreover, Covelluzzo was looked on as rather a credulous person by Feliciano Bussi, the historian, who follows and quotes him (Merlin, Bibl. 6, p. 18, note 2).

Secondly : The analogies between chess and cards dwelt on are worth very little in respect to the question immediately involved, for between all such games there must be certain inevitable approximations, and these are surely insufficient to establish an identity of origin. It is on other conditions than on those on which stress has been laid that correspondence should be sought, and it is there that it fails.

" The game of chess is one purely of calculations and combinations. In cards, on the contrary, the chief part of success depends on chance, the combinations coming into play only after chance has operated, the effects of which latter they serve to correct, diminish, or strengthen. In chess all the pieces are exposed to observation, their positions are equalized, and it is on the after choice made by the player in the movement of his men that their increased or diminished value depends. In cards, on the contrary, a knowledge of the 'hand' of the player is carefully hidden, not only from adversary but from partner. From the moment of dealing the cards the game is unequal, hazard has intervened, and the most skilful player may find himself so scurvily treated by fortune that he may be beaten by a novice without having made a trick." (Merlin, p. 21.)

Further, between the Indian game *Tchaturanga*, described by Sir W. Jones and Mr. Christie, which is a kind of chess, and in the course of which dice come into use, the connection lies rather with backgammon than with cards.

Fourthly : Admitting that between the Muhamedan game of India, *Ghengdifeh* (*Gunjee fu, Gangeefah*) and the Spanish game of *Hombre* there are undoubtedly relations, *quoad* marks of suits and rules of play, it may be inferred, nevertheless, that the Muhamedans of India have imitated, in their game, the game of Europe, rather than that the European game sprang from that of the East. The reason for such inference will be given afterwards when Oriental cards are discussed ; sufficient now to say that the peculiarities which link the European to the Indian game existed in the former in the year 1488, and Europe did not have continuous communication with India until about 1494. Moreover, cards had been known already in Europe for at least a century.

Fifthly : Not any Arabic MS. nor document gives to the word *naïb* such a signification as playing-cards, and the first European traveller, Niebuhr, who recorded having seen cards in Arabia, did so in the second half of the eighteenth century, giving to them the title of *Làb l'kamar*, which means simply " game of chance." The Arabic-French Lexicon of Marcel (1837), who remained in Egypt during the expedition of the first Napoleon, gives to the game of cards the name of *Lab l'oureq, i.e.,* game with leaves of paper (Merlin, p. 18, note). The origin of the modern *naïbis* and *naypes* must be sought elsewhere than among the Arabs, particularly since—

Sixthly : The invention and use of playing-cards would be a direct contravention of two important precepts of the Koran, viz., the prohibition of games of chance, and the representation of human forms. Moreover, not any allusion is made to cards in the " Arabian Nights' Entertainment," a compilation of about the end of the fifteenth century, in which there would have occurred ample reasons and opportunity for mentioning them, had they been known as a popular pastime, at least. Even now those Muhamedans who play openly with cards are of the sect of the Chiites, or followers of Ali belonging to India and Persia, and regarded with suspicion by the more faithful followers of the Prophet. The latter, when they so far forget themselves as to play, do so in secret, and at games they have acquired from the Spaniards.

Seventhly: The derivation of the word *tarot*, from the Egyptian, whether according to the version of Count de Gebelin, or of his correspondent, M. Le C. de M——— (Singer Bibl. 8, Appendix, pp. 303-305), is merely an ingenious play with words, while the interpretation of Eliphas Levi (see " French Cards of Divination," *postea*), is of too mystical a character to submit to be investigated. Again, the word *matto*, signifying foolish, mad, exists in Italian; from it the title of the *tarot, le mat,* is most likely derived, seeing that its significations better apply to the particular emblematic card in question than would those of the Oriental *mat,* which are, killed, slain, dead.

Eighthly: Though it be admitted that the Kabbalah, judicial astrology, and occult science were common to the Semitic nations, there is not any satisfactory evidence that *cards,* or their analogues, were employed by them in the process of divination. The theories of Count de Gebelin, Alliette, Eliphas Levi, Boiteau d'Ambly, and others, in support of the connection of cards with early Eastern occult philosophy and thaumaturgy, however ingenious, are of too recondite and shadowy a character to admit of satisfactory argument.

Ninthly: Whether the Gipsies or Zingari be of Egyptian origin, or have sprung from the Suders of Hindustan, who migrated at the period of Timur Beg, they did not appear in Europe before 1417, a period when cards had been known for some time.

Tenthly: Resorting to China for the origin of cards is only another mission to the " Refuge for the Destitute." At any rate we are justified in assuming that if in the celestial empire cards really had a separate and early birth, Europe had not any more hand in robbing her of this progeny than she had in taking from her gunpowder, printing, and engraving, all of which, with other things, are considered by some to have been originally Chinese inventions. Thus, as we have indicated, may reasons be adduced, which render it very doubtful whether the origin of playing-cards should be looked for in the East.

A far more positive circumstance is that the objects in question made their first appearance in Europe about 500 years back. On this point our knowledge is so sure and varied as to lead some writers to maintain that cards had their *origin* about that time, and in Europe. The latest writer of repute on the subject, M. Merlin (Bibl. 6), may be taken as the chief exponent of this theory.

Whether we regard playing cards as an original invention in

Europe, or as introduced there from some other quarter of the globe, an important question arises: What is the earliest date known at which reference has been made to the existence of these agents? Not any pretence has been made to show that this occurred before 1278, the sixth year of the reign of Edward I. This king, having been in Syria, has been supposed to have become acquainted there with cards, and to have brought them with him into Europe, a supposition which has been supported by the following passage from his Wardrobe Rolls: *Waltero Sturton ad opus regis ad ludendum ad quatuor reyes* viiis. v*d*. ("Archæologia," vol. viii.) Mr. Chatto has, we think, shown satisfactorily that the game of the four kings, played at by Edward I., was chess, and that this name was a literal translation of the Indian one, Chaturaji (Chatto, p. 19). In a MS. of Sandro di Popozzo (*il Governo della Famiglia*), composed, it is said, in 1299, allusion is made to cards. Unfortunately, the copy of it which exists is not of earlier date, according to good authority, than A. D. 1400, and there is not any surety that the allusion in question is not a more recent gloss. The authority of the "Guldin Spil" for 1300, of the statutes of the military order of La Banda for 1332, and of the MS. of "Reynard le Contrefait" for 1341, when carefully weighed, must be admitted as in themselves unsatisfactory (Chatto, Merlin). The same must be said of the MS. "Pélérinage de l'homme" for A.D. 1350, of the Romance, "Jehan de Saintré" for 1367, and of the MS. "Citè de Dieu" (a translation by Raoul de Presle of the "Civitas Dei") for 1375. (Merlin, pp. 7-8.)

Nevertheless, there are reasons for believing that cards made their first appearance in Europe and in Italy about the year 1350, though the earliest direct allusion to them which is acceptable without much demur, is that made by Covelluzzo in the chronicle of Viterbo, quoted by Feliciano Bussi, and before referred to (p. 8). In this chronicle Covelluzzo writes, "Anno 1379. fu recato in Viterbo el gioco delle carti," &c. As respects this date too, it should be borne in mind that Giovanni di Covelluzzo wrote a hundred years after the event in question. It is likewise noteworthy that not any allusion is made to cards, either in the MS. of Hugo von Trymberg, who lived during the second half of the thirteenth and the first of the fourteenth century, or in the MSS. of Petrarch and Chaucer, belonging to the first and second halves of the fourteenth century, in all of which MSS. specific mention is made of other gambling games and agents. According to Passavant (vol. i. p. 7, note) there is in the Library of the Escurial a MS. of the date 1321, composed by order of Don Alphonso the Wise, on the rules of the games of chess and dice; numerous figures are given, but not a word is said in relation to cards. If Breitkopf, Von Murr, and Weigel can be depended on, cards were known at Nürnberg *circa*

1380-1384, since the "Pflicht-buch" of this city is affirmed to allude distinctly to them.

After all, it must be allowed that what may be termed the *positive* history of playing-cards begins in the year 1392. At the beginning of the eighteenth century Le Père Menestrier discovered, in the registers of the Chambres des Comptes of Charles VI. of France, an account of Charles Poupart, the royal treasurer. In this account, commencing the 1st of February, 1392, is the item:—— " Donné à Jacquemin Gringonneur peintre pour trois jeux de cartes à or et diverses couleurs, ornés de plusieurs devises, pour porter devers le Seigneur Roi pour son ebatement LVI sols parisis." This date, 1392, has never been contested, and since—as M. Merlin well points out—Gringonneur is not alluded to as an inventor of cards, but as a *painter* of them, and, considering the price paid, it should be assumed that cards were already known.

From this date (1392) there are certain and many references to playing-cards. The civic archives, guild books, and registers of the German towns, particularly Nürnberg, Augsburg, and Ulm, record early in the fifteenth century the names of both card-makers and card-painters. We know for certain that before the conclusion of the first half of the fifteenth century Germany had established quite a commerce in the production of playing-cards, which were sent to Italy, and against the continued importation of which the Venetian senate was petitioned to interfere. Sermons and edicts against their use, and fiscal regulations connected with them, are of frequent occurrence from the first quarter of the fifteenth century. Bartsch makes the following comment on a print by H. Schaüfelin (n. 36), representing St. John Capistran exhorting by a sermon the inhabitants of Nürnberg to burn their cards and other gambling agents.

" On the impression in the Imperial and Royal Library the subject of the piece is described by a contemporary as follows : ' Anno 1452 sind auf eines Cardinals Nahmens Johann Capistran, Predigt, die er allhier in Nürnberg, unter dem freyen Himmel, ver unserer Frauen Capellen gethan hat, 76 Schlitten, 2,640 Bretspiele, 40,000 Würfeln, und ein grosser Haufen Kartenspiele wie auch unterschiedlich Geschmeide und anderes, so zur Hoffart dienlich auf dem markt öffentlich verbrannt worden;' that is to say,—In the year 1452, in consequence of a sermon delivered in the public place opposite the Chapel of Our Lady at Nürnberg, by Cardinal John Capistran, 76 shovel-boards, 2,640 trictracs (draught and backgammon boards), 40,000 dice, and a great heap of packs of cards, as likewise a variety of trinkets and other objects of vanity, were burnt in the market-place." (Bartsch, vii. p. 256.)

The supposed earliest pictorial representation of persons playing

at cards yet discovered is a miniature in a MS. volume known as
" Le Roman du Roi Meliadus de Leonnoys, par Helie de Borron,"
written for Louis II., titular king of Naples.   This vellum MS. is
now in the British Museum, and may be referred to under " Additional MSS. vol. i. 1828-1841, No. 12,228." The miniature is on
the *verso* of folio 313.   A king and three attendants are at table
playing cards; three other persons are looking on.   One of the
party is playing the five of Deniers with the right hand, exposing,
as he holds his cards in his left hand, a two of Batons to the spectator.   Another holds in his right hand the two of Deniers, as if
ready to follow the lead of the person on his left.   The miniature
is relatively poor in drawing, and but slightly and badly coloured.
Outline facsimiles of it may be seen in Singer's work (Bibl. 8, p. 68),
and in the " Art Journal" for 1859, p. 87.   What is the date
of the MS. ?   The Library Catalogue places it between 1352 and
1362, adding that " the MS. is illustrated by upwards of 350 miniatures, the greater portion of which are by a contemporary hand, but
others have been added at a later period by inferior artists."   Mr.
Wright, in his " Domestic Games and Amusements of the Middle
Ages" (" Art Journal," *ut supra*), places the date of the MS. between
1330 and 1350.   On the fly-leaf of the volume is written *inter alia*,
" Mr. Douce is of opinion that it was executed at least as early as
the close of the fourteenth century.   It has 357 miniatures, in my
opinion of different styles and periods; but in stating this much I
am aware that I am at issue with two powerful authorities — Singer
in his beautiful work on Playing Cards, and Dibdin in his ' Decameron.' "   (G. H. Freeling.)

Unquestionably Singer affirms that the miniatures appear to be
all by the hand of the same artist, and that there is not any reason
to doubt they were executed about the period at which the MS.
was written (*loco* 67).   Dr. Dibdin, however, scarcely advances as
much.   He writes (*op. cit.*), *inter alia*,—" These illuminations are
of two characters or modes of execution," and does not assert them
to be of one and the same period ; nor does he, it is true, directly
deny them this character.   In a note at page ccviii. (vol. i.) he
remarks : " The later illuminations are slightly yet most unskilfully
coloured. . . . The age of the MS. is probably towards the latter
end of the fourteenth century."

Not any opinion is here offered on the date of the MS., but
attention is drawn to the fact that the writers quoted not only
differ sixty to seventy years in respect to it, but do not speak
confidently in any instance.   As regards the miniatures, it may
be stated, they have been carefully examined, and the conclusion
has been arrived at that those from folio 259 to the close of the
volume are not of the same period and style as characterise the

previous illustrations of the MS. Differences in shading and colouring begin about folio 265, with the light red washes and stippling in red of the fortresses, &c. The card-playing miniature appears to have been executed by an inferior hand, not only in colouring, but also in drawing and the ability to produce a neat outline. Folio 259 presents the last of the older style of miniature work common to the MS. Thus it may follow that the date of the " Roman du Roy Meliadus" might be that of the close of the fourteenth century, and the period of execution of the later miniatures might not be earlier than the end of the first quarter of the fifteenth century, or even somewhat later. Should this be the case, this early representation of card-playing cannot be allowed the significance attached to it by Singer, Wright, and others. Nor should the remark of the first-named authority be passed over as unimportant, viz.: " It is remarkable that no mention of the game occurs, as far as we could discover by an examination of that part of the MS. to which the miniature is affixed." (p. 68.)

Mr. Planché has offered strong opposition to the credit of this miniature, and his paper in the " Archæological Journal" for 1871 (vol. xxvii. p. 108) may be consulted with advantage.

In Lacroix and Serre's " Moyen Age et la Renaissance " (t. ii. art. " Cartes à Jouer "), a large chromo-lithograph is given representing a number of royal and noble personages playing and looking on at a game of cards. The print is stated to have been copied from a MS. of the fifteenth century in the Bibliothèque de Rouen (" Salle Leber"), and is entitled, " Le revers au Jeu des Suisses." Le Suisse (B 2) holds three low cards of the suit of diamonds in his hand, and the " Roi de France" (A 1) exhibits three " honours."

Another early representation of a card party is a miniature in a MS. French translation made by Raoul de Presle, between the years 1371 and 1375, of the " Civitas Dei" of St. Augustine. It exhibits two ladies with the steeple head-dresses of 1467, and a gentleman with the small cap and long hair of the same period, playing at a round table with cards, of which the " pips" are visible. Mr. Chatto has given a copy of this miniature (Bibl. 4, p. 72), and Mr. Wright likewise, in the " Art Journal " for 1859.

What is the date of this MS. ? There is not any proof that it is that of the original translation of which it is a copy. Mr. Chatto was of opinion that the costume represented is more like that of 1422 than of 1364 or 1380, while Planché would assign the date to a period not earlier than 1460. However, let the actual date of the MS. be what it may, it is worthy of note that *numeral* cards and " honours" like those now in use were known in France at the time when the miniature was painted.

In the " Magasin Pittoresque" for 1842 (p. 324) is a cut entitled,

" Philippe le bon consultant une tireuse de cartes," copied from a painting ascribed to Jan van Eyck. Though it has been denied that the picture is really by Van Eyck, it has been admitted that the costume is that of the reign of Charles VIII., between the years 1483 and 1498. Supposing that the picture does belong to this period, we have thus evidence of cards having been used for the purpose of divination before the close of the fifteenth century.

Among the prints of the early German masters in the National Collection may be seen a scarce engraving by Israhel van Meckenen, representing a lady and gentleman seated at a table, playing at cards. The gentleman appears to have lost the game. On the table may be seen the three of *eicheln,* or glands, and in the left hand of the lady a figure card, to which she is drawing the attention of her adversary. There is much expression in the faces and actions of both persons. As remarked by Singer, it may be readily seen from their costumes that the players are of no mean rank, and were even in the extreme of fashion, since they wear the strange shoes with long pointed toes, termed by the French *poulains.* At the same time the simplicity of manners and mode of domestic life of the period are obvious from various details in the print. The latter is described in Bartsch, vol. vi. p. 302, n. 114, Passavant, vol. ii. p. 197, n. 251, and a facsimile of it is given by Singer, to whose " Researches," &c., it forms a characteristic frontispiece. The original was produced, probably, during the last quarter of the fifteenth century.

Another interesting representation of card-playing is that given in the *chef-d'œuvre* of the early German master of the initials M Z (Martin Zatzinger). This print is known as "le grand bal" of Bartsch, vol. vi. p. 377, n. 13, and may be seen in the National Collection.

The engraving represents a ball given by the Grand Duke and Duchess of Bavaria. The royal personages have retired from it to a recessed place, where they have seated themselves at table to play at cards. The Duchess is pointing to a five of *roth* or *herzen,* which she has played out on the table, while the Duke, who is about to play his card, looks attentively at the Duchess with an expression which seems to say, " I wonder what you'll think of this." It should be noticed that the players are shown as each keeping a chalked score on the table. On the window frame above the Duke's head is the date 1500. A copy of the portion of the engraving here alluded to is given in Singer's work, p. 274. There is an interesting print connected with card-playing by Anthony of Worms (A.D. 1529), which will be noticed afterwards. The only other representation of card-playing that need be referred to here is that given in cut xli. of Holbein's " Dance of Death " (ed. 1547). It is a gambling party interrupted by Death and the Devil, the latter being in so great a hurry for his prey that he seems desirous of carrying off his victim—

the chief of the party—almost before Death has done his part. On the table the five of diamonds (?) is turned upwards on a pack, and on the floor lie the ace and three of the same suit. The celebrated cuts here referred to were designed during the second quarter of the sixteenth century.

Much controversy has ensued as to whether cards appeared first in Spain, Italy, France, or Germany. Those who have supported the theory of their Eastern origin have allotted them to Spain; such as have maintained their European origin have given them to Italy. There have been writers who have associated them with France, as have a few with Germany. The more satisfactory and direct evidence points to Italy as the European district in which they first appeared.

The particular reasons which have been advanced during the last few years in support of the theory that cards *originated* in Europe will be further alluded to when the old Florentine or Venetian engravings, known as the *Tarocchi of Mantegna*, the *Carte di Baldini*, &c., come under consideration. It is necessary for the proper understanding of our subject that the character and varieties of playing-cards be entered on at once.

SECTION III.

GENERAL NATURE AND VARIETIES OF CARDS.

IRSTLY, of the general nature of playing-cards. All cards in use in Europe at the present day are, as far as can be judged from the rare fragments preserved in a few public collections and private cabinets, and such pictorial representations as have been mentioned, based on the types which prevailed at the time of their origin. These types are two in number, and all true playing-cards may be said to be of two kinds, viz., tarots (proper) and numerals. Tarot cards, or "tarots," constitute a series of pieces generally twenty-two in number, exceptionally forty-one in the *Minchiate* of Florence, and fifty if the early Florentine *Carte di Baldini* be here included. These card pieces are characterised by their having on them whole-length figures or other designs emblematic of various conditions of life, and of certain vicissitudes happening to humanity. These emblematic figures vary somewhat, according to time and country; but taking an early yet still common set, they may be described as representing : [1]—

---

[1] The plates in "Singer" (p. 284) may advantageously illustrate the present text.

No. 1. A juggler.
    2. Female pope.
    3. An empress.
    4. An emperor.
    5. The pope.
    6. The lovers (or marriage).
    7. A chariot with warrior.
    8. Justice.
    9. A hermit.
   10. The wheel of fortune.
   11. Force.
   12. A man hanging by his foot, head downwards (*Le Pendu*).

No. 13. Death.
   14. Temperance.
   15. The devil.
   16. A tower struck by lightning.
   17. A large star, &c.
   18. The moon.
   19. The sun.
   20. The last judgment.
   21. The world, or kosmos.
   22. A fool, generally unnumbered, sometimes placed first.

Though there are Italian, French, Flemish, and German tarots, the titles of these emblematic designs are more frequently in the French language than in any other. Italian titles may be met with, but far less frequently than French ones. As a rule, too, the orthography is wretched. The names, as usually found printed below the figures, are as follows :—

No. 1. Le bataleur.
    2. La papesse.
    3. Limperatrise.
    4. Lempereur.
    5. Le pape.
    6. Lamoreux.
    7. Le charior.
    8. Justice.
    9. Lermite.
   10. La roue de fortune.
   11. La force.
   12. Le pendu.

No. 13. Title often wanting (*la mort*).
   14. Tenperance.
   15. Le diable.
   16. La maison Dieu.
   17. Lestoille.
   18. La lune.
   19. Le soleil.
   20. Le jugement.
   21. Le monde.
   22. Le mat.

These twenty-two card pieces are usually numbered with large Roman numerals in a margin above the design, according to the sequence just given. In those exceptional sets in which the tarots are more than twenty-two in number, symbolic figures of the Muses, sciences, planets, and analogous subjects are introduced (Italian tarots, *postea*). Though the earliest tarots, likewise, were probably more than twenty-two in amount, such as we have described were those chosen out of the lot by more modern card-makers.

These tarots are called likewise *atouts*, *atutti*, and *triomphes*, because in the games played with them, in combination with numeral or common cards, the former override the latter even to the

" kings ;" thus they are *above* and *superior* to all. To these same cards the title *tarocchi* is frequently applied. The origin of the word tarot or tarots has been much canvassed. Some have derived it from Egyptian dialects, others have regarded it as springing from the term *tarotée*, which was applied to cards diapered or marked on the backs with lines crossing lozenge-wise, or dotted diagonally with small spots, as such cards generally were. The earlier ones were often painted with much delicacy, like the miniatures of MSS., on gold grounds. They were also occasionally bordered with a silver margin, on which was represented a spiral or tortuous band, formed by similar dots or points. This band being likened to a *tare*, an " espèce de gaufrure produite par de petites trous piqués et elignés en compartements," the cards possessing it were called tarots. According to Menestrier, " tare " signifies properly a hole— *defaut, dechet, tache, trou*—derived from the Greek τερειν, to bore. The dots, points, &c., in the ornamentation alluded to, simulating little hollows, the cards having them were called tarots, or were said to be *tarotées*. Some of the supporters of the theory of the Oriental origin of cards assign to the word tarot high antiquity, while others of the same school, as well as such as look to Europe for their birthplace, though admitting the cards themselves to exemplify the more ancient type, assert that the term now applied to them is not older than the fifteenth century, their original title being *Naïbis*.

" Tarots " has been said also to have been derived from *tarocchi*, or *tarocchino*, which is properly the name of a game played with tarots combined with numerals, some of the latter being suppressed. The name of the game having been applied to the cards with which it was played, they were hence called " tarocchi cards."

According to M. Merlin, " C'est par corruption que l'on dit le *tarot*, le jeu de *tarot*, il faut dire le jeu des *tarots*." (Bibl. 6, p. 29, note.)

The most ancient cards which have come down to us are of the tarots character. These are the four cards of the Musée Correr at Venice; the seventeen pieces of the Paris Cabinet (erroneously called often the *Gringonneur*, or Charles VI. cards of 1392) fine Venetian tarots of the fifteenth century, in the opinion of some not of an earlier date than 1425 ; and the series of cards belonging to a *Minchiate* set in the possession of the Countess Aurelia Visconti Gonzaga at Milan, when Cicognara wrote. The date of the latter may be concluded from the emblematic design of Love having on it the combined armorials of the Prince Visconti and of Beatrice Tenda, who was married to Filippo Maria Visconti in 1413, and ordained to death by him in 1418. It is true that the cards of the Musée Correr are not emblematic ones, and therefore not in themselves true tarots nor *atutti*, but they are numerals of the particular suit marks, viz., *spade, coppe, danari, bastoni,* which used to accompany the emblematic cards of the old Venetian sets, and hence may be assumed to have formed part of a combined tarots sequence, probably the same to which belong the twenty-three cards once in the cabinet of Cicognara, and now in the possession of MM. Tross Frères at Paris, and described by Merlin in the note at page 90 of his treatise.

These and other early tarots of the first half of the fifteenth century have been drawn and painted by hand, some of them being of very beautiful character. Facsimiles well worthy of attention may be seen in the admirable series, " Jeux de Cartes Tarots et de Cartes Numerales," published by the Society of Bibliophiles Français, 1844, now a difficult work to procure, but a copy of which is in the library of the British Museum. Admirable outline copies of the Correr cards may be found in Merlin (pl. 8 and 9), and of the Visconti pieces in the treatise of Cicognara (Bibl., 6). These and other early cards are larger than the ordinary ones of the present day, some of them being seven inches high by more than four inches broad. Several are likewise very thick, the material of which they are formed resembling the cotton paper of ancient MSS. Others, on the contrary, like the *Carte di Baldini, e.g.,* are on very thin paper, so thin, indeed, that shuffling, dealing, and playing with them, as we do now with cards, would be scarcely possible.

The ancient tarots from which all modern ones have been derived, fragmentary pieces of which have been just adverted to, and *vestigia,* or copies of which may be seen transmitted in the emblems of the *Carte di Baldini* or the *Tarocchi* of Mantegna, constituted the *naïbis* of the early Italian writers. By this term the primitive cards of Europe, if they may be so regarded, were called. Further comment on nomenclature, however, may be dispensed with until the character of playing-cards has been more fully developed, it being sufficient to add that while in accordance with one theory the word *naïbi,* derived from the Arabic, was given first by the Spaniards and transmitted to Italy, as taught by another it originated in the latter country, then passed into Spain, where it is still common, as it is likewise in Portugal in the form of *naypes.*

The other and second kind of playing-cards are *numerals,* familiar to every one, in the modern form, at least, of the cards in ordinary use. These numerals are known also as " suit," " pip cards," and " cartes de points." They are in full sets fifty-two in number, divided into four suits, or colours, of thirteen cards each suit. Each suit is distinguished by a special mark or symbol, which has varied at different times and in different countries. The more general marks of the suits have been cups, money, swords, and clubs. Each suit has three coate, court, or figure cards, likewise called " honours," mostly representing a king, queen, and a valet, or knave, and ten "pip" or "point" cards. The latter commence with an ace, which numbers one pip, the next card has two pips, and so on to the tenth, carrying ten marks on it. The numerals having but few pips are known as " low cards," with the exception of the ace (as), which in some games overrides all other cards; those numerals with several pips are " high cards." In some games the whole fifty-two pieces are not used, certain of the lower cards being suppressed. Sometimes, as will be seen hereafter, there are *four* figure cards or " honours" in each suit, while in other instances a female figure or queen is not allowed, but a " cavalier " is put in her place.

Careful research has proved, we think, that at first all the card germs were purely emblematic in character—*naïbis*—simple tarots, as they are now called—not lending themselves to anything like gambling, whatever they might do towards divinatory purposes. As far as Europe, at any rate, was concerned, it is probable that they were intended for *instructive* diversion, since Morelli, in a chronicle written in 1393, interdicting the use of dice to children, recommends *naïbis* : " Non giuocare a zara nè ad altro giuoco di dadi, fa de giuochi che usano i fanciulli, agli ossi, alla trottola, a ferri, a naïbi," &c. (Merlin, p. 52, note.) Further, in the " Life of the Duke of Milan, Filippo Maria Visconti " (born in 1391), written by Decembrio, his secretary, it is stated that one of the favourite games of this prince, when young, was a game played with painted figures—" qui ex imaginibus depictis fit,"—and which would scarcely be a gambling amusement, since we are informed afterwards that the Duke played sometimes likewise games of hazard on particular occasions : " Solemnibus quoque diebus nonnunquam alea lusit."

Towards the end of the fourteenth century these *naïbis* of instruction were made subservient to the amusement of older persons, probably, as Merlin supposes, by some ingenious Venetians, with the hope of restraining their countrymen from the immoderate use of dice and games of hazard. To effect this intention, and at the same time not to eliminate *in toto* the element of chance from the new amusement, the theory of numerical values was combined with that of emblems or symbolism, these values varying in benefit to the players according as chance might operate in the allotment of the cards. In creating the new game the principle followed apparently was to take about half only (twenty-two) of the original emblematic pieces, and while retaining some of the emblems, as of the *re, imperator, papa, justicia, temperancia, luna, sol,* &c., to have displaced others by emblems of a moral character, more directly bearing on the dangers and consequences of gambling play, such, *e.g.*, as the *roue de la fortune, le pendu, la mort, le diable, le jugement dernier.* The figure of a juggler, placed first in the series, was intended, perhaps, to point as *caution* against the way in which certain dexterous hands might play the cards which followed in the sequence.

A distinct series of fifty-six cards was then added to the above, in which numerical values were to play a part, and into which series four emblematic cards only were admitted, viz., *le roi* (or *re*), *regina, cavalier* (or *chevalier*), *valet* (or *fameio*). These fifty-six cards were divided into four suits of fourteen cards each suit, the latter being distinguished by the symbols of the two theologic and two cardinal virtues of the original *naïbis*, as represented in the fourth decade (B) of the *Carte di Baldini*, viz., *Fede, Charita, Justicia, Fortezza.* One suit had for its mark the cup (*coppa*) of Faith, another the money (*danaro*) of Charity, a third the sword (*spada*) of Justice, and a fourth the club (*bastone*) of Force. Each suit had the four emblematic pieces—*re, regina, cavallo, fante*—king, queen, knight, and knave, the remaining ten numerals of the suit being marked with increasing numbers from one to ten of the particular sign of the suit. These two series—tarots and numerals—being brought together, made up a total of seventy-eight cards. To the first twenty-two emblematic pieces, or tarots proper, was given the privilege of being superior to all the other cards when the game was played, each tarot having a number regulating its order and value in its own suit. To these pieces the name of *atutti* was also applied, and then very commonly the term of tarots was assigned to the general combination of *atutti* and numerals, though properly belonging to the *atutti* only. In this way most probably originated the two characteristic types of playing-cards, which two types were united together at a very early period, or at least as soon as cards began to be used for the recreation of grown persons, or for the purposes of gambling, and the latter was unquestionably soon effected.

It would appear that to this combined series of *atutti* and numerals the original term *naïbis* also continued to be applied for some time after the union, since we find contemporary writers and moralists countenancing one kind of instructive amusement in which chance went for little or nothing as afforded by the employment of *naïbis*, and another game which they reprobated, since it led to gambling as bad and as surely as did the use of dice. St. Bernardin of Sienna, writing and preaching against their use (*circa* 1430), thus expresses himself in a sermon *contra alearum ludos* :—

" Et idem est judicium sicut de tabulariis ita etiam de tabellis taxillis taxillorum, tertii autem participantes sunt qui fiunt participes ex *Naïbis* seu *Charticellas* de quibus innumerabilia mala egrediuntur."

The love of excitement and gambling, however, was too strong for the moralist to subdue; men were captivated by the new amusement, and even the clergy were not always proof against its seductions. The use of tarots (*i.e.*, naïbis combined with numerals) spread rapidly throughout Europe, but each nation soon began to modify and alter the combination and marks of the cards according to its own particular fancy.

It does not seem possible now to determine which was the first, Spain, France, or Germany, to imitate the original Venetian tarots game of seventy-eight cards. The Germans unquestionably were not only very early in so doing, but began to be the card-makers for other nations, favouring Venice in particular with their exportations, against which her own card-makers publicly remonstrated. In Italy itself Florence soon began making alterations in the new and popular game, increasing the emblematic pieces to forty in number, and producing her *Minchiate*. At a later period Bologna suppressed some of the numeral series, reducing the pack of seventy-eight to sixty-two cards, thus establishing her *Tarocchino*, while Venice herself very early instituted changes connected with both *atutti* and numerals under the name of *Trappola*.

Among the various modifications to which the old tarots game was early subjected, the most important was undoubtedly that of the elimination of the whole of the *atutti*, or emblematic series proper, leaving the numeral series to stand and work by itself under some such forms as we have it now. The more men played with cards the more fascinated they became with them, and strove to render them less cumbersome than they were, more amenable to rapid and exciting play, and their games still more dependent on hazard. So the first of the five suits, the true tarots, was thrown aside, the emblems of justice, temperance, death, and judgment not being needed, being, in fact, found *de trop*. The four suits of the numeral cards were taken, and one coate-card or "honour" expunged from each suit; variations were made in the figure designs and in the marks of the suits, while of the thirteen numerals of each suit left different nations suppressed certain pieces in establishing what may be deemed their national games. Spain had its *Hombre*, France its *Piquet*, and Germany its *Landsknechtspiel* or *Lansquenet*. Though such was the rule, some games still retained an emblematic series, and to this day cards may be purchased in Italy and the south of France of the true old tarots character.

The pervading principle throughout all the changes—with one exception, the *Minchiate* of Florence—which the original Venetian game has been made to undergo, has been the principle of *reduction*. Nor is this to be wondered at, considering the purpose to which cards tended at the outset to be popularly applied. As observed by Merlin :—

" The game of tarots with its numerous cards was a game of intricate combinations, which could never please the taste of common players accustomed to dice, in the use of which chance alone generally governed everything. From the new game, therefore, everything that could render its course difficult or slow was eliminated. Its members were reduced to less than half their number [in certain games], and it was at this price that cards became popular." (p. 62.)

Popular indeed have they been, and still are. As these pages are being written remonstrances are appearing in some influential public journals against the continuous and "high play" which is introduced, surreptitiously, as it were, into clubs which have standing rules against the practice. Mr. Chatto pointedly remarked :—

" He who devised the game of cards as now usually played appears to have had a thorough perception of at least two of the weak points of human nature, for next to man's trust in his ' luck ' in all games of chance is his confidence in all games of skill. The shuffling, cutting, and dealing of cards, together with the chance afforded by the turn-up of the trump, place the novice, in his own conceit, on a par with the experienced gamester, who, on the other hand, is apt to underrate his opponent's chance from his over-confidence in his own skill." (p. 79.)

Section IV.

CONNECTION WITH WOOD-ENGRAVING, THE MANUFACTURE OF PAPER, &c.

THE general history of playing-cards thus far developed includes the periods of the last quarter of the fourteenth and the first quarter of the fifteenth century, or a few years more. Within this time is likewise embraced the origin of wood-engraving, the earliest known example of which, with a date to it generally allowed to be authentic, is the " Buxheim Saint Christopher of 1423." Still there is sufficient reason for thinking that the St. Christopher was not the first of its kind, and that for some years before the date connected with it the art of wood-engraving had been known and practised. Nevertheless the *positive* history of wood-engraving can be said to commence A.D. 1423 only as the positive history of playing-cards begins in 1392. In both cases dates are connected with recorded objects. One object, the Saint Christopher, still exists ; while the other, the so-called Gringonneur cards, though questionable, yet unequivocally affords in the history associated with it the record of the precise date of the production of certain cards, and the price paid for them.

It has been maintained by some that wood-engraving must have been known and well practised, too, before 1423, since playing-cards never could have been in anything like general use without their production by some comparatively facile and cheap procedure. That cards were obtainable by the commonalty in 1397, however they may have been manufactured, is unquestionable, for on the 22nd of January in that year, the Prévot of Paris issued a decree forbidding working people to play at tennis, bowls, dice, *cards,* and ninepins on working days.

Heinecken, Von Murr, and Leber advanced the doctrine that the first wood-engravers were card-makers, and that the production of the more profane objects preceded and, as it were, led to that of the *Helgen, Helglein,* or "little Saints" and Scriptural pieces, which were among the earlier efforts of the wood-engraver. Mr. Chatto was once of the same opinion, remarking in his "Treatise on Wood-Engraving" (1836):—

"It has been conjectured that the art of wood engraving was employed on sacred subjects before it was applied to the multiplication of those 'books of Satan'—playing-cards. It, however, seems not unlikely that it was first employed in the manufacture of cards, and that the monks, availing themselves of the same principle, shortly afterwards employed the art of wood-engraving for the purpose of circulating the figures of saints, thus endeavouring to supply a remedy for the evil, and extracting from the serpent a cure for its bite."

At a later period the same authority expressed himself as follows:—

"As there are no cards engraved on wood to which so early a date as 1423 can be fairly assigned, and as at that period there were professional card-makers established at Augsburg, it would appear that wood-engraving was employed on the execution of *Helgen* before it was applied to cards, and that there were stencilled cards before there were wood-engravings of saints. Though this conclusion be not exactly in accordance with an opinion which I have expressed in another work, it is yet that which, on a further investigation of the subject, appears to be best supported by facts, and most strongly corroborated by the incidental notices which we have of the progress of the *Briefmaler,* or card-painter, from his original profession to that of a wood-engraver in general." (Bibl. 4, p. 87.)

It is now impossible to decide whether cards were or were not the first objects on which the wood-engraver practised his art; but taking into consideration what has been already stated, and what has to follow, it must be conceded that while there is much evidence, apparently of a positive kind, against their having been so, there is only presumption, based on hypothetic grounds, that they were.

In the first place, as before observed, the most ancient cards which have come down to us have been executed by hand, and records exist of other early cards having been so executed, as well as for whom, and the price paid for them.

In the second place we are told that when Saint Bernardin, of Sienna, preached at Bologna in 1423 against the use of " Charticellas seu Naibos," and so forcibly that his hearers made a fire in the public place and threw their cards into it, a card-maker who was present and heard the denunciations even against those persons who supplied the obnoxious article, exclaimed : " I have not learned, father, any other business than that of painting cards, and if you deprive me of that, you deprive me of life and my destitute family of the means of earning a subsistence." To this appeal the Saint replied, " If you do not know what to paint, paint this figure, and you will never have cause to repent having done so." Thus saying he took a tablet and drew on it the figure of a radiant sun, having in the centre the sacred cipher, I.H.S.

In the Paris collection of prints, there is a celebrated engraving of the style known as the *Manière criblée*, A. D. 1474, supposed to bear reference to this story. The Saint is holding aloft, in his right hand, the symbol which he recommended to the card-painter. A facsimile of the engraving may be seen among the early pieces in the British Museum.

At the date above mentioned (1423) wood-engraving was already practised, since the Saint Christopher is of the same period ; yet we learn that cards were still painted.

In the third place, though card-making was a regular trade in Germany early in the fifteenth century, and the name of a *Kartenmacher* occurs in the burgess books of Augsburg for 1418, yet the name of a wood-engraver proper, *i.e., Formschneider*, is not to be met with until 1449, when it is entered in the civic archives of Nürnberg, and as for twenty years afterwards it is frequently entered on the same page with that of a card-painter, *Kartenmaler*, there can be scarcely a doubt that there was a distinction between these avocations, though like the barbers and surgeons of former days, the followers of each business belonged to the same guild or company.

" From the circumstance of so many women occurring as card-painters in the town books of Nürnberg between 1423 and 1477, there appears reason to conclude that they at least were not wood-engravers." (Chatto, p. 82.)

In the fourth place, though it be admitted with Lacroix, that " in the interval between 1392 and 1454, means had been discovered of making playing-cards at a cheap rate, and of converting them into an object of commerce," and that painting or hand-work alone could scarcely suffice for this purpose, yet it by no means follows that cards were the work of the wood-engraver. According to Chatto, on the oldest cards he had ever seen the figures had been executed by means of stencils, this being the case both in the cards of 1440 (G 122) and those known as the Stukely cards. The oldest German examples which had come before Passavant belonged to the first half of the fifteenth century, and had been produced from stencils. (Vol. i. p. 12.)

In the fifth place, it is quite possible that more stress has been placed on the statements of the old chroniclers with respect to the extent in which cards were spread among the commonalty than is justifiable. To quote the words of Merlin, " Doubtless cards were then [1397-1423] known, ... but we would add that at the beginning of the fifteenth century they were not in such general use probably as has been supposed." . . . . " Women's labour would then perfectly suffice to keep pace with the demand for them, and if the interdictions launched against their use during the first half of the fifteenth century show that the taste for them made advances alarming to morality, they do not prove that cards were then destroyed as quickly as they are at the present time. The more they cost the more carefully would they be husbanded. Are not houses, and even public places of resort in the country, to be found in our own day, where the same cards have lasted for several years ? To change cards when they have become a little soiled is quite a modern luxury, and a duty to which our ancestors attached but little importance." (p. 68.)

After all that can be said, however, in favour of the opinion that the earlier cards were painted and stencilled, and not the work of the wood-engraver, the question is yet an open one, except as regards such " cartes de luxe " as were executed with great delicacy, like the miniatures of MSS., on gold grounds, diapered on the backs and richly bordered. Leber thus wrote :—

" The greatest adept in a knowledge of the earliest products of xylography, Baron Heinecken, was satisfied that the first impression which appeared in Europe received from a coarsely engraved block, *was a card*. In his opinion, which we think well founded, the engraving of cards led to that of the figures of Saints, which in its turn gave rise to the engraving of inscriptions or legends, from which sprung the art of printing. To think that a card should produce the press ! What a mother, and what posterity ! " ("Etudes Historiques," &c. p. 3.) On this Chatto remarks : " He who can thus persuade himself that the germ of wood-engraving in Europe is to be found in cards, will doubtless feel great pleasure in tracing its interesting development —— 'ce n'est que le premier pas qui coute,' " and therein lies our difficulty.

A circumstance worthy of notice is that cards were in use in certain countries before the manufacture of paper went on there. Such cards must then either have been introduced ready made, or manufactured from paper imported for the purpose.

Exceptionally they may have been made of other material, as we find to be the case still as respects some Oriental cards, which are thin painted tablets of wood, ivory, metal, and even dried leaves. Canvas and leather cards have been recorded, embroidered silk cards have been exhibited at Kensington, and the writer has been assured by a dealer that cards of tortoiseshell and of small tiles had passed through his hands. Both Breitkopf and Merlin refer to cards on silver plates, the latter giving copies of thirty-four such cards in his own possession (plate 68).

Cards were well known in England in 1463, and if they were made of paper, and in this country, the material must have been imported for such purpose, since paper is not considered to have been made here before the reign of Henry VII., or 1485-1509. As late as the reign of Queen Anne (1702) there were imported annually 40,000 reams of Genoa or white paper, chiefly for the manufacture in question. Nevertheless, it is reasonable to suppose that cards were manufactured, as well as imported, in this country during the first half of the seventeenth century, from the circumstance of the tradesmen having petitioned Parliament, in 1643, against their importation, which could matter to them only as interfering with their own monopoly. Further, by a proclamation of Charles I. of June, 1638, it was ordered that all foreign cards should be sealed at London and packed in new bindings or covers (E 227). From Samuel Rowland's satire, the " Knave of Hearts," we may assume that cards were made here in 1612 also (E. 235 —E 239).

Section V.

SIZE AND FORM OF, MARKS AND DESIGNS ON CARDS, DIVISIONS INTO SUITS, TERMINOLOGY, ETC.

F the large size of some of the earlier cards of the tarots character, mention has been already made. A long, narrow form continues to be given to tarots, particularly for the *tarocchino* game. The early cards were often very stout and inflexible, and so have been some of more recent Italian manufacture, which are peculiar likewise in having a narrow layer of paper, sometimes coloured, folded over the edges of the card in front so as to form a slightly elevated border.

Some small metal plates were early engraved in Germany to serve as cards, and in recent times extremely diminutive packs have been manufactured ; the " Cartes Allemandes, jeu Lilliputien en Argent," given by Merlin, pl. 68, measure only $\frac{5}{8}$ of an inch long and slightly more than $\frac{3}{8}$ of an inch wide. Some modern French cards, to be afterwards described (F 63), measure $1\frac{3}{4}$ by $\frac{7}{8}$ of an inch.

The Italian tarots, I. 8, are but $1\frac{1}{16}$ long, by $\frac{4}{8}$ of an inch wide. The *Cartes Suisses,* represented in plate 68 of Merlin's treatise, slightly exceed 1 inch in length and $\frac{5}{8}$ of an inch in width, but whether these are reduced representations, or are of the actual size, we cannot say, but we think the latter. Chinese cards are small and generally narrow in proportion to their length, not being wider than 1 inch and $\frac{2}{8}$ at the utmost. The cards of the Hindus and Persians are often circular, and of an average diameter of $2\frac{1}{2}$ inches. As a contrast to these small examples, the Stuttgart cards, of the end of the fourteenth or of the beginning of the fifteenth century, may be recalled to mind, which measure above seven inches in height and four inches in breadth.

The figures on the coate-cards, or court-cards, or honours, of the numeral suits, represent in the early cards a king, queen, cavalier, and *fante,* or man-servant. When the numeral series was disjoined from the emblematic set or the *atutti,* one of these figure cards was suppressed. The cavalier, or man on horseback, was the piece more generally omitted. The Spaniards, however, would not allow of a lady or dame in their packs, and retained a king and a first and second *caballero* or *caballo,* or a king, a *caballo,* and a *sota,* or valet. The Germans had with the king often an upper and an inferior knave in place of queen and knave. The figures on some of the older coate-cards, as also on certain of the modern ones, have occasionally resemblance to the persons and objects they were intended to represent. But about the latter time of the reign of Charles VII. of France, and the reign of Henry VII. of England, the figures on the honours began to change, and gradually passed into the grotesque and strange-looking things to be seen on the true old-fashioned English cards, and in many foreign packs. For some time past in France, and more recently in England, there has been a tendency to displace the whole-length figures and to substitute for them mere heads or busts, printed double and in reverse on each honour. Whichever way a card may be thrown the design on it thus becomes at once manifest. In most cases the busts have the strange and conventional character belonging to the upper portions of the old full-length figures, but in others it is much modified, and sometimes altogether displaced by a type quite modern or *quasi* historic.

The French appear to have been the first to place on the coate-cards the names of well-known persons, such as David, Hector, Alexander, Rachel, Pallas, Judith, and others. This practice continued from about 1480 to the beginning of the eighteenth century, since which time it has been resorted to only exceptionally.

The suits of the numeral cards from their first introduction have been always *four* in number. The signs or marks of the suits have varied, however. Those of the earliest cards have been *coppe, danari, bastoni,* and *spade,* or cups, money, clubs, and swords. These marks have been very generally retained in all tarots packs and in the cards of the Spanish people, though exceptionally in some modern tarots the marks are spades, clubs, hearts, and diamonds, which is likewise the case in some packs manufactured by the French for the Spanish market.

The Germans early employed other marks for the suits, viz., *herzen (roth,) schellen, laub (grün),* and *eicheln,* or hearts, bells, leaves, and glands (acorns). Some of the more ancient cards existing have these marks of suits.

During the second quarter of the fifteenth century the French adopted the signs of *cœurs, carreaux, trefles,* and *piques,* or hearts, diamonds, clubs, and spades. These marks have been very generally employed throughout Europe for pure numeral sets (*i.e.,* cards without any emblematic figures), and as before remarked may occasionally be found even in tarots packs, and in cards used by the Spaniards.

Germany and England also generally accepted the French symbols. The former nation, however, during the latter part of the fifteenth and the beginning of the sixteenth century, frequently had recourse to animals, real or chimeric, flowers, fruit, and fancy objects for marking the suits, the pieces composing many of which have been termed animated cards.

From some of the few remaining of early hand-executed cards, it is evident that *miniatori* and decorative painters of great ability in their time, were occasionally employed in the production of these objects, both emblematic and numeral. The desirable volume published by the Society of Bibliophiles Français, on the " Jeux de Cartes Tarots et de Cartes Numerales," proves this in its carefully executed facsimiles of the fine Venetian tarots of the fifteenth century, as do also the copies of the four numerals of the Musée Correr on plates 8 and 9 of Merlin's treatise. The four large and beautiful cards of the Stuttgart cabinet, represented on plates 60 and 61 of the same work, are likewise further evidence. These latter examples of early art are supposed by some to have been productions of the end of the fourteenth century, though others with more probability refer them to the commencement of the fifteenth century. How exquisitely the French could work in this way is shown by plates A and B of Merlin's treatise, where fourteen cards of the fifteenth century, in the cabinet of Le Carpentier, are represented.

" The grace and slender delicacy of the figures, the good taste of the ornamentation, the elegance and lightness of the scroll-work and floriation running round the ' pips,' and connecting them together, do not allow us to doubt that they were the work of an artist of talent and belonged to a set destined for some rich and important person." (p. 107.)

It is on record that a set of cards " containing figures of the gods with their emblematic animals and figures of birds likewise," was painted for Filippo Visconti, Duke of Milan (who died in 1447), and cost 1500 pieces of gold. According to Cicognara the piece previously mentioned commemorating the union of Beatrice Tenda with Filippo Visconti belonged to this series, but this is doubtful.

Even as late as the last century playing-cards have been executed solely by hand. A pack was exhibited at a meeting of the Archæological Association, in January, 1857, by Mr. Syer Cuming, the pieces of which had been painted by one E. Locker, in 1799, whose name was inscribed at the lower corner of the ace of diamonds.

" They are not printed but limned—the whole of the figures are spiritedly executed and well coloured—the character of the pack may be described as of the amusing character." (" Archæological Journal," vol. xiii. p. 244.)

In Germany, particularly, some of the best engravers of the time, *i.e.* A.D. 1450 to 1550, undertook occasionally the production of cards. Thus we have the " cards of the Master of 1466," those of

the "Master of the round cards," copies of the latter by Telman von
Wesel, the cards with the signature F. C. Z., the cards by Virgil
Solis, by Erhard Schoen, H. S. Beham, and at a somewhat later
period those from the designs of Iost Amman.   In Italy the beautiful engravings known as the *Tarocchi of Mantegna* (now generally
ascribed to Baldini and Botticelli), were produced, likewise the Venetian tarots of 1491 described by Cicognara, and of the Albertine
Cabinet of Vienna (Pass. vol. v. p. 129), and the tarots of Nicoletto
da Modena (?)   (Pass. vol. v. p. 132.)   In France, at a later period,
the artistic series of card-pieces by Desmarests and Stefano Della
Bella saw the light.   Examples of most of these cards are now of
great rarity, and some realise in the print market extraordinary
prices.

Further details connected with the subjects of this section will
be given when describing the cards of various countries.   The
following tabular arrangement of the chief marks which have been
employed in different places to distinguish the numeral suits, along
with a short commentary, may appropriately conclude the present
division.

Marks and names of the suits in early numeral cards when combined
with tarots (proper) or an emblematic series.

	CUPS.	MONEY.	SWORDS.	CLUBS.
Italy . . .	Coppe . . .	Danari . . .	Spade . .	Bastoni.
Spain. . .	Copas . . .	Oros or Dineros	Espadas . .	Bastos.
Portugal . .	Copas . . .	Oiros—Ouros .	Spadas . .	Paos.
France . .	Coupes . . .	Deniers . . .	Espées . .	Bastons.

Of the early cards of

Germany . .	Roth or Herzen	Schellen . .	Laub or Grün	Eicheln.

Of the suits of numerals from the times of Charles VII. of France
and Henry VII. of England, and when unconnected
with tarots (proper).

France . .	Cœurs . . .	Carreaux . .	Piques . .	Trefles.
Italy . . .	Do. (Cuori) . .	Do. (Quadri) .	Do. (Picche)	Do. (Fiori).
Spain . . .	Do. (Corazones)	Do. (Ladrillos)	Do. (Picas) .	Do. (Palos).
Germany . .	Do. (Herzen) .	Do. (Rauten) .	Do. (Späten)	Do. (Kreuzen).
England . .	Do. (Hearts) .	Do. (Diamonds)	Do. (Spades)	Do. (Clubs).

The following remarks of M. Merlin in connection with this
portion of the subject are worthy of attention.

"That the Italian and Spanish cards have descended in direct
line from the ' Jeux de tarots Vénétiens,' is at once evident from
observation of the cards — the distinctive signs of the suits
are the same; but this is not so apparent as regards the French
and German cards.   Nevertheless, on reflection we may recognise
the parentage of the latter, and show how, in spite of their

differences, the French and German cards may be restored to an Italian origin.

"In the first place, let us determine the geographic distributions of the three types which M. Leber has truthfully arranged in three regions according to their distinctive marks.

"1. Southern region (Italy, Spain, and Portugal), cups, money, swords, and clubs.

"2. Central region (France, England, and at the present day nearly all Germany), *cœurs, carreaux, piques, et trefles,* or hearts, diamonds, spades, and clubs.

"3. Northern region (Ancient Germany, Switzerland), hearts, bells, leaves, and glands.

"At first sight these three families of signs do not appear to have any analogy with each other, but let us study their names and compare their forms, and we shall find the family connections, which were not before appreciable. In the first place, let us compare the names of the suit marks of the French cards with those of the Italian.

"The Italians name their suits	.	Coppe,	Danari,	Spade,	Bastoni.
„ French „	.	Cœurs,	Carreaux,	Piques,	Trefles.
„ English „	.	Hearts,	Diamonds,	Spades,	Clubs.

"The latter a translation of the French terms, as the English adopted our cards from the first.

"Now is it not evident that the word *spades* (*hoyau, bêche*), given by the English to our *piques,* recalls the *spade* of the Italian symbols? That the term *clubs,* by which they distinguish our *trefles,* and which means in English *massue,* is equally a reminiscence of the Italian *bastone?* It is, therefore, more than probable that our last two signs represent weapons like those of the *jeux d'Italie.*

"Another indication:—It has been shown (page 19) that in the *jeux de Tarots,* and afterwards in the national game of the Spaniards, *Hombre,* the four numeral series are divisible in two sections: one composed of cups and money, in which the value of the cards is in an inverse ratio with the number of the pips; the other formed of swords and clubs, where the value is proportionate with their numbers of points.

"This arrangement has passed over in the games which France borrowed from Spain, as in *Hombre,* and in *Quadrille* and *Mediateur,* derived from it; but in order to render it practicable with our cards, it became necessary to divide our four French marks into two groups—a red and a black group. In the red division (*cœurs et carreaux*) the value of the cards in the games mentioned is like that of the Spanish in cups and money, viz., inverse to the number of

D

points ; while in the black division (*piques et trefles*) this value follows the number of points, as in swords and clubs. It may be added, also, that in these games of Spanish origin, the ace of *piques* is called *espadille* (*petite épée*), and the ace of *trefles baste* (*bâton*).

"Thus, then, may be perceived the character of *piques* and *trefles*, which were regarded by our fathers as replacing swords and clubs. Further, there is another proof which does not admit of the least doubt ; when the Portuguese employ our cards, they term our *cœurs*, *copas ;* our *carreaux*, *ouros ;* our *piques*, *espadas ;* and our *trefles*, *paos.*" (Bibl. 6, p. 64.)

Equivalents of the coate, court, figure cards, or honours in the numeral suits.

Italy . . . . Re	. . Regina or Reina . .	Cavallo .	Fante.
Spain . . . . Rey	. . 1st Caballo or Reyna	Caballo .	Sota.
France . . . Roi	. . Reine or Dame		Valet.
Germany . . König	. Ober-mann		Unter-mann.
England . . . King	. . Queen		Knave or Jack.

Terms for Playing-cards.

Italy . . . . . Carte da giuocare.
Spain . . . . Naypes ; Naipes cartas.
France . . . . Cartes à jouer.
Germany . . Spiel-Karten ; Karten ; Briefe.

Terms for a pack of cards.

Italy . . . . . Un mazzo (or pajo) di Carte.
Spain . . . . Una baraja de naypes.
France . . . Un jeu de Cartes.
Germany . . Ein Spiel Karten ; Ein Spiel Briefe.
England . . . A pack of cards.

In a note to a recent edition of Massinger's plays, it is stated that " in our old poets a pack of cards is called a *deck.*" In Shakespeare's Henry VI., part 3, act v. scene i., occurs :

> " The king was slyly fingered from the deck."

And in the well-known song, "The night before Larrey was stretched," it is said that

> " De deck being called for dey played
> Till Larrey found one of dem cheated."

A correspondent in "Notes and Queries" (vol. v. p. 198, 1870 ; vol. ii. p. 405, 1850), informs us that " a pack of cards is so called [*deck*] at this day in the states bordering on the Mississippi river."

Formerly a pack of cards was called likewise a " paier of cards," as by Roger Ascham in his " Toxophilus," *e.g.* (see note in Singer, p. 56).

SECTION VI.

THE CARDS OF VARIOUS COUNTRIES.

ITHOUT considering it *proven* that playing-cards had their origin in modern times and in Europe, and not in remote ages and in the East, we are yet of opinion that there is more direct evidence in favour of the first hypothesis than for the latter, which appears to derive its chief support from theories of a fanciful and romantic character. From what has been already stated, and that which may be found in subsequent pages where tarots and cards of divination come under discussion, it will be seen, however, that the views of those who have adopted the Eastern, and in particular the Egyptian, theory, have not been neglected.

In accordance with the views towards which more decided inclination is here given, Italy will be regarded as the birthplace of cards, as seen in the primitive *naïbis*, and Venice as that particular district which so modified them by changes connected with the emblematic series, and the addition to it of a numeral sequence, as to acquire a right of parentage in respect to modern playing-cards not readily to be set aside. It is true that the earliest engraved examples of Italian cards,[1] the so-called *Tarocchi* of Mantegna, or the *Carte di Baldini*, have more of the feeling of the Florentine school than of any other, though the names below the figures on them are in the Venetian dialect. But these pieces, it must be recollected, transmit a form of the old instructional *naïbis* combined with more recent emblematic figures, constituting a sequence scarcely adapted or intended for the purposes of ordinary play. Between the time of the production of this set of fifty pieces and that of the original or primitive *naïbis* (of which latter many of the former were purely transcripts), there had sprung up a series combining an emblematic virtue and a numeral power, offering the excitements of chance and gambling, along with whatever purpose the emblematic series might subserve. It was to this arrangement that Venice probably gave birth, an arrangement which was the positive source of the playing-cards of modern times, as seen in the

---

[1] The word "cards" is here used in a general sense, not in that of our modern numerals only for games of hazard; the assumption is made likewise that the engravings in question come under this category. The question is discussed further on.

numeral series divested of all association with cards of emblematic character (*antea,* p. 23).

Though various nations hastened to adopt the acceptable modification of the Venetians, they did not hesitate, sooner or later, to make changes of their own, and to stamp their cards and the games played with them with national characteristics. What these were it is now our business to inquire, and we shall first notice how Italy herself undertook to modify the character of her offspring.

It must be admitted that Italy in general long continued to preserve the tarots game, *i.e.,* the game played with both an emblematic and a numeral series, while other nations very soon discarded it for games played with the numeral series only. The latter, however, exceptionally retained the tarots game, and even now tarots packs of cards are published both in France and Germany, while in modern Italy they are still more common. In recent tarots proper the designs, particularly in Germany, are often of a totally different character from those in the older and typical series.

In Italy there were formerly three kinds of tarots games, two of which have been preserved to this day. These games are known as the *tarots* of Venice or of Lombardy, the *tarocchino* of Bologna, and the *minchiate* of Florence. The first of these—the old Venetian *tarots*—is the parent of all. The sequence consisted of seventy-eight cards *in toto, i.e.,* of twenty-two tarots proper (or twenty-one numbered *atutti,* and one unnumbered, the fool), and fifty-six numerals, made up of sixteen figure cards, or " honours," and forty pip cards, *i. e.,* four suits, of four honours and ten plain cards in each suit. As might be expected, the subjects, as well as the actual designs of the emblematic series in the old Venetian sequence, approach more closely those of the encyclopædic or instructive *naïbis,* as seen in the *Carte di Baldini,* than do those in the Florentine modification. The *matto* has a positive resemblance to the *misero* of the *naïbis,* while in the *minchiate* it has the attributes of the true " fool."

" The figures of the Venetian tarots offer but few particularities requiring notice ; still there is one point worthy of remark, which is the introduction among them of a figure entitled *la Papesse.* What motive, it may be asked, could the author have had to prompt him to recall to mind in these designs that absurd fable of a woman asserted to have occupied the Chair of St. Peter, a fable that reasonable Protestants themselves have abandoned ? No doubt the Venetians were often at war with the Popes, but how many times were they not leagued with them against their common enemies ? Besides, the manner in which this design is composed does not reveal any malevolent, nor even an ironical intention. Perhaps the author designed his tarots at a time when the story in question still continued to be generally accepted. Or it might be that this singularity was the result of a contemptuous whim of the artist. The original author of the tarots, after having copied the design in the *naïbis*, where the Pope is represented without a beard, desired to oppose to him the Patriarch of Constantinople, and in order to distinguish the latter adorned his second design with an oriental beard. This explanation receives some support from the fact that in the modern *minchiate* cards where the Pope does not appear at all, an emperor of the west and an emperor of the east are to be found, the first being characterized by an eagle, the second by a star placed above the globe of the world, which the personage holds in his hand. It should be noted also that, like the beardless Pope of the *naïbis*, *la papesse* of the tarots holds a book on her knees. In the case of the old hand-painted tarots, as in the *minchiate* cards of the present day, we do not find any names inscribed on the latter; this want of indication would readily assist in the error of the earlier engravers, and such error might be transmitted without attracting attention." (Merlin, pp. 81-83.)

The Pope in the seventeen tarots of the French Cabinet, known often as the hand-painted cards of Charles VI., is without a beard, while in the *tarocchino* cards of Mitelli there are two bearded Popes, one being seated, the other standing.

The second tarots game—the *tarocchino* of Bologna, though a direct descendant of the ancient Venetian tarots, is not so old as the third game, or *minchiate* of Florence. The *tarocchino* sequence consists *in toto* of sixty-two cards, *i. e.*, twenty-two tarots proper, and forty numerals. The emblematic subjects and designs are nearly identical with those of the Venetian series; slight modifications occur in modern sets, which will be afterwards noticed.

The chief characteristic of the *tarocchino* of Bologna is the suppression in it of the two, three, four, and five of each numeral suit, thus reducing the numeral cards to forty, which in the Venetian series are fifty-six in number. This modification of the tarots game was invented at Bologna, early in the fifteenth century, by Francesco Fibbia (Prince of Pisa), an exile in that city, dying there in 1419. So pleased were the Bolognese civic authorities with the ingenuity of the new game that they awarded Fibbia the privilege of placing his own shield of arms on the queen of *bastoni*, and that of his wife, who was of the Bentivoglio family, on the queen of *danari*. (Cicognara, " Bibl." 5.)

According to Cicognara the emblematic designs of the *tarocchino* remained very similar to those of the Venetian tarots until the end of the fifteenth century. After 1513 the Republic of Bologna passed under Papal domination, and then the designs began to vary slightly. Some of the more modern ones are very bad, and one or two designs have been borrowed evidently from a Florentine *minchiate* set. At the beginning of the eighteenth century an attempt was made by an artist and engraver of Bologna—Giuseppe Maria Mitelli—to introduce a series of *tarocchino* cards of unquestionable artistic merit. This series will come under notice afterwards. (I. 7.)

The word *tarocchino* is a diminutive of *tarocchi*, a name early applied to any game with tarots. Thus may be found in " Costa e Cardinali Dizionario della Lingua Italiana, Bologna, 1826 ; " " *Tarocchi* sorta di giuoco ; ed anche diconsi ' tarocchi ' alcune delle carte, con che si giuoca.

" *Taroccare* dicesi del giuoco delle Minchiate quando alcuno non ha del seme delle cartacce dove sono figurati Danari, Coppe, Spade e Bastoni e conviene che risponda alla data con qualche ' tarocco.' "

The third tarots game is the *minchiate* of Florence. This, instead of being simpler than the old Venetian game, is much more complicated. In place of the twenty-two *atutti* of the latter, there are forty-one in the Florentine series, which contains, with the numerals, ninety-seven cards *in toto*. (See Merlin, p. 87, and plates 13 to 19.)

The designs of several of the Venetian tarots are frequently altered, and the twenty additional ones are often of grotesque character, as, *e. g.*, in the emblems of the four elements of the ancients —fire, air, earth, and water, and in those of the signs of the zodiac. Not any title or name is printed below the subject; the relative value of the card is indicated by a number above. The concluding eight *atutti* are drawn on a red ground.

There are differences in the numeral series likewise. The *cavalli* are chimeric figures composed of human busts on equine or other trunks, with tails, while the *fanti* or valets are warriors in the suits of *spade* and *bastoni*, and servants (*fantiglie*) in those of *coppe* and *danari*. The marks of *danari* have heads in their fields, with the exception of those on the nine, which have birds on them. The marks of *spade* are straight swords instead of curved ones, as in the Venetian numerals. Finally, in some of the blank spaces between the marks of the suits there are all kinds of small ornaments in the way of cats, elephants, monkeys, deer, and other things, though not to the overcrowding of the field. These ornaments would appear to be proper to the *minchiate* cards, since they may be found both in the older and more recent packs. Nevertheless:—

" However numerous have been the additions made by the Florentines to the tarots of Venice in order to devise a new game, these changes cannot prevent us from perceiving that the foundations of the latter exist in the Venetian series. If we take from the Florentine emblems the three theologic virtues, the four elements, and the twelve signs of the zodiac, we arrive very closely to the Venetian tarots from which the other tarots games have descended, as the tarots of Venice themselves have been derived from the fifty encyclopædic *Naïbis.*" (Merlin, p. 87.)

According to Singer, in a comparatively modern version of *minchiate*, published at Munich, the number of cards had been increased to 103 by doubling the twenty-two *atutti*, the king and knave of hearts. (p. 30.)

The derivation of the term " Minchiate" is not known; it is one " dont on ne retrouve aucune trace dans nulle langue connue, et qui par sa structure comme par sa signification accuse pour etymologie le nom du jeu de Florence." (Merlin, p. 85.)

Costa and Cardinali (*op. cit.*) give its character as a game only : " Egli si fa al piu in quatro persone o in partita ai compagni a due per due (e questo è il vero giuoco) ovvero ciascheduno da per se separatamente. Dicesi altrimenti ' tarocchi ' e ' germini.' "

There is a tradition extant that *minchiate* was invented by Michael Angelo to teach children arithmetic.

Information concerning the methods in which the preceding tarots games were played may be obtained on reference to Singer's treatise (notes 12 and 13, pp. 349-354, Appendix).

Venice herself was not long before she modified her original game of *tarots*, and this she did with decision enough, if not with morality. Some of her people were satisfied that they could gamble far more quickly if they suppressed not only all the *atutti*, but likewise some of the numerals. So a game was formed and termed *Trappola*, in which the true tarots were abolished, as likewise the three, four, five, and six of each numeral suit. This game was still in vogue in Silesia when Breitkopf wrote (1784), and according to Merlin packs made up on the *trappola* principle are to this day published at Vienna under the name of *Drapulir Karten*, the suits and figures retaining their old Italian names (modified) and symbols, viz., *reh, reina, cavall, fantell; coppe, danari, spade,* and *bastoni.*

Singer is surely in-error when he states—influenced, it is likely, by the remarks of Gazzoni—that " *Trappola* is probably the most ancient European game at cards " (p. 236), and " probably played with the very cards obtained from the Arabians, if it be not the Eastern game itself." (p. 22.) It may be fairly assumed that the reduction and suppression of the pieces before mentioned were made solely for the purpose that *chance* should play a very important part in the game, and necessitates the previous existence of more perfect series, and of games less hazardous in character. If Singer's supposition be correct, all these changes were made by Muhamedans, and the result—a simple and perfected game for gambling—forwarded as a present to the unsophisticated European! A like priority has been bestowed by others on the games of *Hombre* and *Lansquenet.*

Breitkopf, Leber, and others, have spoken of *trappola* cards as if they were cards having characteristic marks of suits. But they are not so; numerals of any suits, no matter what their marks may be, having the three, four, five, and six of each suit suppressed, are capable of being converted into *trappola* cards, *i.e.*, cards with which to play *trappola* (*postea*, G. 121). The marks usually on the cards are, however, not more necessary for *trappola* than for *hombre*, which the Spaniards play either with the same marks, viz., swords, cups, money, and clubs, or with those of *piques, cœurs, carreaux,* and *trefles,* just as we could play whist with cards the marks of which were *spade, coppe, danari,* and *bastoni.*

With respect to the derivation of the word " trappola," Peignot observes: " Selon le Dictionnaire de la Crusca le mot ' trappola' signifie *cosa ingennese insidia, una sorta di reta,* et *trappolatore* est la même chose que *ingannatore, giuntatore* (trompeur, fripon). D'autres font deriver ce mot de trappe, piége."

It will have been understood from what has been already stated, that the marks of the suits of numerals attached to the Italian tarots proper are *coppe, danari, bastoni,* and *spade.* Italian numerals very often retain these marks when not any longer combined with an emblematic series. Yet modern uncombined Italian numerals have frequently the French marks—*cœurs, carreaux, trefles,* and *piques.* A distinctive character of the marks themselves in the suits *spade* and *bastoni* of Italian numerals, is the mode in which they are interlaced or connected together in place of standing separately or apart. The curved forms, too, of the spade or swords are specially Italian in design.

SPANISH CARDS.—Not any remains of very old Spanish cards have reached our time. It is true that some specimens in the Rouen Cabinet have been accorded by some archæologists to the last quarter of the fifteenth century, but it is probable that Merlin is right in the statement that the earliest examples now known had not an origin before 1600. (Merlin, p. 99, note.) But if there be not evidence in the shape of actual cards of Spain's early possession of the new materials for play, strong proofs of it are apparent in the name which always has been and still is applied to playing-cards, viz., *Naïpes.*

Spain as the *inventor* of cards found a strong champion in the Abbé de la Rive, whose tractate may be found in the appendix to the work of Singer. He maintained that they were given to Italy by Spain at the time when the Spaniards entered Sicily and Calabria under the Castilian princes, in 1267, or under Peter III. of Arragon, *circa* 1282. But although several passages have been brought forward from early MSS. alluding to cards in Spain, they have turned out on close inquiry to have been glosses and interpolations of an after period.   De la Rive stated that Guevara, recording in his " Epistola Familiares" the statutes accorded in 1332 to the military order of La Banda, had mentioned that Alphonso XI. of Castile had included amongst them a prohibition to play at cards. Now it has been found that not one of the earlier Spanish editions of these epistles (1539) contains a syllable about cards, which latter are first mentioned in Gutery's translation of the Epistles into French in 1588, and which it seems the Abbé de la Rive must have made his authority.   Further, in the " Recopilacion de las leyes destos reynos," 1640, a prohibition of John I. of Castile is given— *de jugar dados ne naypes en publico ne escondido*—yet the word *naÿpes* is not to be met with either in the edition of the " Ordenances Reales de Castilla" of 1545 (Medina de Campo), nor in the edition of 1508.   It was simply an *addition* made to the Recopilaciones of 1640.   It must be admitted, nevertheless, that the character of the two national games, *Hombre* and *Quadrille*, proves that they had their origin in a chivalric age, and that the Flemish author Eckeloo, or Pascasius Justus, who lived about 1540, and had travelled in Spain, represents the people as passionately fond of cards, and says that " he had travelled many leagues in that kingdom without being able to procure the necessaries of life, not even bread or wine, yet in every miserable village cards might be met with."   The Spaniards took with them this passion for play to the New World, and finding themselves in St. Dominique unprovided with the necessary agents, they made cards of certain leaves and of leather, according to De la Vega.

" Herrera mentions that upon the conquest of Mexico by the Spaniards Montezuma took great pleasure in seeing them play at cards ; this was in 1519, and it shows that this amusement must for some time previous have been common in Old Spain." (Singer, p. 38.)

Spanish cards are characterised by certain peculiarities evinced to us in actual examples, and by historical allusions.   It should be observed, in the first place, that Spanish tarots are unknown, and it is doubtful if such ever existed.   All Spanish playing-cards are of the numeral kind.   Secondly, in a legitimate Spanish pack there are only forty-eight cards, instead of fifty-two.   This arises from the suppression of the ten in each suit.   Thirdly, in agreement with certain Oriental and some German cards, not any queen, dame, or woman is admitted among the honours.   Her place is supplied by a *caballero* or *caballo*.   Fourthly, the old Italian marks are retained as *copas, oros, espadas,* and *bastos,* but the Spanish designs differ from the former, as they do likewise in the figures on the coate-cards.

" While the Italian kings are seated the Spanish kings are erect,

and their vast mantles are surcharged with large ornaments, as in
the case of the French kings.   As regards the points (pips), the
swords are straight double-edged rapiers, the batons are knotty
branches of trees, and these knotty branches and rapiers are placed
sometimes horizontally, sometimes vertically, close to each other, but
always so arranged that they are never interlaced in the inconvenient
manner common to the numeral cards of the Italian tarots.   Herein
lies an undoubted advantage, as the power to count at a glance
the number of points on each card is much facilitated."   (Merlin,
p. 97.)

It is not known when Spain first began to manufacture her own
cards, but there is evidence to show that France early supplied the
Spanish market.   To some extent she does so now, and this explains why in some modern packs of Spanish cards the marks of
the suits are *cœurs, carreaux, piques,* and *trefles,* and that a *dame* is
admitted in place of a *caballo.*

Referring to plate xxx. in his " History of Playing-cards," Mr.
Taylor remarks that, " though of Parisian workmanship, it is a
Spanish knave of clubs under the form of a Peruvian, with crest of
blue and scarlet feathers.   Singer says that the Spanish government maintains a monopoly of cards, but we have besides this
another proof of that country being supplied from other quarters in
the Senora Morin, who we have seen made *naypes* for the Spanish
market at Paris in the Rue Grenéta, and immense quantities of cards
are produced in London, many of which have the suits of cups,
money, clubs, and swords, those intended for the Spanish settle-
ments being actually marked *de la Real fabrica para las Indias !* "
(p. 177.)   (*postea,* S. 15.)

M. Merlin states that the oldest cards truly of Spanish origin
that he had seen, were four kings kindly presented to him by M.
Carderera, court painter to the Queen of Spain, and author of the
beautiful work on Spanish iconography.

" The pale and slightly bistre-coloured ink with which they have
been printed might, on first inspection, cause them to be attributed
to an early period, did not a circumstance, easily to be overlooked,
betray their more recent origin.   This is the number twelve engraved at the corners of each of these four cards.   We have seen
that the Spaniards have suppressed the tens and the dames, which
reduces their pack to forty-eight cards or twelve per suit, from this
it results that the valet, the cavalier, and the king are the three
cards superior to the *nine,* and possess the numbers ten, eleven, and
twelve.   The custom of inscribing on the cards of each suit the
numbers of their values is comparatively modern, and of which we
are ignorant of any example before the eighteenth century." (p. 98.)
(*postea,* cards of Jehan Volay, S. 15, of the game *alluette,* S. 43.)

PORTUGUESE CARDS.——Copies of Portuguese cards may be seen in the " Jeux de Cartes Tarots et de Cartes numerales." (Bibl. 2.) The coate-cards in this pack, supposed to have been executed in 1693, are king, queen, and cavalier, and the suits money, cups, clubs, and swords. The "honours" and aces have letters on them both at top and bottom indicating the suit, the rank, and names of the cards. The presence of the queen must be regarded as exceptional to the Portuguese series.

" In a pack," writes Chatto, " of modern Portuguese cards now before me, there is no queen, and the suits are hearts, bells, leaves, and acorns. The figures of the coate-cards are half lengths and double, *de duas Cabeças*, so that a head is always uppermost which-ever way the card may be held." (p. 251.)

Was not this pack made in Germany for the Portuguese market ?

FRENCH CARDS.——That France possessed cards very early there is direct historic proof, from the entry in the accounts of the treasurer of Charles VI., A.D. 1392. That she did not have them, of a *gambling* character at least in 1369, is fairly presumable from the circumstance that cards are not mentioned in the long list of games prohibited by Charles V. in that year, while there is an order of the Prévôt of Paris extant of 1397 forbidding their employment.

The earliest French cards known are probably those of the Carpentier collection, described by Merlin, p. 107, and plates, A. B. 38-39. These cards are fourteen in number, painted by hand about the commencement of the fifteenth century. The pieces are numerals, being all the " honours " (except the *dame de cœurs*), with the six of *piques* and the five of *trefles*. The costume is that of the previous century. Not any names are on the cards. The next examples are those of the sheet of strange figure pieces bearing the name of F. Clerc on a scroll held by the valet of *carreaux*, and which are in the collection at Paris. These cards belong probably to the last quarter of the fifteenth century. The third specimens of old French cards which follow, are known wherever the history of playing-cards is studied. They are termed the *Coursube* cards, and belong to the last quarter of the fifteenth century; though it has been maintained by some that they were executed as early as the first quarter.

It is evident from the Carpentier cards that early in the fifteenth century the French cards did not necessarily retain the old Italian marks of the suits, but had new ones of their own. The cups, money, batons, and swords had given place to *cœurs*, *carreaux*, *piques*, and *trefles*, and so persistently were these marks maintained and introduced on cards exported to all countries, that a regular type or class of cards became known as French cards, as opposed to Italian cards on the one hand and to German cards on the other. Thus, in fact, became established the *geographic* types of cards before mentioned (p. 33), at the beginning of what may be termed the second epoch of playing-cards. At this epoch, too, the art of wood-engraving gave to the designer the power of easily and permanently fixing national characteristics.

Our limits prevent all discussion on the origin and hidden meanings of the French marks of suits. These subjects may be found copiously treated in Chatto, p. 206; Merlin, p. 105, and in other systematic writers.

At first the figure cards or honours were without names on them, but about the last quarter of the sixteenth century names were attached, the earliest example of this practice known being found in the *Coursube* pieces before mentioned. These cards belong to the Paris Cabinet; they are ten in number in two rows of five pieces each row, in the following order: *valet, roi, dame (trefles)* ; *roi, dame (carreaux)* ; *valet, dame, roi (piques)* ; *dame, roi (cœurs)* ; on each card-piece, except the *roi de cœurs*, is an inscription in Gothic letters. On the king of *carreaux* is the name *Coursube*, on the king of *piques* is *Apollin*, the queen of *piques* bears the motto *Leauté due* (leal homage), the queen of *carreaux, en toi te fie*, while other cards have other legends (Jeux de tarots, &c., Bibl. 2, pp. 13-17, and plates).

Four very early knaves in the British Museum cabinet (F. 42), bear the names *Lancelot, Hogier, Rolant,* and *Valery.* On other early French cards may be found the names of the Knights of the Round Table, the *Neuf Preux,* and of various heroes of chivalry. Some specimens in the Dijon Cabinet bear historic titles, such as *la Pucelle,* the Dukes of Burgundy, Normandy, Guyenne, the Counts of Flanders, associated with mythologic and legendary personages. Paris, Helene, Venus, La Sybille, Melusine, likewise make their appearance. Some cards found at Narbonne present a very strange mixture, but the only example which need be particularized is the rare sheet of the fifteenth century, in the collection at Paris, and which for the first time bears the names of Alexander, Julius Cæsar, Charlemagne, and David (*neuf preux*), and which at a later period, under Henri IV. and Louis XIII., were definitely adopted as the names of the four kings. Until then, judging "from the often complete absence of names, as likewise from the variety of those which occur, it may be reasonably concluded that the card-makers did not follow any determinate rule nor definite system, and that the Parisians were the only ones who finished by fixing and retaining the names which prevail to the present day." (Merlin, p. 112.)

With these names for the kings, viz., David, Alexander, Cæsar, and Charlemagne, became associated Rachel, Argine, Pallas, and

Judith for the queens, and Hector, Lancelot, Roland, and Hogier, for the valets.

French playing-cards having on them the suit marks, *cœurs, carreaux, trefles,* and *piques,* are often termed *Piquet* cards ; the game of *piquet* being supposed to have originated about the time the *Coursube* cards were made, the latter being considered, therefore, the earliest *piquet* cards known. Nevertheless, there is not satisfactory evidence to show either the date at which *piquet* was first played, or that the ten-figure *Coursube* specimens belonged to a *piquet* pack. The game of *piquet,* it should be borne in mind, is one in which the pack for playing it, up to the beginning of the eighteenth century, consisted of thirty-six cards, *i.e.,* the two, three, four, and five of each suit were suppressed, as in *trappola,* and the *tarocchino* of Bologna. From the date mentioned, the six of each suit has been omitted likewise, so that the *piquet* pack has now but thirty-two cards. The *Coursube* cards, being all figure cards, do not assist us in determining whether the game was in use at their period. Further, *piquet* was clearly not the primitive French game in which numerals having the present marks of suits were used, for the beautiful cards belonging to the early part of the fifteenth century, done by hand and in the Carpentier cabinet, present both a five and six of *trefles.*

Endeavours have been made to associate the origin of this game with the epoch of Charles VII., but a decisive solution of the question cannot be attained. Singer observes : " those who know the game well, agree that it is one of the most amusing and most complete games played with cards." In Macready's Diary is the entry in 1840, " October 9th, played at *piquet* in order to learn the game for the new piece, ' Money.' "

From the circumstance that certain cards dealt may be discarded by the players, and others taken from the stock undealt in their stead, there is a choice, as it were, granted to each player.

" From this *choice* Bullet pretends the game has its name, for *piquo* in Keltic signifies to choose, and the word still preserves the same meaning among the people at Besançon ; choice grapes or choice cherries are called *pique des raisins* or *pique des cerises.* The word is still in use among the military. A *piquet* is a certain number of men chosen by companies, to be ready to mount at the shortest notice."—Singer, Appendix, p. 272.

At the end of the eighteenth century the French Revolution not only changed governments and dethroned kings of the earth, but overthrew those of cards. Yet—

" In effacing the signs of royalty it had not destroyed the passion for play ; indeed, it had never dreamt of doing so, for in granting free trade to cards it had, on the contrary, offered more facilities to players. But it was obliged to pursue royalty vigorously, even on to cards, and it was in the choice of subject that the revolutionary spirit found its scope. Since, however, the imagination of the card-makers was not very fertile, the same circle was continually gone round, but few entirely distinct types were evolved, and fewer still of designs from clever artists. Once more we find the kings dethroned, and by whom ? by emblematic personages, by sages, by philosophers ; the valets are displaced by warriors, or Roman heroes, or by *sans-culottes ;* and the queens have to resign in favour of the virtues and liberties ; and what liberties ! the liberty of marriage, of worship, of the press, and of commerce." . . . . " As soon as the period of sanguinary executions and of public terror had passed by, the passion for play revived, and with it returned the old cards." . . . . " The conqueror of Marengo and of Austerlitz endeavoured to cicatrize the wounds opened by the Republic." . . . . " The civilizing genius, whose glance embraced everything at once, did not pass over the designs on cards, and on the 13th of June, 1808, the painter David was appealed to." (Merlin, p. 114.)

David, Mongez, and Gatteaux obeyed the high decree, and the artistic cards of 1809 and 1811 were the result. (See F. 57 (2) *postea.*) Nevertheless—

" Whether it was that players did not appreciate the changes, or from some other reason, the new designs were not of long duration, and from the year 1813 the old cards reappeared, and triumphing so completely over the innovations, that the official mould was adopted by the Restoration, which contented itself with only substituting the *fleur-de-lys* for the bees and the imperial eagle." (Merlin, p. 114.)

Again, fresh attempts were made in 1816 to introduce other designs, but the enterprise did not succeed, and cost the Government a considerable sum of money. " To-day," says M. Merlin, " we have returned to the mould of 1813, which is multiplied by the galvano-plastic process in sufficient numbers to keep in constant activity three steam presses at the Imperial Printing Office." (p. 116.)

GERMAN CARDS.—It is generally allowed that Germany rightly claims a high place in the early history of playing-cards. According to trustworthy authorities allusion is made to them in the " Pflicht-bücher" of Nürnberg for 1384, and there is extant an ordinance of the Town Council of Ulm for the year 1397, prohibiting their employment. Even by 1441 the Germans imported cards into Venice to such amount that the senate were appealed to to stop the supply, as injurious to the interest of the Italian card-makers.

It is probable that the Germans very soon altered for themselves the Italian marks of the numeral suits, making use of the figures of animals for differentiating the latter. At any rate, the earliest German cards known—those of the Stuttgart Cabinet—have dogs, falcons, stags, and ducks for the suit marks. These " animated" cards were, however, soon followed by a series having the more national signs of *roth* or *herzen, laub* or *grün, eicheln,* and *schellen,* or hearts, leaves, glands, and bells. The latter cards were of smaller size than the first animated ones, which were purely handwork. But though numerals of the national suit marks continued to be manufactured, some of the early German copper-plate engravers of the end of the fifteenth and beginning of the sixteenth century reverted to the animated types, and exercised their talents in designing cards in which all kinds of animals—natural and chimeric—flowers, and fruits, were made to do duty as marks of suits. Some examples of these engraved cards known to the iconophilist are admirable specimens of the early German burin, and are highly prized and paid for by the collector.

The German cards of the end of the fifteenth and of the sixteenth centuries are much more ornamented than are the cards of other countries, for—

" In addition to the pips or the marks of the suits, they frequently contain figures of men and women, quadrupeds, birds, foliage, and such like, introduced by way of ornament at the caprice of the designer. These ornamental appendages are frequently of a grotesque character, and sometimes indecent." (Chatto, p. 236.)

Very peculiar devices were sometimes employed. There is a set of cards by Jost Amman, in which the marks of the suits are books, printers' inking-balls, wine cups, and goblets with bosses of glass or earthenware. Some very pretty diminutive cards, having leaves, bells, hearts, and acorns for the marks of the suits, were produced by the Germans during the sixteenth century.

Much has been written concerning the origin of these national signs, but most interest attaches to the source and meaning of the sign, *schellen, grellot,* or bells. Reference may be made for information to Chatto, pp. 239-245, and to the work of Boiteau D'Ambly.

A peculiarity of the true German pack is that the queen is omitted from the court cards, and an upper valet or *obermann* is put in her place ; thus the honours are composed of king and superior and inferior valets. In modern packs, and particularly those made on the French principles, the queen displaces the superior valet.

A German writer of the seventeenth century, in pointing out that tarots figures should always be regarded as symbolical, observes that even the marks of the German numeral series are intended to have a deeper meaning than is usually supposed. For example, the initial letter of the suit *schellen* (bells), S, with that of the suit *aicheln* (glands), A, of the suit *roth* (hearts), R, and with that of the suit *grün* (leaves), G, compose the German word *SARG*, equivalent for *coffin*.

" Alii ex literis initialibus colorum istorum *aus Schellen, Aicheln, Roth, und Grün einen Sarg,* composuere quia chartæ historiæ sæpe fiunt marsupii et lusoris sepulchrum." (Lehmen, " De Varii Ludendi Generibus.")

Like other peoples, the Germans fashioned a national game of their own. This was *Landsknechtspiel*, or *Lansquenet*. The actual date of its invention is uncertain ; some have stated that it was known in France in 1392, in the reign of Charles VI.; if so, it must be indeed a very old game, since the French borrowed *lansquenet* from the Germans. The military and German origin of the game is evident from its title, which is derived from *landsknecht, lanzenknecht,* or *lanzknecht, i. e.,* a foot soldier armed with a lance, such as may be seen, *e. g.,* playing at cards in the print by Anthony of Worms (Bartsch, vii. p. 491, n. 10), of which a copy is given by Singer, p. 235. *Lansquenet* is still played, and, writes Singer, " if it be the same game which has come down to us, and that now bears the name, its invention required no mighty effort, and it might easily be learned and played by the common soldier." (p. 44.)

" The pipe was not then invented to solace their bivouac, and where so likely an origin of a game requiring so little talent to comprehend it, and yet offering such opportunity for trickery, as a *corps de garde* of these rough warriors ? " (Taylor's Ed. of " Boiteau d'Ambly," p. 279.)

Lansquenet is described in the edition of " Hoyle's Games," published at London in 1786, and must have continued to have been played occasionally as a gambling game in French houses to within the last twenty years, since Paul de Musset, in a " *recit des mœurs contemporains*" (" Histoire d'un Diamant"), in the " Revue des Deux Mondes" for September, 1874, tells us that the hero of his tale, " se laissa mettre à une table de lansquenet. En moins d'une heure il y perdit douze mille francs."

It has been before stated that cards having the old Italian marks of suits, cups, swords, money, and clubs, are still employed in certain parts of Germany in playing a *trappola* game borrowed from the South. True tarots games, also, are yet occasionally played, and modern sets of cards published for the purpose. The designs on these latter cards, however, are often totally different from those of the old emblematic series. They are numbered in the same way, which serves, we presume, the main purpose of the modern player.

Spielhagen acquaints us in his " Aus meinem Jugend Stadt" (1868), *Skitzenbuche,* p. 27, that both *tarots* and *hombre* were played, with other games, at the " *Abendgesellschaften*" in his youthful days.

" The entire company had now placed themselves by threes and fours—according to whether *tarot, hombre, whist,* or *boston* was to be played—at tables."

After the party had broken up—

" The host went from table to table to take up the ' card money' that had been placed in the ' pot'—full price of two packs if the cards had been quite new, if not, *à discrétion.*" (p. 29.)

" We desired," writes M. Merlin, " to be able to point out in a satisfactory manner what were the names and structure of the German games, but have not met with information precise enough on the subject. We must be contented with communicating a few remarks with which the examination of cards has furnished us.

" For figures we meet with kings, superior and inferior valets. Sometimes the kings are seated, sometimes they are on horseback.

" The point cards are the ten, nine, eight, seven, six, and two, a composition resembling our own *Piquet,* in which the ace has been displaced by the two. This structure is that of our own Lilliputian silver series represented on plate 68. It is likewise that of the Saxon game termed *Schwerter Karte—cartes a l'épée.*

" What appears to confirm our conjecture as to the analogy of *piquet* with this *jeu à l'épée,* is the fact that in the modern cards manufactured at Vienna for · playing the German game, and in which the kings are mounted, and we see the flute and the drum (as in the old cards of the Musée Hal at Brussels), the six is suppressed, as it is in the French *piquet* since the end of the seventeenth century." (p. 121.)

The adoption of the French marks of suits is followed in German packs, which often refuse to reinstate the dame or queen in the place of the *obermann* or superior valet. In such cards double busts, in place of whole-length figures on the coate-cards, are usual.

SWISS CARDS.—The old cards of Switzerland were evidently derived from those of Germany at a time posterior to the period of animated cards. " There are always four kings, four superior and four inferior valets, and one, two, six, seven, eight, and nine, in the cards of Schaffouse, and from one to nine in those of Soleure. The marks of the suits are slightly different, for while the glands and the bells are retained, the hearts are displaced by *shields,* and the leaves by *flowers.* Further, the attitudes of the figures, with their naïve and *bourgeoise tournure,* indicate design of the commonest character.

" The Swiss have retained the marks of the aces on banners, such as may be seen for example in the small cards from engraved wood-blocks preserved in the Musée Hal at Brussels." (p. 122.)

Modern Swiss cards are either French or German.

E

ENGLISH CARDS.—It is most probable that cards made their way into England through France, and it must not be forgotten that once Normandy, Touraine, Anjou, Maine, Poitou, and other districts were either in the real or nominal possession of the kings of England for nearly three hundred years. When cards were introduced here is not known, but we are safe in believing they were not in use among us until after the reign of Henry IV. (1405), and that they were certainly employed previous to 1463, for in the Parliament Rolls of that year (Edward IV.) their importation was prohibited. About 1484 they formed a common English Christmas pastime, at least among the upper classes, and in 1495-6 (eleventh of Henry VII.), an edict of the king expressly forbade their use to servants and apprentices, except during the Christmas holidays. That the English made cards as well as imported them by 1463 is clear, or the card-makers would not have petitioned in favour of their own monopoly. Such cards as were home-manufactured must have been made of imported paper, or else of some other material.

England appears to have adopted at once the French suit marks, and the king, queen, and knave of the figure cards or honours. Nevertheless, the names of the suit marks are in part of Spanish descent, *e. g.*, clubs for *bastos,* and not trefoil for *trefles,* and spades for *espadas,* instead of spear for *piques.* Some writers have asserted that Spanish cards, in fact, were introduced into this country before the French, and point out that our *knave* or *jack,* and jack-a-napes have more affinity with the Spanish *sota* or the Italian *fante* than with the French *valet,* which in the earlier French cards bears the name of some person in romance or history. If Spanish cards were introduced early into England they must have soon yielded place to the popular French ones, though at an after period attempts were made to bring them into fashion, as the following from the " Postman," of December, 1702, testifies.

" Advertisement.

" Spanish cards lately brought from Vigo. Being pleasant to the eye by their curious colours and quite different from ours, may be had at 1*s.* a pack at Mrs. Baldwin's, in Warwick Lane."

Most inquirers have failed to meet with any proof that the old tarots cards were ever used, or even known in this country. Singer remarks, p. 240, however—

" We gather from the following passage, in Cleland's 'Institution of a Nobleman,' that *Tarocco* was played in England in the early part of the reign of James I. (1603). Chap. 24 of ' House Games :'—His Majesties permission of honest house games, as Cardes, French Cardes called *Taraux,* Tables and such like plaies, is sufficient to protect you from the blame of those learned men who think them hazards," &c.

The English figure cards or honours retain to the present day more or less of the character and costume marking the reign of Henry VII., when they were probably first designed.

Mr. F. A. Repton in an article on " the costume of Coate-Cards," in the " Gentleman's Magazine " for November, 1843, vol. xx., New Series, p. 471, writes:

" Many of the readers of the ' Gentleman's Magazine ' may not be aware that the dresses represented on our coate-cards are actually the same as those which prevailed about the time of Henry VII. or Henry VIII. The lappets which fall on each side of the faces of the queens are in fact a rude representation of the dress of the females of that period, *i. e.*, about the year 1500-1540. But the crown or coronet as being placed at the *back* of the head, may be traced as late as the reign of Elizabeth or James."

" . . . . The knave of hearts in Rowland's poem (A.D. 1611) complains against the old-fashioned flat caps. These flat caps having several cuts round the rim may be compared with the old paintings and the tapestry of the date 1500-40. . . . . So late as 1585 Strutte, in his ' Anatomie of Abuses,' mentions the flat caps as being ' broade on the crowne like the battlements of a house.' . . . The knave of hearts also complains against the striped stockings, ' My stockings idiot-like red, grene, and yalowe.' These striped stockings may frequently be found in old wood-cuts, particularly in those in the Triumph of Maximilian." (*Op. cit.*)

Mr. Taylor writes :

" The costume and attributes of our modern court-cards vary slightly in different packs, though they have a general similarity. The knave of clubs still holds his arrow, now distorted into a bed-post, with the ' head-end upward,' but with the feathers gone. It has been suggested that the instrument held by some knaves of spades is a kind of *spring fork*, formerly used by constables to catch runaway offenders. Hearts has the ' rustic browne bill,' and diamonds apparently what Falstaff (Hen. IV. Pt. 1, act ii. sc. 4) calls a *Welsh hook*, which Mr. Knight says was a pike with a hook placed at some distance below its point, like some of the ancient partisans." (Bibl. 9, p. 185, note.)

England does not appear to have worked out, at an early period, a national game of her own. The game of *Primero* (Spanish or Italian), was probably one of the earlier games played in this country, and it continued to be the fashionable amusement at cards during the reigns of Henry VIII., Edward VI., Mary, Elizabeth, and James. A game termed *Mawe* succeeded *Primero*, then came *Gleek, Hombre, Quadrille, Reversis*, and *Bassett*. Ruff and Honours introduced *Whist*, now, *par excellence*, the English game.

Some time about 1650, according to Barrington, however, he

" learned from a gentleman, much advanced in years, in 1786, that whist was not played upon principles until about fifty years before, when it was much studied by a set of gentlemen who frequented the Crown Coffee House, in Bedford Row; of these, the first Lord Folkestone was one; before that time it had been chiefly confined to the servants' hall with *All-fours*, and *Put.*"   (Singer, p. 271.)

A tax was levied upon cards first in the reign of James I., 1615 (E. 225, E. 226).   In 1825 the duty was 2*s.* 6*d.* per pack; in 1827 it was reduced to one shilling; it is now threepence.   In 1850, duty was paid on nearly 300,000 packs.   A paragraph in the " Times " of February 20, 1875, is as follows:—

" There was a decrease in the stamp duties on ' playing-cards,' in the year ended March 31st, 1874.   In 1873 the duty was £12,865, in 1874 £12,584."

From the same Journal for November 29th, 1875, we learn that " In the year ended the 31st of March last, the stamp duty of 3*d.* on every pack of cards made for sale in the United Kingdom, amounted to £13,130 9*s.*   The number of packs was 1,050,476."

Sellers are now obliged to take out a licence.

There are two circumstances connected with the history of modern playing-cards particularly noteworthy.   One is that all attempts to improve the *bizarre* figures derived from the coate-cards of the old standard packs have been unwelcomed by the true card-player, whether in France, Germany, or England.   The attempts to effect that object have been manifold, and occasionally the designs desired to be substituted have been good in themselves, and well drawn and coloured.   Not any wide or permanent degree of success has attended them, and, as remarked by Singer, " So pertinaciously have the original figures been adhered to, that although the improvement has been applauded and the cards admired, they have rather been purchased as curiosities than for use, and for the *serious* purpose of card-playing the old figures have ever been preferred."   A sort of compromise between the parties has been sometimes attempted, and even recently one of our first manufacturers attempted the feat, as may be seen in the following passage from the " Athenæum " of October, 1874:—

" Messrs. De la Rue will issue this season a pack of novel playing-cards, in which, whilst historical personages of the present time are introduced as the honours, the traditional quaintness of the old playing-cards is preserved, so that the card-player's attention is not disturbed."   (E. 173.)

Taylor tells an amusing story, illustrative of the Conservative feelings club-players have for the old pack, and nothing but that pack.   (Bibl. 9, p. 450.)

The number of *improved!* Parisian packs is considerable, but their very variety and, after all, much repetition of the new forms, show that not one has any endurancy. Some change no doubt is gradually creeping in, as may be seen in the increasing frequency of figure-cards having on them busts printed double and in reverse, in place of single whole-length figures. Should this change continue to hold its ground, the old, conventional, whole-length figures may disappear, though the busts which displace them may remain of conventional character. Of the substitution of modernised or historic persons on the figure-cards for the old forms, however, we anticipate but little success.

We were informed (1875) at one of the principal card-makers, that they supplied now only two London clubs with cards having the old full-length figures. It would not be surprising, however, to find the old cards re-assert themselves, for it is scarcely to be expected that any compromise which artistic or other merit may offer, will be accepted as a permanent departure from the ancient types, as long as old associations can be cherished and preserved among a brotherhood so exclusively occupied with but one object—that of play—and so intently that not the slightest distraction of thought by any secondary matter could be tolerated for a moment.

The second circumstance worthy of notice is, that all attempts —and they have been many—which have been made in modern times to render cards capable of communicating information and instruction while ordinary games were being played, have never been received with favour beyond that which their novelty would insure. Packs of cards having the ordinary suits and symbols more or less distinctly marked have been devised over and over again, by which, through the addition to them of illustrations and inscriptions, the most varied forms of knowledge were sought to be conveyed. Cards with such a secondary purpose may be met with intended to teach arithmetic, grammar, geography, history, heraldry, mythology, astronomy, astrology, the use of mathematical instruments, and the principles of military science and engineering. Besides such cards as these, others of a satirical, proverbial, caricature, and amusing kind have been produced, provided with the marks of the usual suits so that they might be employed in the ordinary way. In all these endeavours it appears to have been forgotten that those persons who desired to learn grammar, &c., did not want to play at cards; and that such as would willingly play at cards might be blind to the blandishments of grammar. Even were such not the case, it is doubtful whether grammarian or card-player would be more confused in the double duty he undertook to perform, since the definition of the " points" and figure-cards was generally so imperfect, or so subservient to the other illustrations, as to render ordinary play more

a penance than a pleasure, while the grammatical or other knowledge
was given in so concentrated, terse, or tabular a form as not to be
intellectually digestible at a moment's notice.   Be this as it may,
such cards have generally found a resting-place in the cabinets of
the curious, but little favour being shown them by either the student
or the player.   So apparent to many caterers to popular instruction
and amusement has been the inutility of trying to combine information with ordinary play, that they have seized on merely the most
general principles involved in cards, discarding altogether true
playing-card games, and made the pack a vehicle for the relaxation
and laughable amusement only of children or older persons at Christmas, and other festivities.   In such packs the ordinary suits and
marks are unknown, each series forming a special game of its own,
sometimes very simple—mere question and answer—at other times
rather complex in character.   Such cards may be fairly termed
" Cartes de Fantaisie."   Fortune-telling by the Norwood Gipsy,
the Tender Passion, Manners and Customs of the Day, the
Fashions, Charades, Riddles, Pictorial illustrations of an amusing
character, grotesque and laughable changes, and cognate themes
form their subjects.   Of examples of such cards every Christmas
furnishes a new though now limited supply.   Here, as in the previous case, a sort of compromise has been occasionally tried, but not
with more success as regards card-players.   The following extract
from Chatto will help to illustrate it :—

" It was in December, 1692, that the London papers first announced to the world the invention of the ' Game of Carving at
Table.'   This precious announcement is conceived in the following
terms : ' *The Genteel Housekeeper's Pastime,* or the mode of Carving
at Table represented in a pack of playing-cards, with a book by
which any ordinary capacity may learn how to cut up or carve in
mode all the most usual dishes of flesh, fish, fowl, and baked meats,
with the several sawces and garnishes proper to each dish of meat.
Price 1*s.* 6*d.*   Sold by J. Moxon, Warwick Lane."

" In those cards the suit of hearts is occupied by flesh, diamonds
by fowl, clubs by fish, and spades by baked meats.   The king of
hearts presides over a sirloin of beef, of diamonds over a turkey, of
clubs over a pickled herring, and of spades a venison pasty.   A red
stamp on the ace of spades belonging to a pack which I have had an
opportunity of examining, contains the word ' sixpence.'   If this
was the duty on each pack, it was certainly great for the period."
(p. 156.)

It has been supposed by some good authorities that in former
times cards were prepared in a special manner for ecclesiastics to
play with.   The figure cards represented saints and holy persons,
and the latter were introduced even on the pip cards.   Descriptions

of pieces, both from wood and metal engravings, considered to
belong to such packs, may be found in Passavant, vol. i. p. 14;
Weigel's "Anfänge der Drucker Kunst," and Sale Catalogue, Nos.
303-307.

In recent years cards have been prepared in such way that blind
persons might play with them. The marks or pips are slightly
raised, so that touch can distinguish them.

ORIENTAL CARDS. — Between the statement of the Brahmin of
Southern India who, in presenting Captain Smith, in 1816, with a
pack of cards, assured him that it was a thousand years old, and had
been handed down in his family from time immemorial, and that of
M. Merlin, 1869, that " not any historic document, monument, nor
quotation from Eastern writers can be adduced in support of the
theory that cards had either an Arabian or Indian origin" (p. 57) ;
" an attentive study of the various theories of the Oriental origin
of cards will very soon show that they have nearly all been the results of imagination, and that the conjectures on which they have
been based cannot bear serious examination,"—there is ample opportunity for arriving at conclusions of less assured and positive a
character. An attempt to do so here, however, would be a task
beyond both the purpose and limits of this essay. Further, as the
question of the Eastern origin of cards has been touched upon
already, a few remarks on the general characters of Oriental cards
as we know them at present is all that is required.

Cards of India and Persia.—The cards of India are of two kinds ;
viz., those made and used by the Hindus themselves, and those
made and used by the Persian and Muhamedan sects of India, who,
less severe in their observance of the precepts of the Koran than
others of their religion, have recourse to them for amusement. To
these may be added the cards of the Persians of Teheran.

The cards of India, whether having Persian relations or not, are
generally circular in form, while those of Teheran are of the
European shape. The circular cards are about $2\frac{1}{2}$ inches in diameter, and the figures and marks on them are executed purely by
hand. The material of which they have been composed has been
found to be canvas, card, and thick paper, and " in Malacca they
are more cheaply supplied by leaves of the cocoa-nut or palm
tree, dried, and their distinctive characters traced with an iron
style." (Chatto, p. 55.)

The Hindu canvas and paper cards are covered front and back
with a ground of paint, afterwards highly varnished or lacquered.
The Persian cards have on them designs and paintings much ex-
ceeding in merit those on the Hindu pieces. Singer describes and
gives representations of some beautiful Persian cards, painted with

much delicacy on ivory, and as highly illuminated with gold as the miniatures in missals and manuscripts.

The following objects have been met with as marks of suits in Hindu cards, viz.: the ten avatars or incarnations of Vishnu, birds, with two figure-cards also in each suit, certain marks, some of which are of doubtful character, while others are swords (*tulwars*), suns, and money. These marks are painted on different-coloured grounds (red, green, yellow, &c.), which latter also indicate some kind of series or suit. Packs of eight suits, each suit containing two honours and ten common cards, and of ten suits of twelve pieces each suit, have been described.

Persian cards are recorded as having for suit marks crowns, full moons, sabres, slaves, harps, suns, letters (or firmans, or diplomas), and cushions, the pieces being ninety-six in number. Five cards from a Persian pack, very prettily painted on *carton vernis*, are given by Merlin (pl. 74, p. 124), on which are represented the *shah* (king), the *bibi* (queen), the *couli* (dancer), a lion (ace), and *serbas* (soldier). All these figures have been painted on different-coloured grounds, from which it is assumed that the colours form distinctive marks of five suits, and that the entire pack consisted of twenty-five pieces.

Though—as far as our knowledge extends—the true Hindu cards, like the typical Spanish and some other early European sets, do not admit a female, or queen, into the series, it is plain that the Teheran Persians permit of the admission.

Three kinds of games have been described by writers as of Hindu or Persian character. These games are named *Tchaturanga*, *Ghendgifeh*, and *Nâs*, or *Tas*, or *Taj*. Close inquiry has shown, however, that the first is more like European *tric-trac* or backgammon than a game with cards, and though there may be in it a mixture of chance and computation, the evolution of both is effected openly, and the nature of the combinations of hazard and calculation is as different as the objects with which they are associated. (See Merlin, p. 21.) The second, or *ghendgifeh*, which is of Persian origin, is played with a pack of ninety-six cards, *i.e.*, of eight series of twelve pieces, of the suits, crowns (*tas*), full moons, swords, slaves, &c. On reading an account of the details of this game, one is struck first by the circumstance that " the marks of the suits, as well as the rules of play, offer considerable analogy with those of the national game of the Spaniards, *Hombre*. Thus *dineros* (*oros*) is displaced by *moons* and *suns*, but the true character of the latter is recognisable not only by their forms, but likewise by their names, and which are (as already pointed out) simply abbreviations of words signifying in the language of the country, *gold money, silver money* (*zuri soorkh* and *zuri soofed*). *Swords* are equally apparent in the *shumsheer* or *sabres*." (Merlin, p. 15.)

Secondly, from the rules of the game, *ghendgifeh* " appears to bear some resemblance to that which the French call *L'Ombre à trois,* three-handed *Ombre.* In both games the suits appear to be considered as ranged into two divisions, in the Hindostanee game as the Red and the White, and in the European as the Red and the Black. In the Hindostanee game there are eight suits, and six or three players ; and when three play the cards are dealt by fours. In the European game of four suits and forty cards—the tens, nines, and eights being omitted—there are three players, and the cards are dealt by threes. A person who can play at *ombre* will scarcely fail to perceive several other points of similarity between the two games." (Chatto, p. 45.)

To return to M. Merlin :—" In noticing these singular analogies is it not reasonable to suppose that the Hindustani game has been borrowed from the Europeans ? This supposition has not escaped Mr. Chatto, but his conclusion is opposed to our own ; for, while allowing that the resemblances of the distinctive marks and rules observable between *ghendgifeh* and the European games might prove the importation of cards from Europe into India, while admitting that cards had been in use already in the West nearly a hundred years before the Portuguese conquered India, Mr. Chatto nevertheless persists in maintaining their Oriental origin ! And upon what does he rely ? On an imaginary genealogy of cards from chess, and on a pretended Indian tradition, of which not a trace can be found in ancient authors, as even Mr. Chatto himself allows." (p. 16.)

The third game, *As Nas,* is a Teheran one, and according to M. Querry, Secretary to the French Embassy in Persia, it has some analogy with the European game *Trente-et-un.*

Chinese Cards. — Strongly inclined as the Chinese are to gambling of every kind, it would have been surprising not to have found them provided with cards. Those which they employ are much smaller than the cards of Europe, being generally from 2 to $2\frac{1}{2}$ inches in length to $\frac{1}{2}$ an inch or 1 inch in breadth. Some are much narrower than this, while others are of a squarer form ; those represented by Breitkopf on plate 6 of his work, " Versuch den Ursprung der Spielkarten zu erforschen " (1784), being 2 inches long by $1\frac{2}{8}$ wide.

Chinese cards are made of thin cardboard, having the designs and marks printed in black ink on them. The marks of the suits are not easy to define, but chains, money, arms, and typographical characters are decipherable, as well as human busts and whole-length forms. At the upper portion of some cards, particularly those which are figure pieces, a margin is reserved, on which are other marks, and as if writing. The backs are sometimes coloured red, at other times they are black, and frequently quite plain.

Packs of thirty-six cards in nine suits, of thirty cards in three suits, and of thirty-two cards have been described.

The execution is sometimes very clear and distinct, at other times the work is rather heavy.

According to M. Vailsant, the Chinese have a drawing divided into compartments or series, based on combinations of the number 7.

" It so closely resembles the tarot, that the four suits of the latter occupy its first four columns; of the twenty-one *atouts* fourteen occupy the fifth column, and the seven other *atouts* the sixth column. This sixth column of seven *atouts* is that of the six days of the week of creation. Now according to the Chinese, this representation belongs to the first ages of their empire, to the drying up of the waters of the deluge by IAO; it may be concluded, therefore, that it is original, or a copy of the tarot, and under any circumstances that the latter is of an origin anterior to Moses, that it belongs to the beginning of our time, to the epoch of the preparation of the zodiac, and, consequently, that it must own 6,600 years of existence." (!) (" Les Romes, histoire vraie des vraies Bohémiens," Paris, 1857.)

Fancy domino cards have been recorded by Breitkopf, to whose work in particular reference should be made for representations of Chinese cards and games of various descriptions.

Japanese Cards have been stated not to differ in size, but only in marks, from the Chinese varieties.

" Those which I have seen," writes Blomhoff, " are marked with numerical figures, pictures of images, and arms coloured and ornamented with gold and silver; they have as well figured as numerical names, and are somewhat larger than the fourth part of an English card, the same shape, but a little thicker." (Singer, Appendix, p. 364.)

On the subject of Oriental cards generally, reference may be made as follows, with advantage:—Singer, Bibl. 8, pp. 16, 49, 59, 63, 364; Chatto, Bibl. 4, pp. 30-59; Merlin, Bibl. 6, pp. 13, 19, 24, 122.

Some beautiful representations of Hindu, Persian, and Chinese cards are therein given, together with references to the transactions of various learned societies which contain papers on the subject.

PART II.

DESCRIPTIVE CATALOGUE OF PLAYING

AND OTHER CARDS IN THE

BRITISH MUSEUM.

CLASSIFICATION.

THE following arrangement has been adopted in describing the various playing and other cards in the National Collection :—

DIVISION I.—EUROPEAN CARDS.

DIVISION II.—ORIENTAL CARDS.

Division I. includes—

The cards of					Italy.
,,	,,				Spain.
,,	,,				France.
,,	,,				Flanders.
,,	,,				Holland.
,,	,,				Germany.
,,	,,				England.
					(*Varia*).

Division II. includes—

The cards of					India.
,,	,,				Persia.
,,	,,				China.

The cards of each country are divided into *genera*, and described in the following order :—

Genus 1	. . . .	Tarots (pure and combined).
,, 2	. . . .	Numerals (pure).
,, 3	. . . .	Cards with a secondary purpose.
,, 4	. . . .	Cards purely fanciful.

German Numerals are subdivided into—

Cards having national marks of suits.
Cards having animated marks of suits.

Cards with a secondary purpose are arranged as—

        1. Educational, Instructive Cards.
        2. Biographic, Historical.
        3. Politico-Historical.
        4. Satirical.
        5. Divinatory, Astrologic (occult sciences).
        6. Amusing, Humorous.

Under the head *Miscellanea,* various prints, broadsides, advertisements, &c., are referred to, which did not well admit of arrangement elsewhere.

EUROPEAN PLAYING-CARDS.

ITALIAN PLAYING CARDS.

TAROTS.

I. 1.

THIRD QUARTER OF FIFTEENTH CENTURY?
FLORENCE? VENICE?

QUARTO volume containing a series of fifty early Italian engravings, known by the various names of the *Giuoco di Tarocchi di Mantegna, Carte di Baldini, Italian Tarocchi Cards, Ancient Venetian Tarots,* &c.

The sequence of prints to be passed immediately under review is of important and interesting character. Its members are not only among the more ancient examples of the early art of engraving in Italy, but may be considered with much probability direct descendants—as far as their subjects and designs are concerned—from the original source from which the primitive *Naïbis,* tarots, or immediate forerunners of our playing-cards, were derived. They have been long a subject for animated discussion, whether as regards their place and date of production, their author, or their original purport, and their acquisition has continued to be a cherished object of the iconophilist who can afford the means for procuring them. They are of rarity under any conditions, and as a complete series very scarce indeed, but as an uniform and intact sequence in the state in which they were originally published, probably not more than three examples are known; one of these, M. Galichon's copy, was recently (1875), sold by auction, at Paris, for 17,000 francs, or £680, *plus* commissions and duty. This same set realised at the Seratti sale in 1816, £43; and at the auction of Sir M. M. Sykes in 1824, £78 5s. M. Galichon gave for it in 1860 ten thousand francs. It is once more in England, and a choice impression indeed it is.

Detailed descriptions of each engraving of the series, accompanied by more or less critical discussion, may be found under the following heads:—

Bartsch, vol. xiii. pages 120-138.

Ottley's "Inquiry," vol. i. page 379, and "Notices of Engravers," vol. i. art. Baccio Baldini.

Cumberland, "Ancient Engravers of Italian School," pages 51-74.

Passavant, vol. v. page 119.

"Künstler-Lexicon," Meyer's Edition, 1875, vol. ii. page 589.

Merlin, Bibl. 6, page 34.

An accurate copy of the entire sequence of prints is given in the " Jeux de Cartes Tarots et de Cartes Numerales," published by the Société des Bibliophiles Français, in 1844. Copies of one or two pieces may be seen in the treatises of Cicognara and Singer, and reduced representations may be found in the work of M. Merlin.

The series consists of fifty pieces of full-length emblematic figures with their symbols, divided into five sets or suits. Each set contains ten pieces, and has one of the letters A B C D E common to it marked in Roman capitals at the lower left-hand corner of each member of the suit. A continuous numeration runs through the entire sequence from 1 to 50, the numbers being marked at the lower right-hand corner of each piece in Arabic numerals, and also in Roman numbers after the title of the subject, which is engraved at the centre of the lower margin in the Venetian dialect in Roman capitals.

Number 1 commences with the set the diagnostic of which is the letter E; number 11 begins the set D; number 21, C; number 31, B; and number 41 the set A.

The figures represented in the first series, or E, or that commencing with number 1, illustrate various conditions of life, from the beggar and servant to the Emperor and Pope. Those of D (11), portray the Muses and the Arts; of C (21), the Sciences; of B (31), the Virtues; while the members of set A (41) symbolise the Planets, or system of the world. Thus:—

E.	D.	C.
1. Misero.	11. Caliope.	21. Grammatica.
2. Fameio.	12. Urania.	22. Loica.
3. Artixan.	13. Terpsicore.	23. Rhetorica.
4. Merchadante.	14. Erato.	24. Geometria.
5. Zintilomo.	15. Polimnia.	25. Aritmetricha.
6. Chavalier.	16. Talia.	26. Musicha.
7. Doxe.	17. Melpomene.	27. Poesia.
8. Re.	18. Euterpe.	28. Philosofia.
9. Imperator.	19. Clio.	29. Astrologia.
10. Papa.	20. Apollo.	30. Theologia.

B.	A.
31. Iliaco.	41. Luna.
32. Chronico.	42. Mercurio.
33. Cosmico.	43. Venus.
34. Temperancia.	44. Sol.
35. Prudencia.	45. Marte.
36. Forteza.	46. Jupiter.
37. Justicia.	47. Saturno.
38. Charita.	48. Octava Spera.
39. Speranza.	49. Primo Mobile.
40. Fede.	50. Prima Causa.

The emblematic figure " Astrologia " has been numbered in the original by mistake 39 instead of 29.

The pieces vary slightly in size; each is about $7\frac{1}{8}$ inches high by 4 inches in breadth, *i. e.* from the outermost engraved lines. All have good margins in the British Museum example; some pieces, as Euterpe, 18, and Saturno, 47, have margins $\frac{5}{8}$ of an inch wide. To " Zintilomo " (No. 5 E) some gold has been applied on the collars and borders of the draperies, as likewise to the breast of the hawk and the hair of the gentleman.

The technic or manner in which the engraving has been executed is similar in style and equal in merit throughout, while the design and drawing vary in artistic power and taste. The engraving generally may be. described as careful, formal, and dry, the outlines heavier in character than the rest, and of uniform thickness. The shadows are rendered always by means of short strokes, rarely crossing each other or interlaced more than once, the one set of lines being generally horizontal in direction, the other set being oblique, and frequently arrested rather abruptly at the edges of the light parts. The incisions of the burin within the contours are everywhere delicate, and, as observed by Delaborde, "a fleur de peau," the metal being rather scratched, or as one might say, caressed, than incised. The whole design is enclosed within a spirally banded or woven border like that which usually surrounds the Etruscan scarabeus, and having the marks of the holes at the four corners by which the early engravers fixed their plates to a table or board, to prevent their moving when ploughed by the graver. The borders at the upper corners are connected by a four-leaved flower or rosette.

The earlier impressions have been worked off with ink of a bluish or grey tint, which gives a very characteristic appearance to these primitive efforts of the engraver's art. While being printed, the plates were not so carefully wiped or cleaned as was afterwards done, and thus a smear of ink was left upon their surfaces, imparting to the paper a faint bluish *fond sale* which *conoscenti* may at once remark.

Opinions have differed as to whether the earlier proofs were taken off by means of the cylinder or by the hand press. Some persons have seen, as they believe, the marks left by the damp linen layer impressed by the roller, while others have looked in vain for any such *vestigia*, but have easily observed the marks of the plate edges to have been impressed with such strength and distinctness as at once to certify to the use of a press.

The taste and style of some of the designs, as the Fameio, 2 ; Merchadante, 4; Chavalier, 6 ; Doxe, 7 ; Clio, 19 ; Rhetorica, 23 ; Astrologia, 29 (39) ; and Primo mobile, 49, in particular are worthy of much praise ; on the other hand, Caliope, 11, Talia, 16, and Euterpe, 18, are much inferior. Several of the Muse series, D, are the least to be commended of the whole sequence.

According to Kolloff, the impressions in the Paris Cabinet have been delicately gilt with a brush on the hair, wings, weapons, trees, buildings, and symbolic attributes : " a practice adopted only on impressions taken from plates which had already suffered from use." As before observed, the Zintilomo, 5, of the British Museum copy has had gold applied to portions of the drapery and of the hawk ; this piece is one of the faintest impressions in the series, and thus confirms Kolloff's statement. The latter applies in its general bearing, we presume, to the series possessed by the "Bibliothèque" previous to the obtainment of the fine example belonging to M. Gatteaux de l'Institut, and which " *avait une valeur dix fois plus grande*" than the former. (See " Notice Historique suivie d'un Catalogue des Estampes, &c.," par Le Vicomte Henri Delaborde, Paris, 1875, page 165.)

The sequence now before us appears to be composed of impressions in three different states. First, of very early proofs of bluish grey tone, and from the plates before they were either worn or retouched. Secondly, of impressions from the plates when " wear and tear" betrayed themselves, but the metal was as yet untouched. Thirdly, of impressions of a brownish hue, and after the plates had been more or less retouched. Dr. Waagen states that a late Keeper of the prints, Mr. Carpenter, informed him that, judging from other impressions he had seen, the Museum copy of these early Italian engravings should be regarded as only from retouched plates. If this was intended to apply to all the pieces, an examination of the following ones will show, we believe, that the judgment was much too sweeping, viz.:—Misero, E 1; Fameio, E 2; Zintilomo, E 5; Doxe, E 7; Clio, D 19; Rhetorica, C 23; Musicha, C 26; Theologia, C 30; Cosmico, B 33; Luna, A 41; Mercurio, A 42; Venus, A 43; Sol, A 44; Primo mobile, A 49; Prima causa, A 50.

A careful comparison of the Museum specimens with the fine examples which had belonged to M. Galichon did not authorise the conclusion that more than the following pieces were clearly from plates which had been more or less retouched, viz.: Caliope, D 11; Urania, D 12; Erato, D 14; Talia, D 16; Loica, C 22; Geometria, C 24. On the other hand, of the pieces—Clio, D 19; Grammatica, C 21; Rhetorica, C 23; Aritmetricha, C 25; Philosofia, C 28; Cosmico, B 33; Temperancia, B 34; Forteza, B 36; Justicia, B 37; Charita, B 38; Fede, B 40; Octava spera, A 48; and Primo mobile, A 49, some were fully equal to the Galichon impressions, while others very closely approached them in excellence.

It may have been observed that in the preceding remarks certain points have been assumed, for the purposes of general description, which claim to be supported by some show of argument or proof. It may be asked, for instance, to what school of art do these engravings belong, at what period were they executed, and by whom and what was their purport?

In reply to the question—to what school of art do they belong?—it may be said, to the Italian school unquestionably. Not only do the general style and feeling of these engravings at once indicate their birthplace, but certain intentions which pervade them evince a like fact. These latter, as M. Merlin points out (p. 80), reveal the Catholic and Italian ideas of the fourteenth century. The Pope has supremacy over the Emperor, the latter is represented with the attributes of the Empire of the West. The crown of the king is an Italian crown, and the valet, the merchant, the knight, and the gentleman are in Italian costumes. Further, the arts and sciences are arranged in the order of a *trivium* and *quadrivium;* the three theological and four cardinal virtues, Apollo and the Muses, are accompanied by the attributes allotted them in the West during the Middle Ages, and not by those with which they are associated on the monuments of Greece.

As to the particular school of Italy from which these designs and engravings have proceeded, it may be stated that Florence, Venice, and Padua have each had their supporters. From the circumstances that several of the inscriptions are in the Venetian dialect, and that the Venetians are known to have early employed certain emblematic playing-cards, held by some to have sprung from these particular engravings, their birthplace has been assigned to the once luxurious city of the Adriatic. Some authorities, considering them to be the *vechissime carte padovana*, alluded to in " *Le carte parlante* " of Pietro Aretino, have given them to Padua. The weight of authority, however, is in favour of their being of Florentine origin, as based on their general style and feeling. It is not an unfair supposition that the original designs were Florentine, while the series as we now have it was engraved by a Venetian, or by a Florentine with particular adaptations to the Venetian market. Those critics who have looked on these prints as coming from the school of Padua, have usually associated with them the names of Andrea Mantegna and Marco Zoppo, while such as have favoured Florence have considered them as the conjoint productions of Botticelli and Baldini, though the name of Finiguerra has not been without an advocate.

If doubt prevails as to their author, is there more surety as respects the date of their production? All that we are fairly warranted in maintaining is that it was previous to 1485, since in another, and to all appearance later version or edition of the series than the present one, this date is borne on the tablet which the figure of Arithmetic (C 25), holds in her hand (see I. 2.). Taking into consideration the style of design and manner of technic, with their evident assimilation to the period and schools of Botticelli and Baldini, the time allotted to these early Italian prints by Duchesne, viz., *circa* 1470, may be regarded as closely approximate. Kolloff gives them a somewhat later origin, contending that :—

" The engraver must have continued working several years, allowing probably impressions from single plates, or of the various decennary series to
appear before he published them collectively." . . . . " As regards their technic
these pieces have close relationship to the ' Prophets and Sybils,' and the ornamental work of the goldsmiths ; we see the same cold monotone shadows formed
of delicate layers crossed by finer lines in several places, but the line has at the
same time more sharpness and sureness of intention, is more docile and amenable
to the drawing, if not of more aims and of greater variety.   These excellences
are so marked in some pieces, particularly in the angel of the Primo mobile,
that they at once attain the perfected art of the Renaissance period.   These
admirable engravings, therefore, had an origin later than that of the Prophets
and the decorative work of the goldsmiths, an origin somewhere about 1490-
1495." . . . . " The highly graceful and elegant, though occasionally mannered,
but always attractive figures, the character of the beautiful female faces and the
noble heads of the men, the preference for profile, the great delicacy of the
drawing of the hands and feet, the tasteful cast of the draperies, are undoubted
characteristics of Florentine art . . . . nevertheless, inequalities may be
discerned in the composition and drawing which show that the designs for the
engraver proceeded from various hands."   Kolloff in Meyer's " Lexikon," vol. ii.
p. 590.)
    M. Le Vicomte H. Delaborde, in his article on *La Gravure Florentine au XV.
Siecle* (" Gaz. des Beaux-Arts," 1873, vol. vii. p. 99), advocates strongly the
Florentine origin of the prints under notice :—
    " If it be allowable to say that the figures composing the sequence called the
Tarocchi were *designed* by various artists, it is not the less certain that these
productions may be attributed to a single engraver.   There is not any inequality
of merit in the work, nor any difference in the modes of procedure, whether in
defining the contours or indicating the shadows, and the calm serenity with which
it is carried on does not belie itself, even where an energy of technic would
appear to have been natural to the expression, and where the types to be reproduced were those of Saturn, Jupiter, or Mars.   Thus are we led to the conclusion
that the engravings of the *Tarocchi* are not the result of a collective undertaking,
and that he who produced them trusted to his own resources alone to consum-
mate his purpose.   But it is probable we shall not discover anything beyond this,
and must be content to remain ignorant of the name of the engraver, though we
may recognise him elsewhere, and be convinced of his talent and fecundity.
Writers and iconophilists may choose—and most unfortunately in our own
opinion—the names of Finiguerra and Mantegna alternately, or less imprudently
the name of Baccio Baldini.   The Florentine source being once established, we
are satisfied with admiring in themselves these precious examples of primitive
engraving, and refuse to sacrifice to the regret of an absent signature, or to an
obscure inquiry, that which is exacted from us by the picturesque beauty and
unhesitating tokens of ability everywhere present." (*Op. cit.* p. 100.)
    A not less interesting question than any yet replied to is—What was the
general motive in this sequence of emblematic figures, and to what purpose was
it applied ?
    Two chief views have been held.   According to one theory, these symbolic
designs were intended to serve simply as a source of instruction in various ways.
Certain philosophic doctrines and precepts of morality have been supposed to
have been therein illustrated, and likewise the occult sciences of the Middle Ages
to have been therein veiled.
    If each series of the general sequence be closely examined it may be perceived
that the highest or most important subject has the last number—50, and the
least or most subordinate the first number—1.   Thus, *e. g.* the Pope, the highest
dignitary of the Christian world, has the last number—10, of the series E.   Apollo,
chief of the Muses, has the last number— 20, of the series D ; the most important

branch of knowledge, Theology, has the last number—40, of B, and finally, the First Cause, the lowest number of the series—A 50, the terminal of the entire sequence. On the other hand, the order according to which the letters distinguishing the series are placed appears to say—if we begin with the First Cause—" Before all things, think of God who made the world—series A ; next practise the Virtues—series B ; then cultivate knowledge—series C ; seek the Muses, D, and lay stress on the various fortunes of life, last of all—series E."

M. E. Galichon preferred regarding the entire sequence as representing the " Encyclopædic System of Dante, or as being an astrological speculation, striving to assimilate the phases of celestial revolutions to those of terrestrial life ; as constituting a book, in fact, in which the burin of the engraver displaces the pen of the writer, while recounting in five chants, the rewards which await an upright and industrious man."

Lastly, the mystic secrets of the Hebrew Kabbalah have been held by some to have been concealed in certain of the original designs, unfortunately afterwards modified and added to in number, while to others the philosophy of India and the secrets of the Egyptian mysteries lay in them, but hidden, save to the eyes of the *illuminati*, and to the questionings of an unhesitating faith. (*Postea*, " Cards of Divination.")

Under the second head may be classed those theories which involve in the character and purport of these emblematic figures some kind of amusing game. The difficulty of pointing out the exact nature of the game which could be played with such pieces (or cards) as bore on them the symbols of Logic, Rhetoric, Theology, Primo mobile, Prima causa, &c.. has given rise to various conjectures. Some persons, like those who recognise in these emblems the mystic learning of the East, have supposed the sequence to have been used—as the gypsies and others use modern cards—for the purposes of divination and fortune-telling, falling back for support on " Le Sorti di Francesco Marcolini," and Fanti's " Triompho di Fortuna" (A.D. 1526), (Singer, Bibl. 8, pp. 64-66), the latter furnished with the Papal " Privilegium," and dedicated to Pope Clement VII., as proving that analogous emblematic figures were then employed for these purposes.

Other archæologists have regarded the sequence as forming what is now known as a tarots game of cards, or at least some adumbration or modification of it. This school points out that a like general economy pervades the admitted tarots games, and the sequence of the Mantegna *tarocchi.* The latter, *e. g.* is composed of five series, and five divisions go to form a tarots game. Each series of the one is made up of ten pieces, and in the other four series are composed of ten likewise, whose " points " proceed from one to ten. Further, the decades of the *tarocchi of Mantegna* are distinguished by the letters A B C D E, while the five series of more recent tarots are differentiated by objects, the initials of the names of which are the letters A B C D E—*atutti, bastoni, coppe, danari, espada* (*spade,* Ital.). It is true that in the Italian names for the tarots series the E does not occur, since the proper word begins with S, but the Spanish word may have been common at Venice formerly, and thus we find E (*Espada* for *spade,* Ital.) in the early pieces, and it is not the less noteworthy that in the second edition or later version of 1485 the E has been displaced from the last series, and S substituted, as though the engraver, aware of the previous mistake or inconsistency, sought to remedy the error. This view of the matter has been opposed by high authorities. They dwell upon the fact that these early Italian pieces do not bear any of the characteristic marks of suits, even were it to be admitted—which it should not be—that the interpretation of the letters of the several decades above given were in the least satisfactory.

Secondly, the number of the pieces of the sequence—fifty—does not coincide with any combinations involved in the old and true Venetian tarots game of seventy-eight cards.

Thirdly, that in the only two or three truly perfect or originally uniform sets known, the prints are bound together apparently as they were at first, and have large margins, and not any impressions have been met with as yet, printed on paper strong enough to resist the wear and tear of play. Lastly, their size is too great for cards, and they are uncoloured.

To these objections it has been replied that it was not intended to maintain these emblematic engravings were used loose, and were wont to be shuffled like the cards of an after age. On the contrary, they formed originally a sort of book or album, which might be employed by youth and moral persons, but to which, afterwards on other occasions, "suit" members were added, so that they could be used in a game of pure amusement and hazard. Further, their size is not greater than that of the German painted cards of the Stuttgart collection, nor— in height at least—than that of the numerals of the Musée Correr at Venice. Colouring is not essential to a sequence of playing-cards, for several sets of four suits each, evidently intended for play without having been coloured, were delicately engraved on copper before the end of the fifteenth century.

It can be shown in addition that above one-half of the *atouts* of the comparatively modern games of chance called tarots have been borrowed from the figures of the present sequence. Take the tarots (combined) of Besançon, Marseilles, and Geneva, which represent pretty faithfully the older Venetian games, and it may be seen that out of twenty-six figures, fifteen have been borrowed, even to minute details, from the early Italian engravings. Of the cards of the Florentine tarots game, *minchiate*, which are in number ninety-seven (forty being true tarots), having twenty more *atouts* than the Venetian game, it may be seen that the additions have been borrowed really from the same source. Lastly, the general principle of the tarots game appears to have been taken from it likewise. The *atouts*, *e. g.* which have more value in the *jeux de tarots*, are such as have the higher numbers, and these latter belong to such pieces as correspond exactly with the higher numbers of the ancient sequence, and which are included in the numbers 41-50.

We may say—speaking generally—that the relationship of the so-called *tarocchi of Mantegna* to more recent playing-cards, through the medium of the older tarots, has been placed in a clearer light, and has been better defined since 1869 by M. Merlin, the juror who prepared the report on the playing-cards sent to the Parisian Exposition of 1855. According to this authority, long before the production of the fifty early Italian emblematic pieces as a combined series of engravings, and even anterior to the invention at Venice of games of hazard with cards, there existed in Italy a series of pictorial representations called *Naïbis*, which were employed for the purposes both of instruction and simple amusement. The "Chronicle" of Morelli, A.D. 1393, and Decembrio's "History of the Life of Philip Visconti, Duke of Milan," who was born in 1391, afford evidence of this, and also lead to the belief that the subjects of these pictorial representations were the same as those of the *tarocchi of Mantegna*. In other words, it may be implied that the engraver—whoever he was—of the latter copied the devices of the former, just as the authors of the succeeding tarots have copied the emblematic figures of the first engraved sequence.

From this latter circumstance, indeed, the early Italian engravings received the names of tarots and tarocchi, names which there is not any reason to believe belonged to them at first. These early prints, thus derived from the *Naïbis*, cannot, therefore, be regarded as original conceptions of the times at which they were produced, but must be considered as based, at least, on a common type certainly existing a century before. The truth of this is shown, according to M. Merlin, in the critical analysis of a MS. of the early part of the fifteenth century, undertaken by M. Douet d'Arcy, in the "Revue Archéologique" for 1858. This MS. contains, *inter alia*, a treatise on *blazon*—the earliest known. The latter is composed of two portions, one portion consisting of twelve chapters of elementary instruction on the art, and the other being a sort of *petit armorial*, in combination with some rules on heraldic procedures.   The latter section of the *armorial* is as follows :

"Sensuyvent les ditz et armes de ix femmes dictes et appellées Muses.[1]

"Caliope la premiere, porte de synople, une trompette d'argent en bende Son dit : jusques aux nues.

"Uranyes, iie porte de sable, ung cerne dargent ung compas de masson de mesmes Son dit : la non pareille.

"Terpsicore iij[e] porte dargent, ung leut de pourpre Son dit : Seule y suis.

"Erato iiij[e] porte dor, une meule de molin de sable [c'est un tambour de basque] Son dit : jatens l'heure.

"Polymnya v[e] porte dazur, unes orgues d'argent Son dit : moy mesmes.

"Talia vi[e] porte de gueules, une vielle dor Son dit ; a mon devoir.

"Melpomène viie porte de pourpre ung cornet dor Son dit : jamais lasse.

"Euterpe vij[e] porte dargent, une doulcene de sable Son dit : tant mest doulx.

"Clio ixe de sable ung signe dargent Son dit : a la mort chante.

"Sensuyvent les vij ars.

"*Grammaire, la premiere.*—Une vieille ridée, beguinée, esmantelée, porte de pourpre, une lime d'argent, ung pot de mesmes.

"*Logica ii*[e]. Une femme jeune, les cheveux crespés, les bras tout nudz hault recoursez d'une chemise jusques aux piedz, es mammelles et au nombril troussée ——porte de gueules, une serpent volant d'or envelopée d'ung drap d'argent.

"*Rethorica iii*[e]. Une jeune dame, d'ung heaulme et une coronne par dessus sa teste, ung manteau et une riche cotte vestue, en la main dextre tenant une espée—porte de synople, deux enfants nudz d'argent soufflant deux trompettes de mesmes.

"*Geometria iiii*[e]. Une jeune dame issant d'une nue, tenant en sa main une esquarre [une equerre] pour compasser et mesurer pierres—porte d'argent, une nue d'asur.

"*Arismetica v*[e]. Une femme ancienne, de crevechiefs sa teste affublée, d'une robe longue abillée jusques aux piedz, contant argent—porte de sable, six besans d'argent.

"*Musica vi*[e]. Une jeune dame en cheveux, bien adornée, d'une fine chemise vestue les bras tous nudz, assise sur un signe, les jambes entrellées et nudz piedz, unes orgues, ung lehut et plusieurs autres instrumens emprès elle, ung flaiol— porte de synople, deux flaiolz d'argent.

"*Philosophia vii*[e]. Une jeune dame les cheveux pendens, d'ung corset de guerre a escailles, armée d'ung targon, au milieu ung visaige insculpé, tenant en la main senestre, en l'aultre main ung dart ferré et empané—porte de gueles de dars d'argent de mesure.

"Une jeune dame[2] les cheveux pendens, ung chappelet de fleurs par dessus, touchant de la main dextre ung flaiol, de l'aultre main espenchant a ung pot de terre de l'eau qui sourdait d'une fontaine, et en ses piedz le firmament—porte d'assur le firmament d'argent."

It will be at once apparent that in the foregoing descriptions are delineated the emblematic figures of the Muses, Arts, and Poetry, exactly as they are represented in the pieces of the sequence of Mantegna.   If it be a correct opinion

---

[1] "The nine Muses form the subject of the second decade of Mantegna, the seven arts are included in the sciences and arts, the third decade of the same sequence.   The perfect identity may be at once recognised.   The colours and mottoes only are wanting."   (Note by M. Merlin, *op. cit.* p. 48.)

[2] The name of the person is wanting, but on comparing the description with the engraving it will be found that it is—*Poetry.*

that the MS. in question is as early as the first quarter of the fifteenth century, the Italian designs are brought on a level, *quoad* time, with those alluded to by Decembrio as having composed one of the favourite amusements of the young Duke of Milan, born in 1391, an amusement *qui ex imaginibus depictis fit.*

About the end of the fifteenth century some inventive genius, probably Venetian, selecting a certain number—twenty-two—of the original emblematic *Naïbis* (now converted into *atutti, atouts,* or tarots), added to them a series of numeral cards by which the excitement of chance and interest of gain might be added to the instruction, or more innocent amusement, the emblematic series was intended to afford. This modified game, though adopted pretty generally, nevertheless soon underwent a further and most important change. This was the elimination of the whole of the emblematic (*atutti,* tarots) series, leaving the numeral cards alone to play with (*antea,* "General History," p. 23). Some countries, however, still retained an emblematic series in combination with the numeral cards for certain games, though adopting, at the same time, packs of cards made up of numerals only. To this day, even, packs of cards of the true old tarots character may be purchased in Italy and the south of France, and are not unknown in Germany. It is, therefore, through these tarots cards, whether ancient or modern, *i. e.,* the emblematic series conjoined with numerals, that the connection between the *tarocchi of Mantegna* and playing-cards should be sought. Traced as above indicated, the connection is quite apparent, and thus there is not either mistake or exaggeration in regarding the original *Naïbis* transmitted to us through the early Italian engravings before us, as the source from which playing-cards may be said to have sprung, the engravings in question simply representing that series of earlier hand-painted devices from which the old tarots' games of Venice and Florence made a selection for their *atutti* series.

[7 in. × 4 in.]   [Backs plain.]

I. 2.

LAST QUARTER OF FIFTEENTH CENTURY.

FLORENCE? VENICE?

 QUARTO volume of like character to the preceding one (I. 1.), containing forty-five early Italian engravings, known as the *Giuoco di Tarocchi di Mantegna,* ancient Venetian tarots, &c.

The pieces herein contained constitute a second edition or version with numerous variations of the sequence before described. The following pieces are wanting: Misero, 1 ; Fameio, 2 ; Imperator, 9 ; Primo mobile, 49 ; Prima causa, 50. On the tablet held by the emblematic figure C Aritmetricha, xxv.—25, are these figures in the following arrangement :—

```
.1.2.34.5.6*
.7.8.9.10
J 4 ° 8 . 5
```

Duchesne, Passavant, Merlin, and other writers, have considered the lowest row of numerals to imply the date 1485, and the period when the engraving was executed.   Kolloff ridicules this opinion as " an highly wonderful conjecture." . . " The counting-slate is intended to represent a so-called magic quadrature, *i. e.*, a table with numbers so placed, that in whatever direction they may be added up, the resulting amount or sum shall be the same.   Albert Dürer also has represented arithmetic by such a table in his famous piece of the ' Melancholy.' Here the numbers run from one to sixteen, and the sum is forty-four [*sic*] [34]. The Italian engraver was not aware evidently of what he had to represent." (Meyer's " Künstler-Lexicon," p. 594, vol. ii.)

Bartsch looked on the present series as the earlier or original set of the *Cartes de Tarots*, (vol. xiii. p. 120,) and considered the one before described as the second edition or copy of the present sequence.

In connection with this point two questions present themselves for consideration; there is that of priority of production, and that of actual transcription.   The present series may have been, and we believe was, engraved after the preceding one [I. 1.]; but if so it need not have been directly copied from the latter.   The opinion long since broached by Ottley, " that many of the pieces of the one series are rather the repetitions of the same subjects engraved with variations in the designs of the figures than what may be properly called copies," has since been more fully stated by Merlin, who maintains that neither series is a direct copy from the other, but that both have been based on another and more primitive example.   Before referring to the particular marks on which this judgment is founded, it may be well to notice those circumstances in which these two versions or editions differ from each other.

In the first place, the pieces of the present sequence are somewhat smaller in size than are the others.   The initial letter S supplants the letter E of the decade containing the emblematic figures of the various stations of life; the inscriptions and numbers are of heavier, coarser, and apparently of later form, the points or dots before and after them are here absent, and the marks of the nail holes at the corners are wanting.

Secondly, the majority of the figures, which are turned or advance towards the left of the spectator in the former version (I. 1.), are here (I. 2.) turned towards the right, but though thus reversed in direction, the actions are duly performed with the right hand.

Thirdly, though the figures represent like subjects, several of them are of different designs, and are accompanied by symbolic accessories of different character.

Fourthly, there is much disparity between the technical merits of the two sets, the present version being inferior in all respects to the one already described. The expression of the heads is quite changed, the drawing is inferior, and the engraved work is of a harder, stiffer, and inferior kind.   In one instance, however, the author of the second version has improved on the earlier issue, viz., in the drapery of *Temperancia* xxxiiii., which in the present series is superior on the whole to the heavier forms in the figure of the version of 1470.

M. H. Delaborde observes : —

" It is quite certain that one of the two series, that in which the first ten pages bear the letter E in lieu of an S inscribed in like places in the second, has far higher merit as regards drawing and style.   Is not this sufficient to decide the question of priority in its favour, or at least to render it thus highly presumptive ? If, in fact, it be supposed with Bartsch that the inferior one of the two versions is the older one, we shall be forced to admit that, by a singular exception, the first engraver of the *tarocchi* did not know how to profit either from the examples or progress which had occurred during several years.   Further, how could the mediocrity of his work have awakened the spirit of imitation ?   How, at a time and in a country which were cognisant of the *nielli* of a Finiguerra, and the prints of Botticelli, could the desire have arisen to plagiarise pieces which could be made to undergo comparison so easily, and could be so satisfactorily judged ?

At any rate it is at least rare that a copy is better than the original work." (" Gazette des Beaux-Arts," 1873, vol. vii. p. 101.)

Reference may be made now to the data on which Merlin confides, as proving that neither of the editions in question was copied one from the other. This writer proceeds to say, " the comparison which we have made of the first two editions does not allow of our admitting, as is generally done, that one is a copy of the other. The notable differences which may be observed between certain subjects, do not indicate the work of two different burins simply, they reveal a liberty of drawing incompatible with the fetters of a copy. A like circumstance unquestionably happened in connection with these drawings as frequently occurred in respect to MSS., before printing arrived to fix the tests. A first or original model served as a *point de depart*, and the artists who reproduced it, though seizing fundamentals and numerous details, departed more or less from the primitive type, an occurrence attended with far less risk in the case of drawing, however, than as regarded texts.

" A further proof that the two engravers copied a different model is the fact that in the edition of 1485, the first decade of the figures bears as a distinctive mark of the series the letter S, while in the other edition the letter E distinguishes the like series. Now, this difference could not have been the result of chance nor of inadvertence on the part of the engraver, for had it been it would have appeared on two or three only of the subjects of the series, and not on the whole ten.

" Another and a conclusive argument is this : while in the version of 1470 nearly all the figures are turned towards the left of the spectator, in that of 1485 they are directed to the right, yet the care which has been taken by both engravers to preserve the pre-eminence of the right over the left hand in its proper offices, shows that neither of these editions was copied one from the other. Thus, when the person represented uses a weapon or any other object which he should hold in the right hand, it is in this hand that the object is found in both versions, though the figure has a contrary direction in each engraving, and the reversal of position has bestowed occasionally a work of some difficulty on the draughtsman. It may be added, likewise, that several figures, though representing similar subjects, are of quite different designs in the two editions, nor are the accessories always the same. We believe, then, that we are justified in regarding these two editions as perfectly independent one of the other, and as owing their resemblances to the primitive model only from which they originated. Nor is this model anterior to the engravings under consideration a chimera of our imagination, for we have already shown that the types followed by the engravers were common in the fifteenth century. As regards the question of priority of production relative to these two versions, we leave that to competent judges to decide ; it has been sufficient for our purpose to have demonstrated that the two engravers did not copy one from the other, but reproduced anterior or original designs, designs which could not be anything else than the *Naïbis* cited by Morelli in 1393, as objects for recreation fit to be used by children, and exempt from the chances of hazard." (Merlin, p. 78.)

The writer above quoted has the following note at page 79, in reference to the question of priority of production, which is worthy of extract.

" As a proof of the anteriority of the sequence which M. Duchesne supposes to be of the date 1470, that writer observes, that in this edition the figure of Arithmetic (25) reckons with counters, while in that of 1485 this same figure holds a tablet containing the signs of numeration known as Arabic numbers. He adds : ' It is quite certain that when numerals were written with Roman figures, reckoning could be performed with counters only ; the use of Arabic numbers being more recent, they could not be indicated by the engraver before the time at which their employment had become general.' Notwithstanding our high esteem for the learned iconophilist whom we have cited, it is impossible for us to adopt his conclusion. In the first place, the introduction of Indian figures, known under the name of Arabic numerals, was long anterior to 1470. Further, the Arithmetic, to which he alludes, does not reckon with counters, she counts money in her hand, as may be readily seen. M. Duchesne has not borne in mind that calculation with counters can be done only on a table and not in the hand, the value of the counters being subordinate to the respective places which they occupy on the table, and of which we retain the practice in marking games with counters."

On a fly-leaf of the volume containing the present version are the following remarks in MS. :—

" Query—if not *Ant da Brescia.*"   " Wanting Nos. 1, 2, 9, 49, 50."

" Duchesne states that of two sets he had seen, Nos. 1 and 50 were wanting and supplied by facsimile drawings."

In the Slade collection, forming part of the British Museum cabinet, there are two pieces of the earlier edition (1470), and one of the second (1485). The former pieces are the *Astrologia, xxxviiii*, altered to 38 in the restoration of the right-hand lower corner, and the *Octava spera, xxxxviii.—*48. The *Astrologia* is a remarkably fine and early impression, but the *Octava spera* is from a much-worn plate.

The piece from the second edition (1485), is a fine early impression of bluish-grey tint of *Sol, xxxxiiii.—*44.

Besides these *repliche* there are other two pieces of the second edition, viz., the S *Doxe, vii.—*7 and the C *Loica, xxii.—*22. These pieces are fine and early states of bluish-grey tone, but having their surfaces worn and rubbed and being cut down to the innermost lines of the borders. The inscriptions and numbers are thus wanting.

By measurement, these two pieces will be found to be slightly larger, particularly in length, than the engravings contained in the volume of the second edition, I. 2. This is due to the paper having been much damped to receive the impressions, and to the direction of the press or cylinder in motion having been that of the long axis of the plate. Careful comparison of these *repliche* with the other pieces in this volume will show that they are all from the same plates.

In volume I. 1., containing the first edition, may be found a copy of the A SATURNO, xxxxvij.—47 of that series.

This piece is comparatively of modern execution, and of inferior workmanship. We assume it to be one of the " Copie du Jeu des 50 Tarots, par Hans Ladenspelder d'Essen," alluded to by Passavant, vol. v. p. 127.

Passavant remarks :—" Although we have never met with an entire sequence, we have not any hesitation in believing that Ladenspelder engraved one. This copy was made from the original series [*i.e.* of 1470], and all the pieces have the same primitive border, a wound ribbon, the same inscriptions, the same numeration, and the distinctive letters from E to A. Some of the pieces have the mark of Ladenspelder, among others, Hope, Faith, the Sun, and Geometry, on which the monogram is inscribed on a tablet. The master of Essen has not imitated in the least the manner of the old engravers, but has used the burin in the style of the ' Little German masters,' with simple, very fine hatchings, and without much drawing power. The impression is not at all like that of the ancient cards—in pale ink—but in one of a decided black, though not heavily loaded" (p. 127).

Johann or Hans Ladenspelder von Essen, a well-known engraver of the Lower Rhine school, was born in 1511 ; the date of his death is unknown. (See Nagler, "Monogrammisten," vol. iii. n. 1520.)

I. 3.

(Prints of the early Italian School, vol. ii.)

LAST QUARTER OF FIFTEENTH CENTURY.
VENICE.

OUR cards of the numeral series of a tarots sequence, of which as yet but thirty-one pieces have been described.

One card is the *Cavallo di Danari.* It is represented by a thick-set man with a buckler on his left arm, and mounted on horseback. He gallops towards the left. Part of the horse's mouth, chest, and nearly the whole of the forelegs are cut across by the boundary line of the engraving. Below the foot of the horseman, and at the left is the mark of the suit—*Danari.* At the upper right-hand corner is the title, SARAFINO.

A second card is the *Fante di Danari.* A young man stands erect, inclined backwards towards the left of the piece, directing his actions towards the right. Though his back touches the left-hand marginal border of the engraving, his right foot advances so far as to be within three-eighths of an inch of the right border. He holds a bird in his left hand, and points to the ground with the index finger of the right hand. On a large perch, projecting from the right of the engraving, is a hawk, the cord affixed to which is wound loosely round the perch. Below and between the right-hand border of the piece and the valet's left leg is the mark of the suit—*Danari.* Not any title is present.

A third card is the *Cavallo di Spade.* It shows a young man on horseback, advancing towards the left, the right foreleg of the horse being cut across by the left marginal line of the engraving. The man holds with both hands a long drawn sword, as if about to strike some one on the ground. From his left side hangs the long sheath of the weapon. At the upper left-hand corner is the title AMONE.

The fourth piece is the *Dama di Bastoni.* A coroneted female is seated at the left hand in a throne-like chair. She raises her left hand, and is directed and looks towards the right. In her right hand she holds a baton-like sceptre, which she likewise supports by her right shoulder. At the upper right-hand corner is the title PALAS.

Of these designs the *Fante di Danari* is by far the best, and has some resemblance to the style of the Chavalier and Zintilomo in the previously described sequence, I. 1. The technic of these pieces has a strong affinity with that of many of the prints ascribed to Baldini. There is, however, a grotesqueness of design and want of proportion about some figures, and especially the horses, which do not say much for the artistic powers of their author.

These four engravings are very interesting in some respects. They appear to form a portion of the set mentioned by Zani at p. 72 of his "Materiali," by Cicognara, p. 162, and by Passavant, vol. v. p. 127.

The latter writer gives the following account of it under the title, "Venetian Tarot Cards of the year 1070, after the foundation of Venice":—

"The Count Cicognara in his memoirs on 'Nielli and Playing Cards,' alludes to a set of Venetian cards which Zani had met with at Naples dispersed in two collections, but of which a complete series (coloured), was preserved in the cabinet of the Marchioness Busca (born Duchess Serbelloni) at Milan, and some separate pieces in that of the Marquis Durazzo, at Genoa. Cicognara gives in his work, plates xii. and xiii., copies of seven of these cards, offering a fair idea of the manner in which they are engraved. He states afterwards that certain pieces of the series are numbered, while others bear the marks of the suits, swords, money, and cups. He adds further that on the piece of Bacchus, No. xiv., the following inscription may be read: ' *Col permesso del Senato Veneto nell' anno ab urbe condita MLXX.*'; which would assign the execution of these prints to the year 1491, if the date of the foundation of that city be taken as A.D. 421, and not 453, as is usually done.

"The design and composition of these cards is remarkable in this, that the actions of the figures and the play of the muscles have a certain exaggeration which so recalls the style of Pordenone, that in adopting the date 453 as that of the foundation of Venice, one would be tempted to refer their execution to 1523, if the details of costume—which latter is the end of the fifteenth century—did not fulfil better the conditions of the other hypothesis.

"Further, the comparatively poor design and somewhat coarse technical execution by means of oblique hatchings, correspond better with the work of the first epoch of Mantegna.

"We have seen twenty pieces of this series in the Albertine collection at Vienna, these came from the cabinet of Count Fries; three other pieces in the cabinet of the Baron de Haus, in the same city, eventually passing into the Imperial Library, and four others in the British Museum at London. Nevertheless, we could not maintain that all these cards belonged to one and the same edition, though they are of similar dimensions and treated in a like style, since some might be copies only, as would appear to be actually the case with respect to the two numbers 14 afterwards described, and which differ from each other.

"Although Cicognara saw at Naples and Milan two complete series of these cards, he gives but an incomplete account of their number, contours, figures, and design. We would observe only that if the figure of Panfilio be marked with the number 1, it may show that the pieces before us formed part of a *Giuoco del Fante di Spada*, in which, according to the Venetian custom, this card is the highest of all the pieces.

"As far as we can judge from the thirty-one cards known to us, there should be twenty numbered figures, while the other cards (king, queen, knight, and knave) bore the marks of the suits of *spade, coppe, danari*, and *bastoni*." (Pass., vol. v. pp. 127-129.)

[$5\frac{5}{8}$ × $2\frac{7}{8}$ in.]　　　　　　　　　　　　　　　　　　　[Backs plain.]

I. 4.

SECOND HALF OF SEVENTEENTH CENTURY ?

BOLOGNA.

 TAROTS[1] pack, representing the old Venetian tarots set of twenty-two *atutti*, combined with the full numerals, fifty-six in number, *i. e.* seventy-eight *in toto*. As here arranged, the true tarots series is the last series in the book. It begins with "Le Fol," unnumbered as usual, followed by "Le Bateleur," Number i., and terminating in the typical manner with "Le Monde," xxi. Each emblematic card follows

---

[1] The force and meaning of the words tarot and tarots are fully considered *antea*, p. 19, and under French "Cards of Divination," *postea*.

exactly the common old titles and sequences, as are given by Merlin, p. 32. Each of the tarots is numbered at the top in Roman numerals, and has the title below the design.

The numeral suits are of the marks always accompanying the old Italian combined tarots sets, viz. *coppe* (here *coupes*), *danari* (*deniers*), *bastoni* (*baston*), and *spade* (*spee*). Each suit has here of course an additional coate card or honour— the *chevalier*—in accordance with the rule of this typical series. Each numeral card has the number of its value marked in Roman characters at the sides. The coat-cards have their titles inscribed below the designs. On the two of *coupes*— here the first card in the arrangement—is the following inscription at the lower portion: Tarochi Fini Di Francesco Berti in Bologna.

On the two of *deniers* is inscribed "Carte Fine" within an ornamental scroll connecting the marks of the suit, while on the four of *deniers* is "Al Leone" on a tablet in the centre, on which is likewise a large bird pecking the ground.

The back of each card in all the series has a full-length figure of a man with a turban, and in Oriental dress. He holds by the tail a live bird in his left hand, and a dead bird, apparently, in his right. This figure, printed in black, is relieved from off a ground watered or clouded in rose-madder colour. Below it in a margin retained for the purpose is the address al leone.

The whole of the designs, which are from wood-blocks, are of the commonest and coarsest character. The colouring is in keeping with the rest.

This series of cards is noteworthy, as illustrating the following remarks of Taylor, Bibl. 9, ix. p. 229.

"With regard to the tarots, it is singular that so many of the packs, no matter where manufactured, bear French titles, some of them, as we have seen, of very barbarous orthography. A pack, however, in our own possession, inscribed on the deuce of cups, *Fabbricatore Gumppenberg*, and on the backs of the cards, which are *tarottés* in blue, '*in Milano*,' has the titles in Italian, corresponding with those of the French pack of 1500."

In the set under notice, the titles of all the *atutti* are in French, *e.g.* Le *Bateleur, La Imperatrice, Le Empereur, Le Ermite,* &c. The same is the case as respects the honours of the numeral series, as, *e.g. Valet de Spée, Reine de Spée, Roy de Spée*.

These cards are stiffly mounted, and like those of many Italian packs, have the paper of their backs turned over the edges of the front so as to form a border.

[$3\frac{7}{8}$ × $1\frac{7}{8}$ in.]   [Backs figured and coloured.]

I. 5.

SECOND QUARTER OF NINETEENTH CENTURY.

MILANO.

 PACK of seventy-eight cards, representing the old Venetian tarots, *i.e.* twenty-two *atutti* and fifty-six numerals. There are four honours in each suit, which latter are *coppe, danari, spade,* and *bastoni*.

The emblematic figures or true tarots are numbered at the tops in Roman numerals, and have the titles below the designs in the Italian language, viz.: 1. Il Bagattello; 2. La Papessa; 3. L'Imperatrice; 4. L'Imperatore; 5. Il Papa; 6. Gli Amanti; 7. I Carro; 8. La Giustizia; 9. L'Eremita; 10. Ruot. della For; 11. La Forza; 12. L'Appeso; 13. Without title (Death); 14. La Temperanza; 15. Il Diavolo; 16. La Torre; 17. Le Stelle; 18. La

Luna; 19. Il Sole; 20. Il Giudizio; 21. Il Mondo. Il Matto is without number.

The honours bear the titles: Re di Danari, Reg. di Danari, Caval di Dinari, Fan di Danari.

Re di Spade, Reg di Spade, Caval di Spade, Fante di Spade, Re di Bastoni, Reg di Bastoni, Cav. di Bastoni, Fan di Bastoni, Re di Coppe, Reg di Coppe, Caval di Coppe, Fante di Coppe.

On the *Re di Bastoni* is the address GIUS E FELICE ROSSI, and the government stamp, bearing the divided crown of Austria, beneath which is: F. 1. c. 70. Lombardia.

On the two of *coppe* may be read " NUOVA FAB DI MILANO," and on number iii. of the tarots series, " L'Imperatrice," " TAROCCO FINO."

The designs and execution of these cards are common and coarse. The backs are stamped in blue with a lace-work-like ornament, below which is inscribed E DI MILANO.

[$3\frac{6}{8} \times 1\frac{5}{8}$.]   [Backs decorated.]

I. 6.

SECOND QUARTER OF NINETEENTH CENTURY.

BOLOGNA ?

(TAROCCHINO.)

 MODERN pack of sixty-two cards, viz., twenty-two *atutti* and forty numerals, being a perfect set representing the game known as the old *Tarocchino of Bologna.*

This version of the tarots game is stated by Cicognara and others to have been invented in Bologna at the end of the fourteenth or beginning of the fifteenth century, by Francesco Anteminelli Castracani Fibbia, Prince of Pisa, who was an exile in that city, and died there in 1419.

The game of *tarocchino* differs from the typical Venetian tarots series in the number of the numeral cards. In the former, the two, three, four, and five of each suit are suppressed, thus reducing the old Venetian sequence of seventy-eight cards to sixty-two. The true tarots, or *atutti*, are identically the same in number and, speaking generally, similar in design and subjects. In modern sets, however, a modification has been introduced which will be noticed presently.

The authorities of Bologna were so well pleased with Fibbia's alteration of the Venetian game, that they allowed the prince the privilege of placing his own shield of arms on the queen of *bastoni*, and that of his wife, who was of the Bentivoglio family, on the queen of *danari*, a distinction which, as Duchesne remarks, " should not prevent us from hoping that Francesco Fibbia, who had been generalissimo of the Bolognese troops, had rendered his country more important services than teaching it to play at *tarocchino*." (B. 2, p. 11.)

In the pack before us the actual numeration of the *atutti* series begins with the emblem of love, or *L'Amoreux*, as it is often written. This is marked with the Arabic numeral 5 at the upper left-hand and lower right-hand corners in reverse.

The *atutti* continue to receive numbers up to the sixteenth card, *L'Etoile.*

Not any titles nor names occur on the pieces, whether *atutti* or numerals. The peculiar numeration here practised agrees with the account given by Merlin, p. 32. It receives an explanation in the circumstance that this modern pack of *tarocchino* cards has the four " Moor's heads or satraps " in lieu of the emblematic figures *L'Empereur, L'Imperatrice, Le Pape, and La Papesse,* which are present in the old Venetian tarots, and the old *tarocchino* cards of the Paris cabinet. In some still more recent *tarocchino* sets than the present series, the original emblems have been restored (Mitelli cards).

"Several of these variations are due evidently to political circumstances. In 1513 the republic of Bologna acknowledged the sovereignty of the Pope. It was probably after this revolution that the four figures of the tarots were displaced by the four Moors. Other variations have been due to mistakes of the engravers, while changes in costume occurring in time have produced the rest." (Merlin, p. 84.)

All the figures in the present series, both *atutti* and numeral honours, are busts, printed double and in reverse on each piece.

The numeral suits are of course *coppe*, *danari*, *bastoni*, and *spade*. On the ace of *danari*, above and below the symbol of the suit, is a running hare looking behind her as she runs, backed by some bulrush-like plants. On the large central mark itself is a bust, like that on coins. The six of *danari* bears two government stamps, the upper one is inscribed 1827, and has a *baldacchino* with two cross keys below it; on the lower stamp is the word CASE (B), (3). The designs and execution of these cards are of the commonest character. The colouring is in keeping with the rest.

The *Matto* or *Fou* of the *atutti* is a fancifully dressed man playing on a horn and a drum at the same time. The card intended here for the ace of *spade* is peculiar. It is probably a piece of a suit of *bastoni* crept in by mistake.

The long narrow form of these cards is characteristic of a *tarocchino* pack. The backs are stamped in black with a large floriated or arabesque-like ornament, which is the best designed thing in the entire set.

[4⅞ × 1⅝ in.]   [Backs decorated.]

I. 7.

FIRST QUARTER OF EIGHTEENTH CENTURY.
BOLOGNA.

(IL GIUOCO DEL TAROCCHINO DI MITELLI.)

A SET of sixty-two cards, viz., twenty-two *atutti* and forty numerals, representing the *tarocchino* of Bologna. The two, three, four, and five of each numeral suit are suppressed in accordance with the original game.

These cards, well known as Mitelli's, had some repute in their day, and were included by Bartsch in his description of the works of this artist in the nineteenth volume, p. 305, of "Le Peintre Graveur."

Giuseppe Maria Mitelli was born at Bologna in 1634, and died there in 1718. He studied painting in the schools of Albano, Guercino, Torri, and Cantarini, was a proficient in music, and greatly addicted to hunting. Mitelli gave up much time to engraving, but his designs are—as observed by Bartsch—"more remarkable for their strange and sometimes ingenious character, than for the manner in which they are executed. The drawing is not always satisfactory, and the contours want in general purity and taste."—"The works of Mitelli are etched with a light point, but without much feeling, and from the openness of the technic, and the faintness of the shadows formed by simple or but rarely crossed lines, they have a cold look about them. They are, in fact, but designs sketched without force and effect, owing what merit they possess to the subjects they represent." (B. xix. p. 270.)

According to Bartsch, the engravings of Mitelli, after the designs of Titian, Albano, Cagliari, and others, are not superior to those of his own designing. To this judgment objection may be taken. Some of the former are surely very much better than the execution of his own *bizarre* and grotesque compositions. Among the better of the latter and devoid of any extravagance are these designs for a set of *tarocchino* cards, engraved by Mitelli for one of the family of Bentivoglio. The copper-plates were still in the possession of the latter when Cicognara wrote, and who perceived on the designs: " tanta grazia, che può dirsi una delle migliori sue produzioni, salvo quel pò di manierato, del quale ogni opera dell' Arte comincio a risentirsi in quell' epoca" (p. 138).

According to Cicognara, the Mitelli cards had become (1831) scarce, and in request by virtuosi.

Of this series of *tarocchino* cards, the Museum possesses three distinct sets.

Set A.—*Italian School of Engraving. Works of Mitelli.*

(Vol. iii. Nos. 274—277, 308 and 309.)

This is a proof set of impressions from six large plates, varying from 14 in. to $14\frac{1}{2}$ in. in width, by 11 in. to $11\frac{2}{8}$ in. in height. The first or lower plate (275), contains ten of the *atutti* series of emblematic figures in the following order, beginning at the right-hand corner of the lower row: L'Empereur barbu, No. 2; L'Empereur imberbe, 3; Le Pape assis barbu, 4; Le Pape debout barbu, 5; L'Amour les yeux bandés, 6; Venus, 7; La Tempérance, 8; La Justice, 9; La Force, 10; La Fortune, 11. The second or upper plate (274), contains ten other figures, viz.: Le Temps (veillard ailé avec des béquilles), 12; Un homme qui va tuer avec un maillet un jeune homme endormi (Le pendu, le traitre), 13; La Mort, 14; Le Diable, 15; Un homme frappé de la foudre, 16; Un chiffonier et au ciel une etoile (L'Etoile), 17; Diane et la lune au ciel (La Lune), 18; Appollon (Le Soleil), 19; Atlas (Le Monde), 20; Un ange sonnant de la trompette (Le Jugement Dernier), 21.

Each of these plates of unseparated card pieces bears at the upper margin the inscription, " Gioco di carte di Tarocchini," and at the lower margin at the right-hand corner, " *Gioseppe Maria Mitelli, Inv. diss. e. Int.*"

The third plate (276), contains (commencing at the left-hand corner of the upper row), Le Fou qui Saute, Le Bataleur qui joue du tambour de basque 1. Then follow the figure cards or honours of the numeral series in the following order after Le Bataleur: Roi d'Epées, Roi de Batons, Roi de Deniers, Roi de Coupes, Reine d'Epées, Reine de Batons, Reine de Deniers, and Reine de Coupes.

The fourth plate (308), contains ten honours in the following order, commencing at the upper row, left-hand corner: Cavalier d'Epées, Cavalier de Batons, Cavalier de Deniers, Cavalier de Coupes, As d'Epées, Cavalier d'Epées, Cavalier de Batons, Valet de Deniers, Valet de Coupes, As de Batons. On a scroll on the As d'Epées is the motto, " Custodiæ Custos." On the As de Batons is " Ardua Virtus."

Both these plates have inscriptions on the margins like to those previously described.

The fifth plate (277), contains eleven numeral pieces, viz., the *as*, six, seven, eight, nine, and ten of *coupes*, and the six, seven, eight, nine, and ten of *batons*. The *as de coupes* is rather an elegant design, having on it the arms of the Bentivoglio family. The designs of the cups on the other cards are all of different character to each other.

The sixth plate (309), contains eleven numeral pieces of the suits *deniers* and *epées*. The ace of *deniers* bears a female bust in an oval shield, below which on a pedestal is the address, " Gioseppe Maria Mitelli Inv. Dis. e. Int."

The symbols of the six of *deniers* bear birds, those of the seven, grotesque masques, the eight and nine male and female heads. On the ten of *deniers* are small, full-length figures in various actions, such as painting, fencing, shooting, fiddling, &c. Both plates bear inscriptions similar to those on the other impressions.

This particular set is interesting, as showing the actual sequence in which the pieces were executed, and being uncut and uncoloured, admits of a full appreciation of such merits as the designs in it possess. Cicognara remarks:—

" A. Bentivoglio caused it to be engraved, and in this family are preserved the worn plates. The emblems of the armorial bearings of the Bentivoglios may be seen on many of the cards, and in particular the queen of DANARI has all the ornamental portions of her dress cut like a saw, which was the original arms of this signiority." (Bibl. 5, p. 138.)

To the writer above quoted, and to Merlin (Bibl. 6, p. 128), reference may be made for further information.

Set β.—*Tarocchino di Mitelli.*

A pack (62), of the *tarocchino* cards of Mitelli before described. This set is bound up as a book lettered " Playing Cards, Bologna." The pieces are coloured, but in general less carefully and less appropriately than in the set presently to be noticed. The tarots emblematic figure of *La temperance* is uncoloured. The *atutti* series is placed last in the book, and follows a somewhat irregular sequence. The first card of the whole series is here the *as de deniers,* on which, engraved on a pedestal, is the address : " GIOSEPPE MARIA MITELLI INV. DIS. E. INT."

Set γ.—*Tarocchino di Mitelli.*

A pack (62) of the *tarocchino* cards of Mitelli. This set is contained in the original case, lettered : " MITELLI. CARTE DEL TAROC."

The cards are well and carefully coloured. Each piece has the margin edged with a yellow border formed by the overlapping edges of the back-mounting paper of the card.

The *as de deniers* bears the usual address : " GIOSEPPE MARIA MITELLI INV. DIS. E. INT."

[$4\frac{4}{8}$ × 2 in.]   [Backs plain in all the sets.]

Among the works of Mitelli (vol. iii.), are three pieces, representing scenes connected with playing-cards.

No. 227.—A party of four persons is here represented, seated at a table and playing at cards. Twelve others are variously disposed, looking on. Diamonds are being played. On the floor lie some upturned cards ; on a perch, projecting from the wall on the left, sits an owl ; opposite is another bird (? a raven) ; between these are three birds of nondescript character. Two dogs are snarling at each other in the foreground. The centre scene is treated in a grotesque and comic manner. At the upper portion of the print is the inscription : " CONVERSACIONE CONSIDERABILE."

At the lower left-hand corner is the address: " PIETRO DE ROSSI INV."; and at the right-hand corner Mitelli's name, though barely visible.

[$16\frac{2}{8}$ × 10 in.]

No. 243.—Two persons are represented seated at an oval table, engaged with cards. The numeral suit *danari* is being played. The three of *danari* lies upturned on the table, and the person on the left hand is about to play the five of this suit. Cards of the latter (some of which are torn in half) and of *bastoni* are on the table, along with four dice, counters, and a tray.   On the floor lie torn cards.

At the top of the plate is No. 5 ; at the bottom are two verses of fourteen lines each in Italian, showing that a lazy man would gamble away even his patrimony of the sun.

The address of Mitelli is at the lower right-hand corner, and the date 1683 on the support of the bench upon which the man on the left is sitting.

A point worthy of notice in connection with this print is the circumstance, that although Mitelli made himself well-known by his cards for the game of *tarocchino*, the game here being played is a different one, since the small cards which are suppressed in the former are being employed.

[11 $\frac{1}{8}$ × 8 $\frac{2}{8}$ in.]

No. 256.—A gambler is represented holding up in his right hand a pack of cards, with the six of *danari* exposed.   He points with his left hand to a table, on which are cards, counters, dice, and money, together with trays and dice-boxes.

On the floor lie cards of various suits, and balls and racket for playing tennis. On the wall hangs a racket, and three instruments with which gambling may be practised.

At the upper right-hand corner of the print is the number 9.   In the lower margin are two verses of four lines each, in Italian, one verse purporting to be spoken by a gambler and one by Death : the former telling how play has always been his delight, and that without being a Jew, he could live on usury ; the latter replying that if by gambling a fortune may sometimes be gained, it generally follows that the player loses his soul.

Immediately above the verse of the " Giuocatore" is the address of Mitèlli.

[10 $\frac{5}{8}$ × 7 $\frac{5}{8}$ in.]

I. 8.

SEVENTEENTH CENTURY ?

SERIES of diminutive cards, thirty-eight in number.   It is composed of an *atutti* suit (twenty-two), and the sixteen figure cards belonging to the numeral suits, apparently of a *tarocchino* sequence.

The latter may be inferred from the circumstance that two Moors, or satraps, displace *Le Pape* and *La Papesse* in the *atutti* suit.

The designs and execution are of common character ; the pieces are un-coloured.

[1 $\frac{1}{16}$ × $\frac{1}{2}$ in.]   [Backs plain.]

NUMERALS.

I. 9.

SEVENTEENTH CENTURY.

VENICE.

A SERIES of twenty-nine numerals from a pack of fifty-two Venetian cards.

The suits are *coppe*, *danari*, *spade*, and *bastoni*.

The most complete suit is that of *spade*, which wants the seven, nine, and *cavallo*. Judging from the figure cards of the suit *bastoni*, which are *re*, *cavallo*, and *fante*, there was not any queen admitted into this pack, probably from some Spanish influence or fashion prevailing at the time the cards were designed. Nevertheless, this exception may be due only to the "honours" of a tarots sequence having been taken, and the *cavallo* in lieu of the queen retained without any specific intention.

On the two of *spade* is the following address: "Mottavio Cartoler in Piazza di San Marco TIEN in segna La Perleta."

The ace of *spade* bears the motto: "Di Spada Ben Gioca Chi Vince" on a tablet in the centre of the card.

On the ace of *coppe* is the motto: "Chi Coppe Havera Dinari Trovera."

The kings are full-length figures, seated, bearing a sceptre in their left hands, and the symbol of the suit in the right. The *fante* of *spade* is an executioner, having the sword in his right hand, and a decapitated head in his left.

Though the designs and execution of these cards are coarse and commonplace, yet from the mode of colouring which has been followed—bad as it is—a kind of richness of effect is produced, characteristic of the Venetian school of adornment.

Merlin reproduces on the cover of his book (Bibl. 6): "Les deux parties de l'enveloppe d'un jeu du seizième siècle a la perletta." It is evidently Venetian. The present pack was sold at the sign of "*La perleta*."

[$3\frac{4}{8} \times 1\frac{5}{8}$ in.] [Backs plain.]

I. 10.

FIRST HALF OF EIGHTEENTH CENTURY?

PADUA.

A PACK of fifty-two numeral cards, having as the marks of the suits *danari*, *bastoni*, *coppe*, and *spade*.

As in the previous set, a *cavallo* displaces the queen, and the *fante* of *spade* is an executioner.

In the centre of the two of *spade* is the following inscription: "Al Aquila Coronata in Padova per Vicenza."

Within a tablet on the ace of *bastoni* is the motto : " Non ti fidar di me se il cor ti manca."

On the backs of these cards is a full-length figure in outline printed in a carmine ink. It represents a minstrel playing a guitar.

The designs and execution of this pack are in all respects of the most inferior character. Several of the inscriptions are quite undecipherable. In connection with these, however, plate 29 of Merlin's work should be consulted, where a " Jeux a deux Têtes de Vicence, 1602," is represented h ·ving mottoes like the present series.

[3⅝ × 1⅝ in.]   [Back decorated with a figure.]

CARDS WITH A SECONDARY PURPOSE.

EDUCATIONAL, INSTRUCTIVE.

I. ii.

FIRST QUARTER OF EIGHTEENTH CENTURY?

BOLOGNA OR VENICE.

(GEOGRAPHIC AND HERALDIC.)

SERIES of sixty-two cards, viz., twenty-two *atutti* and forty numerals. It represents a comparatively modern version of the *tarocchino* of Bologna. Originally the two, three, four, and five of the numeral suits were suppressed (as in modern *piquet*), but in the present sequence they exist, while the seven, eight, nine, and ten of each suit are absent.

A marked feature of the present series is the intention of it to impart instruction. Each tarots card has a geographic table engraved on it. Above this table is the particular emblematic tarots device, *e. g.*, Love, Justice, Force, &c., with a letter of the alphabet at the left-hand corner. The number of the tarots card is on the left-hand side, at the top of the geographic table. The *matto*, or fool, has the letter O and the number 22 above a table of the " *Regni dell Europa, e citta Regie.*"

In the numeral cards, the place occupied in the *atutti* by the geographic table is filled with shields of armorial bearings. The latter are numbered, No. 1 being on the queen of swords, 175 on the ace of clubs. Above the shields, in separate compartments, are the marks of the suits, which are here money, cups, swords, and clubs.

The honours are indicated by busts, the marks of the suits being sometimes at the left-hand, sometimes at the right-hand corner.

On the ace of cups (No. of shield 174) is the inscription : *In vece del* 7, 8, 9, 10 *di Coppe, si prende il* 2, 3, 4, 5 *e cosi di tutti*, and on the shield, " Libertas."

On the ace of clubs (No. of shield 175) is—*Si stampano da Lelio dall volpe* ; while the ace of money offers—*L'arme sono delli SS^ri. Anziani del* 1670 *smo al* 1725.

The ace of *danari* is here the first card in the series, and has on the shield (No. 175) the cross argent of Savoy.

The cards of the *atutti* series are impressions from engraved metal plates ; the numerals are from wood. The devices and symbols of both are coloured, but the shields on the numerals have been printed off simply in black. Most of the pieces have either dots or ornamental figures on their faces, printed off in red ink.

On the *verso* of each card is an impression of an allegorical figure holding a shield, chequered, in her left hand, and a spear in the right. She is seated, and looking towards the ground. The various portions of the figure are numbered up to twelve, and below, on the pedestal, is the inscription, " DIVISIONE DELL' EUROPA." This figure is from an engraving on wood, and is on all the pieces, both *atutti* and numerals. It is uncoloured.

We presume it is to these cards, and to the book which was published with them, that Cicognara alludes in the following paragraph (Bibl. 5, p. 138) :—

" A short digression relative to what occurred at Bologna in 1725 may not be out of place. A little book was there published, intitled, ' L'utile col diletto ossia Geografia intrecciata nel Giuoco dei Tarocchi,' dedicated to the Marquis Gio. Paolo Pepoli, and issued with the permission of the Archbishop and of the Holy Office. Nevertheless, the little work was severely anathematised a few days afterwards by Cardinal Ruffo, the Papal Legate, by order of the Court of Rome, and the unfortunate game at cards ran a sort of human political career at this epoch, when thoughts and dreams were not wont to be so severely scrutinized as is the case at present. A certain Luigi Montier wrote the dedication of the work, which is composed of twelve pages of text and twenty-two cards, along with those of the *tarocchi* already known. Certainly the adulations of the writer are not to be admired, who imitates the French not only in their invention of games, but likewise in their style of dedicatory address : ' Dedicated to the most glorious King Louis XIV. the Great. I dedicate it,' adds the author, ' to you, most noble Signior, as to a person of blood and royal mind, and as it appears suitable to do so to a monarch of a most flourishing kingdom, and to a conqueror of so many provinces, so does it seem proper to do likewise to a Signior of high and noble race, and to a cavalier who has travelled over so many parts of the world. In the cards dedicated to him we may see those kingdoms, empires, and states, in which from the high prerogatives of his spirit and mind more wonders have arisen than we have been accustomed to observe in other places,' &c.

" But such bombast, very common at that age, and indeed too frequent at all times in which meanness and hypocrisy are the roads to reward, honours, and place, though able clearly to excite a little envy or jealousy, did not necessarily lead to such violent anathemas.

" On reading the text, geography and heraldry were found to be applied to the game of cards, and in the divisions of the four quarters of the world, indicated below the symbols of the *tarocchi*, stood some elementary geographic notices in the form under which, in a table of pedigrees, the noble arms of the Bolognese nobility are printed, and those families who had been *Confalionieri* countersigned with an asterisk."

[$4\frac{7}{8} \times 2\frac{2}{8}$ in.]   [Backs decorated with a figure.]

I. 12.

EIGHTEENTH CENTURY.

BOLOGNA?

(Geographic and Heraldic.)

 SERIES of fifty-nine cards from a *tarocchino* pack, intended to answer the purposes of instruction in geography and heraldry, as well as of ordinary play.

Three coat-cards are wanting in the numeral suit *bastoni*.

These cards form a duplicate set of I. 11. They resemble the latter in all respects but the following circumstance. In the present series the backs of the cards are marked with ten shields, representing the various blazon colours and metals by the respective lines and dots always adopted in such cases. The following inscriptions are contained in five scrolls between the shields of the colours :—

	Colori.	
Azuro.	Oro.	Rosso.
Verde.	Argento.	Porporin.
Armelind.	Nero.	Varri.

The numbers attached to the shields in this and the previous pack may be presumed to refer to the descriptive account alluded to by Cicognara. The pieces are coloured after the method adopted in I. 11.

These cards are contained in the original case, which is lettered, " Montieri Carte del Taroc."

[4⅞ × 2⅜ in.]　　　　　　　　　　　　　[Backs decorated with shields.]

I. 13.

THIRD QUARTER OF SEVENTEENTH CENTURY.

NAPLES.

(Heraldic, Historic, Geographic.)

 SERIES of fifty-two cards of the suits *piques, trefles, carreaux,* and *cœurs.* The pieces are bound up with an explanatory text, the whole being intended to afford instruction in heraldry, geography, and history. The volume is lettered : fine. Giuoco D'Armi napoli. 1677. The card pieces are from engraved metal plates, and are uncoloured.

The original character of this series may be gleaned satisfactorily from the following observations of Taylor (Bibl. 9, p. 197).

" A pack of heraldic cards by M. Claude Oronce Finé, *dit* de Brianville, with a small 12mo. volume as a guide, was published at Lyons in 1659, probably executed for Desmarests, as in a later edition there is printed as an appendix, together with the letters patent before-mentioned, a transfer of his privilege, dated 13th May of that year, to Benoist Coral, Marchand Libraire at Lyons, in so far as relates to the *Cartes de Blason.* The title of this edition, which is the only one we have been able to consult, is ' Jeu d'Armoiries des Sovverains et Estats d'Europe, pour apprendre le Blason et la Geographie et l'Histoire curieuse. A Monseigneur le Dauphin. Par M. de Brianville, Abbé de S. Benoist le Quinçay lez Poitiers. A Lyon, chez Benoist Coral, rue Merciere, a la Victoire, 1672. Avec Privilege du Roy.'[1]

" The author commences with an advertisement to the reader, in which, after professing his obligations to Menestrier and others for their assistance and advice, he gives the following remarks and instructions on the method of play :—

" ' The method of playing this game does not differ from that adopted with the ordinary cards, there being the same numbers of cards and the same points. The only change made is that of valet and ace into prince and chevalier, which is done to prevent any misconstruction (*pour eviter tout equivoque*).[2]

" ' The games of *Hère, Malcontant,* or *Coucou,* are the most suitable, because, being the easiest, they are not so likely to divert the attention needed for the blazonry, geography, and history. The players range themselves around a table covered with a map of Europe, and after the cards are dealt and exchanged to every one's satisfaction, the lowest pays according to the laws of *Hère.* He who is first then describes the blazonry of the card[3] he holds, forfeiting one if he makes an error, either to the player who corrects him, or to the bank, if there is one. The next highest then follows suit, and so on through all the rest. The first round being completed, they then proceed to the second, describing this time the geography of each card, and forfeiting points for mistakes as before. At the third round they take the history in the same manner.' He recommends that at first only the blazon should be attempted, as the game can be played in each division separately, as well as in all three collectively.

" The cards are divided into the four suits, *cœurs, trefles, piques,* and *carreaux,* distinguished respectively by the armorial bearings of the kingdoms, provinces, and great dignitaries of France, Italy, the North (*le Nort*), and Spain. The honours of course contain the most exalted, the King of Great Britain appearing as the prince (knave) of the spade, or Northern suit. . . . . The geographical and historical lessons are very concise and comprehensive, the former giving the latitude, boundaries, chief towns, &c., and the latter entering minutely into the descent of the house whose arms are represented.

" One can easily see that the *utile* in games like this predominates very materially over the *dulce,* and it was doubtless deemed a very sorry recreation by the royal urchin for whose edification it was devised."

Nevertheless, this historico-heraldic game was patronised, and was imported

---

[1] We are indebted for the loan of this rare little work to the valuable heraldic library of A. W. Morant, Esq., C.E., of Great Yarmouth. Notices of other editions will be found in the Bibliographical Appendix. In these, De Brianville is otherwise styled " Mont-Dauphin," and " Conseiller et armoirier du Roy." The third edition (1665) is dedicated " A son Altesse Royale de Savoye." (Note in Taylor, *op. cit.*)

[2] An explanation of this expression, very characteristic of the times, is given by Singer. The aces and valets, it appears, bore in the first edition the arms of certain princes and nobles. This being considered offensive to their dignity, the plates were seized by the magistrates, and only restored on condition that princes and knights should be substituted. (See on this point " The Herald and Genealogist," vol. iii. p. 74. 1866.)

[3] As this could not be done without considerable acquaintance with heraldry, a M. Gauthier devised, in 1686, a new pack of heraldic cards, to serve the purpose of a kind of grammar of the science.

into Naples in 1677, by Antonio Bulifon. Here Don Annibale Acquaviva established a society under the name of "*Armeristi*" to play at *blazon*, its device being a map of Europe, with the motto : "Pulchra sub imagine Ludi."

At Naples, Bulifon published an Italian version of the cards, and the book of instruction edited by Giustiniani, of which the series now before us is an example, cards and book being bound up together. The collective work has the following title : "Giuoco D'Armi Dei Sovrani E Stati D'Europa per Apprendere L'Armi, la Geografia, e l'Historia, loro curiosa. Di C. Oronce Finè, detto Di Brianville. Tradotto dal Francese in Italiano & accresciuto di molte aggiunte necessariè per la perfetta cognitione della Storia. Da Bernardo Giustiniani Veneto. In Napoli 1677 Appresso Antonio Bulifon All' Insegna della Sirena con lic. e Privil."

To this volume of 360 pages there are appended the "Lettera di Alessandro Parthenio intorno alla Società de gli Armeristi et ad un Giuoco detto Lo Spendore della nobiltà Napoletana ascritta ne' cuique Leggi. In Napoli 1678, Appresso Antonio Bulifon."

In respect to the conversion of the valet and ace into *prince* and *chevalier*, alluded to by Taylor, Chatto (B. 4, p. 150), remarks :—

"*Les as et les valets* were represented by the arms of certain princes and nobles. Now, as this was evidently a breach of etiquette and a derogation of heraldic nobility, Mons. de Brianville, like Mr. Anstis, does not seem to have rightly understood his own 'foolish business.' The plates were seized by the magistrates." . . . . "Lord Chesterfield is reported to have said to Anstis on one occasion, when the latter was talking to him about heraldry :—'You silly man, you do not understand your own foolish business.'"

Though each card has a mark of its suit with the value on it at the left-hand upper corner, we presume not any person would attempt to use the set as ordinary playing-cards.

The *roi de trefles*—the first card—bears the arms of Pope Innocent XI. *la dame de trefles*—the second—has the arms of Naples. Some of the pieces have not less than three shields on them, with a description of their blazon in Italian below.

Following the "*Licenze di Superiori Ecclesiastici*" to this Neapolitan version is an engraved sheet, exhibiting the "Primi Elementi o Principy dell' Armi," illustrated with above sixty small shields, representing the various quarterings, &c.

This series, as it exists in the form of a large duodecimo volume, is 5 in. × 3⅛ in. The card-plates are :

[3⅝ × 2⅜ in.]   [Backs plain.]

I. 13. 2.

LAST QUARTER OF SEVENTEENTH CENTURY.

NAPLES.

(HERALDIC, &c.)

LATER edition of the series last described. It is in the form of a bound duodecimo volume, printed at Naples in 1692, by Giacomo Raillard, who dedicates it: "All' illustriss. Signore D. Paolo Mattia Doria Nobile Genovese," &c. "Di Napoli a di I. di Febrajo 1692."

Following the dedication is the third division only of the engraved sheet of the "Primi Elementi o Principy dell' Armi," &c., present in I. 13. Next to this comes "Istruzioni per lo Giuoco." After certain poetic laudatory addresses and epigrams, is printed the original " *licenza de' Superiori* " of the edition of 1677 (I. 13) signed by the Vicar General : "Fr. Scanegata—Joseph imperialis Soc. Jesu Theol. Emin." This is followed by the request of Raillard to the Cardinal Caracciolo, Archbishop of Naples, for permission to reprint the edition previously authorised : "Excellentiss. Signore.—Giacomo Raillard supplicando espone a V E come desidera far stampare un libro intitolato, *Giuoco d' Arme de' Sourani d' Europa*, supplica V E per le solite Regie licenze e l' havera a grazia, ut Deus, &c. R. D."

The former censorship of the Apostolic prothonotary, Pompejus Sarnellius, is referred to, and thus confirmed :

> Visa supra dicta relatione, Imprimatur, et in
> publicatione servetur Regia Pragmatica.
> Galeota Reg. Carillo Reg. Cala Reg. Soria Reg.
> Sebastianus.

Reimprimatur die 28 Januarii 1692. Moles Reg. Montecorvinus."

The first piece in the series is the *Re di fiori*, having on it the arms of Pope Innocent XII. (Pignatelli), below which is the description : " Campo di Oro con tre pentole in mezzo, o vero Pignate nere, due sopra et una sotto in triangolo. Lo Scudo coronato della Tiara, et ornato delle due chiavi della Santa Sede."

The *Giuoco d' Arme* is followed, as in the former edition, by the *Lettera di Alessandro Partenio intorno alla Societa Degli Armeristi*, &c.

The number of pages of the *Giuoco d' Arme* is here 285, in the former edition it is 262.

The card-pieces are uncoloured.

[Size of page, $4\frac{2}{8} \times 2\frac{5}{8}$ in.] [Backs plain.]

I. 14.

LAST QUARTER OF SEVENTEENTH CENTURY.

NAPLES.

(Heraldic.)

A SERIES of fifty-two card-pieces of the suits *cœurs, piques, trefles,* and *carreaux*, intended to afford instruction in heraldry and history.

This set is composed of the card-pieces only of the edition of the *Giuoco d' Arme* just described (I. 13, 2). The impressions have been worked off on very thin paper, and cut down close upon the border lines.

The first piece—the king of clubs—bears the arms with the three black pots of Pope Innocent XII., as in the edition of 1692 (I. 13, 2). Not any book or separate text accompanies this series. It is uncoloured, and the impressions are sharper and earlier than those of I. 13, 2.

It is evident that there were several editions of this heraldic series ; a still later one than that of 1692 was printed at Naples in 1725 by Paolo Petrini.

" The arms of the Pope in this are—Sbarra con una Serpe in campo d' Oro sopra una rosa in campo d' Argento, sotto 4 Sbarre a traverso rosse in campo d' Argente. The first mentioned *Sbarra* is a fess, the *campo d' Argento* a chief ; the lower half of the shield is engraved as if it were (in English blazon) *Gules three bendlets argent*. These were the arms of Pope Benedict XIII. (Ursini) 1724—1730.

" The arms of the Pope were evidently changed for every reign, but no other alteration appears to have been made for the several editions." ("Herald and Genealogist," vol. 3, p. 75.)

The edition of 1725 is supplemented by a geographical discourse from Michele Angelo Petrini.

An interesting and instructive commentary on these and some other historical and heraldic cards may be found in "The Herald and Genealogist," vol. iii. p. 67. 1866. (See *postea*, F. 79, 2.)

[3⅜ × 2 in.]   [Backs plain.]

I. 14. 2.

(*Printed Books Department, Royal or King's Library*, 269. c. 31.)

LAST QUARTER OF THE SEVENTEENTH CENTURY.

(Heraldic.)

BOUND duodecimo volume of 440 pages of text, combined with a numeral series of fifty-two card-pieces and other plates of illustration. The whole is intended to afford information on heraldry.

This series is based on the design of Brianville (I. 13. I. 13. 2, F. 72. 2), and is meant to illustrate the armorials of the Venetian nobility. The author of this adaptation was Casimir Freschot, a Benedictine. The title-page of the work bears the following inscription: "Li Pregi Della Nobiltà Veneta abbozzati in un Giuoco D' Arme di tutte le Famiglie. Presentato al Serenissimo Principe, et Eccellentiss. Senato Da D. Casimiro Freschot. B. In Venezia, M.DC.LXXXII. Appresso Andrea Poletti—con Licenza de' Superiori."

In the "Notitia Succinta Del Blasone, ò Arte Araldica," which prefaces the armorial, the author remarks: "Ho seguitato nel mio Giuoco l' ordine del Signor Oronce Finè Gentilhomo francese nel suo Giuoco de Principi e Stati Sovrani D' Europa cogliendo di più la congiuntura di esporre tutte le specie di Scudi, ed accompagnamenti di essi, che si trovano più usitati, tanto Ecclesiastici quanto Laici, tanto d' huomini quanto di Donne," &c. (p. 11).

Following the "Notitia" is a chapter, "Dell' Origine Della Nobiltà Veneta in generale," which is succeeded by the armorial proper.

The signs of the suits are here *viola, rosa, giglio,* and *tulipano,* on the marks of which are placed letters (R D P) to indicate the coat-cards, and numbers to determine the values.

For the four kings, the dignities of the pope, emperor, king, and doge are taken; for the queens, the armorials of princesses and provinces; and for the princes, the foreign nobility, aggregated to that of Venice. Cavaliers represent the aces, which illustrate the generals of the armies of the Republic.

The first card-piece in the series is the king of violets, on which are the arms of Pope Eugenio IV., of Cardinal Barbarigo, and of the Duke of Parma. On the coat-cards there are generally four shields of arms; on the pip pieces as many as seven. All the armorials, which have been printed off on thin paper, are carefully and distinctly engraved, and are uncoloured. The full page of the volume measures 5½ × 3 in.

[Card-plate, 4⅔ × 2⅝ in.]   [Backs plain.]

SPANISH PLAYING-CARDS.

NUMERALS.

S. 15.

SECOND HALF OF SEVENTEENTH CENTURY.

FORTY-EIGHT cards of a pack of fifty-two Spanish numerals. They are of the usual suits in the cards of Spain, viz., *bastos*, *oros*, *copas*, and *espadas*.

The valet, or *sota*, and eight of *copas* are wanting, as are likewise the four and five of *oros*.

From the circumstance of the suits of *bastos* and *espadas* each being complete—thirteen in number—and from all the four tens being present, it is assumed that the set consisted originally of fifty-two numerals, though the actual number of the cards present, and the substitution of a *caballo* for a dame, might at first sight lead to the idea that the set under notice was an ordinary or typical Spanish one, especially as the marks of the suit are quite of the Spanish character. On the ace of *oros* is a shield with the Spanish arms, and the motto, " Rex Carolus. Dei Gratia Rex Hisbania." Below is the address: Iehan Volay.

On the three of *bastos* are the initials, I V, and on the valet of the same suit is Iehan Volay between the legs of the figure.

On the four of *copas* are I. V in the centre, connected by an ornamental band. Between the marks of the suit on the two of *espadas* is Iehan Volay ; on the five of the same suit is inscribed " Faictes a Tiers," while on the valet of *espadas* the name of Iehan Volay is again repeated.

The designs on these cards are almost exactly such as are given by Merlin, in plates 30, 31, A B, as belonging to the " Cartes Espagnoles, Bibliotheque de Rouen," with the exception of the motto on the shield of the ace of *oros*.

In the Rouen cards the motto runs thus : " Philippus Dei Gratia Hispaniæ Rex," and over the arms of Spain is a shield of pretence of the arms of France, *i. e.*, three *fleurs-de-lis*.

Certain cards and their envelopes bearing the name of Iehan Volay have given rise to some curious discussions.

Mr. Barrington, a well-known antiquary of the beginning of this century, became acquainted—through Mr. Astle, the writer on Caligraphy and MSS.— with an old wood-block, upon which was engraved the cover-design for a pack of cards. This block came afterwards into the possession of Mr. Singer, who gave an impression from it in his work (p. 221). A facsimile was likewise given by Mr. Barrington in his paper in the "Archæologia," vol. viii. p. 144, which was written to prove, *inter alia*, that cards were originally made in Spain. On this cover were engraved the arms of Castile and Leon, together with the marks of the suits, *bastos, copas, espadas*, and *oros*. There was also an inscription in large letters to this purport: "Cartas finnas faictes par Jehan Volay." Below this and between the marks of *copas* and *oros*, there was added in letters of different character, either by a stencil, or by the insertion of a new piece of wood in the original block, the name of "Edward Warman"—probably that of the English vendor of the cards. Mr. Barrington read the above as "Je (or Jean) Hauvola," and the final "y" in Volay as the Spanish conjunction for "and." The whole of the inscription being translated into English was made to run thus: "Superfine cards made by John Hauvola and (Edward Warman)"—the last name being supposed to have been substituted for that of a former partner of John Hauvola. "Now," writes Mr. Singer (p. 221): "Mr. Barrington read the name inscribed on this block erroneously, *cartas finnas faictes par Ie Hauvola y Edward Warman*, whereas it evidently appears Jehan Volay was meant, although the words, from the carelessness of the engraver, are somewhat disjointed."

Mr. Barrington remarks: "I conceive that this advertisement was used by a card-maker, resident in France, who notified the wares he had to sell in the Spanish terms of *cartas finnas*, because those that had been made in Spain at that time were in great vogue. The two words which follow are French, *faictes par*, which were probably in that language that the French reader might more readily understand the advertisement."

Mr. Gough, commenting in the "Archæologia," vol. viii. p. 168, on Mr. Barrington's statement, observes: "The insertion of Edward Warman's name in so very different a type is a proof that he was the vendor of such cards in a far later period. Upon inquiry I am informed by my friend, Mr. Herbert, that a person of the name of Warman kept a stationer's shop somewhere in Bishopsgate Street or Norton Folgate about fifty years ago, and it is not improbable that he sold these cards, and caused this insertion to be made in the block. Mr. Herbert could not recollect his Christian name. If I am not mistaken," continues Mr. Gough, "this extraordinary block once belonged to Mr. Ames, who has, however, taken no notice of it in his History of Printing."

Singer was of opinion that this engraved wood-block might be possibly of English manufacture, and only intended to convey the idea that the cards enclosed in it were foreign in order to obtain a higher price if they were held in greater esteem.

That the entire block was of English fabrication cannot be admitted, though it is clear from the following advertisement, pointed out by Mr. Haslewood to Singer, that Spanish cards were objects of curiosity at the beginning of the last century, and that at this period they were different from our own, and consequently could not be in common use.

" *Advertisement.*

" Spanish cards lately brought from Vigo. Being pleasant to the eye by their curious colours, and quite different from ours, may be had at 1*s.* a pack at Mrs. Baldwins in Warwick Lane."—*Postman*, Dec. 12—15, 1702.

Chatto was of opinion (p. 133), that any vogue Spanish cards might have had in the more northerly countries of Europe during the times of Elizabeth and James I., was probably owing to the circumstance of so many Spaniards being then resident in the Low Countries, rather than to any superiority of the cards manufactured in Spain.

According to Leber, Jean Volay was the most celebrated French card-maker of the sixteenth century, practising his art at the close of the reign of Francis I.

(1515—1547). Volay, no doubt, manufactured for the Spanish market, not only as the engraved envelope-title here under consideration and the inscription FAICTES A TIERS[1] on the five of *espadas* prove, but as the various sheets of Spanish cards, evidently produced in French workshops, show likewise. Such cards are preserved in the collections at Rouen and Paris, and in the cabinets of Michelin, Merlin, and of others.

According to Merlin, however, there is not extant a fragment of the French manufactured Spanish cards, which is earlier than the seventeenth century, and the specimens at Rouen bearing the name "Jehan Volay" are far from having the age attributed to them. "The 'Recueil of the Société des Bibliophiles Français' describes the cards of the Imperial Library bearing the name of Jehan Volay and Jean Goyrand of Paris, as having been made about 1480. Without doubt this is an error, and if we were disposed to discuss the question of date as respects the Rouen block signed Jehan Volay, it would be easy to show, both by certain details of costume, and by the form of the letters, that this block is not older at the furthest than the end of the reign of Louis XIV. The ace of *Deniers* is a large coin, having on it the arms of Spain, the motto of which, engraved in Roman capitals, runs thus: 'PHILIPPUS DEI GRATIA HISPANIÆ REX.' Now the name of Philip II., supposed to be intended by this motto, would no doubt carry back the coin to the sixteenth century, were it not that over all is superposed the shield of France [as a shield of pretence] which was thus placed only on the arms of the kings who were of the royal family of France. It is therefore rather to Philip V. that this coin belongs. The shoes and the entire dress of the valet of *Deniers* of this sheet (pl. 30, 31, A. B.) are of the reign of Louis XIV." (Merlin, Bibl. 6, p. 99, note.)

"These Rouen designs represent, pretty truly we believe, the type in use in Spain at the time when J. Volay flourished. The cards particularly worthy of notice are the king, cavalier, valet, ace, two, and five of *Deniers*."

There does not appear any reason for doubting the correctness of Merlin's interpretation of the blazon on the ace of *oros* in the Rouen (Spanish) cards. It relates to Philip V., Duke of Anjou, grandson of Louis XIV., about the time when arose the "War of the Succession," terminated by the treaty of Utrecht in 1713.

In the pack of Volay cards in the British Museum the shield of France is not present, the arms of Spain standing by themselves. Hence it may be assumed that these cards were produced before the Rouen set, and belong probably to the time of Charles II., the son of Philip IV., the last of the Austrian line.

[$3\frac{2}{8}$ × $2\frac{1}{16}$ in.] [Backs plain.]

S. 16.

FIRST QUARTER OF NINETEENTH CENTURY.

MADRID.

A PACK of fifty-two Spanish numerals of the suits *oros*, *bastos*, *copas*, and *espadas*.

On the four of *oros* is a shield, surmounted by a crown, the former having on it the inscription: "Naypes Finisinos Fabircados En Madrid. H 1801."

On the *cavallo* of *copas*, at the lower left-hand corner, are the capitals A. IVA,

---

[1] The French town now known as Thiers in the depart. Puy-de-Dome, near Clermont.

evidently meant for the A. HIVA, which address occurs on a similar card in another pack, S. 17.

On the ace of *oros*—top and bottom—are inscriptions, of which only the words " Real—Madrid—Pord—Felix—So—, can be made out.

The designs, execution, and colouring of these cards are of inferior character. Some of the figures on the coate-cards are absurd, the horses of the *caballeros* being smaller than their riders. The pieces are thin in texture, and are *tarotées* on the backs with star-like dots of blue colour running diagonally.

[$3\frac{3}{8}$ × $2\frac{1}{16}$ in.]   [Backs decorated.]

S. 17.

FIRST QUARTER OF NINETEENTH CENTURY.

 PACK of Spanish numerals of the typical kind, viz., forty-eight in number, the four tens being suppressed, and the dames, or queens, displaced by *caballos*.

The suits are the usual ones of Spanish cards, viz., *oros*, *copas*, *bastos*, and *espadas*.

Each card is numbered in reverse at two opposite corners diagonally. On the ace of *oros* is the lion of Leon, and the inscription above : R^L. E^A. DE M^D.; below, Año D. 1817.

On the four of *copas* are the words : " NAYPES REFINOS," and on the *caballo* of the same suit are : " A. HIVA," at the lower right-hand corner. The four of *oros* has the initials " R H " in the centre of the card, enclosed within an ornamental frame, while on the five of this suit are the crowned lion and castle on the central and large symbol of the suit.

The designs, execution, and colouring are of inferior character. The backs are marked diagonally with small broad-arrows in black.

[$3\frac{3}{8}$ × $2\frac{1}{8}$ in.]   [Backs decorated.]

S. 18.

SECOND QUARTER OF NINETEENTH CENTURY.

CADIZ.

PACK of numerals of the normal Spanish type, viz., with the tens suppressed, the queens displaced by *caballos*, and the suits, *oros*, *copas*, *bastos, and espadas.*

The large coin-like symbol on the ace of *oros* has on it the initials, " G. A." interlaced and surrounded by flowers. A crown surmounts the whole. Between the marks on the two of *oros* is printed, " 1ER SUPERFINO," while the four of this suit bears the address : " Por Francisco Gonzalez Cadiz," above which is a running stag.

The large central mark on the five of *oros* bears the head of Queen Isabella (?) directed towards the right.

On the two of *copas* is inscribed : " AÑO DE 1848 "; on the four of the same suit is the government duty stamp. In the middle of this latter card are an anchor and caduceus placed crosswise. At the lower left-hand corner of the *caballo* of *copas* are the capitals " A HIVA."

An envelope, with an engraved title and wood-cut printed on blue paper, accompanies the pack. The design is a stag running towards the right. In the background are a well and trees. The marks of the suits *copas* and *bastos* are on one side, and those of *oros* and *espadas* on the other. Above the engraving may be read: "NAPES DE UNA OJA," below it: "DE 1ᴬ. 1ᴱᴿ. Superfino No 5 Fabrica de Barajas, De F. F. Gonzalez. Calle de la Veronica No. 149. En Cadiz."

The backs of these cards are marked with a network of deep pink lines, crossing each other diagonally. The pieces are thin, being of one thickness of paper only —*una oja.*

[3⅛ × 1⅞ in.]   [Backs decorated.]

S. 19.

SECOND QUARTER OF NINETEENTH CENTURY.

CADIZ.

PACK of numerals—forty-eight in number, in accordance with the Spanish type—evidently from the same blocks as is the set previously described, S. 18. The only variations consist in the designs and addresses relating to trade matters. For example, between the marks of the two of *oros* is inscribed, "Naipe de Una Oja," and on the two of *copas*, "1ª EDE 1ª." The four of *oros* bears the address, "J. J. ACUAVIVA CADIZ," below a lion directed towards the right. The ace and five of *oros*, the four of *copas*, and the *caballo* of the last suit are similar to the like cards of S. 18.

An envelope of greenish-blue paper with an engraved title, accompanies the pack. The design of the woodcut is a lion directed towards the right hand, but looking to the left; beneath is the inscription: "Naipes de una oja de vitelade hilo Fabricados por J. Acuaviva En Cadiz. Calle de Juan de Andas Nᵒ. 158 1ᴬ. DE 1ᴬ."

These cards are marked on the backs with dotted stars, printed in blue. They are of thin texture, like the preceding.

[3⅛ × 1⅞ in.]   [Backs decorated.]

S. 20.

SECOND QUARTER OF NINETEENTH CENTURY.

CADIZ.

DUPLICATE set of S. 18, from the same publisher, Francisco Gonzalez, Cadiz, 1848.

An envelope and title, &c., like those of S. 18, accompany the pack. The backs are marked with dotted stars in blue. The pieces are of like texture to those of S. 18.

[3⅛ × 1⅞ in.]   [Backs decorated.]

S. 21.

SECOND QUARTER OF NINETEENTH CENTURY.

MADRID?

(El Hombre.)

 SERIES of forty cards from a pack of forty-eight of the usual kind of Spanish numerals. From the eight and nine as well as the ten of each suit being absent, it is clear that these cards were intended for that particular modification of the old Spanish game, *El Hombre* (or *Ombre*) referred to in the "Compleat Gamester," where it is stated: "there are several sorts of this game, but that which is the chief is called *renegado*, at which three only can play, to whom are dealt nine cards apiece; so that by discarding the eights, nines, and tens, there will remain thirteen cards in the stock."

"Many of our readers," writes Singer (p. 265), "will recollect, we doubt not, to have seen three-cornered tables among old furniture; these tables were made purposely for *Ombre*, and in the print which we have mentioned above (frontispiece to "Compleat Gamester," 1739), the table is of that form. To play this game well, attention and quietness are said to be absolutely necessary, for if a player be ever so expert he will be apt to fall into mistakes if he thinks of anything else, or is disturbed by the conversation of by-standers. There are many ways of playing the game; it is sometimes played with *force spadille*, or *espadille forcè*, sometimes by two persons only, sometimes by three, which is the most general way, but it may be played by four or five persons."

The Spanish game, *El Hombre*, appears to have been well known in England in 1660. A full description of it, under the form of " The English Court Game," may be found in " Macmillan's Magazine" for January, 1874. It is generally considered to be the game described in Pope's " Rape of the Lock," as *Ombre*, as the poet calls it:

> " Belinda now, whom thirst of Fame invites,
> Burns to encounter two adventurous knights,
> At *Ombre* singly to decide their doom,
> And swells her breast with conquests yet to come."

Mr. Pardon considers Pope has described *Quadrille*. The latter game however, is only another species of *Ombre*—supposed to have been an invention of the French nation, and appears to have been a great favourite with the ladies, as requiring much less attention than *Ombre*. There was also a modification of it which might be played by three persons, but it is generally considered far inferior to the game by four, and was only played when a fourth player could not be had. (Singer, Bibl. 8, p. 266.)

There is not any address nor inscription on the present cards. The ace of *oros* has on it a landscape design, in which the sun is setting behind a town backed by hills. A palm-tree is in the middle distance, and water (the sea?) in the foreground. Above the whole is a large sign of the suit, having a radiant sun in the middle, the nucleus of which is a human face. The two of *copas*, four of *oros*, and four of *copas*, have flowers and other ornaments between the marks of the suits. Each card is numbered at two opposite corners diagonally.

These cards are lithographic impressions. The figure cards are wretchedly designed, executed, and coloured. The backs are *tarotées* with pink diagonal dotted lines crossing each other, so as to form large spaces, in which are placed four pink dots.

[$3\frac{2}{8} \times 2\frac{1}{8}$ in.] [Backs decorated.]

S. 22.

SECOND QUARTER OF NINETEENTH CENTURY.

 PACK of forty-eight numerals of the suits *oros, bastos, copas,* and *espadas.* The tens of each suit are as usual suppressed, but there is the exceptional occurrence of a *dama* or queen, instead of the *sota* generally present in Spanish cards.

These cards have been executed either by lithography or zincography, probably the former. The designs of the coate-cards are of a common and theatric character.

The ace of each suit is peculiar. On it is a winged serpent occupying the entire length of the card, and grasping, in three of the suits, the symbol of the suit in its mouth. In the suit of swords is a shield over the spot where the swords cross each other. Medallions, shields, and other ornaments occur on some of the two and three numerals.

On the four of *oros* is the inscription, " Real Fabrica," on a scroll. The four of *copas* bears a similar scroll, but without an inscription.

In the centre of the six of *copas* are the initials " F. B." interlaced, and repeated in reverse ; above them is a crown.

The two of clubs is made up by a figure (?) card from another set.

The backs are marked with small deep blue-coloured dots running diagonally.

[$2\frac{7}{8} \times 1\frac{5}{8}$ in.] [Backs decorated.]

S. 23.

THIRD QUARTER OF NINETEENTH CENTURY ?

BARCELONA.

 REGULAR pack of Spanish numerals (48) mounted in a book of twelve folios, each page containing four cards. It may be recalled to mind that in the typical Spanish set, the tens of each suit are suppressed the *reina* or *dama* is displaced by a *caballo*, and the suits are *oros, copas, bastos,* and *espadas.* Together with these characteristics may be noticed the circumstance that the marks of the suits *bastos* and *espadas* are always distinct and separate from each other, not conjoined nor interlaced, as the swords and clubs are in the like suits of Italian numerals. Further, the figures on the coate-cards are whole-length and erect, the kings being in large and full drapery. Generally, too, in modern packs the cards are numbered at opposite corners diagonally, and in reverse way.

In these cards the suits of *oros* and *copas* are printed in different gradations of red, those of *espadas* and *bastos* in black. The method of technical execution is peculiar; the first *rentré* seems to have been from a roughly etched plate, the second from a wood block.

The ace of *oros* bears the arms of Leon and Castile surmounted by a crown. Around the circular shield of the former is the inscription: " Con privilegio esclusivo de S. M."

On the four of *copas* is the address: " Por Lopez y Comp^a Barcel^{na}."

These cards are numbered in the usual Spanish way, and the kings are covered with long and ample mantles. On the under coat of the king of *copas* is a lion rampant, while the king of *espadas* rests his left hand on a shield which bears a double-headed eagle.

The backs of these cards are marked with a series of zigzag bands, formed of small parallel lines so arranged as to produce a series of diamond-shaped spots, within which are smaller diamonds divided transversely. The whole is printed in black.

[$3\frac{2}{8} \times 1\frac{7}{8}$ in.]   [Backs decorated.]

S. 24.

THIRD QUARTER OF NINETEENTH CENTURY?

BARCELONA.

PACK of numerals of the typical kind, forty-eight in number. The designs of the figure cards differ from those previously described, and there are other variations.

The four of *copas* bears an allegorical winged female figure blowing a trumpet, from which flutters a banderole having on it, " De una Hoja." Her left hand rests on a shield bearing the arms of Leon and Castile surmounted by a crown. Below the figure is the address: " Por Lopez y Comp^a. Barcel^{na}."

On the ace of *oros* are two chimeric or sphynx-like figures bearing a large coin in obverse, surmounted by a crown and standards. Between the marks on the four of *oros* is an emblematic representation of maritime commerce.

The cards are numbered in the usual way. The backs are marked all over with a series of arborescent lines printed in blue.

[$3\frac{2}{8} \times 2$ in.]   [Backs decorated.]

S. 25.

THIRD QUARTER OF NINETEENTH CENTURY.

BARCELONA.

PACK of numerals (forty-eight) of the usual kind, differing slightly in the designs from S. 23 and S. 24.

The four of *copas* bears the allegorical figure and address of Lopez of Barcelona.

On the ace of *oros* the obverse of the coin-like symbol bears the head of Queen Isabella II., who ascended the Spanish throne in 1833, against whom Barcelona revolted in 1841, but was compelled to re-acknowledge her by Espartero in 1842.

The backs of these cards are marked in a similar way to those of S. 23.

[$3\frac{1}{8} \times 1\frac{7}{8}$ in.]   [Backs decorated.]

S. 26.

THIRD QUARTER OF NINETEENTH CENTURY.

BARCELONA.

PACK of numerals of the ordinary Spanish character.

It is a duplicate of the set described under S. 25, with the exception that the backs of the cards are marked in a different manner. In the present series the backs have a network of red lines crossing each other diagonally.

[$3\frac{1}{8}$ × $1\frac{7}{8}$ in.]   [Backs decorated.]

S. 27.

THIRD QUARTER OF NINETEENTH CENTURY.

BARCELONA.

PACK of forty-eight numerals of the ordinary Spanish type.

The designs generally are slightly different from those of the sets before noticed.

The four of *copas* bears the allegorical figure and address of Lopez of Barcelona. At the centre of the four of *oros* is a pine-apple. The figures on the coate-cards of the suit of *espadas* wear armour.

The large symbol on the ace of *oros* is borne by two lions couchant.

The backs of these cards are marked by a network of dull red lines crossing each other diagonally.

[$3\frac{2}{8}$ × 2 in.]   [Backs decorated.]

S. 28.

THIRD QUARTER OF NINETEENTH CENTURY.

BARCELONA.

PACK of the ordinary Spanish sequence of forty-eight cards.

The designs differ slightly from those of the series previously described.

On the four of *copas* are the allegorical figure and address of Lopez of Barcelona. The ace of *oros* bears a medallion head like the obverse of a large coin, surmounted by a crown supported by standards. Below are a caduceus, shell, flowers, and other ornaments.

The cards are numbered at opposite corners diagonally in the ordinary manner. The backs are marked like those of the card of S. 23.

[$3\frac{2}{8}$ × 2 in.]   [Backs decorated.]

S. 29.

THIRD QUARTER OF NINETEENTH CENTURY.

BARCELONA.

 SET (forty-eight) of numerals of the usual Spanish variety. The designs are nearly identical with those of S. 28, but the colouring of the figures on the coate-cards is occasionally different.

The ace of *oros* is analogous to that of S. 28 in design, but is coloured a little differently. The four of *copas* bears the allegorical figure and address of Lopez of Barcelona.

The backs of these cards are marked with a network of blue lines crossing each other diagonally.

[3⅝ in. × 2 in.]   [Backs decorated.]

S. 30.

THIRD QUARTER OF NINETEENTH CENTURY.

BARCELONA.

 SET (forty-eight) of numerals of the ordinary Spanish character, numbered in the usual manner.

The designs differ slightly in some respects from those of the previously described packs.

The ace of *oros* bears the arms of Castile and Leon on a circular shield, surmounted by a crown and supported by standards. Below, on the bar of a large case, are the capitals " A. L. Y. Cᵃ."

The inscription on the circular shield is " Con Privilegio Esclusivo De S. M."

In the centre of the four of *oros* is a basket of flowers. The four of *copas* bears the allegorical figure and address of Lopez of Barcelona.

The backs of these cards are marked with an arborescent network of blue lines.

[3⅝ × 2 in.]   [Backs decorated.]

S. 31.

THIRD QUARTER OF NINETEENTH CENTURY.

PARIS.

 PACK of Spanish numerals of the ordinary kind, manufactured at Paris.

The ace of *oros* bears two large interlaced capital letters ; " A. A." on the mark of the suit. Above, on a scroll, is the inscription : " NAIPES-FINOS."

On the four of *oros* is a chimeric animal—a compromise between a unicorn and a sea monster.

The four of *copas* bears the inscription . " FABRICA DE ALFONZO ARNOULT EN PARIS."

The engraved title of the envelope accompanies this set; on it may be read: " NAPES REFINOS ; " " No. 2 " being on the mark of *oros*.   Below are the marks of the suits *bastos* and *espadas*, placed crosswise, having the foot of a cup (?) placed over the point of decussation ; the backs of the cards are marked with a neat diapered pattern of blue lines forming large diamond-shaped spaces, in the centre of which is a blue dot.

[3$\frac{2}{8}$ × 2 in.]   [Backs decorated.]

S. 32.

THIRD QUARTER OF NINETEENTH CENTURY.

PARIS.

 PACK of forty-eight numerals of the ordinary Spanish kind, manufactured at Paris.

On the ace of *oros* is a head in the centre of a radiant sun, encircled by a wreath of laurel.

On the four of *oros* at the centre is a basket of flowers.   The larger mark on the five of *oros* bears the inscription : " Cartes illustrées.   B. P. Grimaud et Cie. Paris " ; within are the capitals, " B P G," interlaced.

Most of these card-pieces are neatly designed, engraved, and coloured. Where gold is intended to be represented the designs are illuminated.   The ace, two, three, and four of *espadas* are particularly noteworthy.

This pack was manufactured in Paris, evidently for the Spanish market, the cards being in every respect, except commonness or coarseness of execution, truly Spanish in character.

[3$\frac{2}{8}$ × 2 in.]   [Backs plain.]

S. 33.

THIRD QUARTER OF NINETEENTH CENTURY.

MADRID.

SET of Spanish numerals, of different designs to those of the cards before noticed.

The suits are the usual ones, *oros, copas, espadas,* and *bastos*, but the cards are not numbered as in the ordinary manner.

The ace of *oros* bears a large blue eagle, in the middle of which are represented some houses.   On the two of *espadas* is inscribed : " Fabricando in Madrid."   This set of cards offers points of much interest in some respects.   It was manufactured in Madrid, most likely for the use of the provinces Limousin and Bretagne, for the purpose of playing the game known as *l'alluette or la luette*. This game is probably alluded to by Rabelais as among the amusements of Pantagruel, under the term *luettes*.   The pack before us appears to answer so closely in the designs, &c. to the set described by Merlin (p. 102), and to his remarks on the curious early cards found by M. Maurice Ardant (archiviste of Haute Vienne), in the cardboard covers of some old registers of the Hospital of Limoges, that the following extract may be made with advantage : " The cards are in every respect Spanish, unless with the exception that the heavy *caballeros* in their journey through France have become elegant Amazons, whose grace and steadiness in the saddle may defy the most agile *ecuyères* of the circus or hippodrome.

" What was the nature of this game before the Revolution ? We cannot say ; all we know is—it existed. It was known to Court de Gebelin, and exercised the predilections of this *savant* for Egyptian symbolism. Then it had the strange titles of *Monsieur, Madame, la borgne, la vache, grand neuf,* and *petit neuf,* but which not anything in the designs appeared to justify. It was not then played with the cards of to-day.

" Cast but a general glance over plate 37, and you will perceive that the draughtsman was not only inspired with the ideas of the epoch of the Revolution, but endeavoured to make his designs conform to the names previously given to the cards. Thus *e. g.* in the old packs, *Monsieur* was purely and simply the three of *deniers.* The name is here justified by placing the bust of a national guard of 1789 in one of the marks of the three of *deniers. Madame* was the three of *coupes ;* here in one of the cups is introduced a female being crowned by a bird having a long neck and beak, and to whom likewise another bird appears to offer a bouquet of flowers.[1]

" The *fleurs-de-lis* which were distributed everywhere over the *batons* have been here displaced by arrows, and the ' cap of liberty' adorns the four of *coupes,* and decorates the head of the savage who bears the ace of *epées.* Finally the arms of Spain, which in the earlier packs were borne by the ace of *deniers,* have resigned their places to a town in a circle placed on an eagle's breast.

" But what means this savage, belted and crowned with feathers, who supports the enormous trunk of a tree, representing the ace of *batons ?* " If we consult the Limoges cards (pl. 32-36), we shall see on the ace of *batons* two diminutive men, supporting likewise a large branch of a tree. What is the meaning of that shield swinging between the branches of two trees ? It is a reminiscence of the two of *batons* of Limoges, where a little naked man is seen between two knotty clubs. This four of *deniers,* which in the *alluette* of the Revolution is ornamented with a double triangle, so arranged as to represent a star with six points, is it not to be met with in our Limousin cards also ? As to the *robino,* or the *indecorous,* a piece not to be found among the numeral cards of the latter, it is clearly a souvenir of the five of *deniers* of the old Spanish game, in which were represented the heads of the Roman king and queen regarding each other." (p. 103.)

In the present pack, within the double triangle at the centre of the four of *oros* are two cursive capital A's, slightly interlaced. One triangle is coloured yellow, the other green. The symbols of the two of *copas* are peculiar. Each cup has on it a red flat cap, from beneath which at each side projects a bird with long neck and beak. Below the two cups is a recumbent ox, directed towards the right, and looking at a thistle-like plant at his fore feet.

The ace of *espadas* is likewise noteworthy, as is also the ace of *copas.* Although the designs generally are of very inferior character artistically speaking, these cards are well worthy of study in connection with the text and plates of Merlin before mentioned.

The backs of these cards are marked in rather a peculiar manner. They are marbled green, the largest spaces being filled with green dots, the middle-sized are white, and the smallest are of a uniform deep green colour.

[$3\frac{1}{8}$ × 2 in.]   [Backs decorated.]

---

[1] The *alluette* of 1776 came from the workshop of P. Sigogne. Is it not likewise a *cigogne* that is meant to be represented by a bird of long neck to be found also on the breastplate of the *valet de deniers* of 1776 ?

S. 34.

THIRD QUARTER OF NINETEENTH CENTURY.

BARCELONA.

SET of forty-eight numerals of the ordinary Spanish suits and numbered in the usual way.

In opposition to the common Spanish custom, however, a *dama*, or lady, is admitted into the present pack, in place of the *sota* or knave. The tens are suppressed as usual. The coate-cards or honours represent historic personages. In the suit *oros* the *rey* is "D. Taime el conquistador," the lady is a "Dama de la Corte de Fernando III.," the *caballo*, "D. Juan de Austria." In *copas* the *rey* is "D. Pelayo," the lady a "Dama de la Corte de Felipe IV.," the *caballo*, "D. Alvaro de Luna." In *espadas* the *rey* is "Carlos V. Emperador," the lady a "Dama de la Corte de Carlos II.," while the *caballo* is "Gonzalo de Cordova." In *bastos* the *rey* is "D. Pedro el Cruel," the lady a "Dama de la Corte de Alonso XI.," the *caballo* is "El Cid Campeador."

The ace of *oros* bears a large circular shield, having a six-rayed star in the centre of the boss, and being surmounted by a plumed helmet supported by various arms and armour.

The four of *oros* has a shield and crest in its centre, while the four of *copas* bears the address of "Lopez y Compª. of Barcelona."

The designs of this pack are good, and are neatly engraved in different colours. The suit *oros* is yellowish-brown, *copas* rose-madder, *espadas* blue, and *bastos* brown-madder. The execution of the suit *oros* is in particular commendable, the marks having on them well-executed Gothic ornaments. Some of the figures on the coate-cards—as those of *espadas*, for example—are free, artistic, and fairly correct in costume.

Each figure of the "honours" bears the symbol of the particular suit in the right hand. Below the whole-length and flowingly draped figure is the title of the personage it represents.

The backs of the cards are diapered with diagonal lines, comprised of small parallel lines stamped in a dullish-red colour. In the diamond-shaped spaces thus formed are four-rayed stars of like colour.

[$3\frac{2}{3}$ × 2 in.]   [Backs decorated.]

S. 35.

THIRD QUARTER OF NINETEENTH CENTURY.

BARCELONA.

SET of numerals of the ordinary suits and manner of numbering.

The honours of the four suits represent figures illustrative of races typical of the four quarters of the globe.

The suit *oros* typifies Asia in a representation of the Chinese. *Copas* illustrates Africa in three conventional Oriental figures. *Espadas* represents Europe by figures in costume somewhat like that of the early part of the seventeenth century; while the suit *bastos* presents America under the form of what we can only call three Red Indians.

On the mark of the ace of *oros* may be read " Asia;" on that of *copas*, " Africa;" of *espadas*, " Europa;" and on the spiked club of *bastos*, " America." The marks throughout the suit *oros* bear on them what are meant to represent Chinese characters. On the four of *copas* is the allegorical figure and address of Lopez y Comp^a. of Barcelona.

The backs are marked by waved interlaced lines stamped in black.

[$3\frac{2}{8}$ × $1\frac{7}{8}$ in.]   [Backs decorated.]

S. 36.

THIRD QUARTER OF NINETEENTH CENTURY.

BARCELONA.

N ordinary set of Spanish numerals. The peculiarity of these cards consists in the circumstance that the figures on the coate-cards are caricatured or grotesquely represented, while the marks of the suits bear on them laughable ornaments or have ridiculous appendages. The ace of *oros* bears on its grotesque shield the inscription: " Con real Privilegio Esclusivo De S. M.", and on the four of *copas* is the allegorical figure and address of Lopez of Barcelona.

Between the marks of the four of *oros* are two comical figures sitting at a table and playing at cards. The *caballo* and *sota* of the suit *bastos* are particularly absurd.

The backs of the cards are marked by a network of blue lines crossing each other diagonally.

[$3\frac{1}{8}$ × $1\frac{7}{8}$ in.]   [Backs decorated.]

FRENCH PLAYING-CARDS.

TAROTS.

F. 37.

EIGHTEENTH CENTURY.

SOUTH OF FRANCE?

 PACK of combined tarots, *i.e.*, twenty-two *atouts* and fifty-six numerals, but of which two pieces of the latter are here wanting. The absent numeral cards are the ace of *deniers* and the two of *batons*. The true tarots designs are a similar modification of the old French pattern of Besançon, Marseilles, and Geneva, as may be seen in the Flemish series (Fl. 103), bearing the address of "F. J. Vandenbore Cartier a Bruxelles."

As in the Flemish series, No. 2 of the emblematic suit represents *L'Espagnol, Capitano Eracasse*, instead of the typical *La Papesse*. No. v. has on it *Bacus* in lieu of *Le Pape*, and *Le Pendu* (No. xii.) must be reversed in order that the figure may hang in the usual way, head downwards. No. xvi. is here *La Foudre*, a tree struck by lightning, instead of a tower or house, *La Maison Dieu*, and *Le Fol* is numbered xxii.

The suits of the numeral series have the old marks, *batons*, *coupes*, *deniers*, and *epées*, and the marks are like those of the Flemish pack (Fl. 103) before mentioned, with the exception that on the shield in the middle of the four of *deniers* are the letters " I ∗ G " in place of the lion and castle.

The two of *coupes* has a tablet at its lower portion bearing the following inscription :—

> " Pour conoistre que la
> Plus basse de Deniez et
> De coupes enporte les
> Plus hautes quand a
> Fait du Jeu."

The borders of all the cards are slightly different to those of the Belgian pack. The general execution of the pieces is inferior to that of the latter, which is sufficiently bad, while the titles of the subjects are most carelessly spelt. Thus on No. i. is " *Lerateleux*" instead of *Le Bateleur;* on No. iv. is " *Lampereur;*" on v. " *Bacus*," and on No. xiii. is " *Atrempance*" in lieu of *La Temperance*.

The backs of these cards are smooth, and marked diagonally with small stars of four points printed in black, having in their centres a white circular spot.

[$4\frac{1}{2}$ × $2\frac{5}{8}$ in.]   [Backs decorated.]

F. 38.

EIGHTEENTH CENTURY.

SHEET of ten unseparated card pieces from a tarots series. The pieces are in two rows of five cards in each row. The emblematic figures present are *Temperance*, xiiii.; *La Papesse*, ii.; *L'Empereur*, iiii.; *L'Imperatrice*, iii.; and *Le Fol*, i. The other and numeral pieces are the ace of cups, the two of swords, the ace of money, and valet of clubs.

The designs are almost identical with those given by Merlin (plates 20-23). They are from wood blocks, coarsely engraved, and are uncoloured.

The backs are neatly diapered with large diamond-shaped figures, having in their centres stars. The whole is printed in blue.

[$4\frac{3}{8}$ × $2\frac{1}{2}$ in.]   [Backs decorated.]

F. 39.

FIRST HALF OF NINETEENTH CENTURY.

MARSEILLES.

PACK of French combined tarots, *i. e.*, twenty-two *atouts* and fifty-six numerals.

The designs, which are coarsely engraved and coloured, are exactly like such as are represented on plates 20-22 of Merlin's treatise, and plates 1-3 of *tarocchi* cards at page 284 of the work of Singer.

La Papesse (No. ii.) is here present. *Le Pendu* (xii.) hangs head downwards, and *La Maison Dieu* (xvi.) and *Le Monde* are of the typical or old Venetian character.

The marks of the numeral suits are of the Italian character, viz., cups, money, swords, and clubs.

The orthography of the titles is often bad; thus we have " *Limperatrise*," " *Chcharior*," " *Tenperance*," " *Le Stoille*," &c., in place of the proper method.

The suit marks on the two of *deniers* are connected by a scroll bearing the address of " Bernardin Suzanne, Rue Vacon. 1. Marseille."

The backs of these cards are clouded or marbled in rose-madder.

[$4\frac{3}{8}$ × $2\frac{2}{8}$ in.]   [Backs coloured.]

F. 40.

FIRST HALF OF NINETEENTH CENTURY.

PARIS.

SERIES of seventy-eight cards——twenty-two *atouts* and fifty-six numerals.

The designs on the emblematic series are entirely different from those usually met with. They consist in general of animals in various and absurd actions and attitudes, badly and often most ridiculously conceived and coloured. On No. 8 is a rearing unicorn, the head, trunk, and two legs of which are blue, two legs pink, and the mane, tail, and horn yellow. On No. 12 a man plays the flageolet to a dancing bear, while on No. 14 a crocodile with scales of red, blue, and yellow colours, is swallowing a man in red breeches and yellow jacket. The frog on No. 16 is as big as its neighbour, the turtle; but the most extraordinary of all the figures is that of the lion (?) on No. x., which has a yellow body and three yellow legs, one pink leg and tail, a green mane, and green shaggy hair on the right thigh.

No. i., answering to the *Bateleur* of the typical variety, represents a sort of mountebank, or quack doctor, holding up in his left hand a bottle of physic, and grasping with his right the handle of a harlequin's wand. The last *atout* is unnumbered, and shows a man in parti-coloured trousers dancing and playing the flute. He has on a cocked hat with a feather, and carries a sword at his side. This figure answers to the *Mat*, or fool (No. xxii. when numbered) of the ordinary series. Each card of the *atout* series is numbered top and bottom in reverse. The numbers are of extraordinary size, being more than half an inch in height, contained in a margin $\frac{5}{8}$ of an inch wide. The number on 21 occupies a space $1\frac{1}{4}$ inch wide by $\frac{5}{8}$ in. in height.

Not any titles are attached to the *atout* pieces.

The marks of the suits of the numeral series are *piques, carreaux, cœurs,* and *trefles.* The court-cards are *valet, cavalier, dame,* and *roi.* The figures on the latter are whole-length, and the *cavalier* is always mounted on a most absurdly coloured horse. In general, however, the designs are better and less grotesque in conception and execution than are those of the true tarots.

Over the right leg of the king of hearts is a circular clear space left, as if for a duty stamp, but which has been placed instead on the seven of the same suit.

The backs of these cards are marbled in deep green.

The engraved title of the envelope accompanies this set. It is ornamental and printed in black on a buff-coloured ground. At the top is inscribed, " Grand Etteila" in large letters. Below may be read : " Le grand jeu des 78 Tarots Egyptiens ou Livre de Thot Fabriqué et vérifié par Zlismon." (Concerning *Etteila,* see under " French Cards of Divination.")

[$4\frac{2}{8} \times 2\frac{2}{8}$ in.]   [Backs coloured.]

F. 41.

SECOND HALF OF NINETEENTH CENTURY.

PARIS.

SERIES of seventy-eight cards—twenty-two *atutti* and fifty-six numerals.

All the tarots proper are printed double and in reverse, but the designs on each half of the card are different. On one half Chinese figures variously engaged are represented, on the other division are mermaids, tritons, or other sea monsters. On No. i. is a female dancing and playing a tambourine, and a harlequin dancing and playing a harp. The fool, here unnumbered, is represented by the half-length figure of a harlequin in double and reverse. He holds in his right hand a disc, from the centre of which rises a point on which is poised by the left leg the whole-length figure of a diminutive harlequin.

The figure on No. 13 reminds one of the old cut representing Mother Shipton in her favourite conveyance, though here the animal is a camel instead of a stag.

The marks of the suits of the numeral series are *piques, trefles, cœurs,* and *carreaux.*

The designs on the coate-cards, or honours, are busts printed double and in

F. 45.

SIXTEENTH CENTURY.

ROUEN.

OUR sheets relating to a numeral series of the ordinary French suits —*piques, trefles, cœurs,* and *carreaux.* On two sheets are four rows of card-pieces of the suits *piques* and *trefles* alternately. There are generally five perfect pieces and part of another card-piece in each row. The values of the pieces present range from five to ten.

A third sheet consists of the stamped *tarotée* paper, intended for the backs of the cards. It is marked with lozenge-shaped spots, running in slightly curved diagonal lines across the paper, printed in black ink.

A fourth sheet consists of the mutilated wrapper, intended to enclose the cards when perfected for the market. On an upper fragment are parts of a woodcut and inscription, the former exhibits a Sudarium or Veronica, and the latter the words " Sauveur du Monde ✠ ." The whole is printed in black ink. On a lower fragment is a mutilated impression from a woodcut, printed in red ink. Beneath a broad ornamental border is the inscription—

> " Cartes Fines Factes a Rouen
> ⟿ Par Robert Benieres." ⟿

Below are portions of a coat of arms and its supporters, of which three *fleur-de-lis* and the heads of two angels are all that can be seen.

The strange addition of a religious emblem and inscription to the cover of a pack of playing-cards, as shown on this sheet, may be explained by the circumstance that Rouen being a cathedral town, the seat of an archbishopric and college, it bestowed its patronage and certain privileges on a particular printing and publishing-house, which thus provided the inhabitants with amusement or piety according to circumstances.

[$3\frac{1}{2}$ × $1\frac{6}{8}$ in.]   [Backs decorated.]

F. 46.

SECOND QUARTER OF SIXTEENTH CENTURY.

ROUEN.

WO sheets of figure cards from a numeral series of the suits *piques, trefles, cœurs,* and *carreaux.*

On one sheet the pieces are coloured, and have the marks of their suits at the top right-hand corner. On the other sheet the cards have not been coloured, nor have they the suit marks. The coloured sheet has been torn; the upper two rows of figures are imperfect, the lower two rows are nearly entire. Each row exhibits six pieces, composed of the kings, queens, and valets. A queen in the upper row of the coloured sheet is named penthasilee; a king of *trefles,* Hector; and a valet of *trefles* bears on a scroll " Capitaine Vallante," and NB [Nicholas Besniere] on a shield between his legs. A king in the second row is named Charles, a queen of spades Persabee (Bethsabêe), a valet of spades has the address of " Nicolas Besniere " on a scroll, and a king of the same suit is entitled David. On the third row from the top a king of hearts is named Jullius Cæsar; a valet of hearts Siprien Roman; a valet of clubs as before, a queen of clubs Pentaxilee (Pentasilée), and a king of clubs Hector. On the lowest row is a king of diamonds named Charles, a valet of diamonds who is "Capitaine Metely," a queen of diamonds called Lucrelle (Lucresse), a king of spades who is David, and a valet of spades with the address of "Nicolas Besniere."

The other and uncoloured sheet has the four rows in a like sequence of six figures, each nearly perfect. A queen is here present named Heleine, torn away in the other sheet, and the address of "Robert Besniere," instead of "Nicolas Besniere," is on the valets.

These two sheets of card-pieces are interesting as being examples of the cards known as those of Charles, or David, Dubois, slightly modified, as executed at Rouen by the brothers Besniere. The influence of Spanish and Italian types may be seen here in the designs, which belong probably to the second quarter of the sixteenth century, or to about the time of the Battle of Pavia, fought in the early part of 1525, near that town, between the French and the Imperialists. The former were defeated, and their king, François Premier, after fighting with great valour, was obliged at last to surrender himself a prisoner. Francis wrote to his mother, Louisa of Savoy, Regent of the kingdom during his absence, "Tout est perdu, Madame, fors l'honneur."

According to Lacroix, the valet of *piques* in the Dubois cards resembles Charles the Fifth.

[$3\frac{3}{8}$ × $1\frac{6}{8}$ in.]   [Backs plain.]

F. 47.

LAST QUARTER OF SIXTEENTH CENTURY.

 SHEET of figure cards from a numeral series. It is torn at the lower portion. There are two rows of figures of five pieces in each row—king, queen, valet, king, and queen in the upper row, and queen, king, valet, queen, and king in the lower row. The pieces are uncoloured, and the marks of the suits are absent. On the central figure of each row—a valet—is a scroll bearing the address of "Jehan Genevoy." On the breast of the upper valet is a lion, sable, rampant, and on that of the upper king a double-headed eagle.

These cards are more carefully designed and engraved than usual, and appear to have served as a model for an Italianised version, to be immediately noticed.

[$3\frac{6}{8}$ × $2\frac{2}{8}$ in.]   [Backs plain.]

F. 48.

END OF SIXTEENTH CENTURY.

 WO sheets of figure cards from a numeral series of the suits *cœurs*, *carreaux*, *piques*, and *trefles*. Each sheet contains two rows of figures, five figures being in each row. On one sheet the figures are heavily and coarsely coloured, and the signs of the suits are present. The pieces of the other sheet are uncoloured, and are devoid of the marks of the suits.

These two sheets are evidently from different blocks, but which were intended to represent the same designs, the latter being an Italianised version of the French cards previously described—F. 47.

On the scrolls of the valets of both rows of the coloured sheet is the address of "Francesco Franco" very plainly marked, while on the valet of the uncoloured sheet the letters appear to be FRBNSŒ FRENC. The letter F may be seen on the heads of the partisans of the valets in the uncoloured sheet. On the *verso* of the latter is the following memorandum in MS.: "trovate nella fodera di un libro stampato a Torino nel 1600."

Though the execution is here of a heavier and coarser character than in the previous version, the proportions of some of the figures are juster, and the actions of the valets in particular better expressed.

Lacroix remarks :—

"Under Henry II. and his sons as many Italian as French cards were manufactured at Paris. The card-makers were even Italians." ("Le Moyen Age et la Renaissance.")

[$3\frac{5}{8} \times 2\frac{1}{8}$ in.]   [Backs plain.]

F. 49.

END OF SEVENTEENTH CENTURY.

PARIS?

EIGHT figure cards from a numeral series of the suits *cœurs*, *carreaux*, *trefles*, and *piques*.

The cards present are the king and queen of *cœurs*, the king and queen of *carreaux*, another king and queen, and two valets. The kings and queen of *cœurs* and *carreaux* have the suit marks, the other cards are without them. All the pieces are coloured.

The king of *cœurs* is entitled Charles, the queen of *cœurs*, Judic, the king of *carreaux*, Cezar, the queen of *carreaux*, Rachel.

Another king is David, a queen Argine, one valet is named Hogier, while the other has the address of "Jean Lebahy."

On the head of the partisan borne by the latter valet are the initials, J. L.

These cards are of neat execution. The pieces have not been backed nor mounted.

[$3\frac{2}{8} \times 2\frac{1}{16}$ in.]   [Backs plain.]

F. 50.

EIGHTEENTH CENTURY.

PARIS.

THIRTY-FOUR cards from a numeral series of fifty-two of the suits *cœurs*, *carreaux*, *trefles*, and *piques*.

The cards present in the suit of *cœurs* are the ace, 2, 4, 5, 6, 7, 8, 9, 10, *valet*, and *dame*. In *carreaux* the ace, 2, 5, 7, 9, 10, *dame*, and *roi*. In *trefles*, the 2, 3, 4, 5, 6, 7, and 9. In *piques*, the ace, 3, 5, 7, 8, 9, 10, and *valet*.

On the *valet* of *cœurs* is the title, Lahire.

[$3\frac{3}{8} \times 1\frac{6}{8}$ in.]   [Backs plain.]

F. 51.

EIGHTEENTH CENTURY.

PARIS.

IFTEEN cards from a series of fifty-two numerals of the suits *cœurs, carreaux, trefles,* and *piques.*

The cards present are in the suit *cœurs,* the ace, 2, 4, 5, 9, and 10. In *carreaux,* the 5, 7, *dame,* and *roi.* In *trefles,* the 4 and 6, and in *piques,* the ace, 3, and 7.

On the king of *carreaux* there is a monogram at the left-hand lower corner, and one on the head of the partisan on the right hand of the figure; but they are not decipherable.

[3⅜ × 1⅝ in.]   [Backs plain.]

F. 52.

EIGHTEENTH CENTURY.

PARIS.

WO coate-cards from a numeral series of fifty-two.

The cards present are the *dame* of *piques* and the *valet* of *cœurs.*

On the former at the left-hand lower corner are the letters R C on a small shield.

[3⅜ × 2 1/16 in.]   [Backs plain.]

F. 53.

EIGHTEENTH CENTURY.

PARIS.

WO pip cards from a numeral series of fifty-two. The cards present are the nine and ten of *cœurs.*

These cards, along with F. 50, F. 51, F. 52, were found about 1750 behind some wainscoting in a house at Cambridge undergoing repairs.

[3⅔ × 1⅝ in.]   [Backs plain.]

F. 54.

LAST QUARTER OF EIGHTEENTH CENTURY.

PARIS.

NE card from a numeral series manufactured probably for the Spanish market.

The card present is the five of swords. On the front of the card is the address, " Guillau Mandrou," and 1792 has been added in MS. On the back of the card is the following engraved inscription, contained within an ornamental framework, surmounted by the Royal Arms of France : " Eftin Maitre cordonnier de la Reine Demeure rüe Comtesse D'Artois en face de la rüe Mauconseil chez Mᵣ. Corneille Mᵈ. Epicier. a Paris."

The piece is coloured.

[3⅛ × 2 1/16 in.]   [Back decorated.]

F. 55.

EIGHTEENTH CENTURY.

SINGLE figure card—the queen of hearts—from a numeral series of the usual kind.

The queen holds a sceptre in her left hand ; she is turned towards the right.

The piece is coloured. On the back is a study in oil of a head by some artist.

[3⅜ × 2⅞ in.]   [Back decorated by hand.]

F. 56.

FIRST HALF OF NINETEENTH CENTURY.

PARIS.

AN entire set of a numeral series of fifty-two cards of the usual suits. The coate-cards represent full-length figures, the *roi de piques* being entitled David, the *dame* Pallas, and the *valet* Hogier. The *roi de trefles* is Alexandre, the *dame* Argine, and the *valet* Lancelot. The *roi de carreaux* is Cesar, the *dame* Rachel, and the *valet* Hector. The *roi de cœurs* is named Charles, the *dame* Judith, and the *valet* Lahire.

The *valet* of *trefles* holds in his right hand a shield bearing the inscription : "1816 Administ: des Contrib: Indir:" Around the mark of the suit on the ace of *trefles* is a wreath of oak-leaves.

The designs on the coate-cards are from engraved plates of a soft metal, and though stiff are neatly executed, as is likewise the colouring.

[3⅛ × 2 in.]   [Backs plain.]

F. 57.

FIRST QUARTER OF NINETEENTH CENTURY.

PARIS.

AN entire set of a numeral series of fifty-two cards of the usual suits. The pack is a *replica* of the one just described (F 56), but the designs have been printed off on cream-toned paper of considerable *lissage*, and the figure cards coloured in a heavier style.

The engraved title of a wrapper accompanies the pack. On it is inscribed : " Cartes tres-fines de la Fabrique De Jounin. Rue du Four-Saint Germain No. 71. Pres de la Croix-Rouge a Paris."

On one edge of the wrapper is the word " *Piquet*," showing that the same title was used for various sets, the present series not being a *piquet* pack.

[3⅛ × 2 in.]   [Backs plain.]

F. 57. 2.

FIRST QUARTER OF NINETEENTH CENTURY.

PARIS.

A SHEET containing the twelve coate-cards (unseparated) of a numeral series of fifty-two of the suits *trefles, piques, cœurs,* and *carreaux.*

The honours are king, queen, and valet. The kings bear the names of David, Charles, Cæsar, and Alexandre; the queens those of Abigail, Hildegarde, Calpurnie, and Statira, while the valets are entitled Azael, Ogier, Curion, and Parmenion. The *valet* of *trefles* rests his right hand on a shield, in the central circle of which is the address: "Gatteaux, 1811."

These card-pieces are interesting from the circumstance that they form part of the series of designs made by M. Gatteaux (*père*) at the command of the Emperor Napoleon I. who "désirant substituer aux figures bizarres des rois, dames, et valets, un dessin dont l'extrême élégance et la pureté rendent la contrefaçon difficile et qui puisse en même temps, par la fidélité des costumes et l'exactitude des attributs, répondre au but allégorique que paraît s'être proposé l'inventeur de ce jeu," desired that David, Mongez, Gatteaux, and other eminent artists of the time should be requested through the *Conseil d'Etat* to furnish specimens. (*Antea,* p. 46.)

These inventions of M. Gatteaux may be said to be in a general way well conceived, carefully drawn, and neatly executed, but a close examination of them elicits faults which, considering the source of the designs, demand notice. The male forms are heavy and too short for the size of the heads, some of the figures being scarcely more than six and a half heads high. The full and broad draperies, in which the kings particularly are clothed, increase the stumpy appearance of the figures still more. Certain of the female forms also are short for the size of the heads, while at the same time they are drawn on a scale which makes them all as tall as the men. The drawing of the upper extremities of some of the male forms is defective, and the head-dresses of two of the valets (hearts and spades) are mean. As a rule the actions are good, the *poses* statuesque and well-balanced, and the draperies satisfactory and largely designed. The attributes are appropriate and clear in their intentions. The *technic,* or engraving, is of a superior character, though from the closeness of the lines in some of the shadows the former have become clogged in inking, and hence produced a slightly blurred appearance in the impression.

The pieces are uncoloured. Spaces are left at the upper corners of the card for the ordinary suit marks, which in the example before us have not been added. Nevertheless, the suits are indicated, though in a manner very liable to pass unnoticed. The small ornaments in the borders of the draperies are composed chiefly of the marks of the suits, and the ends, or tails, of the chief folds of the mantles and scarves have diminutive pendants, or ornaments, of the form of the marks of the suits.

The card-pieces are here in two rows of six pieces each row. In the upper row are the king, queen, valet of spades, and valet, king, queen of hearts. In the lower row are the valet, queen, and king of diamonds, and valet, queen, and king of clubs. The valet of hearts carries a scroll in his right hand on which is inscribed the word "Ordre."

The designs of M. Gatteaux and others of the First Empire are alluded to by Merlin. (Bibl. 6, p. 114, 115.)

[$3\frac{1}{8}$ × 2 in.]   [Backs plain.]

F. 58.

NINETEENTH CENTURY.

PARIS.

SET of fifty-two numerals of the usual suits.

The coate-cards or honours have full-length figures in national costumes, representing the following personages. In the suit *trefles* the Emperor Napoleon (III.), the Empress Eugenie, and a royal huntsman. In *cœurs*, the Prince Consort of England, Queen Victoria, and a jockey. In *piques*, the Tsar of Russia, the Tsarina, and a royal serf. In *carreaux*, the Emperor of Austria, the Empress, and an imperial groom. On the ace of *trefles* are the imperial arms of France, and the word " FRANCE" at the left-hand lower corner. On the ace of *cœurs* are the arms of England, and the word " Angleterre" at the left-hand lower corner. On the ace of *piques* are the arms of Russia, and on that of *carreaux* those of Austria, with the respective words at the left-hand corner. On a smaller shield, placed like a shield of pretence over the royal arms, is the mark of the suit of each ace.

A wrapper accompanies the set; it is of glazed pink paper, having on it the following inscription, printed in blue and gold:—" Cartes Imperiales et Royales France—Angleterre Russie—Autriche   B. P. Grimaud & Cie   70 Rue de Bondy   Paris   B P Grimaud et Cie."

The designs—particularly the armorial bearings—are neatly engraved and coloured.

The backs are coloured bright rose-colour, and have much *lissage*.

[3⅛ × 2 in.]   [Backs coloured.]

F. 59.

SECOND HALF OF NINETEENTH CENTURY.

PARIS.

PERFECT set of a numeral series of fifty-two cards of the ordinary suits.

The coate-cards of this sequence are full-length figures representing popular characters, in theatrical or quasi-historic costumes. The *roi de piques* is entitled D'Artagnan; the *dame*, Madame Bonacieux; the *valet*, Planchet. In *trefles*, the *roi* is Athos; the *dame*, Lady Winter; the *valet*, Grimaud. In *carreaux*, the *roi* is Porthos; the *dame*, Duchesse de Chevreuse; the *valet*, Mousqueton. In *cœurs*, the *roi* is Aramis; the *dame*, Anne d'Autriche; and the *valet*, Bazin. These figures are well and picturesquely designed; they are printed off in chromo-lithography from several stones in bright and positive colours, and in parts illuminated in gold.

Around the mark of the suit on each ace is an ornamental wreath. The figure cards representing the kings have each a gold coronet at the left-hand upper corner, immediately above the mark of the suit.

The backs of the cards have much *lissage*, and are coloured light blue.

The title of the wrapper accompanies the set. It is printed in gold letters on a blue glazed paper, and bears the following inscription: " Costumes du Temps de Louis 13. Les Mousquetaires B. P. Grimaud & Cie 70, Rue de Bondy."

[3⅝ × 2⅛ in.]   [Backs coloured.]

F. 60.

NINETEENTH CENTURY.

PARIS.

PACK of fifty-two numerals of the usual suits, viz., *piques, carreaux, trefles,* and *cœurs.*

The figure cards or honours have on them busts printed in double and reverse, and bear the names of David, Pallas, and Hogier in *piques ;* Charles, Judith, and Lahire in *cœurs ;* Alexandre, Argine, and Lancelot in *trefles ;* Cæsar, Rachel, and Hector in *carreaux.*

The valet of *trefles* holds a shield in his right hand, on which is inscribed : " Administ. Des Contrib : Indir. 1853."

Around the mark of the suit on the ace of *trefles* is a wreath of oak-leaves.

These cards are after the same designs as those of F. 56, with the exception of the alterations necessary for the coate-cards.

The backs are coloured of a buff hue.

[3⅛ × 2 in.]   [Backs coloured.]

F. 61.

NINETEENTH CENTURY.

PARIS.

SET of fifty-two numerals of the ordinary suits. The coate-cards have busts printed in double and reverse.

The designs in each suit are different. The costumes of the *roi* and *valet* are of earlier character than those of the *dames,* which are quite modern.

On the *valet* of *piques* is the address, " F. d'Alph Arnoult a Paris," printed at the left-hand lower and right-hand upper corners.

The title of the wrapper accompanies the set. It is an ornamental neatly engraved piece, bearing the inscription, " Cartes Fines Allemandes en taille-douce a deux-tetes—No. 5."

It is presumed that these cards are styled *allemandes* because they do not constitute a *piquet* pack, *pure et simple,* and that the figures are double and in reverse.

The backs are marbled pink and white.

[3⅜ × 2⅛ in.]   [Backs coloured.]

F. 62.

NINETEENTH CENTURY.

PARIS.

SET of small-sized cards of the usual suits.

The figure cards have on them busts, printed double and in reverse. The *dame* of *trefles* holds a fan.

The title of the wrapper accompanies the pack. It is printed in black on a pink ground, and bears the following inscription : " Deux-Tetes, Jeu de Patience, Fabrique de Testu Rue Croix-des-Petits champs 37. Paris." The backs are coloured pink.

[2 × 1⅜ in.]   [Backs coloured.]

trefles the *roi* is Bussy d'Amboise, the *dame*, Dame de Monsoreau ; the *valet*, a groom holding a horse, is without title. In *carreaux* the *roi* is Cinq-Mars, the *dame*, Marion Delorme ; the *valet*, bearing glasses on a salver, is untitled. In *cœurs* the *roi* is the Chevalier d'Eon, the *dame*, the Comtesse de Rochefort ; the *valet*, who is footman, is without title, but on the base of a pilaster in the background is the address, " Gibert a Paris."

The marks of the suits on the aces are enclosed within an ornamental frame.

The engraved ornamental title of the wrapper accompanies the cards. It bears the following inscription, printed in black and gold, on a highly glazed and pink-coloured paper : " Entieres illustrées." " Brevet d'invention," " cartes dites opaques, B. P. Grimaud et Cie. Portrait Français Illustré, 70, Rue de Bondy Paris. B. P. Grimaud et Cie." " La transparence des cartes ordinaires est un inconvénient fort grave. Les cartes opaques ont une incontestable supériorité. Elles ne peuvent être reconnues au travers sous quelque jour qu'elles soient placées. Roche inc."

These cards are from neatly etched plates, and are carefully coloured. The backs are coloured pink, and the *lissage* is considerable.

[$3\frac{1}{8}$ × 2 in.]   [Backs coloured.]

F. 68.

NINETEENTH CENTURY.

PARIS.

 SET of *piquet* cards ; being a *replica* of the previously described set, F. 67. Not any title accompanies the pack.

[$3\frac{1}{8}$ × 2 in.]   [Backs decorated.]

F. 69.

SECOND HALF OF NINETEENTH CENTURY.

PARIS.

SET of *piquet* cards of the usual suits. The coate-cards have whole-length figures on them in the costume of the time. Gentlemen in paletots, frock, dress, and hunting coats represent the kings ; ladies in walking, indoor, and dress costumes portray the queens, and persons in the habits of coachmen, footmen, and gamekeepers, signify the valets.

The marks of the suits on the kings have a crown above them, and those on the aces are surrounded by an ornamental framework.

On the *valet* of *trefles* is the address of " O Gibert Fab^t. Paris," at the left-hand lower corner. On the *valet* of *piques*, a footman, is the word *Deposé* at the same place.

The engraved ornamental title of the wrapper accompanies the set. Allegorical female figures are represented emptying from a cornucopœia all kinds of fashions in the way of bonnets, muffs, shoes, &c. Above is printed " Modes, Cartes Parisiennes," below, " Paris Rue des Singes No. 3." The whole is printed in black on a glazed blue paper.

The backs are coloured blue, and are smooth.

[$3\frac{1}{16}$ × 2 in.]   [Backs coloured.]

F. 70.

SECOND HALF OF NINETEENTH CENTURY.

PARIS.

 SET of *piquet* cards of the ordinary character.   The coate-cards have busts on them printed double and in reverse.   They bear the names of David, Pallas, and Hogier in the suit of *piques;* Alexandre, Argine, and Lancelot in *trefles;* Cæsar, Rachel, and Hector in *carreaux;* and Charles, Judith, and Lahire in *cœurs.*

The mark of the suit on the ace of *trefles* is surrounded by a wreath of oak-leaves.

The backs are pink in colour and are glazed.

[3⅛ × 2 in.]   [Backs coloured.]

F. 71.

SECOND HALF OF NINETEENTH CENTURY.

PARIS.

 SET of *piquet* cards of the usual suits.   The coate-cards present busts printed double and in reverse, and are strongly coloured.

[3⅛ × 2 in.]   [Backs plain.]

F. 72.

SECOND HALF OF NINETEENTH CENTURY.

PARIS.

PIQUET set of the usual kind.   The coate-cards have busts printed double and in reverse, of different designs to those in the last set. The costumes are less conventional, and more historic in character, strongly coloured, and illuminated in gold.

The suit marks on the aces are contained within an arabesque ornament. The valet of *trefles* bears a shield, on the border of which is the address, " O Gibert Paris."

The title of the wrapper accompanies the cards.   It is printed in black on a pink ground, highly glazed, and bears the following design and inscription, viz.— two allegorical female figures, one emptying a cornucopœia filled with bonnets, muffs, and other articles of fashionable female attire.   Above them is : " Costumes Historiques Français," " Cartes Parisiennes," " Paris Rue des Singes No. 3."

The backs of the cards are glazed and coloured pink.

[3¹⁄₁₆ × 2 in.]   [Backs coloured.]

F. 73.

SECOND HALF OF NINETEENTH CENTURY.

PARIS.

A SET of *piquet* cards of the usual suits. On the coate-cards are full-length figures of English historic personages. The king of spades represents Buckingham, the queen the Comtesse de Marlborough, the valet, who bears glasses on a salver, is unnamed. The king of clubs is Sir Rhys Thomas, the queen the Comtesse de Salisbury, the valet, who carries a helmet in his hand, is unnamed, but the word FRANCE is engraved at the left-hand lower corner. The king of diamonds is Leicester, the queen the Comtesse d'Oxford, the valet is unnamed. The king of hearts is Mac-Farlan, the queen the Comtesse d'Argyle, while the valet, who bears a falcon on his left hand, is unnamed, but the card has the address, " Gibert Fab^t a Paris," at the background. The costumes are intended to be historic. The marks of the suits on the kings have a crown above them, and those on the aces are contained within arabesque ornaments.

These cards have been carefully designed and etched, and fairly coloured. The backs are coloured blue.

The engraved and ornamental title to the wrapper accompanies the set. It represents the allegorical female figures with the cornucopia of articles before described, and bears the inscription : " Cartes Parisiennes, Paris Rue des Singes. No. 3."

It is printed in black on a blue and glazed paper.

[$3\frac{1}{8}$ × 2 in.]   [Backs coloured.]

CARDS WITH A SECONDARY PURPOSE.

EDUCATIONAL — INSTRUCTIVE.

F. 74. A.

Engravings of the Italian School. Works of Stefano Della Bella,
3rd Volume.

F. 74. B.

(Jeu des Reynes Renommées.)

F. 74. C.

(Les Jeux de Cartes des Roys de France, 1664.)

FIRST HALF OF SEVENTEENTH CENTURY.

PARIS.

THE CARDS OF DESMARESTS AND OF STEFANO DELLA BELLA.

URING the time of Louis XIV. a French academician, Jean Des-marests[1] (born Paris, 1596), undertook, at the suggestion of Cardinal Mazarin, to prepare some series of games with cards, which might serve the purpose of instructing the young king. With this view Desmarests (who died in 1676 at the mansion of the Cardinal, of which he had been made in-tendant), associated with himself Stefano Della Bella, the well-known Florentine artist and engraver. They produced four series of instructive cards, Desmarests undertaking the general designs and arrangements, and Della Bella the particular illustrations and the engraving of them. The various series were afterwards sold by Henri Le Gras, of the Royal Library, letters patent of the date 1644 having been issued to Desmarests, granting him certain privileges and monopolies connected with the cards, and forbidding their sale by any one than his authorized publisher, under a penalty of 3,000 livres and confiscation of the articles.

The first of these instructive or educational cards published, was a set entitled " *Le Jeu des Fables ou de la Metamorphose*," in which were represented " the gods, demi-gods, goddesses, and heroes of antiquity," accompanied by a *précis historique*" at the lower part of each card, illustrative of the mythology of the ancients. Then followed " *Le Jeu des Rois de France*," or " *Le Jeu de l'Histoire de France*," exhibiting the various kings from Pharamond to Louis XIV., and indicating in abridged histories their particular characters, &c. Thirdly appeared " *Le Jeu des Reynes renommées*," in which " is passed under review the queens, heroines, and other illustrious women, from the remotest antiquity until the present time. Some in chariots, some on horseback, others on foot, along with expositions of their characters; and an abridged account of the more striking incidents in their history." (Jombert, p. 28.)

Finally appeared " *Le Jeu de la Géographie*," " the whole forming a series of nearly 200 plates, extremely interesting, and of the best period of the work of S. Della Bella." (Jombert.)

A little explanatory book of sixty pages (F 74, C), was afterwards produced by Desmarests, having the following title : " Les Jeux de Cartes Des Roys de France, des Reines renommées, de la Géographie et des Fables. Cy-devant dédiez à la Reine Régente pour l'instruction du Roy et depuis mis ensemble en un volume portatif pour apprendre très facilement l'Histoire, la Géographie et les Fables. Par IDM. A Paris, chez Florentin Lambert rue Saint Jacques, vis-à-vis Saint Yves a l'Image Saint Paul—M.DC.LXIV. avec Privilége du Roi."

This brochure contains in the first place an address, " A la Reyne Régente," who is informed that " Ce sont des Jeux en apparence que je présente à votre Majesté mais en effet c'est un livre, et une estude pour les Jeunes Princes, aussi sérieuse pour le moins que divertissante. Voicy un nouvel Art qu'a produit une extrème passion de servir mon Roy après avoir considéré ses belles et généreuses inclinations, les beaux fruits que produira cette Royalle plante estant bien cultivée et les biens et la gloire dont vos Majestez et toute la France seront comblées, si l'on adjouste une soigneuse éducation à la grandeur et à la merveille de sa naissance," &c. &c.

Next follows a " Lettre d'une Dame de Rennes a M. Desmarests sur le Jeu des Reines renommées," in which M. Desmarests' selection and rejection of par-

---

[1] Spelt also Des-Marets.

ticular " Dames renommées," and his historical account of the selected ones, are somewhat severely criticised. This letter is signed *M. D. B.*, and is dated " De Rennes ce 27 Décembre 1644." After this comes M. Desmarests' reply, dated " De Paris, ce 10 Janvier 1645." In it the writer makes a strong, but courteous reclamation against the strictures of one whom he believes to be " une Dame de qualité et de très bon esprit."

The following is an analysis of the educational and instructive series of cards by Desmarests and Della Bella (F. 74. A., F. 74. B., F. 74 c.), as preserved in the British Museum.

F. 74. A. 1. " *Jeu des Fables.*"

A sequence of fifty-two separated card-pieces, and a title engraved *au travers*, bearing the inscription, " Jeu des Fables." The series is intended to afford instruction in ancient mythology and fable. Each piece has a figure subject of mythologic character, occupying half the card. Immediately below the design is its title, followed by a short, descriptive summary. Under this, towards the right-hand corner, is the mark of the particular suit to which the piece belongs, and towards the left is the number indicating its value. The intended coate-cards or honours have R, D, and M on them in place of the numbers.

The marks of the suits are *cœurs, trefles, piques,* and *carreaux.*

The coate-cards of the suit *cœurs* represent Jupiter, Juno, and Mars ; those of *carreaux,* Saturn, Venus, and Apollon ; of *piques,* Pluton, Diane, and Bacchus ; of *trefles,* Neptune, Pallas, and Mercury. The ace of *piques* exhibits Amphion seated on a rock overlooking a stream ; in the background are castellated walls. Below is inscribed " Amphion. Roy de Thèbes, bastit les murs de Thèbes au son de sa Lyre, les pierres suivant les cadences et se rangeant d'elles mêmes."

A copy of the ace of *trefles* is given by Boiteau d'Ambly, p. 133, and by Taylor, p. 328, pl. 35. It represents " Arion" seated on a dolphin playing the violin. Below is the following :—" Excellent musicien fut jetté dans la mer par des marchands pour avoir son bien, et ayant joué de sa lyre avant que d'estre jetté, un dauphin le récoit et le mit au bord."

The subjects of " Cephale et Procris," " Jupiter et Danaë," " Thesée et Ariadne," " Hippomène et Atalante," &c., vary the illustrations with " Neptune," " Ceres," " Niobe," " Pigmalion," and others.

Of this particular set, impressions of three different states exist in the collection of the works of S. Della Bella in the British Museum. (Vol. 3.)

1. *First State.*—Brilliant impressions before any inscriptions, marks, and numbers of suits. The card-pieces are unseparated, being contained in four large sheets of twelve cards in three rows of four cards each row, and in two smaller sheets, one sheet having three, the other two pieces engraved on it. A vacant place is on the latter sheet, which contains the title, engraved *au travers*.

2. *Second State.*—Card-pieces separated. Inscriptions and numbers added, together with the marks of the suits. The latter in *cœurs* and *carreaux* are in outline only. The coate-cards are devoid as yet of the letters R, D, A. The title-piece is wanting.

3. *Third State.*—The marks of the suit *carreaux,* before in outline, are now filled up by perpendicular lines, as are likewise the marks of the suit *cœurs.* The letters R, D, A, are added to the coate-cards.

The title-piece is present, and bears the inscription, " Jeu des Fables." The *pieces* are separate. Some of the designs of these card-pieces are very graceful and poetic, and the execution of them admirable, but they should be seen as impressions of the first state to be justly appreciated.

[$3\frac{3}{8} \times 2\frac{1}{8}$ in.]   [Backs plain.]

F. 74. A. 2.   F. 74. C.[1] " *Cartes des Roys de France.*"

A series of forty card-pieces, including a title, the secondary purpose of which is to afford historical instruction. Each piece has on it a figure or figures, equestrian or otherwise, representing kings or regents of France, from Pharamond to Louis XIV., the latter being portrayed as a youth in a stately chariot guided by his mother. Below each design is engraved an historic account of the person represented. Above it is a number (generally at the left-hand upper corner), indicating the person's position in the sequence of the French kings. At the right-hand upper corner is recorded the number of years of the particular reign.

In illustration, the card-piece on which is represented "François 1e" may be taken. Occupying somewhat less than half the card is the figure of a king on horseback, directed towards the left hand. He is in armour, wears a plumed helmet, and extends his right hand, in which is the baton of authority. At the left-hand upper corner is the number 58 in rather large figures, implying that Francis was the fifty-eighth king; at the left-hand upper corner is engraved " regna 32."

Below the design is the following account, engraved on a piece of hanging drapery:—" FRANÇOIS I. Vaillant, libéral, humain, aymant les lettres, il gagna contre les Suisses une grande bataille disputée 2 jours. Il résista à toute l'Europe liguée contre la France, il combatit de toutes partes la puissance de Charles quint, mais sa prise devant Pavie luy fit perdre tous ses avantages."

Though there are but thirty-nine cards (one of the forty being a title), the number of designs proceeds to sixty-five, some of the pieces having four or five figures on them.

On one card are the numbers 6, 7, 8, 9, 14, belonging to " cruel kings," who are Childebert, *cruel et avare*, 6 ; Clotaire, *tué de sa main ses neveux*, 7 ; Cherebert, 8 ; Chilperic, *Il estrangla sa femme*, 9 ; Childeric 2e, *Il fit foueter un gentilhomme qui le tua*, 14.

A copy of one of the pieces, viz. that representing five "*faynéants*," may be seen in Boiteau d'Ambly's work, p. 134, and in Taylor's version, p. 344, pl. xxxvi. The kings selected appear to be arranged in the following manner :— " Good kings,". " simple-minded kings," " cruel kings," " faithless kings," " unfortunate kings," " kings neither good or bad." The latter include Charles the Bald, Francis II., and Louis the Stammerer.

Of the last king, Louis XIV., it is stated :—" Prince longtemps attendu, et qui estant donné de Dieux aux vœux d'une bonne et sage reyne et de tout le peuple faict espérer qu'il possédera toutes les vertus royales et que son regne sera très heureux, puis qu'il a commencé par la bataille de Rocroy et la prise de Thionville."

The ornamental title engraved *au travers*, bears the following inscription : " Cartes des Rois de France. A Paris Chez Henri Le Gras Libraire au troisieme pilier de la grande Salle du Palais."—Avec Privil."

The set of card-pieces under notice has not any indications of suits nor of values. Each piece is separate, and all are neatly designed and engraved.

[$3\frac{3}{8}$ × $2\frac{1}{16}$ in.]   [Backs plain.]

F. 74. A. 3.   "*Jeu des Reynes Renommeés.*"

A set of fifty-two card-pieces with a title, the secondary purpose of which is to afford instruction in history.

---

[1] F. 74. c. The dedicatory and descriptive volume before mentioned at p. 127, refers to all the series in the 3rd vol. of the works of S. Della Bella.

These pieces have on them neatly engraved whole-length figures of renowned women, from Dido to Queen Elizabeth; they are variously engaged, some of them being on horseback and some in chariots. They are classed as follows:—

Saints and holy women	.	.	. as St. Helena, *e.g.*
Good women	.	.	. „ Penelope.
Wise women	.	.	. „ Isabel of Castile.
Clever women	.	.	. „ Catherine de Medici.
Celebrated women	.	.	. „ Dido.
Brave women	.	.	. „ Penthesilea.
Happy women	.	.	. „ Roxana.
Cruel women	.	.	. „ Clytemnestra.
Licentious women	.	.	. „ Messalina.
Capricious women	.	.	. „ Sabina.
Unfortunate women	.	.	. „ Octavia.

The personages chosen under these heads are so arranged in separate classes, as to indicate the ordinary suits and values of playing-cards. In another set presently to be referred to, the four suits are likewise differentiated by the way in which the drapery is coloured. Any attempt, however, to employ these and their congeners as ordinary playing-cards would lead to confusion only.

Each piece of the present series, with the exception of twelve intended to represent the honours, has a number indicating its value at the upper left-hand corner. At the right-hand upper corner is engraved the generic character of the personage represented. Below the design are the title and a description of the " reyne renommée." Thus, *e.g.* on a card intended to form the ten of a suit is the number 10, and the word "*pieuse*" at the upper corners respectively. Half the card is then occupied by a female figure in a religious habit, and carrying a crucifix. At the lower half is engraved " Elizabeth d'Arragon. Femme de Denys Roy de Portugal, elle vescut sainctement et un jour portant dans un coin de sa robe de l'argent pour les pauvres le Roy luy demanda ce quelle portait, elle lui dit, ce sont des roses, le Roy le voulut voir, et l'argent se trouva changé en roses."

A copy of a " reyne galante " is given by Boiteau d'Ambly, p. 136. Some of these female figures are of very elegant design and of careful execution.

The ornamental title is engraved *au travers*, and has on it " Jeu des Reynes Renommées." At the lower portion is the address of Henri Le Gras, " avec Privilége." The address has been cut through, but sufficient remains to permit of the identification.

[$3\frac{3}{8}$ × $2\frac{1}{8}$ in.]   [Backs plain.]

F. 74. B. " *Jeu des Reynes Renommées.*"

Another copy of the set just described, in which the pieces have been coloured so as to indicate the four suits. Boiteau d'Ambly, commenting on this set, observes:—

" Les cartes sont, par couleurs, dorées, ou argentées, ou vertes, ou de teinte dite columbine, c'est-à-dire d'un rose tendre tirant un peu sur le chamois."—(*Op. cit.* p. 136.)

These pieces have been separated, and stiffly mounted like playing-cards. The colouring detracts from the goodness of the designs and engraving, and is but of slight help in the way intended.

The title is absent.

[$3\frac{3}{8}$ × $2\frac{1}{8}$ in.]   [Backs plain.]

F. 74. A. 4. "*Jeu de Cartes de la Géographie.*"

A series of fifty-two card-pieces, without the title, intended to give instruction in geography.

Each card-piece has on its upper half a design or figure in a national costume, emblematic of a geographic division of the globe. Below are the title, and an account of the place represented. Thus, on a card intended to represent an ace is the number 1 at the left-hand upper corner. The upper half of the piece is occupied by a full-length figure with a trailing habit of Mauresque character; he bears a lance with pennon in his right hand, and wears a plumed turban or cap. Below is the following inscription : "BARBARIE. Belle et temperée, s'estend le long de la mer méditerranée jusques au destroit de Gilbratar [sic] les villes Tunis, Biserte, Alger et Tripoly, sont tenues par des pyrates sous la protection du Turc."

The four quarters of the globe represent the four suits, each having twelve divisions, *i.e.* 13 × 4 = 52. In one suit the king is represented by Europe, the queen by France, and the valet by Spain, or their emblematic figures. The numerals of the suit include Sicily, Dalmatia, Greece, Servia, Hungary, Poland, Scandinavia, Great Britain, Germany, and Italy.

The supposition that these cards could be used for the purposes of ordinary play is quite illusory. The designs and executions of this series are very commendable. Some of the former, such, *e.g.* as those illustrating the four quarters of the globe, are rich and pictorial.

[$3\frac{1}{2}$ × $2\frac{1}{8}$ in.]   [Backs plain.]

Of this series, two copies exist in the Museum collection. Both are among the works of Stefano Della Bella, vol. iii. *ut anteœ.*

1. An imperfect set of early impressions of twenty-five of the card-pieces, before the addition of the numbers at the left-hand upper corner. Each piece having been cut away immediately below the design, the places of the inscriptions are wanting.

[2 × 2 in. average.]   [Backs plain.]

2. A full and fine set—*minus* the title, however—having both numbers and inscriptions, as before described.

Charles Antoine Jombert, in his " Essai d'un Catalogue de l'œuvre D'Etienne De la Belle," &c., Paris, 1772, 8vo., has the following note in reference to these various series of cards :—

" In order to be sure of the first states, it is requisite to possess all these small prints, "*avant la lettre*," as they may be seen among the works of Della Bella which are in the cabinet of the king, and which it is almost impossible to gather together. Under any circumstances, these four series should be obtained with the address of Henri Legras at the Palace, and not with that of Florent Lecomte, " Rue St. Jacques au Chiffre Royale," as this author advises in the second volume of his catalogue (second part, p. 117), of the works of Della Bella, since Le Comte did not come into possession of the plates until long after the time of Henri Legras. These four series are very amusing, and are of the best period of the artist. They were designed by Desmarets (author of the poem 'Clovis'), according to the order of Cardinal Mazarin, to facilitate the studies of Louis XIV. when a child." (*Op. cit.* p. 113.)

F. 75.

EIGHTEENTH CENTURY.

PARIS.

(GEOGRAPHIC.)

PIQUET set of card-pieces (thirty-two), the secondary purpose of which is to teach geography.

The suits are distinguished by small squares of colour at the upper corners of each piece. Each square is likewise marked with either the number of the suit or the initial letter of the "honour." The greater portion of each piece is occupied by a neatly engraved geographic map, or a chart having references to a description below.

The aces of the different suits represent respectively a plan of the celestial universe, an armillary sphere, and the two terrestrial hemispheres.

These cards are neatly engraved and coloured, and care has evidently been taken to render them geographically correct. The degrees of latitude and longitude are marked on the maps.

The backs of these cards are marbled with a variety of brilliant colours.

[$4\frac{2}{8} \times 2\frac{3}{8}$ in.]　　　　　　　　　　　　　　　　[Backs coloured.]

F. 76.

LAST QUARTER OF SEVENTEENTH CENTURY.

PARIS.

(MILITARY SCIENCE.)

LARGE engraved sheet, containing fifty-two unseparated card-pieces, intended to serve the purpose of instruction in military engineering science, as well as that of ordinary play.

The marks of the suits are *piques, trefles, carreaux,* and *cœurs;* the figure-cards are *roi, dame,* and *valet.*

There are five rows of cards. Of the upper two rows, each contain eleven pieces ; the middle row has seven, a dedicatory address, and a general bird's-eye view of a " Place Complète des Fortifications." The fourth row has eleven pieces, and the fifth, or lowest, contains twelve.

In a broad margin above the divisions are several inscriptions. The central and titular one is as follows :—" Le Jeu des Fortifications dans lequel les différents ouvrages qui servent à la défense des places et des camps sont exactement dessinés selon la plus nouvelle manière avec toutes leur définitions et une explication courte et facile des termes qui sont en usage dans cet art."

On each side of the above are the " Règles du Jeu," in which it is stated that " ce Jeu souffre toutes les différentes espèces de jeu qui se jouent avec les cartes ordinaires. On le peut jouer aussi avec deux Dés observant les règles marquées cy dessous."

At the left-hand corner of the upper margin is a paragraph pointing out the connection of geometry with military engineering science; while at the right-hand corner of the same, the nature of fortification is pointed out. The dedication in the third row runs thus :—" A L'Illustre Jeunesse élevée dans le collége de Louis Le Grand." Twenty lines of address then follow, with the signature of " Votre très humble et très obéissant serviteur, I. MARIETTE."

The lower portions of these unseparated card-pieces are occupied by engraved and coloured representations of particular details in fortification or engineering work, and of defence.

At the upper part is the title, and a more or less extended description of the design below. At the upper right-hand corner is a diminutive representation of an ordinary numeral playing-card, having a number at the top, proceeding from No. 1 on the ace of diamonds (the first card on the lowest row) to 52 on the king of hearts, the fifth card-piece of the middle row. The figure or coate-cards have on them diminutive full-length figures, standing, and wearing red mantles.

Some of the card-pieces of the lowest series have on them diagrams and descriptions in geometry.

All the designs and descriptions are from neatly engraved copper-plates, and some, like the "Fausse Braye," or the four of *piques*, in the top row, the "Pont Levis," or the nine of *cœurs*, in the second row; the "Ports de Mer," or the two of *trefles*, in the centre row; and the "Chateau," or ten of *cœurs*, in the same series, form agreeable views or landscapes.

A margin is preserved at the left-hand side of the sheet for a "Table Alpha-bétique des Termes contenus en cette carte."

At the bottom, between the broad border-line and the plate edge-mark, is the following address, at the left-hand corner :—"Inventé et dessiné par Gilles de la Boissière, ingénieur ordinaire du Roy."

At the right-hand corner is "A Paris, chez I. Mariette, rue St. Jacques aux Colonnes d'Hercules, avec Privilége du Roy."

The general sheet of card-pieces measures 19½ × 27⅞ in.
[3¾ × 2⅛ in.]   [Backs plain.]

F. 77.

LAST QUARTER OF SEVENTEENTH CENTURY.

PARIS.

(MILITARY SCIENCE.)

LARGE engraved sheet, 19¼ in. high by 27 in. wide, of fifty-two un-separated card-pieces, intended to serve for instruction in the prin-ciples of military science as well as for ordinary play. The suits and honours are of the usual kind.

There are five rows of cards. The upper two rows contain eleven pieces each row; the centre series has seven, and a dedicatory address, together with a repre-sentation of a monarch investing a hero with some dignity. The fourth row con-tains eleven pieces, and the lowest series twelve.

In a broad margin above the upper row of cards are several inscriptions, the central one being titular, and as follows :—" Le Jeu de la Guerre "—" ou tout ce qui s'observe dans les Marches et Campements dans les Batailles, Combats, Siéges et autres actions Militaires est exactement représenté avec les Définitions et les explications de chaque chose en particulier."

At each side of the above are the " Règles du Jeu," which commence with the information that " ce Jeu souffre toutes les différentes espèces de Jeux qui se jouent avec les cartes ordinaires, dont le nombre est représenté par 52 Figures marquées de Pique, de Treffle, de Cœur et de Carreau. Le Chiffre Romain qui se voit dans chaque Carte en marque la Valeur, l' R signifie le Roy, le D la Dame, l' V le Valet.

" Ce jeu se joue aussy avec deux Dez ordinaires," &c. &c.

The dedication in the third row of card-pieces is to " Monseigneur le Duc de

Bourgogne." It contains fourteen lines, and is signed by "Votre très H ét obéis: Serv : I. MARIETTE."

To the left is the representation of the French monarch seated on a throne, the steps of which an officer is ascending to receive a marshal's baton.

Below is the couplet—

> " L'héroïque valeur que ce grand Roy couronne
> N'estime dans ces prix que la main qui les donne."

The upper half of each card-piece exhibits a neatly designed and engraved representation of some military operation ; the lower half has the title and descriptive details.

Some of the designs are very picturesque, forming little bits, much after the styles of Callot and Stefano Della Bella. Each piece has the mark, in outline, of its suit at the upper left-hand corner, containing within it the value of the particular card. At the opposite and upper corner is the general number, rising from 1 on the ace of hearts (the first card on the lowest row) to 52 on the king of clubs, in the middle of the centre series.

At the lower margin of the sheet, at the left-hand corner, is the address : " Inventé et dessiné par Gilles de Boissiére Ingénieur ordinaire du Roy et Gravé par Pierre le Pautre."

At the right-hand corner is " A Paris chez I. Mariette rue St. Jacques aux Colonnes d'Hercules avec Privilége du Roy."

[$3\frac{3}{8}$ × $2\frac{1}{8}$ in.] [Backs plain.]

F. 78.

NINETEENTH CENTURY.

PARIS.

(MYTHOLOGIC.)

PIQUET set of cards (thirty-two), of the usual suits. Its secondary purpose is that of giving instruction in mythology.

On the coate-cards are full-length figures, representing, in *piques*, Pluton, Proserpine, and Minos ; in *trefles*, Neptune, Amphitrite, and a Triton ; in *carreaux*, Mars, Bellone, and Achille ; in *cœurs*, Jupiter, Junon, and Mercure. Each *roi* has a crown at the upper right-hand corner. The aces have a double set of designs, between the upper and lower of which is placed the mark of the suit. On the ace of *piques* are represented the Rape of Proserpine, and the Bark of Charon ; on that of *trefles*, the Nereids and Nymphs; on the ace of *carreaux* are the Trojan War, and the ship Argo, which had an oak for a mast, predicting future events ; while in *cœurs* are Leda and the Swan, and the workshop of Vulcan.

Each pip-card has on it either two circular medallions, or one larger oval medallion, containing a mythologic figure, such as Eurydice, Cerberus, Latona, and Hercules. The names of the subjects and persons represented are placed below them. Between and around the pips runs a delicate ornamental line in blue, having attached to it ornaments illuminated in gold. The medallions have likewise illuminated borders, and the crowns, arms, attributes, &c. of the figures and scenes are also illuminated in gold. All the cards are neatly engraved and coloured, and are printed off on paper having a slight blue tone of colour. The proportions of some of the figures are very bad indeed. The backs are coloured buff and are glazed. On one or two of the pieces is " Lith V^{or} Arouy Rue St. Honoré 67," accompanied on the seven of *trefles* by " V. Lange del et Lith."

The engraved ornamental title of the wrapper accompanies the set. It is printed in blue ink, and bears the following inscription : "Cartes mythologiques V^or Lange Paris V. Lange."

[3⅛ × 2⅛ in.]   [Backs coloured.]

F. 79.

LAST QUARTER OF SEVENTEENTH CENTURY.

LYONS?

(HERALDIC.)

 SERIES of fifty-two cards of the suits *piques, trefles, cœurs,* and *carreaux,* bound together as a small volume. This set is intended to afford instruction in heraldry, and is one of the original French versions of the sequence which originated with Oronce Finé dit de Brianville, an Abbé of Poitiers, and was first published by Benoist Coral, a bookseller at Lyons. A full description of this original edition, and of the Italian versions which succeeded it, has been already given under I. 13, I. 13. 2, I. 14.

In the present series the king of hearts and eight of clubs are wanting; but their places have been filled with hand-drawings of the arms absent.

On the king of clubs are the arms of Pope Innocent XI. (Odeschalci), 1676-1689, with the following description :—"Porte d'argent a six coupes couuertes de gueules posées trois deux et un, entre trois filetes de même mis en face, surmontés d'un lion leopardé aussi de gueles au chef cousu d'or chargé d'un aigle esployée de sable. Lescu tymbre de la Thiare et orné des deux clefs du St Siege."

The present series commences, however, with the king of spades bearing the arms of Leopoldo of the holy Roman empire and of Germany, with a shield of pretence of the arms of the house of Austria.

All the armorials are neatly coloured in their proper blazon, but the technical execution of the copper-plate engraving is but mediocre. The engraved descriptions and titles are in French.

Accompanying these heraldic cards is a curious book-shaped case which formerly contained them. It is of ebony, inlaid with ivory and different coloured woods, and fitted with clasps and hinges of chased steel. The following arms are represented on the external face of each cover by means of the ornamental inlaid ivory and wood, viz.—two lion's jambs couped and crossed in saltire, between an *estoile* of eight rays in chief and a *fleur-de-lis* in base. These are borne on a shield placed between the four letters

in mother-of-pearl.

The author of the article in the "Herald and Genealogist" (vol. iii. p. 77, 1866), alluding to these arms, remarks : "We have not ascertained the name to which the arms on the case belonged. The family of Rasponi of Rome bore Azure two lion's jambs crossed in saltire or, and Raspi of Venice had also lion's jambs in saltire, with a lion's head in chief and an eagle's leg in base. The letters, however, do not point to a name commencing with that initial."

[3½ × 2⅛ in.]   [Backs plain.]

HISTORIC—BIOGRAPHIC.

F. 79. 2.

NINETEENTH CENTURY.

PARIS.

PIQUET set of cards (thirty-two) of the ordinary suits. Biographical and historical information is intended to be conveyed by it, while it is meant also for the purposes of ordinary play.

The coate-cards exhibit full-length coloured figures of eminent male and female personages. In the suit *piques*, the king is Cæsar, the dame Judith, and the valet Guttemberg; in *trefles* the king is Alexander, the dame Saint Genevieve, the valet Christopher Columbus; in *carreaux* the king is Charlemagne, the dame Lucretia, and the valet Moses; while in *cœurs* the king is Homer, the dame Joan of Arc, the valet Napoleon I.

In these "honours" the mark of the suit is placed at the upper left-hand corner; at the right, is either the mark repeated or the word "Héros" on a wreath, to indicate the character of the person represented. The king of *piques*, Cæsar, has "Héros," while the valet, Guttemberg, has a wreath. Below the figure is the name and other information. Thus, below the figure on the *valet* of *trefles* is "Christophe Colomb. 1492-1506. Amérique." Under that of the *dame de cœurs* is "Jeanne d'Arc. 1428-1431. Sauva La France;" and below the *dame de carreaux* is "Lucrece. 509. AV. J.C. Pudeur. Vertu."

Moses holds in his hands the decalogue; Charlemagne a tablet, inscribed "Capitulaires, Ecoles;" and Guttemberg displays a scroll, having on it, "Et la lumière fut."

The ordinary pip-cards have the signs of their suits at each upper corner, the value of the cards being indicated by small medallion heads of illustrious people, in number equivalent to the value of the particular card. Below each medallion is a name and date. Each set of medallion heads is repeated on the corresponding cards of the four suits. Thus, on the seven of *piques* are the heads of Cuvier, Newton, Arago, A. Paré, Archimedes, Plato, and Franklin, which are repeated on the seven of *carreaux*, and on the sevens of the other suits.

The aces have each two designs, the mark of the suit being placed between them. On these pieces the histories of Cain and Abel, of the Creation, the Deluge, the Crucifixion, are portrayed.

All the cards have ornamental borders around the designs.

On the ace of *cœurs* is the address "Mel. G. Deschamps Inv^t. Eng. Moreau Fecit. Minne Sculp."

The ornamental engraved title of the wrapper accompanies the set. It is printed in black and gold on glazed pink paper, and is identical with that described on F. 67.

[$3\frac{1}{8} \times 2\frac{1}{8}$ in.]   [Backs plain.]

SATIRICAL.

F. 80.

FIRST QUARTER OF NINETEENTH CENTURY.
PARIS.

ORTY-FIVE cards from a pack of fifty-two numerals of the usual suits. The four, seven, and ten of *cœurs*, the ace of *piques*, the ace, two, and queen of *carreaux* are wanting.

The secondary purpose of these cards is chiefly of a satirical character, though there prevails much caricature and comic spirit among them. On the other hand, some of the pieces, particularly of the suit *trefles*, are of purely artistic design.

The coate-cards have full-length coloured figures on them, and smaller whole-length figures are introduced on many of the lower numerals. The latter figures are uncoloured, the colour being confined to the marks of the suits variously disposed, which are often made to constitute or fit into portions of the bodies. There is much spirit in some of the designs, and the engraving and colouring has been neatly and carefully executed.

The satire which prevails is directed against the dominant political party of the time. On the king of *trefles* is represented the editor of the " Journal des Débats," endeavouring to carry two large bags, the one inscribed " Empire," the other " Débats." He has a pen behind his ear, and his countenance and action express the difficulty of his labour. Between his legs are two donkeys in the middle distance, caressing each other. On one donkey hang the ribbon and medal of some order.

The *dame de trefles* represents the " Gazette " as an elderly lady, seated at a table writing. She has stopped for a moment to look up at a magpie in a cage hung up above the table.

The valet of the same suit exhibits the person of Talleyrand, under the title of " Clopineau." He carries his cocked hat under his left arm, and supports himself by his left hand on a stick. His left leg is shorter than the right one, and he wears on the left foot a high-heeled shoe. Near the top of the card are the signs of the political zodiac, which the minister has already passed through.

In *cœurs* the king symbolises the popular journal, the " Constitutionnel." He is a figure in Roman costume, with sword and shield, defending a column on which is inscribed " Charte constitutionnel, Liberté de la Presse, Liberté individuelle, Loi des Elections, Tolérance." The *dame* is Minerve, standing on the steps of a temple, and putting to flight certain evil spirits of the *parti prêtre*. The *valet* is Figaro, in character costume.

The king of *piques* is " Conservateur," a Jesuit, at the head of his troop of brethren, carrying a flaming torch and sword. The *dame* is the " Quotidienne," an ugly old woman, with an open book in her left hand, and an extinguisher in the other, which she is about to place on the head of Truth, a nude, good-looking young female, rising, glass in hand, from a well. The *valet* represents Chateaubriand, under the title of Bazile. He is a fine figure, in a clerical habit, hiding under his cloak a Jesuit's cap, which he holds in his left hand. Kneeling at his left side is a donkey, which is looking up at him and braying.

In the suit *carreaux* the king is represented by the " Moniteur," a brazen head on a truncated cone, in which are stuck various flags, indicative of the numerous parties which have been supported by the journal. A figure of Time is at the upper right-hand corner, flying away.   The *dame* is here absent.   The *valet* is " Don-Quichotte" attacking a windmill.

Some of the designs of the pip-cards in *cœurs* and *piques* are laughable enough, while in *trefles* are represented " L'Ange des Ténèbres vaincu par St. Michel," " Le roi Dagobert," " Insectes," " Vases Etrusques," " Tombeau Turc," &c.

These cards have been described by Chatto (p. 264), and alluded to by Peignot (p. 297) in 1826. The latter writer speaks of them as " a very malicious series, published at Paris seven or eight years ago, and, as far as I can remember, during the ministry of M. D. C . . . . , under the title of ' Cartes à rire.'   The pack is attributable to M. A . . . . , C. A.D. C.D.D.O.   All the cards, whether figure or numeral, are of excellent design, with ingeniously grouped figures in agreeable attitudes.   But the spirit of satire is carried to excess, and it is not by such caricatures as these that unanimity can be re-established among the French people."

[$3\frac{1}{2}$ × $2\frac{3}{8}$ in.]   [Backs plain.]

CARDS OF DIVINATION.

THE series of cards now to follow illustrate the application of the latter to the purposes of divination, sortilege, and fortune-telling.

The more important and quasi-scientific—if we may so speak—of such cards have been based generally in modern packs on tarots sequences, and of these latter, such as F. 39 may be taken as a fair example.

Of the tarots, here playing so prominent a part, much has been before stated (pp. 18, 36, 65); but they have yet to be considered under their mystical aspect, which forms so important and curious a branch of their history, as insisted on by some investigators. Their relations in this respect underlie, in fact, according to certain writers, not only a particular branch of thaumaturgic knowledge, but the whole history of playing-cards.   These emblematic figures, the tarots, are asserted to have had a very remote origin; an origin stretching as far back, indeed, as the ancient Egyptians, from whom they have descended to us as a book or series of subjects of deep symbolic meaning.   Some of these subjects have in the course of time, however, become somewhat changed or metamorphosed, yet leaving traces in sufficiency of the original symbols by which those learned in archæology and illuminism may establish their true nature.

The discovery and explication of this supposed source and hidden meaning of the tarots employed in modern times was claimed by M. Court de Gebelin in 1781, who in his " Monde Primitif analysé et comparé avec le Monde Moderne," tome i. p. 363, gave a dissertation, " Du Jeu des Tarots; ou l'on traite de son Origine, ou on explique ses allegories et ou l'on fait voir qu'il est la source de nos cartes modernes a jouer," &c.

In this dissertation M. de Gebelin affirms that the series of seventy-eight Venetian tarots, *i.e.* twenty-two *atutti* and fifty-six numerals, has an unquestionable claim to be regarded as an Egyptian book, which escaped the flames destroying the ancient libraries, and as coming down to us with an epitome of the purest Egyptian doctrine on some of the most important and interesting topics. If, states M. de Gebelin, the tarots game be closely investigated, it must be evident that it is based on the sacred Egyptian number seven. Each suit or colour is composed of twice seven cards. The *atouts* are in number three times seven; the total number of cards being seventy-seven; the fool, or " Matto," being O. If we search the allegories they contain, their ancient and Egyptian source becomes still more evident.

The *atouts* in general represent the spiritual and temporal heads of society, the physical chiefs of agriculture, the cardinal virtues, marriage, death and resurrection, or the Creation, the various aspects of fortune, the sage and the fool, and Time, the consumer of all things.

Let us examine these emblematic figures in detail,[1] commencing with No. 1, *Le Bateleur*, or cup-player (thimble-rigger), and proceed up to No. 21, *Le Monde*, as it is the custom of the present time to begin with the lowest number, though the Egyptians, it would appear, began at the higher and descended to the lower numbers.

The first of the *atouts* in the ascending, and the last in the descending scale, is a conjurer with cups, seen at his table, on which are dice, cups, knives, and balls. He is known also by his Jacob's staff or magician's wand, and by the ball which he holds between two fingers, and which he is going to make vanish. Placed at the head of all estates of men, he implies that our whole life is but a dream, an illusion, a perpetual game of chance, the impulse of a thousand circumstances over which we have no control, but upon which much influence is necessarily produced by an over-ruling administration. Nos. 2, 3, 4, and 5 are the spiritual and temporal heads of society. No. 2, *La Papesse*, is the chief priestess, the wife of the chief priest; No. 5, *Le Pape*.

We know that among the Egyptians the heads of the sacerdotal rank were married. Had these cards been the invention of modern times there would not have occurred any high priestess, far less one under the title *La Papesse*, as the German card-makers have ridiculously entitled the present. The high priestess is seated in an arm-chair, has on a long dress, with a kind of veil behind her head, and which crosses over the chest. She wears a double crown with two horns, as did Isis, holds an open book on her knees, and

---

[1] The study of the following pages, 139-155, should be accompanied by that of a Tarots sequence like F. 39 or of the plates in Singer (Bibl. 8) p. 284.

has two bands adorned with crosses passing like an X over the stomach.

No. 5, the high priest, *Le Pape*, in long dress and large mantle, secured at the neck by an *agraffe;* he wears the triple tiara; in one hand is a sceptre with a triple cross, with the other hand, of which two fingers are extended, he bestows benediction on two persons at his knees.   The Italian and German card-makers have converted these two emblematic figures (2 and 5), upon whom the ancients bestowed the names of father and mother (Oriental terms, signifying *abbé* and *abbesse*), into a pope and popess, in accordance with their own circumscribed knowledge.   As to the sceptre with the triple cross, it is purely an Egyptian relic; it may be seen on the table of Isis, under the form of T T; it is a precious relic, bearing relation to the triple Phallus, carried in the famous festival of Pamylies, representing the recovery of Osiris, and symbolising the regeneration of plants and of the whole of nature.

No. 3, *L'Imperatrice*, represents the queen, and No. 4, *l'Empereur*, the king.   Both have for attributes an eagle on a shield, and a sceptre surmounted by a globe *thautified*, or crowned with a cross, termed " thau," the chief of all symbols.

No. 6, *L'Amoureux*, is marriage.   A young man and woman pledge mutually their faith, a priest blesses them.   The cardmakers name this design *l'Amoreux*, and it would appear they added the Cupid with his bow and arrows in order to make it of a speaking character.

No. 7, *Le Chariot*, is Osiris triumphant.   He advances, sceptre in hand and crown on head.   He is in his chariot of war, drawn by two white horses.   Osiris was the grand and supreme deity, invisible, except as manifesting himself in nature.   He disappeared during winter, but re-appeared in spring with new glory, having in the interim conquered all that opposed him.

Nos. 8, 11, 12, and 14 are the four cardinal virtues.   No. 8 is *Justice* as a queen, or "Astrea," seated on a throne, holding a sword in one hand and a pair of scales in the other.   No. 11 is *Force*, a woman who has overcome a lion, whose jaws she opens with a like facility as she would those of her lap-dog; on her head is the hat of a shepherdess.   No. 12, *Le Pendu*, is in the place of *Prudence*.   Could the Egyptians—it may be asked—have forgotten the latter for this representation of humanity?   Yet we do not find Prudence in the sequence.   Instead of it we find, placed between Force and Temperance, a man suspended by his leg!   What does this mean?   It is the work—writes M. de Gebelin—of some wretched, presumptuous card-maker, who, not understanding the beauty of the allegory contained in the original design, took upon himself to correct it, as he thought, but in lieu disfiguring it *in toto*.

Prudence could be represented to sight satisfactorily only by means of a person erect, who, having one foot firmly fixed on the ground, advances the other, keeping it raised while searching for a spot on which he can place it securely. The original title of this card was equivalent to a man *" pede suspensu."* The card-maker, not understanding the sense of the latter, designed a figure suspended by the foot ! As might be expected, the question has been asked why there is such a strange figure as this *" Le Pendu "* in the tarots sequence ? It has been replied that it represents the just punishment of the inventor of it for having represented therein a female Pope !

No. 14 is *Temperance,* a winged female pouring water from one vessel into another to cool the fluid they contain.

No. 9, *L'Ermite,* is the sage, or seeker after truth and justice. He is a venerable philosopher in long mantle, with a cowl on his shoulders, leaning on a stick as he walks. He holds a lanthorn in his left hand, as he searches for virtue and justice. The card-makers have transformed him into a hermit. There is not any harm in having done so. In the East to become addicted to the occult sciences and *s'hermétiser* is almost one and the same thing. The Egyptian hermits were equal in this respect to those of India and to the Talapoins of Siam, and the same may be said of the Druids.

No. 10 is the *Wheel of Fortune.* Here human beings under the form of monkeys, dogs, rabbits, &c., rise in their turns upon the wheel to which they are attached. It is a satire on Fortune, and on those whom she elevates rapidly into notice, and lets fall with a like rapidity.

No. 13, *La Mort,* is Death mowing down all humanity. Whether kings or queens, rich or poor, none can resist his terrible scythe. Nor is it to be wondered at that Death should be placed under this number, which has always been regarded as of unfortunate character. According to an ancient legend it was on the thirteenth day of the infancy of the world that some great misfortune happened, the remembrance of which had an influence on all the people of antiquity ; on the Jews to the extent that the thirteen tribes have never yet been able to complete more than twelve of their number.

No. 15, *Le Diable,* is Typhon, a celebrated Egyptian personage. He was the brother of Osiris and Isis, the evil principle, the chief demon of Hell. He has bat's wings, the hands and feet of a harpy, and on his head the horns of a stag. At his feet stand two little devils with long ears and tails, and their hands tied behind them. They are secured to each other by a cord round their necks, which is attached at its centre to the pedestal of Typhon. This implies that the latter does not readily allow those to escape who belong to him ; Typhon likes too well his own flock to suffer that negligence.

No. 16, *La Maison Dieu,* is the Castle of Plutus.   It is a tower filled with gold but falling in ruins, and crushing its worshippers as it falls.   It symbolizes the history of the Egyptian Prince Rhampsinit, spoken of by Herodotus.   It is a lesson against avarice.   The moderns added the thunder and lightning of God in bringing to a close the worship of Mammon.

No. 17, *L'Estoille,* is Sirius or the Dog-star.   We perceive a large star having around it seven smaller stars.   Below is a woman resting on one knee while she pours out two streams of water (two rivers) from vases in her hand.   Near her is a butterfly on a flower (or bird on a tree).   It is purely Egyptian all through.   The large star is Sirius, rising as the sun passes from the sign of Cancer (in the next tarots emblem).   The seven smaller stars are the planets, and the woman below so attentive at this moment in discharging the water from her vessels is the Queen of Heaven, Isis, to whose beneficence are to be attributed the inundations of the Nile, which begin at the rising of Sirius.   For this reason the latter star was sacred to Isis; it became her symbol *par excellence.*   The flower and the butterfly on it are emblems of the regeneration and resurrection of nature due to the rising of Sirius and the favours of Isis, causing the naked plains to become laden with fresh harvests.

No. 18, *La Lune,* is the moon following the course of the sun, accompanied by tears of gold and of pearls, showing that she contributes on her part benefits to the earth.   According to the Egyptians it was the tears of Isis which each year increased the waters of the Nile, fertilizing the plains of Egypt.   At the lower part of the design may be seen a crab, which is the sign Cancer, indicating alike the retrograde course of the moon, and that it is at the time when the sun and the moon leave the sign of Cancer that the inundations caused by their tears occur on the rising of the Dog-star represented in number 17.   On each side is a tower, symbolizing the two renowned columns of Hercules, on this side and beyond which these two great luminaries never pass.   Between the towers are two large dogs baying at, and as if guarding, the moon ; an idea perfectly Egyptian, correlative to that which likened the tropics to two palaces, each building guarded by a dog, as if to prevent the sun and moon departing from the centre of the heavens and gliding to the poles.

No. 19, *Le Soleil,* is the sun, here represented as the physical father of man and of all nature ; as enlightening society and as presiding over its communities.   Tears of gold and of pearls drop from his rays, symbolizing the benign influences proceeding from the chief of stars.

No. 20, *Le Jugement,* has been sadly mistaken and metamorphosed by the card-makers, who have thus converted the original emblem into the solemnity of the last day. An angel is seen sounding a trumpet, and at the same time an old man, a woman, and a naked child appear to rise from the earth. The card-makers persisting in their mistake have added tombs to the design. But take away these tombs and the emblem answers to the Creation, taking place in and at the beginning of time typified in the next emblem No. 21.

No. 21, *Le Monde*, properly represents time. In the centre is the Goddess of Time, with her scarf flowing and serving as a kind of *peplum*. She is in the action of movement like Time, within a circle which represents the revolutions of the latter, and also an egg from which everything in the course of time has proceeded. At the four corners are the emblems of the four seasons composing the revolutions of the year. These emblems are like the four heads of the cherubim—the eagle, the lion, the ox, and the young man. The eagle symbolizes spring, when the birds re-appear; the lion, summer, or the fervour of the sun; the ox, autumn, when there are labour and sowing; and the young man, winter, when we re-unite in society.

Leaving the emblematic tarots and passing to the numeral series, four distinct suits may be observed. They are equivalent to the four states into which were divided the ancient Egyptians. The sword (or *epées, piques*, spades) designates the sovereign and all the military nobility; the cup (or *cœurs*, hearts) the sacerdotal rank or clergy; the club (*batons, trefles*, clubs) agriculture; and money (*deniers, carreaux*, diamonds) implies commerce. The name of the sequence—taro or tarots—is pure Egyptian. It is composed of the word TAR, signifying *way*, or *road*, and RO, ROS, ROG, implying *king* or *royal*. The word *taro* meaning, therefore, the "Royal Road of Life." Other Oriental words are still preserved in connection with the cards. The word "mat," *e. g.* the ordinary term for the *fool*, and which exists in Italian as *matto*, is derived from the Oriental *mat*, meaning *assommé, meurtri, fêlé*. Fools have always been considered as having *le cerveau fêlé*. The conjurer with the cups is called *pagad* in the course of the game. This word, which does not resemble anything in our Western tongues, is of purely Eastern origin. It has been well chosen, for PAG means chief, master, Lord, and GAD is fortune. Thus *le bateleur* is represented as disposing of fate with his magician's wand. Further, when the numeral cards are employed for the purposes of divination in Spain at the present time, the three of *oros* (money) is termed the lord (or Osiris); the three of *copas* (cups), the queen (or Isis); the two of *copas*, the cow (or Apis); the nine of *oros*, Mercury; the ace of *bastos* (clubs), the serpent (symbol of agriculture among the Egyptians); and the ace of *oros*, the eye (or Apollo, the sun).

Such is an outline of the views of M. de Gebelin, which received a further development in a memoir with which he accompanied his own dissertation. This memoir may be found printed entire in the appendix to the work of Singer, and is entitled " Recherches sur les Tarots et sur la Divination par les Cartes des tarots Par M. le C. DE M. . . ."

While Court de Gebelin was revealing to the world the origin of tarots, and the treasures of wisdom they contain, there was living at Paris a *perruquier* of the name of Alliette.

" Now *perruquiers*," writes M. Boiteau d'Ambly, " have been, and still are, persons of imagination and of inquisitive spirit. Without dwelling on Tasmin, how many of these hair-curlers have sought to shine by other qualities than the certainty and perfection of the cut of their scissors, and the stroke of their combs! Many have written, even in verse. One lumberingly facetious, wrote over the entrance to his shop this highly distinguished sentence : ' To-day we shave for money, to-morrow we shave gratis.' Another, highly erudite, had verses in Greek inscribed above his door. Alliette was one of the greater men of the caste of *perruquiers*, nay, still more, he was the *Pontifex maximus* of ' cartomancy.' By chance he read the dissertation of Court de Gebelin ; a light flashed across his brain ; he became enlightened. He at once reversed the order of the letters, composing his name, and from Alliette became Etteilla, and prophesied—illustrious Etteilla! One yet finds at thousands of little shops on the quays thousands of atrocious *bilboquets*, having inscribed on their covers : ' The art of Divination by cards according to the rules of the celebrated Etteilla.'

" Alliette was earnest in his inspiration. He gave himself up with his whole soul to the most out-of-the-way studies. He became absorbed in the theory of numbers, according to the system of Pythagoras ; he heard the harmonious murmur of the celestial spheres, and described their courses in space after the formulæ of the sublime arithmetic. He invented mythical calculations, developed them in designs, grouped their numbers, and finally became a professed *kabbalist*. The *Jeu des Tarots* was his chief war-horse. For thirty years he was its apologist, detailing its wonders, and interpreting the secrets it could unveil.

" The more remarkable of his writings is the ' Manière de se récréer avec le Jeu de Cartes nommées Tarots,' 1783 :—

" ' We may well be astonished,' writes Alliette, ' that time which destroys, and ignorance that changes everything, should have allowed a work composed in the 1828th year of Creation, 171 years after the Deluge, and written 3953 years ago, to have descended to our own times. This work was produced by seventeen Magi, including the second of the descendants of Mercury—

Athotis; who was grandson of Cham, and great-grandson of Noè; this Tri-Mercury (or third of the name), decreed the Book of Thot in accordance with the science and the wisdom of his ancestors.'

"It is impossible to be more precise; and how well Alliette knew how to profit by this science! 'I find therein,' he says, 'Time and Place through the discipline of the great Hipparch, the Rhodian, and the just Aristarch, the Samian.'

"Notice Hipparchus and Aristarchus! Alliette adopts an orthography which has an Asiatic, and consequently very religious aspect. He willingly quotes those whom he calls his predecessors, Raymond Lully, Jean Bellot, Duchesne (ordinary physician to the king), Croilus, Agrippa, D'Aubly, and others. Cartomancy thus resting on so fanciful a basis, could not fail to strike the minds of ignorant fashionable women. The *perruquier* Alliette became an important person, the High Priest of a religion. Perceiving this, he assisted Fortune in turning her wheel through his own domain, and straightway installed himself in the 'Hotel de Crillon,' Rue de la Verrerie. Etteilla made disciples, who soon became his rivals. Female ones, especially, were prominent. Under the pretence that Greece had the Delphic priestess, that Judea had the Pythoness of Endor, that Rome had the Cumæan Sibyl, and that their own Gaul had listened to the Druidesses, the women reclaimed their heritage, and began to prophesy" (p. 323.)

The author of the introduction to the "Nouvel Etteilla," (F 82) observes that Alliette, "in rendering justice to the science of Court de Gebelin, overthrew what that grave antiquary had transcribed in his eighth volume of the 'Monde Primitif,' it being nothing more than information obtained from an amateur who himself had gained his knowledge concerning the present subject from his cook only."

If Etteilla and his more recent disciples can be thus severe on De Gebelin, the great man himself, when weighed in the balance by Eliphas Levi, is found not to be perfect.

"The tarot, this miraculous book," writes E. Levi, "the source of inspiration of all the sacred books of the ancient peoples, is the most perfect instrument of divination that can be employed with entire confidence, on account of the analogical precision of its figures and its numbers. In fact, the oracles of this book are always rigorously true, and even when it does not predict anything, it always reveals something that was hidden, and gives the wisest counsel to those who consult it. Alliette, who from a *perruquier*, became a *kabbalist* in the last century, after passing thirty years meditating on the tarot; Alliette, who writing his name backwards, or as we read Hebrew, called himself kabbalistically Etteilla, was very near finding out all that had been concealed in this strange work, but finally succeeded only in displacing the keys of the tarot in lieu of understanding them. He

L

inverted the order and character of the figures, without, however, entirely destroying their analogies, so sympathetic and correspondent are they with each other. The writings of Etteilla—now become rather scarce[1]—are obscure, tiring, and of truly barbarous style. All have not been printed, some MSS. yet existing in the hands of a publisher in Paris, to whom we have been indebted for the means of inspecting them. The more remarkable of their characteristics are the obstinate opinions and the incontestable good faith of the author, who all his life had a presentiment of the grandeur of the occult sciences, yet was forced to die at the gate of the sanctuary without ever having passed behind its veil." ("Dogme et Rituel de la Haute Magie," vol. i. p. 357.) In another work, "Histoire de la Magie," the same writer observes :—

" The cartomancy resuscitated in France by Etteilla was nothing more than the consultation of Fate by means of signs agreed on before hand ; these signs combined with numbers inspired the medium, who became magnetized from looking on them, with oracles. These signs were drawn at hazard after the pack had been slowly shuffled, were then arranged according to kabbalistic numbers, and they always responded to the thoughts of the person who interrogated them seriously and in good faith." " This kabbalistic and wise book—(the " Tarot ")—is in its various combinations a revelation of the harmonies pre-existing among its signs, letters, and numbers, and is therefore capable of truly marvellous application. But we cannot with impunity thus wrest solely for ourselves the secrets of our intimate communication with the universal light. The consultation of cards and of tarots is a veritable conjuration which cannot be prosecuted without danger and crime. In all evocations we compel our astral body to appear before us, and to hold converse with us in the divination which results. We thus give embodiment to our chimeras, and convert into a proximate reality that future which will become veritably our own when we have evoked it by the word and adopted it by faith." (*Op. cit.* p. 465.)

Early in this century Dr. Alexander Buchan read a paper before the Antiquarian Society in reference to the origin and import of cards. The opinions therein broached were communicated by him afterwards to Mr. Singer, who printed them *in extenso* in the appendix to his well-known work. The more important of Dr. Buchan's views were as follows:—

The twelve honours in a pack of cards are emblematic of the twelve signs of the Zodiac—mansions of the sun—and equivalent to the twelve months of the solar year. Each of these signs is divided

---

[1] Two volumes of the early Amsterdam editions are in the British Museum Library—PM. 8630, c. 1, 5. 1, 3.

into three decans or thirty degrees ; each honour is equivalent in value to ten and $30 \times 12 = 360$, the number of the days of the ancient Egyptian year, and equal to the number of degrees into which the equator is still divided. Cards are generally distinguished by the colours, red and black answering to the great division of the year into two equal parts from solstice to solstice, equinox to equinox. The four suits indicate the four seasons, spades represent acorns matured in autumn, while cups—now hearts—mean that wine was ready and fit to be drunk in the winter season. The whole number of cards in a pack, fifty-two, is equal to the number of weeks into which the year is divided, and the number of cards in each suit, viz. thirteen, is equivalent to the number of weeks contained in each quarter of the civil year.

The number of pips on one suit is

	55
Which multiplied by	4
	220
Pips on honours	12
Twelve honours taken at ten each	120
Number of cards in each suit	13
	365 =

to the precise number of days in the solar year.

Cards are usually played and dealt circularly from left to right according to the apparent course of the sun, and when arranged as tricks they amount to thirteen of four suits each ; if each card be considered as representing a week, then the tricks may be regarded as symbolical of the thirteen lunar months composing the year.

Thus cards were originally devised for the purpose of reminding those who understood the allusions, of the system of the universe, a system with which the Magi and priests of ancient Egypt were well acquainted, though they carefully concealed such knowledge from the profane vulgar. Should these and other conjectures be admitted some light may be reflected on the very general employment of cards for the purpose of divination or fortune-telling, particularly by the gipsies. Judicial astrology, or an opinion that the fates and fortunes of the sons of men are influenced by the positions and aspects of the celestial bodies, is one of the most ancient forms of superstition that have prevailed among mankind. But why should cards in particular be employed as the instruments of discovering this mysterious influence unless they were originally supposed to bear some relation to astrology, a science which by the vulgar has always been confounded with astronomy ?

Still more recently views analogous to those of Court de Gebelin, Etteilla, and the divinatory and astrological purposes alluded to by

Buchan, have been advanced by certain writers. In 1857 *e. g.* M. Vailsant, in a work entitled "Les Romes, histoire vraie des vrais Bohémiens," sought to show that in the tarots designs were to be found the highest conceptions of Hindustani wisdom, while M. Eliphas Levi (Alphonse Constant) in his "Dogme et Rituel de la Haute Magie," 1861, and his "Histoire de la Magie," 1860, argues learnedly for the tarots being a revelation of the mysteries of the Hebrew kabbalah. Further, M. Boiteau d'Ambly in his "Les Cartes a Jouer et la Cartomancy," Paris, 1854, seeks to prove that cards were introduced into Europe from India by means of the gipsies for the purposes of divination.

"It is evident that the tarots, altered as they are, nay perverted from their original design, still retain the impress of a civilization which is by no means European" . . . "how comes it about that the tarots series seems based on the combinations of the number *seven,* the sacred number of the East?" . . . "these scraps of Eastern speech, these assumed combinations which centre round a sacred number, these names of certain figures, assuredly all this taken as a whole must be something more than mere speculation" . . . "we can perfectly avail ourselves of these arguments [those of Court de Gebelin], which go to prove that cards are the offspring of the learning of Egypt, and at the same time keep to our own hypothesis of their Asiatic origin—from India, in fact—along with the Gipsy immigration. There is no contradiction involved here. Egypt is the East all the same, and every one knows there is a family connexion between these venerable civilizations of the past —those of Egypt and India. In the ancient legends of Egypt the science of cards is connected even with their divinities." (Taylor's version of "Boiteau d'Ambly," pp. 13-21.)

M. Eliphas Levi (Alphonse Constant) in his extraordinary works "Dogme et Rituel de la Haute Magie" (Paris, 1861, 2 vols.), and "Histoire de la Magie" (Paris, 1860), finds in the tarots a revelation of the mysteries of the Hebrew kabbalah. The key to this revelation "is contained in a word, and in a word of four letters: it is the 'Tetragramma' of the Hebrews, the Azot of the Alchemists, the Thot of the Bohemians or Gipsies, and the Taro of the kabbalists. This word so variously expressed implies God to the profane, signifies Man to the philosopher, and offers to adepts the last word of human sciences, and the key of Divine power. But he alone knows how to employ it who understands the necessity of never revealing it.' ("Dogme," &c. vol. i. p. 90.)

"The incommunicable axiom is kabbalistically included in the four letters of the 'Tetragramma,' disposed in the following way:—

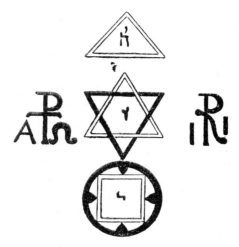

Likewise in the words Azoth and Inri written kabbalistically, and in the monogram of Christ as it was embroidered on the *labarum*, and which the kabbalist Postel interpreted by the word Rota, and from which adepts have formed the Taro or Tarot by repeating twice the first letter to indicate the circle and make it understood, that the word reverts, as it were, upon itself." (*Op. cit.* p. 154.)

Thus we have

"the key of hidden things "—" a word which may be read rota, signifying the Wheel of Ezechiel or tarot, which is then synonymous with the azoth of the hermetic philosophers. It is a word which expresses kabbalistically the dogmatic and natural *Absolute*; it is formed of the characters in the monogram of Christ after the manner of the Greeks and Hebrews. The latin R or the Greek P is placed between the Alpha and the Omega of the Apocalypse : then the tau, the sacred image of the Cross, contains the word in its entirety." (*Op. cit.* p. 341.)

" When the Sovereign Priesthood ceased in Israel, when all the oracles of the world became silent in presence of the Word become Man and speaking by the mouth of the most popular and gentle of sages, when the Ark was lost, the sanctuary profaned, and the Temple destroyed, the mysteries of the Ephod and Theraphim no longer recorded on gold and precious stones, were written or rather figured by certain wise kabbalists first on ivory, parchment, on gilt and silvered leather, and afterwards on simple cards, which were always objects of suspicion to the Official Church as containing a dangerous key to its mysteries. From these have originated those tarots whose antiquity was revealed to the learned Court de Gebelin through the sciences of hieroglyphics and of numbers, and which afterwards severely exercised the doubtful perspicacity and tenacious investigation of Etteilla." (*Op. cit.* vol. i. p. 337.)

" Without the tarot, the magic of the Ancients is a closed book to us, and it is impossible to penetrate any of the great secrets of the kabbalah. The tarot alone affords an interpretation of the magic squares of Agrippa and Paracelsus" (p. 342). " We have stated that the twenty-two keys of the tarots are the twenty-two letters of the primitive kabbalistic alphabet. The following is a table of the variations of this alphabet, according to different Hebrew kabbalists."

" א, Being, Spirit, Man or God, comprehensible object, unity the mother of numbers, the primordial substance.

" All these ideas are hieroglyphically expressed by the figure of the *Bateleur* (No. 1). His body and his arms form the letter א, around his head is a nimbus of the form ∞, the symbol of life and of the universal spirit. Before him lie swords, cups, and pantacles, and he raises his miraculous wand towards the sky. His figure is youthful, and his hair in curly locks like unto Apollo or Mercury. He has the smile of assurance on his lips, and the look of intelligence in his eyes.

" ב. The House of God and of Man, the sanctuary, the law, gnosis, the kabbalah, the hidden church, the binary principle, woman, mother.

" The hieroglyphic tarot is *La Papesse ;* a woman crowned with a tiara, having the horns of the moon or of Isis, the head surrounded by a veil. The solar cross is on her chest, and on her knees a book which she hides with her mantle.

" ג. The Word, the ternary principle, fullness, fecundity, nature, the generative faculty in the three worlds.

" The symbol is *L'Impératrice*, a winged female, crowned, seated, and having at the end of her sceptre the globe of the world. She has for her sign an eagle, image of the soul and of life.

" ד. ' La Porte,' or government among the Orientals, initiation, power, the tetragramma, the quaternary principle, the cubical stone or its base.

" The hieroglyph is *L'Empereur*, a sovereign whose body represents a right-angled triangle and his legs a cross, the image of Athanor of the philosophers.

" ה. Indication, demonstration, instruction, law, symbolism, philosophy, religion.

" Hieroglyph—*Le Pape* or the Grand Hierophant. In the more modern tarots this sign is displaced by the figure of Jupiter. The Grand Hierophant is seated between the pillars of Hermes and of Solomon, makes the sign of esoterism, and rests on a cross having three transverse bars forming a triangle. At his knees are two inferior ministers, so placed that having above him the capitals of the two columns, and below the heads of the two ministers, he becomes the centre of the quinary principle and represents the divine penta-gramma, and of which he thus affords the complete sense. In fact the columns are Necessity or Law, and the heads Liberty or Action. A line may be drawn from head to head, and two lines from each column to each head, thus obtaining a square divided into four triangles by a cross, in the centre of which will be the Grand Hierophant.

" ן. Attachment, entanglement, *lingam*, union, embrace, contest, antagonism, combination, equilibrium.

" Hieroglyph—(*L'Amoreux*), a man between Vice and Virtue. Above him beams the Sun of Truth, from which Love bends his bow threatening Vice with his arrow. In the sequence of the ten Sephiroth this symbol corresponds to Tiphereth, that is, to idealism and to beauty. The number six [of the tarots] represents the antagonism of the two ternaries, *i.e.* of absolute negation and of the absolute affirmative.

" . Arms, sword, flaming sword of the cherub, the sacred septenary principle, triumph, royalty, priesthood.

" Hieroglyph—a cubical chariot having four columns, and azure and starred drapery. In the chariot and between the four columns is a conqueror crowned with a circle, from which rise and radiate three pentagrams of gold. The conqueror has on his cuirass three chevrons one above the other; on his shoulders are the Urim and Thumin of the High Sacrificator, represented by the two crescents of the moon in Gedulah and in Geburah; his attitude is proud and tranquil. A double sphinx, or two sphinxes united by their after portions, are harnessed to the car, he guides a sphinx towards each side, but one of the sphinxes turns its head so that they both look to one point. The sphinx which turns its head is black, the other is white. On the square which forms the fore part of the chariot is the Indian Lingam, surmounted by the flying sphere of the Egyptians. This hieroglyphic is perhaps the most beautiful and complete of all the emblematic designs of the tarots.

" П. Balance, attraction and repulsion, life, fright, promise and menace.

" Hieroglyph—*Justice* with her sword and scales.

" ט. Goodness, horror of evil, morality, wisdom.

" Hieroglyph—a *Sage*, resting on his staff, and carrying a lamp before him. He covers himself closely in his mantle. The inscription is *l'Ermite* or *le Capucin*, but his proper name is *Prudence*, and he thus completes the four cardinal virtues which appeared incomplete to Court de Gebelin and to Etteilla.

" י. Principle, manifestation, praise, manly honour or virility, *phallus*, paternal sceptre.

" Hieroglyph—*La Roue de Fortune*, that is to say, the cosmogonic wheel of Ezechiel, with an Hermanubis ascending on the right hand and a Typhon descending on the left hand. Above is a sphinx in equilibrium, holding a sword with its lion-like claws. An admirable symbol disfigured by Etteilla.

" כ. The hand in the act of taking and holding.

" Hieroglyph—*La Force*, a woman crowned with the vital ∞, and quietly and without effort closing the mouth of a furious lion.

" ל. Example, instruction, public teaching.

"Symbol, a man hanging by a foot, whose hands are tied behind him in such way that his body forms a triangle, with the point downwards, and his limbs form a cross above the triangle. The gibbet has the form of a Hebrew *tau*, the two trees which support it have each six amputated branches. It is a symbol of sacrifice and of work accomplished.

" מ. The heaven of Jupiter and of Mars, domination and force, rejuvenescence, creation, and destruction.

" Hieroglyph—*La Mort*, who mows down crowned heads in a field in which men are seen sprouting.

" נ. The heaven of the sun, climates, seasons, movement, changes of life always new and always the same.

" Hieroglyph—*La Temperance*, an angel having the sign of the sun on his forehead, and on his chest the square and triangle of the septenary principle. He pours the two essences which compose the elixir of life from one vase into another.

" ס. The heaven of Mercury; occult science, magic, commerce, eloquence, mystery, moral force.

" Hieroglyph—*Le Diable*, the he-goat of Mendes, or the Baphomet of the temple, with all his pantheistic attributes. This hieroglyph is the only one that Etteilla perfectly understood and interpreted satisfactorily.

" ע. The heaven of the moon; changes, subversions, weaknesses.

"Hieroglyph— a tower, probably that of Babel, struck by lightning. Two persons, Nimrod without doubt, and his false prophet or minister, are precipitated from the ruins. One in falling represents perfectly the letter ע, gnaïn.

" פ. The heaven of the soul; effusions of thought, moral influence of idea on forms, immortality.

" Hieroglyph— a brilliant star and eternal youth.

" צ. The elements, the visible world, reflected light, material forms, symbolism.

" Hieroglyph—the moon, dew, a crab in the water ascending towards the earth, a dog and a wolf at the base of two towers howling at the moon. A path lost in the horizon is sprinkled with drops of blood.

" ק. Things united—the head, the summit, the prince of heaven.

" Hieroglyph—a radiant sun and two naked children, giving each other their hands within a fortified enclosure. In some tarots the symbol is a woman spinning human destinies; in others it is a naked child mounted on a white horse, and unfolding a scarlet banner.

" ר. The vegetative principle, the generative power of the earth, eternal life.

" Hieroglyph—*Le Jugement.* An angel sounds a trumpet, and the dead rise from their graves. Of these revivified dead we see a man, woman, and child, the ternary of human life.

" ש. The sensitive principle, the flesh, eternal life.

" Hieroglyph—*Le Fou :* a man dressed absurdly, walking at random, carrying a wallet behind him, *i.e.,* loaded with absurdities and vice.

" ת. The microcosm—the recapitulation of the all-in-all.

" Hieroglyph—the *kether* or the kabbalistic crown between the four mysterious animals. In the centre of the crown is Truth, holding in each hand a magic wand.

" Such are the twenty-two keys of the tarot, by which are explainable all the numbers of the latter. The *Bateleur,* or key of the unities, explains the four aces, with their quadruple signification, progressive in the three worlds and in the first principle. Thus the ace of denier or of the circle is the soul of the world; the ace of swords is the combative intelligence; the ace of cups is the animating intellect; the ace of bâtons, the creative intelligence. They are likewise the principles of movement, of progress, of fecundity, and of power. Each number, multiplied by a key, affords another number, which, in its turn explained by the keys, completes the philosophic and religious revelations contained in each sign. So each of the fifty-six cards (that is of the numeral series) may be multiplied by the twenty-two keys in turn; thus results a series of combinations all yielding the most surprising results of revelation and of light. It is a true philosophic machine, preventing the spirit from being led astray, at the same time leaving it its powers of initiation and of liberty. It is mathematics applied to the Absolute, the union of the Positive with the Ideal; it is a lottery of thoughts as rigorously correct as are numbers; in fine, it is perhaps, at the same time, the simplest and the grandest conception of human genius.

" The method of reading the hieroglyphs of the tarot is to arrange them either in squares or triangles, by placing the even numbers in opposition, and in conciliating them by the uneven ones. Four signs always express the Absolute in any order, and are explainable

by a fifth sign.   Thus the solution of all questions in magic is that
of the Pentagramma, and all the antinomies are explained by an
harmonious unity.

"Thus disposed the tarot becomes a true oracle, answering all
possible questions with more preciseness and infallibility than does
the Androidis of Albert the Great.   A prisoner deprived of books
might, in some years' time, if he had only a tarot which he knew how
to employ, acquire the knowledge of an universal science, and discuss
everything with a wisdom which has not any equal, and with an in-
exhaustible eloquence.   This wheel, in fact, is the true key to the
art of oratory, and to the great science of Raymond Lully.   It is the
veritable secret of the transmutation of darkness into light, it is the
first and most important of all the arcana of the great work."

"By means of this universal key of symbolism all the allegories of
India, of Egypt, and of Judea become plain; the Apocalypse of St.
John is a kabbalistic book, the sense of which is rigorously indicated
by the designs and numbers of the Urim and Thumin, of the Theraphim, and of the Ephod all combined and completed by the tarot.
The ancient sanctuaries have not any longer mysteries, and we comprehend for the first time the meaning of the objects in Hebrew
worship.   Who does not perceive, in fact, in the table of gold,
crowned, and supported by the cherubim, and which covered the
ark of the covenant and served as propitiatory, the like symbols as
in the twenty-first key of the tarot?   The ark was a hieroglyphic
résumé of all kabbalistic dogmas.   It contained the *Jod*, or flowering
rod of Aaron; the Hè, or cup, the gomor of manna; the two tables
of the law, a symbol like that of the sword of justice; and the
manna contained in the gomor—four things which translate marvel-
lously the letters of the divine "Tetragramma."   ("Dogme," &c.,
vol. ii. pp. 344-357.)

"The book of the tarot having so high a scientific importance, it
is much to be desired that it should remain unchanged."   "An important work remains to be performed: it is that of engraving and
publishing a tarot, rigorously complete and carefully executed."
"Vestiges of the tarot may be found among every people.   The
Italian tarot is, as we have stated, the best preserved and most faithful; but it may be improved by some valuable hints to be borrowed
from certain Spanish numeral series.   The two of cups, *e.g.* in the
Naïbi, is purely Egyptian; we there observe two antique vases, the
handles of which are formed by Ibises, placed above a cow.   In the
same cards we may see an unicorn in the middle of the four of deniers;
the three of cups represents the figure of Isis emerging from a vase,
with Ibises rising from other two vases; one Ibis bearing a crown
for the goddess, the other a lotus flower, which it appears to offer
her.   The four aces bear the image of the hieratic and sacred serpent;
and in certain packs, in the centre of the four of deniers, may be

found the double triangle of Salomon, in place of the symbolic unicorn.

"The German tarots have undergone more change; little else being found than the number of the keys surcharged with bizarre or pantagruelesque figures. We have before us a Chinese tarot, and some specimens from a like pack may be seen in the Imperial Library. M. Paul Boiteau, in his remarkable work on playing-cards, has given some examples very well executed. The Chinese tarot still preserves several of the primitive emblems; the deniers and the swords are readily to be distinguished, but it would be more difficult to make out the cups and the clubs."

"It was during the time of the Gnostic and the Manichean heresies that the tarot became lost to the Church, and it was at the same period that the meaning of the Divine Apocalypse ceased to be understood. It was no longer comprehended that the seven seals of this Kabbalistic book are seven pantacles explainable by the analogies of the numbers, characters, and figures of the tarot." (*Op. cit.* vol. ii. p. 361.)

As opposed to the preceding recondite and thaumaturgic views, and all such as place the origin of cards in the East, the opinions of M. Merlin (Bibl. 6, p. 37), may be opportunely considered.

According to this writer, if we take the tarots of Geneva, of Marseilles, and of Besançon as more faithfully representing the ancient Venetian tarots, and compare them with the "tarots-images" known as those of Mantegna,[1] we may perceive that of the twenty-six figures [*i. e.* the twenty-two *atouts* and the four additional "honours"] of the modern tarots, fifteen are due to the sequence in question. For example, the

Fou (mat, matto)	. corresponds to the	Misero . .	1,	Series E of Mantegna.
L'Empereur, iv. . .	„ „	Imperator .	9,	„ E „
Le Pape, v. . . .	„ „	Papa . .	10,	„ E „
Le Chariot, vii. . .	„ „	Mars . .	45,	„ A „
La Justice, viii. .	„ „	Justicia . .	37,	„ B „
L'Hermite, ix. . .	„ „	Saturno . .	47,	„ A „
La Force, xi. . .	„ „	Forteza . .	36,	„ B „
La Temperance, xiv.	„ „	Temperancia	34,	„ B „
L'Etoile, xvii. . .	„ „	Venus . .	43,	„ A „
La Lune, xviii. . .	„ „	Luna . .	41,	„ A „
Le Soleil, xix. . .	„ „	Sol . . .	44,	„ A „
Le Monde, xxi. . .	„ „	{ Jupiter . .	46,	„ } A „
		{ Prima Causa	50,	„ }

Among the "honours" of the numerical series—

Le Roi . .	. corresponds to the	RE . . .	8,	Series E of Mantegna.
Le Cavalier . . .	„ „	Chavalier .	6,	„ E „
Le Valet	„ „	Fameio . .	2,	„ E „

---

[1] I. 1. Page 65.

Should scepticism exist in reference to this re-embodiment of the figures of the so-called Mantegna series in the more modern tarots, it should be dissipated on a closer examination of the designs of the former. For example, the Misero, No. 1, of the series E, is being seized at the leg by a dog; so is the mat or fool of the tarots. Venus, 43, of the series A, is represented in the water with a shell or cup in her hand, while L'Etoile, xvii. of the tarots, is likewise a naked woman at the edge of a stream, from which she draws water with one hand to pour over her limbs with the other. Mars, 45, series A, is represented with the attributes awarded him in mythology. He appears as a seated warrior, on a car, sword in hand; both warrior and car are seen direct or in full face. The Chariot, vii. of the tarots, likewise shows a warrior on a car, with crown on head, cuirass on chest, and sceptre in hand. Warrior, chariot, and horses, all are seen direct or in full face. In both designs the car is surmounted by a dais supported by columns. Saturn, 47, series A, is portrayed as the old Saturn of the fable. With his left hand he conveys to his mouth a little child to be devoured, while he supports himself with his right on a staff, holding at the same time a winged serpent with its tail in its mouth— symbol of eternity. The tarot, more human, has made a hermit of him; nevertheless, the profile attitude, the lanthorn held on a level with the head, and the staff which gives support, recall the attitude of the Saturn of Mantegna. Further, the idea of Time has continued to be linked with this figure, for in the so-called " Cards of Charles VI." the hermit holds an hour-glass instead of a lanthorn.

At first sight, but little or no connection may be traced between La Prima Causa, 50, of series A, and Le Monde, xxi. of the tarots, except in the symbols of the four Evangelists, which exist in both, though it must be admitted not in the earlier version of 1470 of the sequence of Mantegna. But if we reflect on the meaning of the series of concentric circles of the design of the Prima Causa, we shall be able to trace the required affinity at once. This design represents the world according to the Ptolemaic system, the only system known in the fourteenth and fifteenth centuries. A like figure may be found in the " Géomance de Cattan" (translated by Gabr. du Preau), having above it the inscription " General figure of the two parts of the elementary and celestial World." In the " Margarita Philosophica" of Reisch, a curious encyclopædia often reprinted during the earlier portion of the sixteenth century, the same design may be observed illustrating a chapter " De Machinæ Mundi partitione." It is likewise the case that Le Monde is the last number (21) of the tarots, as is the Prima Causa the last of the series A. There cannot be any doubt that the author of the former took the title of " The World " from the design of the latter. As to the design of Le Monde of the tarots, which is sometimes a naked woman much like a savage, at other times a naked woman dancing; its explanation is difficult. It may be that its author intended to symbolize " La Volupté" which reigns over the universe; but if so, it must be confessed that the engravers have translated his ideas in a very peculiar way. Perhaps the oval frame, within which this female stands erect, may have been suggested by what may be seen in the Jupiter, 46, of series A.

Finally, look at the " Temperance" of the two series. The attitude and action are alike in each, so are they in the valet of cups in the modern combined tarots and in the Fameio of the ancient sequence.

M. Merlin proceeds to show that for the additional cards going to form the Minchiate of Florence (which consists of forty emblematic cards and fifty-seven numerals), not less than twenty more designs have been taken from the older series, thus forming a theft, if we may so speak, in the total of thirty-five designs towards the composition of modern tarots.

Attention may be called next to the fact that the general economy of the " Jeu des Tarots" appears to have been taken from that of the more ancient game. We find *e.g.* that the atouts of higher value in the former are those, the numbers of which are the more elevated. Now these are precisely such as correspond to the higher numbers of the latter or ancient series, and which are included between numbers forty-one and fifty. The lowest number of the older series is No. 1, the " Misero ; " the figure of the modern tarots corresponding to it is the " Fou," which is the " Zero " of the latter, or their weakest card. It cannot take any other card, and acquires value in a secondary way only, and by favour, as it were, of other cards.

Five series compose the "Tarots-Images" of Mantegna, a like number go to form the " Tarots-Jeux." These five series are each made up of ten pieces in the former, while in the latter four of the series are of ten each, with pips running from one to ten. There is another coincidence, the decades of the old sequence are distinguished by the letters A B C D E; the five series of the "Tarots-Jeux" are distinguished by objects, the initial letters of the names of which are A B C D E, *i.e. atouts, bâtons, coupes, deniers, épées,* and their equivalents in Italian and Spanish. It is true that in Italian the initial letter E does not occur, seeing that in this tongue the word for sword is *spada,* and not *espada,* as in Spanish. But as if this objection had been foreseen, the letter E of the earlier version [1470] has been displaced by the letter S in the version of 1485.[1] Yet once more; if the fourth decade of the ancient sequence be examined—the series of Virtues —it may be noticed that the signs of the four numeral suits of the " Tarots-Jeux," *i. e.* cups, money, swords, and clubs, are to be found among the attributes of the four virtues. Faith, 40, holds a chalice;

---

[1] *Antea,* page 70.

Charity, 38, an inverted purse from which issues money; Justice, 37, is armed with a sword; and Force, 36, with a mace or club. Surely such coincidences, insists M. Merlin, clearly enough indicate the parentage of the "Tarots-Jeux."

In vain may it be objected that differences are to be observed between the modern representations and the designs drawn and painted by hand during the earlier periods, and of which fragments are preserved in some privileged collections. These differences do not offer any satisfactory basis for reasonable doubt, since the cards illustrated by such fragments have been quite exceptional in character, and generally produced for purposes of presentation, or in connection with important circumstances when, as it may be readily conceived, the artists would feel justified in giving full reins to their imaginations.

Finally, to what nation, asks M. Merlin, must we not attribute the parentage of the Naïbis cited by Morelli, the precursors of all? To the Italian, without doubt. Everything in them reveals the Catholic thought and Italian ideas of the epoch [1393]. The pope has in them supremacy over the emperor, who is represented with the attributes of the empire of the West. In the version of 1485 the crown of the king is an Italian crown; the valet, merchant, cavalier, and gentleman all have Italian costumes. Further, the sciences are arranged in the order of the *trivium* and *quadrivium;* we find the three theologic and the four cardinal virtues, and if we meet with Apollo and the Muses it is with the attributes bestowed on them by occidentals of the middle ages, and not with such as accompany them on the ancient monuments of Greece and Rome. (Merlin, Bibl. 6, pp. 38-80.)

Thus, then—if the views of M. Merlin be correct—the "Tarots-Jeux" cards proper have sprung from the old Florentine or Venetian sequence—the cards of Baldini, the *tarocchi* of Mantegna; and this latter had its origin in a series of designs already existing in Italy in the fourteenth century, done by hand and termed "Naïbis." To Italy is likewise due the invention of the latter, and the fable of their Eastern origin must be altogether resigned. "Sic transit gloria mundi," *quoad* the reveries of Court de Gebelin, Etteilla, Levi, Buchan, Vailsant, Boiteau d'Ambly, and others. But it may be asked—is the matter really to be so disposed of?

There still remains to be noticed a view of the origin and meaning of numeral cards, which may be as appositely referred to here as anywhere else. It is that of Saint Bernard and of Saint Anthony. According to the former, who preached at Bologna in 1474, against the use of cards, the latter are the work of the devil. Satan became jealous of the act of Christ in causing the offices of his church to be recorded in books richly adorned with miniatures. He decided therefore, "nec deficere volo officiis meis Breviaria ac Diurna, quæ esse jubeo *char-*

ticellas seu Naibos in quibus variæ figuræ pingantur, sicut fieri solet in Breviariis Christi; quæ figuram in eis mystica præfigurent ut puto: (*i.e.* St. Bernard).

Denarii, avaritiam.

Baculi, stultitiam seu caninam sævitiam.

Calices, ebrietatem et gulam.

Enses, odium et guerram.

Reyes atque *Reginæ* prævalentes in nequitiis supra dictis.

Milites etiam *inferiores* et *superiores* luxuriam et sodomiam aperta fronte proclamant.''—See note in Merlin, p. 51.

It has been the opinion of some authorities that cards were introduced into Europe for the purposes of divination and fortune-telling by the gipsies some time between 1275 and 1325, an opinion strongly opposed by others.[1] The truth is, we are not sure of the exact time when the gipsies entered Europe, of the birth-place of cards, nor of the period when they were first employed for thaumaturgic purposes. But since, as Taylor observes (p. 453), there is so great a faculty of wonder in the uneducated—so infinite a longing for some knowledge of events to come, there can be little doubt that very early, both high and low alike sought oracular responses from any adepts who could be found, and would be satisfied if the replies were only vague enough to give countenance to the hopes they entertained.

According to Chatto (p. 116), there is in the ''Magasin Pittoresque,'' for 1842, p. 324, a cut entitled ''Philipe le Bon consultant une Tireuse de Cartes,'' copied from a painting attributed to Jan Van Eyck. Though it has been denied that this picture is really by V. Eyck, who died in 1467, it is allowed that the costume represented in it belongs to the reign of Charles VIII., between 1483 and 1498. If this be correct, we have thus evidence of cards having been used for the purpose of fortune-telling before the close of the fifteenth century. We have positive evidence that they were applied to this purpose early in the sixteenth century in the publication of the rare and beautiful book known as '' Le Sorti di Francesco Marcolini da Forli, intitolate Giardino di Pensieri, allo illustrissimo Signore Hercole Estense, Duca di Ferrara,'' the colophon of which runs as follows:—'' *In Venetia per Francesco Marcolini da Forli negli Anni del Signore MDXXXX. del mese di Ottobre.*''

It has been supposed that this work was not the first of its kind, and that Marcolini may have been prompted to his undertaking by the treatise of Sigismondo Fanti, of Ferrara, entitled '' Triompho di Fortuna di Sigismondo Fanti,'' and printed at Venice in 1526. But this latter treatise, though professing to teach the art of solving questions by divinations of various kinds, does

---

[1] *Antea,* pp. 8, 11.

not profess to use cards.   The interpreters of fate are the signs of
the zodiac, the constellations, sibyls, and various astrological personages, dice sometimes being used for the direction of the consultant.   The cards employed by Marcolini are the king, knight,
knave, 10, 9, 8, 7, 2, and ace of danari.   Though the ten was employed in Marcolini's system, it appears to have been generally
omitted from the packs used by the Italian jugglers of the sixteenth
century.   The work of Marcolini is known to iconophilists for the
beauty of its woodcuts after the designs of Giuseppe Porta, or
Salviati.   Reference may be made to Singer, p. 64, Chatto, p. 117,
and to Jackson and Chatto's "Treatise on Wood Engravings," p. 390,
for details connected with the treatise of Marcolini.   In Jackson
and Chatto's work copies of several of the cuts are given, accompanied by some valuable criticism.   In vol. i. I. W. 4, folio 136, of
Italian Chiaro-scuros, in the British Museum, may be seen the
engraved frontispiece to Marcolini's book, to which Jackson and
Chatto make particular allusion.

Leber assures us that he had examined "un grand nombre de
tours de cartes," described in the pamphlets of the Italian jugglers
of the sixteenth century, yet he refers to two works only on the subject printed before 1600.   One of them is entitled "Opera Nuova
non piu vista, nella quale potrai facilmente imparare molti giochi
di mano.   Composta da Francesco di Milano nominato in tutto il
mondo il *Bagatello*," 8vo. circa 1550.   The other bears the title
"Giochi di Carte bellissimi e di Memoria, per Horatio Galasso."
Venetia, 1593.   These works, however, together with the *brochure*
"Li Rari et Mirabili Giuochi di Carte da Alberto Francese detto
Perlimpimpim" (Bologna 1622), have more to do really with ordinary legerdemain than with divination.

It appears to have been the case that the recourse to cards for
divinatory purposes gradually declined among the upper classes
until the middle of the eighteenth century, though it was prevalent no
doubt among the lower grades of society frequenting fairs and the
caravans of mountebanks.   About 1750 divination through cards
again became popular—in Paris at least—for in 1751, 1752, and
1753, three persons were publicly known as offering their services
for this intention.   To these adepts were soon added others, since
the venture was profitable, but the cry of sacrilege was raised, and
in order to save—as it was pretended—the card-augurs from the
vengeance of the *dévots*, the former were seized and sent by the
police to the Bicètre, or to the Salpêtrière, unheard in their defence
and regardless of remonstrance.

It was at the latter period, *i. e.* 1753, that Etteilla (Alliette)
made his *début* by superseding the ordinary practice of employing
the cards of a pack singly, and in substituting the art of reading
the mysteries they might unfold when the whole sequence was

arranged upon the table. The former practice was, according to Etteilla, but an absurd imitation of ancient sortilege, or of consulting the oracles through the Odyssey and the verses of Virgil. Etteilla, enlightened—as we have seen—in 1757 by the Piedmontese as to the tarots, and afterwards by the theories of Court de Gebelin on that series of emblematic figures, published in 1783 his work on the "Tharoth or tarots," following it up by additional memoirs on occult and divinatory subjects as connected with "cartomancy." These treatises, when afterwards collected together, bore the title : " Collection sur les hautes Sciences ou Traité théorique et pratique de la sage Magie des anciens peuples absolument complet en douze livres lesquels contiennent tout ce que Etteilla a écrit sur la philosophie hermétique, l'art de tirer les cartes —et notamment le sublime livre de Thot." Paris, 1783-90, 4 tomes, 12° figs.

The part the writings of Etteilla have played in furnishing the stock, and often the whole ingredients of the many popular works and chapbooks on cartomancy and its associated subjects published since his time, may be well judged of—as far as France, at least, is concerned—on reference to the first volume, p. 227 *et seq.* of M. Charles Nisard's interesting work : " Histoire des Livres Populaires ou de la Littérature du Colportage depuis le XV. siècle jusqu'à 1852. Paris, 1854."

The annals of cartomancy, like those of supernatural appearances and second-sight, contain among them a few anecdotes associated with evidence which prevents us either rejecting the relations as false, or of explaining the circumstances in a satisfactory way. For example, Rowland in his " Judicial Astrology Condemned," relates the following in respect to Cuffe, a celebrated Greek scholar, " a man of exquisite wit and learning, but of a turbulent disposition," and secretary to the unfortunate Earl of Essex :—

" Cuffe was told twenty years before his death that he should come to an untimely end, at which Cuffe laughed, and in a scornful manner intreated the astrologer to show him in what manner he should come to his end; who condescended to him, and calling for cards, intreated Cuffe to draw out of the pack three which pleased him. He did so, and drew three knaves, and laid them on the table with their faces downwards by the wizard's direction, who then told him if he desired to see the sum of his bad fortunes, to take up those cards. Cuffe, as he was prescribed, took up the first card, and looking on it he saw the portraiture of himself *cap-à-pie*, having men compassing him about with bills and halberds; then he took up the second, and there he saw the judge that sat upon him; and taking up the last card, he saw Tyburn, the place of his execution, and the hangman, at which he laughed heartily; but many years after, being condemned for treason, he remembered and declared this prediction."

Cuffe was hung at Tyburn on the 13th of March, 1602, for having counselled and abetted the Earl of Essex in his treason. In alluding to this story, Taylor remarks:—

" It is evident that the cards used by the cartomancist on this occasion were tarots. The first drawn was in all probability an *atout*, called the traitor, which in some Italian packs held the place of the devil, the second could be no other than Justice, and the third would be sufficiently shadowed forth by the hanged man (Le Pendu)." (Bibl. 9, p. 456.)

During the exciting periods of the first consulship of Napoleon I., and of the empire which followed, the higher as well as the lower grades of the people eagerly sought to question the augurs of the future. At that time lived a well-known divinitress, named Mademoiselle Lenormand, the believed truth of whose predictions gained her such repute, that crowned heads were not beneath craving her assistance. Herself naturally vain and arrogant, thus flattered, she could scarcely keep at last within decent bounds, and actually attended the Congress at Aix-la-Chapelle, deeming her presence there of the highest importance. She published ten volumes in 8vo. of " Souvenirs Prophétiques," and " Mémoires Historiques," and in 1825 appeared the prospectus of an " Album de Madlle. Lenormand mis en ordre et enrichi de manuscrits autographes, de commentaires, de notes biographiques sur la Révolution Française et sur les Auteurs et les Acteurs de ce Drame politique." This album was intended to form five volumes in 4to. or twenty-eight vols. in 8vo., and to cost 975 francs. Sufficient subscribers were not forthcoming, however, to justify its being given to the world. (Boiteau d'Ambly, p. 330.)

On one occasion, Joachim Murat, when King of Naples, sought the aid of Mademoiselle Lenormand. He was received by the prophetess with her customary haughtiness, who, however, produced the cards. Murat cut the pack. The king of diamonds appeared. Now this card, according to some systems of cartomancy, is regarded as a portent of the extremest ill-fortune, and receives the name of the " grand pendu." Mademoiselle Lenormand told the king that, prosperous as he might then be, an execution awaited him. Murat, disconcerted, laid two Napoleons on the table, and begged for another trial. It was granted. He again cut the king of diamonds. Still more dissatisfied, Murat again produced a similar sum. The Sibyl permitted another trial. The *sortilège* was made, and for a third time the king of diamonds was cut. Bewildered and annoyed, Murat now produced fifty Napoleons, and besought the hesitating Pythoness to grant him one more experiment. It

was at length permitted, when with fatal iteration the same ma-
lignant portent—the king of diamonds—again appeared. In
desperation, the king now offered Lenormand one hundred Napoleons for another and final chance. Angrily she threw the cards
at him, telling him to begone, and turned him out of her sanctum,
with the assurance that his fate would be the gallows or the
musket-ball. It is well known that Murat met his fate by military
execution in Calabria in the year 1816.

Again, Gerard, one of Bernadotte's aid-de-camps, was one day
relating to the latter stories illustrating the strange power of
Mademoiselle Lenormand. Gerard at last asked his superior to
accompany him to the house of the prophetess. Bernadotte agreed,
and they proceeded to the Rue de Tournon. This, it should be
remembered, was in January, 1804. Colonel Gerard presented his
general as a rich merchant, desirous to learn what would be the
issue of some commercial speculations which he was on the point of
commencing in various parts of Germany. Examining her cards,
the sibyl remarked : " Sir, you are not a merchant, but a military
officer, and an officer of very high rank." She was assured that she
was wrong. Lenormand shook her head, replying : " Well, sir, if
you go into commercial speculations, you will be unsuccessful, and
forced to re-enter the career intended by destiny." After examining
the cards again, she continued : " Not only are you of high military
rank, but you are, or will be, related to the emperor." " What
emperor ? " exclaimed Bernadotte and Gerard. " I mean the first
consul," said Lenormand. Then with her finger slowly tracking
the mysterious signs as they opened before her, she answered in a
solemn and as if inspired tone : " Yes, he will be emperor, but here
are some clouds intervening between you." On Bernadotte looking
significantly at Gerard, the sibyl continued : " But there is not any
separation ; you are still attached to him—ah ! how his star is
rising ! " She ceased, as if in surprise, for a moment, and then
resumed : " Sir, be careful not to break with him ; he will be very
powerful, the world will be at his feet, and you—you, far away from
him, will be a king—yes, yes, you will be a king." She stopped.
" Good," said Gerard ; " what then ? " " I cannot perceive anything more, nor can I add anything," replied the prophetess.

Napoleon was crowned emperor by the Pope in December, 1804,
and Bernadotte afterwards became King of Sweden and Norway.

Thus, in spite of the poet's assertion,

" Heaven from all creatures hides the Book of Fate,"

humanity has always persisted in trying to read it, and cartomancy, not unlike other expedients, has had its fortunate episodes,
and occasionally, without intending it, has spoken the truth.

F. 81.

FIRST HALF OF NINETEENTH CENTURY.

PARIS.

(Grand Etteilla.)

SET of emblematic cards based on the designs of the typical tarots, accompanied by a numeral series, the whole being equal in number to the earlier Venetian sequence of seventy-eight pieces. The marks of the suits of the numerals are *batons, coupes, épées,* and *deniers.* The coate-cards have on them whole-length figures holding in their hands the signs of their suits.

This set of cards is designed and arranged for the purposes of divination. It is accompanied by a book of explanations and directions, bearing the title: "Manière de tirer. Le Grand Etteilla ou tarots Egyptiens. Paris, chez tous les marchands des nouveautés."

In the "Notions Préliminaires" with which the book commences, it is stated that *L'art de tirer les tarots,* or the Egyptian cards, is an agreeable science and of exciting interest, but that its results become serious or recreative, miraculous or frivolous, in a ratio with the greater or less degree of faith possessed by those who resort to it. It is a pursuit that merits especially the confidence of amateurs, particularly female ones, who are so partial to secrets.

Directions then having been given *pour tirer les tarots,* the meanings of the latter are explained under seventy-eight heads, and then follow the details necessary to elicit these meanings, and certain other values' appertaining to the numeral series.

All the card-pieces in the set are numbered consecutively from one, *Etteilla questionnant,* to seventy-eight, *Folie,* which seems to correspond to the *Fou* or *Misero* of the older tarots. The designs of the emblematic series of this set are much modified in several instances by Etteilla's interpretation of the older type, as is likewise the order of the sequence. Nos. 1 and 2, the *questionnant* and *feu,* may be said to be equivalent to No. 19, *Le Soleil,* of the ordinary series.

No.	3.	Eau	. . . .	to No.	xviii.	La Lune.
	4.	Air	. . . .	„	xvii.	L'Etoile.
„	5.	Terre	. . . .	„	xxi.	Le Monde.
„	6.	Jour	. . . .	„		
„	7.	Protection	. .	„	} ?	?
„	8.	Questionnante	.	„		
„	9.	La Justice	. .	„	viii.	La Justice.
„	10.	La Temperance		„	xiv.	La Temperance.
„	11.	La Force	. . .	„	xi.	La Force.
„	12.	La Prudence	. .	„ ?	xii.	Le Pendu.
„	13.	Mariage	. . .	„	vi.	L'Amoreux.
„	14.	Force Majeure	.	„	xv.	Le Diable.
„	15.	Maladie	. . .	„	i.	Le Bataleur.
„	16.	Jugement	. .	„	xx.	Le Jugement.
„	17.	Mortalité	. .	„	xiii.	La Mort.
„	18.	Traitre	. . .	„	ix.	L'Ermite.
„	19.	Misere	. . .	„	xvi.	La Maison Dieu.
„	20.	Fortune	. . .	„	x.	La Roue de Fortune.
„	21.	Dissension	. .	„	vii.	Le Chariot.

The designs on these emblematic pieces are mostly full-length figures, and subjects simulating more or less the typical tarots, and are often accompanied by astronomic or astrologic signs. Above and below each design is a title, *e. g.* on No. 5 is *Voyage* at the top and *Terre* at the bottom of the card; on No. 11 is *La Force* above and *Le Souverain* below. Each card is numbered twice, viz. at opposite corners diagonally and in reverse like Spanish cards.

The numeral series begins with the suit *bâtons*. The king and queen are seated and wear crowns, the cavalier is mounted, the valet is on foot. Each personage carries a long wand or staff. Each honour has two titles. Above the king of *batons* is *Homme de campagne*, below, *Homme bon et sévère*. Above the queen is *Femme de campagne*, below, *Bonne Femme*. On the cavalier is *départ* and *désunion*. On the valet is *étranger* and *nouvelle*. The honours of the other suits have like titles of various import.

The marks of the suits are placed in proper number on either blue or green coloured grounds, below the compartments containing which are bright yellow squares, some of them having within astrologic and other symbols or small emblematic figures; other yellow compartments are void of all marks. Each of the pip cards has an upper and lower title printed in reverse like the honours. On the eight of *deniers, e. g.*, is *Fille Brune* above, and *plus* below. On each of the marks of the suit, here coloured pink on a green ground, is Ω (Omega). On the lower and yellow division of the piece is a crescent moon with Venus by her side. On the aces are always a human hand and part of the arm, the former holding up a large symbol of the particular suit. In the ace of *deniers* the hand bears a figure of Apollo with a radiant sun above his head, while below in the yellow compartment is a circle for the mark of the suit. These cards are all neatly engraved and coloured, some of the numeral series being particularly clear and distinct. The backs are ornamented with pink dots.

[$4\frac{1}{2} \times 2\frac{3}{8}$ in.] [Backs decorated.]

F. 82.

FIRST HALF OF NINETEENTH CENTURY

PARIS.

(PETIT ETTEILLA.)

PIQUET set of cards (thirty-two) made subservient to the purpose of divination through dreams.

The series is accompanied by a book of directions and solutions, which bears the following title: "Le nouvel Etteilla ou moyen infaillible de tirer les cartes et de lire dans l'avenir par l'interprétation des songes. Auquel on a joint un tableau alphabétique de tous les objets qui se présentent dans les songes et les visions nocturnes, avec leur signification, traduit d'un manuscrit de Pythagore, commenté par le célèbre Urbain Grandier, l'Iman de la grande mosquée d'Alexandrie, et divers auteurs persans et arabes. Paris, Impr. de Ducessois 55 quai des Gr. Augustins (Près le Pont Neuf)." On the opposite fly-leaf we are informed that " Dans le même magazin l'on trouve : Le grand et le petit Etteilla ; L'oracle des dames ; Les grands tarots italiens et allemands ; et généralement tout ce qui a rapport à la cartomancie."

After an exordium *au beau sexe et à tous les amateurs de la cartomancie*, comes a sketch of what we owe to the " celebrated," the " profound Etteilla," who made his *début* in 1753 by his " L'art de tirer les Cartes." The information also is afforded us that this " learned professor of cartomancy, instructed by a native Piedmont that the book of the first Egyptians, the book named *thot* or *tout*, written in hiero-glyphics and known by the name and game of tarots, or better *tharoth*, contained all the ancient sciences, he made a serious study of it, and in spite of the hinder-ances of the royal censors, of the library administrations, and of the police during

1782, published in 1783 his work on the *tharoth* or tarots, a work which had cost him more than ten consecutive years of study and reflection." (p. 16.)

Page 20 enters on the "Méthode pour tirer les cartes," which extends to page 50, when follows a "Manière simple, naturelle et facile d'expliquer les songes avec les cartes." A "Treatise on Dreams and Visions after the Egyptians and Persians" concludes the book.

Each card-piece, $3\frac{3}{8}$ in. in height by $2\frac{1}{16}$ in. in width, has the representation of a particular card in its centre, $1\frac{5}{8} \times 1$ in. in size. Around this are certain titles, phrases, and numbers, having reference to the mode of employment of the cards, and the details of the divinatory doctrines propounded. Around the quadrangle of the ace of *trefles, e. g.,* are engraved at the upper margin the words, *Bourse d'Argent,* No. 26, *Orphelin,* R 5 *Mauvais,* E Prison; at the lower margin in reverse way, *Noblesse,* No. 26, *Rancune,* R 5 *Mauvais,* E Prison. At the right hand side, 4 As *Lotterie,* 3 As *Petite réussite,* 2 As *Duperie ;* and at the left, 4 As *Déshonneur,* 3 As *Libertinage,* 2 As *Ennemi.* The coate-cards have on them full-length coloured figures in erect attitudes, with titles and numbers similar to the lower cards. Thus on the *Dame de piques* may be read *Femme Veuve,* No. 16 *Vie,* R 13 *Ivrognerie,* E . . . *Cocuage, Femme du Monde,* No. 18, *Avarice,* R 13 *Ivrognerie,* E . . . *Cocuage,* 4 *Dames, grand pour parler,* 3 *D . . . tromperie de femme,* 2 *D . . . amie,* 4 *Dames mauvaise société,* 3 *D . . . gourmandise,* 2 *D . . . ouvrier, ouvrage.* The first card in the series is marked N 1 *Etteilla ou le Questionant,* and has the direction, *Voyez ce que signifie cette carte étant à côté des autres cartes.*

All the cards are from neatly engraved copper plates, and are carefully coloured. The backs are marked with small hexagons formed by dotted lines of a blue colour.

[$3\frac{2}{8} \times 2\frac{1}{8}$ in.]   [Backs decorated.]

F. 83.

FIRST HALF OF NINETEENTH CENTURY.

PARIS.

 SERIES of forty-two separate card-pieces, including twenty-two pure tarots and twenty distinct numerals, the remaining numerals being added to the tarots series, as smaller cards placed at the lower corners of the tarots. In the twenty separate numerals, the pip and honour cards likewise appear only as smaller cards at the lower corners of emblematic designs.

The series is intended to serve the purposes of divination and fortune-telling. It is accompanied by a book of directions, entitled "Le petit Oracle des Dames ou récréation du curieux contenant soixante-douze figures coloriées, formant le jeu complet de cinquante-deux cartes avec la manière de tirer les cartes, tant avec ce jeu qu'avec les cartes ordinaires." Paris Impr. de Ducessois 55 quai des Gr. Augustins (près le Pont Neuf).

An "Epître aux Dames" commences the book, in which we are assured that "lorsqu'une belle prend les cartes magiques, et tache de lever un coin du voile qui couvre l'avenir, elle n'est portée à ce mouvement de curiosité que par une tendresse bien juste, un sentiment bien honorable," &c.

A description of the mysteries symbolized in the tarots cards is next given. These latter are divided into three series, each of the magic number seven. The first series of seven represents the Golden Age of the world, the second series the Silver Age, the third series the Age of Brass.

The first emblematic card of the first series is *terre, voyage, 4ᵉ élément*, corresponding to *Le Monde*, xxi., of the typical sequence, and is thus described, " under the Sign of the Lion:"—" The goddess Isis in the centre of a circle formed by a serpent biting its tail, representing the Universe. The circle is the emblem of the yearly revolutions, and the symbol of eternity, which has neither beginning or end. Isis, whom the Egyptians regarded as the origin of all things, appears ready to run. At the four corners of the design are the emblems of the seasons. The Eagle, under the sign of the Virgin, indicates the Spring, which brings back the birds. The Lion, under its ordinary sign, implies Summer, or the ardour of the sun. The Ox is the allegory of Autumn, when one labours and sows; while the Youth, under the sign of the Twins, represents Winter, the season when we re-unite together. To this design is added the eight of diamonds, which is placed beneath the Ox. It implies the same subjects as before-mentioned—the country, earth, labour. When this design is preceded by the sign of Jupiter, it becomes of very favourable augury."

Details of the various ways in which the cards may be worked are given, along with an account of the pieces, "auxquelles les diseurs de bonne aventure attachent des pronostics."

Some of the tarots proper have each two designs on them, printed in reverse. Thus the piece No. 10 is divided into two equal portions. On the upper portion is a seated female, pouring a fluid from a vase in her right hand into a vase held in her left. At the lower left-hand corner of this division is represented a small numeral card, viz. the four of hearts. The title, *La Temperance*, is engraved above the figure. On the lower division is represented Night, in the form of the moon beaming down from the darkened heavens on the earth.

Some of the tarots designs are almost identical with the typical ones, though bearing other numbers, but several are *sui generis*. No. 21 of the tarots represents *Le Bataleur*, while No. 22 is both *consultant* and *consultante*, with appropriate designs.

All the separate numeral cards have each two emblematic designs on them, printed in reverse. Some of the designs have at the corners the representation of a diminutive pip or honour card; others have not. Above each design is a title. On No. 29, a ship in a tempestuous sea is represented in the upper division of the piece, and a diminutive ten of spades is at the left-hand lower corner. Above is the title *Naufrage, Grand Malheur*.

In the lower division are the arched vaults and staircase of a prison, with the title "PRISON." The number 29 is at the upper left-hand and lower right-hand corner in reverse.

The designs, execution, and colouring of these cards are of inferior character The backs are marbled in madder and white.

[3⅘ × 2⅛ in.]   [Backs decorated.]

F. 84.

NINETEENTH CENTURY.

PARIS.

A SET of seventy-eight cards, viz., twenty-two *atouts* and fifty-six numerals, designed and adapted to the purposes of divination. As far as the twenty-two tarots proper are concerned they may be said to be coarse copies on wood of the designs of the tarots of F. 81. Some slight differences of detail exist, as in No. 1, *Le Chaos*, No. 10, *La Tempérance*, No. 12, *La Prudence*, No. 15, *Maladie*, and No. 21, *Droit*. As in F. 81, the *fou* is No. 78, the last card of the series, and entitled *Folie*.

The marks of the suits of the numeral series are *bâtons, coupes, épées,* and *deniers.* The designs on these pieces differ from F. 81 in certain respects. Each piece is divided into two compartments, the lower and smaller compartment is always coloured yellow, but the upper division is in all instances parti-coloured, pink and blue. The symbols represented in the lower or yellow compartment differ from those of F. 81. In *bâtons,* keys, tablets, cards, lightning, arrows, &c., are to be seen; in *coupes* medallions, within which are various things, as harp, dolphin, bull's head, bee-hive, &c.; in *épées,* busts of men; and in *deniers* whole-length female figures seated, and at various occupations. The honours exhibit like designs to those of F. 81, but are differently coloured.

The titles and descriptions on all the cards differ in certain details from those on the series F. 81. On No. 2, for example, at the summit of the card, is printed *Droit éclaircissement* (1er *jour de la création*); below the design are *Renverse, feu* (2e *élément*); on the right-hand side is *La Lumière,* and the same on the left. At each corner of the piece is the number 2. Each of the numeral series has its suit and value printed on each side of the design, thus on the third figure card in *bâtons, le chevalier de bâton* is printed on each side of the man on horse-back, and on the like card of the suit *coupes,* is *le chevalier de coupe.* But in general, though the marks of the suits are the old Italian ones, as before stated, a twofold description of the suit and value of each card is given, viz., one answering to their actual signs, and the other to the more recent French symbols. Thus on the left-hand of the ten of *deniers* is printed *le dix de denier,* and on the right-hand *le dix de trefles,* on the three of *coupes* is *le trois de coupe* on one side, and *le trois de cœur* on the other.

The book of directions which accompanied this series is wanting.

The backs are coloured blue.

[4½ × 2⅜].   [Backs coloured.]

F. 85.

NINETEENTH CENTURY.

PARIS.

SERIES of seventy-eight cards, viz., twenty-two tarots proper, and fifty-six numerals. The suits of the latter are *bâtons, coupes, épées,* and *deniers.*

These cards are designed according to the principles of Le Grand Etteilla, and adapted to the purposes of divination. Most of the designs are intended to be Egyptian or Assyrian in character.

The first card of the tarots series is *L'homme qui consulte, sagesse, génie.* The last piece, *le fou,* is No. 78 of the whole sequence, and entitled *Folie.*

No. 2 is Osiris *ou le soleil,* No. 3, Isis *ou la lune,* No. 5, Apis *ou les saisons,* (Horus), No. 13, *le premier prophète, gardien des divines paroles,* No. 18, *L'ermite de la grande Thébaïde d'Egypte,* No. 19, *Le Rhamesseium ou Temple funéraire de Rhamses II.* (Mejamoun), No. 21, *le Tyran Busiris.*

The king of *bâtons* is *le Roi Ptolemée Lagus,* the queen *Didon, reine de Carthage,* the cavalier, *le Prince-Gouverneur d'Ethiope,* and the valet is the *Surintendant des Greniers;* the king of cups is *le Grand Prêtre,* the queen *Esther, reine de Perse,* the cavalier *le Prince-Gouverneur de Memphis,* and the valet *le grand Echanson;* the king of swords is represented by *Ninus, roi d'Assyrie,* the queen by *Semiramis, veuve du roi Ninus,* the cavalier by *le surintendant de la cavalerie,* and the valet by *le chef des grammates du palais;* the king of money is *Sesostris* (Rhamses Meïamoun le Grand), the queen *Makeda, reine de Saba et d'Ethiope,* the

F. 88.

SECOND HALF OF NINETEENTH CENTURY.

PARIS.

PIQUET set of cards (thirty-two), of the ordinary suits—*piques, trefles, cœurs,* and *carreaux.*

Each piece may be regarded either as an ordinary playing-card, or as a fortune-telling one, the latter belonging rather to the amusing or comic variety than to the serious divinatory class. A quarter portion of each piece is occupied by the representation of an ordinary playing-card, so large and so distinct that there would not be any embarrassment in using the set in customary play. The remaining portion of the card-piece is taken up with some amusing design, below which is the title. Thus, *e.g.* on the seven of *carreaux* a man's head with a night-cap and large spectacles projects from behind the smaller pip card in the left-hand upper corner ; just below, the man puts out his right hand, holding up the index finger towards a woman, who holds up her's likewise, and appears with open mouth to be arguing with the man above. The woman rests with her left hand on a long birch-broom handle. Below the pip card hangs a red *parroquet* in a cage. Under the design are the words " Bavardage," " Caquets."

On the *reine de trefles* is a very neat design of the honour card at the left-hand upper corner. Below is a three-quarter figure of a young woman, regarding with satisfaction a handful of gold coin, of which there are three piles upon the table over which she leans. Below is engraved " Amour d'Argent."

This set is accompanied by a small ornamental title, on which is inscribed : " Le petit Sorcier composé de 32 Cartes."

These cards are from engraved metal plates of a soft description, such as pewter or zinc. Some of the small figure-pieces or honours are of extremely careful and neat execution. The pieces are gaily coloured throughout.

The backs are marked with dotted arrow-heads, and large stars of a green colour.

[$3\frac{2}{8} \times 2\frac{1}{8}$ in.] [Backs decorated.]

F. 89.

FIRST HALF OF NINETEENTH CENTURY.

PARIS.

PIQUET set of cards of the suits *piques, cœurs, carreaux,* and *trefles*. It is intended for the purposes of fortune-telling as well as for ordinary play, but belongs to the amusing variety of fortune-telling cards, and not to the serious divinatory class.

Each card-piece has a representation of a small numeral card at its upper left-hand corner. Occupying the greater portion of the piece is an emblematic design, including full-length figures and landscapes ; below is the title. The ace of *piques* has on it a Cupid on clouds, about to let off an arrow on some one below. Above him are two billing doves, below is the title, *L'Amour.* The ten of *carreaux* exhibits a large parterre of flowers, from which a serpent protrudes his neck. Over these are some birds hovering, and at a little distance other birds are being caught in a net.   At the lower margin are the words: " Piège ou Trahison."

A book of explication accompanies the set.   It is entitled: " Le Livre de Destin," and commences with an " Epître aux Dames," by M. Violet, éditeur, which begins with the assurance that " L'homme galant doit toujours faire hommage aux Dames du fruit de ses travaux."   After the address comes the " Manière de tirer les Cartes," followed by an " Explication des Cartes," with finally the " Rencontre des Cartes ayant même valeur."

The imprint is " Impr. de Carpentier Mericourt, Rue Trainée S. Eustache, No. 15."

These cards have been carefully designed, neatly engraved on metal, and the impressions coloured.   The costumes and accessories are of modern description.

[4⅛ × 2½ in.]   [Backs plain.]

F. 90.

FIRST HALF OF NINETEENTH CENTURY.

PARIS.

 PIQUET set of cards (thirty-two), of the usual suits, subservient to the purposes of fortune-telling, as well as of ordinary play.

This pack is a *replica* of F. 89, accompanied by the book of directions.

[4⅛ × 2½ in.]   [Backs plain.]

F. 91.

FIRST HALF OF NINETEENTH CENTURY.

PARIS.

PIQUET set of cards of the usual suits, intended for the purposes of fortune-telling as well as of ordinary play.

The set belongs rather to the amusing than to the serious class of divinatory agents, being based on exactly the same principles as are F. 89 and 90.

The greater portion of each piece is occupied by an emblematic design, while the representation of an ordinary numeral of small size is placed at the upper left-hand corner.   The title of the design is engraved beneath the latter.   The emblematic representations, though after the same kind as those of the previous series, are yet different in detail.   On No. 1, the ace of *piques, e.g.* are two Cupids wrestling among the clouds, and around whom roses are scattered.   Below is the title: " La Bagatelle ou L'Amour."   Some of the compositions are very fair, and all are neatly engraved and coloured.   The small numerals and honours at the summits of the large pieces are particularly good.

This set is accompanied by a book of directions, on which is the title in MS. " Cartes du Destins "—(aux Dames)—" Aug. Legrand."   It opens with an account " De la Manière de Tirer les Cartes ;" which is followed by a " Troisième moyen pour connaitre la pensée de quelqu'un," and concludes with an " Explication des Cartes."

The edges of these cards are gilt.

[3½ × 2⅛ in.]   [Backs plain.]

AMUSING—HUMOROUS.

F. 92.

SECOND HALF OF NINETEENTH CENTURY.

PARIS.

FULL set (fifty-two) of numerals of the ordinary suits, *cœurs, piques, trefles,* and *carreaux.*

The series is of an amusing and humorous character.

The court-cards are full-length figures, strongly and positively coloured by chromo-lithography, while the figures which are on the pip-pieces are left in outline and in shadow, the marks of the suits being coloured over them.

The king of spades represents a Red Indian chief with spear and shield, the queen Joan d'Arc, the valet a "Suisse" in the well-known attire; the king of clubs is a tippling Boniface on a donkey, the queen a Swiss flower-girl, and the valet a gardener mowing. The king of diamonds is an inferior Court attendant of the period of long-pointed shoes, the queen a buxom market-woman, the valet a man-servant sweeping the carpet. The king of hearts is Cupid, the queen a "star of the ballet," the valet a porter delivering a letter. A supernumerary piece of this valet commences the series. A variety of amusing and comic designs are on the pip numerals.

Some of the compositions are serious, however, such as the subject on the ace of spades, which represents a nun at devotion before an altar; on the four of clubs is a bishop in full canonicals with crozier, and on the ten of clubs is a monumental effigy of a knight in armour. The way in which the mark of the suit, spades, is made to constitute the head and face of a negro nurse in the four of the suit is admirable.

The backs are of a rose-colour.

[$3\frac{7}{8} \times 2\frac{5}{8}$ in.]   [Backs coloured.]

SIMPLY FANCIFUL.

F. 93.

FIRST HALF OF NINETEENTH CE. TURY.

PARIS.

SERIES of thirty cards, having on them whole-length figures representing eminent personages of the time of Louis XIV.

These pieces are purely *cartes de fantaisie,* not possessing any of the essentials of ordinary playing-cards. A book of biographical summaries connected with the persons represented accompanies the series. It is entitled, "Le Siècle de Louis XIV., ou Vie des Personnages Célèbres qui ont illustré ce Siècle. Paris Librairie de Gide Fils, Rue S. Marc-Feydeau, No. 20."

Among the celebrities are Boileau, Condé, D'Aguesseau, Fénélon, Luxembourg, Mansard, Le Notre, Poussin, Racine, Madame de Sévigné, and Turenne.

The portraits are in general well designed, and neatly engraved and coloured; some, like those of Tourville, Condé, and Racine, are bad in proportions and attitudes. The representations of Flechier, Bossuet, and Fénélon, are particularly good.

The name is engraved in a separate marginal compartment below the design. [$4\frac{2}{8} \times 2\frac{6}{8}$ in.]   [Backs plain.]

F. 94.

FIRST HALF OF NINETEENTH CENTURY.

PARIS.

A SERIES of thirty-eight cards, eighteen of which represent emblematic designs; the remaining twenty giving descriptions of the scenes and persons represented.

These pieces are purely *cartes de fantaisie*, not having any of the essentials of ordinary playing-cards. The character of the amusement offered may be gleaned from the following account given on the introductory piece of the set:

" Jeu de Société: charades en action.

"Chaque charade est composée de trois petites scènes en monologues, renfermant le premier mot, le second et l'entier de la charade. La Société se divise en deux parties, l'une pour jouer et l'autre pour deviner.

" Les charades se jouent comme les 'Proverbes,' autre jeu qu'on trouve chez l'auteur de celui-ci, soit en pantomimes, soit en scènes dialoguées. Il est bon d'avoir les objets et les costumes qui conviennent à la scène que l'on veut représenter. La partie qui a deviné joue à son tour."

The words of the charades represented by the designs on the eighteen cards are *ballot*, *mariage*, *théâtre*, *oranges*, *écriteau*, and *délire*.

The compositions and execution of these pieces are but of mediocre character. [$4\frac{5}{8} \times 2\frac{7}{8}$ in.]   [Backs plain.]

F. 95.

FIRST HALF OF NINETEENTH CENTURY.

PARIS.

A SERIES of fifty-two pieces, having on them emblematic designs with their titles below. The set is purely fanciful, not having any of the characters of true playing-cards. A supernumerary piece has on it " Explication du Jeu de la Sybylle des Salons. Se vend à Paris chez Alph. Giroux & Cie. Rue du Coq. St. Honorè, No. 7; Gihaut Frères, Boulevard des Italiens, No. 5."

This series of designs is excellent in all respects. The compositions are good, and full of meaning: they are etched with freedom and delicacy, and the colouring is tasteful, light, and appropriate. On each piece at the lower left-hand corner is "Mangion, inv^t."

The class of subjects represented may be gleaned from the following emblems. On one card a countryman has brought money to an accountant, which is being sorted in piles on a table, over which the accountant leans; behind the countryman at his feet are bags of money. Below is the motto: "Beaucoup d'Argent." A man closely enveloped in a cloak, from which protrudes a bludgeon, is waiting concealed behind a wall, for a person who is on the point of passing before him. Below is inscribed, "Ennemi." Some of the figures are well worthy of Gavarni, and such pieces as the *Maison de Ville* and *Maison de Campagne* are extremely characteristic of the places represented.

[4$\frac{3}{8}$ × 2$\frac{7}{8}$ in.]   [Backs plain.]

F. 96.

FIRST HALF OF NINETEENTH CENTURY.

PARIS.

A SERIES of thirty-six card-pieces, having on them whole-length figures of persons supposed to be engaged in the furtherance and celebration of a marriage. Accompanying the series is a description of the game, which is entitled: "La Dot. Nouveau Jeu de Société."

Each player must have twenty counters, and be supposed to represent one of the various persons engaged in the ceremony, *e.g., le Prétendu, la Prétendue, le Père, la Mère, le Curé, le Bédeau,* and others. Of these counters the players contribute, according to circumstances, to the "Corbeille de Mariage." *La Prétendue,* a nicely designed and executed *demoiselle,* has *La Demande* made in reference to her, as follows:

> " Un jeune homme bien né, d'une bonne tournure,
> Désirait s'unir à cet objet charmant,
> On dit qu'il le prendrait sans dot assurément,
> Mais il est toujours bon de doter la future."

The above *demande* is engraved on a distinct card, as are likewise *Le Consentement* and *Le Contrat.*

The last card exhibits a table of *Refraichissemens,* which " ayant paru les *importuns* qui restent dans la main des joueurs ne paient rien, et la partie est terminée."

Some of the designs are good, others but mediocre. The execution and colouring are careful.

[3$\frac{1}{2}$ × 2$\frac{1}{8}$ in.]   [Backs plain.]

F. 97.

FIRST HALF OF NINETEENTH CENTURY.

PARIS.

A SERIES of thirty-six cards, having on them whole-length male and female figures, in characteristic costumes.

Four of the cards have each a figure of *Polichinello* in various pantomimic attitudes; one being on stilts. The remaining thirty-two pieces are divided into four suits, distinguished by the colours of the costumes.

The eight cards in each suit have different designs on them, but these designs are repeated in each suit.

In each suit there is a leader of the "troupe" with book and baton; a courtier in full dress, plumed cap, and sword; a countryman by whose side is a diminutive *Polichinello* on stilts; a lady in Court costume with ermined train; a lady in long veil and train; a lady with stomacher and feathered hat; a lady in a bonnet leaning over a parapet, and a country girl with basket on arm.

To each of these suits belongs a *Polichinello*.

It is not easy to make out in all cases the suit to which the card belongs, there being often such a mixture of colours in the costumes as to render the question doubtful. In other cards the distinction is plain enough. The colours distinguishing the suits appear to be brown or violet, blue, red, and green.

Excluding the four *Polichinello* cards, the number of each suit is that of the suit of a *piquet* set of cards, but there are neither pips, numbers, nor any indications on the pieces by which they might be said to simulate ordinary playing-cards.

The designs, engraving, and colouring, are of a superior character, much care and artistic ability being displayed in them.

Accompanying the cards is a title, cut apparently from a sale catalogue. It runs thus: "Jeu des Polichinels Vampires, par A. Giroux. Coloured. Paris, 36."

[$4\frac{1}{8} \times 2\frac{5}{8}$ in.] [Backs plain.]

F. 98.

FIRST HALF OF NINETEENTH CENTURY.

PARIS.

SERIES of thirty-two fancy cards, designed for *Le Jeu de Quilles*. On nine pieces is represented a large skittle in the upright position against a landscape background; then follow nine pieces with skittles on the ground, and landscapes; next come nine bowls; then three pieces, each piece with a running dog on it; and lastly, two cards, on each of which are two prostrate skittles.

Each of the nine pieces having prostrate skittles is numbered at the upper left-hand corner. The cards with the dogs on them are named *Medor*, *Diamant*, and *Mirault* respectively, while those with two prostrate skittles on each are numbered 2, 4, and 3, 6, 9, respectively.

A number of counters must accompany the cards, the game requiring a pool.

A paper of directions and rules is given with this set. The engraving and colouring are careful.

[$3\frac{2}{8} \times 2\frac{2}{8}$ in.] [Backs plain.]

F. 99.

FIRST HALF OF NINETEENTH CENTURY.

PARIS.

SERIES of twenty-four cards, having on them designs and scenes emblematic of the vicissitudes of human life.

These cards are described here as of purely fanciful character, notwithstanding that the marks of the suits, *piques*, *trefles*, *cœurs*, and *carreaux*, are placed at the right-hand lower corner of each piece. There is one mark only on each card, and the same mark extends but to six pieces. The six cards with the mark of *piques*, and the six with that of *trefles, i. e. les douze cartes noires*, represent the troubles of humanity; while those pieces having on them the marks of *cœurs* and *carreaux, i. e., les rouges*, symbolize its joys.

Each card has a number and the title of the design at the lower margin.

On the card numbered 8, with the mark of *trefles*, a young lady in a violent passion is smashing the drawing-room chairs; below is the inscription, "Madame brise Ménage."

On the piece numbered 6, and with the mark of *cœurs*, a marriage ceremony is being performed. Below is the title, "Les Amans à l'Autel."

The game requires to be played with counters, a set of which accompanies the pack. The counters are blue, red, yellow, and white.

An *explication du jeu* is given, entitled, "Jeu des Vicissitudes Humaines, ou les Peines et les Plaisirs."

The designs, execution, and colouring are but of mediocre character.

[$3\frac{1}{2} \times 2\frac{2}{8}$ in.]   [Backs plain.]

F. 100.

FIRST HALF OF NINETEENTH CENTURY

PARIS.

A SERIES of ninety cards, having on them designs representing humorous characters, or laughable incidents. Accompanying these pieces are twenty-four long cards, each card being divided into twenty-seven squares. Some of these squares are coloured, others are left plain; the colours being yellow, green, blue, and red. The fifteen plain squares on each card are numbered with large numerals, varying from one to ninety according to circumstances.

A leaf of instructions accompanies the series, entitled "Règle du Jeu de Loto en Cartes à rire."

Counters are required in the game, as a pool is necessary.

Each pictorial card is numbered at the top, and below the number is the title of the design represented.

On No. 8 is "Le bon Coin," with the representation of a drunken man (whose hat has fallen off) leaning helplessly against the friendly corner of a wine-shop, the owner of which, "Boneau M^d de Vin," is at the door, gazing with astonishment at the drunkard. Some of the designs are comical enough in intention, but the artistic power displayed is in many instances but of very mediocre character. All the pieces are coloured.

[$3\frac{7}{8} \times 2\frac{3}{8}$ in.]   [Backs plain.]

F. 101.

FIRST HALF OF NINETEENTH CENTURY.

PARIS.

A SERIES of thirty-six cards, having on them whole-length male and female figures, in national costumes.

These pieces are for the purpose of playing the *Jeu du Nigaud*, the performance of which is described on an accompanying sheet. Counters are required in the amusement, a set of which goes along with the cards. These square counters are numbered with large figures up to 36, and correspond to like numbers on the cards.

Some of the designs are admirable in respect of drawing, engraving, and colour.

[$3\frac{1}{2}$ × $2\frac{5}{8}$ in.] [Backs plain.]

F. 102.

NINETEENTH CENTURY.

PARIS.

SERIES of twenty-eight cards, representing the pieces of a set of dominoes. Each card is divided into six equal compartments. In the middle white space are marked the values of the pieces by the usual black dots, here having a white star in the centre. In the lateral divisions at the corners, opposite diagonally, are shields with castellated crowns, and arabesque ornaments are at the other corners. Each shield is divided longitudinally, having the domino points of the central compartments repeated in its divisions.

On the first card is inscribed across the upper central compartment: "Propriété de l'auteur."

The engraving of these cards is very neatly executed; the shields and ornaments being relieved white off a black ground.

[$3\frac{3}{8}$ × $2\frac{1}{8}$ in.] [Backs ?]

FLEMISH PLAYING-CARDS.

TAROTS.

Fl. 103.

EIGHTEENTH CENTURY?

BRUXELLES.

COMPLETE set of combined tarots, *i. e.* twenty-two *atouts* and fifty-six numeral cards. The marks of the latter suits are *coupes*, *épées*, *deniers*, and *bâtons*. The designs of the tarots proper are like those of the French set, F. 37, before described. No. 2 has on it a whole-length portrait of *Le Spagnol Capitano Eracasse*, in place of the typical *La Papesse*. On No. 5 is *Bacus* in lieu of *Le Pape*, and No. 12, *Lepen-du*, must be reversed in order that the figure may hang in the usual way, viz., head downwards. No. 16 is *La Foudre*, a tree struck by lightning, instead of *La Maison Dieu*, and *Le Fou* bears a number—xxii. The title on No. 1 is spelt *Le Bataleux*, on vi. *Lamour*, and No. 13 has here a title—*La Mort*.

On the ace of *deniers* is inscribed—top and bottom and in reverse—" Cartes de Suisses, fabriquées par F. I. Vandenborre Cartier à Bruxelles." On the two of *deniers* is "F. I. Vandenborre" on a scroll between the marks of the suit, and on the two of *coupes* on a broad margin at the bottom may be read : " Pour conoistre que la plus basse de Deniez et de Coupes, en porte les plus hautes quand au fait du jeu." On the shield in the middle of the four of *deniers* is a lion rampant with a castle on his right paw, in place of the letters I ＊ G in the pack F 37.

Though the designs and execution of these cards are poor enough, they are not so bad as those of the French set.

M. Merlin, alluding to the old Venetian or Lombardian tarots, draws attention (p. 83) to the constancy with which the primitive types have been preserved and transmitted without notable change to the south and east of France, as likewise to Switzerland. " The alterations produced by time have done scarcely more than affect the costume of the figures belonging to the numeral series, the cavaliers and valets of which on entering France relinquished undoubtedly the iron armour of the fifteenth century for the garments of a more recent epoch. It is not implied that the engravers have been always faithful to the primitive models; they have swerved from them but rarely, however, and in the rich collection of tarots in the Imperial library scarcely three or four examples of such a liberty are to be seen. . . . The Swiss had a *jeu de tarot*, however, slightly different from the Venetian tarot, at least in the eighteenth century, for some engraved wood-blocks preserved in the 'Musée de la porte Hal' at Brussels yield the figures of a series, the ace of *deniers* in which bears the following address, viz. : 'Cartes de Suisse, fabriquées par T. S. Vanden Borre Cartier à Bruxelles.' " In this set, No. 2, instead of representing *La Papesse*, is *L'Espagnol Capitano Fracasse*, while on No. 3 the Pope is displaced by a Bacchus astride on a barrel and holding a bottle in his hand."

The backs of these cards are marked with a net-work of hexagonal moniliform meshes, within which are radiant suns printed in black.

[4⅜ × 2⅜ in.] [Backs decorated.]

NUMERALS. FULL SET (52).

Fl. 104.

NINETEENTH CENTURY.

LIEGE.

 SET of fifty-two numerals of the suits *trefles, cœurs, piques,* and *carreaux.* The figures on the honours are whole-length and bear titles. In *trefles* the latter are Alexandre, Argine, and Lancelot; in *cœurs* Charles, Judith, and Lahire; in *piques* David, Pallas, and Hogier; and in *carreaux* Cæsar, Rachel, and Hector.

The valet of *trefles* holds a shield in his right hand, on the border of which are the words, "Administ. des Droits Réunis, 1813." On each coate-card the mark of its suit is placed both at top and bottom, the bottom mark being reversed. Below each mark are black circular spots, three in number on the kings, two on the queens, and one on the valets.

[3⅛ × 2⅛ in.] [Backs plain.]

Fl. 105.

FIRST HALF OF NINETEENTH CENTURY.

BRUXELLES.

SERIES of fifty-two numerals of the usual suits—*piques, cœurs, trefles,* and *carreaux.*

The coate-cards have on them whole-length figures in semi-historical, semi-theatrical middle-age and subsequent costumes. The kings of *piques* and of *carreaux* wear armour, the queen of *cœurs* has a high pointed head-dress and long veil, and the queen of *piques* an elevated cap with large veil. The designs and execution are very mediocre. An introductory or supplementary card accompanies the set; on it are represented a hand displaying a pip card of each suit, a large mark of a suit at the corners of the piece, and a flower at each side of the hand. The impression is in black from either stone or a zinc plate, probably from the latter.

The backs are dotted in pink.

[3⅞ × 2⅞ in.] [Backs decorated.]

Fl. 106.

NINETEENTH CENTURY.

BRUXELLES.

SERIES of fifty-two numerals of the ordinary suits.
The coate-cards have busts printed double and in reverse. The queens hold roses in their right hands. The designs and execution are of mediocre character. Engraved on zinc probably.
The backs are dotted and starred in black.
[3⅜ × 2⅞ in.]   [Backs decorated.]

Fl. 107.

SECOND HALF OF NINETEENTH CENTURY.

BRUXELLES.

SERIES of fifty-two numerals of the ordinary suits.
The figure-cards have busts printed double and in reverse.
This set appears to be a *replica* of Fl. 106, somewhat differently coloured. It is accompanied by a supplementary piece, on which is represented a boy dancing, and holding up in his right hand a seven of diamonds. He holds a cap with feather in his left hand. The backs are like Fl. 106.
[3⅜ × 2⅞ in.]   [Backs decorated.]

Fl. 108.

NINETEENTH CENTURY.

BRUXELLES.

SET of fifty-two numerals of the ordinary suits.
The figure-cards have on them busts printed double and in reverse. On a tablet in the middle of the *roi de cœurs* is the title "Hubertus Agneessens." The aces are illustrated in an exceptional manner. They have each two landscapes printed in reverse, neatly engraved and coloured, the truthfulness of which, however, is less than doubtful. Within a circular space in the middle of the card is placed the mark of the suit. On the ace of spades are portrayed the "Conté de Fife" and the "Conté de Perth;" on that of clubs the "Chateau de Ribnian" and the "Bord du Rhin." On the ace of diamonds are the "Chateau de Finckenstein" and the "Chateau de Ribnian;" on that of hearts the "Bord du Rhin" and "Saint Leonard." The backs are marked with blue vermiform lines.
[3½ × 2⅜ in.]   [Backs decorated.]

Fl. 109.

NINETEENTH CENTURY.

BRUXELLES.

A SET of fifty-two numerals of the usual suits.
The honours exhibit busts printed double and in reverse.
The *roi de carreaux* represents Napoleon I. crowned with a wreath, and holding an eagle in his left hand. The valet of the same suit is a Turk with a scimitar. The king of spades is Henry IV. of France, crowned with a wreath, and holding a drawn sword in his left hand. On the belt of the valet of clubs is the name VEYRAT F. The backs are marked with a blue vermiform line.

[$3\frac{1}{2}$ × $2\frac{2}{8}$ in.]   [Backs decorated.]

PIQUET.

Fl. 110.

NINETEENTH CENTURY.

BRUXELLES.

A *PIQUET* set (thirty-two) of cards of the suits *piques, trefles, carreaux,* and *cœurs.*
The honours are whole-length figures in conventional costumes, very poorly designed and coloured. The king of hearts rests his right hand on a shield bearing a double-headed eagle. One or two of the designs have a slight Spanish look about them. Part of an engraved wrapper accompanies this set. It exhibits a valet in conventional costume, having a drawn scimitar in his right hand and a shield on his left, bearing what look like three marks of the suit *trefles* with feathered tails. The backs are marbled in Vandyke brown colour.

[$3\frac{2}{8}$ × $1\frac{7}{8}$ in.]   [Backs coloured.]

DUTCH PLAYING-CARDS.

NUMERALS—FULL SET.

D. 111.

FIRST HALF OF NINETEENTH CENTURY.

AMSTERDAM.

 PACK of fifty-two numerals of the suits spades, hearts, diamonds, and clubs.

The coate-cards or honours have on them whole-length, standing figures, in full characteristic costumes, representing historic personages, whose arms are borne by the valets on shields placed on their chests. The king of spades is Godefroid de Bouillon; the Queen, Richilde, the valet is unnamed. The king of hearts is Baudouin de Constantinople, and the queen, Marguérite d'Autriche. The king of clubs exhibits Philippe le Bon, the queen Marie de Bourgogne. The king of diamonds is François Premier; the queen, L'Infante Isabelle. On the king of each suit a crown surmounts the mark of the latter. The marks of the suits on the aces are surrounded by ornamental and arabesque framework, printed in blue. On the ace of spades is inscribed "Cartes Déposés;" on the ace of hearts, "Daveloy," "Breveté."

All the designs are neatly executed and coloured. The *lissage* is considerable, the cards working most freely in the hand. The backs are marked with blue dots.

The engraved ornamental title of the wrapper accompanies the set. On it is the inscription: "Supra Fijne Speelkaarten Erve Wijsmuller Amsterdam."

[$3\frac{1}{2}$ × $2\frac{2}{8}$ in.]   [Backs decorated.]

D. 112.

FIRST HALF OF NINETEENTH CENTURY.

AMSTERDAM.

PACK of fifty-two numerals of the ordinary suits.

The figure cards have on them busts, printed double and in reverse. The same bust is printed twice on each card. That on the king of spades represents Prins Willem III.; that on the queen of this suit, a lady of Friesland; on the valet, a field labourer of Noord Brabant. The king of diamonds exhibits Prins Willem I.; the queen, a young woman of Eiland-marken; the valet, a boatman of Zeeland. On the king of clubs is Prins Frederick Hendrik; on the queen, a lady of Kamper-eiland; on the valet, a countryman of Eilandmarken. On the king of hearts may be seen Prins Maurits; on the queen, a young woman of Zuid Holland; and on the valet, a fisherman of Scheveningen. On each of the aces are two landscapes in reverse. On the ace of clubs are representations of Zaandam and Scheveningen; on that of diamonds are Leyden and Utrecht. On the ace of spades are Amsterdam and Sgravenhage, and on that of hearts are Rotterdam and Dordrecht.

All the figures and landscapes are neatly engraved and coloured, the cards generally being of superior manufacture. The backs are coloured blue, and over them runs a lace-like pattern of leaves and flowers in white.

An engraved ornamental title of a wrapper accompanies the pack. It bears the inscription, " Nederlandsche Speelkaarten. Supra fin."

Below are the arms, with supporters, of Holland, and the motto, "je main-tiendrai."

[$3\frac{6}{8} \times 2\frac{1}{2}$ in.]   [Backs decorated.]

D. 113.

FIRST HALF OF NINETEENTH CENTURY.

AMSTERDAM.

 PACK of fifty-two numerals of the usual suits.
The figure cards have on them busts, printed double and in reverse. The kings hold sceptres, the queens flowers, and the knaves partisans. The aces are plain

The backs are marked with oak-leaves (?), printed in blue.

The engraved title of the wrapper is present, and bears the inscription: "Supra Fijne Speelkaarten Erve Wijsmuller Amsterdam."

[$3\frac{1}{2} \times 2\frac{3}{8}$ in.]   [Backs decorated.]

CARDS WITH A SECONDARY PURPOSE.

SATIRICAL.

D. 114.

Number 1642 of Political and Personal Satires.

FIRST QUARTER OF EIGHTEENTH CENTURY.

 SERIES of fifty-two numerals and two supplementary card-pieces, printed off on a large sheet, $21\frac{2}{8} \times 17\frac{6}{8}$ in. in size.
The marks of the suits are spades, diamonds, clubs, and hearts. The marks are placed at the upper right-hand corners of the cards. The values are indicated by Arabic numerals placed at the sides of the marks in the suits spades and clubs, and in the centre of the marks in diamonds and hearts. The figure cards are *Heer, Vrouw*, and *Knecht*, the names of which displace the Arabic numerals.

The major portion of each piece is occupied by a figure and its accessories below which is a couplet in Dutch verse, referring to the emblematic sense of the figure.

This set is made subservient to satire on the South Sea, Mississippi, and other bubble companies of the year 1720. Besides the present copy there is another which may be found as No. 8, in vol. i. of " Het Groote Tafereel Der Dwaasheid," a collection of Dutch satires on those schemes in the Library of the Print Room.

One of the supplementary pieces bears a large, strutting cock, holding by its beak a placard, on which is represented a horse grazing. Below is the following inscription :—" Dese fyne modese kaarten worden gemaakt to Schothauenburg bӱ Lawrens Bombarist in de Wroetende droom goud-mӱn graver." (These fine, fashionable cards were made at Schothauenburg at Lawrence Bombarist's in the rooting dream (of the ?) digger of gold mines.)

On the other supplementary piece is the title to the series. A man holds extended a piece of drapery having on it, " April-Kaart of Kaart Spel van Momus Naar de Nieuwste Mode."

Below is a couplet, having reference to Law and to Frederick Henry's ghost.

These card-pieces have been ably designed and engraved; they are not coloured. A set was exhibited before the Archæological Association by Mr. Patin ("Herald and Genealogist," v. 3, p. 72, 1866; "Notes and Queries," I. v. 217).

A detailed description of each of the fifty-two pieces, and other information connected with the satire therewith conveyed, may be found in the second volume of the " Catalogue of Political and Personal Satires," p. 648, No. 1642.

[$3\frac{3}{8}$ × $1\frac{7}{8}$ in.]   [Backs plain.]

MISCELLANEA.

D. 115.

THE WORKS OF REMBRANDT.

Etchings, vol. V. folio 3.

 N an impression of the scarce landscape known as the " Vue d'Omval près d'Amsterdam " (Ch. Blanc, No. 312, Wilson, No. 206) in one of the sets of the etchings of the great master in the National Collection, three designs have been superadded, which were etched by some strange hand on the original copper after it had become worn, apparently for the purpose of destroying the plate, or preventing further impressions of its original state being taken.

These designs are an eight of clubs, $3\frac{1}{8}$ × $2\frac{6}{8}$ in. in size ; a woman carrying milk or water-pails, $2\frac{2}{8}$ × $1\frac{6}{8}$ in., and a boy blowing soap-bubbles, $2\frac{2}{8}$ × $1\frac{6}{8}$ in. in size. The first two compositions occupy places at the upper right-hand corner of the impression lying transversely, and the piece having the milk-woman on it is so drawn as to appear lying partly over the eight of clubs. The upper right-hand corner of the card touches the right-hand side of the plate mark of the landscape, and the lower left-hand corner of the piece of the woman approaches the upper margin of the landscape. A branch of the large tree on the right is intruded on by the card and the woman. The naked boy blowing bubbles is placed obliquely across the deep mass of foliage, beneath which sit the two figures near the lower left-hand corner of the piece. The composition of the boy is represented as lying on a large piece of green-coloured paper.

On the piece of the milk-woman is the word "Boerinne 5," at the upper part of it; her boddice is tinted yellow, as are likewise the pails, while the skirt of her dress is light red. A wash of the latter colour has been thrown over a portion of the boy, the flower-pots on each side of him being coloured yellow. Above the boy is inscribed "Leven 2." The marks of the suit in the card are coloured black.

In reference to this peculiar impression M. Charles Blanc remarks: "I saw a singular impression of this plate at the British Museum. In place of the two figures which are on the left, those of the young girl and young man who places a garland on her head, is a small coloured engraving of a child blowing soap-bubbles between a vase of flowers, and another vase from which smoke escapes. Above is inscribed the word "Leven" (*la vie*) and the numeral 2. On the right above the two mills a card—the eight of clubs—is drawn diagonally, and on this card appears to be thrown a coloured figure of a woman after the style of the boy and equally coarse. Above the figure is inscribed "Boerinne" (*paysanne*), and close to it is the number 5. At first I supposed that I had before me simply an impression disfigured by some barbarian, but on closer examination I perceived that the original plate had been scraped, and that another hand had engraved these designs, of which two are coloured, on the veritable copper of Rembrandt.

"This is the only example I have seen of this disfigurement of the plate. Who could have been the unhappy person that, possessing a plate of Rembrandt, could have permitted or have perpetrated such an act of Vandalism?" ("L'œuvre complet de Rembrandt," vol. ii. p. 291.)

Wilson, in his "Descriptive Catalogue," p. 150, writes: "There are impressions of this plate when worn, on which an eight of clubs is engraved at the top on the right." Whether Wilson here speaks of "impressions" from actual observation, or from hearsay only, is not determinable. The present impression belonged to the Slade collection, and was formerly in the possession of Deighton, his mark being at the lower right-hand corner of the landscape. It has been recorded here chiefly on account of its peculiarity and rareness.

GERMAN PLAYING-CARDS.

TAROTS.

G. 116.

EIGHTEENTH CENTURY.

STUTTGART?

COMPLETE set of combined tarots, seventy-eight in number, or twenty-two tarots proper and fifty-six numerals.

The marks of the numeral suits are hearts, diamonds, clubs, and spades, and the figure-cards are king, queen, cavalier, and valet.

The designs on the tarots represent a wedding procession, each card-piece having on it either figures on horseback, or groups of the marriage guests drawn in festively decorated cars. Below each composition is a couplet in German; above is the number of the tarot in numerals five-eighths of an inch long.

The piece corresponding to the *Fou* is unnumbered, and appears first. It exhibits two persons: a man in rather a comical costume standing and playing a harp, a woman semi-recumbent playing a guitar. The couplet is as follows:—

> " Da wenn unsre Saiten klingen
> Müs das Herz vor Freüde springen."

No. 1, equivalent to " Le Bataleur," is a trumpeter on horseback, holding up a large glass of wine, and has below:—

> " Ihr Hochzeitgäste kombt herbey
> Damit der freude volkom sey."

The clergyman is represented on No. 6, and has below the following couplet:—

> " Der Pastor warü heüt so schön
> Will er zu frau Pastorin gehn."

On No. 21 are wedding guests in a decorated car, with the verse below:—

> " Brüder läst uns lustig sein
> Denn die freüd ist allgemein."

The designs on these cards are but of mediocre character, but the technical execution of them is rather peculiar. They are from engravings on metal, are coloured and illuminated both in silver and gold. The marks of the suits in spades and clubs have a few gold lines on what may be considered the shadow side, here the left ; the marks in hearts and diamonds have them likewise, but on the right side.

The figures on the coate-cards are whole-length and heavily draped. In spades, the king is in conventional costume, holds a sceptre in his right hand, beneath which is a harp. In diamonds, the king wears a turban with a plume and aigrette, and carries a sceptre surmounted by a crescent. In hearts, the cavalier is a mounted Tartar (?). Below the figure of the valet of clubs is the address— " Andreas Benedictus Göbel."

The backs of the cards are diapered with stars and cross-lines printed in blue.
[$4\frac{1}{2} \times 2\frac{3}{8}$ in.] [Backs decorated.]

G. 117.

EIGHTEENTH CENTURY ?

SET of combined tarots, or twenty-two *atutti* and fifty-six numerals. The suits of the latter are spades, clubs, diamonds, and hearts. The figure-cards are king, queen, cavalier, and valet.

The designs on the proper tarots are very poor in character, being chiefly animals in ludicrous actions or positions. The *matto* or *fou* is without number, and is represented by a violin-player in fantastic dress. No. 1 is a harlequin, having a child-harlequin perched at the end of the conventional flat sword of the former.

These cards are numbered at both top and bottom with large numerals in margins an inch wide ; the designs occupying the spaces between. The design on No. 7 is an unicorn. At the lower part of the valet of clubs is the address— " I. M. BAKOFEN."

The backs are marbled in rose-madder.
[$4\frac{3}{8} \times 2\frac{3}{8}$ in.] [Backs coloured.]

G. 118.

EIGHTEENTH CENTURY ?

REGENSBURG.

PACK of combined tarots, seventy-eight in number. The suits of the numeral series are spades, clubs, diamonds, and hearts. Two cards are wanting, viz., the queen of diamonds and valet of spades.

The designs on the tarots proper are landscapes and sea-pieces of the most inferior design. They are printed double and in reverse on each card, above and below the designs being the numbers in wide margins.

The *fou* is a plumed Indian warrior, discharging an arrow from his bow. No. 1, equivalent to the *Bataleur*, is a harlequin holding a human head in his right hand, which is extended upwards. The landscapes, &c., on most of the *atouts*, though double, vary in composition on each card. On No. 2 is the address— " Wolfgang Scheidl. B. und Karten fabricant in Regensburg."

The figure-cards of the numeral series have on them busts, printed double and in reverse.

All the cards have an ornamental border.

The backs are marbled in rose-madder.

[4 × 2⅖ in.]   [Backs coloured.]

G. 119.

THIRD QUARTER OF NINETEENTH CENTURY.

POMERANIA.

 PACK of modern North German tarots, seventy-eight in number. The marks of the numeral suits are spades, clubs, diamonds, and hearts. The tarots proper have each two different designs on them printed in reverse. Each design is numbered in large, open, Arabic figures within the composition. All these tarots designs are from neatly engraved metal plates, and remain uncoloured, with the exception of the "fool," which is a double bust of a man with cap and bells neatly coloured. The compositions vary much in character. On No. 15 is a stout gentleman hailing the train on a railway; on No. 10 is a scene reminding one of that in "Auerbach's Keller" (Faust) and likewise a joust at a tournament. No. 19 represents Napoleon I. the night before the battle of Austerlitz, and No. 11 a countryman having the grease removed from his coat by a man at a stall, who is vaunting his wonderful composition. The words "Flek Seife" are on an advertisement board by the table of the renovator of soiled garments. On one of the designs of No. 13 is a young girl in sorrow at a tomb, near which on a monumental cross is the word "Pommer" and the date "1852."

The figure-cards of the numerals have on them busts printed double and in reverse, and are coloured.

Most of the compositions are carefully drawn and neatly engraved. The true *fou* of the tarots is remarkably good.

The backs are marked with sinuous dotted lines terminating in three larger dots, printed in blue.

[4⅖ × 2⅜ in.]   [Backs decorated.]

NUMERALS. SUIT MARKS, ITALIAN.

G. 120.

SECOND HALF OF FIFTEENTH CENTURY.

 BOUND volume (in a case) lettered "Trappola Cards," (and having the press number 94), containing forty-seven card-pieces lightly mounted on its pages. These cards are from a series of fifty-two numerals, the suits of which are swords, cups, fruit, and batons; the fruit being a pomegranate. The pieces wanting are the three of cups, the nine, ten, valet, and king of pomegranates.

This is an important and interesting sequence, and one, though very rare, well known both to the archæologist and iconophilist from the references made to it by various writers. The designs are from engravings on copper, the productions of a very early master of the German school, who worked with a goldsmith-like technic. They have been attributed by some writers to Israhel van Meckenen, an ascription, however, not acquiesced in by others. There are good reasons for believing that these cards cannot be more ancient than the time of Martin Schongauer—the last quarter of the fifteenth century—since the design on the two of batons of the figure of the naked female with a child upon her knees, and having her right hand on the top of an escutcheon, appears to be taken from a circular print—B. vi. p. 161, No. 100—by this master. The idea of the sow and young pigs on the three of swords surely has also a connection with the design of Martin Schongauer, B. vi. p. 160, No. 95.

The figure-cards, or " honours," are king, queen, and valet, proving that in some early German cards a second valet did not displace the *dame*, a circumstance here, perhaps, in unison only with the adoption of the Italian marks of suits, *coppe*, *spade*, and *bastoni*; the fruit, or pomegranate, being substituted for the sign *danari*. This fruit " was perhaps intended by the artist to commemorate the marriage of Philip the Fair, son of the Emperor Maximilian, with Joanna, daughter of Ferdinand and Isabella, King and Queen of Spain, who on their subjugation of the kingdom of Granada in 1497 appear to have adopted the Granada, or pomegranate, as one of their badges. The cards unquestionably belong to that period, and in support of the speculation it may be further observed that they are generally ascribed to Israel van Mecken, who, as a native of Bocholt, was a subject of Philip, who inherited the Netherlands in right of his mother Mary of Burgundy." (Chatto, Bibl. 4, p. 226.)

The figure-cards are decidedly better designed and executed than any of the other pieces. In some of the former may be perceived the work both of a superior artist and engraver to that of the authors of the ordinary numerals. The queen of swords is an admirably designed and executed figure, and the arabesque work below is delicately and carefully engraved. When placed by the side of the six of batons, for example, the contrast is very marked. The king of swords, valet, queen, and king of cups, and king and queen of batons may be instanced as noteworthy pieces.

The valet is always represented on horseback ; the kings, bearing the symbols of their suits in their hands, are seated on rich thrones of Gothic character, and the queens are slender and elegantly draped forms.

All the cards are richly ornamented with groups of figures, often of a burlesque or grotesque character, and with a variety of arabesque-like ornaments. Some of the latter, however, are too large in proportion, and look heavy in work for the size of the card. On the tens and aces are scrolls or banners, on which are letters and inscriptions more or less distinctly engraved, but to which it is difficult to give any meaning. On a scroll on the ace of swords are the following letters, some of which, too, it must be admitted, are of doubtful definition :— C. T. A. O. T. S. E. S. H. D. On the three of swords are " Ante, Motorum, Meus." On the ten of swords, H. Z. D. H., on the ten of cups C. B. F. S. A., on the ten of batons J N R. Z. Q. Some of these inscriptions are printed in reverse.

In the Suit of Swords,

On the ace are a large scimitar and scroll, having on one side an unicorn, on the other a bird on a shrub.

On the two, the pictorial design is a man kneeling, and asking alms of a lady.

On the three is a sow with her pigs.

On the four are birds, and armed men on horseback.

On the five are monkeys and flowers.

On the six is large arabesque ornamentation.

On the seven are two naked children playing with a stag, and plants.

On the eight is a peasant addressing a lady.

On the nine, St. George killing the Dragon.

On the ten a man in armour, holding a large banner, having below a tree and an escutcheon.

In the Suit of Cups,

On the ace is an ornamental fountain, on the brink of which are two falconers, and above are two Cupids, discharging arrows.

On the two is a fool below, a lady and gentleman are above.

On the four above is a man kneeling, below is a nondescript animal's head.

On the five are two armed men.

On the six are four naked children playing.

On the seven are only seven cups, each cup being of a different design.

On the eight is a lady in the middle, playing with a bird.

On the nine is a grotesque figure, into whose mouth falls a stream from one of the cups.

On the ten is a banner carried by a lion.

In the Suit of Pomegranates or Fruit,

On the ace are two children, seated within the opened fruit, above which are five birds.

On the two are two naked children below, one of whom emerges from the fruit; above are three children, one of whom is entering a fruit.

On the three are three naked children, and birds and flowers.

On the four are five naked children, two of whom are seated within pomegranates, and threaten each other with bows and arrows.

On the five are two wild hairy men, and a child in a pomegranate.

On the six are various fanciful figures, among which are a naked man, woman, and a monkey.

On the seven is a fool below, and above are two boys fighting.

On the eight are eight birds.

In the Suit of Batons,

On the ace are two men sawing the trunk of a tree.

On the two is a naked woman with a child on her knee, and her right hand on the top of an escutcheon. Birds are above the marks of the suit.

On the three is a centaur fighting against two dragons.

On the four are five naked children; playing on the back of the central figure is a bird.

On the five are two birds, and three naked children.

On the six are birds, and three playing children.

On the seven are birds, flowers, and arabesque ornamentation.

On the eight are two playing children above, and arabesques below.

On the nine is a scroll at the summit of the central mark of the suit.

On the ten is a banner carried by a griffin.

The tens in each suit are distinguished by the Roman numeral **X** only, which is placed, as in all the other pip cards, at the upper margin of the piece.

The example in the collection of the British Museum of this rare series was formerly in the possession of Dr. Silberrad, of Nürnberg. It afterwards passed into the cabinet of Count de Fries at Vienna, next into the hands of the Messrs. Woodburn, and finally into the keeping of Messrs. Smith, of Lisle Street, from whom it was purchased by the authorities of the British Museum.

Breitkopf has inserted copies of nine of these engravings in his work on the origin of playing-cards; Chatto has given four, including the ten of pomegranates, which is wanting in the present series, and Mr. Ottley, in his "Facsimiles of Scarce and Curious Prints," London, 1828, has introduced the entire sequence of forty-seven pieces, accompanied by descriptions of each engraving.

These cards are described by Bartsch, vol. x. p. 76, No. 2, under the title of "Cartes allemandes, avec les marques de la trappola," and are referred to by Passavant, vol. ii. p. 246, as "Cartes à Jouer Allemandes Anciennes."

The series of pieces before us has been called erroneously one of "Trappola cards."

Breitkopf described the engravings as "German *Piquet* Cards of the 15th Century with Trappola Characters;" then Von Murr termed them "Trappola Cards;" Bartsch, "Cartes allemandes avec les marques de la Trappola;" while Passavant wrote of them as "Cinquante-deux cartes d'un jeu de Trappola."

The truth is, there are not any marks special to *trappola* cards, and that these cards were not intended simply for the game of *trappola*, nor for that of *piquet*. The game of *trappola* is played with a series of numerals, of which the 3, 4, 5, and 6 of each suit are suppressed, and as long as this is done, *trappola* may be played with cards showing no matter what marks of suits. Now the series under consideration has all the low cards, and therefore could not have been intended solely for the game of *trappola*. The latter might be played with them, no doubt, if the low cards mentioned were rejected.

From the circumstance of *trappola* being a Venetian game, the original marks of the suits were naturally the Italian ones, viz. *spade, bastoni, coppe,* and *danari.* Since like marks, or slight modifications of them have been retained for the cards in Silesia, and a few other places where the game has been practised in more recent times, the idea arose that these marks have some essential connection with the game in which such cards are employed.

[5 × 2⅝ in.]   [Backs plain.]

G. 121.

SECOND HALF OF FIFTEENTH CENTURY.

SINGLE figure-card—the valet of cups—from the numeral series before described. A young gentleman on horseback advances towards the left hand carrying the symbol of the suit in his right hand. The cavalier wears a low, plumed cap, his hair over his shoulders, and looks downwards towards the right side. Beneath the feet of the horse is arabesque ornamentation, having in the centre a bird.

This piece belonged to the Slade Collection, and is among the works of the early German masters.

[5 × 2⅝ in.]   [Back plain.]

SUIT MARKS, NATIONAL.

G. 122.

SECOND QUARTER OF FIFTEENTH CENTURY.

ULM?

BOUND quarto volume, on the pages of which are mounted eight small sheets, containing generally three perfect card-pieces and portions of others. The cards are numerals of the suits *herzen, schellen,* and *eicheln;* both court and pip-cards are present.

The first sheet contains a perfect knave of *eicheln* and king of *schellen,* with portions of other five figure-cards. The second sheet exhibits a perfect knave of *herzen,* king of *schellen,* knave of *eicheln,* and portions of other four figure-cards. On the third sheet are the four of *herzen,* and the two and five of *schellen.* On the fourth sheet are the two, three, seven, and nine of glands; while the fifth sheet contains a king of glands or *eicheln,* a king and knave of *herzen,* with parts of other pieces of the suits *herzen, schellen,* and *eicheln.* The sixth sheet contains the knave of *eicheln,* and portions of four other pieces, and the seventh presents the five and six of *eicheln,* with parts of four other pieces. The eighth and last sheet presents the ten of *herzen,* the ten of *schellen,* the king and knave of *herzen,* and parts of other two pieces.

In the figure-cards the kings are seated, the king in the suit of *schellen* having a sceptre in the left hand.

The *Untermänner,* or lower knaves, or inferior valets, have either a crossbow or scimitar in their raised hands. On sheet 3, the two of *schellen* shows the figure of a lion below the marks of the suit. On the first piece (two of *eicheln*) of sheet 4, likewise, is a lion and part of an inscription in a scroll. The latter is not satisfactorily decipherable; it may be read perhaps as either *niulner, inwiner,* or *in*(or *zu*)*ulm.*

These card-pieces are uncoloured, stencilled in black, and of stiff, archaic design. There is, nevertheless, expression in the head of the king of *schellen* on sheet 5, and the designs of the suit marks are of good character.

These cards, along with F. 42, are in an archæological aspect two of the more interesting series in the national collection. The present set constitute probably the most ancient playing-cards in the Museum Cabinet.

Facsimiles of sheets 2 and 5 are given by Chatto, p. 88, accompanied with the following observations :—[these old cards] "formed part of the covers or boards of an old book, and were sold to the British Museum by Mr. D. Colnaghi. Looking at the marks of the suits in these cards, the character of the figures, and the manner in which they are executed, I should say that they are not of a later date than 1440. Though cards of only three suits occur, namely, hearts, bells, and acorns, there can be little doubt that the fourth suit was leaves, as in the pack described by Mr. Gough in the eighth volume of the 'Archæologia.' As in Mr. Gough's cards, so in these there is no queen, though like them there appears to have been three coate-cards in each suit, namely: a king, a knight or superior officer, and a knave or servant; in other words, king, jack, and jack's man. The lower cards, as in Mr. Gough's pack, appear to have been numbered by their pips from two to ten without any ace.

"That these cards were depicted by means of a stencil is evident from the feebleness and irregularity of the lines, as well as from the numerous breaks in them, which in many instances show where a white isolated space was connected with other blank parts of the stencil. The separation seen in the heads of the figures in No. 1 of the facsimiles here given would appear to have been occasioned by the stencil either breaking or slipping, while the operator was passing the brush over it.

"From the costume of the figures in these cards I am inclined to think that they are the production of a Venetian card-maker. A lion, the emblem of St. Mark, the patron saint of Venice, and a distinctive badge of the city, appears as in the annexed cut in the suit of bells, and a similar figure with part of a mutilated inscription also occurs in the suit of acorns. . . . . From repeated examination of them I am convinced that they have been depicted by means of a stencil, and not printed nor 'rubbed' off from wood-blocks." (Bibl. 4, pp. 88-90.)

A close examination of these card-pieces along with the copies of the "Stukely Cards" given by Singer, p. 172, *et seq.* leads to the belief that they were meant to be a like series with the latter, with the exception of the emblematic figure on the two of glands, which figure in the "Stukely cards" is a unicorn couchant, having below a shield bearing a pick and hammer crosswise, probably the arms or mark of the card-maker. The resemblance between the present cards and the

" Stukely " ones had struck Mr. Taylor also, who referred to it at page 114 of the work he edited.

The remarks of Passavant in respect to the present subject may be quoted here appositely.

" In the Royal Library at Berlin are thirty-one German playing-cards, which belong to the fifteenth century. They have been engraved on wood in a rather coarse manner, in simple outline, the figures being coloured in red and green. The sequence appears to have consisted of forty-eight cards, in four suits of twelve pieces each suit, the latter being hearts, bells, leaves, and glands.

" The king is seated, the two valets are erect, the remainder being numerals from two to ten. The ace is wanting, but the two has on it a shield bearing *en saltire* a pick and a hammer. On the two of glands is a unicorn whose horn is edged like a saw; the intended meaning here of this animal, usually a symbol of chastity, it is not easy to divine. The pick and the hammer are connected with miners' labour, and these coarsely executed cards may have been intended for the amusement of those persons who worked in the mines. The Berlin specimens came from the Hoffmann-Fallersleben Library, and are for the most part in bad condition. The card least mutilated measures still 2 inches 8 lines in length, and 1 inch 9 lines in width. Dr. Stukely, of London, possessed in 1763 forty similar cards, which Chatto, who gives *facsimiles*,[1] regarded as ancient Venetian cards, but they are only copies of those at Berlin, and of very inferior character." (Bibl. vol. i. p. 15.)

In connection with the present series it may not be out of place to consult the remarks of Singer, pp. 172-7, upon the Stukely sequence.

[3 × 2 in.] [Backs plain.]

G. 123.

WO *facsimiles* of card-pieces in the set before described, G. 122. The pieces here present are the seven of *eicheln* and the king of *schellen*.

[3 × 2 in.] [Backs plain.]

G. 124.

SECOND HALF OF FIFTEENTH CENTURY.

HREE cards from a numeral series, the suits of which are *schellen*, *herzen*, *eicheln ?* and *laub ?*
One of the pieces is the king of *herzen*, another the superior valet of *schellen*, and the third is the three of *schellen*.

The king is seated, and holds up the index and third finger of the left hand as in the act of benediction; his right hand rests upon his knee. These card-pieces are not from stencils but from engraved wood-blocks, and are slightly coloured. They are from a very early series unquestionably, and appear to have been removed from the binding of a book.

[3⅛ × 2 in.] [Backs plain.]

---

[1] Singer gives facsimiles of the " Stukely cards," Chatto facsimiles of the *present series*, which are like the Stukely ones.

G. 125.

FIRST HALF OF SIXTEENTH CENTURY.

NÜRNBERG OR ULM?

TWO pieces of four unseparated cards, each piece belonging to a numeral series of the suits *eicheln, laub, roth,* and *schellen.*

The cards present are the three of *eicheln,* three of *laub* or *grün,* six of *eicheln* and six of *laub* on one sheet; and the three of *roth,* three of *schellen,* four of *roth,* and four of *schellen* on the other sheet.

On the pieces of *eicheln* and *grün* are arabesque-like or ornamental trees to which the suit marks are attached, while on *roth* and *schellen* at the lower half of the cards are animal and other figures, but so indistinct, from imperfect printing and mutilation, that they cannot be described.

These card-pieces have been printed from engraved wood-blocks and coloured in an inferior manner. They are of stout consistence, and appear to have been removed from the binding of a book. They were formerly in the Weigel collection. See Weigel, "Die Anfänge der Druckerkunst," vol. ii. p. 186, n. 311.

[3 × 2 in.]   [Backs plain.]

G. 126.

FIRST QUARTER OF SIXTEENTH CENTURY.

ULM.

FIVE card-pieces, two of which contain two cards each, the other piece is a single card.

The cards are numerals of the suits *eicheln, schellen,* and *herzen,* or *roth.* On one piece are the kings of *eicheln* and *schellen,* on a second the six and eight of *roth,* and the third is the nine of *roth.*

The kings are seated, holding the symbols of the suits in their hands. The king of *eicheln* is bearded, and turned towards the right, the king of *schellen* is bearded, and directed to the left. On a broad margin to the left of the king of *eicheln* is the inscription ZU VLM ⊞. On a scroll on the eight of *herzen* is the date 1504, and below the marks of the six of *herzen* is a dog running towards the right. On the separate card of the nine of *herzen* is the monogram, ⊞.

The cards appear to have been executed from stencils, and are of neat and careful design. They are uncoloured. Weigel, of whose collection they formed part, remarks: "We do not know anything respecting the author of these cards. On *roth* nine there is a monogram, which refers probably to the printer or publisher of the cards, and not to the designer of them. If this be the case, the monogram is perhaps that of the well-known Ulm printer, Johannes Zainer, or of a son of the latter, who was living in 1523, and printed not only books but woodcuts." (*Op. cit.* p. 183.)

These pieces have been removed evidently from the binding of a book.

[3⅝ × 2⅛ in.]   [Backs plain.]

G. 127.

FIRST QUARTER OF SIXTEENTH CENTURY.

ULM.

 PIECE of three unseparated numeral cards of the suit *roth* or *herzen*. The cards are the six, seven, and nine of *herzen*.   On the six is the figure of a dog running towards the right, with his head raised, and on the nine of the suit is the monogram ⊞.   Below the latter, which is on the central card, is the address ZU VLM ⊞ , in a broad margin.   These card-pieces are from a series of the same designs as those before noticed—G. 126. They are not from the same stencils, however, which have been here of a heavier or coarser kind.   The stencil plate appears to have undergone a slip angularly during the working-off the design, and so doubling the lines; the right-hand lower corner having been the more fixed point.

The cards are uncoloured, and have been removed from the binding of a book.

[3⅜ × 2⅛ in.]   [Backs plain.]

G. 128.

NE entire card and part of another of the suit *herzen*.   The entire piece is the six of the suit, the other is probably the seven.

Below the marks of the suit on the first card is the figure of a dog running with his head downwards, towards the right hand.   In outline only, and from stencils, uncoloured.

This specimen is from a series after the designs of G. 126 and G. 127, but not from the same stencil plates.

[3⅜ × 2⅛ in.]   [Backs plain.]

G. 129.

SECOND HALF OF SIXTEENTH CENTURY.

EN more or less perfect cards of the ordinary old German suits, glands, hearts, leaves, and bells.   Seven of the ten pieces exhibit the fronts, three the *versos* of the card-pieces.

The numerals present are the three and four of leaves, the four and nine of glands, the five and six of hearts, and the three (?) of bells.

In several of the pieces below the suit marks are ornamental designs and figures, difficult to define satisfactorily, however, from the bad condition of the cards.

The backs of the cards shown are diapered with *fleurs-de-lys* running diagonally, and printed in black.

The cards are from wood-blocks, and are uncoloured.

[3⅛ × 2 in.]   [Backs decorated.]

G. 130.

SECOND HALF OF SIXTEENTH CENTURY.

SOUTHERN GERMANY.

MUTILATED sheet, containing portions, more or less perfect, of sixteen card-pieces; nine cards are in tolerably good condition. The suits are *eicheln, roth, laub,* and *schellen.* A noteworthy circumstance is that seated queens occupy the places of the superior valets, or *obermänner*, in the suits of acorns and hearts. It may be remarked also that while in the suit of glands or acorns, and probably in leaves, the suit-marks are connected by arabesque or ornamental trees, the marks in hearts and bells are not so connected.

The kings of hearts, glands, and bells are in the central row of pieces; each king is mounted on a rearing or curvetting horse, and holds a sceptre in the left hand. On the horses behind the kings of bells and glands are sows rearing up on their hind legs. The king of bells rides towards the right hand, the king of glands towards the left. The eight of hearts and eight of bells are perfect pieces.

In the upper row the lower portions only of the *untermänner*, or inferior valets, can be seen.

The queens of glands and hearts and the king of leaves in the lower row are entire, with the exception of the feet.

The costume of the figures points to the second half of the sixteenth century. The designs are but of mediocre character, and the execution, as regards the printing, is bad. The pieces are uncoloured.

Formerly in the Weigel collection.

[3 × 2⅜ in.]   [Backs plain.]

G. 131.

FIRST HALF OF SIXTEENTH CENTURY.

NÜRNBERG OR ULM?

SIX pieces of four cards each piece, of the suits *herzen, laub, schellen,* and *eicheln.*

Eight figure-cards are present, viz., the under valets of leaves, glands, bells, and hearts, the kings of glands and hearts, and the queens of bells and leaves; queens in this series displacing the superior valets. The queen of bells is represented by a young female turned towards the left, in a long, stiff robe, bordered at the lower part, and with puffy sleeves. On her head is a narrow dentated crown, and in her raised right hand she holds the symbol of the suit. The queen of leaves is a nearly naked female, having a little drapery around her waist only, one end of which scarf is thrown over her right forearm. Around her neck are a ribbon and medal, on her head a narrow crenated crown, and in her right hand the symbol of the suit. The kings of glands and hearts are on horseback, holding swords in their right hands. Narrow crowns are on their heads. The horses are slightly caparisoned. The valets of leaves and hearts have drawn swords in their right hands, while the valet of glands bears an arquebus on his left shoulder, and the valet of bells holds a cup in his left hand, which is raised.

The pip-cards present are the four, five, six, and nine of leaves; the seven, two, three, and eight of leaves; the three, five, seven, and nine of glands; and the four, six, eight of glands, and the three of bells.

The suit marks are connected by arabesque-like work. Below the marks on the three of bells is a running stag followed by a dog. On the two of leaves is a stag crouching on his hinder quarters, from whose muzzle springs an arabesque stem, supporting and connecting by its branches the marks of the suit.

The artistic value of these card designs is but slight. The figure-cards are uncoloured. The pip-pieces are coloured green and red.

The costume points to the second half of the sixteenth century. The backs of the figure-cards are diapered with large black squares or lozenges, running diagonally, each square containing four white pearl-like drops.

These cards were formerly in the Weigel collection, and three of them may be seen figured in the second vol. p. 184, of the "Anfänge der Druckerkunst."

[3⅛ × 2 in.]   [Backs decorated.]

G. 132.

FIRST HALF OF SIXTEENTH CENTURY.

ULM ?

SEVEN cards from a numeral series, the suits of which are leaves, bells, glands, and hearts (?).

The cards present are the four, six, seven, and nine of leaves; the six and seven of bells, and the ten of glands.

The marks of the suit of leaves are connected by a tree-like stem; those of bells are not so connected. The marks on the ten of glands are connected, and two birds are perched on the base of the flower-like stalk.

The impressions are from wood-blocks, and scarcely more than in outline; the shadow sides of the leaves being indicated by distant lines, and those of the cups of the glands by punctations.

On the backs of some of the pieces are the remains of the *tarotage*. It consists of alternate figures of *fleurs-de-lys* and flowers, running diagonally, in large diamond spaces across the back of the card. They are printed in black.

[4 × 2⅝ in.]   [Backs decorated.]

G. 133.

SEVENTEENTH CENTURY ?

TWELVE cards from a numeral series of fifty-two, the marks of the suits being leaves, glands, hearts, and bells.

The cards present are the king, four, and seven of leaves; the three and nine of glands; the five, seven, eight, and nine of hearts; and the upper valet, seven, and eight of bells.

These cards have on them either figures or arabesque ornaments, along with the marks of the suits.

On the king of leaves is a whole-length figure in armour, with large plume to his helmet, and long straight sword by his side. He extends his left hand, and looks upwards towards the left, to which his steps are directed.

Below is the couplet,

> "Ein könig aufrichtig ūn grecht
> Ein löblich gdechtn9 enpfecht." [*sic.*]

At each of the upper corners of the piece is a mark of the suit.

At the base of the tree-like stem, uniting the marks on the four of leaves, are two naked children at play. One is drawing the other in a sledge. At the bottom of the seven of leaves are two arabesque dolphins.

The marks on the three of glands rise on a stem from a large vase, on each side of which is a small whole-length figure; a female on the right, a man on the left-hand side.

On the five of hearts is a group of armed men, fighting; on the seven of the suit there appears to be an ogre or giant about to devour a boy; on the eight of hearts is a large vase-like ornament; and on the nine are a man and a woman, as if warming their hands over a cylindrical German *ofen*.

The *obermann*, or superior valet of bells, is represented by a military officer in puffed sleeves and breeches, and with a single stiff feather in his cap.

Below is a couplet, undecipherable, with the exception of the words—

" Eines hauptmãs gerechte —
———— feld gut regiment."

On the seven and eight of bells are grotesque faces and arabesque ornaments.

The coarse and slovenly colouring of these cards hinders a full appreciation of the designs.

On the back of each card-piece is a musical score of three lines. On that of the king of leaves is likewise the inscription, " Pacienciã mus ich han." On the seven of hearts may be read also, " Sie ist mein Bül." 1 2 ; while on the *obermann* of bells are the words, " So wünsch ich Ihm ein güte nacht."

[$3\frac{7}{8}$ × $2\frac{2}{8}$ in.] [Backs decorated.]

G. 134.

SEVENTEENTH CENTURY.

SINGLE figure-card, apparently; but there is not any title or indication of suit.

The design is a whole-length figure of an Oriental, with spear and shield. The figure is in outline, enclosed in broad dotted border, and of inferior workmanship.

[$3\frac{7}{8}$ × $2\frac{3}{8}$ in.] [Backs plain.]

G. 135.

FIRST HALF OF SIXTEENTH CENTURY.

NÜRNBERG ?

(Cards of F. C. Z.)

SHEET of ten unseparated card-pieces in two rows of five pieces each row. The marks of the suits are hearts, bells, leaves, and glands.

The upper row contains the sixes of the four suits and the nine of glands; the lower row the fives of the four suits and the nine of hearts.

These cards are highly ornamental, the marks of the suits being connected or accompanied by decorative stems and foliage, having below groups of figures of very varied kind.

The designs and technical execution are of very superior character, recalling to mind the best period of the school of German wood-engraving.

The pieces are uncoloured. Commencing at the left-hand corner of the upper row is the six of hearts. On it is a standard-bearer in a landscape, who raises a standard with his right hand, between the marks of the suit. Next comes the six of bells, having below the marks, a fool with the cap and bells on the left hand, and a female on the right hand of an ornamental pedestal which springs from a female head, and has on the top the head of a cherub. On the six of leaves are seated an amorous couple. The man has his right arm around his companion's waist, to whom he offers something to drink from a large cup. At the base of the six of glands is a wedding (?) procession, preceded by a fool with cap and bells, who plays a violin. On the nine of glands are two boars seated, with an open backgammon board between them. The left-hand boar has one foot on the board and appears to be addressing his opponent, who is in the attitude of listening. In both animals there is much expression. On the lower row, beginning at the left, is the five of hearts, having a couple at a fountain. The woman has her back to the spectator. She holds a vase-like pitcher in her left hand, and keys in her right. On the next card—the five of leaves—are a richly dressed burgher and his wife, followed by a female servant, having a pannier-basket at her back, and a large pitcher in her right hand. Below the marks on the five of bells are four naked children dancing in a circle. One child has the back turned to the spectator, and holds a flaring torch in the right hand. In the centre of the group is a pedestal, at the top of which is a child blowing two horns. On the five of glands is a man mounted on a goat, and tilting with a spear against a boar. Behind a contiguous tree is a woman attentively regarding the result, and holding up a laurel crown in her left hand. The whole appears to be a travesty of St. George and the Dragon.

The last card of the row is the nine of hearts, having on it the figure of a naked child who fondles a dog with each hand. From the boy's head springs an ornamental pedestal, which rises among the signs of the suit.

A point of interest in connection with the present sheet of cards is that it forms part of a sequence of fifty-two numerals, known as the cards of F. C. Z., copies of thirty-six of which are given in the work of the Bibliophiles Français (Bibl. 2, pp. 92-95,) of four in Singer, pp. 210-213, and of two in Chatto, pp. 236, 237. Thirty-four pieces were in the Weigel collection. In commenting on them in his larger work, "Die Anfänge Der Druckerkunst" (p. 191, vol. ii.), Weigel makes the following remarks:—

"No. 314. German Playing-cards with the signature, F. C. Z. 36 pieces (A.D. 1525-1550). These interesting specimens, which are among the best of the German playing-cards of the sixteenth century, are most probably of Nürnberg origin, since the ace of hearts, or *roth*, bears the arms of the city. Chatto places their origin in the year 1511. We are not aware of the source from which Chatto draws this deduction. On the examples before us there is not any date, but we believe we may, without hesitation, assign their origin to the second quarter of the sixteenth century.

" The technic and costume of the figures point to that period, and particular figures, as the king of bells, for example, strikingly recall certain ones in Dürer's woodcuts. The king of glands would appear to be the portrait of the Emperor Maximilian I. The designer of the cards has placed his monogram, F. C. Z., on the ace of glands [on the two ?] We have searched in vain Murr and Baader's catalogue of old Nürnberg's *Formschneider Kartenmacher* and *Illuministen*, for the meaning of the signature. A *Formschneider* of the name of Christ. Zell lived during the second half of the sixteenth century, but it might be too venturesome to look for the author in him, or even in one of his ancestors.

" The series, of which we possess thirty-six pieces, is of the ordinary suits ; the pieces are five pip-cards, vi.-x., under and upper valets, king, and ace of each suit. The pip-cards are ornamented with figures overstepping occasionally, in their actions and stories, the bounds of propriety. The drawing is of considerable delicacy, spirit, and firmness, and full of appreciation of the forms and costumes it is intended to portray. The technic is decided, and that of a practised hand. Two examples of these cards, viz., under valet of glands and upper valet of leaves, are given—but not very accurately—by Chatto (pp. 236-7), who finds therein a resemblance to the style of Lucas Cranach. Two other copies may be seen in Singer's 'Researches,' and in the beautiful French work, 'Jeux de Cartes Tarots, par la Société des Bibliophiles Français;' other representations may be found on plates 92-95."

" In the latter work the series is more complete, since, including the pieces now detached, but evidently formerly present, it contains forty-eight cards. Nevertheless, we are inclined to believe that our own series, which—as before stated—contains but thirty-six pieces, is a complete set, since each suit begins with the pip-card *six*. We have here evidently two different editions of one and the same series of cards, intended perhaps for different countries and places, just as we have at the present day. This is clear from the complete difference of the ace of leaves in our own set from that in the Paris example; in the latter it bears the arms of Saxony, which probably induced Chatto and others to look on these cards as of Saxon manufacture, and as related to the style of L. Cranach." (*Op. cit.* pp. 191-6.)

We may remind the reader that numerals of five pips are present in the British Museum example, and of two, three, four pips in the Paris series. It is noteworthy, also, that the piece bearing the arms of Saxony in the Paris version, has on a shield below them a pick and mallet in saltire, resembling those in the Stukely cards before mentioned (p. 193).

On a shield borne by a lion on the two of glands, in the Paris set, is another mark, impossible to describe by words, however. This is the same card which bears the signature F. C. Z., the last letter implying *zeichnet*, probably.

These card-pieces are uncoloured, and the backs free from any decoration.

[3⅝ × 2⅜ in.]   [Backs plain.]

G. 136.

FIRST QUARTER OF SEVENTEENTH CENTURY.

WO pieces, exhibiting fragments of four numeral cards on each piece. On one piece are the aces of glands and of bells, and the seven of glands and of bells. On the second piece are the aces of leaves and of hearts, the seven of leaves, and the six of hearts.

The suit marks are connected by neatly engraved arabesque ornaments. On the aces are large scrolls bearing inscriptions, but of which WIS ; IS ; NI only remain. The marks of the suits have been coloured—but not carefully—green and red.

In these pieces the divisions between the cards, where the latter should be separated, are indicated by crosses, and not by the usual border lines.

One piece has been backed with printed paper, having a Latin text on it. From the Weigel Cabinet.

[3½ × 2⅜ in.]   [Backs plain.]

G. 137.

FIRST QUARTER OF SEVENTEENTH CENTURY.

ULM?

TWO sheets of numeral cards, each sheet having three rows of three cards each row, of the usual suits.

In the upper row of the first sheet are the under valet of leaves, the king of leaves, and the king of bells. In the second row are the under valets of hearts and bells, and the upper valet of bells. On the lower range are the five, ten, and eight of bells.

On the second sheet, upper row, are the kings of hearts and of glands, and the upper valet of leaves. Second row, the under valet of glands, the upper valet of glands, and upper valet of hearts. Lower row, the seven, nine, and six of bells.

All the kings are seated, and bear sceptres in their hands ; those of leaves and glands wear turbans, and semi-Oriental costumes. The valets in the central rows have drawn swords in their hands, and are represented in various actions, and positions of attack and defence. The under valet of glands has a sword in each hand. The under valet of leaves (first row of first sheet), is a standard-bearer ; he rests the colours on his left shoulder. The upper valet of leaves (first row of second sheet), is an officer directed towards the left; he wears a plumed hat, carries a commander's baton in the right hand, resting the former on his right hip, and his left hand on the other hip. He stands with outstretched legs in a formal manner.

Below the marks of the suit on the five of bells, a female is represented sitting in a large bath-tub, leaning over which is a fool with cap and bells, and harlequin's wand(?) in his right hand. At the bottom of the ten of bells sits a hare, turning round a dog on a spit over a fire. On the eight of bells is a goat, and a tub before him. On the seven of bells a fox is seizing a duck ; on the nine of the same suit is represented the fable of the " Fox and the Stork." On the six of bells is a naked woman astride on a hedgehog or porcupine, and holding a mirror in her left outstretched hand, while she seizes with her right the ear of the animal.

On the right-hand margin of the first sheet runs an inscription in Roman capitals, but too mutilated to be decipherable.

The technical execution of these card-pieces is of an inferior character in all respects. They are from wood-blocks, and are uncoloured. They formed part of T. O. Weigel's collection, who observes of them :—

" In R. v. Eitelberger's Essay on Playing Cards (Wien, 1860), at p. 16, two examples are given, viz. the two of leaves and upper knave of bells, which closely resemble our own set; for the soldier on the upper valet of bells is represented in a like offensive position, and the general intention of the figures and the costume are substantially of the type of our own cards. Both examples are in the fine Hauslab collection at Vienna, and belong to a series of *kemptener* origin, bearing the address of the designer, George Schachomair. The date of their production is about the end of the sixteenth century. Our own set appears, from the costume of the figures, to belong to that period, and is probably likewise of Kemptener or Ulm origin, since, as before observed, the whole type of the series strikingly coincides with the cards of the Hauslab collection." (*Op. cit.* vol. ii. p. 197.)

These cards are very thickly mounted, and the backs are diapered with large rosettes, running diagonally. Printed in black.

[$3\frac{7}{8} \times 2\frac{3}{8}$ in.]   [Backs decorated.]

G. 138.

THIRD QUARTER OF SIXTEENTH CENTURY.

FRANKFURT?

(CARDS OF H. S. BEHAM?)

THREE large sheets of unseparated card-pieces, of the suits leaves, glands, flowers, and fruits.

The marks of the latter two suits are somewhat of a conventional character, the flower being something like a rose, and the fruit having a distant resemblance to a poppy capsule, or a pomegranate with a slit in it.

The first sheet contains the twelve figure-cards, and below them the twos of the four suits.

In the first row are the four under valets, in the second row are the four kings, and in the third row from the top are the four upper valets. The kings are mounted; the horse of the king of leaves is standing quiet, the horses of the kings of glands and of flowers are rearing, and that of the king of fruit trotting forwards. The king of leaves has on a crown with a convex top, surmounted by a small cross. The other kings have simple dentated crowns. The king of leaves, directed towards the right hand, bears the symbol of his suit in his left hand. The king of glands, advancing in the same direction, bears it in his right hand. The king of flowers, advancing towards the left, carries the long-stalked rose in his left hand; while the king of fruit, trotting towards the right, turns round in his saddle to the left, and elevates the large capsule with both hands.

The valets of leaves are military figures in large plumed hats, like the designs of Burgkmair and of the time of Maximilian. Those of glands are adorned as dissolute rustic Bacchuses; the valets of flowers are running peasants, with cowl-like caps on their heads, the upper valet blowing a horn as he advances. The valets of fruit are characterised by their jerkin boots with large overlapping tops. The marks of the suits, glands, flowers, and leaves, are borne on long curved stalks by the valets. The stalk of the rose on the under valet of flowers is broken and separated from the blossom.

The marks of the suits on the pip-cards are throughout the series connected on each piece by a central stout, arborescent, and leafy stem, having lateral branches. Slight variations, however, occur on two cards. On the two of glands (first sheet), at the lower part, is a shield bearing a large pine-apple or fircone-like fruit. This shield hangs from the neck of a winged child, who is holding it with his left hand while he kneels and extends the right arm. From the child's head springs a short stem, bearing the dependent symbols of the suits. At the base of the three of glands (second sheet) is a hog, supporting the short leafy stem which bears the signs of the suit.

The second sheet presents the three, four, five, and six, seven, eight, nine, and ten, of fruit and glands.

The third sheet bears the three, four, five, and six, and the seven, eight, nine, and ten, of the suits flowers and leaves.

All the aces of the series are absent or have been originally suppressed.

Each pip-card has its value indicated in Roman numerals at the top, and in Arabic ones at the bottom.

These card-pieces are from well-engraved wood-blocks, and are of superior character. They have been attributed to Hans Sebald Beham, a distinguished engraver, born at Nürnberg 1500, and dying there about 1550. As far as the designs alone of the marks of the suits are concerned, there is much similitude between them and the designs of the suit marks in the series of cards ascribed to

Errhard Schön (Singer, pp. 42-3). The groups below the connecting stems in the pip-cards, present in the E. Schön series, are wanting in the present or " Beham " sequence.

These cards are uncoloured; the figure pieces are devoid of names or titles, and not any address or inscription is present.

$[3\frac{5}{8} \times 2\frac{3}{8}$ in.] [Backs plain.]

G. 139.

FIRST QUARTER OF NINETEENTH CENTURY?

PRAG.

TWO sheets of sixteen unseparated card-pieces in each sheet. The cards absent are the four aces, and the three, four, and five of each suit.

Each sheet has three rows of six card-pieces on each row. The suit marks are leaves, glands, bells, and hearts.

The first sheet contains all the figure-cards, and the six, seven, eight, nine, and ten of hearts, and the seven of bells. In the first row are the four superior valets, in the second row are the four kings, in the third row are the four inferior valets.

The superior valets of bells and leaves are whole-length figures in Oriental costume, those of glands and hearts are in dresses of Frederick the Great's time. The valet of hearts carries a letter in his right hand, in his left a footman's cane with tassel.

All the kings are on horseback, advancing towards the left hand. The horse of the king of hearts is rearing on his hind legs. The king of leaves is in Oriental costume, and wears a turban surmounted by a crescent. In his left hand is a sceptre, having at the top a radiant sun. The other kings are crowned and carry short sceptres. The king of bells alone has spurs.

The under valets of leaves and hearts are in Oriental costume, directing their gaze upward. The under valet of bells is a postilion in " Kannonen Stiefeln," and with a whip in his right hand. The under valet of glands is a " jäger," holding a hawk in his left hand.

Each figure-card has the mark of the suit at the proper corner. On the six of hearts—the first card in the upper row of the first sheet—is a monumental erection, having an urn at the top and large tablet at the base, on which is inscribed—" Feine Teische Karten zu finden Bei Anton Herbst. IN Prag. No. 257."

On the eight of hearts are two half-draped semi-savage figures, with bows and arrows in their hands. Below the marks on the seven of hearts are two female figures, one carrying a large jug, the other having a tray upon her head. On the seven of bells—the sixth piece in the upper row of sheet one—are two men, having between them a couple of posts, connected by a cord at the top, from which hangs a bird. The man on the right is running towards the latter, while he on the left appears as if shooting or pointing with a stick upwards. On the ten of hearts is an Indian woman, reclining in a sort of hammock supported by palm trees; below, seated on the ground and raising his left hand, is an Indian, with the conventional circle of feathers around his head. On the nine of hearts is a drummer and another person in a dancing attitude; both have feather headdresses.

The second sheet contains the six, eight, nine of bells, seven and nine of glands, and seven of leaves in the first row. On the second row are the eight of glands, two of hearts, glands, bells, and leaves, and eight of leaves. On the third row are the six of glands, the nine of leaves, the ten of glands, the ten of bells, the ten of leaves, and the six of leaves. On each of these card-pieces are figures or scenes of a grotesque character. Monkeys wear cocked hats and ride dogs, carry lant-horns, umbrellas, &c. A mermaid is on the two of bells; a sea-dog or lion, from whose fish-like tail rises the stem bearing the symbols of the suit, is on the two of glands, while on the seven of leaves a man rides astride on the trunk of an ele-phant. A rearing tiger, muzzled, and led in chains by a man in Oriental dress, is on the eight of leaves. The tens are the only pip-cards which have their values expressed in Roman numerals placed at the top of the pieces. Each card has an ornamental border.

This series consists of very inferior designs from wood-blocks engraved in an equally bad manner, as far, at least, as the decorative figures and scenes are con-cerned. The suit marks themselves have been executed in a neater manner. All the pieces are uncoloured.

[$3\frac{6}{8} \times 2\frac{1}{8}$ in.]   [Backs plain.]

G. 140.

FIRST HALF OF NINETEENTH CENTURY.

PRAG.

 SHEET containing eighteen unseparated card-pieces of the suits, bells, leaves, hearts, and glands. There are three rows, each row having six cards. The upper row exhibits the under valet of leaves, the upper valets of bells and glands, the ten of hearts, the nine of hearts, and the six of this suit.

On the second row are the kings of leaves, bells, and glands, the two of hearts, with the under valet and seven of the same suit.

On the third row are the upper valet of leaves, the under valets of bells and glands, the king of hearts, the upper valet, and ten of hearts.

The designs on this sheet of card-pieces have been suggested evidently by those in G. 137—the sequence containing the fighting figures. The valets of bells, glands, and hearts have swords in their hands, and are in either offensive or defensive postures. The valets of glands carry a sword in each hand, as do the valets of the like suit in G. 137. The under valet of leaves is here a military fifer, the upper valet a drummer.

The four kings are in Oriental costume and seated, as in G. 137. The costume of both kings and valets is based clearly on that in the previous series. The pip-cards have ornamental designs on them. On the ten of hearts a Cupid holds his bow towards a flower; on the nine of the same suit is a cone, around which is spirally twisted a branch of leaves.

On the two of hearts is a shield of armorial bearings, crested by a bird and leaves. The seven of hearts exhibits a tub, from which rises a small tree, while the six of hearts bears on a shield the following inscription—

" HIR KARDEN FEIN
ZU FINDEN SEIND
IM. PRA."

On the ten of hearts is the value in a Roman numeral at the top of the piece.

All the pieces are uncoloured, the drawing, technic, &c., being even worse than in the preceding series, G. 139.

[$3\frac{6}{8} \times 2\frac{2}{8}$ in.]   [Backs plain.]

G. 141.

FIRST QUARTER OF NINETEENTH CENTURY.

FRANKFURT.

PACK of fifty-two numerals of the suits hearts, clubs, spades, and diamonds. The coate-cards are king, queen, and valet, as busts printed double and in reverse.

All the aces bear two designs (in reverse) of battle scenes, white circular spaces being reserved in the centre of the card for the mark of the suit. On the ace of hearts are represented an attack on Frankfurt and the battle of Hanau. ·On the upper division is the following address, on a pedestal surmounted by a shield bearing an eagle and machiolated crown—" Zu finden bei E L Wüst in Frankfurt a/m." The word Frankfurt is at the upper right-hand corner, and that of Hanau at the lower left-hand corner (in reverse) of the card-piece. Within the space for the suit mark is " J C F Neubauer fec."

The battle of Leipzig and " heiliger augenblick," or prayer before action, are represented on the ace of diamonds; on the ace of spades are the engagements at Brienne and Katzbach. On the ace of clubs are the attack on Montmartre and the entry into Paris.

The busts on the figure-cards are intended to be in the costume of the time. Mr. Chatto, who was cognisant of this series, remarks, " The Duke of Wellington figures as the knave of diamonds, and Marshal Blucher as the knave of clubs " (p. 260).

An ornamental engraved title of a wrapper accompanies this set, having on it the following inscription :—" Feine Spiel-Karten in Staats Militair Costum, dem Andenken in die merkwürdigen Jahre 1813 und 1814 gewidmet. Von. Corn, Ludw., Wüst in Frankfurt a.M."

The above is encircled in a wreath of oak-leaves, at the top of which is an eagle displayed with the letter F on its breast; below are a sword and conqueror's palm within another wreath. The whole is printed in blue ink.

These cards are neatly engraved and coloured, but the compositions on the aces are destitute of any artistic merit.

The backs are adorned with blue dotted lines and oval ornaments.

[$3\frac{1}{2}$ × $2\frac{3}{8}$ in.]   [Backs decorated.]

G. 142.

SECOND QUARTER OF NINETEENTH CENTURY?

VIENNA?

LL the coate-cards, with the exception of the valet of spades, of a numeral series of fifty-two (?).

The figures are king, queen, and valet, in busts printed double and in reverse.

On one of the divisions the name of the person represented is engraved in modern Greek, on the other in Roman characters. Thus, the king of spades is Σουλιμάν on one bust, and Soliman on the other. The queen of the same suit is Θεοδωρα and Theodora. The king of hearts is Aρουν αλ ρασχιδ and Harun al

Rashid, the queen Σαββαῖδε and Sobbaide, the valet Βοτσαρις and Botsarys. The king of diamonds bears Μεχμεδ and Mohammed II., the queen Ρωξανη and Roxane, the valet Πυρρος and Pyrrhus. The king of clubs is Τιμουρ-Βεγ and Timur Beg, the queen is Φατιμα and Fatima, and the valet Σκανδερ-Βεγ and Skanderbeg.

On a transverse space between the busts on the valet of clubs is the address, "Niederlage am Peter, No. 577."

These cards are neatly engraved and coloured, though without any particular artistic merit. The backs are *tarotées* with pale blue dots in diamond shapes, within dotted circles.

The series was probably published at Vienna for the Greek market.

[$3\frac{2}{8}$ × 2 in.]   [Backs decorated.]

SUIT MARKS ANIMATED.

G. 143.

SECOND HALF OF FIFTEENTH CENTURY.

COLOGNE.

(Circular Cards.)

THREE circular card-pieces of a numeral series, the exact number of the suits of which is, in the opinion of some persons, undetermined. The cards here present are the upper valet of parroquets, the under valet of roses, and the under valet of columbines.

The upper valet of parroquets is a single piece; the two other pieces are on one sheet, having been engraved on the same plate. They touch each other by the outer borders.

The valet of parroquets is an armed man, running towards the right hand. He bears on his right shoulder a mace-like flail, having a spiked iron globe attached. A long curved sword is at his side. On a level with his shoulder, at the right-hand upper part of the field, is the mark of the suit.

The valet of roses is a man proceeding towards the right. He bears a crossbow on his left shoulder, and holds an arrow in his right hand. From his left side, and projecting from behind his back, is a bundle of arrows. The mark of the suit is on a level with his knee, at the right-hand lower part of the circular field.

The valet of columbines is an armed man dressed in a long slit coat, and walking towards the left. He bears a long spear or halberd on his left shoulder, and from his left side projects a long straight sword. He carries the mark of the suit in his right hand.

The groundwork of each piece is formed of hillocks with plants on them. The field of each card-piece is enclosed within a border of three circles.

Considering their time of production the designs on these cards are good, as is also the technic.

Though the three specimens here present are of the same set as regards design, it may be doubted if they have all been engraved by the same hand. The lower two cards appear to be the work of a heavier burin than that which produced the upper valet.

Much interest attaches to these specimens of early German metal engraving, and rare examples of playing-cards; they are three of a sequence described by Bartsch, vol. x. p. 70; Singer, pp. 45, 205; Passavant, vol. ii. pp. 176-7; alluded to by Chatto, p. 223, and by Taylor, p. 119.

The following quotation is from Passavant, under "Le Maître des Cartes à jouer de forme ronde" (*Op. cit.*):—

"The originals of these cards are to be ranked among the finer engravings, *au burin*, of the fifteenth century. The inscription, *Salve Felix Colonia*, accompanied by three crowns, which is on the titled wrapper, informs us that these cards had their origin at Cologne. We must conclude, at the same time, that they appeared between the years 1461 and 1483, if we accept the figure of the mounted king of columbines as representing Louis XI. of France, who reigned at that period. Up to the present time we have remained in ignorance as to the master who executed these engravings, and further, it is almost impossible to point out any other engraving which could be safely attributed to him. His manner resembles that of John of Cologne, from Zwolle, though it cannot be said to be identical with it in details. The five suits—each suit having thirteen pieces—contain nine pip-cards in each suit, an upper and under valet (*ober et unter*), a dame, and a king, as was formerly the practice in Germany.

"Hitherto but a few incomplete specimens of the original series have been recorded, as those, *e.g.*, at Oxford and Dresden. They are executed with much delicacy of drawing, the etching generally terminating with points or dots, and some impressions being printed off in a pale black ink.

"There are two copies of the original cards.

"(A). The first copy, that by Telman de Wesel, bears at the lower portion of each piece the initials T. W.

"(B). The second, by an engraver of Upper Germany, is treated in a stiff and very inferior manner to the former by Telman. The king of pinks (Bartsch, N. 39 of the original series) bears on the bridle of the horse the inscription: 'Demi. Ich. War. Gertei (Getrei?).' In the Albertine collection.

"Heinecken ('Neue Nachrichten,' p. 353), mentions a mounted king of the suit of pinks, who bears on his crown the inscription, 'Ich. Win,' &c." (*Op. cit.*)

From the scattered and imperfect sets of these cards which exist, two deductions have been drawn, one of which is no doubt right, but the other we think rather questionable. The first conclusion has been that not any pip-cards of the value *ten* entered into either of the suits. Nevertheless, the number of pieces in each suit was the regular one, viz. thirteen; but this was made up by there being *four* figure-cards or honours, viz., a king, queen, and two valets.

The second conclusion has been that this series consisted of *five* suits, viz. hares, parroquets, pinks, columbines, and roses. It is true that some pieces of a suit of roses exist, as likewise of suits of pinks and columbines, and which appear to be undoubtedly the work of the same engraver, as proved by the examples in the British Museum collection. This suit of roses was intended, we think, to displace, as occasion or taste might demand, the suit of pinks, and not to be added to it. Singer's belief that tens existed in the sequence, that there were five suits of fourteen cards each suit, and that the series belonged to Tarocchino, does not merit discussion.

Mr. Chatto writes in connection with these examples:—

"In the circular cards described by Bartsch and Singer the inscription on the ace of hares is in Latin, and the initials of the engraver, T. W. are wanting. (See next series, G. 144.) From a wrapper, of which a facsimile is given by Singer, it would appear that those cards were engraved at Cologne, and it has been supposed that they are of as early a date as 1470. They are unquestionably the work of either a German or a Flemish artist; and some amateurs of engraving have erroneously ascribed them to Martin Schöngauer. Bartsch, in his description of them, includes a fifth suit—namely, that of roses—and says that each suit consisted of thirteen cards, which would thus give sixty-five pieces for the complete pack. Mr. Singer also, in his account of such of those cards as were formerly in the collection of Mr. Douce, gives it as his opinion that the complete pack ought to consist of five suits of fourteen cards each—in all seventy pieces. Mons. Duchesne, however, thinks that those authors were wrong, and that the complete pack consisted of only four suits of thirteen cards each, as displayed by those preserved in the Bibliothèque du Roi.   But as he entirely overlooks the difficulty of accounting for a suit of roses engraved in the same style, he does not seem to be justified in pronouncing so decisively that Bartsch and Singer are wrong in supposing that a complete pack consisted of five suits, for it is by no means unlikely that a fifth suit might have been introduced by the artist with a view of giving variety to the game, but which might have been subsequently discarded as inconsistent with the old established principles of the game, and as only making it more complicated, without rendering it more interesting." (*Op. cit.*)   These cards are uncoloured.

[2⅝ in. diameter.]   [Backs plain.]

G. 144.

FIRST QUARTER OF SIXTEENTH CENTURY.

(Circular Cards by Telman von Wesel.)

BOUND folio volume, lettered "Cartes à jouer du XVI. Siècle," with the press mark, "Sheepshanks Cabinet, 23, No. 2."

It contains a series of fifty-two circular card-pieces of the suits hares (or rabbits), parroquets, pinks, and columbines.   Of the specimens present, twenty-six are genuine pieces, and twenty-six are facsimile drawings.   The card-pieces are unseparated, with the exception of two—the queens of hares and columbines—appearing as they came from the hands of the printer in separate sheets, either of four or six cards each sheet.   The original or genuine pieces are the four aces on sheet 1; the two and three of columbines on sheet 2; the nine of hares on sheet 4; the four, five, six, seven, eight, and nine of pinks on sheet 6; the four, five, six, seven, eight, and nine of parroquets on sheet 7; the six valets on sheet 8; and the queen of hares, number 9.

Within the outer circle of the border at the lower part of each card are the initials T. W.   This circumstance, combined with the style and technic of these rare and interesting objects, has led to the opinion that they are copies by Telman von Wesel, generally in reverse, and with certain variations of the series last noticed (G. 143).

The values of the pip-cards are given in Roman numbers at the lower portion, and in Arabic figures at the upper part of each piece close to the inner circle of the border.   In the Arabic numbering the numerals 4 and 7 are of the old forms: λ (4) ꝗ (7), and the 5 is 7.

The figure-cards have not either titles or numbers.   On the first sheet are the aces of the four suits—rare, genuine pieces.   In the first ace, that of hares, the hare sits upright in the centre of the circle, having above a long waved scroll or banderol, on which is the inscription in *Platt-Deutsch:*

"AVE. MI. DRINT. ME. VIN
DAEROM. MOT. IC. EN. LEPUS. SIN."

The precise meaning of this it is not easy to determine.   Passavant read it thus:

" O weh! mich drängt man fein,
Darum muss ich ein Hase sein."

i. e. Alas! men hotly me pursue,
I am a hare it is most true.

P

Chatto remarks : " Taking the contracted $\overset{\Omega}{ave}$ to have been intended for *auwe*, a meadow, the couplet may be thus done into English—

> ' Me o'er fields men keen pursue,
> Therefore I'm the hare you view.'

But supposing the word $\overset{\Omega}{ave}$ to have been meant for *augen*, the eyes, and giving a slight turn to one or two other words, the meaning would be that the hare was called *lepus*, quasi *lippus*, on account of its blear eyes" (p. 222).

On the ace of hares in the original set, from which the present is supposed to have been copied, is the following inscription, according to Bartsch (vol. x. p. 75) : " Felix medic, quisquis turba parte quiet," which favours rather Passavant's reading than that of Chatto.

On the second ace is a parroquet perched on a stumpy tree ; above in a waved scroll is the inscription—" QUIDQUID FACIMUS. VENIT. EX ALTO."

On the ace of pinks, above the large flower in the centre, on a very long waved scroll is : " FORTUNA. OPES. AUFERRE. NON. ANIMUM. POTEST."

On a scroll around the drooping flower on the ace of columbines may be read—" PAR. ILLE. SVPIS [superis] CVI PAR$\overset{\Omega}{TT}$ (? Parturiunt) DIES. ET FORTVNA. FVIT."

On sheet 2 are inlaid the two and three of columbines, genuine pieces, and the two and three of hares, facsimile copies. On the two of hares is a large leaf below the marks of the suit.

On sheet 3 are copies only of the two and three of parroquets, and of the two and three of pinks.

On sheet 4 the only genuine card is the nine of hares, the four, five, six, seven, and eight of hares being copies. The hares on the four, five, and six are represented eating leaves.

On the fifth sheet all the pieces are copies, and consist of the four, five, six, seven, eight, and nine of columbines.

The six cards of the sixth sheet are genuine, and include the four, five, six, seven, eight, and nine of pinks.

On sheet 7 all the pieces are genuine, and comprehend the four, five, six, seven, eight, and nine of parroquets.

Sheet 8 includes six valets in two longitudinal rows of three each row. All the pieces are genuine. The first valet is the *ober* of hares. His dress is peculiar : he has a long-tailed cap on his head, carries a large arrow in his right hand, and runs towards a hare on a bank on the right. The hare jumps towards the man. The *unter* of parroquets has been discharging an arrow at the bird sitting on the ground at the right hand ; the bird has caught the arrow in its mouth. The third valet is the *unter* of hares. He is in oriental costume, bears a lance on his left shoulder, and carries a hare head downwards by the hind legs in his right hand. The first card in the lower row is the *ober* of columbines. His back is turned to the spectator. He advances towards the right, bearing a lance on his left shoulder, and a long sword projecting backwards from under his right arm. The *untermann* of columbines follows ; he is a young man of condition advancing in front, extending the left hand, and supporting some object—difficult to define—with the right against his chest. The symbol of the suit is at the right hand. There are some peculiar marks immediately in the foreground at the feet of the young man ; they may be intended for ants, upon which the student-like youth may be moralising. The *unter* of pinks is a stooping figure in a large cloak directed towards the left, and contemplating with raised hand the flower, the mark of the suit. Below this sheet (8) of valets is a single card, No. 9, representing the queen of hares. It is genuine. The lady is mounted and rides towards the left ; she wears a coronetted head-dress, rich drapery spotted with *fleurs-de-lys*, and having peculiar leafy appendages to the arms. The palfrey is richly caparisoned, and has a tuft of hair with a cross upon it projecting from the brow. Behind the queen on the left hand a

hare is seated on a bank level with the lady's shoulder.   On sheet 10 are four
facsimiles of the kings of hares, parroquets, columbines, and pinks.   The king of
hares is a mounted Turk galloping towards the right.   The hare is behind, springing towards his back from a bank.   The king of parroquets is mounted on a
rearing horse turned towards the left.   The bird is perched on a branch behind
the horseman.   The king of columbines on horseback advances towards the
right ; the mark of the suit is behind him on the left.   The king of pinks mounted
rides towards the left.   The flower of the suit is on the right.   The king of pinks
is a youthful and graceful figure with long wavy hair, the king of columbines is
an old man.

Sheet 11 contains facsimiles only of the queens of pinks and parroquets, and
of the upper valets of the same suits ; both queens are on horseback advancing
towards the left hand.   The flower of the suit is on the right, and behind the queen
of pinks ; the bird of the queen of parroquets is on the left in front of the lady.
The two valets are armed men running towards the left ; one bears a halberd, the
other a mace-like flail on his shoulder—long swords are at their sides.   The
marks of their suits are on the left hand, *i.e.* in front of them.

Below is No. 12, a single card, being a facsimile of the queen of columbines.
She is seated on a mule advancing towards the right.   Her full-front is towards
the spectator.   The head-dress is peculiar.   The flower-mark of the suit is on
the left-hand side of the circle.

It should be remarked that in the present sequence there are not any tens, but
that there are *four court-cards*—king, queen, and upper and under valets.   In
reference to this circumstance Chatto observes : " The third character in those
coat-cards cannot properly be called a cavalier, and has indeed very little pretensions to the designation of squire.   The knaves are evidently common foot-
soldiers, such as were known in Italy by the name of *fanti*."—" The distinction
between the two latter is not, indeed, very clearly expressed in the costume,
though there cannot be a doubt that the lowest character is that which in each
suit is represented as running, and thus plainly corresponding with the Italian
fante."   (p. 221.)

Though a full and regular numeral sequence is here present, viz., fifty-two
cards divided into four suits of thirteen cards each suit, some authorities consider that the series has properly five suits of fourteen cards each suit ; *in toto*,
seventy pieces, similar to the sequence G. 143.   According to this view the
original sequence is supposed to have possessed the tens and a *fifth* suit, the suit
of roses.   The number being thus increased to seventy, the multiplicity of suits
and the circular shape of the pieces have been assumed to show in this example,
not only the Oriental origin of playing-cards, but the Persian characteristics of
the latter in the style and decorations of the pieces.

" Demandez "—writes M. B. d'Ambly—" au Cabinet des Estampes l'exem-
plaire des *cartes rondes*.   Elles sont à peu près du même temps, car on croit y
lire la date 1477, ce sont les seules que j'aie vues avec cette forme.   En Orient
on aime, on adore véritablement cette forme-là, qui est la forme symbolique du
panthéisme.   En Europe on n'en a pas voulu ; nous aimons les angles."   (Bibl.
3, p. 85.)

A complete set of genuine impressions—fifty-two in number—of these card-
pieces is preserved in the Paris Collection.   It formerly belonged to a Monsieur
Volpato, " Amateur distingué attaché au Théâtre Italien à Paris." (Bibl. 2, fol. 2
verso, No. 10), and were purchased of him for the Bibliothèque du Roi in 1833.
M. Volpato received in exchange twenty-six genuine cards of the same series,
and twenty-six facsimile drawings of other pieces necessary to complete the set,
along with a sum of money.   M. Volpato afterwards sent his copy to the Messrs.
Smith of Lisle Street for sale.   It passed into the Sheepshanks Cabinet, and from
thence to the Collection of the British Museum, being the series now under
examination.

Accompanying the latter is the legal agreement to the transaction just referred to, having attached to it M. Guizot's signature. It is as follows :

" Entre les Soussignés Letronne Directeur de la Bibliothèque royale agissant au nom du conservatoire de la dite Bibliothèque et avec l'autorisation du Ministre de l'Instruction publique, à lui donnée par la lettre en date du 22 Décembre, 1832, d'une part.

" Et Jean Antoine Vincent Volpato artiste graveur demeurant à Paris, rue Godot Mauroy, No. 36, d'autre part.

" Il a été convenu de ce qui suit, savoir moi Volpato, je cède au département des estampes cartes et plans de la Bibliothèque royale, un jeu de cartes complet de 52 cartes gravé vers 1477, toutes dans un état de parfaite conservation et à pleine marge. Ces cartes proviennent de la vente du Cabinet de M. Bitter, Peintre, faite à Bercy en 1832, sont en forme de medallions ronds et portent au bas la marque T. W.; elles sont au nombre de six sur six planches, et de quatre sur quatre autres planches.

" La quelle cession en faite par moi pour le prix de deux mille cinq cents francs.

" Et j'accepte pour le prix de la même jeu—1°, une somme de mille huit cents francs qui me sera fournie en deux payemens ; 2°, pour les sept cents francs restant je m'engage à prendre vingt-six cartes de ce meme jeu, savoir, trois planches entière de six medaillons chaque, mais sans marge et avec quelques détériorations, une planche contenant les quatres As, enfin quatres autres cartes séparées et rognées.

" Et moi Letronne m'engage à faire payer à M. Volpato la somme de mille huit cents francs en deux paymens, savoir, le premier sur les dépenses de Janvier, 1833, et le second sur celles d'Avril, 1833, et à lui livrer pour solde du prix total de 2,500 francs les vingt six cartes ci-dessus mentionnées pour la valeur de sept cents francs les dites cartes provenant, vingt quatre du volume No. 624, pages 13, 14, 15, et 16 de la collection donnée par M. Begon en 1770, la vingt cinquième du No. 57, page 10 de la Collection acquise de M. de Marolles en 1666, et la vingt sixième d'une donation faite par M. Delamotte en l'an 9.

" Après que le Présent Marché aura été soumis à l'approbation du Ministre de l'instruction publique, conformément à l'ordonance du Roi en date du 14 Septembre, 1822.

" Le présent Acte Fait double, Paris, Bibliothèque royale, le 10 Janvier, 1833. " VOLPATO.

" LETRONNE Directeur de la B. Rᵉ.

" Vu et approuvé Paris, le 22 Janvier, 1833. Le Ministre Secrétaire d'Etat au département de l'Instruction publique. " GUIZOT."

The set thus acquired by the Parisian authorities from Volpato has been copied in entirety by the Bibliophiles Français for their work on " Jeux de Cartes Tarots et de Cartes Numerales" (pl. 71-80).

[2⅝ in. diameter.] [Backs plain.]

G. 145.

FIRST QUARTER OF SIXTEENTH CENTURY.

FRANKFORT ?

TWO circular card-pieces of a numeral series of fifty-two. The cards present are the under valet of hares and the upper valet of parroquets. Within the circle of the border at the lower part of each piece are the letters T. W.

These examples are from the series just described (G. 144), supposed to have been engraved by Telman von Wesel, after an older sequence (G. 143). The description of the two valets of hares and parroquets, under that number, may apply to the present examples, which formed part of the Willet Collection.

[2⅝ in. diameter.] [Backs plain.]

G. 146.

FIRST QUARTER OF SIXTEENTH CENTURY.

FRANKFURT ?

TWO circular card-pieces of a numeral series of fifty-two. The cards present are the six of hares and the seven of columbines. Within the circle of the border at the lower part of each piece are the letters T. W.

From the series previously described, as engraved by Telman von Wesel (G. 144). The examples formed part of the Slade collection.

[2⅝ in. diameter.] [Backs plain.]

G. 147.

LAST QUARTER OF FIFTEENTH CENTURY?

A CARD-PIECE from a numeral series, one of the suits of which had chimeric animals for its sign.

The example present is a three of animals, the latter being a frog and two dragons.

The animals are represented as on the declivity of a hill on which grow a tree and plants. A large dragon with spotted body and jagged curled tail is in the centre. To the left is another dragon with small body, but a longer neck and tail. Its head is at the bottom of the piece, the tail extending upwards to the spot on the side of the hill from which the tree springs; above the central dragon and near the top of the hill is a large frog, directed towards the left.

This example was formerly in the Weigel cabinet, into which it had passed from that of Quandt. It is No. 446 in Weigel's large work.

"Its period of production may be assumed to have been from 1470 to 1480. The somewhat awkward and laboured technic implies the hand of the goldsmith. The print is interesting from the circumstance that it appears to be not an impression from one plate simply, but from two superimposed plates." (Vol. ii. p. 379.)

This piece is referred to by Passavant, vol. ii. p. 243, n. 226, but neither he nor Weigel alludes to it as a *card*. Bartsch, however, recognized its true character, and as such described it (vol. x. p. 103, No. 8).

[3⅞ × 2⅝ in.] [Back plain.]

G. 148.

SECOND HALF OF FIFTEENTH CENTURY.

PORTION of a card-piece of a numeral series, one of the suits of which were quadrupeds—bears and lions.

The part present represents a bear sucking his left fore-paw, and scratching himself with his right hind claw.

In the sequence of which this card-piece forms part, the suits appear to have been—bears and lions, stags, birds, and flowers and leaves (*laub* or *grün*). A somewhat different view is taken by Chatto, pp. 224, 225. We are of opinion, however, that the strange little figures in the numeral piece five of plate 91, in the " Jeux de Cartes Tarots," &c. of the Bibliophiles Français (Bibl. 2), belong to the suit of leaves.

The present example appears to be an impression from a card-plate which had been cut down to form a separate print, on account of the admirable technical execution and truth to nature exhibited in the design, or for the reason adduced by Wilson, presently to be noticed.

The sequence, of which it is supposed to be an unit, may be found described by Passavant, vol. ii. p. 73, as the work of "Le Maître aux cartes à jouer," who is presumed to have belonged to the school of the Master of 1446.

In the work of the Bibliophiles Français, forty pieces of the sequence are represented by lithographic facsimiles. We believe that twenty-nine of the cards in the Paris Cabinet were procured at the sale of Mr. Wilson's collection, and are described by the latter writer in his " Catalogue Raisonné of the Select Collection of Engravings of an Amateur," London, 1828, p. 87.

In Mr. Wilson's cabinet and in the Dresden Collection were several pieces of separate figures of the suit marks to which the present specimen belongs. Mr. Wilson remarks in connection with these pieces: "All these plates are of an irregular form, several of them the exact shapes of the figures which they contain; those indicating the suits on the court-cards are all impressed in spaces curiously left for the purpose in the work of the larger plates."

Bartsch alludes in vol. x. p. 80, *et seq.* to some pieces of this series.

[$1\frac{7}{8}$ × $2\frac{4}{8}$ in.]   [Back plain.]

G. 149.

LAST QUARTER OF FIFTEENTH CENTURY.

SINGLE piece from a numeral series, the mark of one of the suits of which was deer.

The example present is the three of deer.

To the right is a stag, full horned, raising his right fore and hind legs ; a fawn is grazing in the foreground, and behind and above, on a gentle elevation, is a doe looking towards the left. Large plantain-like herbs are on the ground.

The impression is from a copper plate, and the technic that of the goldsmith engraver. It is described by Bartsch, vol. x. p. 103, n. 6.

[$3\frac{5}{8}$ × $2\frac{6}{8}$ in.]   [Back plain.]

G. 150.

LAST QUARTER OF FIFTEENTH CENTURY.

SINGLE card-piece from a numeral series of which dogs formed the mark of one of the suits.

The example present is the four of dogs.

The animals are placed two above and two below. The left lower one sits on his hind quarters and looks towards the right. The right lower dog lies and licks himself. The upper left animal turns towards the right upper one, who rears on his hind legs and regards his neighbour.

The engraving is from a copper-plate, and evidently the work of a firm and practised hand. It is described by Bartsch, vol. x. p. 106, n. 15; Pass. vol. 2, p. 249, n. 4.

Accompanying this card are two photographs of a five of dogs and an eight of the same suit, contained in the Douce Collection, now at Oxford. These pieces are evidently by the same able hand, whether as respects design or technic, as the four of dogs here described; but they are not of the same dimensions as the latter, nor as regards each other. The five of dogs is $4\frac{3}{8} \times 3\frac{3}{8}$ in., the eight of dogs $5\frac{1}{8} \times 3\frac{5}{8}$ in. The originals are described by Bartsch, vol. x. p. 106, n. 16; 108, n. 20.

[$4\frac{3}{8} \times 3\frac{1}{8}$ in.]   [Back plain.]

G. 151.

LAST QUARTER OF FIFTEENTH CENTURY?

SINGLE card from a numeral series having a suit of birds.

The example present is a three of birds, two of which are chimeric cocks opposed to each other on a hillock. The other is a large crow flying above towards the left. The cock on the right hand has the crest erected, and elevates his right leg as if in anger; the one opposite regards him with disdainful astonishment.

From a copper-plate coarsely engraved in the style of a goldsmith engraver. Described by Bartsch, vol. x. p. 112, No. 10.

[$3\frac{5}{8} \times 2\frac{5}{8}$ in.]   [Back plain.]

G. 152.

LAST QUARTER OF FIFTEENTH CENTURY.

SINGLE card-piece of a numeral series of which one of the suits was birds.

The example present is the three of birds.

In the upper part of the field is a parroquet, perched on an ornamental scroll-like branch, seizing one end of it by the mouth. Below, to the left, a sort of eagle bites his own right wing; while at the base, towards the right hand, another eagle-like bird seizes by the beak an ornamental branch.

From a copper-plate, heavily and coarsely engraved in the goldsmith style. Described by Bartsch, vol. x. p. 112, n. 9.

[$3\frac{1}{2} \times 2\frac{5}{8}$ in.]   [Back plain.]

G. 153.

FIRST QUARTER OF SIXTEENTH CENTURY.

SINGLE card-piece from a numeral series having a suit of birds.
The example present is a three of birds, or chimeric eagles. One
of the latter flies off above with a small ornamental branch in his
claws; below, at the left hand, a long-necked chimeric raptorial
scratches his raised right leg with his beak, while to the right hand another bird
raises his right leg and looks upwards.

From a copper-plate which, though heavily and stiffly engraved, has been
rather more carefully worked than the preceding.

Described by Bartsch, vol. x. p. 111, n. 7.

[$3\frac{1}{2}$ × $2\frac{5}{8}$ in.]   [Back plain.]

G. 154.

LAST QUARTER OF FIFTEENTH CENTURY.

SINGLE card-piece from a numeral series, having birds for one of its
suits.
The example present is a four of birds, from a different series to
any of the preceding.

At the upper part of the field two parrot-like birds fly, the bird on the left
hand downwards, that on the right upwards. Below, on the right, is a chimeric
cock, strutting towards the left hand. On the left is a fanciful, peacock-like bird
walking towards the left, but looks back at his neighbour the cock.

From a copper-plate engraving, the technic of which is more delicate and re-
fined than that of any of the previous bird-pieces. The plate appears to have been
very irregularly cut in a circular form by the artist, previous to having it more
carefully trimmed by the coppersmith.

Described by Bartsch, vol. x. p. 90.

[$3\frac{1}{2}$ in. longest diameter.]   [Back plain.]

G. 155.

LAST QUARTER OF FIFTEENTH CENTURY.

SINGLE card-piece from a numeral series, one of the suits of which
is birds.
The example present is the eight of birds.
At the upper part of the piece are three parrots; one has a long
tail, another scratches his head with the right claw, and at the extreme right is a
pelican (?). In the centre is a parrot with a long tail extended horizontally.
At the lower part is a heron-like bird on the left, and to the right are two nondescript birds, one of which has a long tail extended horizontally.

The design and technic of this piece are evidently from the same hands to
which we owe the suit of dogs, G. 150.

Described by Bartsch, vol. x. p. 116, No. 20. Pass. v. 2, p. 250, n. 8.

[$3\frac{2}{8}$ × $4\frac{6}{8}$ in.]   [Back plain.]

G. 156.

SECOND HALF OF SIXTEENTH CENTURY.

NÜRNBERG?

(CARDS BY VIRGIL SOLIS.)

FIFTY-ONE card-pieces from a numeral series of fifty-two, the suits of which are lions (for *schellen*), monkeys (for *eicheln*), peacocks (for *grün*), and parrots (for *herzen*).

The suits of lions, monkeys, and parrots are complete; the suit of peacocks wants one coate-card, viz., the queen.

Certain pieces of the sequence under consideration are original impressions, others are copies only. All the members of the suit of lions here present are genuine, as are likewise those of the suits of peacocks and monkeys. In parrots, all the pieces are copies, except the nine and king of the suit.

This is an important and interesting series of card-pieces. It forms one of the better examples of card-engraving produced during the sixteenth century, and one of the chief efforts of the well-known designer and engraver, Vergilius (or Virgil) Solis, who was born at Nürnberg in 1514, and died in 1562. Though not at the summit of his art, V. Solis, like Jobst Amman, his follower, produced among the almost innumerable prints which bear his mark, some very good engravings, both on wood and copper. His engravings on metal as designs for gold and silversmiths, and his friezes and scrolls are very beautiful, and probably represent the master at his best. Impressions from many of these plates have now become scarce in good states and condition, and command high prices. The set of cards under notice is extremely rare as a complete sequence, and when of fine impression is of proportionate price. In the Weigel cabinet was a choice set in admirable condition. The possessor of it observed:

"This series belongs to the more interesting and beautiful German playing-cards of the sixteenth century. It includes four suits and fifty-two pieces, but these are not expressed by *schellen*, *eicheln*, *grün*, and *roth*, but by animals; by lions, monkeys, peacocks, and parrots. There is another peculiarity to be noticed: instead of upper and inferior knaves, queen and valet appear. This departure from the usual custom appears to show that this 'tarocks pack' was not intended for the commonalty, but for the higher classes of the community at the time of its production.

"Since but a small part of that mannered and marked handicraft style which pervaded his [V. Solis] later productions appears in these cards, and as they bear the impress of a fresh and youthful spirit, they must have been produced at his earlier and better period, a time when he was more sensibly affected by the influence which Dürer and his pupils produced on German art. The drawing, making allowance for some hardness of line, is in general sure and masterly, and recalls to mind, in the figures particularly of the soldiers, the manner of Aldegrever. The technic is careful and clean, the composition full of taste and rigidly symmetric, the actions of the animals natural, and often not without humour; and moreover there is less of that vulgarity and grossness which the master afterwards introduced often in his playing-cards.

"In R. Eitelberger's 'Memoir on Playing-Cards, with special reference to some examples of old packs existing at Vienna' (Wien, 1860), may be seen a faithful copy in wood of the ace of lions." ("Anfänge," &c. vol. ii. p. 207.)

The pip-cards in the various suits have their values in Roman numerals marked at the tops; the figure-cards are devoid of marks and inscriptions. On the aces of the four suits, the titles of the suits and the cipher of the master are placed.

The symbols of a suit are symmetrically and harmoniously connected by a variety of arabesque and ornamental work. On the ace of lions the upper half of the piece is occupied by a lion seated on his hind quarters. He holds in his extended fore paws an ornamental bar, to which is suspended a shield, on which is inscribed the word, " Schelen," below which is the master's cipher. The lower third of the piece is filled up with arabesques, and the number I. is above the head of the lion.

The queen of lions (*schellen*) exhibits a richly costumed, coronetted lady on horseback. She holds in her left hand a long sceptre, and the horse, richly caparisoned, curvets and directs his steps towards the left. On a fallen tree at the right hand behind the horse is a lion gazing at the lady.

The upper third of the ace of monkeys is occupied by an ape seated on an ornamental frame between two baskets of fruit. Above is the number I. Below the monkey, and in the centre of the card on a shield, is the word *aicheln,* having under it the cipher of the master. Three ornamental human masks disposed triangularly occupy the lower part of the card. The knave of monkeys represents a soldier in a landscape and walking towards the right. He carries an ape astride on his right shoulder, who bears a musket on his left shoulder, the stock of which is supported by the left hand of the man. The queen of monkeys is a lady mounted on a richly caparisoned horse advancing to the right hand. She is crowned, bears a sceptre in her left hand, and has her back turned towards the spectator. Behind her on the hind quarters of the horse stands an ape extending his right arm to the lady's shoulder, and micturating on her dress. The king of monkeys is mounted on a decorated charger, advancing to the right. A plume of feathers is on the forehead of the horse. The king has on a crown, over which falls the tasselled end of a cap. He carries a sceptre in his right hand. On the horse's hind quarters stands an ape, leaning with the right arm on the king's left shoulder. The ape holds a whip in his left hand and raises his left leg towards the king.

On the ace of peacocks, the sign bird stands with outspread tail on some ornamental foliage which is at the centre of the piece. Below is a shield, on which is the word *gruen,* having under it the cipher of the master. Vine-leaves and grapes are on each side of the shield.

On the ace of parrots the bird stands with outspread wings on some flower-stalks at the upper part of the piece. The tail of the parrot descends to the beginning of the upper third of the card, where is a shield having inscribed on it ROT, and below the cipher of the master.

All the pieces of the suit of parrots are but copies, it should be remembered, except the nine and king. The knave is a soldier advancing towards the left, where may be seen the symbolical bird perched on a branch, and stretching towards the man. The latter carries a halberd on his left shoulder and a long, straight sword at his left side. The cipher of the master has been added at the lower left-hand corner. The queen is mounted and turned towards the spectator; the horse advances towards the left, she carries a sceptre in her left hand, at the upper right-hand corner is the bird of the suit, perched on a slender branch. The cipher of the master has been added at the left-hand lower corner. The king of parrots is mounted on a charger and trots towards the left. He carries a sceptre in his right hand, and from his left side hangs a sword, at the upper right-hand corner is the bird of the suit.

The impressions, both originals and copies, are from metal and are uncoloured.

This series of playing-cards is described by Bartsch, vol. ix. p. 282, No. 300-351; is alluded to by Chatto, p. 238; and by Taylor, p. 124.

Why Weigel should term this sequence a " Tarocks-Spiel " is not apparent.
[3⅝ × 2⅜ in.]   [Backs plain.]

G. 157.

SECOND HALF OF SIXTEENTH CENTURY.

NÜRNBERG?

TWENTY-FOUR card-pieces from a numeral series of fifty-two, the suits of which are lions, monkeys, parrots, and peacocks.

These examples are from the sequence designed and engraved by Virgil Solis, before described (G. 156).

The cards present are the three, eight, nine, and ten of lions, the entire suit of monkeys, the one, two, three, six, and ten of peacocks, and the nine and king of parrots.

The members of the suit of lions are all genuine, those of monkeys are copies, the pieces of the suit of peacocks are from the original plates, and those of parrots are copies.

The impressions in the suit of peacocks have, it must be admitted, a somewhat suspicious look; but this is explained by their having been taken after the original plates had been re-worked and rather heavily inked.

[$3\frac{5}{8}$ × $2\frac{3}{8}$ in.]   [Backs plain.]

G. 158.

SECOND HALF OF SIXTEENTH CENTURY.

NÜRNBERG?

FOUR card-pieces from the numeral series, designed and engraved by Virgil Solis (G. 156).

The examples present are the two, three, and four of monkeys, and the nine of lions.

The pieces of the suit of monkeys are genuine, the nine of lions is a copy.

[$3\frac{5}{8}$ × $2\frac{3}{8}$ in.]   [Backs plain.]

CARDS WITH A SECONDARY PURPOSE.

EDUCATIONAL, INSTRUCTIVE.

G. 159.

LAST QUARTER OF SEVENTEENTH CENTURY.

NÜRNBERG.

(GEOGRAPHIC.)

A SEQUENCE of fifty-two numerals, the suits of which are spades, clubs, hearts, and diamonds.

The honours are *könig*, *dame*, and *knecht*, indicated by these titles only.

This series is intended to be subservient to the purpose of instruction in geography.

Each piece, with the exception of an upper margin rather more than an inch wide, is occupied by a map or chart of a particular country or sea-board.

Above it, in the upper margin, is the name of the place represented, and generally a scale of miles. Above these are the name and mark of the suit in the "honours," and in the pip-cards the particular number of marks placed in a single horizontal line, with their value in Arabic numerals at the left-hand corner.

The ace of spades has on it "Typus Orbis Terrarum," with the address : " I. H. Seÿfrid delineavit. Wilhelm Pfaun Sculpsit."

The suits of spades and hearts are occupied with the various regions and districts of Germany, Austria, and Prussia, as formerly recognized.

On the suit of diamonds are maps of Switzerland, Belgium, Holland, Flanders, Spain, and other places; while the king of clubs shows Anglia, the dame Scotia, and the knave Hibernia.

Norway, Poland, Italy, &c. &c. are likewise in the suit.

A volume of more than 230 pages, bound in vellum, gilt edged, and illustrated with maps, accompanies this set of cards. The whole is enclosed in an old-fashioned leathern slip-case, above five inches high and more than three inches in width. This case is probably two hundred years old. The volume in question has the following title:—" Europæisch-Geographische Spiel-Charte/ Darinnen Vermittels LII Sonderbarer Blätlein alle in Europa befindliche Königreiche und Länder, samt deren Vornemsten Städten, zu des curiosen Lesers Sonderbarer Belustigung und anmuthigen Zeitkürtzung in möglichster Nettigkeit præsentiret werden; worzu noch über das V absonderliche Land-Chärtlein gefüget worden welche Solche Oerter vorstellig machen die nicht füglich unter die andern haben können gebracht werden. Samt einer Kurtze Beschreibung aller vorneemsten und notablesten Sachen so in denen berühmtesten Ländern und Städten theils zu sehen sind; theils sich vor langer und kurzer Zeit ereignet und zugetragen. Nürnberg. In Verlegung Johann Hoffmann Buch und Kùnsthandlers. Anno 1678."

In a " Kurtze Voransprache an den Hochgeneigten Leser " we are informed that the credit of the invention is due to the learned and well-known author " Herrn M. Johann Pretorio," to whom, as likewise to his associated and able representative Hn. I. H. Seyfrieden, not a small amount of thanks is due. To Franciscus Nigrinus the reader is indebted for the geographic descriptions which follow.

An engraved and coloured frontispiece precedes the title page. It represents eight persons seated at a long table covered with green cloth, playing with the geographic cards. At the top of the print is the following title on a scroll, borne by a figure of Mercury, descending with a pack of cards in his right hand:— " Europäisch Geographische Spiel-Charte." At the bottom is the couplet—

> " Durch Spielen das Land
> Wird werden bekannt."
> —HINSCHMAN.

This series of cards was known to Mr. Taylor, who writes :—" Mr. Quaritch has a German geographical pack, in which the marks of the suits are arranged in the same way as the above, in a row at the top, but of the French order and pattern —*könig, dame, knecht*, and *Asz*, and the full number of pips. The ace of spades is entitled " Typus Orbis Terrarum," and contains a map on Mercator's projection, the longitude calculated from Ferrol. It bears the designer's and engraver's name, I. H. Seÿfrid and Wilhelm Pfaun. Each card has a coloured map of one of the countries of Europe, without apparent preference, except that the ace of hearts is Europe and the king Germania. The cards are of larger size than the ordinary sort, their backs marbled, and the edges gilt. As Livonia is not included in ' Muscovia,' and St. Petersburg not mentioned, they are probably of the latter part of the seventeenth century, and anterior to Peter the Great." (Bibl. 9, p. 213.)

[$4\frac{6}{8} \times 2\frac{1}{2}$ in.]   [Backs marbled.]

G. 160.

NINETEENTH CENTURY.

SIX cards from a numeral series, the marks of the suits of which are clubs, diamonds, spades, and hearts.

The cards present are the two, four, and seven of clubs, the seven of diamonds, and the seven and ten of spades.

The whole field of each piece is occupied by representations of animals of various kinds, in a landscape. The designs, which are from engraved metal plates, are coloured, and over these the marks of the suits are stamped in the ordinary way.

The secondary intention of these cards is to afford instruction in natural history.

On the two of clubs is a stag in the foreground ; in the distance a stag hunt is represented. On the four of clubs is a mountain huntsman, accompanied by his dog. On the seven of the same suit are two rabbits, each animal showing different aspects. Two dogs of different kinds are on the seven of diamonds, as is the case also with the seven of spades. On the ten of the last suit is a dog jumping towards a monkey with whip in hand on horseback.

[$3\frac{6}{8} \times 2\frac{2}{8}$ in.]   [Backs plain.]

AMUSING.

G. 161.

(Printed Books Department, 554, b. 38.)

LAST QUARTER OF SIXTEENTH CENTURY.

NÜRNBERG.

(Cards by Jobst Amman.)

A BOUND small quarto volume of sixty-four leaves, containing a sequence of fifty-two card-pieces of a numeral series, along with dedicatory, poetic, and other printed matter.

The marks of the suits are printers' ink-balls, books, wine-cups of metal (*i. e.* formed by the skill of the goldsmith), and vases or goblets studded with large bosses.

The figure-cards or honours are kings, upper and inferior valets.

The page, or each card-piece is $7\frac{3}{8}$ in. high by $5\frac{3}{8}$ in. wide. The central portion, to the extent of 4 in. and $2\frac{3}{8}$ in., is occupied by the card design itself, above which are four lines of Latin verse, and below from four to eight lines of German verse, which are generally a free translation of the Latin superscription, explanatory of the design.

The suit marks are large in size, and occupy the upper portion of the card-space ; below are figure compositions, representing nobles, burghers, and artisans at various occupations, either of duty or amusement.

The value of the ten of each suit is indicated by the Roman numeral X on a small scroll at one of the upper corners; the mark of the suit (one in number only), is held by a female (whole-length figure) in rich costume.

All the kings are mounted. On the three and five of books, the eight and nine of cups, animals form the subjects of the compositions, and play parts likewise in some of the other pieces. The designs on the six of printers' balls, the five of books, and the ace of goblets, have incidents of a vulgar, gross, or even obscene character.

On the aces of printers' balls and of books are shields of armorial bearings below the marks of the suits. On the nine of cups are the letters I A (Iobst Amman), on an ornamental tablet in the centre of the field, between the two rows of suit marks. On the ace of printers' balls are represented the arms of " *Sigmundt Feyrabend—weit gepreist.*"

The title-page of the volume bears the inscription printed in black and red ink :—Iodoci Ammanni, Civis Noribergensis *Charta Lvsoria* Tetrastichis illustrata per *Ianum Heinricum Scroterum de Gustrou* Megalopolitanum, Equitem & P, L, Cæsarem 𝔎𝔲𝔫𝔰𝔱𝔩𝔦𝔠𝔥𝔢 𝔳𝔫̃ 𝔴𝔬𝔩𝔤𝔢𝔯𝔦𝔰𝔰𝔢𝔫𝔢 𝔉𝔦𝔤𝔲𝔯𝔢𝔫 𝔦𝔫 𝔢𝔦𝔫𝔫𝔢𝔫 𝔎𝔞𝔯𝔱𝔢𝔫 spiel durch den Kunstreichen und Weitberümteu Jost Amman, Burger in Nürnberg,—Allen vnd jeden der Kunst liebhabenden / zu besonderm nutz / liest und wolgefallen jetzund erst new an tag geben.   Und mit Kurtzen latienischen und teeutschen Verslein illustrirt.   Durch Ianum Heinricum Schröterum von Güstrow/ Kayserlichen Coronirten Poeten. Gedruckt zu Nürnberg/ durch Leonhardt Heusler.   Anno M.D.LXXXVIII."

Then follows a dedicatory address in Latin poetry—"Vere nobilibus magnificis etq. clarissimis viris ac Dominis D. Hilario Rulando—D. Gerhardo Rulando—D. Oswaldo Rulando—Fratribus Germanis, Dominis et Patronis suis perpetua observantia reverenter colendis.—Sigmund."

This is succeeded by laudatory verses to the same.

After the dedicatory and laudatory addresses, we have the following from the " Liber de Leipso :"—

> " Charta mihi titulum tribuit Lusoria ; lusus
> Et Chartæ in pretio munera vulgus habet
> Sed nec ego laudes moror aut convicia vulgi
> Sit mihi sat claris posse placere viris
> Hos rogo, ut a rerum quandam graviore vacantes
> Cura, si chartis ludere forte velint
> Colludant nostris : sine rixis vulnere morte
> Ludenti quoniam lucra benigna dabunt."

Then follow the fifty-two card-pieces. After which come two compositions : the first representing a lady and gentleman, seated on a garden seat, embracing each other ; the second, a whole-length figure of a richly dressed female playing on a guitar.   On the first piece is the following inscription : " Duas sequentes Tabellas addimus ne vacarent chartæ," with six lines of Latin verse referring to the design.   On the second piece are eight lines of Latin verse.

Finally comes " Eiusdem Scroteri Carmen in laudem jodoci Ammanni hujus Chartæ inventoris ad Candidum Lectorem."

The short colophon runs thus : " Noribergæ Excudebat Leonhardus Heuslerus."

As an example of the character of the pages of the volume we may instance the three of printers' inking-balls.   Below the marks of the suit a gentleman and his wife are represented as seated at a table, on which is a lighted candle and a pack of cards.   A large dog is by the side of the lady.   The latter holds a goblet in her right hand, and a card in the left, which she appears to be showing to her husband, who, while regarding it, seems about to play his card with the right hand, as he holds some pieces in the left.   Above the composition are the following lines :—

"Sum tua, vicisti, vitæ o mihi dulce levamen
Sit tibi cura mei, sit mihi cura tui
O suave imperium, vel nectare dulcius unum
In geminis ubi cor, mens amor et studium."

Below are these lines in German :—

"Du hast gewonnen edler Hort
Ich will nun dein sein hic et dort
Da lebet Gott wo Mann und Weib
Zwey menschen sein, ein Seel, ein Leib."

This rare and choice volume (formerly in the Praun collection) is a good example of design and wood-engraving. The artist, Jobst Amman, was born at Zürich in 1539, and died at Nürnberg in 1591. He was one of the most prolific designers of his time for engraving, both in wood and metal.

The rarest of all the works of this master is the present book of cards. Becker ("Jobst Amman Zeichner und Formschneider Kupferätzer und Stecher von C. Becker nebst Zusätzen von R. Weigel mit 17 Holzschnitten und Register," Leipzig, 1854) remarks : "Although it is probable that an average number of impressions was printed, few examples are known. Among them, however, is a very well-coloured copy. The separate woodcuts are not to be met with in other books, the opposite of which occurrence mostly happens in the case of the other works of Amman. One or two copies only are known in which the wood-blocks have been worked off on sheets to the number of six on each sheet. The technic of these highly humorous woodcuts is so peculiar and masterly that one cannot help believing the engraving itself must have been executed by the hand of Amman, a belief supported by the circumstance that the mark of a *formschneider* is not to be found on any of the blocks, while it is usually to be met with in most of the woodcut books of the master." (p. 140.)

Becker concludes by stating that "this rare work has not been described by any writer on art." Becker is wrong in this statement. The book was fully described nearly half-a-century before Becker himself did it. It is true that the work escaped Bartsch's notice, nor is it alluded to by Nagler in his "Künstler-Lexicon;" but Singer in his well-known work devotes nearly twenty pages to its consideration, and gives facsimiles of eight entire card-pieces and groups from five others. (Bibl. 8 pp. 180-197.)

From Singer's commentary on Amman's book the following is extracted.

"The beautiful pack of cards engraved by Jost Ammon, of which the succeeding pages afford specimens, is accompanied by moral distichs in Latin and German, and were published in the form of a small volume in 4to. as well as for the purpose of playing-cards. Their moral intention was apparently to inculcate the advantages of industry and learning over idleness and drunkenness. The subjects are for the most part treated humorously ; the four suits are books, printers' balls, wine-pots, and drinking-cups. We shall give a brief description of the subject on each card, and proceed to present the reader with facsimiles of some of the most interesting cards of each suit, beginning with that of books, emblematical of learning, the deuce of which suit contains the following spirited representation of the ancient bookbinder, accompanied by Latin and German verses by H. S. de Gustrou.

". . . . . De Murr in his 'Bibliothèque de Peinture, de Sculpture, et de Gravure,' Francfort, 1770, 12mo. v. 2, p. 470, mentions them among the works of Jost Ammon, thus : 'Charta Lusoria tetrastichis illustrata per Janum Heinricum Scroterum de Gustrou Noribergæ,' 1588, 4to. It seems, however, probable that they had been some time used as playing-cards before they were thus collected together in a volume and accompanied by metrical inscriptions, and Sigismund Feyrabend's name occurs in the German verses under the ace of printers' balls, so that he was most probably the publisher. It has been already mentioned that Jost Ammon was principally employed in decorating books printed by him. . . . We had omitted to notice that the set of these cards which we here describe have been formed from the little book before mentioned; the accompanying verses are pasted on the backs of the cards. Notwithstanding the numerous impressions which it is most likely were taken off, copies of this little book or complete packs of the cards are at the present day of the utmost rarity, even in Germany. We were assured by the parties from whom the present set were obtained that another complete copy would with difficulty be found, even in the most celebrated collections in that country. Single cards of various packs are to be found in the cabinets of some curious collectors, but we know not of any other complete set of these decorated cards in this country." (*Op. cit.*)

Though it is possible that these cards may have been used for the purposes of ordinary play, as suggested by Singer, yet we think it not very probable, and should accord with Chatto's opinion, that judging from the verses, " Liber de Leipso " previously quoted, they were not originally designed with that intention.

[4 × 2⅜ in.]   [Backs plain.]

G. 162.

FIRST QUARTER OF NINETEENTH CENTURY.

TÜBINGEN.

 SERIES of fifty-two numerals, the suits of which are clubs, spades, hearts, and diamonds. The figure-cards or honours are, *roi, dame, valet.* Each piece is occupied by a composition, over which are placed the marks of the suit in the usual form. The designs are of very varied character; instructive, amusing, laughable, &c.

This series is interesting, as being the first which appeared of Cotta's " Karten Almanach " at Tübingen in 1806. The latter continued to be published for several years " as a small pocket volume of a square form, and the illustrations consisted entirely of fanciful cards, the mark of the suit being always introduced into each subject either by hook or by crook. The designs for the cards in the first four volumes, from 1806 to 1809 inclusive, are said to have been made by a lady." (Chatto, p. 259.)

In the present sequence the *roi de trefles* represents Pirrhus, the *dame*, Ester, the *valet*, Arcas. In *piques* the *roi* is Assuerus, the *dame*, Andromaque, the *valet*, Burrhus. In *carreaux* the *roi* is Agamemnon, the *dame*, Agripine, the *valet*, Oreste. In *cœurs* the *roi* is Ulisse, the *dame*, Iphigénie, the *valet*, Mardochée. The words *roi, dame, valet* are engraved above the whole-length figure on each coate-card, the symbol of the suit being at one of the upper corners, and the title at the bottom of the piece.

The ace of *trefles* bears the address : " A Tubinge chez ·T. G. Cotta, Libraire."

On the six of *carreaux* is a representation of the *ponte rotto*, formerly the *pons palatinus* or *senatorius*, the first stone bridge built at Rome, and half of which was destroyed by an inundation of the Tiber in 1598. Some of the cards, *e. g.* the five and seven of *trefles* and of *piques*, the three and eight of *piques* have on them designs of a religious character. On others are domestic scenes; the ten of *carreaux* exhibits a Christmas tree with children amusing themselves. On the seven of *cœurs* is a family tea-party. Several of the pip-cards of the suit *cœurs* have purely fanciful or ideal subjects, in which Cupids play an important part. The design on the nine of *piques* is comic in character, and includes two boys playing at cards.

The members of this series have been executed in the " stipple " manner by means of the *roulette* on copper, and afterwards coloured carefully and delicately.

An explanatory little book accompanies the set, having as title, " Karten Almanach, Tübingen, in der J. G. Cotta' schen Buchhandlung, 1806."

An ingenious conversation is represented as being carried on between several male and female persons, which serves to elucidate the subjects treated on the cards of the various suits. The researches of Breitkopf are specially alluded to, and the theory maintained that playing-cards owe their origin to chess.

" The knight, however, was suppressed, and the gallant French people changed the commander, a second Tiresias, into a lady."   (Explanatory Book.)

[$3\frac{6}{8}$ × $2\frac{1}{2}$ in.]   [Backs plain.]

MISCELLANEA.

G. 163.

(*Print Room, Library, German Books, No.* 7.)

SMALL octavo volume, bound, and lettered "Schopferi ΠΑΝΟ-ΠΛΙΑ 1568."

The title-page bears the following inscription :—" ΠΑΝΟΠΛΙΑ Omnium illiberalium mechanicarum aut sedentiarum artium genera continens " ——— " accesserunt etiam venustissimæ Imagines omnes omnium artificum negociationes ad vivum Lectori representantes ante hac nec visæ, nec unquam editæ : per Hartman Schopperum Novoforens, Noricum.   Francofurti ad Mænum cum Privilegio Cæsareo MDLXVIII."

This work is generally known as " Iobst Amman's Book of Trades."   The cuts in it were designed by the artist, and the descriptions in Latin verse were by Hartman Schopper.   It issued from the press of " Sigismundus Feyrabend civis et Typographus Francfurdianius.   Calend. Januarii Anno MDLXVIII."

The volume contains cuts of a *Formschneider* and a *Briefmaler*.   The first appears to be engraving on wood, and the second to be colouring certain figures by means of a stencil.   Up to the latter end of the fifteenth century a distinction was preserved between the calling of a *kartenmaler*, and that of a *form-schneider*, though persons following either belonged to the same guild.   A few years subsequent to the *formschneider*, the *briefmaler* occurs in the civic books of various German towns, but though his designation has the same literal meaning as that of the *kartenmaler*, his business seems to have been more general, including that of the card-painter, and of the wood-engraver.

" About 1470, we find the *briefmalers* not only employed in executing figures, but also in engraving the text of block books ; and about the end of the fifteenth century, the term seems to have been generally synonymous with that of *form-schneider*.   Subsequently, the latter term prevailed as the proper designation of a wood-engraver, while that of *briefmaler* was more especially applied, like that of the original *kartenmaler*, to designate a person who coloured cards and other figures.

" Though we have positive evidence that about the year 1470, the *briefmaler* was a wood-engraver as well as a colourer of cards, and though it be highly probable that the outlines on the figures on cards were then engraved on wood, and that from this circumstance the *briefmaler* became also a wood-engraver, yet we have no proof that the earliest wood-engravers in Europe were the card-makers."   (Chatto, p. 84.)

Notwithstanding that at the time when the work now under notice was published, the business of a *briefmaler* was considered as distinct from that of a *formschneider*, there is reason to believe that the old *briefmalers* continued both to engrave and to print wood-cuts. On several large cuts, bearing the dates 1553-1554, may be read: "Gedruckt zu Nürnberg durch Hanns Glaser Brieff-maler."

The following illustrations in the ΠΑΝΟΠΛΙΑ should be referred to:—
Adumbrator—Der Reisser, folio C.
Sculptor—Der Formschneider, folio C. 2.
Illuminator imaginum—Brieffmaler, folio C. 6."

G. 164.

SECOND HALF OF EIGHTEENTH CENTURY.

 POLITICAL broad-side sheet, having on the upper half a represen-tation of a party seated at a round table playing at cards (*hombre*), in a drawing-room of the "Frau Germanin." On the lower half is a descriptive account in sixteen verses, of the sentiments supposed to be expressed by the various persons engaged at the game.

On an ornamental scroll at the bottom of the engraving is the inscription: "Abbildung des Jetzigen Politischen L'Ombre Spiels in Hause der Frau Ger-manin. 1757."

Six persons are seated, playing, viz. a Prussian officer, who holds up the ace of spades, an English nobleman, a French marquis, a son of the *Frau Germanin*, an Hungarian magnate, and a Swedish baron. Standing by, or sitting and over-looking the players, are a Danish cavalier, the *Frau Germanin* herself, a Saxon officer, and a Russian tourist. Behind, and away from the table, are a Dutch sea-captain, a Swiss proprietor, a Polish *woywod*, an Italian nobleman, and a grandee of Spain. Through an open window a Turkish night patrol looks into the room.

A number is affixed to each member of the group, which corresponds to a verse below—the supposed sentiments of the person indicated.

Heaps of money and bags are on the table. A chandelier with eight lighted candles illuminates the scene, while three other lights project from the ornamental scroll-work frame with which the engraving is bordered. Mirrors and a sword hang up against the walls of the room.

The *Frau Germanin* (No. 15), is represented as coming forward and ad-dressing the players at the table in the following words:—

> "Ich bitt die Herren doch dem Spiel ein end zu machen
> Es ist doch an der Zeit; statt schlafen muss ich wachen
> Sie seyn mir liebe Gäst; wenn sie mir lassen Ruh
> Und wenn sie einmal fort, mach ich die Thüre zu."

The Turkish patrol calls out (No. 16):

> "Ihr Herren machts sein End, und geht einmal nach Haus
> Wo nicht, so komme ich, und lösch die Lichter aus."

An engraved ornamental frame borders the letter-press.
[18 × 13 in.]　　　　　　　　　　　　　　　　　　[Back plain.]

G. 165.

Engravings by early German Masters, vol. vi.

FIRST QUARTER OF SIXTEENTH CENTURY.

THE rare engraving known as "Le grand bal," by the Master MZ, described at page 16 of General History, and in Bartsch, vol. vi. p. 377, No. 13.)

The Grand Duke and Duchess of Bavaria are represented playing at cards, and keeping their scores marked upon the table. A five of hearts is exposed. The date 1500 is on the engraving.

Singer, page 274, may be referred to.

G. 166.

LAST QUARTER OF FIFTEENTH CENTURY?

AN engraving by Israhel Van Meckenen, representing a lady and gentleman playing at cards. The three of glands is exposed on the table, and a figure-card is in the lady's hand.

This piece has been described previously—General History, p. 16.

See the frontispiece to Singer's "Researches," also Bartsch, vol. vi. p. 302, n. 114.)

ENGLISH PLAYING-CARDS.

NUMERALS.

E. 167.

(MS. Department, Sloane Collection, 1044, fol. 93 verso, art. 421.)

LAST QUARTER OF SEVENTEENTH CENTURY.

LONDON.

SHEET of ten unseparated card-pieces, in two rows of five pieces each row.

The cards present are king, queen, knave, king, and queen in the first row; and king, queen, knave, king, and queen in the second row.

Not any marks of suits are present, but the examples may be assumed to belong to a numeral series of fifty-two, of the suits spades, clubs, hearts, and diamonds.

On a tablet between the feet of the knave in the upper series is the address: "C. Hewson."

The designs are of the conventional character; the queens bear flowers in their hands.

The impressions are from wood-blocks, and are entirely uncoloured.

[$3\frac{2}{8} \times 2\frac{1}{8}$ in.]   [Backs plain.]

E. 168.

(MS. Department, Harleian Collection, 5947, fol. 2 verso, fol. 3.)

LAST QUARTER OF SEVENTEENTH CENTURY.

LONDON.

TWO sheets of card-pieces, each sheet containing nine cards arranged in three rows.

The pieces present are all figure-cards, a king, queen, and knave being in each row. Not any suit marks are present.

The designs are of the conventional character, and the impressions remain entirely uncoloured.

These examples closely approach the series before mentioned, E. 167; the address of C. Hewson is not present, however, and the engraving of the wood-blocks has been somewhat coarser and the printing less careful than in E. 167.

[$3\frac{2}{8} \times 2\frac{1}{8}$ in.]   [Backs plain.]

E. 169.

LAST QUARTER OF EIGHTEENTH CENTURY.

LONDON.

PACK of fifty-two numerals, the suit-marks of which are in reality spear-heads, diamonds, trefoils, and cups, though intended to imply spades, diamonds, clubs, and hearts.

The series is interesting from the attempt shown in it to make the card-emblems and the names *piques*, *trefles*, *cœurs*, and *carreaux* more consistent with each other than is usually the case.

On the ace of spades or spear-heads is the duty stamp of the reign of " G. III. Rex." The piece is marked No. 10, and bears the address of " Rowley and Co."

On the ace of diamonds is the design of a precious stone cut in facets. It is enclosed within an ornamental oval frame-work of oak-leaves, surmounted by the winged cap of Mercury, supported by a trident and caduceus.

In the centre of the ace of trefoils is the ternate leaf of a *trifolium*, surrounded by an ornamental frame, above which appear the heads of a scythe, rake, pitchfork, and reaping-hook. The marks of this suit are printed of a green colour.

The ace of cups or hearts has a sacramental-like chalice in the middle of the card, having within it a heart. An ornamental frame-work, into which olive-leaves and fruit enter, surround the emblem; above which is a bishop's mitre, a pastoral staff, and a cross. The figure-cards—king, queen, and knave—are three-quarter figures contained in ovals, and having flat ruled backgrounds.

The king of spades wears a crown, carries a sceptre in his right hand, and his mantle is marked with *fleurs-de-lys*. The queen of this suit wears a crown, and *fleurs-de-lys* are on her dress. The knave is a soldier, with wig and pig-tail, and carrying a lance. He looks towards the right.

The king of diamonds is dressed like one of the German monarchs, wears a crown, carries a sceptre erect, and looks towards the left. The queen is crowned, and her dress adorned with ermine; the knave is a soldier in cloak and circular-frilled collar, conical hat and feather, and carrying a partizan in his right hand.

The king of trefoils is dressed in a mantle adorned with crowns; the queen has a veil, descending from the back of the head over her right shoulder; while the knave is a soldier, having a double-headed black eagle on the front of his tall cap, and carrying a spear in his right hand.

The king of the suit of chalices or hearts evidently implies England, from the mantle and order which he wears. The queen intends the same, and the knave is meant for one of the well-known Tower " Beef-eaters." On his chest below a crown is the letter G.

All the figure-cards are printed in bluish-black ink. Throughout the series the ace of spades alone is in pure black.

The impressions are from engravings on copper, done in a neat but formal style.

This series was known to Taylor, who observes :—" We have already noticed an attempt (p. 183) to make our card emblems and their names more consistent with each other, but an earlier and more complete essay in the same direction occurs in a pack, date 1790, by Rowley and Co. Here again the spade is a kind of dagger, of a clumsy and inconvenient form, the ace of the suit being, however, a regular duty-card. The ace of clubs is a clover leaf in an oval, surmounted by agricultural implements. 'Diamonds' clearly points to the original conventional form of representing this gem, being a veritable diamond, lozenge-shaped, with the facets of the cutting shown in relief. This idea of a quadrangular shape is involved in all the names of the diamond suit, whether it be panes of glass (*rauten, ruyten,* &c.), or paving-tiles (Spanish, *ladrillos*), a sense also given to *carreaux* by Menestrier. The ace of hearts in the same pack is represented by a chalice, with a heart engraved on the front, an irreverent introduction characteristic of that epoch, for we are left in no doubt as to what is meant, for the oval in which it is contained is surmounted by a mitre, cross, and crozier. The court-cards appear to be portraits, and the costumes are of the period." (Taylor, p. 232.)

The intention of the cup or chalice in this suit was, we assume, to link the suit with the *coppe* or cups of the early Italian numerals, which were believed to have originally symbolized the clergy, the *coppe* themselves descending from an emblem symbolizing the ancient Egyptian hierarchy. In the same way swords, *piques*, spades, symbolized the military class; money, *deniers, carreaux*, diamonds, the mercantile; and *bastoni, trefles*, clubs, the agricultural communities.

[3½ × 2½ in.]   [Backs plain.]

E. 170.

LAST QUARTER OF EIGHTEENTH CENTURY.

LONDON.

PACK of fifty-two numerals of the suits spear-heads (spades), diamonds, trefoils (clubs), and cups (hearts).

This series is a duplicate of the one last described, G. 169.

The duty-card—the ace of spades—bears the number 16, with the address of Rowley and Co.

[3⅛ × 2⅛ in.]   [Backs plain.]

E. 171.

LAST QUARTER OF EIGHTEENTH CENTURY.

LONDON.

PACK of fifty-two numerals of the usual suits, spades, diamonds, hearts, and clubs.

The designs on the figure cards are of the old conventional character, but there are certain variations in those of each suit.

The king of spades has a three-quarter face turned towards the right; the kings of clubs and of hearts have three-quarter faces turned towards the left. The kings of spades and of clubs hold swords erect in their left hands, the king of hearts holds a sword in guard across the head, while the king of diamonds carries a partizan.

All the queens have three-quarter faces; those of spades and hearts are turned towards the left, those of diamonds and clubs to the right hand. Each queen holds a rose (?) in her left hand.

The knaves of spades and of hearts have profile faces to the right, those of diamonds and clubs have three-quarter faces, one to the right, the other to the left hand. The knave of spades holds a spear in his left hand, the other knaves have spears in their right hands. The knave of spades has a curved sword, the knaves of diamonds and of hearts straight weapons. The knave of clubs is without a sword.

The decorations of the dresses differ somewhat in each figure.

The ace of spades is the " duty-card."

The mark of the suit on the latter is on a large oval shield, surmounted by a crown, having below the motto, " Dieu et mon Droit." Around the shield is the motto of the Order of the Garter, " Honi soit qui mal y pense." The card bears the inscription : " G. III *Rex.*   No. 6.   Exportation 1. Hardy."

$[3\frac{5}{8} \times 2\frac{1}{2}$ in.]   [Backs plain.]

E. 172.

TIME OF GEORGE III.

LONDON.

PACK of fifty-two numerals of the usual suits.

The coate-cards have figures on them, nearly similar to those on the cards last described (E. 171), but they are not from the same blocks, and may be perhaps of a somewhat earlier date than E. 171.

The ace of spades is the " duty-card," of the same character as that of E. 171.   The inscriptions are " Sixpence additional Duty " above the crown and at the sides of the shield.   Below is the address, " Gibson."   The number of the pack is 150.

$[3\frac{5}{8} \times 2\frac{1}{2}$ in.]   [Backs plain.]

E. 173.

THIRD QUARTER OF NINETEENTH CENTURY.

LONDON.

PACK of fifty-two numerals of the ordinary suits.

The figure-cards are king, queen, and knave, represented in busts printed double and in reverse.

Accompanying the pack are two wrappers, an outer and inner one.   The last is of bright green glazed paper, having on it a bust of the " Great Mogul," printed in gold ; below which is the inscription, " International Playing-Cards.   Ent. Sta. Hall."   At the right-hand margin is " Designed by Reuben Townroe for Felix Summerly's Art Manufactures."   On the left margin is the address, " De La Rue and Cº 110 Bunhill Row London."   The outer envelope is the stamp or duty cover, ornamentally engraved, and printed in light blue.   On the central fold may be read, " De La Rue & Cº. 110 Bunhill Row London.   The seller is to cancel the Stamp by writing in Ink or printing his name upon it.   Penalty for omission £5."   Below this is elaborately engraved, by machine, the stamp of four circles, having at the top " Card-Stamp," at the bottom " Three pence," and the letters " V R " in large open capitals at the sides.

On the left lateral fold is engraved, in open letters, the following caution : " On opening a pack of cards, the wrapper is to be destroyed.   Penalty £20, if retained for use again."

A notice of these cards reprinted from the "Times" of December 3rd, 1874, accompanies the pack, from it the following extracts are taken :

"The well-worn adage as to the non-existence of novelty under the sun does not altogether apply to the international cards, since we find that although national, political, and educational cards have been produced, the notion is original of making international cards. In giving effect to this idea it is satisfactory that the general appearance of the cards is not sacrificed to the temptation of rendering them confusingly picturesque. The leading conventional features of ordinary playing-cards are retained, while an interesting *cachet* of the period of production is given to the international cards which will not, as might be apprehended, distract the most solemn of whist players. . . . The idea of international playing-cards, as now carried out in this production, was recently originated by Mr. Felix Summerly, with the aid of Mr. Reuben Townroe, an artist whose originality in design and its varied forms of treatment is testified to by the ornamental terra-cotta work on the centre of the Royal Albert Hall, and many decorative works at the South Kensington Museum.

"At first glance, if we overlook the aces the cards have the appearance of the modern stereotyped form of cards, a style which we adopted from the French cards made at Chartres in 1702 ; but on closer inspection we find his Royal Highness the Prince of Wales doing duty as the king of diamonds, the King of the Belgians as the king of hearts, the Crown Prince of Prussia as the king of spades, and the King of Italy as the king of clubs. The likenesses are fairly good, especially that of the King of Italy.

"The aces are allotted to the greatest potentates—thus, Her Majesty, as Empress of India and Queen of the United Kingdom, appears as the ace of hearts ; the President of the United States is the ace of spades, the Emperor of Russia is the ace of diamonds, and the German Emperor is the ace of clubs. But Mr. Felix Summerly, with perhaps a pardonable *penchant* to pay an irreproachable compliment, has allotted to her Royal Highness the Princess of Wales the high office of queen of hearts, while to the Crown Princess of Germany he assigns the dignity of the queen of clubs. The Queen of Greece appears as queen of diamonds, and the Empress of Austria as queen of spades. The four knaves have a more original character about them than the other court-cards. The square and blocky conventionality is maintained, although the actual details are totally different from what are used in ordinary playing-cards. A Scotch piper with distended cheeks vigorously blowing his pipe, the utmost determination of purpose shown in his features, appears as knave of hearts. An officious and splendid functionary, obviously a *gendarme*, is the knave of spades. A yellow-bearded Swiss guide with his rope on his shoulder, and clenching a spiked staff, is the knave of clubs ; while Spain is represented by a keen-eyed and carefully coifed matador as knave of diamonds. As a number of portraits some of the cards are less successful than others. Looking, however, to the restrictions as respects attitude and form which were imposed on the designer, Mr. Reuben Townroe, we must congratulate him upon the success he has obtained in his portraits of Her Majesty the Queen, the Emperors of Austria and Russia, the Princess of Wales, King Victor Emmanuel, the King of the Belgians, and the Crown Prince of Germany."

The backs of these cards are of a deep blue colour of extreme *lissage*, having on them printed in gold the royal arms of England, with those of Saxe-Coburg-Gotha on a shield of pretence. Below is the double-headed eagle of Prussia, with the George and Dragon on a shield of pretence. The whole is surrounded with an ornamental design composed of oak-leaves, acorns, thistles, shamrocks, and roses.

It is right to observe that as far as the *idea* simply of international playing-cards is concerned, it had been previously illustrated by the French. See F. 58.

[$3\frac{5}{8} \times 2\frac{1}{2}$ in.]   [Backs decorated.]

CARDS WITH A SECONDARY PURPOSE.

EDUCATIONAL—INSTRUCTIVE.

E. 174.

LAST QUARTER OF SEVENTEENTH CENTURY.

LONDON.

(Grammatical.)

SET of fifty-two numerals of the ordinary suits and honours. The marks of the suits are relatively large, and placed at the upper left-hand corner of each piece. The values of the pip-cards are indicated by large Roman numbers at the upper right-hand corners. On the honours are busts of king, queen, and valet, mostly of different designs in each suit, they are from engraved wood-blocks, are of inferior character in all respects, and remain uncoloured.

This series is intended to serve the purpose of teaching the rules of grammar, as comprised in the four principal parts of "Lillie's Grammar." All the rules and instructions are in the Latin language, and occupy in print of different sizes the greater portion of each card.

Ten pages of descriptive matter and address in English precede the cards. On the title-page is the inscription: "Grammatical Cards. Imprimatur. June 1, 1676. J. Jane. London. Printed for S. Mearn and A. Clark, and are to be sold by J. Seller, at the Hermitage Stairs in Wapping, and J. Hill, in Exchange Alley, 1677."

Then follows the dedication and address: "To all ingenious gentlemen, the perusers of these Sciential cards." The gentlemen have advice addressed them, based on the following quotation from Plutarch: "Proinde recte monebat PLATO ut neque corpus exerceremus sine animo neque animum sine corpore, sed veluti conjugii cujusdam æquilibrium teneremus corpori." This address is signed "yours, T. B." Next comes "A short tract tauching (*sic*) the use of these Grammatical cards," in which the reader is assured that "All games may be played thereon with witty jests, sweet flowing Latine and great understanding." "In fine and to conclude all briefly, the use and practise of them shall perform more than I will or can speak in praise of them."

The suit of spades teaches "Orthographia," that of clubs "Etymologia," hearts "Syntaxis," and diamonds "Prosodia." Below the bust of the smiling knave of spades is inscribed, "Mel in ore, Orthographia. Cavendum est ab iis vitiis quæ vulgo propria videntur, viz:

Iocatisimus.   Lit. 1. nimia extensio.
Lambdacismus.   Lit l. nimis operosonus.
Ischnotes.   Loquendi exilitas.
Traulismus.   Oris hesitantia.
Plateasimus.   Vocis crassa et rustica expressio.

Below the knave of clubs is "Omnium horarum homo, Etymologia," &c. &c. On the knave of hearts is "Syntaxis," "Grata Novitas," and the names of the "Dictionis sex" and "Constructionis 8," the "figura novata arte aliqua dicendi forma." The knave of diamonds bears "Prosodia. Palinodiam Canit," &c.

[$3\frac{5}{8} \times 2\frac{3}{8}$ in.]   [Backs plain.]

E. 175.

LAST QUARTER OF SEVENTEENTH CENTURY.

LONDON.

(GRAMMATICAL.)

FORTY cards from a numeral series of fifty-two pieces of the usual suits and honours.

The cards wanting are the four of spades, king and five of hearts, the king, three, four, six, seven, eight of clubs, and the king, ace, and ten of diamonds.

This imperfect sequence is a duplicate of the set last described, E. 174, wanting the introductory descriptive pages. In place of the latter is a supplementary card, having on it the following inscription :—

" These cards are ingeniously contrived for the comprising the general rules of Lillie's Grammar, in the four principal parts thereof, viz. *Orthographia, Prosodia, Etymologia,* and *Syntaxis,* thereby rendering it very useful to all Persons that have already the Latine Tongue, for the recollecting their memories, and also for the better Improvement of such as have made some beginnings in the study thereof, besides the Divertisements they afford in all our English games as other common cards.

" *Advertisement.*

" These *grammatical,* as also the *geographical* cards so ingeniously contrived for improvement of Geography, with any sorts of maps both great and small, and Atlas's both for sea and land, and all the Maps, Charts, Books, and Atlas's made by *John Seller,* the king's *Hydrographer,* are sold by John Hills, Stationer, in Exchange Alley, near the Royal Exchange in London."

[$3\frac{5}{8} \times 2\frac{3}{8}$ in.]   [Backs plain.]

E. 176.

EIGHTEENTH CENTURY.

LONDON.

(ARITHMETICAL.)

A PACK of fifty-two numeral card-pieces of the ordinary suits.

This series is made subservient to arithmetical instruction.

In the upper right-hand corner of each piece is a reduced representation of a particular card of the usual design. On the remaining portion of the piece an arithmetical question is proposed and the sum worked out in detail. The whole is enclosed in a frame-like border.

The ace of diamonds, which commences the series, has on it the " numeration table," and a " duty stamp (?) " in red. Below is the inscription, " This table shows how to express properly the true value of any number whatsoever whether it be written or named."

The ace of hearts illustrates the " Substraction of Cloth Measure," the ace of spades the " Reduction of Money," and the ace of clubs the " Reduction of Cloth Measure." The knave of clubs, the last card of the series, works out " Question 5 " in " Practice." The whole sequence is thus made to include the arithmetic of addition, subtraction, multiplication, division, reduction, the rule of three, and practice.

These cards are, as respects both designs and text, impressions from neatly engraved copper-plates.

[$3\frac{2}{8} \times 2\frac{3}{8}$ in.]   [Backs plain.]

E. 177.

LAST QUARTER OF SEVENTEENTH CENTURY.

LONDON.

SERIES of thirty-one card-pieces from a numeral set of fifty-two of the ordinary suits.

This sequence is more like a shopkeeper's illustrated catalogue of mathematical instruments than anything else. More than $2\frac{1}{2}$ inches of each piece is occupied by a neat engraving from copper of persons engaged in the use of various astronomic, mathematic, and other scientific appliances. At the upper right-hand corner of each piece is the diminutive representation of an ordinary playing-card, similar to E. 176. On a shield to the left of the small card is the name of the instrument represented in use below. At the lower portion is a description of the design above. Thus on the six of clubs is "baro-meter," on a shield above four standard barometers, backed by numerous enquiring personages. Below is inscribed: " An instrument shewing the gravita-tion of ye Air (invented by Torricellus) being altered by the different compres-sions of ye Atmosphere it foretells (☿ riseing) Fair or Frost (☿ falling) Rain, Snow, Wind, or Storms."

The first card of the series is the king of clubs, which bears the following :—

" These cards, globes, spheres, mathematical Books, and instruments for Sea and Land, with many other curiositys in Gold, Silver, Steell, Brass, Ivory, and Wood, and the best Charts, Maps, and Prints at ye King's Armes and Globes at Charing Cross, and against the Royal Exchange in Cornhill, by Tho. Tuttell, Mathematical Instrument maker to the King's most excellent Majesty, where are taught all parts of the Mathematics."

Above this account are the arms of England with the motto, " Je maintien-dray ;" from which it may be concluded that the series was published during the reign of William III.

On the ace of spades is a list of "Books and Instruments for Navigation."

Chatto has the following remarks :—" In the reign of Charles II. or James II. was published a pack of mathematical cards by Thomas Tuttell, ' Mathematical instrument maker to the king's most excellent Majesty.' These cards were designed by Boitard, and engraved by J. Savage, they represent various kinds of mathematical instruments, together with the trades and professions in which they are used. They were evidently ' got up ' as an advertisement. A few years afterwards Moxon, also a mathematical instrument maker, followed suit." (Bibl. 4, p. 155.)

These cards are neatly designed and executed. See *postea*, E. 222. MS. Depart. Harleian MSS. No. 5947, fol. 6.

[$3\frac{1}{2} \times 2\frac{2}{8}$ in.]   [Backs plain.]

E. 178.

LAST QUARTER OF SEVENTEENTH CENTURY.

LONDON.

(Geographic.)

SERIES of fifty-two numerals of the ordinary suits. These cards are intended to convey geographical information. The greater portion of each piece is occupied by a geographical account of various countries, a systematic classification of which is given in a tabular form on the ace of each suit. At the left-hand upper corner of each card is the mark of the suit, and at the right-hand upper corner is the value of the card in Roman numerals, while a small Arabic number is below the mark itself. Each coate-card has a bust within a circle at its upper portion. In the case of the kings there is a crown on the right of the circle, the mark of the suit being on the left. The king of clubs represents John IV. of Portugal for Brazil, the queen Elizabeth for English Plantations, the knave a cannibal for Caribee Islands. The king of diamonds is Vanlie for China ; the queen Statira for Persia, the knave a janissary for Turkey in Asia. The king of hearts is Charles II. for the British Isles, the queen Rhea Silvia for Spain and Portugal, the knave a Greek for Turkey in Europe. The king of spades is Zaga Chris for Ethiopia, the queen Candace for Nubia, the knave is a Negro for " the country of the Negros or Blacks."

The ace of clubs is the first piece of the series, and has on it a table of the divisions and subdivisions of Septentrional and Meridional America. Above the table is marked *Lat. N.* 80, below *Lat. S.* 54, *Long. W.* 235, *Long. E.* 350.

This sequence was known to Taylor, who notices it at page 195 (Bibl. 9.) He gives the following note in reference to the king of spades, Zaga Chris. " See ' Une Relation Véritable de Zaga-Christ, Prince d'Ethiope,' in a curiously illustrated work called ' La Terre Sainte, 4to., Paris, 1664.' "

The medallion busts on the figure-cards are coloured.

[3⅝ × 2¾ in.] [Backs plain.]

E. 179.

THIRD QUARTER OF SEVENTEENTH CENTURY.

LITTLEBURY, ESSEX.

(Geographic, &c.)

FORTY-ONE card-pieces from a series of fifty-two numerals of the usual suits. The ace, two, and ten of spades, the two, three, seven, and king of diamonds, the six, seven, and queen of clubs, and the ten of hearts are wanting.

This set is intended to afford instruction in geography and ethnology. Each card-piece has a descriptive account of one of the states of the four quarters of the globe. On the upper part of the card is the symbol and value of it, or the name of the honour, supported by two figures representing the inhabitants of a particular portion of the world. Between these figures and as a background is a landscape or view of some town. The lower half of each piece is occupied with a general account of the place and persons represented above.

The ace of hearts appears to have been intended as the first piece of the set, since it has the address of " H. Winstanley, at Littlebury, Fecit " on it, below the descriptive account of Europe, which is as follows:

" Europe is the least of the four parts of the world, and yet it is not much inferior to any at this present, for containing many nations, most polished and ingenious where arts and sciences flourish and are cherished, trading abounding and conversation without danger. Shee may boast her riches, fruitfulness, and stately towns and palaces, but above all in that the Christian religion is wholly professed in her bounds, whereas the rest of the world is for the most part ignorant of a true Deity, but what they learn of Christian colonies that have seated themselves amongst them, to force as it were a tribute of the best of all that Europe can be sayd to want; of which nations the situation, the chief citys and habits, and religions, and fruitfulness, &c. see the following cards for all the world. Europe is distinguished with roses, Asia with suns, Africa with moons, and America with stars."

The king of hearts represents London and the English, and bears the duty stamp in red. On the king of spades are " Tangier and the Tingitanians," on the king of clubs " James Town and the Verginians," while on the knave of hearts are " Rome and the Italians," and on the knave of diamonds " Babylon and the Babylonians." These card-pieces are from neatly engraved copper-plates, and are uncoloured.

[3⅝ × 2½ in.]   [Backs plain.]

E. 180.

THIRD QUARTER OF NINETEENTH CENTURY.

SERIES of fifty-two card-pieces of the usual suits. A preliminary card of information accompanies the set, which is composed, we are informed, of " Instructive Playing-cards. The object of these cards is to convey instruction while seeking amusement. To play the game of stops, &c. The cards may also be used for any other game known."

In the game of stops a pool with counters is necessary, and " whoever holds the ace of diamonds and plays it, wins the pool."

Each card has its mark and value printed double and in reverse, as also an account of the object under description. Thus "Ace of diamonds" is printed in red at the upper part of the card, below which may be read : " Diamonds were formerly called adamant." On the same card in reverse are the words, " Ace of diamonds ; " diamonds are the most costly of gems." Below the nine of diamonds are the words " The nine of diamonds is called the ' Curse of Scotland ; ' "[1] in reverse, " There are thirty-three counties in Scotland." On the seven of spades is printed " Side-saddles were first used in England in 1380," and in reverse, " Saltpetre was first made in England in 1625." On the three of hearts may be read " Hans Holbein, historical and portrait painter, died in 1554," in reverse, " Hogarth, the painter and engraver, died in 1764."

It may be observed that the information intended to be conveyed is of the most opposite and varied kind. The coate-cards are without designs, the titles king, queen, and Jack being used instead.

The title of the wrapper accompanies the set, the following inscription being printed in black and red on a rose-coloured ground : " Moral and Instructive Playing-cards. Amusement and information combined. London : Dean and Son, Ludgate Hill." At each corner of the title is a mark of one of the four suits.

[2⅞ × 2⅜ in.]   [Backs plain.]

E. 181.

SECOND HALF OF EIGHTEENTH CENTURY.

LONDON.

FORTY-NINE card-pieces from a series of fifty-two numerals of the ordinary suits. The cards absent are the seven of diamonds, the king of spades, and the nine of clubs. At the upper part of each card is the mark of the suit, and the value in Roman numbers of the particular piece. Below, and occupying generally more than half of the card, is a whole-length allegorical figure, with emblems in a circle, followed by a description of the symbolical de-

---

[1] See Chatto, p. 266.

sign. The honours are not otherwise distinguished than by having the words king, queen, knave at the upper left-hand corner of the card.

The ace of hearts has on it, within the circle, an emblematic figure of Religion; below which is the following account :—

" Religion.

" A woman veiled, a Book in her right, and a flaming fire in her left hand. The Veil informs us that Religion has its mysteries. The Book expresses the Divine Law, and the flaming Fire the utmost ardency of Devotion."

On the knave of clubs is an emblem of Deceit, described as " a monstrous old man, with tails of serpents twining instead of legs; three hooks in one hand, a bag of flowers with a snake issuing from it; and behind him, a panther hiding his head, and shewing his beautiful back.

"His Humane shape and Flowers denote his specious pretences; the Serpents' tails, the Hooks, and the Snake, his villanous intentions; the Panther hiding his ugly head, his Subtelty."

The figure designs are from engravings on wood; some of those in the suits of hearts and diamonds being of a superior character. Both text and designs in these suits are printed in red.

[$3\frac{6}{8} \times 2\frac{1}{2}$ in.]   [Backs plain.]

E. 182.

EIGHTEENTH CENTURY.

LONDON.

TWO large sheets of card-pieces, each sheet containing twenty-six pieces. Of the latter there are four rows, of six in each row, and two in a middle row. The lower row in each sheet is appropriated to the honours, the other rows to the point numerals.

There are not any marks of suits present. The impressions are from neatly engraved wood-blocks, scarcely more than in outline, and are uncoloured.

The series is intended to serve the purposes of instruction, but the designer does not seem to have been overburdened himself with that which he desired to bestow on others : for example, on a three pip-card in the central row of sheet 1, is inscribed within an oval in the centre :

> " These cards was truely well designed
> To ground all Letters in youths minde."

On the adjacent four pip-card may be read:

> " Both youth and age may learne hereby
> All sorts of Letters speedily."

On an ace in the central row of sheet 2 is :

> " These cards are good, well understood;"

while on the adjacent two we are told :

> " Her's Criscross Row for thee to know
> Thy Letters all both greate and small."

Below on a ten is :

> " These cards may be a Scoole to thee
> If you deserne what you may Lerne."

The subjects intended to be taught are the letters of the alphabet, in their black-letter, Roman, and italic forms, a few words of one syllable, and some moral axioms worthy of remembrance by the card-player.

Each point numeral has a large central oval, surrounded by ornamental work, generally of a floral character, but occasionally birds and butterflies are introduced. On the third row of the second sheet human figures, of a fanciful or poetic kind, may be seen.

In the central ovoid spaces are upper and lower-case examples of the letters of the alphabet in three forms, viz. 𝕬a, Aa, *Aa*.

Above the oval is a square space, at the left-hand corner of which the value of the piece is indicated in Roman figures, room being reserved towards the right for the mark of the suit, here absent.

On four pieces of the fourth row of sheet 1 are the words: Ab, eb, ib, ob, ub, and so on, there being five words of one syllable in each oval.

The ovals on the honours contain moral axioms, like the following on sheet 2 :—

> *Knave.*—" A gamester that doth play for gaine,
>   Is but a knave and that is plaine."
> *King.*— " Play faire Do not sweare,
>   From Oaths forbeare."
> *Queen.*—" Cards may be used but not abused
>   And they used well all games exell."
> *Knave.*—" Play not for Coine in these regards,
>   Men loose and then they curs the Cards."

On a king on sheet 1 may be read:

> " When these cards are understood,
>   You'l say that my design is good."

In the lower rows, or coate-cards, the Roman numbers in the square spaces above the ovals are displaced by half-length figures of king, queen, and knave, the titles of which are given below.

[$3\frac{2}{8} \times 2\frac{1}{8}$ in.]   [Backs plain.]

BIOGRAPHIC—HISTORIC.

E. 183.

FIRST QUARTER OF NINETEENTH CENTURY.

LONDON.

(Baker's Eclectic Cards.)

PACK of fifty-two numerals, having as marks of suits swords (*spata*), hearts, glands (acorns), and diamonds.

The figure cards are king, queen, and knight, and represent historic personages in assumed costumes of their times, the marks of their suits being distinctly indicated at one of the upper corners of the cards. The marks of the suits are large and plain in all the pip-pieces, but particularly so in the aces and lower cards.

The sword or *spata* is a broad, double-edged one. The heart is larger on its left than on its right side, which is under-cut towards the apex, and is pierced longitudinally by an arrow in the ace. The diamond is a lozenge divided into four smaller lozenges, while the gland is an acorn) in the ace pedicled, and having diminutive acorns and oak-leaves bi-laterally. All the pip-cards have the margins ornamented with floral designs, those on the right-hand side of the piece being emblematic of the country which the suit is intended to represent. On the suit of swords, which represents Wales, there is a leek on the right and mistletoe on the lower edge of the card. On diamonds, typifying Scotland, is a thistle. On hearts, implying Ireland, a shamrock ; and on glands (acorns), by which England is represented, there are oak-leaves and roses. On each ace are the letters " B. & C°."

A supplementary card introduces the series. On it is inscribed—" Baker & Co". Eclectic Cards. In England, Ireland, Scotland, and Wales. Sold Wholesale and Retail at their Manufactory, No. 2. King Arthur or New Card Court, York Street, Black Friar's Road, London. N.B. To be had of all Respectable Stationers in the United Kingdom."

Above this inscription is a whole-length figure of Sir John Falstaff, contained in an octangular frame, within the angles of which, at the upper and lower portions, are the marks of the four suits.

Accompanying this series is a pamphlet of twelve pages, the title page of which bears the following :—" A short account of Baker and Co.'s Complete, Grand, Historical, Eclectic Cards, for England, Ireland, Scotland, and Wales, being a selection or an Eclectic Company of Twelve of the most eminent personages that ever distinguished themselves in those respective Countries for Heroic Deeds, Wisdom, &c." ; and the other forty cards descriptive of the local and national emblems of the four nations.

> " Historian, Poet, Painter, all combine
> To charm the eye, the taste and mind refine ;
> Fancy and sentiment their aid impart
> To raise the genius and to mend the heart."

" Price, third class, 15s.; second class, 17s. 6d.; first class, 20s. London. Printed by Theodore Page, Blackfriars Road. 1813."

Then follows the dedication :—" With most humble submission to every respectable person in the British Empire." After which is the description of " Baker's and Co.'s complete, grand, Imperial, historical, eclectic cards for England, Ireland, Scotland, and Wales, which are designed, drawn, engraved, and now finished at a very great expense by some of the most eminent artists in England, being copper-plate engravings, beautifully executed, and pencil-coloured, upon an entire new and elegant plan, especially intended for the circles of taste and fashion, and peculiarly calculated for the encouragement of youth to study the interesting history of their native country.

" In the selection which we have made to form our set of court-cards, we have, as we before observed, chosen them from among those characters who have rendered themselves most conspicuous in the history of the United Kingdom. In this particular we have had recourse not only to historical truth, which we have rigidly observed, but we have taken care to fix upon personages who lived at different periods, and which are calculated in colour, variety of dress, and characteristic features, to form an agreeable and elegant contrast, and to avoid that unpleasant monotony which must have taken place if they had all been selected from the same period of time, and it will be a peculiar gratification to us in our attempts to form a set of cards should we contribute in the smallest degree to augment the elegant and rational amusement of taste and fashion.

" Nor have we been inattentive to minor objects in our anxiety to complete the plan. We believe it has never been attempted to be explained why the coarse and vulgar appellation of knave was originally given to the card next in degree to the queen. Perhaps the following demonstration is the most plausible way in

R

which it can be accounted for. It was usual with kings in ancient times to choose some ludicrous person, with whose ridiculous and comical tricks they might be diverted in their hours of relaxation from the cares and formalities of royalty. This person was generally chosen from among men of low condition, but not wholly destitute of talent, particularly in that species of low cunning and humour calculated to excite mirth and laughter, and the tricks of knavery (in which he was allowed free indulgence in the presence of the king) gave him the appellation of the king's fool or knave.

" Whether this explanation be really the origin from whence the knave in the old cards is derived may still remain undetermined, but it appears to us the most rational way of accounting for it. Nor is it, indeed, essential to our present purpose. The name of knave, in our opinion, is vulgar, unmeaning, and inconsistent, and being, moreover, absolutely incompatible with the dignity of our characters and the uniformity of our plan, we have entirely rejected it and substituted a knight in its stead, this being a title of honour not only in immediate succession to that of king and queen, but is ever considered as an honourable appendage to royalty itself.

" And as we have now restored that most ancient and most honourable order of the Knights of the Round Table, under its great patron and founder Prince Arthur of immortal memory, the great champion for chivalry, religion, and liberty, the Briton's king and emperor, we here insert a list of this our first installation, with a brief account of their history, and cause of selection.

" Personæ, or the Eclectic Company of Knights.

" For England.

" King of clubs (glands)—Arthur, the great and victorious hero, king of Britain.

" Queen of clubs—Elizabeth, the wise and virtuous queen of England.

" Knight of clubs—Sir John Falstaff, the facetious knight, and companion of Henry V., knight of England.

" For Ireland.

" King of hearts—Gathelus, the Grecian prince, king of Ireland.

" Queen of hearts—Scotia, his wife, the Egyptian princess, queen of Ireland.

" Knight of hearts—Ossian, the warrior and poet, son of Fingal, knight of Ireland.

" For Scotland.

" King of diamonds—Achajus, the fortunate contemporary and in alliance with Charlemagne, king of Scots.

" Queen of diamonds—Mary Stuart, the unfortunate dowager-queen of France, and queen of Scots.

" Knight of diamonds—Merlin, the magic prophet, cabinet counsellor to Vortigern, Aurelius Ambrosius, Uter Pendragon, the father of King Arthur, and to King Arthur who was his pupil, knight of Scotland.

" For Wales.

" King of *spata*—Camber, the third son of Brute, king of Cambria.

" Queen of *spata*—Elfrida, the beautiful queen of Mona and of the mountains.

" Knight of *spata*—Thaliesson, the Welsh bard and poet, dressed like a herald or king-at-arms of the divine and ancient Druids, as he sung to King Henry II. of the great deeds of Arthur, the justly-termed hero of the British Isle, knight of Cambria.

" A description of these twelve plates and the history of them; also an account of the emblems and wreaths of the numerical cards, with our reasons for appropriating the different suits to the different nations, and for altering the pip or numerical cards by substituting the acorn, which is the offspring and seed of our invulnerable oak, for the black mark denominated club in the old cards. Also for producing the true representation of the real *spata*, which is not a coal-heaver's spade, but a two-edged heavy sword without a point, as used by the ancient Britons to fight with, cut, hew, and slash down either enemy or tree. So says our ancient history.

"The alterations in the hearts and diamonds are equally beautiful, both in form and colour. To the history is added a new and most interesting game, called 'Courtship and Wedding,' in which is shown the absurdity of many of the words and terms now used at cards which ought not to be heard in genteel company."

Chatto had cognizance of this series, of which he observes (p. 261) :—

"These cards, which are considerably larger than those in common use, display considerable skill and fancy in the designs, and are beautifully coloured."

These card-pieces are of a very stiff and stout character.

[$4\frac{1}{2} \times 2\frac{5}{8}$ in.]   [Backs plain.]

POLITICO-HISTORICAL.

E. 184.

Manuscript Department, Harleian MSS. No. 5947 (51. F.)

Bagford Collection.

THIS volume of the Harleian MSS., forming part of the "Bagford Collection," contains some curious and interesting "cuttings" and advertisements connected with playing-cards. Among the advertisements is one having immediate reference to the particular class of playing-cards to come under immediate notice.

On the *verso* of folio five is "An advertisement concerning a new Pack of Cards," which would seem to have appeared in more than one newspaper of the latter part of the year 1679.

From which paper John Bagford's example was cut we do not know. Taylor refers (p. 168) to the first number of "Mercurius Domesticus" for December 19th, 1679, as containing a modified form of the advertisement. We have met with it, however—as will be shown presently—as early as October 21st, 1679, in the thirty-first number of the "Domestic Intelligence." Bagford's copy runs as follows :—

"There is newly published a Pack of cards, containing a History of all the Popish Plots that have been in England, beginning with those in Queen Elizabeth's time, and ending with this last damnable plot against his sacred majesty, King Charles the Second, whom God long preserve ; wherein are an exact account of the Spanish Invasion of 1588, the manner of their attempting England, and their being almost all burnt and taken by Sir Francis Drake. The conspiracy of Dr. Parry to kill Queen Elizabeth, his confessing the design upon his Tryal, and his Papist-like denying it at his Execution. The History of the horrid Gunpowder plot to blow up the King, Lords and Commons, when they were all sitting in the Parliament House ; the manner of its discovery by a letter sent to the Lord Monteagle, the Papists rebelling upon it, their being routed, and the Tryals and Executions of the several accomplices. And lastly, a true account of this present hellish plot against the life of his Present Majesty, the murdering of Sir Edmondbury Godfrey, the several meetings, Tryals and Executions of the Traytors, with all other material passages relating thereto. All of them so contrived that a child that can but read English will be acquainted with a chronicle for above 100 years past of all the bloody purposes and devilish designs of the Papists against the Protestant Religion and the true Professors of it, all excellently engraved on copper-plates, with very large descriptions under each card. The like not extant.

" Some persons that care not what they say so they can get by it, lying being as essential to them as eating, for they can as soon live without the last as the first, have endeavoured to asperse this Pack by a malicious libel intimating that it did not answer what is proposed : the contrary is evident to any person that shall peruse them, there being not one material passage in any of the above mentioned plots, but is neatly engraven and exactly described in writing to the great satisfaction of all who have seen them. But malice must shew itself most where the least reason, the aspersors of this Pack do plainly show themselves *Popishly Affected* in that they would not have the English World know that the Papists have been always as well as now ennemies to the Protestant Religion.

" They are to be Sold by Randal Taylor near Stationer's Hall and at the Harrow in Fleet Street, at the Three Bibles on London Bridge, at the Feathers at Pope's Head Alley, and in Cornhill at the Ship in S^t. Pauls churchyard, at the Three Flower-de-Luces in Little Brittain and at the Bell in Duck Lane and by most other Booksellers. The price of each Pack is one Shilling."

During the year 1679, there was published in London among other newspapers the " Domestick Intelligence or News both from City and Country. Published to prevent False Reports," and also " The True Domestick Intelligence or News both from City and Country. Published to prevent False Reports." In one or other, and sometimes in both of these papers, during the months of November and December, some advertisements connected with the subject of politico-historical cards occur, and which merit particular notice here.

The first advertisement we have met with—as before remarked—is in No. 31 of the " Domestick Intelligence " for Tuesday, October 21st, 1679. This is frequently repeated, and does not need repetition here.

In No. 35 of the " True Domestick Intelligence " for November 4th, 1679, is the following : —

" The Horrid Popish Plot lively represented in a Pack of Cards Printed for Jonathan Wilkins and Jacob Sampson."

In No. 50 of the " True Domestick Intelligence" for December 26, 1679, occurs this advertisement : —

" There is lately published a new Pack of Cards neatly cut in copper, in which are represented to the life the several consults for killing the King and extirpating the Protestant Religion, the manner of the murthering Sir Edmondbury Godfrey, the Tryals and Executions of the Conspirators, and all other material designs relating to the contrivance and management of the said horrid Popish Plot, with their attempt to throw it on the Protestants. These have something more than the first have, and yet nothing left out that was in them nor any old impertinent things added. Printed and sold by Robert Walton at the Globe, on the north side of St. Paul's Churchyard, near the West end, where you may have a pack for eightpence of the very best, you may have them in sheets fit to adorn studies and houses. There is likewise a broadside with an almanack, and some of the aforesaid pictures about it, which may not unfitly be called the Christian Almanack fit for Shops, Houses and Studies. Sold as above said, the price Sixpence."

This was repeated in No. 53 for January 6th, 1680 : —

Mr. Chatto, who was acquainted with the copy of the advertisement preserved by Bagford, and before given, thus comments on it (p. 153) :—

" In a ' puff collusive,'[1] forming a kind of postscript to this announcement, approbation of these cards is thus indirectly made a test of staunch Protestantism.

" Such a pack of cards as that announced in the advertisement referred to— containing an history of all the popish plots that have been in England, beginning with those in Queen Elizabeth's time—I have never seen, and from the objection which was made to it at the time, namely, 'that it did not answer what was proposed, I am inclined to think that it was the same pack as that which relates entirely to the pretended Popish Plot of 1678, and the murder of Sir Edmondbury Godfrey."

Certainly the British Museum collection of playing-cards does not contain any single pack illustrating all the events and plots above mentioned, but it has several distinct series of cards referring to many of them. Thus, it has a pack relating to the Spanish Armada, one in connection with the " Popish Plot," and other sequences illustrative of the " Rye House Plot," the victories of Marlborough, and events of the Reign of James II., with the arrival in England of the Prince of Orange. The Rebellion of 1698, and the story of Dr. Sacheverel are likewise portrayed.

In order that those persons who may refer to these politico-historical cards in the national collection, may have at hand a ready key in the catalogue to their descriptions and devices, it has been deemed advisable to supply here a succinct account of the various events and plots which the series of cards in question illustrate. As Locke elegantly expresses it : " The pictures drawn in our minds are laid in fading colours, and if not sometimes refreshed, vanish and disappear." ("On Human Understanding," b. ii. ch. 10.)

HISTORIC INTRODUCTION.

URING the Parliamentary Session of 1584-5 a stringent law was passed relative to Catholics. All Jesuits and secular priests were ordered to quit the kingdom within forty days ; those remaining after that time were to be held guilty of treason, and such as harboured or relieved them guilty of felony. All students at foreign Catholic seminaries were to return home within six months, or be considered treasonable if not doing so, and those who supplied them with money were to be liable to a *præmunire*. This bill was strongly opposed by one William Parry, a Doctor of Civil Law, who declared " the bill savoured of treason, was full of blood and danger, of despair and terror to the English subjects of this realm, and spoke with so much passion and vehemence that he was committed to custody." (Old-

---

[1] " The *puff collusive* is the newest of any, for it acts in the disguise of determined hostility. It is much used by bold booksellers and enterprising poets." " The Critic," act i.

The " puff collusive" was not an invention of Sheridan's time, but merely the revival of an old trick.

mixon, vol. i. p. 520.)   Being commanded to give his reasons for what he said, he obstinately refused, unless before the Privy Council.   Upon his submission after a few days' time he was re-admitted to the House of Commons.   Scarcely at liberty, however, than Edmund Nevil (who claimed the inheritance of the fugitive Earl of Westmoreland, lately dead in Flanders) accused him of conspiring against the Queen, and upon this he was committed to the Tower. Parry's confession was in substance as follows.   We follow Keightley, " History of England," v. ii. p. 220.

He was in the Queen's service from 1570 to 1580, when having attempted to kill a man to whom he was in debt, and having obtained a pardon, he went to Paris, where he was reconciled to the Church of Rome.   At Venice, some time after, he hinted to a Jesuit named Palmio, that he had found a way to relieve the English Catholics if the Pope, or any learned Divines, would justify it as lawful.   Palmio extolled the project (which was to kill the Queen) as a pious design, and recommended him to the Nuncio.   Letters of safe conduct for Parry to go to Rome were sent by Cardinal Como. Parry returned, however, to Paris, and there conversing with his countryman Morgan, the agent of the Queen of Scots, he declared himself ready to kill the greatest subject in England in the cause of the Church.

" Why not the Queen herself ? " said Morgan.   But of this Parry now had doubts, as Watts, an English priest, and Creighton, the Scottish Jesuit, had assured him it was not lawful.   The Nuncio Raggazzoni, however, confirmed him in his design, and he received, after his return to England, a letter from Cardinal Como, in the Pope's name, recommending his project and giving him absolution. He had communicated this letter to some at Court, and though he had had several interviews with the Queen, he went on such occasions always unarmed, lest he might be tempted to injure her, for such was the force of his natural feelings.

A book which had been written recently by Dr. Allen, however, had again confirmed him in his earlier resolution.   He had hence communicated it to Neville, and they had arranged their plans, but Lord Westmoreland dying at the time, Neville, in hopes of obtaining the family estates, had betrayed him.

Without stopping to inquire how far this confession was true or false, " we will only observe," writes Keightley, " that the world had just had a convincing proof that the Catholic party scrupled not at assassination.   On the 10th of July, 1584, the Great Prince of Orange was shot by a man named Balthazar Gerard, who confessed that he had been kept for some time in the Jesuits' College at Treves by one of the brotherhood, who approved of his design and instructed him how to proceed.   Philip II. had set a large reward on the Prince's head, and his great general the Prince of Parma sullied his fame by personally examining the qualifications of the assassins who presented themselves." (Keightley, v. ii. p. 221.)

Oldmixon tells us that "Parry was condemned, as a traitor, to be hanged, drawn, and quartered, and a gallows was put up in the Palace yard at Westminster, near the Parliament House, to which he was drawn through the City of London from the Tower, and there executed on the 2nd of March."

Spanish Invasion in 1588.—The execution of Mary, Queen of Scots, in 1587, formed an excuse for the Catholic powers, under the pretence of avenging her treatment, to attempt the overthrow and destruction of Elizabeth and the Protestant faith. But it happened that Philip II. of Spain was the only Prince who could, at the time, venture openly to turn any true force against the Queen and her kingdom. That designs against the latter were being made by Spain was soon known, for, says Welwood, "Walsingham had intelligence from Madrid that Philip had told his council he had despatched an express to Rome with a letter in his own hand to the Pope, acquainting him with the true design of his preparations, and asking his blessing upon it, which, for some reasons, he would not yet disclose to them till the return of the courier. The secret being thus lodged with the Pope, Walsingham, by means of a Venetian priest retained at Rome as his spy, got a copy of the original letter, which was stolen from the Pope's cabinet by a gentleman who took the keys out of the Pope's pocket while he slept."

On this becoming known in England, Sir Francis Drake went out to Cadiz and other places and inflicted such damage on the Spaniards that they postponed their intended invasion for a year. Consequently, in 1588 was fitted out what was termed the "Invincible Armada." "This boasted fleet," writes Oldmixon (v. i. p. 584), "consisted of 150 sail, great and small, containing near 60,000 tons of shipping, and had on board about 20,000 soldiers, 8,450 marines, 2,088 slaves, 2,630 great brass guns, &c. Farnese had ready to join them 13,000 foot, and 4,000 horse soldiers." Thus the Spanish army when united would have consisted of about 37,000 men, horse and foot. The Duke de Guise, to encourage the Spaniards, had brought 12,000 men to the coast of Normandy. These forces belonged to the League, who could very ill spare them out of France. The command of the Spanish fleet was designed for the Marquis of Santa Cruz, but he dying soon after he had been punished the previous year by Sir Francis Drake, the Duke of Medina Sidonia, a freshwater admiral, was appointed in his place.

Besides Philip's whimsical pretensions to the crown of England he made use of another thing not more rational and solid than that, to support him in his undertaking. This was a Bull of Pope Sixtus

V., which he thundered against Queen Elizabeth, absolving her subjects from their oaths of allegiance, and giving her kingdoms to the first who should seize them. The Bull of Pope Gregory XIII. was renewed also by William Allen, priest, to whom the Pope had given a cardinal's cap, and sent him into Flanders to be nearer at hand to England, and to stir up the Catholics there to rebellion by his missionaries. Allen brought the Bull of Sixtus with him into the Netherlands, and wrote an admonition to the English to adhere to the Pope and the Spaniards. Upon York and Stanley's betraying their garrisons in the Low Countries to the Spaniards, Allen wrote a libel entitled, " Epistolæ de Daventriæ Ditione," wherein he highly commended their treason, exciting others to do likewise, as they were not bound to serve or obey the Queen, she being under excommunication. Allen despatched several priests to Rowland York, whose regiment of 13,000 men, English and Irish, needed them as chaplains and confessors. He published his admonition under the protection of Alexander Farnese, Prince of Parma, governor of the Spanish Netherlands. To the latter Queen Elizabeth sent Dr. Valentine Dale mildly to expostulate against the treasonable attempts of Allen. Farnese pretended that he knew nothing of them, dismissing Dale without any satisfactory reply.

Nevertheless, while all these preparations were going on, the Prince of Parma endeavoured to amuse and beguile Elizabeth with negotiations for an amicable settlement of all difficulties between England and Spain. But neither England nor her sovereign were to be entrapped. At the beginning of November, 1587, orders had been given to prepare resistance.

" All the men from sixteen to sixty were enrolled and trained by the Lords Lieutenant of counties, who were directed to appoint officers and provide arms. One army of 36,000 men under Lord Huntsdon was to be assembled for the guard of the royal person; another of 30,000 men, under Leicester, was to be stationed at Tilbury to protect the city. The seaports were required to supply shipping according to their means. On this occasion the city of London set a noble example; being called upon to furnish 5,000 men and fifteen ships, the citizens voluntarily pledged themselves to send double the number of each. The royal navy consisted of but thirty-four ships, but many noblemen fitted out vessels at their own expense, and the whole fleet numbered 181 ships of all kinds, manned by 17,472 seamen. The chief command was entrusted to Howard of Effingham, Lord High Admiral of England; the three distinguished seamen, Drake, Hawkins, and Frobisher, held commands under him. The main fleet was stationed at Plymouth; a squadron of forty ships under Lord Henry Seymour lay off Dunkirk, to watch the motions of the Prince of Parma." (Keightley, vol. ii. p. 241.)

After some hindrances to its progress, the Armada was seen on the 19th of July, 1588, off the Lizard Point at Cornwall, by one Fleming—a sort of Scottish pirate—who quickly conveyed the news to Plymouth.

"The admiral got his fleet out to sea, though with great difficulty, as the wind blew strong into the port. The instructions of the Spanish admiral were to avoid hostilities till he had seen the army of the Prince of Parma safely landed in England; he therefore rejected the advice of his captains to attack the English fleet, and the Armada proceeded up the Channel in the form of a crescent, of which the horns were seven miles asunder. The motion of the fleet, the greatest that had ever ploughed the ocean, was slow, though every sail was spread. 'The winds,' says Camden, 'being as it were tired with carrying them, and the ocean groaning under their weight.'

"The plan adopted by the English admiral was to follow the Armada and harass it, and cut off stragglers. During six days, which it took the Spaniards to reach Calais, the annoyance was incessant, and several of their ships were taken or disabled, the superior seamanship of the English, and the agility and low build of their ships giving them great advantage over the unwieldy galleons and galleasses. At length (27th) the Armada cast anchor near Calais, and the admiral sent off to the Prince of Parma, requiring him to embark his troops without delay. But this it was not in his power now to do; his stores were not yet prepared, his sailors had run away, and the Dutch blockaded the harbours of Dunkirk and Newport. The Armada itself narrowly escaped destruction. On the night of the 29th the English sent eight fire-ships into it; the Spaniards in terror cut their cables, the English fell on them in the morning when they were dispersed, and took two galleons, and the following day (31st), a storm came on and drove them among the shoals and sands of Zealand. Here, in a council of war, it was decided, as the navy was now in too shattered a condition to effect anything, to return to Spain without delay. But the passage down the Channel was so full of hazard that it was resolved in preference to sail round Scotland and Ireland, dangerous as that course appeared. The Armada set sail, the English pursued as far as Flamborough Head, where want of ammunition forced them to give over the chase. Storms assailed the Armada in its progress, several ships were cast away on the west and south coasts of Ireland, where the crews were butchered by the barbarous natives, or put to the sword by orders of the Lord Deputy. The total loss was thirty large ships and about 10,000 men."—"The Queen of England had shown throughout the spirit of a heroine. She visited the camp at Tilbury (Aug. 9), rode along the lines on a white palfrey with a truncheon in her hand, and animated the soldiers by her inspiriting language. When the danger was over, she went in state to St. Paul's to return thanks to Heaven. She then granted pensions to the disabled seamen. She bestowed her favours on the admiral and his officers, and she had actually caused a warrant to be prepared, appointing Leicester to the office of Lord Lieutenant of England and Ireland, but the influence of Burleigh and Walsingham prevented her from signing it, and as Leicester was on his way to Kenilworth after disbanding his army he fell sick and died at Cornbury Park, in Oxfordshire (Sept. 4). The Queen lamented him, but she caused his goods to be seized for payment of his debts to the Crown." (*Op. cit.* v. ii. p. 243.)

The Gunpowder Plot.—In 1605, at the end of October, the Lords of the Council became suspicious of a plot, which on the 4th of November following was completely discovered by the Lord Chamberlain, Lord Monteagle, and others, on examining the cellars under the Parliament-house. These they found stuffed with billets, fagots, and coal, from under which was finally brought to light thirty-six barrels of gunpowder, and Guy, or Guido Fawkes was seized as he was slipping out at the door of the cellar with a dark lanthorn, tinder-box, and matches in his possession. By these and a slow match he was soon to have fired the mine, to have escaped by a small vessel then lying in the river, and have carried the news over to Flanders.

Many of the conspirators in this plot, originally concocted by Robert Catesby, known to and agreeable to the Jesuit party, but not, it is probable, to the Catholics generally, nor to the secular priesthood, were convicted and condemned, and others were shot while being arrested. Fawkes avowed and gloried in the design contemplated, that, viz., of blowing up the Parliament-house with all assembled in it.

The Great Plague and Fire in London.—In 1665 (5th year of the reign of Charles II.), during a period of great and long summer heat, the plague ravaged London. About this time some "sham plots," as they have been termed, were supposed to have been discovered. They were thought to have for their object the overthrow of the Government in England, through means of the discontented Presbyterians and Republicans exiled in the Dutch States, and of others secretly abiding at home. De Witt entered into correspondence with Ludlow, Sidney, and other exiles for this purpose, Lord Say and others forming a council at the Hague to correspond with their associates in England. The result was that when Parliament met at Oxford at the end of the year (1665) to grant supplies, an Act was passed for attainting all British subjects who should continue in the service of the States.

During the next year—1666—the "Great Fire" took place, destroying 13,000 houses, 89 churches, and necessitating 20,000 persons to lie in huts or in the open air in the fields between Islington and Highgate.

"It is not to be supposed that the real simple cause would be assigned for this calamity. Incendiaries, it was averred, were seen firing the city in various parts. Some laid it on the French, some on the Republicans, but it was finally fixed on the general scapegoat, the Papists, and the beautiful column raised by authority on the spot where the fire commenced long

'Like a tall bully lifted its head and lied'

in the inscription which it bore." (Keightley, *Op. cit.* vol. iii. p. 125.)

The Popish Plot.—In 1678, while the kingdom was at peace, what is known as the "Popish Plot" was discovered during the recess of Parliament. As King Charles II. was walking in the Park on the 12th of August, a person named Kirby, who was accustomed to assist the King in his laboratory, approached him, and said, "Sire, keep within the company, your enemies have a design upon your life; you may be shot within this very walk." Kirby was placed under examination, the result being the arrest of Dr. Tonge, or Tongue, the Rector of St. Michael's, Wood-street, and the coming forward of Titus Oates, who had taken orders at Cambridge, been indicted for perjury, had been a chaplain in the Navy, charged with sodomy, and obliged to quit his ship. He was appointed, nevertheless, one of the chaplains of the Duke of Norfolk, became a real or pretended convert to the Catholic faith, went over to St. Omer, thence to Spain, and had returned to England just at this period. Previously to having Oates examined before the Council, he was sent before a magistrate (Sept. 6th) named Sir Edmond Berry (Edmondbury is wrong) Godfrey, when he made oath to the truth of a narrative extending to eighty-one articles. Before the Council, Oates (dressed in a clergyman's gown) deposed to the following effect:—

"The Jesuits" (we quote from Keightley) "had resolved by all means to re-establish the Catholic religion in the British dominions. They were organising a rebellion and massacre in Ireland; in Scotland, disguised as Presbyterian ministers, they were opposing episcopacy; here they proposed to assassinate the King, and then to offer the crown to the duke, provided he would consent to hold it of the Pope, and aid in extirpating Protestantism; if not, 'to pot James must go,' was their expression. They had abundant funds, having £100,000 in bank, £60,000 a-year in rents, &c. Father Leshee (La Chaise), the French king's confessor, had given them £10,000, and they were promised an equal sum from Spain.

"In March last, two men named Honest William (Grove) and Pickering (the last a lay-brother of the Order), were often directed to shoot the King with silver bullets at Windsor, for which the former was to have £1,500, the latter 30,000 masses, and on their neglecting to do so William had been reprimanded, and Pickering had received twenty lashes on his bare back.

"On the 24th of April there had been a great meeting of the Jesuits at the White Horse Tavern, by St. Clement's in the Strand, to deliberate on the assassination of the King and two Benedictines, named Coniers and Anderton, and four Irishmen, whose names he knew not, were added to the former two. £10,000, and afterwards £15,000, had been offered to Wakeman, the queen's physician, to poison the King, and he had reason to believe he had undertaken it. He had also learned since his return that the Jesuits had caused the fire in 1666, on which occasion they had expended 700 fire-balls; and they would then have murdered the King, but they relented when they witnessed his zeal and humanity. They had secured amidst the conflagration diamonds to the value of £14,000; ten years afterwards they had made £2,000 by setting fire to Southwark; and they had now a plan for burning Westminster, Wapping, and the shipping. Finally, the Pope had lately issued a Bull, appointing to all the dignities in the Church of England, as the Catholic religion was sure to triumph as soon as the King was taken out of the way."

Oldmixon, in his "History of England during the Reigns of the Royal House of Stuart," observes, vol. i. p. 612:—

"The Pope, in a congregation *de propaganda fide*, consisting of about 300 persons, held about December, 1677, declared the King of England's dominions to be part of St. Peter's patrimony, as forfeited to the Holy See for heresy, and to be disposed of as he should think fit. Cardinal Howard, nominal Archbishop of Canterbury, was accordingly appointed Legate of England, to take possession of it in the Pope's name; he was also to have 40,000 crowns a year augmentation for the maintenance of his legatine authority.

"Perrot was made Archbishop of York; Corker, Bishop of London; Whitebread, Bishop of Winchester; Strange, Bishop of Durham; Godden, Bishop of Salisbury; Napper, Bishop of Norwich; Lord Arundel of Warder, Lord Chancellor of England; Lord Powis, Lord Treasurer; Sir William Godolphin, Lord Privy Seal; Edward Coleman, Esq., Secretary of State; Lord Bellasis, General of the Army; John Lambert, Esq., Adjutant-General; Richard Langhorne, Advocate-General.

"The lay officers had all commissions sent them ready sealed by

Joannes Paulus de Oliva, Father-General of the Jesuits' Society, residing at Rome, who was to give directions to the Provincial of the Jesuits residing at London how to proceed in this affair. Pedro de Jeronimo de Corduba, Provincial of the Jesuits in Spain, was to assist with counsel and money, and misrepresent the actions of his Britannic majesty to the Spanish court, which likewise was to be done by a Jesuit confessor to the Emperor in relation to England and that court. The correspondence for France was carried on between Coleman and Father Terriers first, and afterwards Father La Chaise, confessor to the French king."

To revert to Keightley's history, it may be remarked that, though Oates by his own account had feigned to be a convert, with the sole purpose of discovering the secrets of the Jesuits, and betraying them, though, as he said, he was so highly in their confidence that numerous documents had been in his hands, he had not retained a single one of them, and there was nothing but his bare assertion for the truth of the almost incredible circumstances which he related. His only chance, therefore, was that something of a confirmatory character might be found among the papers of those persons who were committed on his information. And here fortune stood his friend. Notwithstanding that little trust can be attached to Oates' assertions, the following passage in Burnet (vol. ii. p. 159) is worthy of attention :—

" Tillotson told me that Langhorn's wife, who was still as zealous a Protestant as *he* was a Papist, came off to him, and gave him notice of everything she could discover among them, though she continued a faithful and dutiful wife to the last minute of her husband's life. Upon the first breaking out of the plot, before Oates had spoken a word of commissions, or had accused Langhorn, she engaged her son in some discourse upon those matters, who was a hot, indiscreet Papist. He said their designs were so well laid that it was impossible they should miscarry, and that his father would be one of the greatest men in England, for he had seen a commission from the Pope constituting him Advocate-General. This he told me in Stillingfleet's hearing."

Among the persons accused by Oates was Coleman, the Duchess of York's secretary. Though the son of a Protestant clergyman, he had become a Catholic, and exerted himself greatly for the propagation of his faith. In connection with this endeavour he was in correspondence with La Chaise, and his successor in office, St. Germain. Hearing of the danger which threatened him from the statements of Oates, he hid his papers, but forgot a drawer which contained some correspondence carried on during 1674 and the following two years. In one of the letters therein deposited he had written, " We have here a mighty work upon our hands, no less than the conversion of three kingdoms, and by that, perhaps, the utter subduing of a persistent heresy which has a long time domineered over a great part of this northern world. There were never such hopes of success since the days of our Queen Mary as now in our days," &c.

In other correspondence Coleman alluded to the interests of the crown of England being inseparable from those of France and the Catholic religion, and describes the king as inclined to favour the Catholics, but at the same time as being thoroughly venial. As Keightley observes, when we consider the language of Coleman, and add to it the other evidence we possess, we may venture to say that the following assertion of Hallam is probably correct: " There was really and truly a popish plot in being, though not that which Titus Oates and his associates pretended to reveal; but one alert, enterprising, effective, in direct operation against the established Protestant religion in England. In this plot the King, the Duke of York, and the King of France were chief conspirators; the Romish priests, and especially the Jesuits, were eager co-operators." (" Constitutional History," vol. ii. p. 570.)

It has been stated that Titus Oates made his first averments before the magistrate, Sir Edmond Berry Godfrey. Though the latter was a zealous Protestant he kept on good terms with the Catholics, and warned Coleman of his danger. Nevertheless, he appears to have become impressed with the belief that some trouble would befall him on account of the matter in hand, telling Dr. Lloyd (the rector of his parish) and Dr. Burnet that he had been informed he would "be knocked on the head." To a person who inquired of him if he had had any hand in taking the informations concerning the plot, he replied in the affirmative, adding, " I know not what will be the consequence of them, but I believe I shall be the first martyr."

On the 12th of October—a Saturday morning—not a month after the interview with Oates, Sir E. Godfrey left his home, going to various parts of the town. He was met in St. Martin's Lane by persons of whom he inquired the way to Paddington Woods, and was seen by others in Marylebone Fields and Soho. At one o'clock he was seen in the Strand, was afterwards recognised in Lincoln's Inn Fields, and a person supposed to be he was seen in Red Lion Fields on the way to Primrose Hill, and finally in a field near the latter eminence. He continued absent from home, however, which " caused great uneasiness to his family and friends, and various conjectures were made to account for it. Some thought he was gone out of the way from his creditors, others gave out that he was married, and 'that not very decently,' or that he was run away with a harlot, but the more prevalent report was that he was murdered by the papists. For some days no account could be got of him, but on Thursday evening (the 17th), as two men were going towards the White House at Primrose Hill, they saw a cane and a pair of gloves lying on a bank by a ditch, and on searching further they found in the ditch the dead body of a man, with a sword run through him.   His rings were on his fingers, and his money was in his pocket.   There was a double crease round his neck, which was so limber that the face might be turned round to the shoulder.   The body was at once recognised to be that of the missing Justice.   A coroner's jury, swayed by the opinions of two ignorant surgeons, brought in a verdict that he had been strangled, and it was supposed that the assassins had run his own sword through him that he might be supposed to have killed himself. That the papists had done the deed was a point about which few had any doubt, and those who had, thought it most prudent to confine their suspicions to their own bosoms."   (Keightley, *Op. cit.* vol. iii. p. 170.)

According to Oldmixon (vol. ii. p. 614), the body was seen by Drs. Lloyd and Burnet, the late Bishops of Salisbury and Worcester, and their evidence tended to more than a suspicion that *priests* were concerned in the murder, for "there were many drops of white wax-lights on his breeches, which he never used in his house, and since only persons of quality or priests use these lights, this made all people conclude in whose hands he must have been.   'Twas visible he was first strangled and then carried to that place."

A reward of £500 having been offered for the arrest of the murderer of Sir E. Godfrey, a letter dated from Newbury was received by the Secretary of State the day after the funeral, requesting that the writer of it—William Bedloe—might be arrested at Bristol and conveyed to London.   This was accordingly done, and Bedloe examined on November the 7th in the presence of the King. Bedloe said that he had seen the body of Godfrey at Somerset House (the residence of the Queen), where he had been smothered between pillows by two Jesuits, and that he had been offered two thousand guineas to help remove it.   At a subsequent examination he said that Godfrey had been inveigled into Somerset House about five in the evening, and there strangled with a linen cravat. But it happened that at that very hour the King was visiting the Queen, that the place was full of guards, and the room in which he said he saw the body was one appropriated to the Queen's footmen, who were always in it.   At first, too, he knew nothing of the plot, but having read Oates' narrative, his memory brightened, and he called to mind many circumstances learned from English regulars and other religious persons he had met on the Continent.

The fact is, Bedloe was, if possible, a greater liar than Oates. Originally a servant of Lord Bellasis, he had travelled chiefly as a *courier* over much of the Continent, had been guilty of many acts of robbery and swindling, had been often the inmate of a prison, and had but recently come out of Newgate.

"The plain truth, however, appears to be that in this instance the unfortunate Papists were perfectly innocent, and that Godfrey died by his own hand. There was an hereditary melancholy in his family, and for some days before his disappearance a strangeness in his manner and behaviour had been observed. The apprehension of being brought into some trouble on account of having taken the deposition of Oates, probably led to the catastrophe. As by the law the property of a *felo de se* was forfeit to the Crown, it was the interest of his brothers to have it believed that he had been murdered. The report, laying the guilt on the Papists, was traced to them; they kept back important evidence, and they dealt with the coroner and the surgeons."

However, the result was that Lord Danby was impeached, Coleman, Grove, Pickering, and Ireland a Jesuit, were brought to trial along with Hill, Green, and Berry, and all, with the exception of Lord Danby, were condemned upon the evidence of Oates, Bedloe, Prance, and Carstairs, and executed, though protesting their innocence, whether in the general plot or Godfrey's murder, to the last. Some time after, five Jesuits, Whitebread (Provincial), Fenwick, Gavan, Turner, and Harcourt were condemned and executed; then followed Langhorne to share their fate. Sir George Wakeman, Croker, Marshall, and three Benedictine monks were next tried, but were acquitted by the jury, when the two chief and now baffled informers, Oates and Bedloe, had the audacity to declare "that they would never more give evidence in a Court where Scroggs presided," and actually exhibited articles against him to the Council (Keightley, *Op. cit.*) The writer here referred to observes with justice that when we consider how universal and strong was the belief in the plot, and how artful the modes adopted by some profligate politicians to exaggerate its activity, we shall find here as in the civil war grounds for admiring the freedom from bloodthirsty characteristics of the English people. Respecting the execution of the Catholic priests, for instance, Sir William Temple has informed us that " upon this point Lord Halifax and I had so sharp a debate that he told me if I would not concur in points that were so necessary for the people's satisfaction he would tell every body I was a Papist, affirming that the plot must be handled as if it were true, whether it were so or no."

On the accession of James II. (1685) the tide turned completely against Oates. He was indicted for perjury, thrown into prison, convicted, sentenced to stand in the pillory five times a year during his life, and to be whipped from Aldgate to Newgate, and thence to Tyburn. Though he suffered considerably from the latter part of his punishment, which was severely carried out, he recovered, regained his liberty, and found confiders, if not in his veracity, at least in his services to faction, who procured him in the reign of William III. a pension of £400 a-year for his life. T. Oates died in 1705.

Meal-Tub Plot.—Dangerfield and Madame Cellier.—1679-1680.—— While the various political intrigues connected with the Popish plot and Titus Oates's affairs were going on, a man named Dangerfield and a Madame Cellier, a midwife, started the idea of fabricating a plot of the Presbyterians against the Government.

Madame Cellier introduced Dangerfield to Lady Powis, who procured him interviews with Lord Peterborough, and finally obtained him communication with the Duke of York. The latter gave Dangerfield twenty guineas, and secured for him an interview with King Charles, from whom Dangerfield received forty guineas for the information he had offered.

Dangerfield advised that revenue officers should be sent to the lodgings of a certain Colonel Mansel, the intended quarter-master of the future Presbyterian army, to search for smuggled lace. On search being made treasonable documents were found concealed behind his bed. But these turning out to have been only forgeries, Dangerfield was committed to Newgate. While in prison he averred that he had been bribed by the Catholics to invent the plot to assassinate the King and Lord Shaftesbury. To confirm the truth of his statements Dangerfield requested that Madame Cellier's rooms should be searched, where in a meal-tub might be found documents which would prove the truth of his story. In such a place were discovered papers seemingly confirmatory of Dangerfield's statements. Nevertheless, on the trials both of Madame Cellier and of Lord Castlemain the juries declined to give credit to his assertions.

" The whole affair is as usual involved in mystery ; the Catholics may have endeavoured to get up a counterplot, the Monmouth party may have sought by means of a sham plot to cast odium on the Duke of York. All parties at this time, in their anxiety about ends, were but too indifferent as to means." (Keightley, vol. iii. p. 191.)

The Rye House Plot, 1683.——After the dissolution by King Charles of the Parliament which had met at Oxford in 1681, the leaders of the popular party began to confer seriously among themselves as to what should be done in opposing the Government, should it appear to aim at a despotic authority.

Shaftesbury was impetuous, and advised instant action, but this was deemed inadvisable by the rest of the party, which resolved to proceed with caution, and only after further deliberation.

Shaftesbury dying at the Hague in 1683, his old associates felt now at liberty to proceed from words to action. A council, composed of the Lords Monmouth, Essex, and Russell, of Howard, Algernon Sydney, and John Hampden (grandson of the " great Hampden "), was formed, for the purpose of arranging matters for a general rising. But it would seem after all, that when the plot was discovered in the summer of 1683, not anything very determinate or practical had been consummated.

The discovery of this conspiracy, known as the " Rye House Plot," was made as follows:—

" Rumsey, West, and other satellites of Shaftesbury used to hold meetings of their own, in which there was frequent talk of ' lopping the two sparks,' as West expressed it, that is, killing the King and Duke. West spoke of doing it as they were going to or from the play-house, then he said ' they would die in their calling.' There was one Rumbold, an old officer of Cromwell's army, who had married a maltster's widow, and thus become master of a house called the Rye, near Hoddesden in Herts, close by which the King used to pass on his way to Newmarket. He happened to say how easy it would be for a man to shoot the King at that place. West caught at the idea, and hence the plot was named the ' Rye-house plot.'

" In this case, also, although there was a real conspiracy, nothing would seem to have been actually determined on, and things remained in this state till the month of June, when on the very day (12th) that judgment was given against the city, one Josiah Keeling, a sinking merchant, who was one of the confederates, resolved to turn informer. He went to Legge (now Lord Dartmouth), who sent him to secretary Jenkins, and on the information which he gave, rewards were offered for nine of the conspirators, but they had been forewarned by Keeling's brother, and had concealed themselves. Two days after West and Rumsey came in and surrendered, and on their information, together with that of one Shephard, a wine merchant, Russell and Sidney were arrested and sent to the tower. Lord Grey was arrested, but he contrived to escape from the messengers, the Duke of Monmouth also escaped, but Howard was taken concealed in a chimney in his own house. To save his life he discovered all that he said he knew, and on his information Lord Essex and Hampden were arrested." (Keightley, *op. cit.* vol. iii. p. 209.) Essex committed suicide, Russell suffered decapitation, as did Sidney. Monmouth was pardoned on condition that he acknowledged in a letter to the King the truth of the conspiracy. King Charles II. died on February the 6th, 1684-85.

The Committal of the Seven Bishops, 1685-1688.—On the death of Charles II. his brother James ascended the throne without opposition; but, soon after his accession, the Duke of Monmouth (natural son of Charles by Lucy Waters) who had been banished the kingdom on account of his connection with the Rye-house plot, landed in England with 100 men, had himself proclaimed king at Taunton, and set a price on the head of King James. He was soon defeated at the battle of Sedgemoor, when finding himself abandoned he knelt to the King for mercy, but in vain. He was beheaded a few days after on Tower-hill.

James having caused his " Declaration for liberty of conscience " to be republished with additions, he, by the advice, it is said, of Father Petrie, made an order in council (May 4th), that it should be read out in the churches during the time of Divine Service, and the bishops were required to distribute it for that purpose.

The Archbishop of Canterbury (Dr. Sancroft) and the bishops of Asaph, Ely, Bath and Wells, Peterborough, Chichester, and Bristol declined to carry out this order, affirming, writes Burnett, that " they could not in prudence, honour, and conscience make themselves so far parties to it as the publication once and again in God's house and in the time of Divine Service must amount to."

The bishops were at length cited to appear before the council, and were afterwards committed to the tower for their contumacy.

" A week after their commitment they were brought upon a *habeas corpus* to the King's Bench, where their counsel offered to make it appear to be an illegal commitment, but the court allowed it in good law. They were required to enter into bonds for small sums to answer to the information that day fortnight. When the day fixed for their trial came on, there was a vast concourse—the trial did last long, above ten hours—the court sat again next day, and the jury came in with their verdict (acquittal), upon which there were such shoutings, so long continued, and as it were echoed in the city, that all people were struck with it, every man seemed transported with joy." (Burnet's " History of his own Times," vol. iii. p. 225.)

As the result of this trial, which was considered all over Europe, according to Burnet, to determine whether the King or the Church were more likely to prevail, the King was defeated.

The birth of a son, however, might appear to have been a sufficient consolation under his disappointment; but here, too, the King's usual misfortune attended him, for both his own paternity and the origin of the child were among certain parties equally disputed. Yet if ever there was a prince about whose birth there should seem to have been not a shadow of doubt, it was this particular Prince of Wales.

The Warming-pan Plot, 1688.—King James was twice married, his first wife was the daughter of the Earl of Clarendon, and died in 1671. His second wife was Mary Beatrice, Princess of Modena, daughter of the Duke Alphonse d'Este. Mary of Modena had several children, but they died soon after birth. In 1687 it was reported that the Queen was again pregnant; this was news much astonishing the people. Extraordinary surmises were slowly mooted about, but which led generally to the opinion that the Catholic party, prompted by the Jesuits, was determined to have by some means or other an heir to the throne, trained up in their own doctrines.

On the birth of the child, James Francis Edward Stuart (June 10, 1688), it was asserted by some that he was really the son of a miller's wife, the child having been procured by Father Petre, who had him brought to the Queen's bed in a warming-pan, and then passed off as an actual child of King James and Mary of Modena.

According to a ballad of the time ("Roxburghe Ballads," vol. iii. p. 724.—B. M. C 20 f) :—

"A NEW SONG ENTITULED, THE WARMING-PAN—

*　　　　*　　　　*　　　　*　　　　*

since it was determined an heir must be got,
No matter from *Kettle* from *Pan* or from *Pot*,
In mettles fertile the old Jesuit's clan
Produced a brave boy from a *brass Warming-pan.*
　　　　　　　　　　　　Derry-down," &c. &c.

*　　　　*　　　　*　　　　*　　　　*

Another party had not any hesitation in awarding the Church a still more direct hand in the production of the young prince, whom they called the "spawn of a Fryer," describing his origin in a series of obscene and blasphemous jokes, inexcusable even in an age of free thought and very open expression.

Father Petre, whose name so frequently recurs in connection with the Warming-pan Plot, was a Jesuit of noble family, and had been long in the confidence of the king. Shortly before the pregnancy of the Queen he had been made a privy-councillor. The following is from Burnet's "History of his own Times," vol. iii. pp. 236-246 ; Clarendon Press edition.

"The Queen had been for six or seven years in such an ill state of health, that every winter brought her very near death. Those about her seemed well assured that she who had buried all her children soon after they were born, and had now for several years ceased bearing, would have no more children. Her own priests apprehended it, and seemed to wish for her death."———"In September (1687) the queen went to Bath, where as was already told, the king came and saw her, and stayed a few days with her ; it was said that at the time of her coming to the King, her mother, the Duchess of Modena, made a vow to the Lady Loretto that her daughter might by her means have a son, and it went current that the Queen believed herself to be with child in that very instant in which her mother made her vow. A conception said to be thus begun looked suspicious. It was soon observed that all things

about her person were managed with a mysterious secrecy, into
which none were admitted but a few Papists. She was not dressed
nor undressed with the usual ceremony. The thing upon this
began to be suspected, and some libels were writ treating the
whole as an imposture. Those about the Queen did all of the
sudden change her reckoning, and began it from the King's being
with her at Bath. It was given out by all her train that she was
going to be delivered. Some said it would be next morning, and
the priests said very confidently it would be a boy. The next
morning, about nine o'clock, she sent word to the King that she was
in labour. The queen-dowager was next sent to ; but no ladies
were sent for, so that no women were in the room but two dressers
and one under-dresser, and the midwife. The King brought over
with him from Whitehall a great many peers and privy-councillors,
and of these eighteen were let into the bed-chamber, but they stood
at the furthest end of the room. The ladies stood within the alcove.
The curtains of the bed were drawn close, and none came within
them but the midwife and an under-dresser. The Queen lay all the
while a-bed, and in order to the warming one side of it a warming-
pan was brought. But it was not opened that it might be seen
that there was fire and nothing else in it. So there was matter for
suspicion with which all people were filled. A little before ten the
Queen cried out as in a strong pain, and immediately after the midwife said, aloud, she was happily brought to bed. . . No cries were
heard from the child, nor was it shown to those in the room ; it was
not known whether the child was alive or dead, it looked like the
giving time for some mismanagement; all that concerned the milk
or the Queen's purgations was managed still in the dark. This
made all people inclined more and more that there was a base
imposture now put on the nation." [It was soon reported that the
infant prince was dead,] "and it looked as if all was ordered
to be kept shut up close till another child was found. One that
saw the child two days after, said to me that he looked strong, and
not like a child so newly born. It was said that the child was
strongly revived of a sudden. Some of the physicians told Lloyd,
Bishop of St. Asaph, that it was not possible for them to think
it was the same child. They looked on one another, but durst
not speak what they thought. What truth soever may be in these
[reports], this is certain, that the method in which this matter was
conducted from the first to last was very unaccountable, if an
imposture had been intended it could not have been otherwise
managed." (*Op. cit.*)

The note in the Clarendon Press edition referring to the preceding account is in part as follows :—" So here are three children "
[Swift], " first the Queen is surmised not to have been with child ;

secondly, to have miscarried ; thirdly, a child in a warming-pan is supposed to have been conveyed into the bed-chamber; fourthly, perhaps no child to have been carried into the next room ; fifthly, the child seen by all in the room to have died ; sixthly, a substituted child to have died. Thus, as Swift observes, we have three children, the new-born infant, seen by all, the substituted child, and the Prince of Wales. It is lamentable that such a man as Burnet should have disgraced himself by the recital of these stupid and inconsistent falsehoods." (*Op. cit.* p. 245.)

Descriptions of several satirical prints referring to the " Warming-pan Plot " may be found in the first volume of the " Catalogue of Prints of Political and Personal Satires," Nos. 1156-1166, and 1177, 1211, page 710 *et seq.*

Marlborough. The Flight of James. The Prince of Orange.—On the accession of King James II. (1685), Lieutenant-Colonel Churchill had been sent to France to announce the occurrence. On his return from this duty he was raised to the English Peerage, with the title of Baron Churchill of Sundridge. By his vigilance and skill he contributed greatly to the suppression of the insurrection of Monmouth, which occurred shortly.

As the behaviour of the King, on the suggestions of the Earl of Sunderland, and of others of the Catholic party, had soon rendered James unpopular with the Protestants, overtures were made by influential members of the latter to William Prince of Orange, that he should rid them of a sovereign so inclined towards Rome, and if all went satisfactorily, take the vacant office on himself. The Dutch fleet, with the prince on board, anchored at Torbay on the 5th of November, 1688. On landing, the prince and his retinue proceeded towards London. The success of the Dutch invasion was such as to lead King James to mistrust the fidelity of his army, to fly from England, and seek an asylum at St. Germain from the King of France.

The Prince of Orange then issued writs for the election of members to a national convention, and on the 13th of February, 1689, he, along with the Princess of Orange, received the two Houses of Parliament at Whitehall, by which was made, through Lord Halifax, a solemn tender of the Crown of England. The same day the prince and princess were proclaimed as King William III. and Queen Mary II.

During the revolution of 1688, which banished James and secured the Prince of Orange, Churchill behaved towards the former with a duplicity and treachery deserving severe condemnation. While professing to support James he entered the service of his rival.

On the coronation of the latter, Churchill assisted at the ceremony, and was created afterwards Earl of Marlborough and a Privy

Councillor. In 1689 he received the command of the English forces in the Netherlands. He next served in Ireland, but was recalled to Flanders. Being suspected of a traitorous correspondence with the exiled King (James II.), he was deprived of his command and imprisoned in the Tower. He was soon released, however, but did not regain the favour of William until 1697.

On the outbreak of the war connected with the Spanish succession, Marlborough received the chief command of the forces of the United Provinces, and was named Ambassador to France. He became master of several places in the Netherlands by 1702, gained (under Prince Eugène) the battle of Blenheim in 1704, defeated Villeroy at Ramillies in 1706, was victorious at Oudenard in 1708, and at Malplaquet in 1709. By 1712 Marlborough's fortune had changed, and he was dismissed from all his offices at the beginning of this year.

To escape the charges of having prolonged the war, of peculation, and the disquietudes of home, he went abroad with the duchess, who also had been displaced at Court. In 1714, Marlborough returned to England, and was restored by King George I. to office; but an attack of apoplexy soon compelled him to retire once more, and he died at Windsor Lodge in 1722.

" The character of Marlborough presents a perplexing combination of noble and base qualities, which have served as the groundwork of extravagant eulogy and fierce invective. His rare ability as a general, his skill and success as a diplomatist, are unquestionable. No less so are his vast ambition, his avarice, and his treachery." (" Dictionary of General Biography," Coates.)

Dr. Sacheverell, 1709-1710.—Henry Sacheverell, an English divine, was educated at Oxford, where in 1708 he obtained the degree of Doctor of Divinity. In 1709 he was appointed preacher at St. Saviour's, Southwark. On the 5th of November of that year, having become a willing tool of the party then opposing the administration of Marlborough and Godolphin, he preached a violent sermon at St. Paul's before the lord mayor and aldermen, on " The Perils of false Brethren both in Church and State," and " Perfidious Prelates and false Sons of the Church." He assailed the Government, declaring it tended both in ecclesiastical and civil affairs to the destruction of the constitution; called Godolphin Volpone, asserted that the toleration granted by law to the Protestant dissenters was both unreasonable and unwarrantable, maintained the doctrine of "passive obedience," and called on the people to stand firm in the defence of principles which the crown and its advisers tended to overthrow and destroy. Forty thousand copies of the printed sermon are stated to have been circulated by the political party of its author.

Godolphin resolved on Sacheverell's impeachment, and the Serjeant of the House of Commons delivered him to the custody of the Deputy Usher of the Black Rod on the ensuing January 14th, 1710. Sacheverell was admitted to bail. On the 27th of February he was brought to trial at Westminster Hall, Queen Anne being then and every day of the trial present—*incognita.* As she approached the hall in her sedan chair the people crowded around it, exclaiming, " God bless your Majesty and the Church, we hope your Majesty is for Dr. Sacheverell." As the latter descended from the coach in which he was brought daily from the Temple, the persons near him tried to kiss his hands.

The trial continued for three weeks, being prosecuted by Sir Joseph Jekyl, General Stanhope, Walpole, King, and others. Sacheverell was defended by Sir Simon Harcourt and Phipps, assisted by Drs. Atterbury, Smallbridge and Friend. He was declared guilty by sixty-nine lords against fifty-two, who pronounced him not guilty.

" Accordingly sentence passed upon him—that Henry Sacheverell, Doctor in Divinity, shall be and is hereby enjoined not to preach during the term of three years next ensuing. That Dr. Henry Sacheverell's two printed sermons, referred to by the impeachment of the House of Commons, shall be burnt before the Royal Exchange in London, between the hours of twelve and one on Monday, the 27th of this instant March by the hands of the common hangman, in the presence of the lord mayor of the city of London, and the two sheriffs of London and Middlesex." (Oldmixon, vol. iii. p. 438.)

" This gentle sentence," writes Keightley, " was regarded by the Tory party as a triumph, and such in fact it was. Bonfires and illuminations in London and all over the kingdom testified to their joy, and addresses in favour of non-resistance poured in from all quarters. But the other side was greatly annoyed."

" 'Twill be astonishing to posterity," writes Oldmixon, " that so many noblemen and gentlemen should countenance such an insignificant tool in his seditious and insolent behaviour, or endeavour to screen him from punishment—the merciful sentence past upon him for which the Whigs have paid dearly from that time to this." (*Op. cit.* vol. iii. p. 442.)

E. 185.

LAST QUARTER OF SEVENTEENTH CENTURY.

LONDON.

(SPANISH ARMADA.)

PACK of fifty-two numerals of the ordinary suits and honours. This series illustrates the chief events connected with the history of the Spanish Armada, of the English Fleet engaged in its overthrow, of the Acts and Progresses of Queen Elizabeth, of the Earls of Oxford, Northumberland, and Cumberland, of the Lord High Admiral Howard, and of others.

The greater portion of each card-piece is occupied by a design illustrating some of the events mentioned. Above the pictorial composition a broad margin is left clear, at the right-hand corner of which is the mark of the suit, and at the left-hand is indicated in Roman numbers the value of the particular number of the series. The coate-cards or honours have busts in circles at the left-hand upper corners in place of the Roman numerals. The title of the honour is engraved between the bust and the mark of the suit. Below the design is a description of the events therein represented. The events are not recorded in the perfectly systematic order of their actual occurrence, but are variously placed through the different suits.

On the knave of hearts is shown "the Pope consulting with his Cardinalls, and contributing a million of gold towards the charge of the Armada."

The Holy Father is seated with four cardinals at a table on which are several bags of money. An attendant is approaching with more bags. A mitred bishop forms the bust in the medallion above.

On the nine of hearts are represented " the twelve Spanish Shipps caled the 12 Apostles."

The ten of hearts exhibits " The Spanish Armada consisting of 130 Shipps where of 72 were Galleasses and Galeons, in wh^{ch} were 19290 soulders 8359 marriners, 2080 gally slaves, and 2630 great ordinance, ye Navy was 3 whole yeares preparing."

On the eight of hearts may be seen " The Spanish Fleete weighing Ancor from the River Tagus the 20th of May, 1588."

The king of clubs presents us with " The English Fleet whereof the Ld Charles Howard was Ld Admirall and Sir Fran. Drake vice-admirall."

The five of clubs represents " The Earle of Oxford, Northumberland, Cumberland, with many more of the nobility and gentry going to visit the English Fleet."

On the queen of hearts is shown " Queen Eliz : visiting her Camp at Tilbury, being mounted on Horseback with a truncheon of an ordinary Captain in her hand."

The queen of clubs represents " Queen Eliz : walking up and downe ye Camp at Tilbury, and encouraging the Captaines and Souldiers."

In both these compositions the queen wears her crown.

On the ace of clubs we see how " The Admirall ye Ld Sheffield S Tho : Howard and others joyn with Drake and Fenez ag^t ye Spanish Fleet & worst them."

On the three of clubs are shown the " 8 Fireships sent by ye English Admirall towards ye Spanish Fleet in ye middle of ye night under the conduct of Young and Prowse."

The two of clubs exhibits " The Spaniards on right of the Fireships weighing Ancors, cutting cables, and betakeing themselves to flight with a hideouse noise, & in great confusion."

On the eight of clubs is represented "The third fight between ye Eng^h and Spanish Fleetes, being the 25th of June, 1588, where in the English had again ye better."

The ten of spades describes " The Spaniards consulting and at last resolving to return into Spain by the North Ocean, many of their Ships being disabled."

On the eight of spades are shown " The Spanish Ships lost on the coast of Scotland, and 700 souldiers and marriners cast ashore."

The seven of spades shows the " Spanish ships castaway on the Irish Shoare with marriners and seamen."

The nine of spades exhibits the " Spanish Commanders taken prisoners and brought into England."

The knave of diamonds tells how " The Spanish fleet that remained returned home disabled or with much dishonour."

A monk forms the bust in the medallion above.

On the two of spades we have " The Spaniards bewailing yᵉ misfortune of their friends."

The scene now changes on the three of spades, for here is " Queene Eliz : with Nobles and Gentry and a great number of people giving God humble thanks in Sᵗ. Pauls church and having set upp the Ensignes taken from the Spaniards."

On the four of spades is " Queene Eliz : Riding in Triumph through London in a chariot drawn by two Horses, and all yᵉ companies attending her with their Baners."

The sequence of events may be said to conclude on the knave of spades, on which are exhibited " Severall Jesuits hang'd for Treason against the Queene, and for having a hand in the Invasion."

The bust of the knave in the medallion is that of a Jesuit.

According to Taylor (p. 409) these cards were issued as " quiet reproofs to the mendicant priests who haunted England previous to the abdication of the King, to whom his brother, himself a King of England, said, ' Never mind York, they will never shoot *me* to make a way for you.'   When said York was perhaps anxious to make an illicit way to the throne, please the Pope, satisfy the Presbyters and otherwise cool down the Nonconformists to a reasonably tepid point.   No, no, Vagabond Charles was perhaps not the most moral, but inconfutably the best of the later Stuarts, and he saw through York's ' diminutive game.'"

It has been stated that this series of cards was formerly exhibited by Sir Joseph Banks before the Society of Antiquaries.

These card-pieces are from neatly engraved copper-plates, and are uncoloured.

The backs are marked by an hexagonal network in pale black ink, a St. Andrew's cross within a circle forming the centre of the several hexagonal meshes.

In connection with the Spanish Armada Series, the prints and medals numbered from forty-one to fifty-four inclusive, described in the first volume of the Catalogue of Prints relating to ' Political and Personal Satires,' may be consulted with advantage.

[$3\frac{1}{2}$ × $2\frac{1}{8}$ in.]   [Backs decorated.]

E. 186.

LAST QUARTER OF SEVENTEENTH CENTURY.

LONDON (1679 ?).

(POPISH PLOT, &c.)

 PACK of fifty-two numerals of the ordinary suits.

This series illustrates the events which took place, or were assumed to have taken place, in connection with what are known as the Popish Plot, the Titus Oates and Sir Edmond Berry Godfrey's Affairs.

Each card-piece is occupied in its greater portion by a design illustrating an occurrence of the before-mentioned narratives.   Above it, in a reserved and broad margin, are the mark of the suit at the left-hand corner, and the value of the piece in Roman numerals at the right-hand corner. In the " honours " a title displaces the numerical value.

Below the pictorial design is engraved a description of it. The ace of hearts may be said to begin the drama, and represents " The plot first hatcht at Rome by the Pope and Cardinalls, &c."

The holy father, three cardinals, and a bishop, are seated at a table, beneath which the devil is crouching and grinning.

On the nine of clubs a monk is declaiming from a pulpit to a mixed audience; from his mouth proceeds a scroll on which is inscribed " Extirpate Hereticks root and branch."

Below the composition may be read, " Father Connyers preaching against ye Oathes of Alejance and Supremacy."

On the five of hearts, " Dr. Oates receives letters from ye Fathers to carry beyound Sea."

Two Jesuits and two conspirators are shown, the latter handing despatches to Oates, while the Jesuit fathers look on.

On the eight of clubs may be seen " The conspirators Signeing ye Resolve for Killing the King."

The knave of diamonds shows how " Pickerin attempts to kill ye K. in St James Park."

Pickering is crouching gun in hand behind a tree while the king passes with his attendants. His majesty has on his hat, the attendants wear large wigs.

The three of this suit tells how " Ashly received instructions of White-bread for the Society to offer Sir George Wakeman £10 000 " [to poison the King.]

A Jesuit is seated at a table listening to the arguments of Ashby and point-ing his finger at a document.

On the king of hearts, " Dr. Oates discovereth ye Plot to ye King and Cown-cell," while the two of this suit represents " Sr E B Godfree takeing D^r. Oates his depositions."

The queen of spades exhibits " The Club at ye Plow Ale house for the murther of S. E B Godfree"; and the nine of the same suit represents " Sir E B Godfree strangled—Girald going to Stab him."

On the three of spades may be seen " The execution of the Murtherers of Sir E B Godfree." The criminals are hanging on the gallows, and the cart in which they are standing is in the act of being drawn away.

The ace of clubs exhibits " The Consult of Benedictine Monks and Fryers in the Savoy."

On the six, " Capt^t Berry and Alderman Brooks are offered 500 £ to cast the Plot on the Protestants."

On the nine of hearts we have, " The seizing severall conspirators."

On the four of the clubs comes " The tryall of Sir G Wakeman and 3 Benedictine Monks."

And on the five of clubs is " The Execution of the 5 Jesuitts."

On the six of hearts is " Coleman drawn to his Execution."

On the two of diamonds may be seen " Ireland and Grove drawn to their execution."

And on the knave of clubs is " Reddin standing in ye Pillory."

The six of diamonds exhibits " Pickerin Executed." His body is on the ground and about to be " quartered " by the executioner.

The events now change to the Great Fire of London.

On the three of clubs is shown that " Gifford and Stubbs give money to a made to fire her master's house," while on the two of the same suit, London is re-presented in flames, beneath which design is inscribed—

" London remember } 1666."
    The 2nd of September, } 1666."

This interesting series has been noticed more or less in detail by various writers, and the cards have been exhibited before several antiquarian societies.

Mr. Chatto refers, at p. 154 (Bibl. 4), and Mr. Taylor at p. 169 (Bibl. 9), to the present sequence. In the first volume of the "Catalogue of Prints relating to Political and Personal Satires," descriptions of several prints and broadsides relative to the events illustrated by these cards may be found, from Nos. 1,057-1,068, 1,073-1,078, 1,135-1,142, pp. 601-702.

A detailed list of the various subjects treated of in the order of the suits, beginning with the ace of hearts and ending with the king of spades, together with copies of eight of the cards, may be found in the "Gentleman's Magazine" for September, 1849, vol. xxxii. New Series, p. 265. In this article reference is made to a pocket volume published in 1681, bearing the title, "The Plot in a Dream; or, the Discoverer in Masquerade, in a succinct discourse, and narrative of the late and present designs of the Papists against the King and Government. By Philo-patris." In the course of this work are several copper-plate engravings, the designs of which, in some cases, closely follow those of the present series of cards, though on the whole, they are much inferior to them. The writer in the "Gentleman's Magazine" instances the "attempted assassination of the King in St. James's Park; the carrying of Sir E. B. Godfrey's body to Primrose Hill; Reading's standing in the Pillory; and the Papists hiring servants to fire houses," as examples of such imitation.

In the "Catalogue of a Collection of Printed Broadsides in the Possession of the Society of Antiquaries of London" (Printed Books Department, B. M. 1,190, 2. h. [academies]), are the following records :—

"1679, June.   581.—A true Narrative of the Horrid Hellish Popish-plot. To the Tune of Packington's Pound.   The second part.

"Describing in Verse, and in a series of twelve coloured engravings, the principal points of the Jesuits' or Oates's Plot.   Thomas Whitbread, the Provincial of the Jesuits in England, and four others of that order were executed at Tyburn on the 20th June, 1679.

"582.—Specimens of a part of a series of Historical cards, some of the subjects and costumes being evidently taken from the above broadside. They were published in the 'Gentleman's Magazine' in 1849, and are inserted in this collection in illustration of the preceding article. The idea of making playing-cards a vehicle of amusement, instruction, or political satire, has been a favourite one at all times. In 1812 the late Queen Charlotte, for her own amusement, had a private printing press at Frogmore Lodge, and one of its productions was a series of five sets of historical and chronological cards." (*Op. cit.* p. 134.)

Mr. S. A. Hankey exhibited a pack of these cards before the Royal Archæological Institute in March, 1873. In the paper read in connection with it, the author drew attention to the "very singular (and possibly unique) example of the display of popular feeling as stamped upon the ordinary appendages to mere play or amusement. And the publication of a series of plates so intensely partizan in their character, affords a remarkable testimony to the agitated state of the public mind while under the influence of the stirring revelations of Titus Oates, Bedloe, and the other informers. This pack was published in the year 1679 or 1680, when the excitement and apprehension of the alleged Popish plot was at its highest, and it contains the history of all the imputed conspiracies 'excellently engraved,' as the advertisement runs, 'on copper-plates, with very large descriptions under each card.'

"This class of cards will be found to be the offspring of periods of extraordinary political or party excitement. They were the caricatures of the day, and it may be doubted if their publication had any other object than the expression of popular feeling in a form which, if convenient for general circulation, must have been objectionable to players, as likely to distract their attention from the game.

"I have vainly essayed to discover a connection between the sequence of the cards under their respective suits and the order of the events which the several plates record. For the personal history of the informers is so intermingled with the story of the plot, that it is difficult even to set out the cards in their historical order, and, except in the account of Sir Edmondbury Godfrey, such an effort at arrangement only brings about a hopeless confusion in suits and numbers. Godfrey's prominence in these events is, however, well sustained, for his tragic history occupies nearly the whole of the suit of spades, the description of which section may serve as a fair sample of the entire series.

"Beginning with the queen, and following in order downward to the two of spades, we find pictorial representations described as follows :—

" 1. The Club at the Plow Alehouse for the murther of Sir E. B. Godfree.

" 2. He is dogg'd by St Clement's Church.

" 3. He is persuaded to goe down Sommerset house yard.

" 4. He is strangled. Girald going to stab him.

" 5. The eight of spades missing. [Sir E B Godfree carrying up into a Roome.]

" 6. The body is shewed to Capt. Bedlow and Mr Prance.

" 7. The dead body conveyed out of Sommerset house in a Sedan.

" 8. The body carry'd to Primrose Hill on a horse.

" 9. The Murtherers are diverting themselves at Bow after the Murther.

" 10. Next, but out of its historical place, comes the three of spades, showing the execution of the murtherers.

" 11. (And after that) The Funerall of S^r E B Godfree.

" The two of hearts actually opens this story, the description at the foot being, 'Sir E. B. Godfree takeing Dr. Oates his depositions,' while the king of spades, which in the natural order should have commenced the history, only represents an after event, viz. 'Mr. Prance discovering the Murther to the King and Council.' Not less than six of the cards represent capital executions, and the spirit of the whole series may be observed in the ace, or one of hearts, which represents 'The plot first hatcht at Rome by the Pope and Cardinalls, &c., in which his Holiness appears sitting key in hand, with three Cardinals and a Bishop, while the Devil is seen crouching under the Council table.'

" Besides this there are depicted several 'Consults,' or minor plots, among Jesuits and others, in various localities. In one plate Father Conyers occupies the pulpit, preaching disloyalty, and in several others bribes are being offered or money distributed to forward the designs of the conspiracy. Coleman, Whitebread, Langhorne, and Dugdale have each their respective histories, while two of the cards bring into the plot the guilt of the Fire of London, one of these representing ' Giffard and Stubbs bribing a made to set fire to her Master's House,' and the other shewing London in flames, with the inscription at the foot—

" London remember
The second September (date)
2 September, 1666.' "

The Archæological Journal for 1873, vol. xxx. p. 185.

The designs and inscriptions on these card-pieces are from engraved copperplates. The cards are uncoloured.

[3½ × 2⅛ in.]   [Backs plain.]

E. 187.

LAST QUARTER OF SEVENTEENTH CENTURY.

LONDON.

(Popish Plot, &c.)

SERIES of fifty-one card-pieces from a numeral set of fifty-two.
　　The card wanting is the four of diamonds.
　　This is a duplicate of the series last described (E. 186) relating
to the Popish Plot and the murder of Sir Edmond Berry Godfrey.
$3\frac{1}{2} \times 2\frac{1}{8}$ in.　　　　　　　　　　　　　　　　[Backs plain.]

E. 188.

(*Printed Books Department*, 1754. c.)

LAST QUARTER OF SEVENTEENTH CENTURY.

LONDON.

(Popish Plot, &c.)

SERIES of fifty-two numerals of the usual suits, but having the ace
of spades, the ace of clubs, the queen of hearts, and the knave of clubs
belonging to a different set.
　　The present is another sequence of the cards previously described
relating to the Popish Plot and the murder of Sir Edmond Berry Godfrey. E. 186.
E. 187.
　　The exceptional pieces, the two aces, the queen and the knave before men-
tioned, belong to a series to be presently described, illustrating the " Rye House
Plot."
　　These cards are contained in a folio volume (1754. c.), in which are several
prints and broadsides relating to persons and subjects of the time.
　　There are two titles in MS. to the volume, which run thus :—" A Pack of
cards of the reign of Charles 2nd, Engraved by Faithorne, Illustrating the Great
Fire of London, the horrid Popish Plot, Executions, Murder of Sir Edmondbury
Godfrey. London : 1684."
　　Facing the first title is a portrait bust of Charles II. in a large oval. He
looks towards the left. He wears a large wig, breastplate, slashed sleeves, collar
and tassels. Below are the royal arms with the inscription, " Carolus secundus
Dei Gratia Magnæ Britaniæ Franciæ et Hiberniæ Rex."
　　The print has been cut down, so that both painter's and engraver's names—if
they existed—have been removed.
　　Following the first title is " England's Mournful Elegy for the Dissolving
the Parliament ; " it consists of eighty-two lines, beginning with—

　　　　" Are all our hopes thus on a sudden dashed ?
　　　　Our trust confounded and rejoicings quashed."

And ends with—

> " Good counsel she doth on her sons bestow,
> Bids them be bold but not with rage to swell;
> Petition, pray and all their griefs to tell
> To Heaven and their King, but not rebel.
>
> London: printed for S. N."

On the following page are two woodcuts. One represents the execution of Thomas Venner (the religious enthusiast) and his disciples, in January, 1660-1661 (Grainger, vol. vi. p. 9), the other an attack by armed horsemen on the coach of Charles II.

On the opposite page is an impression from a copper-plate engraving of four card players sitting at table. Clubs are being played, the ace and four of the suit are out, and the five is shown in the hand of one of the party. A person is looking on, another is dancing and holding up a bag of money in his left hand, while a third person is sitting in a pensive mood at a side-table on which is a decanter and wineglass. Below is the couplet—

> " Who has the better Game still *Fears* the end,
> Who has the worst still *Hopes* his game will mend."

On the page opposite the folio containing the eight, nine, ten, &c., of spades, is a broadside entitled " Merlin revived; or an old prophecy, lately found in a manuscript in Pontefract Castle in Yorkshire."

The prophetic verses are divided into five sections, one section relating to A.D. 1650, another to 1660, a third to 1666, a fourth to 1680, and a fifth to 1682.

The verses commence—

> " When M D C shall join with L,
> In England things will not go well.
> A body shall without an head,
> Make all the neighbouring Nationes dread.
> The Lyon's whelps shall banished be,
> And seek their prey beyond the Sea;"

and end thus—

> " A triple league shall then be made
> And Rome of England be afraid;
> And he who lives till eighty three,
> All this to come to pass shall see."

On the *verso* of the folio last-mentioned is a printed sheet having the title, " A new *Ignoramus*, being the second new Song to the same old Tune, *Law lyes a Bleeding*." There are eight stanzas, of twelve lines each stanza, beginning—

> " Since Popish plotters
> Joined with Bogg-Trotters,
> *Sham-plots* are made as fast as pots are formed by potters,"

and concluding—

> " They sham us and flam us,
> They ram us and damn us,
> When, according to the Law, we find *Ignoramus*.
>
> London: printed for Charles Leigh, 1681."

On the *verso* of the next folio is " A Dialogue betwixt H. B.'s Ghost and his Dear Author R. L. S." The Ghost enters with—

> " Be not afraid, its kindness brings me here,
> And makes me leave a while the lower sphere,
> That I in time may warn thee of the wrong
> Done by thy scribbling pen and Lying tongue."

The conclusion is by R. S. in the following words :—" So he's gon ; I hope he'l now be quiet: This is, I think, the nine and thirtieth warning I have had and to as little purpose as all the rest, and so I'le let 'um know in my next pamphlet, which shall out as soon as I can agree with a Bookseller. 'Tis good to be true to one's principles.

> " Let ghosts talk what they will of Hell and Pain,
> From real pleasure they shan't me restrain
> The itch of scribbling and the sweet of Gain.
> Finis.   London : printed for J. M."

The volume concludes with another copy of the broadside, " Merlin revived ; or, an old prophecy Lately found in a manuscript in Pontefract Castle in Yorkshire."

To this copy are added in MS. the names of the persons alluded to and satirized under fictitious titles in the prophetic verses.   Thus—

" A *man of cole* shall plots design," is Coleman.

" When *Janock* and the *Truckle-Couch*," may be read, Dr. Oates and Bedloe.

" And when the *Valley of the Breast*," implies Dugdale.

" The *son of Jane* shall first relate," is Jannison.

> " An officer to tell his tale
> In wooden house shall hither sail,"

implies Serjeant who came from Flanders.

> " Through *Loop-hole* shall a Lawyer look,
> And *Vulcan's son* shall write a book ;
> A *Willow* to a *Field* shall change,
> And shew things dangerous and strange ;
> Then shall a *Price* be strongly pre
> To buy the *Valley of the Breast*,
> And *Mother-Midnight* shall declare
> She for religion will make war."

The names to be supplied are Reading, Smith, Willoughby *alias* Dangerfield, Mrs. Price, who would suborn Dugdale, and Mrs. Celair, a midwife.

To the following :
> " *Janock* shall go nigh to be slain,
> And *Knockt* down in a Dirty *Lane ;*
> But *Janock* shall escape at last
> And see the dangers he had past."

the comment is, " Dr. Oates was accused of Sodomy by one Knox and Lane."

> " Superstition shall have a fall,
> Its trinkets hung out *on a Wall*.
> The *Whore of Babylon's* attire
> Shall *by the Wall* be burnt ith' Fire,"

refers to Sir William Waller, who " burnt Papist garments."

In connection with—
> " Then from three there shall arise
> A flaming Meteor in the Skies,
> Which shall to England threat much Woe,
> And down the Miter overthrow,"

is the gloss, " The biggest Comett yt ever was seen on Dec: 1680.

All the MS. annotations present refer to the lines which include the year " MDCLXXX.—1680."

In connection with Titus Oates, reference should be made to the following prints and to the comments upon them in the first volume of the " Catalogue of prints relating to Political and Personal Satires," p. 615 *et seq.* Nos. 1073, 1078, 1134-1139, and 1142.

[Cards 3½ × 2⅛ in.]   [Backs plain.]

E. 189.

LAST QUARTER OF SEVENTEENTH CENTURY.

LONDON.

(RYE HOUSE PLOT.)

 SERIES of fifty-two numerals of the ordinary suits. It illustrates the conspiracy known as the "Rye House Plot." Each card-piece is occupied by a design connected with the history of the plot, and has below the requisite description. At the upper right-hand corner, in most instances, is the mark of the suit; sometimes the latter is placed at the left-hand corner. At the opposite upper corner is the value of the card in Roman numbers. The illustrative designs extend to the upper edge of the card-pieces; hence the marks and numbers are printed on the faces of the former. In the honours the titles are given in place of the Roman numbers.

Allusion is made to this series by Chatto, who observes: " Another pack of historical cards, apparently published in the same reign, but of inferior execution to the former (E. 186), appears to have related to the Rye House Plot. As these cards are even of greater rarity than those relating to the Popish Plot, the following description of four of them is here given as a stimulus to collectors." (p. 155.)

On account of the rareness of this sequence, a list of all the subjects illustrated in the order of the suits will be given here, premising that a consecutive historic order in the occurrence of the events has not been followed by the designer.

DIAMONDS.—Ace. Lord Shaftsbury going for Holland. Ferguson taking leave.

2. Walcot coming from Ireland.

3. Walcot and Ferguson coming from Holland.

4. The Counsell of Six sitting.

5. Colliford standing in the Pillory.

6. Rump Officers ready to take command on them.

7. Blunderbusses sent downe to Rumbold's House.

8. Walcot, Hone, and Rouse executed.

9. Walcot and other conspirators ready to charge ye King's Guards.

10. The designe of shooting the K^s Postilian.

Knave. Rumbold the Malster [who is exclaiming, " They shall dye "].

Queen. The designe of shooting into the K^s Coach.

King. The places mentioned for killing ye King [one conspirator names " Bedford Wall," a second " from Newmarket," a third " bull feast," and a fourth " downe ye river "].

HEARTS.—Ace. The King's declaration read in churches, 9th of Sept^{br}.

2. Goodenough and Nelthrop flying away in disguise.

3. Conspirators viewing the city and deviding it into 20 pr^s [one of the persons exclaims, " Wapping, &c., is ours "].

4. Dr. Smith sent into Scotland to invite comissinors [he exclaims, " I question not a Scott "].

5. Mon, Arms, and Grey viewing the Guards [one of them observes, " They may be seized "].

6. Lord Russell beheaded in Lincolne Inn Fields.

7. Hone and Rouse going to be executed.

8. Walcot going to be executed.

9. Rumbolds Houss.

T

10. Conspirators waiting for ye K. coming by Rumbole^{ds} House [one conspirator says to the other, " Faile not "].

Knave. Nelthrop [who exclaims, " here's a modell "].

Queen. Thompson, one of ye Conspirators, taken at Hamersmith.

King. E. of Essex cutting his throat in ye Tower.

CLUBS.—Ace. Keeling troubled in mind [he utters, " King killing is Damnable "].

2. West going downe to White hall.

3. Keeling going to the Ld Dart.

4. Keeling examined by Sr L. Jenkins.

5. C. Rumsey delivering himself [he exclaims, " I beg the King's mercy "].

6. Rumsey examined by the King and Councell.

7. West writing a Letter to Sr G. J. [he mutters, " I must discover all "].

8. Lord Grey apprehended.

9. Lord Grey making his escape.

10. Lord Grey sent Prisoner to the Tower.

Knave. Ferguson, the Independent Parson [who declaims, " Fight the Laird's battel "].

Queen. A conspirator overturning a cart to stop the King's coach.

King. The Lord Shaftsbury [he says, " Assist me freind "].

SPADES.—Ace. Hone taken prisoner at Cambridge.

2. Hone and Rouse sent Prisoners to Newgate.

3. The fire at New-Market.

4. Walcot taken in Southwarke.

5. Walcot sending a letter to Sr L. I.

6. Rumsey sent by Shaftsbury to the Consult at Sheaphard.

7. Lord Russell apprehended.

8. Ld Howard Writing an account of the Plot.

9. Walcot and Hone tryed at the Old Bayly.

10. Lord Russell tried at the Old Bayly.

Knave. Goodenough [he exclaims, " The Jury is ours "].

Queen. West bying of Armes.

King. Ferguson paying West £100.

The designs and technical execution of these cards are inferior in all respects to those of both E. 185 and E. 186. The impressions are from engraved metal plates, and are uncoloured.

The ace of spades, ace of clubs, queen of hearts, and knave of clubs of this set may be found making up deficiencies in the previous sequence of the Popish Plot, E. 188 (P. B. Dep. 1754 c.)

Reference may be made to No. 1129, in the first vol. of the " Catalogue of Prints relating to Political and Personal Satires."

[3½ × 2⅛ in.]   [Backs plain.]

E. 190.

LAST QUARTER OF SEVENTEENTH CENTURY.

LONDON.

(REIGN OF JAMES II.)

TWENTY-EIGHT cards from a numeral series of fifty-two of the ordinary suits.

The two and three of clubs, four, eight, nine, ten, and king of hearts, four, five, six, seven, eight, nine, ten, and knave of spades, and the two, three, five, six, seven, eight, nine, ten, and king of diamonds are wanting.

This sequence is intended to illustrate events during the reign of King James II. (1685-1688).

Each piece is occupied for the greater portion by an illustrative design, beneath which is its description. Above in a broad margin is the mark of the suit at the right-hand corner, and at the left the value of the piece is indicated in Roman numbers. The suit marks in hearts and diamonds are in simple outline, on the coate-cards the titles in large letters displace the Roman numbers.

The twenty-eight pieces here preserved relate to the following circumstances: —

CLUBS.—Ace. A new comishond Court for the inquier into the Ecclesiasticall Afairs.

4. About 200 ministers suspended in ye countey of Duram for not reading the Kings Declaration.

5. The Archbishop of Canterberey with 6 more Bishops Deliver a petishon to the King.

6. The Bishops are sent to the Tower by Watter.

7. The Bishops are cleared at their triall 2 of ye judges, were after displaced they giving for the Bishops.

8. The Keys of the Tower sent to the Lord Major.

9. Judg Harbert writing a book in Defence of the King's dispensing Power.

10. Oxford and Winchester Declared to be Desolved from being a bodey politik.

Knave. The French wayting an apertunity to Land in England, but are prevented by the Dutch.

Queen. The F. King and ye K. of Spain with other Princes ingaging to root out ye Northern herisey.

King. Comishoners sent into ye cuntry to perswade ye people to choose such men as shall take of ye pen^l Laws.

HEARTS.—Ace. The King leaving London about three a clock in the morning in his barge.

2. The King—— and with 2 more are stoped by rude Seamen being in an hoy by the Isle of Shipey.

3. The Chancellor taken in Wapping in Disguise.

5. The Chancellor going to the Tower, and is followed by many more of ye Brethren.

6. The Prince of Orange going into Exeter.

7. The Prince of Orange coming to St. Jameses, is received with great Joy.

Knave. The Queen and child and father Peters going away in the night.

Queen. A fight at Reding, wherein the Irish souldiers suffred most, the people firing out at window on them.

SPADES.—Ace. 500 thousand pounds sent from France yearly to Charls the 2 to keep the sitting of the Parliament of.

2. Severall persons sent to Newgate for murdering the E^l of Essex.

3. The Duches of Modena Presenting a wedge of gold to the Lady of Loreta that ye Q. might conceive a Son.

Queen. Severall firebauls found on severall persons in Southwark yet sum were cleared.

King. Strikt watch kept by the Inhabitants of London.

DIAMONDS.—Ace. Many witnesses sworn before a great body of ye Peers that ye child was a Lawfull Prince of Wales.

4. The Dutch flett put out to Sea, and are driven back by a Tempest.

Knave. The King coming from Salisbury, the Armie following in hast, the Enemy not being near.

Queen. The King going to Salisbury.

These card-pieces are poor in design, and are coarsely executed. They are from copper-plates, and are uncoloured.

The orthography is very bad.

[$3\frac{1}{2} \times 2\frac{1}{8}$ in.]   [Backs plain.]

E. 191.

FIRST QUARTER OF EIGHTEENTH CENTURY?

LONDON.

(Reign of James II. Rebellion, &c.)

FIFTY-TWO card-pieces of a numeral series of the usual suits. This series illustrates events of the reign of James II., more particularly such as relate to the attempts to restore Catholicism in England, and to the Rebellion which followed.

Each card is occupied in greater part by a design commemorating the events in question. Below is a description of the design, and above the latter in a broad margin is the mark of the suit at the left-hand corner, and the value of the piece at the right-hand corner in Roman numbers. In the coate-cards titles displace the value numbers at the right-hand corners. At the centre of the upper margin each card is marked with an Arabic numeral—the number going from one to fifty-two—indicating its place in the sequence of events.

The series begins with the knave of clubs—which represents the L⁴ Chancellor condeming Protestants in West.

CLUBS.—Ace (2). The Earle of Essex's throat cut.

Two (3). The inscription taken out of yᵉ monument.

Three (4). Oates whipt from Algate to Tyburn.

Four (5). Drinking the King's Health in the West, L⁴ Chᵉˢ, &c.

Five (6). Hanging Protestants in yᵉ West.

Six (7). Two Bᵖˢ and Judge Jenner speake rudely to Dʳ Huff [one of the Bishops exclaims, " I'le huff yᵉ Dʳ Huff for all your huff"]

Seven (9). The Tryal of the Seaven Bishops.

Eight (8). Magdalen Colledge Scholars turned out.

Nine (10). The Seaven Bishops going to the Tower.

Ten (12). Refuseing to assist at yᵉ Entrance of yᵉ Pope's Nuncio.

King (11). The Earle of Castlemain sent Embassador to yᵉ Pope.

Queen (13). The Midwife cutting her Husband to pieces.

SPADES. Ace (14). The Popish midwife putting his quarters in yᵉ Privy.

Two (15). The Popish midwife burning.

Three (16). Whiping Heresy out of Windsor chaple.

Four (17). The Procession of yᵉ Host through Sᵗ James's Park.

Five (18). Doing of Penance up a high hill with Peas in his Shoos.

Six (19). A Lady going to S Winifrids well for Penance.

Seven (22). Praying to yᵉ Lady of Loretto for a Prince of Wales to be born.

Eight (23). From Rome a consecrated smock.

Nine (25). Prince of Wales dressing by yᵉ Fire.

Ten (26). P. of Wales baptizd yᵉ Nuncio stands Godfather for yᵉ Pope.

Knave (20). A Jesuit preaching against our Bible [one of the audience exclaims, " You lie "].

Queen (21). Madam W—ks at Confession.

King (24). My Lord Chancellor at the Beds feet.

DIAMONDS.—Ace (39). T. Ellis in Grocers Ally entertaining his Friends [the host raising a glass in his right hand exclaims " to yᵉ P. of Orange."]

Two (38). Lime Street Chaple pulling down and burnt.

Three (37). Burning yᵉ Popish Chaple in Lincoln's Inn Fields.

Four (35). Bucklers Berry Popish Chaple burnt in the Stocks Market.

Five (34). The Prince of Orange coming to London.

Six (33). Father Peters burning his papers.

Seven (36). The Fight at Redding.

Eight (29). Mortar peices put upon the Tower.

Nine (30). The Prince of Orange Landing.

Ten (28). The Mass house at St. Jones's pulling it down, &c. [one of the destroyers calls out, " Capt. Tom "].

Knave (31). Singing of Mass thinking that the French had landed.

Queen (32). The Queen and Prince of Wales making their escape.

King (27). Prince of Wales giving audience.

HEARTS.—Ace (52). My Lord Chancellor in the Tower.

Two (51). L. P. taken in disguise going to Sea.

Three (50). A Papist of quallity taken at Wapping.

Four (49). A papist in disguise taken at yᵉ Tower.

Five (47). A preist marching off with bag and baggage.

Six (46). A preist hard very hard at Work.

Seven (45). A preist selling of Relicks by auction [he exclaims, " Thos. a Becket's old stockins 5s. once "].

Eight (42). Singing of Lilly bullero.

Nine (41). Cry yᵉ Prince of Orange's third Declaration.

Ten (40). The Army going over to yᵉ Prince of Orange.

Knave (48). Tyrconel arming yᵉ Papists in Ireland.

Queen (43). Singing O brave popery, delicate Popery, oh.

King (44). My Lᵈ Mayor & Sheriffs wait on yᵉ Prince at Windsor.

The designs on these card-pieces are in general good, as is also their technical execution. The orthography is better as a rule than in the previous series. The impressions are from engraved metal plates, and are uncoloured.

[3½ × 2⅜ in.]   [Backs plain.]

E. 192.

FIRST QUARTER OF EIGHTEENTH CENTURY.

LONDON.

(MARLBOROUGH AND HIS TIME.)

A SET of fifty-two numerals of the ordinary character. These cards illustrate the victories of Marlborough, and the political events of his time. Satirical designs relating to the contemporary history of France and Germany are also included.

Each piece is chiefly occupied by an illustration, having its description below.

The suit mark is above at the right-hand corner, and the value of the piece is shown by Roman numbers at the left-hand upper corner.

The marks and values have been engraved on the field of the compositions, not any separate margin having been retained for them.

Some of the compositions are of a very curious character, perhaps more being attempted to be conveyed in them than in the designs of any of the other politico-historical cards.

The following pieces may be cited as worthy of particular notice :—

Ace of Spades.—The French King (Louis XIV.) is in bed, three large cats are on the floor of the chamber. Below is the following inscription :

" The French King's Dream. The fat cat denotes the Partisans fatten'd with ye substance of ye nation, ye lean cat ye People of France exhausted by heavy Impositions, and ye blind cat ye K^s Councel who are at their witts end."

Queen of Spades.—Represents the French King and Madame de Maintenon driving turkeys. From the King's mouth, " How do you sell your Turkeys now " ? and from Madame de Maintenon, " To ye old trade again."

Below the composition may be read—

> " At first dishonest when I Turkeys fed,
> Little I thought t' enjoy a Monarchs bed,
> But now ye dotard's glutted with a baddy reign
> I may to Turkey keeping go again."

Two of Clubs.—Represents the siege of Dendermond, below which is: " Septr ye 5, 1706, Dendermond surrenders to General Churchill his Grace ye Prince and D. of Marlboros Brother."

Three of Clubs.—" The French abandon Ghent at the approach of Marlb'ro, June 2, 1706."

Eight of Clubs.—" The Duke of Marlboro obliges Limburg to surrender at discretion, Sept. 28, 1705."

Ten of Diamonds.—Here is represented " The Battle of Ramillies, where ye D. of Marlborough, &c. took 26 standards and 63 ensigns, the French loosing 20,000 men, all their Baggage, Ammunition, &c."

Eight of Diamonds.—" The Burgomasters and Magistrates of Brussells present the D. of Marlborough with ye Keys of ye City in a Gold Bason, Oct. 27, 1706."

Ace of Hearts.—Exhibits Queen Anne in a triumphal chariot, the horses of which are trampling on the arms, crown, and insignia of the King of France and the Pope. Below are the lines—

> " As ye bright chariot of the quickening Sun
> Dos over noisome Clouds and Vapours run,
> So mighty Anne on Victory dos ride,
> And tramples down ye Pope's and tyrant's Pride."

On the ace of clubs is an equestrian portrait of " Joseph, Emperour of Germany, born July 16, 1678."

On the ten of clubs is a portrait bust of " Prince Eugene of Savoy, born October 18, 1663."

The queen of clubs presents a large portrait bust of " Anne by ye Grace of God, of Great Britain, France, and Ireland, Queen Defender of ye Faith."

On the king of clubs is the companion portrait of " Charles III. King of Spain, born October 1^s, 1685."

While the queen of diamonds presents us with " The Princess Roy^l of Prussia."

The last cards of the sequence are the king and queen of hearts. On the first piece is a portrait bust of " His Royal Highness, George, Prince of Denmark," born 1653. On the second, one of " The most Illustrious Anna Sophia of Hannover, born 1630."

The impressions are from engraved metal plates, the technic of which, is laboured, and heavy, and but of mediocre character. The cards are uncoloured.

[$3\frac{3}{8}$ × $2\frac{2}{8}$ in.]   [Backs plain.]

E. 193.

FIRST QUARTER OF EIGHTEENTH CENTURY.

LONDON.

(MARLBOROUGH AND HIS TIME.)

SERIES of fifty-two numerals of the usual suits. These cards illustrate the victories of Marlborough, and the events—both domestic and foreign—of his time.

This set is a duplicate of that last described (E. 192).

[3⅜ × 2⅞ in.]   [Backs plain.]

E. 194.

(Prints relating to Political and Personal Satires, No. 1546.)

FIRST QUARTER OF EIGHTEENTH CENTURY.

LONDON, 1710.

SERIES of twenty-six card-pieces of the suits of hearts and diamonds, engraved on a single sheet, 17⅛ in. wide by 14 in. high.

The greater portion of each piece is occupied by a design illustrating some event in the career of Dr. Sacheverell. Below is a couplet referring to the design above. At the upper right-hand corner of each piece is the representation of a diminutive playing-card of the ordinary kind.

On the two of diamonds Dr. Sacheverell is shown in his coach, attended by a crowd which cheers him ; below is the verse—

" Others would swell with pride if thus cares'd,
But he bears humble thoughts within his breast."

The ace of hearts exhibits Dr. Sacheverell walking towards a pulpit, and below the lines—

" From hence the Church's restoration rose,
And made Discovery of her secret Foes."

The knave of hearts represents Mr. Dolben, son of a former Archbishop of York, presenting the Articles of Impeachment against Dr. Sacheverell to the House of Lords. Below may be read—

" Here an Archbishop's son yᵉ Church impeaches,
Whose sire, if living, would abhor such speeches."

A detailed account of each of these twenty-six card-pieces may be found in the second volume of the " Catalogue of Prints relating to Political and Personal Satires," p. 332, No. 1546. The impressions are from copper-plates. The designs and technic are of mediocre character. The card-pieces are uncoloured.

[3⅜ × 2⅞ in.]   [Backs plain.]

E. 195.

SECOND HALF OF SEVENTEENTH CENTURY.

LONDON ? HOLLAND ?

(Rump Parliament.)

SET of photographs from a numeral series of fifty-two card-pieces of the ordinary character.

The rare originals from which these photographs were taken were presented by Thaddeus Hyatt, Esq., of Gloucester Gardens, Hyde Park, to the late Hon. Charles Sumner, of Boston, U.S., in the possession of whose executors these cards now are, it is believed. Before they left England these photographs were allowed to be executed, as records for the National Collection by permission of Mr. T. Hyatt.

A pack of the original cards was exhibited before the Archæological Association by Mr. S. L. Tucker in 1854, on which a paper was read by Mr. Pettigrew, to be found in the "Journal of the British Archæological Association," vol. ix. pp. 121, 308, 1854. Mr. Pettigrew remarked on the originals before the Association, that "These cards are to be considered as belonging to a political game, and are especially illustrative of the Rump Parliament and the private actions and conduct of several of the individuals most conspicuous during the Commonwealth. The nature of the subject clearly fixes the period to which they belong. They must be assigned to the time of Charles II., and it may be presumed that they were executed in Holland, and that they formed a source of amusement to the royalists at the Hague during that sovereign's residence in that country, on the captivity and execution of his father. The history of them, as far as I have been able to obtain it, is but meagre. They were purchased by the late — Prest, Esq., of Connaught Place. He obtained them at the Hague, for the sum of thirty-five guineas, of a gentleman who stated that they had descended in his family from the time of their fabrication, and they have been in Mr. Prest's family for upwards of thirty years. It is not a little singular that no other copy is known, and that hitherto no notice of such a pack has appeared. As an addition, therefore, to the materials of the history of playing-cards, a description of these, illustrated by historical notes and references, may not be inappropriate in the pages of our *Journal*, and useful to future labourers in this branch of inquiry.

"The pack consists of fifty-two cards, measuring $3\frac{1}{2}$ in. in length by 2 in. in breadth. They are engraved on copper, and their execution exhibits no deficiency of talent on the part of the artists employed. The suits are marked, and the number of the suit on the upper corners of the cards, and the description of the subject occupying the body of the card is engraved at the bottom."

Mr. Pettigrew's paper is accompanied by copies of eight of the original cards. On the first sheet is given the eight of diamonds, which represents " Don Haselrig K^t of ye coddled braine ;" the nine of diamonds, showing how " Lenthall runs away with his Mace to the Army ;" the queen of diamonds illustrating " the takeing of the Holy League and Covenant ;" and the five of hearts, portraying " The E. of Pem. in ye H. of Com. thanks ye Speaker for his admission."

On the second sheet are the seven of hearts, representing " Nathaniel Fines, whereby hangs a tale ;" the eight of hearts, having a full-length figure of " Lambert, K^t of y^e Golden Tulip ;" the knave of the same suit, whereon " Hugh Peters shews the bodkins and thimbles given by the wives of Wappin for the good old cause ;" and the five of spades, where stand figured " Nye and Godwin, Oliver's Confessors."

[$3\frac{3}{8}$ × 2 in.]   [Backs plain ?]

E. 196.

LAST QUARTER OF EIGHTEENTH CENTURY.

LONDON.

 SMALL sheet, $8\frac{1}{8} \times 9\frac{6}{8}$ in. wide, having engraved on it a knave and a king, between which is an ordinary figure in Oriental costume, kneeling on one leg, and holding a diamond (card suit mark) up in each hand towards the figure on each side of him.

The king is in profile and in the usual conventional card-costume of the time, but the face is intended to be a portrait of George III. The knave has a three-quarter face—a portrait of Lord Chancellor Thurlow—looking towards the king and the diamond held by the central figure. The knave wears a large wig and broad hat. Below the coate-card, the king, is engraved "Geo. III.," below the knave, " Thurlow," while beneath the central figure may be read " Hastings."

At the base of the sheet is the inscription, " Court cards the best to deal with." At the right-hand corner is the address, " BOYNE. Price 3^s. the P^r. col^d."

The impressions are from aquatinta plates, and are strongly marked and coloured. On the *verso* of the sheet is written in MS. " Pub^d. Feb. 8th. 1788, for S. Doughty and Co. No. 19 Holborn, London."

See Taylor Bibl. 9, pp. 433, 520.

$[3\frac{5}{8} \times 2\frac{1}{2}$ in.] [Backs plain.]

SATIRICAL.

E. 197.

FIRST QUARTER OF EIGHTEENTH CENTURY.

LONDON.

 SERIES of thirty-four cards from a numeral set of fifty-two pieces of the usual character. The cards wanting are the four, five, six, seven, eight, nine, ten, knave, queen, and king of spades, and the ace, two, three, four, five, six, seven, and eight of diamonds. This sequence is of a satirical character. Each of its members is occupied by a figure subject, having its explanation in verse below the design. Above at the left-hand corner is a representation of a small playing card of the ordinary kind. The small coate-cards are of the conventional forms.

On the nine of diamonds five ladies are represented in a saloon seated at a card-table. Two cards are displayed, one is an ace. Below is the couplet—

" Whilst fields of blood ye Heroes do delight,
The Fair at Oumber wast ye tedious night."

On the ten of diamonds the interior of a shop is exhibited ; articles of plate are on the shelves, and a dice-box and dice are on the counter, by which stand two ladies and a gentleman. Below may be read—

" At Epsom oft these Rafflings I have seen
But assignation's w^t they cheifly mean."

On the knave of the same suit a quack, standing on a platform, is exhibiting and praising his nostrum before a crowd. The accompanying lines are—

" Give me the gold cryes quack heres my Pills,
You think for cure, no, to increase your Ills."

On the four of clubs a ruined gambler is returning in despair from a club-house. He has thrown down on the ground cards, dice-box, and dice. A jeering companion is holding a money-bag towards him and exclaiming—

" You seem to be craisy at y[e] loss of your coin,
If you want money take some of mine."

On the king of clubs are shown a man and his wife dancing together; a fiddler is playing to them; on a table is an overturned empty wine-jug, by which stands a large glass. Below is the couplet—

" A well matched pair they'l never freet,
For a pound of greif woint pay an ounce Debt."

On the four of hearts is a lady petting a parrot, and the lines—

" Phillis thy lovers I'm affraid have left you,
That Poll's so much in favour to divert thee."

On the five of hearts is a widow being visited by a female friend; they are taking a glass of cordials together, while the latter exclaims—

" No more wth deep Concern y[e] dead lament,
A living Husband's w[t] we Ladys want."

The ten of hearts shows us Jupiter descending on an eagle towards a seated woman; below is the verse—

" Jove for a mistres down to Earth does come,
And like a london Rake leaves his poor wife alone."

On the three of spades may be seen four billiard-players engaged at their amusement; the accompanying lines are—

" Think not a lossing gamester will be fair
Who at y[e] best ne're play'd upon the square."

Mr. Chatto alludes to these satirical pieces, observing—

" A pack of satirical cards, belonging to W. H. Diamond, Esq. Frith Street, Soho, appears to have been executed about the same time (Reigns of Queen Anne and King George I.) All the subjects are coarsely engraved, though some of them display points of character very much in the style of Hogarth.

" In the ten of spades a Moorfields Quack is seen pointing to his sign, with the inscription—

' To famed Moorfields I dayly do repair,
Kill worms, cure itch, and make y[e] ladies fair.'

" In the ace of diamonds a lady is seen showing her palm to a fortune-teller, with the inscription—

' How can you hope this Gipsey drabb should know
The Fates' decrees and who was made for you.'

" In the four of diamonds a lady is seen exchanging some of her clothes for china ware with an itinerant dealer. The inscription is—

" Your pockets madam surely are wondrous bare,
To sell your very clothes for china ware.' (p. 158.)

In the pack alluded to by Mr. Chatto there was a red duty stamp on the ace of spades; it is not present here.

[3⅜ × 2⅞ in.]   [Backs plain.]

E. 198.

(Prints of Political and Personal Satires, vol. i. No. 81.)

FIRST QUARTER OF SEVENTEENTH CENTURY.

LONDON.

SATIRICAL print representing James I., Henry IV. of France, Prince Maurice (Stadtholder), and Christian IV. of Denmark, playing at cards and backgammon against the Pope and his ecclesiastical brethren. King Henry is playing a trump card—the ace of hearts ; his antagonist, a monk, having the knave only. A five of hearts is displayed upon the table as mark of the trump suit.

This print bears at its upper margin the title of " The Revells of Christen-dome." At the lower right-hand corner is " T. Cocksonus Sculp."

The lower portion of the sheet is occupied by forty-eight lines of verse, in four columns of twelve lines each. Below these is the address, " Sould by Mary Oliver in Westminster Hall."

Thomas Cockson, the engraver of this print, flourished *circa* 1620 ; his better works, at least, are dated 1620-1630.

" He worked exclusively with the graver in a neat, finished, stiff manner, and engraved a great variety of portraits, among them of James I. sitting in Parliament, his daughter, the Princess Elizabeth, Charles I. in Parliament, Louis XIII., Mary de Medicis, also the ' Revels of Christendom,' and some pieces with shipping." (Redgrave " Dictionary of Artists of the English School," p. 87.)

The " Revels of Christendome" was probably " of German origin, and published in 1609, when England and France were negotiating the peace between the United Provinces and Spain. This peace was a severe blow to the Pope, and Maurice was watching the game which promised so much benefit to his country. See ' Royal and Ecclesiastical Gamesters,' No. 101, 1626, which was imitated from this print." (Catalogue of Prints, &c., relating to " Political and Personal Satires," vol. i. p. 42, No. 81, where this piece is described in detail.)

[13⅞ × 8⅜ in.]

E. 198. 2.

SEVENTEENTH CENTURY.

REDUCED copy with several alterations of the piece just described. Four verses in Dutch displace all other inscriptions. The technic is of an inferior character to that of E. 198.

[10⅝ × 7⅞ in.]

E. 199.

(Prints of Political and Personal Satires, vol. i. No. 101.)

SECOND QUARTER OF SEVENTEENTH CENTURY.

LONDON (1626).

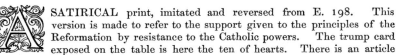 SATIRICAL print, imitated and reversed from E. 198. This version is made to refer to the support given to the principles of the Reformation by resistance to the Catholic powers. The trump card exposed on the table is here the ten of hearts. There is an article on this print in the "Gentleman's Magazine" for July, 1853. The print is also fully described in the first volume of the "Catalogue of Prints relating to Political and Personal Satires," page 61, No. 101.

[14⅘ × 10⅔ in.]

E. 200.

(Prints of Political and Personal Satires, vol. i. No. 1033.)

THIRD QUARTER OF EIGHTEENTH CENTURY.

LONDON.

PRINT executed in aqua tinta, representing "Hans Buling, a mountebank of great notoriety, who frequently exhibited in Covent Garden." The design is copied from a Delft dinner-plate, on the back of which are the initials "B. S. 1750." The centre of the plate is occupied by Buling with a monkey, &c. Coming towards him, as he enters from the left, is a harlequin grotesquely draped. On the broad edge of the plate are four groups of playing-cards, two groups containing four cards each group, and two having five cards. Immediately below the inferior margin of the plate is the address: "I. R. Cruickshank fecit."

This piece is described in the first volume of the "Catalogue of Prints relating to Political and Personal Satires," p. 584, No. 1033.

[10 × 8⅚ in.]

E. 201.

(Prints of Political and Personal Satires, vol. ii. No. 1407.)

FIRST QUARTER OF EIGHTEENTH CENTURY.

LONDON.

 LARGE woodcut with letterpress, coloured in red, crimson, and blue, representing "A prodigal sifted and found out in his several Debaucheries. With a lively representation of the many inconveniences and trains of Evils attending Idleness, Tipling, Gaming, and Drunkenness, &c."

The composition represents a room, on the walls of which hang pictures of the evil events in the life of the prodigal. Among these, gambling is portrayed on the fourth design from the left. The prodigal is being held on a large sieve by his father and mother, through the meshes of which his actions are being sifted. As the latter fall, cards and dice, among other symbols of prodigality, may be observed. The ace of hearts and the three of clubs are displayed. The kneeling and repentant prodigal is supposed to exclaim—

> "Pardon, dear Parents, and I'll tell the truth,
> What I have done in my debauched Youth."

The print is stated to have been "Published in Love to those concerned, and recommended to them as a tender caution to avoid the same excess. London: Sold in Aldermary Church yard."

This piece is described in the second volume of the "Catalogue of Prints relating to Political and Personal Satires," p. 153, No. 1407.

[$17\frac{1}{2} \times 12\frac{5}{8}$ in.]

E. 202.

SECOND HALF OF EIGHTEENTH CENTURY.

LONDON.

A SHEET of eight card-pieces, representing caricatured figures of well-known personages. Two figures in the lower row are designed as knaves; the first, directed towards the left hand, is entitled "Monsr le Dupe," the other, turned to the right, is "Monsr Sure Card," the name "Fox" being at the upper right-hand corner, and the knave's face fox-like in character. Above these knaves are caricature representations of Fox and Welbore Ellis. Fox is exclaiming, as he marches to the left, "Military Government—no Militia," while he holds in his left hand papers marked "Irish Reversions," "Peerages," "1400 in Agent." Welbore Ellis, with a drum, cries out, "No, no Militia, by Gad." A figure of S. Anson follows; he remarks, "Deep play this, or nothing." Winchelsea succeeds, muttering, "I'll walk on over to Germany." In the lower row are a statue of "Cumberland" beneath an architectural canopy, and a figure of an armed man standing on a prostrate skeleton, which points at him a dart. A bag, from which money has escaped, lies in the foreground of the latter composition.

The *fleurs-de-lys* on the ground of the two knaves are noteworthy. The impressions are from etched plates of a soft metallic character, and are uncoloured.

[Knaves, $3\frac{1}{2} \times 2\frac{2}{8}$ in.]　　　　　　　　　　　　[Backs plain.]

AMUSING.

E. 203.

LATTER PART OF SEVENTEENTH CENTURY.

LONDON.

 PACK of fifty-two numerals of the usual suits, the honours having on them full-length costume figures. The suit marks are placed upon the cards in the ordinary positions, those of spades and clubs being engraved, those of hearts and diamonds being stamped in red colour. On the general face of the card various animals with landscape backgrounds are represented.

Accompanying the series are two supplementary pieces, on which is engraved the following inscription : " The Use. These cards of all sorts of Birds and Beasts are very ingeniously contrived, and very diverting to young Gentlemen and Ladys who are Lovers of ingenuity. The suites of Harts and Diamonds contain all sorts of Birds. The Clubbs and Spades all sorts of Beasts. Sold by John Lenthall, stationer, at ye Talbot, agst St Dunstan's church in Fleet Street, London. Where are sold the severall Fine Sorts of Pictured Cards following, viz : The Whole World described, each card being a compleat map, neatly engraved and corrected by ye best Geographers, &c."

A few of these card-pieces are of a somewhat amusing character, *e. g.* the ten of spades has on it a " cat a fidling and mice a dancing." On the four of spades is represented " Orpheus playing to the Wild Beasts." On the two of clubs is an unicorn, while on other pieces bulls are fighting, bears are being hunted, &c.

Lenthall, the publisher of these cards, carried on business at the before-mentioned address from 1665 to 1685. He professed to be related to William Lenthall, speaker of the House of Commons-during the Long Parliament (1641-1653), which opposed Charles I. at the beginning of 1642. This, however, did not prevent him, as Taylor remarks, from figuring " one-eyed Hewson " as the knave of clubs, accoutred in a leather apron, in allusion to his original trade of a cobbler, the subject of many a satire in the songs of the Cavaliers.

> " And here are old Noll's brewing vessels,
>   And here are his dray and his slings,
> Here are Hewson's awl and his bristles,
>   With diverse other odd things."

(" The Sale of Rebellious Household Stuff," Percy's Reliques, ii. b. iii. 14.)

See Taylor, Bibl. 9, p. 209, and " Journal of the Archæological Association," vol. ix. p. 316, concerning " Huson the Cobbler."

The duty stamp in red is placed on the ace of spades, above the head of the lion thereon represented. Taylor has a note to the following effect : " After the 11th of June, 1711, for thirty-two years, the Act directs there shall be a duty on each pack of cards made of sixpence, and one of the cards stamped on the spotted side, as the commissioner of stamp duties shall direct, under a penalty of £5. Lenthall's cards, however, which were certainly before 1685, bear a red stamp with a crown, and that sum stamped over the design on the ace of spades, as do also more than one other pack of that period mentioned in the course of this history." (*Op. cit.* p. 225.) Though the *crown* can be made out on the present ace of spades, the inscription above it is not apparent.

The designs on these cards are bad, and the execution of them is of a very inferior character. The impressions are from metal plates, and are coloured occasionally in a most absurd manner. Around each piece is an ornamental frame-like border. The names of the animals delineated are placed above the latter, often a very necessary procedure for their due recognition.

$[3\frac{1}{2} \times 2\frac{2}{8}$ in.] [Backs plain.]

E. 204.

LAST QUARTER OF EIGHTEENTH CENTURY.

 PACK of fifty-two numerals of the usual kind. Each card has the suit mark stamped at the upper right-hand corner, of a size much larger than the design traced out by the engraver. The value of the piece is indicated by Roman numbers at the left-hand upper corner. On the honours the titles are engraved at the tops of the pieces in the centre.

The greater portion of each card is occupied by an engraved design, mostly of a laughable or grotesque character, intended to illustrate some humorous proverb which is inscribed below. For example, on the five of clubs a woman has rushed into a house in search of her daughter, whom she discovers in a cupboard bed-place. In the room are a man's hat and cloak on a stool. Below the design is the following proverb : " The old woman had never lookd in the oven for her Daughter had she not been there herselfe." The five of spades illustrates the saying : " Every one as they like, said the old woman when she kissed her cow." On the nine of spades is a party drinking, fiddling, and dancing, to the proverb : " An ounce of mirth is worth a pound of sorrow." On the eight of diamonds are portrayed women and geese quarrelling, below may be read : " Where there are women and geese there wants noe noise." The king of diamonds exhibits three persons in doctors' robes at a table, above which are books on a shelf, below are the words : " If you'l avoid old Charon, the fferry man, consult Dr. Dyett, Dr. Quiett, and Dr. Merryman." The design on the five of diamonds shows the devil sitting by a cauldron over a fire, from which he has taken a bowl of soup, and with which he regales himself. Cautiously approaching the bowl on the devil's knees is a man with a long-handled spoon, by which he trusts to obtain a mouthful of the savoury potage ; below is the proverb : " A good stomach is the Best Sawce." This has not appeared to some former possessor of the cards to be sufficiently to the point so he has written the following around the foregoing motto : " There's need of a long spoon to eat with the devil." The proverb illustrated on the eight of hearts is the following : " He y^t Letts his wife go to every wake, and his Horse drinke at every Lake, sháll never be without a Jilt and a Jade."

One or two of the compositions are of a gross and repulsive kind. All are uncoloured, and mostly poor in design and technical execution.

$[3\frac{1}{2} \times 2\frac{2}{8}$ in.] [Backs plain.]

E. 205.

FIRST QUARTER OF NINETEENTH CENTURY.

LONDON.

SERIES of fifty-two numerals of the usual suits.

The card-pieces composing this sequence are of artistic as well as of amusing character. Each member of it exhibits one or more figures and accessories with good architectural backgrounds. The subjects illustrated are of very varied and opposite kinds. Egyptian, classic, Gothic themes occur; events in ancient and mediæval history, of the modern stage, and pantomimes.

The full-length figures on the coate-cards are carefully coloured, the kings having a crown above the mark of the suit, which is placed at the upper right-hand corner. The designs, composition, drawing, and engraving on these card-pieces have been well studied and carefully executed. The technic is chiefly in the stippled, dotted, or Bartolozzi manner.

This set is alluded to by Chatto, Boiteau D'Ambly, and Taylor. The latter gives two illustrations from it, accompanied by the following remarks :—

"Specimens of pictorial cards designed by a Viennese artist, and published four at a time in the 'Repository of Arts' for 1818-19, and as a pack afterwards, two editions of which are in the Paris library. We should need the entire set to be engraved to give a full idea of the variety of the very original and fantastic designs on these cards—knights in armour, Eastern warriors, figures of the classic mythology, scenes from modern tales and dramas, costumes of every age and clime, well drawn, and displaying great versatility of talent, but with no apparent order or object, and crowded with accessories of every conceivable kind, in which the marks of the suits are introduced in the most ingenious manner possible. The descriptions in the original work are by the late J. B. Papworth, Esq., architect,[1] from which we extract the one explanatory of Plate xxxii.

"The six of diamonds represents the characters of a pantomime, and the several personages of the scene will be easily recognised. The emaciated and decrepit debauchee is still assuming the gallant, and mixing the habiliments of the soldier with the airs and manners of a youthful *petit maître*. He is gazing on a distant lady, while she whom he vainly fancies he possesses in perfect security, is bestowing her favours on the first idiot that solicits them. The female is wantonly attired, and holding in her right hand a mask, the emblem of her duplicity, and from the other arm suspends a ridicule, the type of her condescensions. The diamond forms an ornament to a fan, ridicules and the furniture of the apartment. The descriptions of the two succeeding contain no more than the prints themselves will suggest. Only the marks of suits are coloured, and even this hardly redeems them from the charge of being too indistinct for use." (Bibl. 9, p. 181.)

These card-pieces are of very limp texture, large in size, and undecorated backs.

[$3\frac{5}{8} \times 2\frac{1}{2}$ in.]   [Backs plain.]

---

[1] John Buonarotti Papworth, who, on the establishment of the Government School of Design in 1837, was appointed director. He fitted up and arranged the schools. ("A Dictionary of Artists of the English School," &c., by Samuel Redgrave. London : 1874.)

E. 206.

SECOND QUARTER OF EIGHTEENTH CENTURY.

LONDON.

(*Musical.*)

A SERIES of forty-eight cards from a set of fifty-two of the ordinary suits.

The pieces here absent are the ten of spades, the four and eight of diamonds, and the four of clubs.

This sequence is composed of musical cards. Most of the pieces have on them four lines of music, commencing at the top; following these is a verse of a song, to which succeeds two more lines of music, for accompaniment by the flute. Between the upper lines of music are words of the song, of which the verse in the centre of the card is a continuation.

A few of the cards have eight lines of music with accompanying words, in place of six lines, and verse in the centre. The lower lines are of flute accompaniment.

At the upper left-hand corner of each piece is the representation in miniature of an ordinary playing card. The designs on the honours are of the conventional character, and are uncoloured. The whole designs, music and words, are from neatly engraved copper-plates. The orthography is often very bad. The duty stamp of "vi Pence" has been impressed in red on the ace of spades, immediately on the small card design at the upper left-hand corner.

The king of spades commences the series, to the music and words of "The First King:"

> " When Adam was the King of Spades,
>   And Eve his wife did sew ;
> Then delving was the best of Trades,
>   No pride no Fraud they knew."

The queen of the same suit follows to the tune, &c., of "The Fair Jade," and the knave to that of the "Miser."

The other cards of the suit produce the "Fair Ingrate," "Little Jeny," "Dispairing Lover," "Lovers' Resolution," "All Must Love," "Pritty Cloe," "Dying Lover," "Advice to Celia," and "Vain Pursuit."

In the suit of diamonds, the king appears under the aspect of "True Lover," assuring his beloved that

> " Not all the Diamonds, all the gold
> That all the Mines on Earth can hold,
> Should tempt me to resign my right
> To the my Diamond, my Delight."

The queen represents "The Lover's Treasure;" and from the knave, who is Jack Shepherd, we learn that

> " The People lament, alack and alack,
> 'Twas pity to hang up their Favourite Jack ;
> For Britains hate thinking, and all would be dumb,
> But for Shepherd and Faux, Faustus, Wild, and Tom Thumb."

U

The pip-cards of the suit of diamonds have on them " The Fool's Thought," " The Fickle Lover," " A Merry Song," " The Critical Minute," " Damon and Phillis," " Bright Cloe," " Coy Celia," and " The Jovial Soul."

The king of clubs appears as Sir Oliver Rant, and—

> " Sir Oliver Rant is a Terrible fellow,
> He drives all before him when'er he is Mellow ;
> He Scowers the Watch, and he ranges the Town,
> And all that resist him he strait knocks 'em down.

> " The Baliffs and Marshalls men dare not come nigh him,
> Free masons and Mollies and Schemers all fly him ;
> The Bullies he kicks and their Harlots he drubs,
> And all round ye Hundreds he's cal'd King of Clubs."

The queen is the " Bewitching Charmer," and the knave all " Contradiction."

Then follow " No Fault in Loving," " Cupid's Snare," " Jovial Toper," " Drinking Song," " Faithful Love," " Sally's Dart," " Love for Love," " Lover's Wish," " Brisk Joan."

In hearts, the king shows Cupid's dart useless ; but the queen supplies the refrain of a " Broken Heart :"

> " Oh what Heart but needs must yield,
>   When like Pallas you advance,
> With a Thimble for your shield,
>   And a Needle for your Lance.
> Fairest of the Stitching Train,
>   Ease my Passion by thy Art ;
> And in pity to my Pain,
>   Mend the hole that's in my Heart."

The " Sly Knave " succeeds, followed by " The Faithful Lover," " The Unconstant Lover," " Tender Heart," " The Happy Swain," " Young Damon," " Beauteous Celia," " Dejected Cloe," " Charming Cloe," " Sly Cloe," and the " True Lover," who wisely concludes the general lament,

> " I'll hast to some far distant shore,
> And never, never, never, never think of Woman more."

[$3\frac{6}{8} \times 2\frac{3}{8}$ in. without margin.]   [Backs plain.]

E. 207.

FIRST QUARTER OF NINETEENTH CENTURY.

LONDON.

SERIES of fifty-one cards from a numeral set of fifty-two of the ordinary suits. The ace of spades is here absent. The designs are of a humorous character. The marks of the suits of clubs and spades are in white, on a deep blue ground. Within each mark a grotesque face is etched in imitation of a pen-and-ink drawing. The diamonds and hearts are on a light madder-coloured ground, and treated in a similar manner. The coate-cards are the king, queen, and knave of conventional character, with laughable expressions in their faces. A printed title-card accompanies this set, which is described as composed of "Imperial Royal Playing-Cards," and as being of a serious and Historic character!

The discrepancy which exists between the description of the cards and their actual character, can only be explained by assuming that a wrong supplementary descriptive card has become accidentally attached to the series.

The latter was published by "S and J. Fuller, at the Temple of Fancy, No. 34, Rathbone Place."

The cards are stiff, and marked on the backs with large stars, made up of dull red spots.

On the whole they form a very poor effort, whether as relates to design or execution.

[$3\frac{5}{8} \times 2\frac{1}{2}$ in.]   [Backs decorated.]

CARDS PURELY FANCIFUL.

E. 208.

LAST QUARTER OF EIGHTEENTH CENTURY.

LONDON.

TWELVE card-pieces of emblematic character.

In the centre of each piece on a large shield, the emblematic object is represented. Above the shield is the crest of the Prince of Wales; a motto scroll, curtain-like drapery and palm branches are other accessories. On the lower part of each card is a verse of four lines, referring to the emblem above.

The designs and inscriptions are from engraved copper-plates, the former being coloured. Each card has a yellow border between engraved lines.

A wrapper, with engraved ornamental title, accompanies the set. It bears the following inscription within a large oval, surmounted by the crest of the Prince of Wales:—"Wallis's Emblematical Cards for the Amusement of Youth. London. Published Sept. 15th, 1788, by J. Wallis, No. 16, Ludgate Street, J. Binny, Leeds, and L. Bull, Bath. Price one Shilling, neatly coloured."

Card No. 1 has on it a crown for the emblem. Below is the verse:—

> "Crowns are ambitious gilded toys,
>   As blessings never meant,
> Know that the greatest Joys on Earth,
>   Are plenty and Content."

On No. 2 is a clock; below which is:—

> "The Clock a daily monitor,
>   Points to each passing Hour,
> And bids you well employ the time
>   Which now is in your pow'r."

No. 3 has a ship, No. 4 an anchor, No. 5 a cannon, No. 6 a basket of flowers, No. 7 a horn, No. 8 a guitar, No. 9 a harlequin, No. 10 a rocking horse, No. 11 a kite, and No. 12 a boy with a whipping-top.

Below each emblem are appropriate lines.

Though devoid of any artistic merit, the designs have been neatly and carefully engraved.

[$3\frac{1}{2} \times 2\frac{1}{2}$ in.]   [Backs plain.]

E. 209.

THIRD QUARTER OF NINETEENTH CENTURY.

LONDON.

 SERIES of forty-five card-pieces, nine of which have text alone on them, the rest have full-length figures of historical personages.

A descriptive pamphlet accompanies the sequence, which is entitled " The Royal Historical Game of Cards, invented by Miss Jane Roberts. London. Robert Hardwicke, 26, Duke Street, Piccadilly, and all Booksellers."

After " Directions for playing the Game," " the inventor hopes that this Simple Division of the thirty-five reigns, or thirty-six periods of English History, between the nine centuries which have elapsed since the Conquest, will enable the players with a little practice to remember the exact line of succession to the British Throne."

The figures are in the assumed costume of their times ; the designs and proportions of the former are often of very inferior character.

Printed with bronze powder. The backs of these cards were marked by deep blue and light red lines, forming bands running across the card diagonally.

[4 × 2½ in.]   [Backs decorated.]

E. 210.

SECOND QUARTER OF NINETEENTH CENTURY.

ROMSEY.

SERIES of fifty pieces, having historical problems in printed text on them, which have to be solved by the players. Two supplementary cards accompany the set, having on them "Rules for playing the Game," and the " Key" to the historical problems.

These card-pieces are here arranged as a bound volume, bearing the following inscription :—" Darvall. Historical, Biographical, and Geographical Cards. Romsey. 1830."

Not any pictorial designs nor marks are present.

[3½ × 2⅜ in.]   [Backs plain.]

E. 211.

SECOND HALF OF NINETEENTH CENTURY.

LONDON.

FIFTY-TWO card-pieces, of which fifty-one have on them printed problems connected with literature, which have to be solved by the players. One card-piece is occupied by the " Rules and Regulations."

The title of the wrapper accompanies the set, and bears the inscription, " Price 2s. 6d. An Evening Game of Cards on a Novel and Interesting Plan. Poetry and Literature. London : Hamilton, Adams, and Co., and all Booksellers."

It has here " been an object to prepare such questions as shall be full of interest and freshness to those who enjoy and appreciate English Poetry and Literature."

Not any pictorial designs nor marks are present.

[3½ × 2⅜ in.]   [Backs plain.]

E. 212.

SECOND HALF OF NINETEENTH CENTURY.

MANCHESTER.

SEQUENCE of thirty card-pieces, of which fifteen have riddle questions derived from Shakespeare on them, and fifteen have their answers. Ten other and larger pieces are present, entitled " Key to the Riddles." A supplementary card of directions accompanies the set, as likewise a title bearing the following inscription, " [Entered at Stationer's Hall.] Shaksperian Playing-Cards. Shakespere's Riddles. Selected and arranged by John B. Marsh. Examiner and Times Office, Manchester. One Shilling. Manchester: John Heywood, 143, Deansgate. London: Simpkin, Marshall, and Co. and sold by all Booksellers."

Not any pictorial designs nor marks are present.

[3 × 1⅝ in.]   [Backs plain.]

E. 213.

SECOND HALF OF NINETEENTH CENTURY.

MANCHESTER.

SEQUENCE of thirty card-pieces, the latter having love letters printed on them.

A " Card of Directions " accompanies the set, as does likewise a title bearing the following inscription : " [Entered at Stationer's Hall.] Shakesperian Playing Cards, No. II. Shakespere's Love Letters. Selected and arranged by John B. Marsh. Manchester, One Shilling. Manchester: John Heywood, 143, Deansgate. London: Simpkin, Marshall, and Co. and sold by all Booksellers."

Not any pictorial designs nor marks are present.

[3½ × 2⅜ in.]   [Backs plain.]

E. 214.

SECOND HALF OF NINETEENTH CENTURY.

LONDON.

SERIES of thirty-six card-pieces, eighteen of which have a question in the form of two lines of poetry on each of them, and eighteen have the answers in four or more lines.

The ornamental title of a wrapper accompanies the set, and bears the following inscription :—

" Shuffle and cut, question as you will,
Yet every answer shall prove fitting still."

" Comic Conversation Cards, by Joyce Jocund, Esq.

" Most Packs are in full cry when game they're after,
This Comic Pack now try,—whose game is laughter."

"London : Published by Reynolds and Son, Playing Card Manufacturers By appointment to his Majesty, 29 and 30, Vere Street, Lincoln's Inn Fields. Ent. at Stat. Hall. Price 1ˢ. 6ᵈ."

The only pictorial design is on the title of the wrapper. It represents two knaves in attendance upon two Kings and two Queens seated at table.

[3⅛ × 2⅜ in.]   [Backs plain.]

E. 215.

LAST QUARTER OF EIGHTEENTH CENTURY.

LONDON.

 SEQUENCE of thirty-two card-pieces, having on them emblematic designs of various character, and below moral apophthegms to which the designs have reference. Each piece has a number at the upper left-hand corner, answering to certain explanatory and descriptive tables given in a book of directions, which here accompanies the cards. The title-page of this book of 31 pages bears the following inscription :—

" Les Amusemens des Allemands, or the Diversions of The Court of Vienna, in which the Mystery of Fortune-Telling from the Grounds of the Coffee-Cup is unravelled, and Three pleasant Games, viz. :—

" 1. Fortune-telling from the Grounds of the Coffee-Cup.
2. Fortune-telling by laying out the cards.
3. The new Imperial Game of numbers
are invented.

Admirably calculated to promote Useful reflections and Innocent Festivity, By the means of Extempore Composition. The whole illustrated with a Pack of Thirty-Two Emblematical Cards.

" Here fertile fancy may amuse the mind,
With moral truths and sprightly wit combined."

London : Printed for Champante and Whitrow, Jewry-Street, Aldgate, And may be had at every Booksellers and Toy Shop in the Kingdom, 1796. Entered at Stationer's Hall."

According to an advertisement on the back of the title-page, " these entertaining games first made their appearance at Vienna in 1794, where they still are the favourite amusement of the Empress of Germany and the Imperial Court. They have since been diffused through all the fashionable circles in that country. The Editor therefore has to hope that in a country where the liberality and curious discernment of its inhabitants is so conspicuous as that of Britain, they will not be held in less estimation."

Designs and text are from engraved copper-plates ; the former are uncoloured and of mediocre character.

[3⅝ × 2⅝ in.]   [Backs plain.]

E. 216.

NINETEENTH CENTURY.

LONDON.

A SERIES of thirty unseparated card-pieces. The latter are here contained in six sheets of three rows of two pieces each sheet.

Below the cards is the inscription on each sheet: "March's Conjuring Cards. No. 1. Price one Halfpenny. Directions—Cut them apart through the lines, then with a pin bore holes where dotted, tye a thread in each end and twirl the card quickly round, when the goat will have a monkey on his back, the gridiron 3 mackerel, and so on with the others. J. March, Publisher, 12, Webber Street, New-Cut."

The back of each card-piece has on it a design in reverse to that which is on the front. The design on the latter is uncoloured, that on the back is coloured.

[$1\frac{1}{8}$ × $1\frac{3}{8}$ in.]   [Backs with designs on them.]

MISCELLANEA.

E. 217.

SECOND QUARTER OF EIGHTEENTH CENTURY.

LONDON.

Prints of the English School.

Works of and after Francis Hayman. B. 1708—D. 1776.

THIS piece represents one of a series of paintings executed by Hayman for Vauxhall Gardens, and by which chiefly he is celebrated.

The design of the present work appears to have been suggested by a composition of Gravelot, of which Hayman fully availed himself.

In the print before us, a young lady and gentleman appear seated at a round table " Building Houses with Cards," at another and small side-table are two little girls following a like amusement. Four persons are looking on. The card-house of the first group is tumbling down. The gentleman holds the five of hearts in his right hand, and towards which the attention of the lady is directed. Below the composition are the following lines :—

" Whilst innocently youth their hours beguile,
And joy to raise with cards the wondrous pile,
A breath, a start, makes the whole fabric vain,
And all lies flat to be began again.

Ambition thus erects in riper years,
Wild schemes of power, and wealth, and endless cares,
Some change takes place, the labour'd plan retards,
All drops—Illusion all—an House of Cards."

Immediately below the engraving are the inscription and addresses : " Building Houses with Cards. H. Gravelot, Invenit ; F. Hayman, Pinx. ; L. Truchy, Sculp. From the original Painting in Vaux-hall Garden. Published according to Act of Parliament, 4ᵗʰ April, 1743."

[11¾ × 13⅝ in.]

E. 218.

SECOND QUARTER OF EIGHTEENTH CENTURY.

LONDON.

Prints of the English School.

Works of and after Francis Hayman. B. 1708—D. 1776.

THE composition represents a lady and two gentlemen seated at a card-table playing Quadrille. Two ladies and a gentleman are looking on. A female servant and a negro page are at a side-table engaged with tea-things. The two gentlemen who are playing are showing their cards to the ladies seated near them; the cards are of the suit of hearts. The ace of spades (?) is on the table, together with other cards and counters.

The inscription and addresses at the lower margin are as follows : " Quadrille. Engraved from the original Painting in Vaux Hall Garden. F. Hayman, pinxᵗ· C. Grignion, Sculpᵗ· Printed for John Bowles, at the Black Horse in Cornhil, and Carington Bowles, in St. Pauls Churchyard, London."

In reference to the game of Quadrille as here played by three persons, the following extract from Singer (p. 266) is worthy of attention. " Quadrille, which is only another species of Ombre, appears to have superseded it, and to have been very popular in England until whist began to be played upon scientific principles. Although this game has a Spanish name, it is supposed to be an invention of the French nation, and appears to have been a great favourite with the ladies, as requiring much less attention than Ombre ; there was also a modification of it which might be played by three persons, but it is generally considered far inferior to the game by four, and was only played when a fourth player could not be had."

[9⅜ × 13⅝ in., without margin.]

E. 219.

SECOND QUARTER OF EIGHTEENTH CENTURY.

LONDON.

A SMALL engraving from a copper-plate representing two ladies and two gentlemen seated at a table playing cards. Below is the inscription, " The Quadrille Party."

This appears to be after a design of Gravelot, otherwise Henri D'Anville and Hubert François Bourguignon. He came to England in 1733, and for a time kept a drawing school in the Strand. He was largely employed by the London booksellers, and his assistance was likewise sought by various artists. " He attempted small compositions and conversation-pieces, and is said to have been a designer by choice, an engraver by necessity." " He was born in Paris, March 26, 1699, died in Paris 1773. (Redgrave's " Dictionary of Artists of the English School.")

[5⅝ × 3½ in., without margin.]

E. 220.

Drolls published by Robert Sayer, Laurie, and Whittle,
1792-1803, *No.* 168.

LONDON.

 PRINT representing two ladies and three gentlemen playing at loo. One of the latter is scratching his head in desperation, another and one of the ladies are regarding with vexatious astonishment the cards —(a flush of diamonds)—which their successful antagonist displays in her hands. Her opposite neighbour smiles with complacency as he shows the knave of clubs.

Below, in the margin, may be read " Loo. Pam saves me. A Flush. Published 20th Febr., 1796, by Lawrie and Whittle, 53, Fleet Street, London."

On the table are cards and counters or money.

Loo or lanterloo was at one period a very fashionable game, but began to go out soon after the time when whist began to be played on scientific principles.

" If you are acquainted with my Lady Barrymore," writes H. Walpole to his friend Montagu, " pray tell her that in less than two hours t'other night, the Duke of Cumberland lost four hundred and fifty pounds at loo ; Miss Pelham won three hundred, and I the rest. However, in general loo is extremely gone to decay. I am to play at Princess Emily's to-morrow for the first time this winter, and it is with difficulty she has made a party." This was in December, 1761.

In 1759 Walpole wrote : " Loo is mounted to the zenith. The parties last till one and two in the morning. We played at Lady Hertford's last week, the last night of her lying-in, till deep into Sunday morning, after she and her lord were retired. It is now adjourned to Mrs. Fitzroy's, whose child the Town calls ' *Pam-ela.*' "

At certain games the knave of clubs is called PAM. In the " Toast," a satirical poem, written about 1730, by Dr. William King, Principal of St. Mary's Hall, Oxford, Dr. Hort, Archbishop of Tuam, is called " Lord Pam." He is also called Pam by Swift.

" A few years ago the name was applied to the celebrated public character, whom Byron is supposed to have designated as ' a moral chimney-sweep ' in one of the cantos of Don Juan." (Chatto, p. 269.)

[6½ × 9⅛ in. without margin.]

E. 221.

SECOND HALF OF SEVENTEENTH CENTURY.

LONDON.

 BROADSIDE sheet of politico-satirical verses, headed by three lines of music, and entitled " A New Game at. Cards." The words within the lines of music are as follows :—

" Ye merry hearts that love to play at Cards,
See who hath won the day ;

You that once did sadly sing
The Knave of Clubs hath won the King;
But now more happy times we have,
The King hath overcome the Knave,
The King hath overcome the Knave."

Then follow eight verses of seven lines, each verse in two columns. The verses refer to Cromwell and the Rump Parliament.

The second verse runs thus:—

"Old Noll, he was the Knave o' th' Clubs,
And dad of such as Preach in Tubs;
Bradshaw, Ireton, and Pride,
Where three other Knaves beside,
And they Plaid with half the Pack,
Throwing out all Cards but Black."

The last of the sequence is:—

"After this Game was done, I think
The Standers by had cause to drink,
And the Loyal Subjects sing
Farewell Knaves, and welcome King,
For till we saw the King returned
We wish'd the Cards had all been Burn'd,
We wish'd the Cards had all been Burn'd."

The whole of the music and typography of this broadside is from an engraved copper-plate.

[$12\frac{6}{8} \times 7\frac{1}{2}$ in. without margin.]

E. 222.

Manuscript Department.

Harleian MSS. No. 5947 (51 F.)

THIS volume of "Bagford's Collection," previously alluded to (E 184) as containing the advertisement relating to the "Popish Plot" cards, has, in addition, the following "cuttings":—

On folio 4, a wrapper or introductory title to a pack of cards as follows: "The Scientiall Cards, or a new and ingenious knowledge, gramatically epitomised, both for the plea ure and profit of Schollers and such as delight to recollect (without any labour) the Rudiments of so necessary an art as Grammer is without hindring them from their more necessary and grave studies: Offering them as a second course unto you which in all points and suites doe represent your vulgar or common cards: So that the perfection of the Grammer principles may hereby be easily attained unto both with much delight and profit, Together with a Key shewing the redy use of them. Written by a Lover of ingenuity and Learning. And are to be sold by Baptist Pendleton, Cardmaker, at his House neere S^t^. Dunston's Church in the East, or by John Holden, at the Anchor in the New Exchange. 1651."

Referring to this advertisement, Mr. Chatto remarks (p. 140):—"Of those cards or of the key showing how they are to be used, I know nothing beyond what is contained in the title above given. I, however, greatly suspect that the 'lover of learning and ingenuity' who devised them was specially employed for the purpose by the maker, Mr. Baptist Pendleton, who, sensible of the decline of his regular business, and noting the signs of the times, might think it both for his interest and credit to manufacture cards which might serve indifferently for the purposes of instruction, but equally as well for play as ' your vulgar or common cards,' which were then in very bad repute. The Scientiall cards would appear to have been well adapted for the use of persons who wished to save appearances with the Puritans, and yet had no objection to play a quiet game with the profane."

Secondly follows the envelope of a pack printed in blue ink, bearing in the centre the inscription, "trielles [?] des fines de Jacques Legras faites à Morlais." On the upper border in reverse is "à bon jeu bon argent," and on a plain margin at the left hand is the mark of the suit *piques* in the centre.

Thirdly. The title of a wrapper, printed in black ink, from a coarsely engraved wood-block, having as a device Diana seated, an unicorn standing and gazing at her with much expression of admiration and curiosity. Below is the couplet :

" The Unicorn tho deafe to Subtle Charmes,
A Virgin's Smiles allayes his Furious Stormes."

Then follows " Fine cards made by John Savage."

On folio 4 comes the titled cover of a pack of cards, printed in black ink, from a carefully engraved metal plate. The chief part is occupied by a medallion portrait of Edward VI., below which is the following inscription : " These superfine cards are sold by Richard Fountaine only, at the Golden Lion, in St. Lawrens Lane, London." Below this are the marks of the suits of hearts and spades, having between them the letters " R. ✳ F." as ornamental capitals. The whole is enclosed in a frame-like border.

The next cutting is the ornamental title of a wrapper, printed from a neatly, but rather stiffly engraved copper-plate. In the upper portion are the royal arms of England, with supporters and mottoes, while the lower part bears the following inscription, within an ornamental shield with scrolled edge, viz.: " Cards containing the arms of the King, and all the Lords Spirituall and Temporall of England. This may be printed. Norfolke and Marshall."

In the " Herald and Genealogist," vol. iii. p. 358, 1861, may be found an elaborate paper on the cards referred to in the present title:—

" It is supposed that these cards, which thus appeared with the *imprimatur* of the Earl Marshal, were edited by Gregory King, then Somerset Herald, as ' A Pack of Cards containing the arms of the English nobility. Lond. 1684,' is attributed to him in Watt's ' Bibliotheca Britannia.' "

These cards, known as " Gregory King's Peerage Cards," are fully described (*loco cit.*), from a pack in the possession of Evelyn Philip Shirley, Esq., F.S.A., and the remark is made that they " are now so exceedingly scarce as to be almost unknown."

At page 79 of this volume of the " Herald and Genealogist" is the following statement:—

" In the ' Observator,' No. 239, for Feby. 12, 1686-7, are advertised cards containing the arms of the King and all the Lords Spiritual and Temporal of England. Printed for John Nicholson, and sold by E. Evets, at the Green Dragon and St. Paul's Church Yard." (See Chatto, p. 152.)

On the *verso* of folio 4 is an ornamental title of a wrapper, with a device from an engraving on a copper-plate. It represents a black man standing with his right arm extended, in a tropical landscape. Above the figure on a scroll is the title " Prince Giolo." Below the device is the inscription : " These principal superfine large cards are made by me, Andrew Layton."

Then follow the marks of the suits of diamonds and clubs, having between them the ornamental capital letters " A ✳ L."

Adjacent is the mutilated cover of a pack of cards, having on it a device from a coarsely engraved metal plate.   The device is a man in a jockey-cap on horseback, with a hunting-whip in his hand.   The horse is at full gallop.   The hind-quarters of the horse are torn away.   At the left margin, towards which the figure is directed, appears a hand in the sky holding a large double-handled vase or tankard towards the rider, near whose head is the inscription : " The Joc—" (The rest is torn away.)

On another piece of paper, which apparently formed part of this envelope, are the words : " Of London — Master Card-maker of England.   E. I." Between these latter capitals is a horseman in a gallop towards the right hand.

On folio 5 is the title of a wrapper, printed from a wood-block bearing a crown, having below and within a motto-garter the device of a falcon seizing another bird.   Beneath is the inscription : " Superfine cards made by Nicholas Faulcon."

The motto on the garter seems to be " The Faulcon playing—Takes me Flying."

At one of the margins of the cover are the capital letters N. F., with the marks of the suits of diamonds and clubs.

On the *verso* of folio 5 is the " Advertisement concerning a new pack of cards," previously alluded to. [E. 184.]

On folio 6 is the engraved title to " Tuttle's Mathematical Cards."   This is inscribed on a shield surrounded with figures and designs symbolical of mathematic forms and instruments.   At the lower margin of the plate are the addresses : " Boitard Delin.   J. Savage Sculp."

It may be here noticed that on folio 33 is the following intimation : " John Savage, Engraver, who bought Mr. Isaac Beckett's mezzo-tinto plates and prints, and lived at his House at the Golden Head in the Old Bayly, is removed to ye Golden Head in S^t. Paul's Churchyard, where you may be furnished with all sorts of Mezzotints, Prints, Frames, Glasses, &c."

John Savage resided in London about 1680, and was noted for engraving the portraits of malefactors.   (See Walpole's " Anecdotes," and Bryan's " Dictionary.")

Following the title to Tuttle's cards on folio 6 is the following " Advertisement " :—

" There is now published a pack of Proverb Cards with Figures on each card, lively representing the Proverbs.   A Design, altogether new and very diverting to the Fancy of all Lovers of ingenuity, the whole curiously engraved on copper-plates.   Price 1*s.* 6*d.* per pack.

Where you may likewise have *Frost-fair*, or an exact and lively Mapp or Representation of Booths, and all the Variety of Shows and Humours upon the Ice on the River of Thames by London, during that memorable Frost in King Charles the Second's Reign, curiously engraven on a copper-plate, with an Alphabetical Explanation of the most remarkable figures.   Price 1*s.*

Both of which are to be sold by W. Warter, Stationer, at the Sign of the Talbot, under the Mytre Tavern in Fleet Street, London."

JOHN BAGFORD.

OHN BAGFORD, to whose collection among the Harleian MSS. we are indebted for the preceding and other fragments, was born in London about 1675, and died at Islington in 1716. He was buried in the cemetery of the Charterhouse. Originally a shoemaker, he began in early life to interest himself about antiquarian subjects, particularly such as related to printing and old English literature. He travelled in Holland and elsewhere in search of literary curiosities, which he managed to pick up at low prices, and re-sold them honestly at moderate profits. With many of these he enriched the library of Dr. John Moore, Bishop of Ely, through whose influence Bagford was admitted a Carthusian.

"Most of the very many [literary curiosities] in the British Museum under the general title of 'Bagford's Collectanea' consist of printed title-pages, advertisements, hand-bills, fugitive papers of all kinds, vignettes, prints, &c., pasted into paper books, sometimes with MS. notes interspersed, but oftener without any. Bagford's MSS., properly so called, are comparatively few, intermixed with the numerous volumes above-mentioned, and promiscuously arranged and deposited along with them in the department of MSS. Besides these there are very many MSS. in the same rich repository that have printed papers and tracts bound up with them."—(Nicholl's "Literary Anecdotes of the Eighteenth Century," vol. ii. p. 462.)

A portrait of Bagford may be seen in Dibdin's "Bibliographical Decameron," vol. iii. p. 28, and much about him in a note on that page where he is styled the "faithful book jackal of Lord Oxford." In his "Bibliomania" also, first edition, Dr. Dibdin is not sparing of his animadversions. Among them is the following :—

"A modern collector and lover of perfect copies will witness with shuddering among Bagford's immense collection of title-pages in the Museum the frontispiece of the 'Complutensian Polyglot' and Chauncy's 'History of Hertfordshire' torn out to illustrate a history of printing."

Dr. Dibdin admits, nevertheless, that Bagford's "enthusiasm, however, carried him through a great deal of laborious toil, and he supplied in some measure by this qualification the want of other attainments. His whole mind was devoted to book-hunting, and his integrity and diligence probably made his employers overlook his many failings."

In the third edition of the "Bibliomania" (1842), (note to p. 326), John Bagford is again discussed at some length, and, on the whole, with rather more favour, as based chiefly on the accounts of Thomas Hearne.

Bagford described himself as " Dr. John Bagford, patron of printing." Howard painted his portrait and Vertue engraved it,[1] while one of his friends found a coat of arms for him in this wise:

" For my Lovinge friend Mr. Jno. Bagford—you having shewed me so many rebuses, as I was returning home I thought of one for you—a bagge, and below that a fourd or passable water." (Harl. MSS. No. 5910.)

In the Sloane collection of MSS. vol. 1044, folio 1, is the following in Bagford's handwriting, which well indicates both the ambitious character and extensive scope of the author's intentions:—

" Proposals for the Printing an Essay for the Famous Art of Typography & Calcography from ye first Invention of it by Coster at Harlem, with Blocks or Molds of Wood collected from the most approved Authors and the Observation of ye books themselves first printed therewith, with a discourse of the several ways of printing by the Antient Chinese.

" An Acc^{tt} of the Invention of Matrices of Single Types at Mentz by Joh: Fust & Peter Sceffer & not by Guttenburg as shall be made plainly appear.

" Also a Catalogue of what books were printed from ye year 1450 to 1500 in several parts of ye World, viz. Germany, Italy, Holland, Flanders, France, Spain, Portugal, Denmark, Swedland, Switzerland, East and West Indies, Turkey, and Russia.

" Some observations on the Antiquity of Paper made with rags. When Invented where made & ye Places most famous for making the same with the Maker's marks.

" An Acco^{tt} of the bringing printing into England first to Oxford by Nicolas Corselis, & St. Albans, Westminster, London, Southwark, Greenwich, York, Canterbury, Worcester, Ipswich, Tavistock, Cambridge, Chester, Bristol, Exeter, &c.

" Scotland at Edinburgh, Glasgow, Aberdeen.

" Ireland at Dublin, &c.

" The Lives and Effigies of our most celebrated Printers.

" The whole Interwoven with a description of the manner of making books, first MSS. and the several materials they certainly wrote on, as vellum, Parchment, Paper, &c.

" The Instruments used in writing, viz., Styles, Pens, Reeds, &c.

" The Ink used by the Antients both in Writing and Printing with an account of Book Binding in all its Parts.

" To which shall be added a catalogue of such books as early appear

by John Bagford."

---

[1] Brit. Mus. Coll. " English Portraits." (Bromley, vol. i. p. 232.)

E. 223.

Newspapers. Printed Books Department.

Public Advertiser, *Saturday, December* 1, 1759. *No.* 7812.

"*Advertisement.*

THIS day is published Price 5s plain each pastime improved by a new pack of cards called Beau Monde, or the Bath, Tunbridge, and Scarborough portraits engraved from particular persons and their likenesses to Beasts and Birds by Figures, and have Pips like common cards; likewise new and curious. Pack of regimental cards with the words of command under each card containing portraits of the Pretty Smarts belonging to the Army and the Militia; Stampt for George Bickham in Mays Buildings Covent Garden."

The George Bickham here mentioned must have been G. Bickham, Junior, it is presumed. He was one of our earlier caricaturists, and engraved the humorous pieces published by the Messrs. Bowles, and analogous subjects. It is true that this advertisement appeared in 1759, and George Bickham died in 1758, but a pack of cards having humorous subjects, portraits, &c., on its pieces would take some time to prepare.

"Public Advertiser, *Monday, December* 17th, 1759, No. 7816.

"*Advertisement.*

"This day is published price 5s. each. Three packs of diverting cards curiously engraved. On one corner of which is the court-card and pips, painted so striking that they may be played with as ready as common cards, which renders them liable to a duty of a 1s. a pack. On one pack the various passions of Love are emphatically represented with a title and four lines in verse entirely new and explanatory of the design. Another the cries and Humours of London, finely copied after nature with their proper mottos, the other Æsops fables, exactly copied after Barlow, the Fables and Morals in Verse.

"To be had of the proprietor I Kirk, at the Grotto Toy Shop in St. Paul's Churchyard, and at I Kirk's Toy shop in St. James' Street. Also the impenetrable secret or the Proverb Cards, price 1s. to be had as above.

"Of all the passions that possess mankind
Love is the noblest when with Virtue joined
To guard the Fair, the Lover swiftly flies
And all the danger that surrounds defies.
"*Love cards.*"

A small woodcut design of the nine of clubs heads the above advertisement.

Public Advertiser, *Wednesday, December* 26th, 1759, No. 7823.

"*Advertisement.*

"This day is published and sold in May's Buildings, Covent Garden, Price 5s. each Pack. Some of them coloured.
"1. Knowledge improved by County-cards describing the Cities and Towns.

"2. Drollery improved by a New Pack of Picture cards from Erasmus' Folly.

"3. Pastime improved by a curious pack of cards called the Beau Monde.

"4. Militia Cards or the Pretty Smarts of the Army and Militia with Regimentals."

A diminutive representation of the nine of clubs heads this advertisement.

E. 224.

(Printed Books Department, 505, f. 4.)

LAST QUARTER OF FIFTEENTH CENTURY.

LONDON.

THE volume here referred to is that of the "Nova Statuta," printed by William of Mechlin, or Machlinia, as he is generally called, about the years 1482-3.

It is a folio volume of Statutes, without date, place, or name of printer.

According to Dibdin ("Bibliotheca Spenceriana," vol. iv. No. 896), "This is the most elaborate production of the press of Machlinia, and must be considered no mean acquisition to the library of the legal antiquary. The type is exactly similar to that of the Tenures described in the preceding page, and leaves no doubt of the printer by whom this volume was executed. The ink and the paper merit more commendation than the type, indeed the paper is of no ordinary excellence."

In this work the first printed allusion to playing-cards occurs in relation to England. It may be found "Anno tercio Regis Edwardi IV., Cap. iiij." The statute here quoted is one of the year 1463, prohibiting the importation of playing-cards.

Since an act was passed in the eleventh year of the reign of Henry IV., 1409, A.D. directing the penalties to be inflicted upon persons offending against a statute of 12 Richard II. cap. 6, anno 1388, forbidding certain games, as "coytes, dyces, gettre de pere, keyles, and aultres tielx jeues importunes," and not any mention is made of cards, it may be assumed that the latter were not in use in England in 1409. It must have been some time between this date and 1463 that playing-cards found their way into this country. The Statute of the 3rd of Edward IV. allows it to be presumed, however, that the prohibited article was known some years before its importation was made illegal.

The extract from the Statute of Edward IV. relating to cards is given here from the following work.

E. 225.

(Printed Books Department, 505, h. 11.)

LAST QUARTER OF FIFTEENTH CENTURY.

LONDON.

THIS is a reprint by Richard Pynson of the "Nova Statuta" of Machlinia previously referred to.

It is a folio of statutes, commencing with the first year of the reign of Edward III., and concluding with the twelfth of Henry VII.

There is not any title-page to the volume, nor is any date given in the colophon, which runs thus on sig. G. 2. i. :

℩. Emprynted by my Rycharde Pynson.

On the *verso* is the device, No. 5 of Johnson's "Typographia," having on it a shield bearing as a monogram R. P., and below, in stout Gothic letters,

" Richard Pynson "

There are running titles and signatures, but neither catch-words nor numerals. The book commences with a blank leaf, which is followed by a full alphabetical table on sig. a. ii. The statutes are generally in Norman-French, but some are in Latin, *e.g.*, " Anno xxxiii Henrici Sexti," " Anno xxxix Henrici Sexti," while from the first of Henry VII. to the end of the volume the statutes are in English.

This work is supposed to have been the first statute-book printed by Pynson.

That portion of the statute of the third year of Edward IV. relating to the prohibition of the importation of playing-cards is as follows :—

¶ Anno tercio.   Edwardi iiij.

*   *   *   *   *   *   *

" Noſtre treſredoute ſouerayn ſeignour le roy les premiſſes conſiderant & voillant & en ceo cas puruoir de remedye del adups aſſent & auctoriſe ſuiſdites ad ordeigne enacte & eſtablie que nul marchant nees ſubjet de noſtre ſeigneour le roy dein= zein neſtrange ne alcun autre perſone apres le Feſte de ſeynt Mychell 'larchaungel proſchein auſignir ameſne mande ne conuoſe ne cauſe daſmener maunder ne conuoyer en meſme ceſt royalme Dengleterre & Seignourye de Gales aſcunes de ceſtez chaffares wares ou choſes deſoubz eſcriptez ceſt aſſauoir aſcunes bonettes launz aſcuns draps launz laces corſes rybans frenges de ſoie / & de file laces de file ſoye en fille / ſoye en aſcune maner enbraudes laces dor Tires de ſoye ou dor Selles eſtriuens ou aſcune herneiſe regardaunt as Sellers Eſperons moleins pur fremes aundirens gredirnes aſcunes maners ſerures martens vulgarement nommes hamers pynſons fire= tonges dreppyngpannes diſez tenys balles poyntes laces burſes grauntz ceintez harneis pur ceinctes de ferre De laton daſſer deſtain ou de alkempne choſ ouer daſſ quirre Tawe aſcune maner pellure tawe huſeous ſolers galoges ou corkes cotelr daggers woodknyues botkyns Sheres pur Taillours Ciſours Raſours Shetes Cardes a Juer Eſpinges Patins Agules pur Sakkes vulgarement nommer paknedels aſcune maner chaffare ou ware depeynte Forcers, Caſketles."

Mr. R. P. Cruden, referring (in a letter to the late Mr. Singer) to this statute making it illegal to import cards, remarks, " I should like extremely to know the result of an inquiry into the manner of making playing-cards in England imme- diately after the year 1463, when they were no longer to be obtained from abroad. That they were used is not to be doubted. The Act afterwards restraining the use of them did not pass till the 33 Henry VIII. cap. 8, anno 1541."

" It is a curious fact that a tax was first levied upon cards anno 1631, in the reign of Charles I. ; it was one of the impositions complained of as arbitrary and illegal, being levied without consent of Parliament, and which complaints terminated in the sacrifice of the monarch and his minister (Strafford)." (Singer, Bibl. 8, p. 365, appendix.)

The last statement is erroneous, as to the first imposition of a tax on playing-cards, as the following records under E. 226 will show, a tax being levied in 1615, though not by parliamentary statute, which was first done during the reign of Queen Anne, session 1711.

The Company of Card-makers was incorporated by letters patent of Charles I. the 22nd of October, 1629, under the title of "the Master, Wardens, and Commonalty of the Mistery of the Makers of Playing-cards of the City of London."— Rec. Roll, Pat. 4, Car. i. p. 22, No. 6. (See Singer, p. 226, Note.)

E. 226.

(*Printed Books Department*, 2076. 6.)

FIRST QUARTER OF SEVENTEENTH CENTURY.

LONDON.

INGER, in his researches, observes (p. 223) that towards the close of Elizabeth's reign patents were so frequently granted by favour, that the House of Commons deemed it necessary to make some inquiries respecting them. At this period a patent was granted to one Edward D'Arcy for cards.

"On the mention of the monopoly of cards Sir Walter Raleigh blushed. Upon reading the patents, Mr. Hakewell of Lincoln's-inn stood up, and asked thus, ' Is not bread there ?' ' Bread !' quoth one. ' Bread !' quoth another. ' This voice seems strange,' quoth another. ' No,' quoth Mr. Hacket, ' if order be not taken herein, bread will be there before the next Parliament.' " (Singer, p. 223.)

The volume referred to under the present head, E. 226, is the " Calendar of State Papers," Domestic Series, James I. A.D. 1611-1618, from which the following minutes are selected :—

" 1615. July 20, Westminster.—(19.) Letters Patent granting to Sir Richard Coningsby, for a rent of £200 per annum, the imposition of 5*s.* per gross on playing-cards, and the office of Inspector of all playing-cards imported in recompense of £1,800 due to him from the king, and of his patent for the sole export of Tin granted by the late queen."—Warrant for the above granted July 19. (Sign. Man., vol. v. No. 41.)—(Page 296.)

" 1615. July 21.—(19) Proclamation of the Patent granting to Sir Rich. Coningsby the right of searching and sealing all playing cards made in England or imported printed." (Proc. Coll., No. 44 A.)—(Page 297.)

" 1616. (124.) Reasons against the Suit of the Card-makers who remonstrate against the exercise of Sir Richard Coningsby's patent for importation of playing-cards."—(Page 420.)

" 1617. Dec. 21.—(75.) Petition of Sir Thos. Smythe and the merchants trading to France to the Council to renew their order to the Lord Chief Justice of the King's Bench to stay a suit commenced against them by Radnor, an informer, for importing playing-cards, and to permit the importation of the same on payment of the usual duties."—(Page 504.)

Among the valuable series of proclamations preserved in the Library of the Society of Antiquaries is that alluded to previously (July 20, 1615), as granting the right to Sir R. Coningsby of imposing a duty of 5*s.* per gross on playing-cards :—

"𝔚𝔥𝔦𝔠𝔥 𝔣𝔯𝔬𝔪 𝔞𝔫𝔡 𝔞𝔣𝔱𝔢𝔯 𝔱𝔥𝔢 𝔗𝔴𝔢𝔫𝔱𝔦𝔢𝔱𝔥 𝔡𝔞𝔶 𝔬𝔣 𝔍𝔲𝔩𝔶 𝔱𝔥𝔢𝔫 𝔫𝔢𝔵𝔱 𝔠𝔬𝔪𝔦𝔫𝔤 𝔰𝔥𝔬𝔲𝔩𝔡 𝔥𝔞𝔭𝔭𝔢𝔫 𝔱𝔬 𝔟𝔢 𝔟𝔯𝔬𝔲𝔤𝔥𝔱 𝔣𝔯𝔬𝔪 𝔞𝔫𝔶 𝔬𝔣 𝔱𝔥𝔢 𝔭𝔞𝔯𝔱𝔰 𝔟𝔢𝔶𝔬𝔫𝔡 𝔱𝔥𝔢 𝔰𝔢𝔞𝔰 𝔦𝔫𝔱𝔬 𝔬𝔲𝔯 𝔯𝔢𝔞𝔩𝔪𝔢 𝔬𝔣 𝔈𝔫𝔤𝔩𝔞𝔫𝔡 𝔇𝔬𝔪𝔦𝔫𝔦𝔬𝔫 𝔬𝔣 𝔚𝔞𝔩𝔢𝔰 𝔬𝔯 𝔓𝔬𝔯𝔱 𝔞𝔫𝔡 𝔗𝔬𝔴𝔫𝔢 𝔬𝔣 𝔅𝔢𝔯𝔴𝔦𝔠𝔨𝔢 𝔟𝔶 𝔞𝔫𝔶 𝔓𝔢𝔯𝔰𝔬𝔫 𝔬𝔯 𝔓𝔢𝔯𝔰𝔬𝔫𝔰 𝔈𝔫𝔤𝔩𝔦𝔰𝔥𝔪𝔢𝔫 𝔡𝔢𝔫𝔦𝔷𝔢𝔫𝔰 𝔬𝔯 𝔖𝔱𝔯𝔞𝔫𝔤𝔢𝔯𝔰 𝔱𝔬 𝔱𝔥𝔢 𝔢𝔫𝔡 𝔱𝔬 𝔟𝔢 𝔲𝔱𝔱𝔢𝔯𝔢𝔡 𝔰𝔬𝔩𝔡 𝔬𝔯 𝔭𝔲𝔱 𝔱𝔬 𝔰𝔞𝔩𝔢 𝔞𝔰 𝔟𝔶 𝔱𝔥𝔢 𝔰𝔞𝔪𝔢 𝔬𝔲𝔯 𝔏𝔢𝔱𝔱𝔢𝔯𝔰 𝔪𝔬𝔯𝔢 𝔞𝔱 𝔩𝔞𝔯𝔤𝔢 𝔦𝔱 𝔡𝔬𝔱𝔥 𝔞𝔫𝔡 𝔪𝔞𝔶 𝔞𝔭𝔭𝔢𝔞𝔯𝔢."

Following this proclamation is

" *The Copie of the Lord Treasourers Letter.*

"After my heartie commendations, whereby it hath pleased his Majestie to direct a Privy Seal to me, touching the imposition of five shillings upon every grosse of Playing Cards that shall be Imported into this Kingdome or the Dominions thereof by vertue of his Majesties Letters Patents granted to Sir Richard Coningsby knight under the Greate Seale of England. In regard whereof These are to wil and require you to take notice thereof and not to suffer any merchant to make any entry of Playing-Cards until the same impositions be payed according to the said Letters patents. Provided that the Patentees give caution for maintayning the Custome and Import according to a Medium thereof to be made as in such cases is used; And so having signified his Majesties pleasure to you in that behalfe I bid you heartily farewell.

"Your Louing Friend,
"Tho : Suffolke.
"From Northampton House the 29th of October, 1615."

Numerous other references to the subject of playing-cards may be found in the "Calendar of State Papers, Domestic Series," particularly in the volumes relating to the latter part of Queen Elizabeth's reign. The details connected therewith, however, falling beyond the scope of the present work, further allusion here to the records of the "Calendar" would be out of place.

E. 227.

(*Printed Books Department, Tracts relating to Trade, vol.* 12, 816. *m.* 12/72.)

SECOND QUARTER OF SEVENTEENTH CENTURY.

(King Charles I.)

LONDON.

IN this volume of "Notabilia" may be seen, as above indicated, the Proclamation referred to by Chatto, p. 137. It is as follows :—

"BY THE KING.

" A Proclamation concerning playing-Cards and Dice.

" Whereas the kings Majeſtie having lately ſettled a courſe for the conſtant weekly buying and taking from the Card

makers and Dicemakers, such of them as are his naturall born
subjects, their manufactures of Cards and Dice, by his Proclama=
tion published the fifteenth day of May in the thirteenth year of
his Reign (whereby they might be enabled to live of their trades)
did therefore require and command that all Cards and Dice
made here or otherwise imported from foreign parts should be
brought to his Majesties officer in London, appointed for the
searching and sealing of such as should be found good and
merchantable before the same Cards or Dice should be sold or
disposed of: But his Majestie now finding that sundry wayes
of deceipt have been and are daily practised as well by the
makers of Cards and Dice as by those that import the same, is
pleased to ratifie and confirme his said Proclamation and again
to declare his further Royall pleasure therein and doth therefore
straitly charge and command that no person or persons whatso=
ever (other than his Majesties said officer) shall hereafter pre=
sume to seal or mark any Playing=Cards or Dice or to fix thereon
any seals or printed papers now used or which hereafter shall
be used by the said Officer; And that none but such as he shall
appoint, do engrave, cut, or print any of the said seals for the
sealing of Cards or Dice or do imitate or counterfeit the same;
And that no foreign Cards or Dice imported or to be imported
shall be from henceforth landed in any other of his Majesties
Ports in England or Wales, then in the Port of London only.
And that upon the landing thereof in the same Port or within
two dayes after notice be thereof given by the Importers or
Owners to his Majesties said Officer of the just quantities
thereof, and that none of the Officers in any other of his
Majesties Ports (under pain of losse of their office) shall suffer
any Cards or Dice to be imported or landed contrary to his
Majesties command but shall seize the same and give notice of
such seizure within convenient time after.

"And further his Majestie doth straightly charge and com=
mand, That no Merchant Master or Owner of Ships Mariners
or others shall hereafter import or suffer to be imported any
foreign Cards or Dice to any other Port than the Port of
London only and thereof duly to give knowledge as aforesaid.
And for the better discovery of deceipts herein his Majestie doth
hereby straightly charge and command, That all foreign Cards
after Michaelmas next shall be brought to the office in London
for Sealing of Cards where they shall be put into English
Binders, or new bound by his Majesties said Officer or his
Deputie, before the same shall be sold; and that no person or

perſons of ƿhat condition or qualitie ſoeber after Michaelmas next ſhall buy ſell uſe utter keep or diſpoſe of any Cards ƿhatſo= eber, that he or ſhall be put in foreign Binders before the ſame ſhall be neƿ bound, or put in Engliſh Binders, and be ſealed by his Majeſties Officer or his Deputie upon pain of the forfeiture thereof.

And to theſe his Maieſties Royall commands he requir= eth all due conformitie and obedience of all ƿhom it ſhall con= cern upon pain of the loſſe and forfeiture of all ſuch Cards or Dice as ſhall be Sealed Marked Counterfeited Imported or otherƿiſe bought ſold or diſpoſed of contrary to his Majeſties pleaſure herein declared and upon ſuch further penalties and puniſhments as by the Laƿes or Statutes of the Realm or otherƿiſe may be inflicted for their contempt or negleɛt herein.

" Given at our court at Greenwich the eighteenth day of June, in the fourteenth yeer of our Reign.

" God Save the King.

" Imprinted at London by Robert Barker, Printer to the Kings moſt Excellent Majeſtie : and by the Aſſignes of John Bill. 1638."
[$25\frac{6}{8} \times 10\frac{2}{8}$ in.]

E. 228.

(*Printed Books Department, Single Sheets, vol.* 3, 669. *f.* 7/28.)

SECOND QUARTER OF SEVENTEENTH CENTURY.

(CHARLES I.)

LONDON.

THE following order of Parliament is contained as above indicated :—
" *Die Martis* 11 *Julii* 1643.
" Committee appointed by Parliament for the Navy and Customes.
" Upon the Humble Complaints of severall Poore *Cardmakers* of London, who having beene bred up in their Trades of making Playing-Cards are likely to perish with their families by reason of Divers Merchants secretly bring- ing in Playing-Cards into this Kingdome, contrary to the Lawes and Statutes of this Realme ; It is this day ordered by this Committee, That the Officers of the Custome House of the Port of *London* and likewise of the Out Ports within the Kingdome of *England* and Dominion of *Wales* and all other Officers whom it doth concerne respectively do seize and put into safe custody all sorts of Playing-Cards of Forraigne making which are or hereafter shall be brought into this Kingdom or Dominion of *Wales.* And that they doe thereupon proceed against the parties so offending according to the Lawes and Statutes in that case provided.

" And it is further ordered That the Copy hereof be sent unto the Custome House of the Port of *London* and unto all other the Outports within the King- dome of *England* and *Wales,* that the Officers may take notice thereof accordingly.
" *Treasury Chamber,* Westminster.

" *Giles Grene.*
" *London,* Printed by F. R. for *Joseph Hunscott.* July 12, 1643."
[$14 \times 9\frac{1}{2}$ in.]

E. 229.

(*Printed Books Department, Tracts relating to Trade, vol.* 12, 816. *m.* 12/73.)

LAST QUARTER OF SEVENTEENTH CENTURY.

(King Charles II.)

LONDON.

HE following proclamation succeeds in the present volume the previous one of King Charles I. of the year 1638 (E. 227):—

"BY THE KING.

" A Proclamation

Prohibiting the Importation of Foreign Playing-Cards and for feizing fuch as are or fhall be IMPORTED.

"Charles R.

" Whereas by the Laws and Statutes of this our Realm, all foreign Playing Cards (amongst divers other foreign manufactures) are prohibited to be imported, under penalty of forfeiture; Yet notwithstanding, as we are given to understand by the humble petition of the Master, Wardens, and Assistants of the Company of Cardmakers of London, divers of Our Subjects and others, are so hardy, to bring into this Kingdom great quantities of foreign playing=Cards and publickly to expose the same to sale in contempt of us and our Laws and to the great impoverishment of the poor artificers of the said com= pany and other our subjects imployed in making the said manu= facture; We taking the same into our serious consideration and being desirous in this particular, as we always hitherto have been in the whole course of our Government, to encourage manufactures within this Our Kingdom, whereby our subjects are maintained in good estate, and Trade increased, are gra= ciously pleased with the advice of our privy council by this Our Royal Proclamation to command and direct; That all laws now in force prohibiting the importation of any Foreign Playing=Cards be duely put in execution by all our Officers and other persons concerned : And that all foreign playing-cards already imported be forthwith searched for, seized and con= demned, and all such as make resistance therein proceeded against according to the utmost rigour of Law: hereby strictly commanding and requiring all Justices of the Peace, Mayors,

𝔖𝔥𝔢𝔯𝔦𝔣𝔣𝔰, 𝔅𝔞𝔶𝔩𝔦𝔣𝔣𝔰, 𝔠𝔬𝔫𝔰𝔱𝔞𝔟𝔩𝔢𝔰 𝔞𝔫𝔡 𝔬𝔱𝔥𝔢𝔯 𝔬𝔣𝔣𝔦𝔠𝔢𝔯𝔰 𝔴𝔥𝔞𝔱𝔰𝔬𝔢𝔳𝔢𝔯 𝔱𝔬 𝔟𝔢 𝔣𝔯𝔬𝔪 𝔱𝔦𝔪𝔢 𝔱𝔬 𝔱𝔦𝔪𝔢 𝔄𝔦𝔡𝔦𝔫𝔤 𝔞𝔫𝔡 𝔄𝔰𝔰𝔦𝔰𝔱𝔦𝔫𝔤 𝔦𝔫 𝔞𝔩𝔩 𝔱𝔥𝔦𝔫𝔤𝔰 𝔯𝔢𝔮𝔲𝔦𝔰𝔦𝔱𝔢 𝔣𝔬𝔯 𝔞𝔫𝔡 𝔱𝔬𝔲𝔠𝔥𝔦𝔫𝔤 𝔱𝔥𝔢 𝔡𝔲𝔢 𝔬𝔟𝔰𝔢𝔯𝔳𝔞𝔱𝔦𝔬𝔫 𝔞𝔫𝔡 𝔢𝔵𝔢𝔠𝔲𝔱𝔦𝔬𝔫 𝔬𝔣 𝔱𝔥𝔢 𝔰𝔞𝔦𝔡 𝔏𝔞𝔴𝔰 𝔞𝔫𝔡 𝔬𝔣 𝔱𝔥𝔦𝔰 𝔒𝔲𝔯 𝔯𝔬𝔶𝔞𝔩 𝔓𝔯𝔬𝔠𝔩𝔞𝔪𝔞𝔱𝔦𝔬𝔫 𝔞𝔱 𝔱𝔥𝔢𝔦𝔯 𝔓𝔢𝔯𝔦𝔩𝔰.

"Given at our Court at *Whitehall* the feventh day of *November* 1684. In the fix and thirtieth year of our Reign.

"God Save the King.

"London.

"Printed by the Affigns of *John Bill,* deceafed: And by *Henry Hills* and *Thomas Newcomb,* Printers to the Kings moft Excellent Majefty. 1684."

[$13\frac{1}{2} \times 10\frac{6}{8}$ in.]

E. 230.

(Printed Books Department, Tracts relating to Trade, vol. 12, 816. *m.* 12/68.)

FIRST QUARTER OF EIGHTEENTH CENTURY.

(QUEEN ANNE.)

LONDON.

N the volume here referred to are:

"CONSIDERATIONS
In Relation to
𝔗𝔥𝔢 𝔍𝔪𝔭𝔬𝔰𝔦𝔱𝔦𝔬𝔫 𝔬𝔫 𝔠𝔞𝔯𝔡𝔰,
Humbly submitted to the
Honourable HOUSE of COMMONS."

"Nine parts in Ten of the Cards now made are sold from 6*s.* to 24*s.* per gross, and even these six shillings in Cards by this Duty are subjected to pay £3 12*s.* tax.

"This with humble submission will destroy Nine Parts in Ten of this manufacture for those Cards which are now bought for 3*d.* can't then be afforded under 10*d.* or a shilling, for every hand through which they pass will add a gain in consideration of the Tax imposed and therefore the generality of the people will buy none at all.

"If any of your Honours hope by this Tax to suppress expensive Card-playing, It is answered, That the Common sort who play for innocent diversion will by this tax be only hinder'd; for those sharp gamesters who play for money but do not use the Twentieth part of the Cards sold, will not by this Tax be discouraged; for those who play for many Pounds at a game will not be hindered by paying 12*d.* per pack: And the destruction of this manufacture will be attended with these ill consequences:—

"*First.* Nothing (in comparison) will be (clear of all charges) raised by this duty imposed.

"*Secondly.* All that depend upon this manufacture will be rendered incapable to maintain their numerous families or pay their debts.

"*Thirdly.* The English paper manufacture (which is the middle of the Cards) will be extreamly prejudiced.

"*Fourthly.* The importation of the *Genoa* White Paper (with which the Cards are covered) will be very much diminished; and in the consequence thereof,

" *Fifthly and lastly*, Her Majesty will lose as much Paper duty as the clear Duty on the Cards to be sold will amount unto."

" And if it be intended to charge the Stock in hand, then the present Possessors will be thereby obliged to pay a Duty for Ten times more Cards than ever they will sell.

" *Wherefore it is humbly hoped, That your Honours will not lay a Duty which it's humbly conceived will bring no profit to the* QUEEN, *but inevitably ruin many hundreds of her subjects.*"

[12⅜ × 7⁶⁄₈ in.]

E. 231.

(Printed Books Department, Tracts relating to Trade, vol. 12, 816. *m.* 12/69.)

FIRST QUARTER OF EIGHTEENTH CENTURY.

(QUEEN ANNE.)

LONDON.

" THE case of the Merchants Importing Genoa paper, the Stationers, Haberdashers of small ware, the English Paper-Makers and Card-makers,"

" In relation to the Intended Duty on Cards, humbly submitted to the Honourable House of Commons."

The first portion or preamble of this petition against the duty on cards is the previous one, 816. m. 12/68, as far as the words " duty imposed," with a few slight alterations. The petition then proceeds to point out as ill consequences:

Secondly. " The English Paper-Manufacture extremely prejudiced, because by a modest computation there are 150 Paper Mills in England and each of these one with another Annually make 400 Rheams; one-Fourth of which is now used in the ordinary cards, and none of these will (when this great Duty is imposed) be ever made.

" *Thirdly.* Her Majesty's Customs arising from the Importation of Genoa Paper will be extremely lessen'd: for it is reasonably supposed that there are 40,000 Rheams of Genoa paper annually used in this manufacture, which already pays Custom 10*d.* per Rheam, amounting to £1666 13*s.*, which by this intended duty will be quite lost, the said Genoa paper being of little use but in Card-marking.

" *Fourthly.* Three parts in four of the card-makers, and the many families which depend upon them, will by this intended Tax be inevitably ruin'd, for those Card-makers depend upon their credit and work 8 months in 12 for the Winter-Season, and during those 8 months scarce receive enough to find their families with Bread, and therefore can never pay this *great Duty*, and consequently not follow their trade.

" Seeing by this intended Duty her Majesty's loss in her Customs, the loss of the Merchants importing paper, of the Stationers who credit the Card-makers, of the Wholesale Haberdashers who sell the Cards, and of the Card-makers, will amount to five times more than this designed imposition can clear of all charges be suppos'd to raise; and five parts in six of the Card-makers and their numerous *Dependents* inevitably ruined.

" *It is therefore humbly hop'd this* Honourable House *will give relief in the* Premisses."

On the back of this petition is the inscription: " The many Losses from severall Trades and Manufactures attending the great Imposition on CARDS."

[12⅞ × 7⁶⁄₈ in.]

E. 232.

(*Printed Books Department, Tracts relating to Trade, vol.* 12, 816. m. 12/70.)

FIRST QUARTER OF EIGHTEENTH CENTURY.

(Queen Anne.)

LONDON.

" REASONS Humbly offer'd by the Card-makers against the Tax upon Playing-Cards."

"The Card-makers in and about the City of London are about One Hundred Master Workmen. For some time past (Paper having been double the Price as formerly) the trade is much Decayed.

"The most they sell their Cards for to the Retailers (one sort with another) is Three Half-pence the Pack, and their Profit not above one Half-penny. So that the Tax intended will be double the value of the Cards and six times their gain.

"The generality of these Cardmakers are Poor men and out of the Small Gains above can hardly maintain their families : And therefore to impose a Tax to be immediately paid upon making by the Cardmakers (whose Stocks and Abilities are so very mean, that they now make hard shift to forbear the Retailers the ordinary time of Credit) will be a direct way to Ruine these Poor Men.

"Besides there is at present a Stock of Cards in the retailers hands sufficient for the consumption of Four or Five years ; and they will assuredly sell all the old stock off before they take any at the New advanced rate : The consequence whereof will be :

"*First.* That the Cardmakers till that stock be sold off can make no new ones.

"*Secondly.* That during that time they and their Families must needs starve.

"*Lastly.* That until the card-makers can make new ones no money can arise by such Tax."

[12 × 7 in.]

E. 233.

(*Printed Books Department, Tracts relating to Trade, vol.* 12, 816. m. 12/71.)

FIRST QUARTER OF EIGHTEENTH CENTURY.

(Queen Anne.)

LONDON.

" REASONS humbly offer'd to the Honourable House of Commons by the Company of 𝕮𝖆𝖗𝖉-𝕸𝖆𝖐𝖊𝖗𝖘 against the Tax upon Playing-Cards."

This petition of the "Company" itself varies, but very slightly, from the one previously given (816. m. 12/70), viz., that of the "poor Card makers."

[12⅛ × 7 in.]

E. 234.

(*Printed Books Department*, 1076, i. 10.)

FIRST QUARTER OF SEVENTEENTH CENTURY.

(KING JAMES I.)

LONDON.

PRINTED book of forty-four pages containing satirical poems in reference to characters of loose or immoral kind.
The title-page bears the inscription :

"The Knave of Clubbs.
'Tis Merry when Knaues Meet.

"Printed at London by E. A. Dwelling nere Christ-Church 1611."
The central part of the title-page is occupied by a wood-cut, with a device of two full-length figures representing the knaves of clubs and of hearts.   The knave of clubs on the left holds a long arrow-like lance in his left hand, the knave of hearts supports a partisan in his right hand, while he raises his left and addresses his companion.   The knave of hearts is seen in profile.
The first page (A. 2.) has an address by the author S. R.

"To Fustis Knave of Clubbs,"

who is asked to

"March in the forefront of my Booke
And say I use thee kinde
A crew of madmen, knaves and fooles
Thy fellowes, come behinde."

The last page informs the reader that

"The knave of *Clubs* his part hath plaid,
But now wee want *Hart, Diamond, Spade*,
To shew themselves like in true shape,
The reason why they doe escape
Is this : of late they fell at iarre,
Disperst asunder very farre,
Harts in the Country at new-cut,
And *Spades* in Newgate safe is shut,
And *Diamonds* he is gone to seas
Sick of the scurvy which disease
If he escape, and get on shore
We will present you with all foure
And make them march unto the presse
To utter all their roguishnes,
So till they be together drawne
Pray keepe the Knave of *Clubs* in pawne.
FINIS."

[7 × 5 in.]

E. 235.

(Printed Books Department, 1076, i. 11.)

FIRST QUARTER OF SEVENTEENTH CENTURY.

(King James I.)

LONDON.

PRINTED book of forty-eight pages, each page containing about twenty lines of satirical verse. The title-page bears the inscription : " The Knave of Harts, Haile Fellow, well met. London : Printed for John Bache and are to be sold at his shop at the entring in of the royall Exchange, 1613."

The central part of the title-page is occupied by a wood-cut, representing the knaves of hearts and of clubs as soldiers, one of whom bears a partisan in his left hand (hearts), the other (clubs) a long arrow-like lance in his right hand. The figures regard and address each other, and have the marks of their suits placed at the side of their heads. The knave of hearts wears likewise a sword and buckler. A second block has been stamped in red over the greater portion of this last figure and the sign of the suit. On the first page (A. 2.) is an address of " The knave of Harts to his three Brethern Knaves," and on the last is the " Epilogue," concluding with the lines :

> " Farewell, farewell in haste adue
> The cardes want Harts to make them true."

[7 × 5 in.]

E. 236.

(Printed Books Department, c. 32. b. 17.)

FIRST QUARTER OF SEVENTEENTH CENTURY.

(King James I.)

LONDON.

PRINTED volume of forty-eight pages, consisting of satirical poems referring to various characters and customs of loose or questionable description. The titlepage bears the inscription, "More Knaves yet? The Knaves of Spades and Diamonds. London : Printed for John Tap, dwelling at Saint Magnus." The central portion of the title-page is occupied by a representation of two full-length figures, personifying the knaves of spades and diamonds. The knave of spades is seen in profile on the left hand addressing his companion, who carries a partisan and wears spurs.

On the first page (A. 3.) is, " The epistle to any man but especially to Fooles and *Mad-men.*" On the last page is concluded a poem on " The seaven deadly Sins all Horst and riding to Hell," following which is the verse :

" The knaves are delt, the game is plaid,
And with this wish concludeth spade,
I would all knaves who ere they bee
Were knowne by sight as well as wee.
Finis."

The previous two volumes, E. 234 and E. 235, are the original editions of the series of " Rowlands' Knaves." The present work is but a reprint, the *verso* of the supplementary leaf to which bears the following inscriptions : " Vereor ne hæc forte nimis antiqua, et jam obsoleta videantur."—*Cicero in Verrem.* " Reprinted at the Beldornie Press, by G. E. Palmer for Edwd. V. Utterson, in the year MDCCCXLI."

E. 237.

(Printed Books Department, c. 32. b. 20.)

FIRST QUARTER OF SEVENTEENTH CENTURY.

(King James I.)

LONDON.

PRINTED volume of forty-two pages of satirical verse. It is entitled, " The Knave of Clubbs, 'tis merry when Knaves meet. Printed at London by E. A., dwelling nere Christ-Church, 1611." This volume is a modern reprint of E. 235.

On the last page of the present work is the inscription, " Reprinted at the Beldornie Press, by G. E. Palmer for Edwd. V. Utterson, in the year MDCCCXLI."

E. 238.

(Printed Books Department, c. 32. b. 15.)

FIRST QUARTER OF SEVENTEENTH CENTURY.

(King James I.)

LONDON.

PRINTED volume of forty-six pages, consisting of satirical verse. It bears the title, " Knave of Harts, Haile Fellow, well met. London : Printed for John Bache, and are to be sold at his shop at the entring in of the Royall Exchange, 1613."

This volume is a modern reprint of E 235. " Reprinted at the Beldornie Press by George Butler, for Edwd. V. Utterson, in the year MDCCCXL."

E. 239.

(*Printed Books Department*, A. c. 9480.)

SECOND QUARTER OF NINETEENTH CENTURY.

LONDON.

HIS, is the ninth volume of the " Early English Poetry, Ballads, and popular Literature of the Middle Ages. Edited from original Manuscripts and scarce publications by the Percy Society. London, MDCCCXLIII". It contains reprints of " The four Knaves. A series of satirical tracts by Samuel Rowlands. Edited with an Introduction and Notes by E. F. Rimbault, Esq., Ph.D., F.S.A., Member of the Royal Academy of Music in Stockholm, &c."

These " four Knaves " are the works previously described, viz., E. 234, E. 235, E. 236. Dr. Rimbault in his introduction remarks : " Samuel Rowlands, the author of the (foregoing) tracts, was a prolific writer of the end of the sixteenth and early part of the succeeding century." . . . . " Excepting that he lived and wrote nothing is now known of his history." . . . . " All his productions have now become exceedingly rare, but perhaps none more so than the series of quaint satirical tracts reprinted in the following pages. The first, 'The knave of Clubbs, 'tis merry when Knaves meete,' upon its appearance in 1600, gave such offence on account of the severity of its satire and the obviousness of its allusions, that an order was made that it should be burnt, first publicly, and afterwards in the Hall Kitchen of the Stationers' Company.'

" In accordance with a promise given at the end of the ' Knave of Clubbs,' Rowlands went on with his series of Knaves, and in 1612 gave to the world, ' The Knave of Harts, Haile Fellowe well met.'——' The last of the series of Rowlands' Knaves was ' More knaves yet ? The Knaves of Spades and Diamonds.' It was printed without a date, but in all probability (from allusions to Ward and Dansikar, two famous pirates whose story was then popular) about the same period as the preceding tract."

Another tract by Rowlands bears the title : "A paire of spy-knaves." Between the publication of the first and second tracts (E. 234, E. 235) an anonymous writer, without (according to Dr. Rimbault) a particle of wit or drollery, endeavoured to take advantage of Rowlands' popularity by imitating the title-page of one of the most successful of his publications. The work alluded to is entitled, " Roome for a messe of knaves, &c. *London : Printed by N. F.*, 1610."

From the remarks by Mr. Utterson, appended to his various reprints of these knave tracts, the following has been taken. Samuel Rowlands "appears to have visited the haunts of profligacy and vice, in search of objects for his sarcastic Muse, and the result of such Enquiries communicated in his various pieces, is productive of amusement as well as instruction to modern readers."——" All his productions are now become very rare, although most of them went through repeated editions."——" There are copies of the three several volumes of ' Knaves' in the Malone collection in the Bodleian Library ; in the British Museum are the knaves of Harts and Clubs, and the *three* works bound together were in Mr. Heber's collection, having been purchased by him at Mr. Brindley's sale.[1] The present reprint is limited to fifteen copies, none of which are intended for sale."

On folio B of the " Knave of Harts," E. 235, is " The knave of Harts his suppli-

---

[1] For £35 3s.

cation to card makers," in which the petitioner, on behalf of himself and his brother knaves of clubs, diamonds, and spades, complains of the way in which the card-makers persist in dressing them, and that they

> " Are kept in pie-bald suites which we have worne
> Hundred of yeares, this hardly can be borne.
>   *   *   *   *
> How can we choose but have the itching gift
> Kept in one kinde of cloaths, and never shift ?
>   *   *   *   *
> How bad I and my fellow Diamond goes
> We never yet had garter to our hose
> Nor any shooe to put upon our feete
> With such base cloaths, 'tis e'en a shame to see't
> My sleeves are like some Morris-dauncing fellow
> My stockings ideot like, red greene and yeallow
> My Breeches like a pair of lute-pins be
> Scarse Buttocke-roome as every man may see
> Like three-penie watch men, three of us doe stand
> Each with a rusty Browne-bill in his hand
> And Clubs he holds an Arrow like a Clowne
> The head-end upward and the feathers downe
>   *   *   •   *
> Shew us (I pray) some reason how it haps
> That we are ever bound to wear flat caps
>   *   *   *   *
> And some because we have no beards do thinke
> We are foure Panders with our lowsie lockes
> Whose naked chinnes are shaven with the ——
>   *   *   *   *
> Good card-makers (if there be any goodnes in you)
> Apparell us with more respected care
> Put us in hats our caps are worne thread-bare
> Let us have standing collers in the fashion
> (all are become a stiffe-necke generation)
> Rose Hatbands with the shagged-ragged Ruffe
> Great cabbage shooe-strings (pray you bigge enough)
> French Dublet, and the Spanish Hose to breech it
> Short cloakes old Mandilions (we beseech it)
> Exchange our Swords, and take away our Bils,
> Let us have Rapiers (Knaves love fight that kils)
> Put us in Bootes and make us leather legs
> This *Harts* most humbly and his fellowes begs."

On the title-page of " More knaves yet? The knaves of Spades and Diamonds," E. 236, the figures appear, clad in a different costume to those of the knaves making the above complaint, E. 235, and to the conventional dress derived from the time of Henry VII. The dress in E. 236, has been modernized by the card-makers. For the change, as far as it went, the knaves of spades and diamonds thus return thanks :

> " As now the honest Printer hath bin kinde
> Bootes and stockins to our legs doth finde
> Garters, polonia heeles, and rose shooe-strings
> Which, somewhat us two knaves in fashion brings

From the knee downeward, legs are well amended
And we acknowledge that we are befrended
And will requite him for it as we can
A knave some time may serve an honest man."

It is open to question, we think, whether the knaves have profited by the changes following their complaint. The knave of spades is rather smart about the legs with his garters and shoe-strings, and the knave of diamonds is booted and spurred, but on the whole we would have preferred, had we been the knaves, remaining as we were. Even the latter are not wholly satisfied, and evince desire

" For the great large abominable breech
Like brewers hop-sackes ; yet since new they be
Each knave will have them, and why should not wee ?
Some laundresse we also will entreate
For bannes and ruffes, which kindnes to be great
We will confesse yea and requite it too
In any service that poore knaves can doe
Scarffes we doe want to hang our weapons by
If any puncke will deale so courteously
As in the way of favour to bestow them
Rare cheating tricks we will protest to owe them
Or any pander with a ring in 's eare
That is a gentleman (as he doth sweare)
And will affoord us hats of newest blocke
A payre of cardes shall be his trade and stocke
To get his lyving by, for lack of lands
Because he scornes to overworke his handes
And thus ere long we trust we shall be fitted
Those knaves that cannot shift, are shallow witted."

Impressions from the wood-blocks belonging to the Percy Society, illustrating the costume of the " Four Knaves," may be found in Chatto's treatise, Bibl. pp. 133, 136.

E. 240.

(*Printed Books Department*, e. 246, Tract xi.)

SECOND QUARTER OF SEVENTEENTH CENTURY.

(KING CHARLES I.)

LONDON.

N this volume is a tract (No. xi.) entitled, " The Bloody Game at Cards as it was played betwixt the King of Hearts and the rest of his Suite, against the residue of the Packe of Cards wherein Is discovered where faire play was plaid and where was fowle. Shuffled at London, Cut at Westminster, Dealt at Yorke, and Plaid in the Open fiel by the City-clubs, the country spade-men, Rich-Diamond men, and Loyall Hearted Men."

In the centre of the title page is the representation of the honour card—the king of hearts—in the conventional way. It is from a wood-block, the design on which has been carefully drawn and engraved. It is uncoloured.

On the eighth page—the last—the account concludes as follows :—" The King of Hearts as his suit is best in colour and in courage, so they are such understanding gamesters that they will not be taken in any over-sight, there are no bunglers there, nor any fumbling in all their play, but all expert and cunning gamesters; it is, therefore, no wonder if successe doth attend them and that they still come winners off in all the games they play. The rest of the pack have therefore done very well and wisely to crave a truce of the King of Hearts who is more willing to forgive them then they have bin apt to oppose him.

> " Since they on both sides have been cross't
> And both have wonne and both have lost
> It now is thought high time of Day
> Friendly to part and leave off play.
> *Finis."*

E. 241.

(*Printed Books Department*, e. 309, *Collection of Pamphlets*, 233.)

SECOND QUARTER OF SEVENTEENTH CENTURY.

(KING CHARLES I.)

LONDON.

RACT No. 19 in this volume is one entitled, " Chartæ Scriptæ, or a New Game at Cards called Play by the Booke, printed in the year 1645."
In the dedication, " To the most Vertuous and therefore most accomplished Lady, the Lady V. M.," allusion is made to the well-known French card-maker, Nicholas Besniere, (*antea*, F. 46.)

> " Madam,—Though other cards passe here and there
> Under the name of Nicholas Beniere,'
> And his Protections good (unless it be)
> From the Exciseman or Monoply," &c.

The aces and honour cards are here first personified, and made to express half-moral, half-satirical sentiments in verse. Then follow the tens with ten poetic apophthegms, the nines with nine, and so on, concluding on p. 24 with " Duo sacramenta."

E. 242.

(*Printed Books Department*, e. 983, *Collection of Pamphlets*, 790.)

THIRD QUARTER OF SEVENTEENTH CENTURY.

LONDON.

HIS volume contains a tract (No. 9) entitled, " Shufling, Cutting, and Dealing in a Game at Pickquet, being Acted from the Year 1653 to 1658, by O. P. and others; with great Applause. Tempora mutantur et nos. Printed in the year 1659."
Oliver Cromwell is represented after the dissolution of the Long Parliament (20th April, 1653), playing at cards along with certain of his old officers and

friends, together with his opponents and some public offices personified, such as the Exchequer, Common Pleas, Presbyterianism, &c. All these persons as they sit at piquet are supposed to express sentiments in respect to the political transactions previously and then taking place. The game opens with—

" Oliver P.—I am like to have a good begining on't; I have thrown out all my best cards, and got none but a company of wretched ones, so may very well be capetted."

It concludes with the

" Divines.—I was pickquet the last, but am now rejoicing."

" Papist.—If you all complain, I hope I shall win at last."

Following the game is the " Epilogue. It is to be noted that the gentlemen that have been eminent in this last dealing of the cards playd very fair in the former game here described. With a Plaudite." " Sic transit gloria mundi."

These politico-satirical tracts (E. 240, E. 241, E. 242) were known to Chatto, who remarks in regard to them:—" When the civil war commenced and the people became interested in a sterner game, card-playing appears to have declined. The card-playing gallant whose favourite haunts had been the play-house and the tavern, now became transformed into a cavalier, and displayed his bravery in the field at the head of a troop of horse, whilst his old opponent, the puritanical minister, incited by a higher spirit of indignation, instead of holding forth on sports and pastimes, and household vices, now thundered on the ' drum ecclesiastic ' against national oppressors, urged his congregation to stand up for their rights as men against the pretensions of absolute monarchy and rampant prelacy, and to try the crab-tree staff against the courtier's dancing rapier."

" Among the numerous pamphlets which appeared during the contest, there are a few whose titles show that the game of cards, though not so much in vogue as formerly, was still not forgotten."

Besides these " A Murnival of Knaves " (1683) " Win first lose at last, or the game of cards which were shuffled by President Bradshaw, cut by Col. Hewson, the Cobler, and played by Oliver Cromwell and Ireton till the Restoration of Charles II. (1707)." A " Lenten Litany," " Poems on State Affairs" (1704), " Jamesanna, or a Pythagorical Play at Cards," are politico-satirical literary ventures which may be here recorded. (See Chatto, p. 138.)

E. 243.

Printed Books Department, Roxburghe Ballads, vol. ii. pp. 81, 243, 360, also p. 149, Edited by Mr. Chappell.

(Published by the Ballad Society), Hertford, 1873.

N this volume there is a quaint wood-cut heading three ballads, pp. 81, 243, and 360. Among the figures on the cut is a great rabbit holding up in each front paw a card with the pips exposed to the spectator, viz. the three of spades and the five of clubs.

Mr. Chappell remarks in reference to this cut, that it is probably derived from one of Robert Greene's books on " Coney-Catching."

Heading another ballad at p. 149 is a cut representing a sot standing near a table on which, among other things, is an upturned card.

VARIA.

V. 244.

SECOND QUARTER OF NINETEENTH CENTURY.

RUSSIA.

PACK of fifty-two numerals of the suits, diamonds, hearts, spades, and clubs. The honours are king, queen, and knave figured in busts, printed double and in reverse.

The individual marks of the suits are characterized by their very acute or prolonged forms, where their contour lines meet or decussate. The ternate form of the sign for clubs is also noteworthy. The mark on the ace of diamonds is surrounded by a sinuous border, having large dots in the hollows of its curves.

The designs on the figure-cards are from metal plates of soft character. The knave of hearts bears a shield, on which is the double-headed eagle of Russia.

On the two of diamonds is the Russian duty stamp.

This series should be compared with V. 246.

The backs of these cards are very neatly diapered with dotted lines, forming the Greek key ornament running diagonally, and printed in blue.

[3½ × 2⅜ in.]   [Backs decorated.]

V. 245.

SECOND QUARTER OF NINETEENTH CENTURY.

PORTUGAL.

PACK of fifty-two numerals of the suits, hearts, diamonds, spades, and clubs. The honours are king, queen, and knave, figured as busts, printed double and in reverse.

Each ace has on it two landscapes printed in reverse, a central circular space being kept clear for the symbol of the suit.

On the four of diamonds are the arms of Portugal, having inscribed below : "Thesouro Publico, Pagou quarenta reis de Sello."

The designs on the figure-cards are of half costume, half modern character, strongly coloured. The landscapes on the aces are heavily coloured.

The marks of diamonds, spades, and clubs, approach those of the before-mentioned set, V. 244.

The backs are marked with sinuous dotted lines, printed in red.

[$3\frac{3}{8}$ × $2\frac{2}{8}$ in.]   [Backs decorated.]

V. 246.

SECOND QUARTER OF NINETEENTH CENTURY.

SWITZERLAND (?)

PACK of fifty-two numerals of the suits, spades, hearts, diamonds, clubs. The honours are represented as busts, printed double and in reverse; the designs being of half historic, half costume character.

The general design of the whole series approximates to that of V. 244. It is presumed that the Swiss relationship of these cards recorded on the title has been inferred from their having been procured from Switzerland.

The backs are marked with sinuous, dotted red lines, and large red stars.

[$3\frac{7}{8}$ × $2\frac{3}{8}$ in.]   [Backs decorated.]

V. 247.

THIRD QUARTER OF THE NINETEENTH CENTURY.

NEW YORK.

SET of fifty-two numerals, the marks of the suits and designs of the figure-cards being of a special character, and designed for American feeling and taste.

The intent of this series may be accurately learnt from the following address printed in red, on a buff-coloured ground, and which accompanies the cards :—

" The American Card Co., confident that the Introduction of National Emblems in the place of Foreign, in Playing Cards, will be hailed with delight by the American People, take pleasure in presenting the Union Playing Cards as the first and only Genuine American Cards ever produced, in the fullest confidence that the time is not far distant when they will be the leading card in the American market.

" *Explanation.*—The Union Cards are calculated to play all the games for which the old style of Playing Cards are used. The suits are Eagles, Shields, Stars, and Flags. Goddess of Liberty in place of Queen, Colonel for King, Major for Jack. In playing with these cards they are to be called by the names the emblems represent, and as the emblems are as familiar as household words everywhere among the American people, they can be used as readily the first occasion as Cards bearing Foreign Emblems."

An engraved title is present, representing the " Goddess of Liberty," enclosed within a framework of the following inscriptions : " Nationality everything." [Two marks of admiration follow.]   " National Emblems, something new in the card world. Time for a change. Foreign Emblems used long enough in the U. S."

Then succeeds : "Entered according to Act of Congress in the year 1862, by Benj. W. Hitchcock, in the Clerk's Office of the District Court of the United States for the Southern District of New York."

The ace of eagles also bears the above authorization below an eagle and cage. From the mouth of the bird proceeds a scroll having on it *E pluribus unum.* Above is a larger scroll, bearing the address of the "American Card Company. Below on a third scroll, may be read : "14 Chambers S^t. & 165 William S^t., New York."

The eagle is backed by a radiant sun. The suits of eagles and of shields are printed in blue, those of stars and flags in red colours.

The "colonel" (king) of the suit of eagles is a three-quarter figure in a blue military surtout, with epaulettes, sword, and sash. He stands in a hilly landscape, having tents in the background.

The queen of the same suit is represented by the Goddess of Liberty, bearing a red Phrygian cap at the end of a lance, and extending her left hand towards the mark of the suit. By her right side is an eagle perched on a shield, bearing the stars and stripes. The goddess bears a radiant star on her head, and her drapery (decorated with stars and stripes), is raised above her knee, so as to expose the whole of the left leg.

The major (Jack), is represented by a person in jack-boots, Tyrolean hat, blue jacket, and red breeches, holding a lance in his right hand. Behind him is a gun and carriage, and in the middle distance is an orderly bringing forward the major's horse. In the distance a steamer is seen descending a river. At the right-hand upper corner is the mark of the suit.

The backs of these cards are marked with an elaborate design, printed in blue, made up of shields, banners, anchors, oak leaves, stars, stripes, &c. &c. The whole is of very vulgar character.

[3½ × 2½ in.]   [Backs decorated.]

V. 248.

THIRD QUARTER OF NINETEENTH CENTURY.

LONDON.

 THIN quarto volume of sixteen leaves, having fifty-two divisions, representing the pieces of a numeral series of the ordinary character, together with descriptions and blank divisions. Each leaf has four equal divisions ; on the first compartment of the first page is the following account :—

"Marginal Index or Self-sorting and Distinguishing Safety Playing-Cards.— Your Hand at Whist, and all other Games distinguished at a glance by yourself alone, without the trouble of sorting. All risks of Revokes and Involuntary play of winning Cards Effectually prevented. Whether playing at Cards for Love or Money, *no* others should be used.

" To be had at all Licensed Vendors of Playing Cards throughout the Kingdom. London : Printed by John A. Rufus, Cross Street, Finsbury Square, E.C. 1869. Entered at Stationers Hall, and right of Translation Reserved."

The method here adopted will be satisfactorily explained by the following reduced copy of one of the compartments, viz. that which represents the eight of hearts

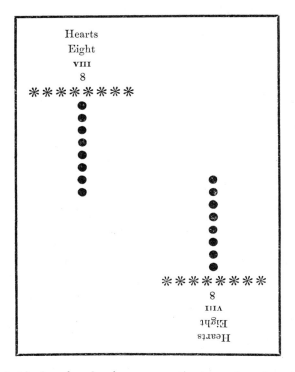

On the last leaf are four drawings representing by marks and numbers the six of hearts, the nine of spades, the seven of diamonds, and the ten of clubs after the following manner:

Then succeeds the note in MS. :—

"N.B.   The foregoing Marginal Marks (or any of them) are intended to denote the suit and the number of Pips on Playing-Cards, and to be conveniently placed on the margins or corners of the Cards.   In the margin under the first corner pip, and its corresponding pip, will be found a very appropriate position for indication of the number, or the numbers may be marked on the pip itself as illustrated in the sketch.

The Author."

On the general field of the card-piece, within the marginal index, the marks of the suit, or the design of the figure-card, are to be represented in the ordinary way.

V. 249.

THIRD QUARTER OF NINETEENTH CENTURY.

LONDON.

 FOLDED sheet, on the first page of which is a description of " Four colours or new Playing-cards, by Francis John Bettles," and on the second and third pages are " Drawings of Eighty-one Cards, Forming the four Colours or New Playing-cards, by Francis John Bettles."

In his account of the new cards the author remarks, " it had occurred to me that there was a much greater fund of amusement to be obtained from playing-cards than by those at present in use, and this has induced me to turn my attention by trying if something simpler, and more diversified, could not be introduced, and the result is my present ' Four Colours, or new Playing-Cards,' which I beg to bring to the notice of the public. I call them new, as I am not aware of any similar cards having ever been used, and I believe the result will be, that any of the games at present played with the existing playing-cards, can be played with them, and an entirely new scope of games and diversions, simple or complicated, can be added. I will, therefore, commence with a description. First of all, each of these cards will have on the face a line drawn across the middle, on each side of which there will be either a blank, or one or more stars, (or any other mark instead of a star which the taste of the printer may prefer) ; there will be only one card a double blank, and four sets of the following, each set being distinguished by a different colour, thus say, Red—blank one side of the line and one star on the other, blank and two, blank and three, blank and four, blank and five, one and one, one and two, one and three, one and four, one and five ; two and two, two and three, two and four, two and five ; three and three, three and four, three and five ; four and four, four and five ; five and five ; thus twenty cards of one colour, and the foregoing twenty cards repeated in three other different colours, say Green, Blue, and Black (or other colours if preferred by the printers), there being eighty-one cards in all, as seen in the drawing annexed."

The method of using these cards in playing what is termed by the deviser the " Matching Game," is described to " show the diversified amusement that may be afforded with them."

Entered at Stationers' Hall, 27th October, 1871.

---

[1] The three of diamonds is employed here twice over on account of the facility of printing the suit mark ; the marks and values furnished in the original being the three of diamonds and the five of spades.

ORIENTAL PLAYING-CARDS.

ORIENTAL PLAYING CARDS.

HINDUSTANI.

O. H. 250.

SECOND QUARTER OF NINETEENTH CENTURY.

AHMEDABAD (?).

 SET of Hindustani cards ninety-six in number.

There are three suits of different colours, viz. red, green, and yellow. The red and green suits have each three series, viz. a deep green, a medium green, and light green sequence. The yellow suit has but two series, a light yellow and orange yellow sequence. Each of the eight series has ten point cards and two figure cards. The marks of the suits are birds on the various coloured grounds, in number according to the value of the card; No. 1 having the mark in the centre of the piece similar to the European ace.

The first rank of the red (chocolate) suit has a peacock (?) for the sign; the second rank (deep red) has a black bird; the third (light red) has a white bird with slate coloured wings.

The first rank (deep green) of the green suit has a large white bird of the goose tribe for its sign; the second (medium green) has the same; while the third rank (light green) has a red bird for its symbol.

The first rank of the yellow suit has the black bird symbol. The second rank (orange yellow) has the goose for its mark.

Each rank has ten point or pip cards, and two figure-cards or honours; the latter being represented by a *Wusseer* and a mounted *Schah*, or king. The *Wusseer* is mounted on a white horse in five of the ranks, and on a camel (medium green) or a tiger (light green) or a bull (light yellow) in the others. He gallops always towards the left, extending the arm and hand towards the sign of the rank to which he belongs, and which is represented above the horses' head. The white horses have large black spots on the necks and flanks. In six of the ranks the king is seated under a canopy in the centre of the card. He is turned towards the left, apparently addressing an attendant, towards whom he extends his right arm. Behind the king stands another attendant, waving a large fan. Above the attendant standing opposite the king, the sign of the rank is represented.

In the third rank of the green suit (light green) the king is a radiant sun face above the back of a tiger, preceded by an attendant, and followed by another servant with a fan. Above the sun-like full face is an umbrella, and above the tiger's head is the mark of the rank. This honour closely resembles figure No. 6 on plate 2 of Chatto's work (Bibl. 4), page 42, there said to be the king of the suit—*soorkh*, red, or *Zur i soorkh*—gold coin, figuratively the sun.

The king of the light yellow rank is seated on an elephant. Before him is the driver, behind is the attendant with the fan. Above the head of the elephant is the black bird, the mark of the rank. This card closely approximates the figure, No. 4, of plate 1, in Chatto as before mentioned, and there stated to represent the king of *Gholam*, or of the suit, slaves. Reference may be made with advantage to plate 70 in Merlin's Treatise (Bibl. 6)—the lowest card on the left hand.

Alluding to Hindustani cards, Merlin observes : " They are generally on lacquered cardboard. They are curious, but the painting on them is of a primitive kind ; the Hindu draughtsmen do not know how to represent the eyes. One class of artists always draws profile eyes, even in a full face ; another class always portrays a full eye, even in a profile face." (p. 123.)

In the pack now under consideration there is but one full face represented, viz. the green king of the third rank ; and here the eyes, as respects the position of the cornea and pupil, are evidently of profile character.

The cards of the present series are circular in form, and seem to be made of thick paper or thin pasteboard. They are painted on both faces, and highly varnished on the front face, by which process the pieces have been made very stiff and firm. The colour of the ground stops short about one-eighth of an inch from the circular margin of the card, which is edged red, with a narrow light yellow line within the circle.

On the figure-cards or honours, within the yellow and inner circle, is another and gilt circle, from which, in places, slight leaf-like ornaments occasionally project within the field of the card.

The backs of all the pieces are coloured red, of the same depth as the ground of the third rank of the red suit. A light yellow circle forms a border to them.

Whether this set of Indian cards should be described as above, or, rather, as consisting of eight suits of twelve cards each suit, is, it must be admitted, open to question.

Colours, or red, green, and yellow, are the more general *differentiæ*, but then they are not equally divided among the eight ranks. Red and green have each three ranks ; yellow has but two. If the birds be taken as marks of the chief divisions, a like inequality may be found: *e. g.* there are three ranks of geese, two of black birds, one of red birds, one of white birds, one of peacocks. Further, the geese occupy both the green and the yellow colours, and the black birds the red and the yellow. There is a green peacock (?) on the red ground, and a red bird on the light green colour.

Accompanying this set of Indian cards is a memorandum in MS. as given below :—

" The following is an extract from William Carpenter's letter, dated Ahmedabad, Sept. 22nd, 1851, relating to the Playing-Cards used in India.

" ' I write you what little information I have obtained about the cards. One contains 120 pieces of the Avatars of Krishna, ten suits of twelve each. There are twelve figures painted on —— (?), from one to ten in number, like our playing cards :

" ' 1. Horse.
  2. Gholaum.
  3. Fish.
  4. Tortoise.
  5. Lion.

  6. Umbrella,
  7. Fusee—a piece of iron Goseins carry.
  8. Flag.
  9. Sword.
  10. Bow.

" ' The other contains eight suits of twelve each, from one to ten—a King and a Wuseer. They are divided into two sets, and have different coloured grounds. The first set is this, and counts from ten to one in playing:

" ' Samseer—dark red (or a sword). This signifies bravery and is expressed symbolically.

Rupee—black.

Taj—green.

Gholaum—yellow (for slave)—a little animal having a faint resemblance to a human being.

Brath—light red.

Cit er note.

Kumach—orange. This, with the first, is Persian, and I don't know the meaning.

Asrafee
Sooruk } —light green—a gold coin.

Chan
Bell (?) } —dark green.

" ' This set reckons from one to ten. With regard to the method of play I can tell you nothing till I have seen it, as these natives I am acquainted with, and who speak English, do not understand it.' "

The whole is contained in an oblong wooden box, with sliding lid, ornamented with flowers painted on a green ground ; gold also has been used in the decoration. The box is coarsely made, and is nearly $4\frac{1}{2}$ in. long, $2\frac{1}{2}$ in. wide, and $2\frac{3}{8}$ in. deep.

[Circular, $1\frac{7}{8}$ in. diameter.]   [Backs coloured.]

CHINESE.

O. C. 251.

NINETEENTH CENTURY.

CHINA.

 SERIES of thirty-eight cards from a set of forty-five apparently. It is probable that in the perfect sequence there are five suits of nine pieces each suit, the marks of which are bags, money, batons (or bows), swords, and a fifth mark not satisfactorily demonstrable.

The pieces of the suits of bags and money have on them the marks only in proper number—from one to nine—according to the value of the piece. Those of batons and swords have full-length figures, bearing in their hands the symbols of the suits. The pieces of the fifth suit have figures on some, at least, of their number.

The suits of bags and money are presumed to be complete, *i.e.* of nine pieces each suit. The suit of batons is assumed to want two cards, the suit of swords one, and the fifth suit wants four pieces, at least this is according to the arrangement which appears to be the more satisfactory.

On No. 2 of the suit of batons the figure holds a bow in a state of tension, in place of a baton or spear. The latter, however, may be intended for an unstrung bow, yet it should be remarked that on the six of the suit the mark has decidedly a partisan-like head to it. Above the marks and figures of the suits are Chinese characters. The eight and nine of bags have been stamped in red over the part occupied by the Chinese writing. The six, seven, and eight of swords have been stamped in the same way, as well as four of the cards which appear to belong to the fifth suit. On one of the latter the red stamp has been twice impressed. This stamp is composed of four semi-circular irregular lines one within the other and connected at the extremities. One of the red stamped pieces in " swords " has characters above the usual ones, and outside the border line of the engraving. Those suits having figures on the pieces have small characters near the heads of the figures as if indicating the title of the person represented.

Mr. Chatto, alluding to Chinese cards, remarks, " In a pack of the Chinese cards called Tseen-wan-che-pae, the mark of the suit of Nine Cakes is nearly the same as that of the old Italian *danari*, which Galeottus Martius, in his treatise ' De Doctrina Promiscua,' written about 1488, considers to have been meant for a loaf."———" The Chinese name for a card considered singly, or as one of the pieces of a pack or set, appears to be *Shen*, a fan " (p. 59).

The relative values of the cards of four of the suits are easily to be surmised, such is the purpose and distinctness with which the designs have been executed.

The impressions are on thin flexible card-board, the backs of the pieces being of a deep red colour, and very smooth.

[$2\frac{2}{8} \times 1$ in. size of impression.]   [Backs coloured.]
[$2\frac{5}{8} \times 1\frac{1}{8}$ in. whole card.]

O. C. 252.

NINETEENTH CENTURY.

CHINA.

TWENTY cards from a numeral series of probably thirty pieces, the marks of the suits of which appear to be chains, money, and heads.

The cards present are the one, three, five, six, seven, and eight of chains, the two, three, four, six, and others of money (?), seven pieces of the suit of heads, one piece of which is a full-length figure-card having on it two red stamps. The five of money (?) bears two red stamps as it does in the series O. C. 255. In the suit of chains there are characters above the marks of the suit in the pieces one and five as is the case in O. C. 255 on the one and nine. The series is made of thin card-board, and the backs of the pieces are of a deep orange colour and smooth.

[$2\frac{2}{8} \times \frac{1}{2}$ in. size of impression.]   [Backs coloured.]
[$3\frac{1}{16} \times \frac{5}{8}$ in. whole card.]

O. C. 253.

NINETEENTH CENTURY.

CHINA.

EIGHT cards from a numeral series, probably of thirty pieces, the suits of which are chains, money, and heads.

The cards present are the six of chains, the two, three, six, and another of money, and three pieces of the suit of heads.

[$2\frac{2}{8} \times \frac{1}{2}$ in. size of impression.]   [Backs coloured.]
[$3\frac{1}{16} \times \frac{5}{8}$ in. whole card.]

O. C. 254.

NINETEENTH CENTURY.

CHINA.

THREE cards from a numeral series, probably of thirty pieces, the suits of which are chains, money, and heads.

The cards present are the six of chains, the six of money, and a piece of the suit heads (?).

[$2\frac{2}{8}$ × $\frac{1}{2}$ in. size of impression.]   [Backs coloured.]
[$3\frac{1}{16}$ × $\frac{5}{8}$ in. whole card.]

O. C. 255.

NINETEENTH CENTURY.

CHINA.

A SEQUENCE of thirty cards, forming probably a perfect set as regards number, but one at least of the suits is made up of pieces from another set.

The marks of the suits are chains, money, and heads. There are three separate superior cards. Each suit has nine numeral members ; the suit of money is here a made-up suit.

On the nine of chains is an oval stamp in red over the centre of the card. This stamp is twice repeated on two other cards. On the one and nine of chains are Chinese characters above and outside the border lines of the impressions, as is likewise the case in two other pieces. Certain of the heads have characters immediately above them, as if indicating their titles.

These cards are much like those represented in the work of Singer, page 59, and some of the lower cards at p. 60.

As far as relates to the characters above the heads, these cards accord like-wise with the two figured in Chatto, p. 57, the first and third of the suit— Nine Myriads of Kwan.

One of the three separate cards in the present series is similar in its upper portion to that of No. 6, p. 58, of Chatto's Treatise, representing one of the superior members called " Pih-hwa," the White Flower.

M. Boiteau d'Amly justly observes that engraved representations of some narrow Chinese cards go far towards reminding one of cakes of Indian ink.

The narrow size of these cards is remarkable. They are of thin card-board, rounded at both ends, and have their backs coloured deep orange.

[$2\frac{2}{8}$ in. × $\frac{3}{8}$ in. size of impression.]   [Backs coloured.]
[$3\frac{3}{8}$ × $\frac{1}{2}$ in. whole card.]

APPENDIX.

APPENDIX.

CHRONOLOGICAL TABLE.

SERIES OF EARLIER CARDS, ETC., ARRANGED

CHRONOLOGICALLY.

(The dates are approximative only in several instances.)

Cards of the					Cards of the				
2nd quarter,	15th century,	G. 122.			2nd quarter,	16th century,	F. 43.		
3rd	„	15th	„	I. 1.	2nd	„	16th	„	F. 46.
3rd	„	15th	„	G. 120.	3rd	„	16th	„	G. 138.
4th	„	15th	„	I. 2.	4th	„	16th	„	G. 161.
4th	„	15th	„	I. 3.	4th	„	16th	„	F. 47.
4th	„	15th	„	F. 42.	4th	„	16th	„	F. 48.
4th	„	15th	„	G. 147.	1st	half,	16th	„	G. 125.
4th	„	15th	„	G. 149.	1st	„	16th	„	G. 132.
4th	„	15th	„	G. 150.	1st	„	16th	„	G. 135.
4th	„	15th	„	G. 151.	2nd	„	16th	„	I. 4.
4th	„	15th	„	G. 152.	2nd	„	16th	„	G. 129.
4th	„	15th	„	G. 154.	2nd	„	16th	„	G. 130.
4th	„	15th	„	G. 155.	2nd	„	16th	„	G. 131.
4th	„	15th	„	G. 166.	2nd	„	16th	„	G. 156.
4th	„	15th	„	E. 224.	2nd	„	16th	„	G. 157.
4th	„	15th	„	E. 225.	2nd	„	16th	„	G. 258.
2nd	half,	15th	„	G. 124.	2nd	„	16th	„	G. 163.
2nd	„	15th	„	G. 143.	?	?	16th	„	F. 44.
2nd	„	15th	„	G. 148.	?	?	16th	„	F. 45.
1st	quarter,	16th	„	G. 126.	1st	quarter,	17th	„	G. 136.
1st	„	16th	„	G. 127.	1st	„	17th	„	G. 137.
1st	„	16th	„	G. 128.	1st	„	17th	„	E. 198.
1st	„	16th	„	G. 144.	1st	„	17th	„	E. 198. 2.
1st	„	16th	„	G. 145.	1st	„	17th	„	E. 234.
1st	„	16th	„	G. 146.	1st	„	17th	„	E. 235.
1st	„	16th	„	G. 153.	1st	„	17th	„	E. 236.
1st	„	16th	„	G. 165.	1st	„	17th	„	E. 237.

Cards of the				Cards of the			
1st quarter,	17th century,	E. 238.		4th quarter,	17th century,	E. 184.
2nd ,,	17th ,,	E. 199.		4th ,,	17th ,,	E. 185.
2nd ,,	17th ,,	E. 228.		4th ,,	17th ,,	E. 186.
2nd ,,	17th ,,	E. 240.		4th ,,	17th ,,	E. 187.
2nd ,,	17th ,,	E. 241.		4th ,,	17th ,,	E. 188.
2nd ,,	17th ,,	S. 15.		4th ,,	17th ,,	E. 189.
3rd ,,	17th ,,	I. 13.		4th ,,	17th ,,	E. 190.
3rd ,,	17th ,,	E. 179.		4th ,,	17th ,,	E. 203.
3rd ,,	17th ,,	E. 242.		4th ,,	17th ,,	E. 229.
4th ,,	17th ,,	I. 13. 2.		1st ,,	17th ,,	F. 74.
4th ,,	17th ,,	I. 14.		1st ,,	17th ,,	E. 226.
4th ,,	17th ,,	I. 14. 2.		2nd half,	17th ,,	G. 159.
4th ,,	17th ,,	F. 76.		2nd ,,	17th ,,	E. 195.
4th ,,	17th ,,	F. 77.		2nd ,,	17th ,,	E. 227.
4th ,,	17th ,,	F. 79. 2.		? ?	17th ,,	I. 8.
4th ,,	17th ,,	E. 167.		? ?	17th ,,	I. 9.
4th ,,	17th ,,	E. 168.		? ?	17th ,,	F. 49.
4th ,,	17th ,,	E. 174.		? ?	17th ,,	D. 115.
4th ,,	17th ,,	E. 175.		? ?	17th ,,	G. 133.
4th ,,	17th ,,	E. 177.		? ?	17th ,,	G. 134.
4th ,,	17th ,,	E. 178.				

NOTEWORTHY SERIES.

SERIES OF CARDS, ETC., TO WHICH SPECIAL INTEREST IS ATTACHED.

1. The so-called (erroneously) Tarocchi of Mantegna, or *Carte di Baldini*, I. 1, page 65.

2. Venetian Tarots of the Marchesa Busca Serbelloni, I. 3, p. 77.

3. Early Stencilled Cards of 1440 (?), G. 122, p. 192.

4. The "Chatto Cards," (or the cards of the binding of the *Sermones M. Vincentii*) of the last quarter of the 15th century, F. 42, p. 110.

5. The so-called (erroneously) "Trappola Cards," of the last quarter of the 15th century, having the *Granada* as a mark of a suit, G. 120, p. 189.

6. Circular Cards of Cologne, with animated marks of suits, G. 143, p. 207.

7. Telman von Wesel's version of the Circular Cards of Cologne, G. 144, p. 209.

8. Cards having chimeric animals as marks of suits, G. 147, p. 213.

9. Cards having animated marks of suits, from G. 148, to G. 155, inclusive, pp. 214-216.

10. German Numerals, from G. 124, to G., 132, inclusive, pp. 194-198.

11. The "Jehan Volay," Spanish numerals, S. 15, p. 93.

12. The several series of French numerals, from F. 43, to F. 49, inclusive, pp. 113-116.

13. French Tarots, F. 37, p. 107.

14. Flemish Tarots, Fl. 103, p. 179.

15. The Cards of Stefano della Bella, F. 74, p. 126.

16. F. C. Z. Cards, G. 135, p. 199.

17. The Beham Cards, G. 138, p. 203.

18. The Jobst Amman Cards, G. 161, p. 221.

19. The Virgil Solis Cards, G. 156, p. 217.

20. German Tarots, G. 116, p. 187.

21. English Cards, E. 167, p. 229.

22. Spanish Armada Cards, E. 185, p. 265.

23. The Popish Plot Cards from E. 186, to E. 188, inclusive, pp. 266-270.

24. The Rye House Plot Cards, E. 189, p. 273.

25. The Seven Bishops' Cards, E. 190, p. 274.

BIBLIOGRAPHY.

THE following works will prove amply sufficient for those persons who may desire further information on the subjects treated of in the preceding pages, but yet who do not purpose entering into a minute and critical investigation of the whole History of Playing-Cards. Such as intend to do so, however, may find all the necessary sources of instruction referred to in the bibliographical lists appended to the treatises of Chatto (No. 4), of the Bibliophiles Français (No. 2), and of Boiteau d'Ambly (No. 3).

The " Analyse critique et raisonnée de toutes les Recherches publiées jusqu'à ce jour sur l'origine et l'histoire des Cartes à Jouer," which forms the second portion of the " Recherches Historiques et Littéraires sur les Danses des Morts et sur l'origine des Cartes à Jouer, par Gabriel Peignot. Dijon et Paris. MDCCCXXVI." may be also consulted.

No. 1. Bartsch (Adam). Le Peintre-Graveur. Leipsic, 1803-21-54, 8vo. Vol. vi. p. 55; vol. x. pp. 70-120; vol. xiii. pp. 120-138.

No. 2. Bibliophiles Français (Société des). Jeux de Cartes Tarots et de Cartes Numerales du Quatorzième au Dix-huitième Siècle. Paris, 1844, folio.

No. 3. Boiteau d'Ambly (P.). Les Cartes à Jouer et la Cartomancie. Paris, 1854. 8vo.

No. 4. Chatto (William Andrew). Facts and Speculations on the Origin and History of Playing-Cards. London, 1848, 8vo.

No. 5. Cicognara (Leopoldo). Memorie spettanti alla storia della Calcografia. Prato, 1831, 8vo., tavole in foglio.

No. 6. Merlin (R.). Origine des Cartes à Jouer. Recherches Nouvelles sur les Naïbis, les Tarots, et sur les autres espèces de Cartes. Paris, 1869, 4to.

No. 7. Passavant (J. D.). Le Peintre-Graveur. Leipsic, 1860, 8vo. Vol. i., pages 6, 208, 213, 243; vol. ii., pages 66, 70, 100, 176, 205, 242, 246, 247; vol. v., pages 11, 119, 126, 129, 132, 134.

No. 8. Singer (Samuel Weller). Researches into the History of Playing-Cards, with Illustrations of the Origin of Printing and Engraving on Wood. London, 1816, 4to.

No. 9. Taylor (Rev. Ed. S. and others.) The History of Playing-Cards, with Anecdotes of their Use in Conjuring, Fortune-Telling, and Card-Sharping. London, 1865, 8vo. This work forms an English version, with additions and changes, of Boiteau d'Ambly's treatise, No. 3.

INDEX.

INDEX TO PROPER NAMES.

INDEX TO SUBJECTS.

CHISWICK PRESS :—PRINTED BY WHITTINGHAM AND WILKINS,
TOOKS COURT, CHANCERY LANE.

DESCRIPTIVE CATALOGUE OF PLAYING AND OTHER CARDS IN THE BRITISH MUSEUM.

(SUPPLEMENTARY PORTION.)

HE arrangement adopted in describing the various playing and other cards in the national collection may be found detailed at pages 61 and 62 of the first part of this Catalogue.

The contraction Bibl., accompanied by a number, in the following pages, refers to the " Bibliography," vol. i., p. 343.

PREFACE.

 FEW prefatory remarks are necessary on this supplementary portion of the " Descriptive Catalogue of Playing and other Cards." It was not until the first Division was ready for publication that the Trustees decided to issue this supplementary part, which should include an account of several items acquired by the Museum since the former part had been completed. It was also determined that advantage should be taken of this supplement to include in it a series of illustrations by which a fuller explanation of several of the topics discussed in the first part of the Catalogue might be given and the reader's interest in them be thereby increased.

This subsequent decision will account for the absence from the first part of all reference to the commentary and plates in the present portion of the Catalogue.

The present supplement to the Catalogue has been executed by the author of the former portion, under the supervision of the Keeper -of the Prints and Drawings.

March, 1877.

GEORGE WILLIAM REID.

TABLE OF CONTENTS.

PART I.

EUROPEAN PLAYING-CARDS.

ITALIAN PLAYING-CARDS.

TAROTS.

I. 256.

LATTER THIRD OF SEVENTEENTH CENTURY.

FLORENCE.

(MINCHIATE.)

N imperfect sequence of combined tarots, *i. e.*, an emblematic series along with numerals, constituting a modification of the old Venetian tarots, known as the "Minchiate of Florence." A perfect set of Minchiate playing-cards is composed of ninety-seven pieces, viz., forty-one tarots proper and fifty-six numerals. The present incomplete set includes twenty-six tarots proper and thirty-nine numerals; it is hence deficient of thirty-two pieces.

The "Minchiate" is alluded to in vol. i. p. 38 as the third tarots game, or that modification of the early Venetian *tarocchi* which became the national game of the Florentines and Tuscany, a game not any longer one of simple combinations like its parents, but one of arithmetical perplexity.

An account of the "Valore di Tarocchi" in this complex amusement, and of the numerical combinations arising out of them, may be met with in the following treatise by a professor of mathematics at Rome:—

"Giuochi delle Minchiate, Ombre, Scacchi ed altri d'ingegno, Dedicati Alla Illͫa, ed Eccͫa Signora la Signora Principessa Donna Guilia Albani Chigi Da D. Francesco Saverio Brunetti Da Corinaldo. In Roma, per il Bernabo, e Lazzarini, 1747. Con licenza de' Superiori," 8vo, pp. 128.

A copy of this uncommon work is in the Library of the British Museum, 7915 a a a.

In the treatise by Brunetti may be found a full description of the way in which Minchiate should be played, the laws relative to the game, as also "Avvertimenti per giuocar bene." Following each notice of particular details is a "Nota Allegorica," with quotations from Latin and Italian writers. The Nota Allegorica to the "Capo Primo" on the "Mazzo delle Carte" is as follows:—

"This extensive series of cards may be likened to the catastrophes and casualties of mankind; the whole is analogous to the Human race, which lives mixed up together on this earth. The four suits represent the four early monarchies of the Assyrians or Chaldeans, which commenced with Ninus, the father-in-law of Semiramidis, in the year of the world 1944, contemporaneously with Deborah, and ended with Darius Medus, the son of Astiagus, contemporaneous with Daniel, in the year of the world 3450. The second monarchy of the Persians commenced with Cyrus, the nephew of the sister of the before-mentioned Darius, and ended with Darius Codomanus, who was conquered by Alexander the Great. With the latter commenced and finished the third monarchy of the Greeks, since the latter were afterwards broken up into several kingdoms. These latter gradually succumbed to the Roman power, which culminated gloriously in the fourth monarchy."

" The forty *tarocchi*, which are superior to or 'take' all the other suits, may be likened to the fifth universal monarchy, which brought together every nation under its ægis. We have at last the 'Matto' which responds to every other card, but never takes nor can be taken unless all be lost. Perhaps we should bear in mind that the human race became mad from its origin; and that, nevertheless, fools will last to the end of the world, when more men will not be produced any longer. *Stultorum plena sunt omnia* (Cic. Ep. ix.)."

" I have desired to point out the above in order that, with the opportunity of playing *Minchiate*, those engaged in it should desire to obtain a knowledge of history and above all of chronology, because *nescire quod anteaquam natus sis acciderit, id est semper esse puerum.* Cic. in Oratore." (Brunetti, *op. cit.* p. 15.)

There is a tradition that the game of Minchiate was invented at Sienna by Michael Angelo to teach young persons arithmetic, but that it did not become fashionable until the time of Pope Innocent the Tenth (1644 A.D.), whose portrait is that of the Pope of these cards. (Gough, in " Archæologia," vol. viii. p. 172.)

In the " Regole Generali del Giuoco delle Minchiate," etc., a work to be presently alluded to, is the following statement :—

" Ebbe, questo Giuoco a sua prima origine in una conversazione de nobili Cittadini Fiorentini che studiosi nell' aritmetica lo inventarono per occuparsi con util diletto nell' ora di loro recreazione."

The precise origin of the term Minchiate is not known, but is probably from the old Italian word *Menchia*, signifying game, sport, etc. It was obligingly pointed out to the author by C. Knight Watson, Esq., of the Society of Antiquaries, that in the old " Vocabolario Italiano e Inglese," by Florio, London, 1659, the name of the game is spelt *Menchiatte*.

Florio gives also *Menchia*, game, some sport, etc. In more recent dictionaries the word is always spelt *Minchiate*.

In the latter part of the year 1803 a paper was read at the Society of Antiquaries by Mr. J. Smith, describing " Minchiate," who, at the same time presented the Society with a pack of the cards. In this paper, which may be found in the fifteenth volume of the "Archæologia" (for 1806), p. 140, Mr. Smith observes :—

" I have the honour to present to the Society a complete set of Minchiate cards such as have been long in use at Florence, and with it a small treatise, in the Italian language, containing the rules of the game and directions for playing it, both of which I have brought from the Continent some years ago, and have had them by me ever since.

" There is no game on the cards of which I have any knowledge that requires closer attention, a more ready talent for figures, or greater exercise of the memory than this of Minchiate. It is held in high estimation among the fashionable circles in Tuscany, where almost everybody exclaims in the language of the treatise, 'E senza dubbio il più nobile di tutti i Giuochi che siensi mai potuti inventare colle carte.' "

Opportunity has been afforded the author of examining Mr. Smith's gift to the Society. He has found the set of cards to be complete and in good condition, and the little work accompanying it to bear the following title :—

" Regole Generali del Giuoco delle Minchiate con Diversi Istruzioni brevi, e facili per bene imparare a giuocarlo,

" In Firenze mdcclxxxi.

" Nella Stamperia Vanni e Tofani. Con Approvazione.

" A Spese de Vincenzio Landi." (8vo, pp. 70.)

The characteristics of the Florentine Minchiate may be thus described :—

In place of the twenty-two *atutti* of the old Venetian sequence there are forty-one tarots proper, *i.e.*, nineteen of the older series, or what are equivalent to them, and twenty-two additional tarots, including the *matto* or *fou*. The chief modifications of the old Venetian sequences are as follows, viz. : the figure of *Le Pape* (No. v.) is withdrawn ; *La Papesse* (No. ii.) becomes " Le Grand Duc " ; *L'Impératrise* (No. iii.) and *L'Empereur* (No. iv.) represent the " Emperor of the West " and the " Emperor of the East " respectively ; *L'Hermite* (No. ix.) becomes an old man upon crutches (*le Sablier* No. xi.), having behind him a star and above his shoulder an hour-glass transfixed by an arrow ; while *La Maison Dieu ou la Foudre* (No. xvi.) is discarded, or, perhaps, is metamorphosed into *L'Enfer* (No. xv.). *L'Etoile* (No. xvii.), *La Lune* (No. xviii.), *Le Soleil* (No. xix.), and *Le Monde* (No. xxi.), are retained.

To this slight modification of the old Venetian tarots are added the three theological Virtues—*Faith* (No. xviii.), *Hope* (No. xvi.), and *Charity* (No. xix). Other additional pieces are, one of the four cardinal virtues, *Prudence* (No. xvii.) ; the four elements of the ancient philosophers, as *Fire* (No. xx.), *Water* (No. xxi.), *Earth* (No. xxii.), *Air* (No. xxiii.) ; the twelve signs of the Zodiac (Nos. xxiv. to xxxv.) ; the remainder of the series concluding with the *Star*, the *Moon*, the *Sun*, the *World*, and *La Renommée*.

A peculiarity of the emblematic series in the Minchiate sequence is that the cards do not bear any titles nor names below the subjects represented on them, as they are borne in the other tarots sets. The subjects can be known by their attributes only.

The cards are numbered above in Roman numerals.

Another characteristic of the Minchiate tarots is that the concluding eight of the series—viz., the *Lion* (No. xxxiii.), the *Bull* (No. xxxiv.), the *Twins* (No. xxxv.), the *Star*, the *Moon*, the *Sun*, the *World*, and *La Renommée*— have the designs on them relieved from a red or rose-coloured ground.

The numeral series consists of four suits of fourteen cards each suit, as in the other tarots sequences. Here, as in the case of the emblematic series, certain peculiarities may be observed.

The *cavalli* of the court-cards, or " honours," are chimeric or centaur-like figures, composed of human busts, on equine or other trunks with fantastic tails.

The *fanti*, or valets, are warriors in the suits of spade and *bastoni*, and *fantiglie*, or servants, in those of *coppe* and *danari*.

The suit-marks of *danari* on the pip-cards have heads in their fields, with the exception of the *nine*, on which are birds.

In spade the swords are straight and pointed for thrusting with, except as regards the *cavallo* and *fante*, whose weapons are scimitars.

In the suit of spade particularly the designer of the Minchiate variation has placed various animals, such as cats, elephants, monkeys, and other creatures, with now and then objects, such as stars, etc., on the faces of the cards, as ornamental additions. These would appear to be proper to the Minchiate pieces, since they may be seen both on the older and more recent versions.

Breitkopf would appear, from an observation he makes (" Versuch," etc., p. 27, note *m*), to award to the Neapolitans the increase of the old tarots sequence to the number of ninety-seven pieces, as found in the present Minchiate ; and though he refers to the " Regole Generali del Giuoco delle Minchiate," published at Florence in 1781, and before alluded to, the author did not observe therein any warranty for such award while examining this little treatise at the Society of Antiquaries. The same writer observes, also, that at Munich a modification of the series might be met with, in which the pack consisted of 103 cards, a result obtained by doubling the twenty-one tarots proper and the *fou*, as also the ace, king, and knave of *cœurs* [sic] *i.e.*, 42 tarots, 2 fous, 1 ace, 1 knave, 1 king = 47, added to the 56 numerals = 103.

The present series is of very inferior character as respects design, execution, and colouring—so inferior, indeed, that the subjects on some of the cardpieces are with difficulty made out.

The backs of the cards are marked with the arms, apparently, of Cosmo de Medici the Third, *i.e.*, *circa* the latter end of the seventeenth century. The shield is surmounted with a ducal crown, and has below the motto " FORTUNA."

The armorial bearings are enclosed within a broad border, composed of small points or dots. The whole is printed in very faint black ink. A like but narrower border encloses the designs of the faces of the cards.

[4 × 2⅖ in.]   [Backs decorated.]

I. 257.

LATTER THIRD OF SEVENTEENTH CENTURY.

FLORENCE.

N imperfect sequence of combined tarots, constituting " Minchiate," a Florentine modification of the old Venetian series of emblematic cards.

Of the perfect set of ninety-seven pieces the present series contains the following eleven tarots and eight numerals = 19 *in toto*.

Tarots proper	. . .	Le Bataleur	. . .	Number	i.
		La Force	. . .	„	vii.
		Le Pendu	. . .	„	xii.
		La Mort	. . .	„	xiii.
		L'Eau	. . .	„	xxi.
		L'Air	. . .	„	xxiii.
		La Balance	. . .	„	xxiiii.
		La Vierge	. . .	„	xxv.
		La Capricorne	. . .	„	xxviii.
		Les Poissons	. . .	„	xxxi.
		Le Lion	. . .	„	xxxiii.
Numerals		Coppe	. . .	Reina and the 6.	
		Danari	. . .	Cavallo and the 9.	
		Spade	. . .	Ace and the 8, 9 and Re.	

On the " Balance " (No. xxiiii.) is a modern stamped cipher of " F.C.S."

The backs of these cards are marked with the same armorial bearings as are the previously-described set (I. 256), though the supporters or decorative *encadrement* of the shield are slightly different. Below the arms is the motto " COLOMBA."

Dotted borders are present as described in the set I. 256.

The designs, etc., are slightly better in the present set than they are in I. 256, and much more easily decipherable.

[4 × 2⅖ in.]   [Backs decorated.]

SPANISH PLAYING-CARDS.

NUMERALS.

S. 258.

EIGHTEENTH CENTURY?

A PACK of numerals of the normal Spanish type, viz., forty-eight in number, having the queens displaced by *caballos*, the tens suppressed, and the suits being *copas, oros, bastos,* and *espadas*.

One piece, the three of *oros*, is here wanting.

The ace of *oros* has a large coin-like sign, having on it the arms of Spain, over the centre of which, on a shield of pretence, are the *fleurs-de-lis* of France. A crowned eagle is a supporter (vol. i. p. 95).

On scrolls above and below the mark of the suit is the address of "GIO. BARTOLOMEO BOCCIARDI."

On the four of *oros* is a double interlaced triangle, having in the hexagonal centre the initial capitals " G.B.B."

On the large central mark of the five of *oros* are busts of Ferdinand the Second of Aragon and Isabella of Castile, his consort. By the marriage here in question the union of Castile with Aragon was perpetuated (A.D. 1479-1512).

The device appears to have been taken from an old coin of the period mentioned. It became a frequently employed sign for the mark of the suit *oros* in Spanish playing-cards. Yet there is some obscurity about this device as used for Spanish cards. For example, on the central mark of the five of *oros* in the oldest Spanish playing-cards which have reached our time, viz., the " Rouen cards of Jehan Volay " (vol. i. p. 93, S. 15), the busts of Ferdinand and Isabella may be seen surrounded by the inscription: " + GROSSUS. VSNONUS. IMPERATORIS. ROMANORUM."

We are informed by numismatologists that there was an old German coin named " Grossus," and it is therefore presumable that " imperatoris romanorum " has also German relations. What " VSNONUS "—for it certainly is that—may imply is not apparent. At one time we were inclined to read these words as signifying, *Crassus nonassis, i.e.,* a large nine "As" piece, but such a rendering is, we are told, out of all question.

Across the middle of the two of *copas* is the address, " GIO. BAR : BOCCIA." On the four of the same suit are the initials " G. B. B." enclosed within the loops of a central ornament.

The designs, execution, and colouring of the cards are of mediocre character. There is one border line only on each card, and it remains continuous in each suit. (*Postea*, S. 259.)

The backs of these cards are marked by a series of broad arrow-heads running transversely across the pieces. Printed in black ink.

[3½ × 2⅛ in.]   [Backs decorated.]

S. 259.

FIRST QUARTER OF NINETEENTH CENTURY.

MADRID.

PACK of Spanish numerals of the full sequence of fifty-two cards. One card, the two of *oros*, is here wanting.

The suit-marks are of the typical character, and the *dama* is displaced by a *caballo*, but the tens are not suppressed.

A common characteristic, though by no means a universal one, of Spanish cards, is here present, while another and frequent one is absent. It may be observed that the border lines on each of the pieces of the suit of *oros* are continuous and perfect. In the suit of *copas* the upper and lower portions of the border lines are each broken by a single gap. In the suit *espadas* the upper and lower portions of the border lines are each broken by two spaces, while in the suit of *bastos* the like lines have each three solutions of continuity. Thus the character of a suit may be at once known by not exposing anything beyond the upper and lower margins of the cards. In many Spanish packs each pip-numeral has the value of the piece marked with an Arabic figure in reverse, at two opposite corners, diagonally. This peculiarity is here wanting.

On the four of *oros* is a central shield surmounted by a crown. The shield bears the inscription: " Naypes finisinos [finisimos] Fabircados [Fabricados] en Madrid. H. 1801."

Above the mark of the suit on the ace of *oros* is the inscription: " Real Fabrica De Madrid;" below is, " Por D Felix Solesioe H.   .   .   ."

On the *caballo* of *copas* is " A IVA " at the left-hand lower corner, and across the middle of the two of *copas* may be read, " Para Caracas."

The backs of these cards are marked with a series of blue stars, having central white spaces in them; between the stars are series of small blue dots.

[3½ × 2⅛ in.]   [Backs decorated.]

S. 260.

FIRST QUARTER OF NINETEENTH CENTURY.

MADRID.

PACK of Spanish numerals, having several of the ordinary characters of Spanish playing-cards. The pieces are forty-eight in number—the tens being suppressed, and a *caballo* displaces the *dama*. The border lines of the cards in three of the suits are broken after the manner described under S. 259.

The figures on the coate-cards are not after the usual Spanish type (vol. i.

p. 41), but are busts printed double, and in reverse. The pip-cards have not their values marked on them at the corners.

Within a scroll above the mark of the suit on the ace of *oros* is the word "Fabrica;" below are the letters, "D Dⁿ C . . ." On the mark itself is a shield of the arms of Castile and Léon. On the four of *oros* is a central shield surmounted by a crown. On the shield is inscribed, "Roxas a nu de 1814."

The backs of these cards are marked with a series of large rayed stars, having between them small dots. The whole is printed in blue.

[3½ × 2⅔ in.]   [Backs decorated.]

S. 261.

FIRST QUARTER OF NINETEENTH CENTURY.

MADRID.

PACK of cards of the ordinary Spanish character, viz., the tens are suppressed, the *dama* is displaced by a *caballo*, and the border lines in three of the suits (S. 259) are broken up into parts; but the pieces have not their values marked at the corners.

On the sign of the ace of *oros* is a shield of the arms of Castile and Léon, surmounted by a crown. Above, on a scroll, is the address, "Calle de las MAL," and below is "Donad a' ad 1811." (?)

On an ornamental shield, surmounted by a crown, on the four of *oros*, is inscribed, "Fabrica d Madrid 1811."

On the *caballo* of the same suit is the word "aiva," at the lower left-hand corner.

These cards are of small size, and of mediocre execution.

The backs are marked with a series of small arrow-heads running across the cards diagonally and reversed in position. They are printed in blue.

[2½ × 1½ in.]   [Backs decorated.]

S. 262.

FIRST QUARTER OF NINETEENTH CENTURY.

MADRID.

PACK of fifty-two numerals, the suits of which have the French marks, viz., *cœurs, carreaux, piques,* and *trèfles. Damas* are present among the "honours."

On the ace of *carreaux* is the inscription, "Fabrica de Madrid," within a scroll at the upper part of the card, and below are the words, "Por D Clemente Roxas."

On the four of *carreaux*, in the centre, is the figure of a horse galloping to the right. The *sota*, or valet, of *carreaux* is a whole-length standing figure of a soldier, with a halberd in his left hand; the title of "Hector" is marked at the left-hand lower corner of the card. The *dama* of the same suit is a whole-length standing figure, entitled "Rachel," while the *rey*, or king, is "Cezar." On the lower part of the tunic of the latter personage is a medallion head of a grey-hound, with crown on the head.

On the ace of *trèfles* is a large brown eagle, bearing on its breast the symbol of the suit. The head of the eagle is crowned. On the four of *trèfles* is an elephant in the centre of the card, and the valet of the same suit carries a mirror (?) by a ribbon in his right hand, and a halberd in his left. He is un-named. The *dama*, or queen, is entitled "Argine," and the *rey* is "Alegandre."

On the ace of *cœurs* is a large yellow eagle, holding a thunderbolt in its claws and the symbol of the suit in its beak. On the four of this suit is the figure of a lion directed towards the right hand. The valet of the suit is a whole-length figure, "Lahire," the *dama*, "Judic," and the *rey* is "Charles."

The ace of *piques* is decorated with two geese, regarding each other, and hold-ing the symbol of the suit between them. On the four of this suit, in the middle of the card, is a leopard, directed towards the right hand.

The *sota*, or valet, is "Hogier," bearing a halberd in his left hand, while a dog, supporting himself by the forepaws against the man's thigh, looks inquiringly up at him. The *dama* is "Pallas;" the *roi*, "David," having his right hand on the top of a large harp.

The border lines of the cards in all the suits are continuous, and the values of the pieces are not marked at the corners.

The backs of these cards are marked with diagonal rows of large diamonds or lozenges, having dots in their centres. The whole is printed in blue.

[$3\frac{2}{8} \times 2\frac{1}{8}$ in.]   [Backs decorated.]

S. 263.

FIRST QUARTER OF NINETEENTH CENTURY.

MADRID.

 PACK of numerals of the usual Spanish type, viz., forty-eight in number, with the tens suppressed, the *dama* displaced by a *caballo*, and the top and bottom border lines of each card in three of the suits broken up in divisions. The values of the pieces are not marked at the corners.

The coate-cards have on them whole-length costume figures, intended to symbolize the four quarters of the world. It is not easy to recognize America, however, except by assuming Spanish America only to be represented, a not unlikely circumstance, considering the series of cards is of Spanish origin.

On the *rey* of *oros* are the letters "Dⁿ. C. R." upon the pedestal supporting the symbol of the suit, which latter represents America.

Europe is represented by the "honours" of the suit of *espadas*, Asia by those of *bastos*, and Africa by the honours of the suit of *oros*.

On the ace of *oros* the mark of the suit bears the arms of Castile and Léon, surmounted by a crown. Below, a lion grasps a sword and ball. Columns and drapery serve as decorative supports to the arms, and a tower and ship are repre-sented in the distance. Throughout the suit *oros* the marks bear in their centres the castle and lion alternately.

On the ace of *copas* a satyr supports on each side the symbol of the suit.

The figures on the honours of the suit *espadas* are clothed in more or less of armour.

The fours of each suit have ornamental designs in their centres. On the four of *espadas* is Mars, aroused by a genius holding a blazing torch, the god is about to assume the helmet of war. On the four of *copas* are two *amorini* reclining on a bank; on that of *bastos* is a circular group of naked children dancing; while the four of *oros* has, in the middle, a group of four naked children seated at a table playing with cards.

The central mark of the suit on the five of *oros* is a large circular shield, having on it a Mercury's head and a horn of plenty at each side.

On the ace of *bastos* two turbaned figures raise up the mark of the suit.

The designs, engraving, and colouring of these cards are of a superior character to the usual run of Spanish sequencies, though, in some pieces, the colouring is rather heavy and opaque, and detracting from their appearance. The backs of the cards are marked with a reticulation of neatly-engraved ivy leaves, printed in a slightly greenish-blue colour.

[$3\frac{1}{2}$ × $2\frac{2}{8}$ in.]   [Backs decorated.]

S. 264.

FIRST QUARTER OF NINETEENTH CENTURY.

MADRID.

PACK of forty-eight cards according to the rule of Spanish numerals. The tens are suppressed, *caballos* displace the *damas*; the upper and lower border lines of the pieces in three of the suits are broken, and the values of the pieces are marked in Arabic numbers in reverse, at two opposite corners diagonally.

The "honours" are whole-length costume figures of an historic character, with the exception of the suit of *bastos*, which represents Africa.

The ace of *oros* bears a large medal or coin, on which is a bust of " Ferdinando VII. Rey de Esp. E. YND." This medal is surrounded by an ornamental design, of which flowers, coins, a harp, etc., are the components. All the signs of the suit *oros* have on them busts of the Kings of Spain, with the name, etc., accompanying them as on the obverse of a coin.

The designs, engraving, and colouring of this series are of a superior character. Several of the compositions are quite artistic, and some of the groups of animals and flowers are worthy of commendation. The central portions of the fours in each suit are occupied with ornamental designs. On the four of *copas* a satyr plays a Pandean pipe beneath a bower of fruits and flowers; on the four of *oros* two swans are floating on a reedy stream; on the four of *bastos* dogs are hunting a wild boar; and on the four of *espadas* is a group of military weapons, musical instruments, etc.

The backs of these cards are marked by a series of small diamond-shaped figures, arranged in diagonal lines very neatly engraved, and printed in a warm, black ink.

[$3\frac{5}{8}$ × $2\frac{2}{8}$ in.]   [Backs decorated.]

S. 265.

FIRST QUARTER OF NINETEENTH CENTURY.

BARCELONA.

 PACK of forty-eight numerals of the ordinary Spanish character, viz., the tens are suppressed, the *damas* supplanted by *caballos,* the border lines of the cards of three of the suits are broken up into divisions, and the values of the pieces are marked in numbers at the corners diagonally. An exceptional feature in this pack is, the *sota,* or valet, being represented by a female.

'The coate-cards are whole-length figures emblematic of the four elements of the ancient philosophers. The "honours" of the suit of *oros* symbolize *Water.* The *sota,* or valet, is a "Sirena" in the sea, holding in her right hand the sign of the suit, and in her left hand a harp. The *caballo* is a "Triton" on a sea-horse; he holds the sign of the suit in the right hand, and a shell which he is blowing in his left hand. The *rey* is "Neptuno," standing on a shell, bearing a trident in his left hand, and in his right the symbol of the suit.

The *sota* of the suit of *copas* is "Venus," by whose side is Cupid with flaming torch, typifying the *fire* of love. The *caballo* represents "Faetonte" on one of the horses of the sun—"C. Flegon," with flaming feet; while the *rey* is "Jupiter," holding in his right hand a thunderbolt and in his left hand a winged sceptre. *Air* is symbolized by the suit *espadas;* the *sota* is "Belona," about to rush through the air with shield and sword; the *caballero* is "Marte," mounted on the horse "El Terror," and galloping through the air; the *rey* is "Eolo," towards whom Eolus is blowing a favourable wind. *Earth* is typified in the suit *bastos;* the *sota* is "Cercs;" the *caballero,* "Belerofonte" mounted on "C. Pegaso," riding over the hills; while the *rey* is "Hercules" trampling the serpent on the earth. On the ace of *oros* the mark of the suit is borne on the mast of a ship. Above is a scroll having on it the inscription; "Fabrica de Forns y Compania." On the four of *copas* is a central ornament bearing the inscription, "Barcelona en Cataluna."

The designs, engraving, and colouring of this series are far inferior to the sets (S. 263, S. 264) last described. The backs of the cards are marked by alternate series of stars and small bars printed in black.

[$3\frac{3}{8}$ × $2\frac{1}{8}$ in.]   [Backs decorated.]

S. 266.

SECOND QUARTER OF NINETEENTH CENTURY.

BARCELONA ?

 PACK of forty-eight cards of the usual Spanish character. The tens are suppressed, the *damas* displaced by *caballeros ;* the upper and lower border lines in the pieces of three of the suits are broken into divisions, and the values of the pieces are marked in numbers at opposite corners.

The whole-length figures on the coate-cards typify the four quarters of the globe, the *sota* of each suit having on it the designation of that part of the world the suit is intended to signify. "Europa" is illustrated by the "honours" of *copas*, "America" by those of *oros*, "Asia" by those of *espadas*, and "Africa" by the honours of *bastos*.

The large mark of the suit on the ace of *oros*, containing the arms of Castile and Léon, is supported by conventional American figures. Above it is a winged genius blowing a trumpet, and holding in the right hand a scroll, on which is inscribed, "Fabrica de Forns." The figures supporting the mark of the suit hold a scroll between them, on which may be read, "Y Compania."

The designs, engraving, and colouring are only mediocre. The backs of these cards are marked with alternate series of stars and bars printed in black, similar to the sequence last described.

[3⅜ × 2⅛ in.]   [Backs decorated.]

S. 267.

SECOND HALF OF NINETEENTH CENTURY.

NAPLES.

 PACK of modern cards of Spanish character fabricated at Naples, and adapted to playing the Spanish game *El Hombre* (vol. i. p. 98). The sequence is composed of forty cards only, the eight, nine and ten of each suit being suppressed. There is not any *dama*.

The cards are not numbered, nor are there any border lines; the backing of each piece is folded over the edges of the front of the card, forming an ornamental border after the manner to be seen in many Italian packs.

The marks of the suits *espádas* and *bastos* are discrete, or separate, as they are in all true Spanish cards (vol. i. p. 42), and not interlaced as in the Italian series.

The ace of *oros* bears the duty stamp, on which is a head of Mercury, having inscribed around it, "Regno d'Italia." "Centesimi 30." This stamp has been impressed for the mark of the suit on the breast of a double-headed eagle, below which is the address, "Luigi Pignalosa" "STR. Mercantial Cerriglio 7."

The designs, etc., are of an inferior character.

The backs are stamped with a representation of the Royal Palace, printed double and in reverse, surrounded by a border marked with diagonal lines. Between the two designs on the back of the card is printed on a transverse band "P. Reale," and the same in reverse. The whole has been worked off in blue ink.

These cards are of stiff and firm character and small in size.

A decorative envelope accompanies the pack. In the centre is a circular shield within a wreath surmounted by a crown. Above may be read, "Napoli;" below, "Carte Correnti Napoli." At the sides is the address, "Luigi Pignalosa Strada Cerriglio A Mercanti No 7."

[3⅛ × 2 in.]   [Backs decorated.]

FRENCH PLAYING-CARDS.

NUMERALS.—PIQUET.

F. 268.

NINETEENTH CENTURY.

PARIS.

 SET of *piquet* cards, *i. e.*, thirty-two numerals only, the two, three, four, five and six of each suit being suppressed (vol. i. pp. 45, 123). The coate-cards have on them whole-length figures entitled, Hogier, Pallas, and David in the suit of *piques;* Argine and Alexandre in the suit of *trèfles;* and Judic and Charles in the suit of *cœurs.*

The valets in the suits *trèfles, cœurs* and *carreaux* are unnamed, as is also the *dame* in *carreaux.* On the *roi* and *dame* of each suit is the word *ridan* at the lower margin, and on the valet of *trèfles* is the address, "A Paris." The valet of *piques* bears the word *ridan* as well as "Hogier," and holds in his right hand an oval shield with a flower on it. On the *roi de cœurs* also is the word *ridan.*

The designs and execution are of an ordinary and conventional character. The fabrication and *lissage* are good.

[$3\frac{2}{5}$ × $2\frac{1}{8}$ in.] [Backs plain.]

CARDS WITH A SECONDARY PURPOSE.

AMUSING.

F. 269.

FIRST QUARTER OF EIGHTEENTH CENTURY.

PARIS?

SERIES of 181 cards belonging to the suits *cœurs, carreaux, trèfles,* and *piques.* In each suit there are several duplicate pieces both figure and pip-cards, and there are two different sets of the suit *trèfles.*

In the suit *cœurs* there are 54 pieces, in *piques* 42, in *carreaux* 42; in one set of *trèfles* there are 33, in the other set of that suit only 10 pieces. It would appear that the cards of two or three different sets are here intermingled.

The designs on the coate-cards are whole-length figures of the old conventional kind, and bearing the well-known names of David, Charles, Alexandre, and Cezar for the kings ; Pallas, Judic, Argine, and Rachel for the queens ; Hogier, Lahire, and Hector for the valets.

On some of the figure-cards of the suits *piques, cœurs*, and of one set of *trèfles*, is the address " Maudrou " at the lower margins, and on the valets of one set of *trèfles* is the word " Caen " at the bottom, while close by the side of the right leg of the figure is a duty stamp (?), on which is a crown above two hands grasping each other ; below is an inscription not decipherable.

On the backs of all these cards are printed either amusing questions or answers in red, or blue, or black ink. These are contained within ornamental borders stamped in variously coloured ink. The designs and colouring of these borders show that the cardpieces of various sets go to form the collection. The character of the questions propounded may be gleaned from what follows : —

On one of the *dames de piques* is the question,

" Etes vous mon ami ? "

on another is,

" Me croyé vous ingrates ? "

on a *roi de cœurs* is,

" Aimez vous les Soupirs d'un Amant ? "

on a six of *piques* is,

" Pensez vous souvent à moi ? "

Some of the questions are rather free and gallant, and might be replied to by certain of the answers in a manner which should forbid the indiscriminate use of the cards among young people.

The designs and execution are of a conventional character.

[$3\frac{2}{8}$ × $2\frac{1}{8}$ in.]   [Backs decorated.]

MISCELLANEA.

F. 270.

FIRST QUARTER OF EIGHTEENTH CENTURY.

PARIS.

N octavo volume, in which are bound up together the following works :—

1. Le jeu de L'Hombre, augmenté des Décisions Nouvelles sur les difficultez et Incidens de ce Jeu.

Le prix est de 30 Sols.

A Paris. Chez Pierre Ribou, à la Descente du Pont Neuf, sur le Quay des Augustins, à l'Image S. Louis. M.DCC.IX.

Avec approbation, et Privilége du Roy, (pp. 166).

2. Décisions Nouvelles sur les difficultez et Incidens du jeu de l'Hombre.

Le prix est de dix Sols broché, et quinze Sols, relié en veau.

A Paris chez Pierre Ribou à la Descente du Pont Neuf, sur le Quay des Augustins, à l'image S. Louis. M.DCC.IX.

Avec Permission, (pp. 36).

The first treatise opens with an address of "Le Libraire au Lecteur," of which the following is a translation :—

"Here is a new game of Hombre, which I present to you, friendly reader. That which I laid before you previously has become so different from the manner in which the game is now played that it is not of any use. This one has been described under the form of subject-paragraphs, so that the attention may be kept within bounds, and not be led to jump from precept to precept without any profit being reaped.

"Endeavours have been made not to omit anything that might facilitate the understanding of the matter by those who have not the least smattering of it, and would desire to learn it nevertheless. Such as are instructed in it may find, at least, hints to guide them through the difficulties which a different mode of play may originate at any moment. Perhaps it may be thought strange that things sufficiently explained before have been here repeated, but it should be borne in mind that such repetitions have been made in consideration both of beginners and of the essentials of the game.

"To this sixth edition have been added several examples of the most advisable methods of play under particular circumstances. These methods may be accepted as rules, and as indicating the proper manner of playing the cards under the most puzzling combinations. New decisions, relative to the difficulties and incidents of the game, have been also appended.

"Further, as there are terms which are not understood by everybody, and which lead those ignorant of them to believe that they are derived from 'la magie noire,' they, along with explanations of them, have been added at the end of the volume. Thus may be effaced the idea held by many, viz., that the game of Hombre is a barbarous game, the very language of which is unchristian."

The chapter "Du Jeu de l'Hombre" informs the reader that—

"It is useless to ponder over the etymology of the game of Hombre : it is sufficient to say that the Spaniards were the authors of it, and that it is stamped with the temper of the nation from which it has been derived.

"It is a game which necessitates close attention, and, however quick one may be, many errors will be infallibly committed by those who think of something else while at play, or who are distracted by the conversation of lookers-on.

"Therefore, for playing satisfactorily, silence and quietude are indispensable. Those present, then, should be careful not to engage in anything beyond observation of the play, if such thing cannot be done without distracting the players.

"But what I say should not make those who desire to learn the game believe that it will be a task of more trouble than pleasure, for it is without contradiction the finest and most diverting of all games for such as possess what is usually called the 'spirit of play.'

"Further, if under ordinary circumstances it is played in a way by which little money is lost, this rule is not inviolable.

"There are various modes of playing Hombre. Sometimes *espadille forcé* is played ; occasionally two persons play at the game, at other times five persons play, but ordinarily the game is played by three persons."

Of the modifications of the game of Hombre discussed in this volume, the following may be noticed :—

Des pertintailles.	La partie quarrée des dames du temps.
La consolation.	La triomphante.
Le bon air.	L'estrapade.
Le parfait contentement.	Le dégoût.
La guinguette.	Les yeux de ma grand'mère.
Le mirlino.	La chicorée.
Les fanatiques.	L'espadille forcé.
Le charivary.	L'hombre à deux.
La discorde.	L'hombre à cinq.

The more important sections of the treatise are accompanied by diagrams of both figure and pip-cards from neatly engraved wood-blocks.

In the second treatise in this volume, " Décisions Nouvelles, etc.," there is an " Avertissement de l'Auteur " which states that " The game of Hombre, being one of the most entertaining and ingenious of amusements, has become also one of the most fashionable and most in vogue at all assemblies and companies where it is desired to pass time in play, involving but little risk and expense."

" Fashionable and amusing as the game is, and to many persons as agreeable to be seen played as to be played at, it would be still more popular if fewer difficulties and incidents occurred causing disputes and contestations going to greater lengths than desirable."

To obviate this drawback the present work was undertaken, so that by it most doubts and difficulties might be readily solved. Nevertheless, "There yet remain many difficulties which have occurred, and which could not be recorded in these pages. Fresh ones happen indeed every day. But all such may be readily solved when they bear any relations to those mentioned in this repertory, where such only are recorded of which actual examples have occurred, giving rise to disputes which have been definitely settled."

Thus the author " Des Décisions du Jeu de l'Hombre " does not hesitate accepting the address on his work :—

> " Ah ! que les amateurs de l'Hombre et de la Paix
> Vous seront obligez, sçavant Jurisconsulte
> Parceque votre code en bannit pour jamais
> Tout procès et toutes disputes."

FLEMISH PLAYING-CARDS.

NUMERALS.

Fl. 271.

FIRST QUARTER OF NINETEENTH CENTURY.

LIEGE.

 PACK of fifty-two numerals of the suits *piques*, *trèfles*, *cœurs*, and *carreaux*.

The coate-cards are busts printed double and in reverse.

The *valet of piques* is entitled Hogier, *the dame* Pallas, the *roi* David.

In *trèfles* the *valet* is Maior, the *dame* Argine, the *roi* Alexandre.

In *cœurs* the valet is unnamed, the *dame* is Judic, the *roi* Charle.

In *carreaux* the valet is unnamed, the *dame* is Rachel, the *roi* Cezar.

The designs are of the usual conventional character. The make and *lissage* are good.

The backs of these cards are marked with parallel series of stars with four points and open centres, between which run waved lines of small dots. The whole is printed in pale black.

Accompanying this set is the engraved ornamental title of a wrapper. On an oval shield is the inscription, "Fabrique de **J T** Dubois, Rue Souverain-Pont No. 314, a Liege." Above, on an ornamental scroll, borne by a winged **Fame**, are the words " Cartes Fines ; " at each corner of the design is the mark of a suit. The whole is printed in red.

[$3\frac{2}{8} \times 2\frac{2}{8}$ in.] [Backs decorated.]

GERMAN PLAYING-CARDS.

TAROTS.

G. 272.

COMPLETE sequence—wanting one card—of combined tarots, *i.e.*, seventy-eight pieces, composed of a set of twenty-two emblematic cards and fifty-six numerals.

The marks of the suits of the numeral series are hearts, spades, clubs, and diamonds.

The designs on the tarots are whole-length coloured figures in the national costumes of Turkey.

The figure occupies the central and chief division of the cardpiece, above and below which, in a broad plain margin, is the number of the tarot in large Roman numerals. Close to either the right or left margin of the border line of each card is engraved the title of the character and costume represented.

The only piece in which the spirit of the old emblematic tarots is preserved is the unnumbered piece (22), answering to the *fou*, or *matto*, of the latter. In the present sequence the *fou* represents a harlequin dancing to the music of his cymbals.

The " honours " of the numeral series are also whole-length coloured figures in the national costumes of Turkey. The king of spades represents " Le Grand Seigneur ;" the king of diamonds, " Le Grand Pacha ;" the king of clubs, " Capidje Pacha ;" and the king of diamonds, " Le Reis Effendi."

At each of the upper corners of the king-cards is the mark of the suit with a crown above it.

The equestrian knave of spades signifies " Le Grand Vizir à Cheval ;" the titles and descriptions of all the pieces being given in French.

The designs on the cards are of a superior character, and are carefully engraved and coloured. On some of the *atutti* two figures are introduced.

The piece wanting in this pack is the seven of hearts.

The backs of these cards are marked by a series of hexagonal figures, having dots in the centres, and are printed in blue. The make and *lissage* are good.

The set is contained in a green case, on which is a title in red, bearing the following inscription : " Extra Feine Tarok-Karte mit Türkischen National-trachten. Leipzig im Industrie Comtoir."

[4⅜ × 2⅜ in.]   [Backs decorated.]

G. 273.

FIRST QUARTER OF NINETEENTH CENTURY.

LEIPZIG.

A SET of combined tarots, *i.e.*, twenty-two *atutti* and fifty-six numerals. The emblematic series illustrates some of the well-known fables of Æsop and of other writers.

In the centre of each cardpiece is the pictorial composition; above and below in wide margins is the number of the tarot.

As examples, reference may be made to No. ii., which illustrates the fable of " The Boy who cried Wolf;" No. v., representing " The Rabbits of La Fontaine;" No. vi., " The Fox and the Pitcher;" No. vii., "The Fox and the Crow with the Piece of Cheese;" No. x., " The Stag and the Stream;" No. xi., " The Wolf and the Crane;" No. xii., " The Fowler and the Wolf;" No. xiii., " The Gourd and the Pine;" No. xiv., " The Stork and the Frogs;" No. xvi., " The Men and the Bear;" No. xvii., " The Frog and the Well;" and No. xxi., which represents " The Dog and his Shadow."

The *matto*, or *fou*, has on it the bust of a harlequin with cymbals in his hands, printed double and in reverse.

The suit-marks of the numeral series are of French character, viz., *piques*, *trèfles*, *cœurs*, and *carreaux*.

The figures on the "honours" are costume busts printed double and in reverse.

The designs (which are either from stone or zinc), are, as respects composition, technic, and colour, of an ordinary description.

The backs of these cards are marked with rows of four-rayed stars and dots, printed in a dull red colour. The make and *lissage* are good.

The title of a wrapper accompanies the set. It bears the following inscription: " Feine Tarochkarte mit Doppelten Figuren. Leipzig. Industrie-Comptoir."

[$4\frac{2}{8} \times 2\frac{3}{8}$ in.]   [Backs decorated.]

NUMERALS.

G. 274.

FIRST QUARTER OF NINETEENTH CENTURY.

FRANKFURT-AM-MAINE.

TWELVE coate-cards and four aces of the suits of a numeral sequence of which the signs are spades, clubs, hearts, and diamonds.

The figures on the "honours" are busts printed double and in reverse. The costume is intended to represent that of the time of the persons represented, who belong to different segments of the Germanic empire.

On each ace is an ornamental design made up of armour, instruments of warfare, banners, etc., in the centre of which is the mark of the suit.

On the banner of the ace of hearts is the double-headed black eagle; on that of spades, the single-headed black eagle; on the banner of clubs, the black eagle with a crown; and on the flags of the ace of diamonds is a leopard, and " G iii." with a crown above.

The engraving and colouring of these cards are of a better description than usual, though the latter is occasionally opaque and heavy. A narrow ornamental border runs along the margins of each cardpiece.

The backs are marked with sinuous dotted lines printed in light rose colour. [$3\frac{1}{2} \times 2\frac{3}{8}$ in.]   [Backs decorated.]

G. 275.

FIRST QUARTER OF NINETEENTH CENTURY.

FRANKFURT-AM-MAINE.

 PACK of fifty-two numerals of the French suits *piques, trèfles, cœurs,* and *carreaux.*

The coate-cards have on them busts printed double and in reverse, and are *valet, dame,* and *roi.* The designs are of the modernized conventional character.

The backs are marked with stars and double sinuous lines of dots printed in blue. [$3\frac{5}{8} \times 2\frac{1}{2}$ in.]   [Backs decorated.]

G. 276.

FIRST QUARTER OF NINETEENTH CENTURY.

FRANKFURT ?

PACK of fifty-two numerals having the French marks of suits, viz., *piques, trèfles, cœurs,* and *carreaux.*

The "honours" have on them busts printed double and in reverse. The figure-designs are of inferior character, and the marks on the pip-cards are equally bad.

The backs of these cards are marked with stars and sinuous lines of small bars printed in a light pink colour. [$3\frac{1}{2} \times 2\frac{2}{8}$ in.]   [Backs decorated.]

G. 277.

FIRST QUARTER OF NINETEENTH CENTURY.

BERLIN.

 PACK of fifty-two numerals having French suit-marks.
The figure-cards have on them busts printed double and in reverse. The designs are of semi-historic costume character, and are much inferior to those of the previously described sequence, as are also the technic and colouring.

The valet of clubs bears on his right arm an oval shield, having on it the Prussian eagle, around which is the motto, " Unter seinem Schutze sind wir sicher."

On the valet of hearts is the address, " F. G. B. in Berlin."

The backs of these cards are marked with rows of stars printed in red.

[$3\frac{3}{8}$ × $2\frac{2}{8}$ in.]   [Backs decorated.]

G. 278.

FIRST QUARTER OF NINETEENTH CENTURY.

LEIPZIG.

PACK of fifty-two numerals of the suits spades, hearts, diamonds, and clubs.

The coate-cards have on them whole-length costume figures of good design and of careful technic and colour. The valets of the suits are soldiers in armour bearing partisans.

The valet of clubs points with the index finger of his right hand downwards to an oval shield, on which is inscribed, " Industrie Comptoir Leipzig."

The " honours " have their titles, viz., *roi*, *dame*, *valet*, engraved at the lower left-hand corners of the cards.

The *dames* are dancing females with wreaths and flowing scarves. The kings are crowned, and have on long trailing robes.

The backs of these cards are marked with alternate rows of stars and perpendicular bars, printed in a blue colour.

[$3\frac{3}{8}$ × $2\frac{3}{8}$ in.]   [Backs decorated.]

CARDS WITH A SECONDARY PURPOSE.

AMUSING.

G. 279.

FIRST QUARTER OF NINETEENTH CENTURY.

TÜBINGEN.

 SERIES of fifty-two numerals, contained in a book of 102 pages, which has on the title-page the following inscription : "Karten-Almanach, Tübingen in der J. G. Cotta'schen Buchhandlung, 1810." The marks of the suits are *cœurs, treffel, pick,* and *karo, i.e.,* hearts, clubs, spades, and diamonds.

Each ordinary numeral consists of a more or less humorous composition of several figures connected with the military or with subjects of domestic life. The marks of the suits are so placed over these designs as to fit in, as it were, naturally to particular portions of the body, and as if forming parts of the original design.

The engraving is executed in a half stippled and line manner, and is uncoloured ; the marks of the suits hearts and diamonds only are coloured.

The "honours" are placed together at the end of the volume, and represent whole-length figures, which travesty the heroes and heroines of ancient mythology. The king of clubs has been removed from its natural place in the sequence to form a frontispiece to the book, and represents a travesty of Jupiter, smoking, seated in an arm-chair, and wearing a large wig. The *dame* of this suit is Juno, with parasol and feathers, and the valet is Momus, or an enraged author, holding open a book, on which may be read, "Schlag ihm nur todt den Hund, er ist ein Recenseur."

The title of the honour is placed at one of the upper corners of the piece, and the mark of the suit at the other corner. Below the designs are the names of the characters travestied, some of which are so effected in a most ludicrous manner.

On the valet of *karo,* which concludes the series, is represented Paris as a capering French dancing-master, with cocked hat and fiddle under his arms.

Accompanying each cardpiece is a humorous poem or description in prose connected with the pictorial composition opposite.

At p. 78 of the volume the pip-numerals finish with the *ten* of *karo,* and its description.

Following these are the honours, accompanied by " Neue Mythologische Briefe an Emilie," in which some of the chief points in the histories of the Olympian heroes here burlesqued are jocosely referred to.

The present series of amusing playing-cards is interesting, from its being the fifth issue of the work once well known as " Cotta's Card Almanack." The latter was referred to at p. 224 of the first volume, where the first issue in 1806 is described (G. 162).

The almanack now under consideration is dedicated to " Ihrer Majestät

Louisen Königinn von Preussen seiner Erhabenen Landes Mutter, in tiefster Ehrfurcht gewidmet von G. Reinbeck."

Following the dedication is a poem relating how "Jokus und Phantasus" wove a wreath of flowers, and bestowed it on a poet, who places it, in the form of the present work, at the feet of Louisa.

A preface follows, to this purport :—

"The Card Almanack may boast of having received for four years the distinguished favour of the public. The witty ideas, so ingeniously developed and embodied by female hands, deserved this encouragement. On the present occasion, the fifth yearly issue, the work appears under another form, and by other hands. That which the designer, 'Herr Osiander in Tübingen,' evolved, with rich, if often wayward fancy, from the simple card-marks, the poet undertook to describe in his own way. Designer and poet worked, in other respects, quite independent of each other. As the latter received the designs from the artist as soon as they were ready, without any understanding with him, it remained free to the genius of the writer to make out of them what he could, as well as to infuse into them any fancy of his own. Thus originated this 'quod libet,' which the author commits in full trust to the forbearance of the public.

"The whole should not be regarded otherwise than as an amusing game of jest and fancy, and, indeed, of that kind, in its own way, which *bouts rimés* are in theirs. Not any higher credit is to be attributed to the author. The poet, therefore, entreats that he be not judged by any other standard; in particular he deprecates any comparison with Lichtenberg's celebrated commentary to Hogarth's engravings, with which the present work, either as regards matter or object, has nothing in common, and he declares—since, alas! such declarations are requisite in our own times—that he himself is determined not to enter the lists with such a master. What would alone entitle him to do otherwise he knows better, perhaps, than many who would impose on him such a comparison. . . . The plates have been engraved by Herr Bissell, in Manheim."

The volume consists of 102 duodecimo pages, independent of the card-pieces.

[$4\frac{5}{8} \times 3\frac{3}{8}$ in.]   [Backs plain.]

ENGLISH PLAYING-CARDS.

NUMERALS.

E. 280.

FIRST QUARTER OF NINETEENTH CENTURY.

LONDON.

PACK of fifty-two numerals of the usual suits, viz., spades, diamonds, clubs, and hearts.

The figure-cards have on them busts of the conventional type, printed double and in reverse.

The marks of the suits are modified slightly in design. Around the ordinary sign of the spade, at the sixteenth of an inch distance from it, runs a black line, following the form of the symbol itself, a narrow white space being thus preserved between the two.

In the suit of diamonds there is a rather small white mark of the suit in the centre of a larger red one.

In clubs there is a small white mark of the suit enclosed within a larger black one.

In hearts there is an outside line around the symbol, as in the suit of spades.

The designs on the aces bear reference to the four chief orders of knighthood in this country.

The ace of spades bears the sign of the suit within the insignia and mottoes of the Order of the Garter, "Honi . Soit . qui . Mal . y . pense ;" below which is the motto, "Dieu et Mon Droit." The date of the year, 1344, in which the first step was made by Edward III. towards founding the Order, is placed below the mark of the suit, the Order being definitely constituted a.d. 1349.

On the ace of spades are also the inscriptions: "G iii. Rex," "Sixpence additional Duty" (repeated three times), "T. Wheeler, No. 56."

On the ace of diamonds the mark of the suit is surrounded by the insignia and motto of the Order of the Bath, "Tria Juncta in Uno," below which is the date 1399, and "Ich dien." This Order, though stated to be of early origin, was for-mally constituted only by Henry IV. two days previous to his coronation in the Tower. He conferred the honour of fellowship upon forty-six esquires who had watched the night before and had bathed. After the coronation of Charles II. the Order became neglected, but was revived by George I., a.d. 1725.

On the ace of clubs the Order of the Thistle is represented with its motto,

" Nemo me impune lacessit." Below is the date of its revival by Queen Anne, viz., 1703.

The Order is considered to have been of very ancient date, as early, indeed, as the year 800; but its usual recognition is only from the year 1540, when James V. definitely founded it. After the death of James, in 1542, the Order was discontinued. It was renewed by James VII., King of Scotland, and II. of England in the year 1687, increased by Queen Anne in 1703, and again augmented by George IV. in 1827.

On this cardpiece—the ace of spades—is also the inscription, " Ludlow and Cº. Patent Knight's Cards," with the date below, " 1800."

On the ace of hearts are the insignia and motto of the Order of St. Patrick, " Quis Seperabit," and the date below of 1783. This was an Order instituted by George III. in 1783, and in 1784 the establishment of the St. Patrick Benevolent Society of London was effected. The Order was increased in the years 1821, 1831, and 1833. The Prince of Wales was installed a Knight of the Order in April, 1868.

The designs, particularly of the aces, have been carefully engraved, but the colouring of the figure-cards is opaque and heavy.

A wrapper, with duty stamp on it, accompanies the sequence. On one face is a bust of the " Great Mogul," below which is the address of " Thos. Wheeler, from Gibson, No. 27, opposite Fetter Lane, Holborn, London."

The duty stamp of sixpence has been affixed on the front of the Great Mogul.

On the other face of the wrapper is an ornamental design printed in red and inscribed, " Stamp Office." " £10 penalty selling any playing-cards unlabelled. £20 penalty selling or buying any Label or Wrapper used before."

The backs of these cards are quite plain, but the edges are coloured green. The manufacture is good.

[3⅝ × 2½ in.] [Backs plain.]

E. 281.

FIRST QUARTER OF NINETEENTH CENTURY.

LONDON.

 PACK of fifty-two numerals of the several suits, spades, hearts, diamonds, and clubs,.

On the coate-cards, or " honours," are whole-length figures of the conventional kind.

The ace of spades bears the duty stamp of " George iii. Rex," and the number 10.

The execution of the figure-cards is of an inferior character.

A peculiarity of these cards is the relative small size of the figures on the honours. They are barely 2⅜ of an inch high by 1½ in. wide, and are contained within a clear border of ⅝ of an inch wide.

An engraved wrapper accompanies the pack. On the former is a bust of the " Great Mogul," having below the address of " Hall and Bancks, Card-Makers to her Majesty and their Royal Highnesses the Prince and Princess of Wales, No. 23 Piccadilly London." A duty stamp of sixpence has been placed over the bust of the Great Mogul. On one end of the wrapper is the warning, " £10 Penalty selling any playing-cards unlabelled, £20 Penalty selling or buying any Label or Wrapper used before."

[3⅜ × 2⅜ in.] [Backs plain.]

E. 282.

LAST QUARTER OF NINETEENTH CENTURY.

LONDON.

SINGLE card—the three of hearts—from a numeral series of fifty-two pieces. It serves as a specimen of a variety of the ornamental devices recently introduced for the backs of playing-cards.

In the middle of the card, on the *verso*, is a bust of Shakespeare, placed within a double and acuminated oval frame. The points of the external frame nearly touch the upper and lower edges of the card. Between the inner and outer frames are small designs of the seven ages of man, with their titles, and on a mark of the suit of spades at the bottom is inscribed, " We are all players." Within the lines of the outer framework or oval border may be read—

"All the world's a stage, and all the men and women merely players,
"They have their exits and their entrances, and one man in his time
plays many parts."

Leaves and flowers of ornamental character form parts of the general design. All is printed in black and red, on a yellow ground.

The fabrication and *lissage* are good, but such adornments will not meet with the patronage of regular card-players. (See vol. i. p. 52.)

[$3\frac{5}{8}$ × $2\frac{1}{2}$ in.] [Backs decorated.]

PIQUET.

E. 283.

FIRST QUARTER OF NINETEENTH CENTURY.

LONDON.

PIQUET set of cards of English manufacture.

The pack consists of thirty-two numerals of the suits hearts, clubs, spades, and diamonds. In accordance with the game of *piquet*, the two, three, four, five, and six of each suit are suppressed. (Vol. i. p. 45.)

The coate-cards have on them whole-length figures of the conventional kind, and of a like size, character, and execution as those of E. 281, or even inferior to them.

Around the mark of the suit on the ace of spades are a garter and crown. Within the former is inscribed, " Duty—VI. Pence."

[$3\frac{3}{8}$ × $2\frac{2}{8}$ in.] [Backs plain.]

CARDS WITH A SECONDARY PURPOSE.

EDUCATIONAL, INSTRUCTIVE.

E. 284.

LAST QUARTER OF EIGHTEENTH CENTURY.

LONDON.

(GEOGRAPHIC.)

A SERIES of fifty-two cardpieces of the suits spades, clubs, hearts, and diamonds.

This set is intended to afford instruction in geography and ethnography.

Each card is occupied with a general account of various portions of the earth's surface. At the upper left-hand corner of each piece, in a space about $\frac{6}{8}$ of an inch square, is the mark of the suit, in its proper colour, and having stamped on it, in Arabic numerals, the value of the particular card.

The mark on the ace of each suit bears the name of that quarter of the globe which is described on the cards of the particular suit to which the ace belongs.

The figure-cards, or "honours," are indicated by the letters J, Q, and K, for Jack, Queen, and King, placed on the marks of the suits. These marks have also ornaments, as crowns, flowers, etc., above and below them.

A narrow ornamental border or edging printed in the colour of the suit runs round each card.

Accompanying the pack is a supplementary cardpiece explanatory of the intention of the series. It bears the following inscription:—

" A Systematical Compendium of Geography on the face of 52 cards."

The four quarters of the globe are thus arranged:—

" Asia under Spades; Africa under Clubs; Europe under Hearts, and America under Diamonds.

" The Cards with the names of the quarters in the pips give an account of each and take the rank of Aces; those of kings have a K in the pips and contain the Kingdoms, to which figures are annexed referring to cards of the same suit (ranking according to their number) which describe them; the Q and J cards rank as Queens and Jacks or Knaves, and contain all the Islands.

" If the reader wishes to find any Island, if in Asia look on the Q and J of Spades; if in Africa look on the Q and J of Clubs, and so of the others.

" Note.—The kingdoms between two lines on the K cards are described on those cards of the same suit which the figures denote—for instance, China on the K of Spades has 2 and 3; its description begins on 2 (where Tartary ends) and finishes on 3. Turkey in Asia with its provinces have 8, 9, and 10. See 8, 9 and 10. Guinea and its divisions on the K of Clubs have 8 and 9, look on those numbers of that suit. Spain and Portugal on the K of Hearts have 6, look on 6, and so of all the other kingdoms.

" B stands for bounded; N for north, &c.; O for ocean; R for river; M for miles.

" Entered as the Act directs, February 17 . . . ."

[$3\frac{5}{8} \times 2\frac{1}{2}$ in.]   [Backs plain.]

AMUSING.

E. 285.

FIRST QUARTER OF NINETEENTH CENTURY.

LONDON?

TWENTY-FOUR numeral-cards of the suits diamonds, hearts, and clubs.

Of these suits only the aces, the twos, threes, fours, fives, sixes, sevens, and eights are present. In the middle of each cardpiece is a large X nearly an inch square, stamped in a red colour. The backs of the cards are both undecorated and uncoloured.

Of the nature of the game intended to be played with these cards, and as to whether the series is complete or not, we are ignorant. It is assumed the former must have been of the amusing character.

[$3\frac{5}{8}$ × $2\frac{1}{2}$ in.]   [Backs plain.]

HUMOROUS.

E. 286.

FIRST QUARTER OF NINETEENTH CENTURY.

LONDON.

A SERIES of forty-eight numerals from a sequence of fifty-two cards of the suits hearts, diamonds, spades, and clubs.

The pieces absent are the five of clubs, the eight, ten, and queen of spades.

These cards are of a half-jocose, half-satirical character. On each piece are designs of various kinds treated in a humorous manner and associated with descriptions, exclamations, etc. The marks of the suits are made to fit into particular portions of the bodies of the figures. Thus on the upper part of the four of hearts is a gentleman bowing like a dancing-master to a lady opposite. He is represented as saying, "Madam, I am eternally yours." The lady replies, "Are you in earnest, Sir?" Below is the bust of a male person, who exclaims to that of a lady hiding her face with a fan, "Angels are painted fair, to look like you." The lady replies, "Spare my blushes."

On the seven of clubs is represented "Miss Pricilla Prickfinger, Milliner and Fancy-dress maker," etc., with three of her young ladies at work. Miss Priscilla herself appears to be engaged on a pair of man's small-clothes. A pug-dog is seated on the work-table.

On the six of spades is represented the "Englishman in Paris." A lady and gentleman are at dinner in a restaurant. The gentleman holds up a frog on his fork and addresses a waiter, who replies, "Ils sont les veritables grenouilles monsieur." "Green owls," replies the gentleman; "D——e they're nothing but frogs."

It is not unlikely that the cards here wanting to complete the set had on them designs of more than equivocal character, and were destroyed by a former possessor on account of that circumstance. It is assumed that this may have been the case from the fact that the four of spades had been torn in six pieces, and the design on it is such as we have stated.

The designs are in general of a common description, except those on the figure-cards, which are superior in every respect. On the latter are whole-length figures of the conventional form, with the countenances made humorous.

In the suits diamonds and hearts, the faces remain human but laughable. In the suit clubs, the knave has the face of a ram, the queen the head of a parrot (?), and the king the head of a bull.

In spades, the knave has the head of a dog, and the king that of an ape.

Each figure on the coate-cards is enclosed within a border, ornamented with small designs of pip and figure-cards.

The marks of the suits on many of the higher pip-cards remain uncoloured.

Some of the pieces bear the name of " Cowell " at the bottom, as that of the etcher of the compositions.

[$3\frac{5}{8}$ $\times$ $2\frac{3}{8}$ in.]   [Backs plain.]

MISCELLANEA.

E. 287.

SECOND HALF OF EIGHTEENTH CENTURY.

LONDON.

 SMALL octavo volume of fifteen printed pages, and seventy-five engravings, having on the title-page the following inscription: " A Political and Satyrical History of the years 1756 and 1757. In a series of Seventy-five Humorous and Entertaining Prints, containing All the most remarkable Transactions, Characters, and Caricaturas of those two memorable Years. To which is annexed an explanatory Account or Key to every Print which renders the whole full and significant. The Second Edition. London: Printed for E. Morris, near St. Paul's."

Among the engravings in this volume, plates 7, 14, 15, 26, and 38 have on them satirical designs under the guise of cards.

On plate 7 is represented, according to the " Explanation ": —

" A remarkable Caricatura compounded of several Species, being by some supposed to be a Sea-Calf, by others, a Sea Lion ; after having been tossed about on its native Element for some Years it was cast ashore on a gaming Island, where it was so captivated with Cards and Dice, that it was Naturalized, commenced *gamester*, and fixed upon the Island ever since."

On the plate above the figure is inscribed, " The Sea Lyon ; " below, " Mores Homines." On the ground lie several figure-cards.

On plate 14 is the knave of spades, having below the title, " Monsr Dupe." Along the bottom of the piece run three *fleurs-de-lis*. According to the " explanation," this plate " expresses by the Flower de Luce how much the caricatura was connected with our enemies, and was even a dupe to them against the interest of his country."

On plate 15 is the knave of hearts with a fox's head, having below the title, "Mons' Surecard." This figure " infers by the sharpness of the Nose that Craft and Subtilty that is natural to creatures of a similar kind known by the name of Foxes, and is here pointed out as a k——e."

On plate 26 is the knave of clubs, having inscribed below, " Null Marriage." " This caricatura was esteemed the most atrocious knave in the Pack and the worst of the *black sort*."

On plate 38 is the knave of diamonds, having above, " Hic niger est ;" below, " Acapulca."

" This caricatura's propensity to gaming tells us at once how valuable he must be to a shipwrecked state, and that he deserves (like a drunken pilot in a storm) to be thrown overboard to make room for one of clearer brains and more integrity."

The last plate (75) in this volume represents " The true Patriot," and is dedicated " To the R^t Honble the Lord Mayor Aldermen and Common Council of the City of London " " by their humb^le servants Darby and Edwards " " To be had at the Acorn facing Hungerford Strand."

E. 288.

SECOND HALF OF EIGHTEENTH CENTURY.

LONDON.

SMALL octavo volume of eight printed pages and twenty-five engravings, having on the title-page the following inscription :—
" A political and Satyrical History of the Years 1758 and 1759 In a series of Twenty-five Humorous and Entertaining Prints containing all the most remarkable Transactions Characters and Caricaturas of those two memorable years. To which is annexed an explanatory Account or Key to every Print which renders the whole full and significant.

" Part II. London. Printed for E Morris near St Paul's."

The plates in this volume are numbered so as to follow in sequence those of the work last described (E. 287). They commence therefore with No. 76, and end with No. 100.

Plates 79, 80, and 90, convey their satire under the guise of cards. On plate 79 are two knaves of clubs as supporters to a shield of armorial bearings, the components of which are dice and dice-boxes on a chevron, two cards (aces of hearts and diamonds) in chief, one card (ace of spades) in base. The coat is an arm with dice-box in hand rising from a coronet. The motto is " Claret," " Cogit," " Amor," " Nummi." The " explanation " (p. 4) is as follows :—" The arms of two great gamesters well-known at *Arthurs* and the *Cocoa-tree*."

On plate 80 are " The court-cards or all trumps 1756," under the guise of the twelve figure-cards of the ordinary numerals. From the mouth of each figure proceeds an exclamation : such as, " I'll have England," from the French king, the king of clubs ; and " I'll stick to France," from the king of Spain, or the king of diamonds. Below each figure is the title of the person intended to be represented. The " explanation " of this plate is the following :—" The different resolutions of the great personages of that time is here represented according to the appearance they then made in the affairs of Europe."

On plate 90 are " the court-cards of 1759, a heart is trumps, and has won the game." , The figures are the twelve " honours " of a pack of cards, designed on the same principle as are those on plate 80. Of the present it is remarked in the " explanation " : " The labels and characters here represented are sufficient to explain the meaning of the print with the least application " (p. 6).

The series terminates with an engraving described below : " 'Tis a Christians duty to show mercy to his enemys." For a full account of the literary and politico-satirical history of these works (E. 287, E. 288) the reader should refer to the third volume of the Catalogue of " Political and Personal Satires," " The 2 H, H's " (No. 1), March, 1756, by Mr. Frederic George Stephens.

It may be remarked here, however, that Mr. Stephens points out that there are copies of two earlier editions of the work now described in the general library, and two more versions occur in the Grenville Library, the latter includ- ing a series of copies from the engravings on new plates, of which last there is an imperfect series in the Print Room.

Reference should be made also to the first volume of the present Catalogue on Playing-cards, where at p. 285, E. 202, are described some prints of cardpieces which seem to be re-engraved versions of some of the pieces connected with the present series (E. 287, E. 288).

VARIA.

VARIA.

V. 289.

MIDDLE OF FIFTEENTH CENTURY?

GERMANY.

(Number 305 of the Weigel Collection, and now in the British Museum. Early German prints from metal in relief and wood.)

AMONG the rare and interesting examples of early German cuts obtained at the sale of the Weigel collection, at Leipzig, in 1872, was the piece marked No. 305 in the large work of Weigel and Zestermann,[1] and in the sale catalogue.

This piece bears on it a design of the Holy Cross, and cipher "y h s"—*in hoc signo*, or, *Jesus Hominum Salvator?* treated in a floriated ornamental manner.

The cross is in the middle of the composition, and forms the upright portion of the letter "h"; on the left of the latter is a large "y", and on the right an "s". Above the cross is a large crown, from which, at the upper part, spring three branches, bearing at their extremities appendages of an acorn-like character. The centre and shortest of these branches bears three glands, the two others one acorn each. Other two branches run out from beneath the crown, having acorns at their ends. The latter branches are longer than the upper ones, and are each looped once.

Below the cross and cipher is an inverted lily (?), embedded in much ornamental leaf-work. The whole composition is enclosed within a double-lined border, and has been coloured. The border and crown are yellow, the cross crimson-madder, the letters crimson-madder, yellow, and green.

"These colours point to Swabia. The paper has not any water-mark. The piece was produced probably towards the middle of the fifteenth century—at least, the style and treatment of the ornamental portions tend to such an inference."

"The decoration of the crown with *eicheln* (glands, acorns) is peculiar, such has not previously come before us on analogous prints, and the symbolic meaning of which, in relation to the general design, is less clear and apparent than would have been that of ordinary leaf-work employed in its place. Perhaps it may be inferred from this that we have here to do, not simply with a representation of the

---

[1] Die Anfänge der Druckerkunst in Bild und Schrift. Leipzig, 1866. Vol. ii. p. 175.

religious symbols, but with a playing-card for the ecclesiastical orders, other examples of such cards being present in our collection. The *eicheln* would then not appear out of place, and would simply illustrate the suit of "glands" in German playing-cards." (*Op. cit.*)

The view here taken by Weigel we find difficult of acceptation. In the first place, the size of the piece, though not positively negativing it, is certainly against it; in the second place, a gold-thread, or otherwise composed acorn-like ornament, is an old and still frequent termination to decorative bands and cords. (Vol. i. p. 54.)

[8 × 5⅜ in.]   [Backs plain.]

V. 290.

PEN and ink facsimile drawing of the piece numbered 199, p. 88, in Wilson's "Catalogue Raisonné of the Select Engravings of an Amateur." London. MDCCCXXVIII.

The same piece, a five numeral-card, may be found represented on plate 91 in the "Jeux de Cartes Tarots," etc., of the Bibliophiles Français. (Bibl. 2.)

The character and relations of this cardpiece have been previously alluded to in vol. i. p. 214, G. 148.

V. 291.

LAST QUARTER OF SEVENTEENTH CENTURY.

LONDON.

T pp. 234 and 235 of the first volume are described (E. 174, E. 175) two series of the educational and instructive cards issued by John Seller. These series are of a grammatical character. The present volume is "A Book of Geography, shewing all the Empires, Monarchies, Kingdoms, Regions, Dominions, Principalities, and Countries in the whole World. By John Seller, Hydrographer to the King, and are sold at his House at the Hermitage at Wapping."

It is presumed that this book of cards with a secondary purpose is composed of "the geographical cards" alluded to in the advertisement quoted under E. 175, vol. i. p. 235.

Appended to the geographic cardpieces are several tables, almanacks, astronomic diagrams, and representations of the surface of the moon.

This volume came into the possession of the Museum too late to admit of its insertion and full description in the proper place.

ORIENTAL PLAYING-CARDS.

ORIENTAL PLAYING-CARDS.

HINDUSTANI.

O. H. 292.

PLACE AND DATE UNCERTAIN.

SEQUENCE of ninety circular cards from a series apparently of ninety-six pieces. There are three suits of colours, viz., red, yellow, and green. These colours in different shades form the grounds of the various cardpieces. The red and green suits have each three series, ranks, or grades of colour, viz., a chocolate-red, a deep red, and a light red colour; a deep green, a medium green, and a light green colour. The yellow suit has but two grades, or ranks, viz., an orange-yellow and a light yellow colour.

Each of the eight suits should have normally ten pip or point numerals, and two figure-cards, or "honours." There being, as in the set described in vol. i. p. 331, O. H. 250, eight suits of twelve cards each suit. In the present set five of the suits are incomplete in their numbers, and in two there are duplicates apparently by mistake. Thus, e. g., the deep green-coloured rank of the green suit wants the one, or ace, and there are in it two seated *schahs*, or kings, instead of one king and one *wusseer*.

It is extremely difficult to define the nature of the symbols on the various ranks of the coloured suits. The symbols here are totally different to those in O. H. 250. The first rank (chocolate) of the red suit has a small green disc with three dark spots on it, and a series of white spots below it, or reversed it may be likened to a purse, the white spots representing the open and beaded mouth.

The second rank (deep) of the red suit has a long leaf, or *tulwar* or sword, for its sign; while the third rank (light red) has a parallelogram with dots, and a curved line on it, as if to represent writing.

In the orange rank of the yellow suit the symbol, or mark, is a small green oval body, having one white and two dark spots on it; in the light yellow rank of this suit it is a man's head and shoulders.

In the deep-coloured rank of the green suit the mark is a circular white spot—perhaps silver coin. There is a *three* in lieu of an ace, or one, and a second *schah* in place of a *wusseer*.

In the second rank of the green suit the ten is wanting. The *wusseer* is mounted on a camel.

In the third rank, or light green suit, the number of pieces is complete. Both *wusseer* and *schah* are mounted on tigers running towards the left hand. The *schah* has a full radiant sunlike face, but with profile eyes. On the latter peculiarity, see Merlin, Bibl. 6, p. 124.

On comparing the present set with the one previously described (vol. i. p. 331, O. H. 250) it may be observed that the more important details connected with the figure-cards, or honours, are alike. Thus, in each set, the *schah* is seated under a sort of canopy and attended by slaves in the three red ranks. In each set the *schah* of the light yellow rank is mounted on an elephant, and in the light green rank of each set he is a radiant sun, also mounted.

In the second rank (medium green) of this suit the sign may be intended for a flower (?), and in the light green rank it represents, perhaps, a gold coin or money.

In connection with the marks or symbols in the suits of these cards, the observations of Mr. Chatto (Bibl. 4, pp. 35, 46-50) may be referred to with advantage.

In the chocolate-red rank the pieces here present are the one, three, four, five, six, seven, eight, nine, and ten point-cards, and two figure-cards, or honours, viz., a mounted *wusseer* galloping towards the left, and a seated *schah*, or king.

In the second rank of the red suit the pieces present are the one, four, five, six, seven, eight, nine, and ten numerals, and the two figure-cards, or honours, a mounted *wusseer* and seated *schah*.

In the light red rank the number of pieces is complete—ten pip-cards and two honours.

In the orange rank of the yellow suit the six and seven pip-pieces are wanting. In the second rank (light yellow) of this suit the number is entire, and the *schah* is not seated in the usual way, but is mounted on an elephant.

In the first rank (light) of the green suit there are twelve pieces, and both *schah* and *wusseer* are mounted on tigers.

In each set the *wusseer* is mounted on a horse in the three red and in the two yellow ranks, while in the medium green he is on a camel, and in the light green on a tiger.

The present cards are circular in form, as are those of O. H. 250, but are of larger diameter. They appear to be made of a similar material, or else of canvas, are painted red on the backs, and are highly varnished or lacquered on both faces. The designs and execution of the present set are inferior to those of O. H. 250.

These cards are contained in a box of corresponding character to that of O. H. 250.

[$2\frac{1}{8}$ in. in diameter.] [Backs coloured.]

CHINESE.

O. C. 293.

NINETEENTH CENTURY.

CHINA.

SERIES of cards consisting of thirty pieces, probably complete. There appear to be five suits—viz., a suit of chains (?), of ten pieces; a suit of heads, of ten pieces; a suit of money or cakes, of five pieces; a suit of three pieces, the sign of which we are scarcely able to decipher, but designate tables; and a suit of two pieces, on one of which latter are several Chinese characters. It is possible, however, that there may be in this series three suits only, the five, three, and two cards last mentioned belonging to one suit, thus making it to consist of ten pieces, in conformity with the suits of chains and heads. This is the more likely, since one of the card-pieces of the lot containing two cards bears on it a red stamp.

The signs and values of the one, two, three, four, five, six, seven, eight, and nine of chains are easily to be distinguished, but not so those of the piece assumed to represent the ten. This numeral piece has on it five marks only of the suit, and it bears a large red stamp. The outer broad black margin of the one and nine of chains is cut off in an oblique manner at the upper right-hand and lower left-hand corners; the two has an arched notch at the upper right and lower left-hand corners of the inner edge of the broad black border; the three has a needle-shaped slit at the same places; the four has an arched notch in the middle of the inner edge of the same border; the five has two arched notches outerly, top and bottom; the six has two slits in the margin, top and bottom, at opposite corners, diagonally; the seven has three oblique notches on the black margin, top and bottom, directed in reverse way; the eight has a notch centrally, top and bottom; the nine has the corners of the outer margin cut off obliquely, as in the one of the suit (chains); while the tenth cardpiece, with the red stamp, has a slit in the margin at the upper left-hand and lower right-hand corners of the broad black border.

The pieces of the suit of heads are marked with slits and notches in a manner almost identical with that common to the suit of chains. The tenth cardpiece has a red stamp covering its face and Chinese characters at the upper margin.

The designs have been stamped off in deep black ink, and belong to the heavier and coarser variety of Chinese cards.

The texture is that of thin cardboard. The backs of the pieces are smooth, and of a brownish-yellow colour.

Two cards from the suits of heads and of tables (?) are represented on plate 21.

[$2\frac{1}{8}$ in. × o$\frac{5}{8}$ in., size of impression; $2\frac{3}{8}$ in. × o$\frac{6}{8}$ in., whole card.]

[Backs coloured.]

O. C. 294.

NINETEENTH CENTURY.

CHINA.

SERIES of twenty-eight cards, composed of seven suits of four pieces each suit.

Each cardpiece is divided into three parts, enclosed in a general broad outer border and in a narrow inner one. In the centre of each piece is the representation of an animated sign (vol. i. p. 47) of a division, above and below which is the name of the suit in Chinese characters. Through the obliging assistance of Professor Douglas, we are enabled to state that the names of the seven primary suits are as follows :—viz., scholars, generals, knights (probably, or a grade equivalent to that of the knights in chess), soldiers (equivalents to pawns in chess), elephants, horses, carriages.

In the centre of the pieces of the suit of "scholars" is what looks like a *crab*, in that of "generals," a *scarabæus*, in "knights," an *escalop* or *limpet shell*, in "soldiers," a *snail*, in "elephants," a *dragon*, in "horses," a *fish*, and in the middle of the pieces of the suit of "carriages" is something like a *tick*.

The designs are stamped in deep black ink, and belong to the heavier or coarser kind of Chinese playing-cards.

The texture is that of thin cardboard. The backs are smooth, and of a brownish-yellow colour.

Cards from the suits of "horses" and "carriages" are represented on plate 21.

[2 × $0\frac{5}{8}$ in., size of impression ; $2\frac{2}{8}$ × $0\frac{6}{8}$ in., size of card.]   [Backs coloured.]

O. C. 295.

NINETEENTH CENTURY.

CHINA.

SERIES of fifteen cardpieces, having their imports denominated in Chinese characters, painted in a water-colour of "Chinese vermillion," some of the characters being six-eighths of an inch in length.

There is a card entitled leader, or commander, or black king, two cards representing "aids to the black king," two cards are "black knights," four are "soldiers," two represent "black elephants," and four other pieces—two of a kind—are too obscure to decipher, or the characters designating them are contractions.

The texture is that of thin cardboard. The backs are smooth, and of a deep reddish-brown colour.

Two cards from the suits of black knights and the contracted characters are represented on plate 21.

[$3\frac{1}{8}$ × $0\frac{6}{8}$ in.]   [Backs coloured.]

O. C. 296.

NINETEENTH CENTURY.

CHINA.

HIRTY-TWO cardpieces, consisting apparently of three suits. One suit is of figures, a second of animals and of flowers, and a third of boxes or cases.

Each cardpiece is divided into three portions. The centre is occupied by the mark of the suit, the upper and lower parts are marked with round domino-like dots of different values, on some cards in red, on others in black ink, and on some pieces both red and black dots are present. The exact numerical progression and sequence of these domino points are not easily determinable, though they no doubt indicate the values of the pieces on which they occur.

In the suit of figures there are five designs, once repeated. These figures are whole-length males and females, carrying various devices. The first two cards have figures of men, carrying small banners, and are dotted like each other at top and bottom. The next two figures are females, bearing flags and provided with swords ; then follow two males carrying whips, next two females, each carrying a child, and lastly two males with swords (?) and flags.

In the suit of animated cards (vol. i. p. 47) there are here eight pieces only ; three have on them flowers, two have fishes, two butterflies, and one bears a tiger.

In the third suit, or that of boxes, there are fourteen cards ; in the middle of each piece is an open ornamental box or case, on the lid and inside of which are repeated the domino points in like value to those marked on the upper and lower portions of each card.

All the figures or designs are neatly executed and coloured. The texture is that of thin cardboard, the *lissage* is considerable, and the backs are marked with hexagonal figures stamped in black ink.

Two cards from the suits of animated signs are represented on plate 21.

It is doubtful if this series be complete, and whether or not the cards to be next described belong to it.

[$3\frac{2}{8}$ × $0\frac{7}{8}$ in.]   [Backs decorated.]

O. C. 297.

NINETEENTH CENTURY.

CHINA.

WENTY cardpieces, marked with domino points in black and red ink at their tops and bottoms in reverse way. The middle portion of each cardpiece is quite plain.

It is not improbable that these cards may form a plain suit in the foregoing sequence (O. C. 296), as the backs are marked in a like way.

The texture is thinner than that of the previous series, the *lissage* is good, and the cards are marked with hexagonal figures in black.

[$3\frac{3}{8}$ × $0\frac{7}{8}$ in.]   [Backs decorated.]

PART II.

COMMENTARY ON AND DESCRIPTION OF THE PLATES.

DESCRIPTION OF THE PLATES.

IT has been stated at p. 35, vol. i., that although it be *not proven*, playing-cards had their origin in Europe, and in modern times, yet that there is more direct evidence in favour of such opinion than can be adduced in support of the hypothesis that they have descended to us—in the form of the tarots or emblematic series, at least—from remote ages, and had their birth in the East. While maintaining here a like doctrine, and laying stress on the obscure and recondite character of the data on which the belief of an Oriental source of the tarots has been based, it is nevertheless freely admitted that the meaning of many of the relations and peculiarities of these cards are left quite unexplained by the theories of their European origin, while those affirming their Eastern source do really attempt some elucidation of them, however fanciful and mystical it may be considered to be by the opponents to the theories from which it springs.

While feeling satisfied then that there is not any direct proof of the Oriental origin of playing-cards, and that not any *documentary* evidence can be produced for their existence before the second half of the fourteenth century, we cannot refuse to allow that the theory which regards the numeral playing-cards of Europe as having been invented either in Spain or Venice, for the purpose of displacing the emblematic tarots (which had become prohibited from their connection with the practice of " la magie noire " and divination derived with them from the East), has been supported by much ingenious illustration, obtained from translating the emblems in question through the doctrines of the Hebrew Kabbalah and of the Egyptian mystics.

The entire displacement of the tarot cards has not only not been accomplished, but even their fusion with the numeral series has not been prevented : that series which, according to the theory last referred to, was invented to supplant them, and in connection with which they continue to exist in some countries to the present day. To such as carry out the theory of the Oriental origin of cards to the still greater extent of tracing the original conception of the true numerals as well as of the emblematic series to India or Egypt, this persistency of union will not be surprising. Perhaps, too, it might be difficult to show a valid reason why acceptance should not be given to the hypothesis in its entirety, if given to it at all. (Vol i. pp. 20, 73.)

However this may be, we find that for five hundred years have endured, with some slight modifications of design, a series of cards of emblematic composition; the source, exact meaning, and original intention of which have been variously interpreted, and concerning which we are in darkness at the present time.

Details connected with this series—the tarots—formed an important part of the history and examples recorded in the previous volume. It has been felt that, notwithstanding the attempt made to render their nature and symbolical meanings, as derived from the Oriental and Kabbalistic theories of their source, tolerably clear by the disquisition on Divination and Cartomancy, etc. (pp. 138-163, vol. i.), that a fair idea could be formed of them by those strange to the subject, only by having before them while studying the previous pages an actual tarots sequence, or carefully executed plates illustrative of the symbolic designs therein contained.

As these advantages might not be always at hand, and that the labour already performed should not remain more fruitless than it need, it has been deemed advisable to supplement the text of vol. i. by a series of plates illustrative of this obscure subject.

It must not be assumed—it is once more insisted—from the comments which follow, and from what has been previously stated (vol. i.), that the occult and thaumaturgic doctrines touched on are here accepted as verities, or even as probably hidden or intended to be expressed in the emblematic composition of the tarots. They have been brought forward simply as a necessary part of the scheme proposed in this work, of illustrating the general history of playing-cards. Without viewing these objects under their aspect of emblematic cards or tarots, and these again, in connection with their Oriental and mystical relations, the consideration of the subject would have remained imperfectly performed.

PLATES I., II., III., IV., V., AND PART OF VI.

N these plates are represented the twenty-two emblematic cards or tarots described at pp. 18, 36, 38, 150, and 155 of vol. i.

In these designs the oldest typical forms, as far as they can be attained to now, of the yet comparatively modern renderings of a supposed ancient hieroglyphic and kabbalistic alphabet are given, in order that the interpretations of the symbolic figures, and their accessories, according to the recondite theories of Court de Gebelin and others detailed at p. 138 *et seq.* of vol. i., may be easily followed. The cardmakers have generally caused these designs to be drawn, engraved, and coloured in so coarse and careless a manner, and with such small amount of regard to essential details, that direct facsimiles of any actual sequence in the Museum collection would not have answered the purpose of illustrating the esoteric doctrines of those who would derive the tarots from the patriarchal East, so well as will the compositions here placed before the reader. Nevertheless, on comparing them with those of any actual tarots sequence of the fifteenth and sixteenth centuries, and of such more recent series as have imitated the older emblematic cards, it may be seen at once that like emblems and objects are intended to be represented, though on a smaller scale in our illustrations than is usual in the cardpieces of ordinary tarots. The earliest known tarots have been supposed to be after all but comparatively modern renderings, during the latter portion of the fourteenth and beginning of the fifteenth centuries, of other forms gradually vanishing in the twilight of Oriental obscurity; and however close the esoteric doctrines themselves, as taught in modern times, may be to those inculcated originally, through a series of hieroglyphs and emblems, it is quite impossible that the latter could approach but in intention, and as translated by modern art and influences, the assumed original symbolical designs.

Egypt is to us the cradle of wisdom and science, since it clothed in hieroglyphic forms the ancient dogmas of the first and true Zoroaster, forms purer and more exact, if not richer than those of Hindu birth. The right expression of these symbolic forms and

E

their interpretation constitute the kabbalistic and thaumaturgic science of hieroglyphs, which in Egypt had for its basis an alphabet in which all the gods were letters, all the letters were ideas, all the ideas were numbers, and all the numbers perfect signs. This kabbalistic alphabet was in one of its forms, according to certain writers, the famous book of Thauth or Thot,[1] to be found broken up and scattered amongst the *débris* of Egyptian monuments, and from it have descended, they affirm, the spirit and intention of the tarots of the fourteenth century. These latter, along with the numeral series, in the opinion of the extremer theorists, constitute, in the eyes of the initiated, an alphabet of twenty-two allegorical letters, and of four series of ten hieroglyphs relating to the four letters of the name of Jehovah or the *tetragramma*. The various combinations of these signs, and of the numbers corresponding to them, compose so many kabbalistic oracles, which may become in the hands of such as belong to the higher initiation the exponents of all wisdom and science. (Eliphas Levi, "La Clef des Grands Mystères," etc. p. 208.)

According to Levi, the best key to the primitive hieroglyphic alphabet on which this tarot sequence has been founded, was to be met with in the *mensa isiaca*, formerly belonging to Cardinal Bembo, but afterwards unfortunately destroyed. This table was of copper, having on it engraved figures filled with a sort of incrusted enamel. A copy of the table with an interpretation of its hieroglyphs and emblems, etc., may be seen in the following work of the learned Jesuit Father Athanasius Kircher, viz.:—

"Ædipi Ægyptiaci. Athanasii Kircheri. Romæ 1652." t. 3. cap. v. p. 123.

A fine copy is in the Library of the British Museum— 87.1.4.7.

According to Kircher, this table contained the hieroglyphic key to the sacred alphabets of Egypt.

If the table—as given in Kircher's treatise—be placed by the side of our present tarots not any similarity of actual pictorial designs can be found, it is true. But if the intention of the emblems of the former or their interpretation by Kircher be considered, it may be readily conceived in what way the followers of the schools of De Gebelin and Levi have been led to borrow an origin so remote as they have done for the tarots of the fourteenth century.

To the statement that there is not any likeness between the figures of the modern tarots and the emblems of the Egyptian hieroglyphs, whatever there may be between the dogmas which have been extorted from the esoterism of each, reply may be

---

[1] The Egyptian Hermes or Mercury, and the patron deity of scribes and writing.

made in inferring a continuedly advancing metamorphosis as necessarily involved in the varying iconic phases of the tarots as they have come down to us on the stream of time.

It is advisable that the series of tarot figures contained in Breitkopf's work[1] be consulted side by side with that presented here, as certain modifications of the ordinary designs proper to be noticed are therein given, and which do not exist in the present illustrations.

To the general account which has been laid before the reader in vol. i. p. 138 *et seq.* of the emblematic figures represented on plates 1, 2, 3, 4, 5, and 6 in this appendix, the following remarks on some particular tarots will not be out of place, for the more perfect explanation of them in their connection with occult philosophy, and with the theories of De Gebelin, Eliphas Levi, and others.

On the kabbalah generally the following work may be advantageously consulted :—

" The Kabbalah. Its Doctrines, Development, and Literature. An Essay by Christian D. Ginsburg, LL.D. London, 1865."

TAROT NUMBER II. LA PAPESSE.

In this design the binary principle is intended to be symbolized as represented by the High Priestess of the Egyptians, now metamorphosed into a female Pope in certain tarot series (vol. i. pp. 36, 37), and reverting in others to the true correlative, the goddess Hera of the Greeks and Juno of the Romans. (Breitkopf, *op. cit.* Tarot No. 11.) In the latter, the figure properly follows what is more likely to have been the normal action of the antiquer emblems in elevating one hand towards heaven, and pointing downwards with the other towards the earth, formulating by this gesture the dogmas of unity and dualism, which constitute the basis of " la haute magie," and commence the symbols of the emerald table of Hermes. (Breitkopf, *op. cit.* Tarot No. 11. Eliphas Levi, "Dogme et Rituel," etc. vol. i. p. 133. Desbarrolles, " Chiromancie Nouvelle," "Les Mystères de la main révélés et expliqués." Paris, 1859, p. 33.)

TAROT NUMBER V. LE PAPE.

The Pope of the ordinary emblematic cards is the grand hierophant of the Egyptians, and changes in certain Italian sequences to his correlative, Zeus of the Greeks and Jupiter Optimus Maximus of the Romans. As the latter, he descends from heaven on an eagle,

---

[1] " Versuch den Ursprung der Spielkarten, die Einführung des Leinenpapieres und den Anfang der Holzschneidekunst in Europa zu erforschen." Leipzig. 1784. Erster Abschnitt, p. 20.

bearing thunderbolts and lightning in each hand.   (Breitkopf, Tarot
No. V.)

In accordance with the mystical and Oriental theory of the
import of the tarots, it has been presumed that the normal form of
this present emblem, in which the Pope is seen extending the
fingers of the right hand in benediction, showed the hierophant
making the sign of esoterism which prescribes silence, and which
may be observed also in the accompanying figure of ADDHA-NARI,
the Isis of the Hindus, a pantheistic emblem typifying Nature, Truth,
and Religion.

The hand which holds the wand has the first three fingers
extended, signifying Force, Power, and Fate; the annular and
auricular fingers, which typify science and light, are hidden or bent.
This gesture may be translated as implying—" I speak thus to the
initiated." " Unite together, for so you have strength and dominion
to guide the fatality which is in your hands; but from the un-
initiated—since they are the vicious, the unintelligent of men—

hide (esoterism) all light and science ; " such teaching being quite in accordance also with the doctrines of Egyptian philosophy.

In this Hindu emblematic figure the four symbols of the ancient tarots, now the suit-marks of the numeral series of the playing-cards of Italy and Spain, are placed in the hands ; viz., the cup, the circle or money, the sword, and the wand or club. These attributes will be again referred to (*postea*, p. 62).

TAROT NUMBER VII. LE CHARIOR.

This emblem represented normally the advance or triumph of Osiris ; afterwards the chariot of Hermes, then the *Marte* of the *Carte di Baldini,* and finally "Le Charior" of the modern tarots.

It symbolizes the septenary principle, or the No. 7, representing the universal synthesis.

The number seven was *absolute* among the Eastern magi. The *seventh* year was a jubilee with the Jews, and the *seventh* day, the end of the week, was consecrated by them to rest and prayer.

" In Septenario (qui sacratissimus est in oraculis numerus et mysteriorum plerissimus) tam sacrum augustumque decus in est, ut inter eos numeros qui concluduntur in denario singularem eximiam præ cæteris rationem habent." (Petri Bungi, " Bergomatis Numerorum Mysteria," etc. Bergomi iↃXCi. De Numero vii. p. 282. Which see also on other numbers. There is a copy in the Museum Library, 529, c. 8.)

" On the *seventh* day God ended his work which he had made —and God blessed the *seventh* day, and sanctified it because that in it he had rested from all his work." (Genesis, chap. ii. v. 2, 3.)

Noah was directed to take the clean beasts and birds into the ark by *sevens,* " and it came to pass after *seven* days that the waters of the flood were upon the earth." (Genesis, chap. vii. v. 2-10.)

So holy was the *seventh* day to be regarded that on the sixth day a double quantity of manna was given to the Israelites on their journeyings, as the bread of two days, with the order, " Abide ye every man in his place, let no man go out of his place on the *seventh* day ; so the people rested on the *seventh* day," and thus not any infraction of its repose ensued. (Exodus, chap. xvi. v. 29, 30.)

The Hebrew slave became free on his attaining his *seventh* year of service. " Six years he shall serve, and in the *seventh* he shall go out free for nothing." (Exodus, chap. xxi. v. 2.)

There was the " mystery of the *seven* stars," of the " *seven* golden candlesticks," and there were " *seven* churches which are in Asia." (Apocalypse, chap. i.).

There were " *seven* lamps of fire burning before the throne, on which are the *seven* spirits of God," and the book " sealed with *seven* seals " (Apoc. chap. v.). There were the " *seven* angels which had the *seven* trumpets " (chap. viii.), and there was " a beast rise up from out of the sea, having *seven* heads " (chap. xiii.). There were " *seven* angels which had the *seven* vials full of the *seven* last plagues " (chap. xxi.).

In the days of Elisha there were yet " *seven* thousand in Israel " who had not bowed unto Baal. (1 Kings, chap. xx. v. 18.)

When Elisha " said to his servant, Go up now, look towards the sea ; and he went up, and looked, and said, There is nothing." Elisha replied, " Go again *seven* times ; and it came to pass at the *seventh* time," etc. (1 Kings, chap. xix. v. 43, 44). The same prophet also declared that " the Lord hath called for a famine, and it shall also come upon the land *seven* years." (2 Kings, chap. viii. v. 1.)

When Elisha restored the dead son of the Shunamite he " prayed unto the Lord, and he went up and lay upon the child— and the flesh of the child waxed warm—and the child sneezed *seven* times, and the child opened his eyes." (2 Kings, chap. iv. v. 33-35.)

It was said by Jesus to the anxious nobleman of Galilee, " Go thy way, thy son liveth ;" and when " he enquired of them the hour when he began to amend, they said unto him, At the *seventh* hour the fever left him." (John, chap. iv. v. 50-52.)

On the stone laid before Joshua were to be " *seven* eyes." (Zechariah, chap. iii. v. 9.)

There were *seven* chief Archangels—Michael, Gabriel, Raphael, Anael, Samael, Zadkiel, and Oriphiel, the latter four being the Uriel, Barachiel, Sealtiel, and Jebudiel of the Gnostic Christians. To these the *seven* Christian sacraments are correlates, and unite with the *seven* Virtues (the seven cords of the human lyre), having their analogues in the *seven* colours of the prismatic spectrum and the *seven* notes of the musical octave. With these were included by modern kabbalists the *seven* precious stones, viz., the carbuncle, crystal, diamond, emerald, agate, sapphire, and onyx ; and the *seven* chief metals, gold, silver, iron, copper, mercury, tin, and lead. Finally came the kabbalistic signs of the *seven* spirits, the symbols of all these being to be found on the stones graven by the ancients, particularly on the talismans known as *Abraxas* of the Gnostic epoch.

This number *seven* rules, in a mysterious way, the numbers of the tarots sequence, according to certain writers. There are in this sequence twenty-one pieces (the *matto* being unnumbered, or zero), *i. e.*, the sacred number *seven* multiplied by the ternary principle, which is the universal dogma, the perfect word, the fulness of unity.

Even the numerals in the combined tarots sequencies are fifty-six in number, *i.e.*, eight by *seven*, making in the old Venetian series a total, with the tarots proper, of seventy-seven, *i. e.*, eleven by *seven*, rejecting the unnumbered *matto* or fool.   (Taylor, Bibl. 9, p. 19.)

In an ancient design of this emblematic figure the symbolic *lingam* of the Hindus, surmounted by the flying sphere of the Egyptians, was represented on the front panel of the car in place of the varying marks now to be met with. (See the representation of " Le Charior d'Hermes, Suprême Clef du Tarot," in Eliphas Levi's "Dogme et Rituel," etc. vol. ii. p. 332.)

TAROT NUMBER X. LA ROUE DE FORTUNE.

This emblem has its analogue, according to Levi, in the wheels of Ezekiel and of Pythagoras.   (" Dogme et Rituel," vol. i. p. 333. " La Clef des Grands Mystères," p. 117.)

Etteilla, in his cards for divination, displaced the original descending typhon on the left by a man ; the ascending Hermanubis on the right by a rabbit, mouse, or nondescript animal ; and the sphinx above by an ape. (See the figure of " La dixième Clef du Tarot " in " La Clef," etc. of E. Levi, p. 116.)

TAROT NUMBER XII. LE PENDU.

According to E. Levi (" Dogme et Rituel," vol. i. p. 255), this emblematic figure has been misunderstood by Court de Gebelin and by Etteilla, who perceived in it merely an error committed by a German cardmaker. This design represents a man having his hands tied behind his back, and with two bags of money attached to his armpits in certain of those tarots in which the figure has the hands tied behind. In " Le Pendu " of the series of cards known as those of Charles the Sixth, or of Gringonneur (vol. i. pp. 13, 14), the arms are free and dependent, and the figure holds a large bag of money in each hand. (See Bibl. 2, plate 35.) In " Le Pendu " of the *Minchiate* series also, described under I. 256 and I. 257 of the present volume, pp. 3, 6, the arms are free and dependent, and a bag hangs from each hand. The man is suspended by one foot to a gibbet composed of the trunks of two trees, each trunk showing the roots of six truncated branches and being surmounted by a transverse beam completing the figure of the Hebrew Tau, ת. The legs of the culprit are crossed, and his elbows form a ξ angle with his head. Now the triangle surmounted by a cross signifies in

alchemy the end and the perfection of the Great Work, a signification identical with that of the letter ת, which is the last letter of the
sacred alphabet.

"'Le Pendu,' then, is the adept bound by his engagements,
spiritualized, or with the feet turned towards heaven. The emblem
typifies also the ancient Prometheus suffering in everlasting torture
the punishment of his glorious larceny. Vulgarly it represents
Judas the traitor, and his execution menaces the revealers of the
Great Secret." ("Dogme et Rituel," vol. i. p. 255.)

"In the ancient writings, anterior to the captivity, the Hebrew
tau had the form of a cross, a circumstance further confirmatory of
our interpretation of the twelfth piece of the kabbalistic tarot. The
cross, generatrix of four triangles, is also the sacred sign of the duo-
denary principle (the cyclical number and that of the universal
symbol), called the 'Key of Heaven' by the Egyptians for that
reason."

"Thus Etteilla, embarrassed in his protracted endeavours to
reconcile the analogical requirements of the figure with his own
personal views, placed in the hands of his reversed *pendu*, with
which he symbolizes prudence, an hermetic caduceus formed of
two serpents and a Greek *tau*. Since he had comprehended the
necessity of the *tau*, or cross ("Book of Thot," p. 12), he ought to
have understood the multiple and magnificent symbol of the hermetic
pendu, the Prometheus of science, the living man who touches
earth by thought only and whose base is in heaven; the free and
sacrificed adept, the revealer, menaced with death." ("Dogme,"
etc. vol. i. p. 258.)

TAROT NUMBER XIII. LA MORT.

In accordance with the misfortune and ill-fatedness attached
to the number thirteen, the present member of the emblematic
series represents *Death* in each of the chief tarots sequencies, viz. :
the old Venetian sequence, the *tarocchino* of Bologna and the
minchiate of Florence. (Vol. i. p. 141, No. 13.)

"Juxta Hœbreorum traditionem anno a mundo condito tertio-
decimo primus reproborum exemplar, primus parricida, civitas
diaboli et regni impiorum conditor, Cain nascitur." (Petri Bungi,
op. cit. de num. xiii. et xiv. p. 401.)

"This idea of misfortune attached to the number thirteen is
essentially Oriental. The symbolical *atouts* are numbered, so to
say, from low to high, just as certain modes of Asiatic writing proceed from right to left. Has this also not some hidden meaning?"
(Boiteau d'Ambly, *op. cit.* p. 21.)

A striking series of coincidences has been recently recorded in an account of one of the more remarkable of the Arctic expeditions of modern times.[1]

" At last," writes Commander Payer, " every trace of land disappeared from our gaze, a hopeless waste received us, in which no man could tell how long we should be, nor how far we should penetrate. . . A change, however, was soon to come over the scene. . . A dreadful day was the 13th of October—a Sunday—it was decisive of the fate of the expedition. To the superstitious amongst us the number 13 was clothed with a profound significance : the committee of the expedition had been constituted on February 13 ; on the 13th of January the keel of the 'Tegetthoff' had been laid down; on the 13th of April she was launched ; on the 13th of June we left Bremerhaven ; on the 13th of July, Tromsoe ; after a voyage of 13 days we had arrived at the ice ; and on the 13th October the temperature marked 13 degrees below zero. In the morning of that day, as we sat at breakfast, our floe burst across, immediately under the ship—just as in the risings of a people, the wave of revolt spreads on every side, so now the ice uprose against us, mountains threateningly reared themselves from out the level fields of ice, and the low groan which issued from its depths grew into a deep rumbling sound, and at last rose into a furious howl, as of myriads of voices. Noise and confusion reigned supreme, and step by step destruction drew nigh in the crashing together of the fields of ice." (Vol. i. pp. 161-4.)

It may be observed *en passant,* that in the sequence known as " Charles the VIth cards " (vol. i. pp. 13, 19), *Death* is mounted and on a black horse instead of on a white one (Bibl. 2). The like emblematic figure is also mounted in the two *minchiate* tarots (sets I. 256, I. 257) described at pp. 3, 6 of the present volume. Here the horse being unshaded is probably intended to be white.

TAROT NUMBER XVI. LA MAISON DIEU.

Herein is symbolized an event in the life of the Egyptian Prince Rhampsinitus, or Rameses the Second, which is alluded to in vol. i. p. 142.

The history of this event is given in detail by Herodotus, whose account of the end of the thieves differs in some particulars from the following version, taken from Court de Gebelin.

According to the latter, the Prince Rhampsinitus ordered a great

---

[1] " New Lands within the Arctic Circle. Narrative of the Discoveries of the Austrian ship 'Tegetthoff.' " By Julius Payer, one of the Commanders of the Expedition. Translated from the German. London. 1876.

tower to be built, for the purpose of containing his treasures. Though he alone possessed a key to it, he found his treasures daily diminish, and yet not anyone passed the door. In order to discover the adroit thieves, the Prince placed snares around the vases containing his money; by these the robbers were indicated, and turned out to be the two sons of the architect who had built the tower. The latter person had so disposed a stone that it might be easily removed and replaced at will, without risk of discovery. This secret he intrusted to his sons, who availed themselves of it as related. Having been betrayed while at their work, through the Prince's arrangements, they threw themselves down headlong from the summit of the tower.

TAROT NUMBER XXI. LE MONDE.

Eliphas Levi, in his chapter (" Rituel," etc. p. 172) on " Le Grand Œuvre," remarks: " The twenty-second key, which bears the number 21, because the *fou* which precedes it in the kabbalistic order is not numbered, represents a youthful female divinity, slightly veiled, running within a blossoming wreath, supported at the four corners by the four animals of the kabbalah. The goddess holds a wand in each hand, in the Italian tarots; while in the tarots of Besançon she retains both wands in a single hand, placing the other hand on her thigh; symbols equally indicative of the magnetic action, whether alternate in its polarization, or simultaneous by opposition and transmission."

In an article " Sur la Kabbale," in the supplement to " La Clef des Grands Mystères," the author writes: " That which most attracted the attention of Court de Gebelin, when he discovered the tarot, were the hieroglyphs of the twenty-first piece, which bears the title of ' Le Monde.' This card (which is nothing but the same key of William Postel) represents Truth, naked and triumphant, within a wreath divided into four portions by four flowers of the lotus. At the four corners of the card may be seen the four symbolic animals, which are afforded by an analysis of the sphinx, and which Saint John borrowed from the prophet Ezekiel, as Ezekiel himself had taken them from the bucephalous or other sphinxes of Egypt and Assyria. These four figures—which a tradition, uncomprehended even by the Church, still allots to our four Evangelists—represent the four elementary forms of the kabbalah; the four seasons; the four metals; in fine also the four mysterious letters of the TORA of the Jews, of the wheel of Ezekiel, ROTA, and of the TAROT, which, according to Postel, is the key of things hidden from the beginning of the world."

PLATES VII. AND VIII.

N plate 7 is a facsimile of the piece No. 1, the *Misero* of the series E of the *Carte di Baldini*, or the so-called *Tarocchi* of Mantegna. (Vol. i. pp. 66, 155.)

On comparing this emblematic figure of the Italian sequence with the *mat, matto*, or *fou*, the unnumbered piece or zero of the tarots on plate 6, it may be seen how in both examples a dog is seizing the man by his left leg. In this instance the descent of both symbolical designs from some earlier type is certainly fairly presumable, and if it be admitted with Merlin and others, that the engraved Italian version of 1470 (?) was derived from a pictorial series of emblematic representations existing long anterior to the invention at Venice (?) of games of hazard with cards, there cannot easily be placed any limit to the *traditional* origin—if we may so speak—of the common type of both examples. (Vol. i. p. 71.)

On the other hand, the opponents to the theory of the Oriental source of cards, and their original mystical teachings, may point to the resemblance in question as proof simply of the fact that the *matto* of the old Venetian tarots was borrowed directly from the Florentine sequence of 1470, and, therefore, as helping to support the doctrine that the twenty-two old Venetian emblems are of more recent origin than the *Carte di Baldini*. (Vol. i. p. 156.)

It should be noted also that in some of the tarots versions the *matto*, or *fou*, is represented like the *Misero* of the Florentine sequence, that is, more of a beggar than a fool, as which latter he is given in other tarots.

According to one system of interpretation the unnumbered emblem, the *matto*, or *fou*, of the ordinary tarots (plate 6) is to be regarded as symbolizing Folly with a sackful of faults on his back, while the animal biting him signifies the pangs of conscience and of remorse which so often attack the possessor of such a burden.

In the *Misero* of the *Carte di Baldini* (plate 7) are portrayed the want and destitution to which such faults have brought their owner.   Conscience yet pricks him—in the biting dog—though the faults be gone, while the leafless barren trees and broken wall typify the fruitlessness and waste of such a fool's existence.

On plate 8 is a facsimile, the actual size, of No. 45 the *Marte* of series A of the *Carte di Baldini*.   (Vol. i. p. 66.)

This design should be compared with No. 7 of the tarots figures on plate 2.

In the former or present emblem the figure appears as a sedate warrior in helmet and armour, bearing in his right hand a sword, and bending his left arm on his left thigh.   He is observed to be seated in direct or full face on a car, having an architectural canopy above, supported by columns.   A dog is at his feet.

In the tarot piece No. 7 (plate 2), we have Osiris advancing in his chariot, bearing a sceptre in his right hand, and bending his left arm on his left thigh.   The figure is in direct or full face to the spectator, and the car has a canopy above supported by columns. Two animals are in front of the car.

The same kind of comparison is applicable here as in the case of the *matto* and *Misero* just noticed.   The resemblance between the two emblems testifies either to the descent of both compositions from an antecedent and common type, or to the fact that the piece No. 7 of the old Venetian tarots is simply a modification of No. 45 of the Italian sequence.   (Vol. i. p. 156.)

PLATES IX., X., XI., AND XII.

EPRESENT the marks, signs, or symbols of the suits of the numeral playing-cards of Italy, Spain, France (England), and Germany, whether uncombined or combined with an emblematic series. A general rule prevails, however, that when numerals are conjoined to an emblematic series the suit-marks of the former are of the Italian character.

In the typical and full numeral series of each country there are always four suits.

Plate 9 exhibits the marks of the suits of Italian numerals. (Vol. i. pp. 32, 85.) These are *coppe* (cups), *spade* (swords), *danari* (money), and *bastoni* (clubs).

It should be observed that the marks of the suits *spade* and *bastoni* are crossed or interlaced among themselves, and that the narrow width of each piece in proportion to the length indicates that these particular numerals belonged to a combined tarots or *tarocchino* sequence. The proportions of these cards are true, but the general size is smaller than that of the originals.

Plate 10 represents the marks of the suits in Spanish numerals. (Vol. i. pp. 40, 93.) There are *copas* (cups), *espadas* (swords), *oros* (money), and *bastos* (clubs).

It should be noticed that the marks of the suits *espadas* and *bastos* are discrete or separate, which circumstance along with the numbers at opposite corners diagonally, and the divisions of the inner border lines on the pieces in three of the suits into separate portions of different number (*antea*, p. 8), distinguish the Spanish numeral pip-cards from the Italian numerals.

Plate 11 shows the marks of French numerals, viz., *cœurs* (hearts = cups), *piques* (spades = swords), *carreaux* (diamonds = money), and *trèfles* (clubs). (Vol. i. pp. 46, 50, 111.)

These suit-marks have always been adopted for English numerals, frequently for Italian, occasionally for Spanish, and in modern times pretty constantly for the numeral playing-cards of Germany. France and Belgium manufacturing cards for various countries naturally introduce these symbols, except when fabricating to order what may be turned factitious Italian, Spanish, and other cards.

Plate 12 represents the national suit-marks of the earlier cards of Germany, viz., *roth* or *herzen* (hearts = cups) ; *laub* or *grün* (leaves = swords, spades) ; *schellen* or " grelots " (bells = money, diamonds), and *eicheln* (glands = *trèfles*, clubs). (Vol. i. pp. 47, 192.)

EXPLICATION OF THE SYMBOLS OF THE NUMERAL SUITS.

THE SUIT-MARKS OF ITALY AND SPAIN.

NOT only has the series of emblematic cards, or tarots, been translated into the dogmas of an ancient and recondite philosophy, but the symbols of the numeral-cards accompanying them in combined or compound sets have been also interpreted in a similar manner. As a natural consequence a like interpretation was afterwards applied to the same marks of the suits of numerals, when the latter appeared unconnected with an emblematic sequence. Remarks relative to this point may be found on reference to vol. i. pp. 143,153-155. To these we shall add the following observations.

On examining such numerals as are found first to have been conjoined with the tarots proper they may be observed to bear the ordinary marks of the four suits of the playing-cards of Italy and Spain, viz., the cup, money, sword, and club.

It was at an after period that the French and other symbols were so employed, but even then, as far as our own experience extends, quite exceptionally.

According to the schools of the occult philosophy, the four thaumaturgic signs of the tarot may be seen in the hands of the Hindu symbolic figure ADDHA-NARI, which was given *antea*, p. 52.

These signs represent also the symbols of the four numeral suits, and correspond to the four elements of the old philosophers. There is the *cup* in the lower right hand of the figure, which in other emblems when held by a man = *aquarius*, typifies *water ;* there is the staff or club of wood in the upper right hand, signifying the *fire*, which it feeds; in the lower left hand is the circle (afterwards meta-morphosed into the form of money), emblematic of *air*, while the upper left hand grasps the sword or knife of Mithra, which immo-lates yearly the sacred bull, whose blood causes the sap to flow and fill all the fruits of the earth. (E. Levi, "Dogme," etc. vol. ii. p. 333.)

If we pass from India to Egypt and its occultism and then to the Hebrews and their theosophy, it may be assumed that the symbols of the numeral suits are the hieroglyphs of the *tetragramma.* (Vol. i. pp. 148, 154.)

The "club" is the *phallus* of the Egyptians, and the *jod* of the Hebrews; the "cup" is the *cteis*, and the primitive *hé;* the "sword" is the conjunction of the *phallus* and *cteis* represented in Hebrew anterior to the captivity by the *vau;* while the "circle" (pantacles) and money (vulgarly the emblem of the world) is the final *hé* of the Divine name. Thus we have הוהי, *jod hé vau hé,* or, as we conventionally pronounce it, JEHOVAH. ("Dogme et Rituel," etc. vol. i. p. 230.)

Some adherents to the theory of the Oriental origin of cards, refusing to admit such extremely transcendental views as those just mentioned, nevertheless go to the extent of recognizing in the symbols of the numeral suits the *four chief castes* into which men were divided on the banks both of the Nile and the Ganges. Ac-cordingly, the "cup" denotes the sacerdotal rank, or *priesthood;* the "sword" implies the king, warrior, or *military rank;* the "circle" typifies the world, or *commercial community,* of which money is the sign; and the "club" is emblematic of agriculture, or of the *tillers of the soil.*

THE SUIT-MARKS OF FRANCE AND GERMANY.

THE origin and meaning of the marks of the suits of the numeral playing-cards of France and Germany have been variously determined, and much research and ingenious attempts expended on their elucidation.

The adherents to the theory of the Eastern source of cards have assumed the like intentions to be conveyed in them as in the suit-marks of Italy and Spain. It has been urged against such a view that the signs of France and Germany do not accord with each other, or ostensibly only in respect to one sign, viz., *roth* or *herzen,* and *cœurs.* How, then, can these signs make common cause to-gether, and link themselves with those of Italy and Spain? It has been replied that a sufficient analysis will show that the three other suit-marks of Germany and France are modifications one of the other.

But, if so, which were the originals? It is probable, we think, that the German signs were first in the field, though Leber and Merlin are not of this opinion. Be that as it may, in the suits *roth* or *herzen,* and *cœurs,* may be found the analogues of the vase or " cup," the emblem of the sacerdotal rank or clergy, with its irreproachable, unworldly *heart. Laub* or *grün,* and *carreaux,* are modifications of the " circle " or *money,* typical of *commerce* and wealth ; in *schellen* (bells) and *piques* (spades) may be found the spade or swords of the nobles and *military ;* while in the suits *eicheln* (glands) and *trèfles* (clubs) is signified the agricultural status.

In tracing the connection between the suit-marks of France and Germany and those of Italy and Spain there does not arise much difficulty, except in the case of the *schellen* and *piques* of the former and the *spade* and *espadas* of the numerals of the latter countries. In respect to *schellen,* or bells, the difficulty is not insuperable, if it be borne in mind that bells were the insignia of rank and importance in the East from the earliest times. They were the signs of worldly position before the second epoch of heraldic distinctions (A.D. 1152), and at an after period the bell was used in Falconry[1] by princes and nobles of the highest class. The *bell* thus became the emblem first of the falcon and afterwards of the upper and richer grades, to which its employment was confined.

The robe of Aaron, the high priest, was directed to be thus adorned :—

" A golden bell and a pomegranate upon the hem of the robe roundabout." (Exodus, chap. xxviii. v. 34.)

" And they made bells of pure gold, and put the bells between the pomegranates upon the hem of the robe." (Exodus, chap. xxxix. v. 25.)

" It is probable, however, that these bells had a *symbolical* announcement, like all the other parts of the high priest's dress. The pomegranate was the emblem of *fulness,* and the bell of *announcement,* and the alternation of these on the *meïl* indicated the wearer's function as the preserver of the Divine Word in its fulness, and the announcer of it to the people. It is remarkable that there is no appearance of any kind of bell in the Egyptian monuments." (Kitto, " Cyclopædia of Biblical Literature.")

It may be added that the decoration of their idols with bells was a common practice with the Hindus.

---

[1] It is not implied that the bell was thus made use of at the earlier period of that sport.

Breitkopf gives ("Versuch den Ursprung der Spielkarten zu erforschen," taf. iv. s. 33) representations of Wulphild, the Emperor Henry VI., and Otto IV., the draperies in which are all adorned with small bells exactly like those on German playing-cards. In connection with these illustrations and the argument maintained by Breitkopf, viz., that the German suit-marks are older than the French ones, and date at least from the fourteenth century, the author observes, in the following notes (pp. 33, g. ; 116, s. 33, anmerk. g.):—

"In GABR. BUCELINI Germaniæ Topo-Chronostemmato-graphicæ Sacræ et profanæ ; Parte altera ; Aug. Vindel. 1662. fol. von pp. 346-423, where are introduced *Agilolfingicæ familiæ Principum Guelforum veterum*, etc., *generis deductione*, are also representations of various emperors and princely personages of the Guelpho-Brunswick houses, who are clothed with these once princely adornments. Among them are Guelpho II. and his consort Ermengarde, who lived about the years 1002-24, adorned with waist-girdles of bells ; Wulphild, the wife of Rudolph Com. Brig. *circa* 1138, with a necklace of bells ; the Emperor Henry VI., who died in 1197, with a waist-girdle of bells ; and the Emperor Otto IV., who died in 1218, with a collar of bells, which hangs behind him from across the shoulders to the calves of the legs. Since, then, this old princely clothing was worn from the eleventh to the thirteenth century, we may infer that these alterations of the suit-marks must have been made soon after the introduction of cards into Germany, and that the French *piquet*, which first appeared during the fifteenth century, is only a copy of the German changes, unless it be assumed that this old decoration, becoming recalled to mind, was ingeniously made to serve the purpose of the present argument." . . . .

. . "The figures in question were most likely taken from the old German chronicle of the Guelphs, preserved in the convent of Weingarten, and from which Eccard also took them for his ' Orig. Guelf.' t. ii. pp. 279, 323, 357. At the earliest they were not executed before the beginning of the fifteenth century, as may be presumed from the presence of the *Saxon rue*, but they were taken, probably, from older originals. Keysler, in his recent travels (' Hannover, 1751-4,' 1 ster Theil, vi Schreiben, s. 27), alludes to these figures of the Dukes of Brunswick as statues placed in the ' autorshofe ' at Brunswick, and at the same time refers to the previously-mentioned work of Bucelini, and to the portraits of princely personages in the ' Rathhaus ' at Lüneburg."

Leber and Chatto treat Breitkopf's theory of bell decoration very slightingly, the former remarking on the costume of Breitkopf's illustrations: " Il est hors de toute vraisemblance qu'on y ait supposé une parure de grelots étrangère au monument original." Chatto observes : " Breitkopf's conjecture is undeserving of remark ; had

F

he asserted that his old German emperors and princes were adorned with bells to indicate their rank and precedence in the manner of leading pack-horses he would, perhaps, have been as near the truth." (Bibl. 4, p. 240.)

The form of the *schelle, grelot,* or bell, on the " old German princely-bell costume" of Breitkopf, and on the numeral cards of Germany, is denied by Lampe ("De Cymbalis Veterum") to bear resemblance to the κρόταλον, κρὢσμα, *crotalum et crusma,* of the Greeks and Romans, which are frequently translated by the word *grelot,* " et en effet la figure du grelot ne se retrouve dans aucun monument d'une antiquité bien établie." (See note 4, p. 242, in Chatto, Bibl. 4.)[1]

Some writers make the *schellen* of the German numerals answer to the *danari* (money) of the Italian suits, and to the *carreaux* (diamonds) of the French cards, instead of to the *spade* and *espadas* of the southern numerals, and the *piques* of the French series. *Laub* or *grün,* they regard as the correlate of spade and *pique,* while others compare the former with *bastoni, trèfles,* and clubs.

Three well known writers—Daniel, Bullet, and Leber—propounded theories of which the following are short abstracts.

According to Père Daniel, the signs of the French suits are emblematic of the necessities of war. *Trèfles*—trefoil, or the clover-plant—symbolize "forage;" *piques,* "pikes and powder-shovels;" *carreaux,* arrows, stones, etc., shot from crossbows—the *carreau* being a kind of heavy arrow having the head *carré,* or squared. *Cœurs* signify the bold hearts and courage of soldiers.

Bullet accepts with some modifications Père Daniel's theory. He supposes that the sign *piques* represents offensive weapons, like the pique or lance, and that of *carreaux,* defensive arms, as represented by a lozenge-shaped buckler.

In Leber's opinion, the sign *cœurs* explains itself, being a symbol of the nobler sentiments, and especially indicative of intrepidity and courage. *Trèfle* is a flower, or *fleuron,* with three branches, symbolical of the mysterious number 3, or the sacred ternary. It is the three-branched *fleuron* which appears on the monuments of the early French kings, but in consequence of its having been badly designed, and worse understood, it became confounded with the heraldic *fleur-de-lis,* and is now in fact displaced by it. *Carreau* is a square placed lozenge-wise, as an emblem of constancy and firmness. The genius "Fortune" is always represented as standing by one foot on a wheel or globe to signify her instability. The oppo-

---

[1] In an engraving by Mantegna (B. xiii. p. 240, n. 19), known as "La Bacchanale à la Cuve," two figures may be observed decorated with *grelots;* at least, in the copy by Zoan Andrea (?) now before us such is the case.

site idea to unstableness was attached to a square or cube, considered as a firm and immovable base. It was for this reason that the ancients placed the figure of Wisdom and Firmness on a cubical support, and Aristotle speaks in a like sense when he tells us that a true philosopher should be square—*carré*—that is to say, immovable in courage and virtue.

The *pique*, according to Leber, represents the head of a lance, and signifies the warrior force, or soldier, and is the equivalent of the *spada* of the Italian numerals.

Thus the French suits typify four monarchies or political societies. The suit *cœurs* signifies a State governed by a generous and courageous prince; *trèfles*, one ruled over by a sovereign wise and just; *carreaux* signifies a community swayed over by a king both consistent in principle and decided in action; while the suit *piques* implies the appanage of a warlike ruler, who owes his territory to his arms.

THE SUIT-MARKS OF ENGLISH CARDS.

WHILE the English names of the suits are in part adopted from those of the Italian and Spanish cards, the signs or marks of them are exactly those of the French numerals. It is most probable that the term "spade" given in England to the French sign *pique*, is derivable either from the *spada* of Italian, or the *espada* of Spanish numerals; while the term " clubs " is related to *bastone* of the Italian, and to *basto*, or *baston*, of the Spanish suit, though here applied to the French sign *trèfle*. (Vol. i. pp. 33, 240, E. 183.)

"The Hon. Daines Barrington, in his paper in the eighth volume of the 'Archæologia,' ' On the Antiquity of Card-playing in England,' maintains the probability that cards of the Spanish type, and bearing the marks of cups, money, clubs, and swords (of the Spanish names of the last two, *bastos* and *espadas*, our clubs and spades are certainly of the one a translation, and of the other a corruption), preceded the adoption of French cards in this country; and he endeavours to connect them with the arrival of Philip the Second and his suite; though an equally plausible argument might be founded on the marriage of Henry VIII. with a Spanish Princess, Catharine of Aragon, of whom it is recorded by Sir William Forest, that in her youth—

> " ' With stoole and with needyl she was not to seeke
> And other practiseings for ladyes meete
> To pastyme at tables, tick tacke, or gleeke
> Cardis and dyce ' &c.

" Mr. Chatto, in support of this assumed priority of the Spanish cards, remarks that the knave, or jack, of our popular game, the meaning of which he defines to be ' a servant of low condition,' has more affinity in character with the Spanish *sota*, or the Italian *fante*, than with the French *valet*, which, in the earliest French cards, always bears the name of some person in romance or history. This sense of knave, however, which is curiously parallel to the modern sense of *valet*—like the still earlier one of ' man-child,' soon became obsolete, and the word came to be used exclusively to denote a cheat or dishonest person. According to the same author, the original of the English term ' Jackanapes,' was in all probability Jack-a-naïpes, *i. e.*, a buffoon in a parti-coloured dress, like a knave on cards. (See a very interesting discussion in Mr. Chatto's ' Facts and Speculations,' p. 230.) The earliest use of this appellation occurs in a ballad in the British Museum, date about 1450, where Jac Napes is applied as a term of reproach to the unfortunate Duke of Suffolk, then lately murdered." (Taylor, Bibl. 9, p. 140.)

On the other hand, Singer refers (Bibl. 8, p. 37) to a volume of Latin Dialogues, printed at Antwerp in 1533, in which the suit of *piques*, or our own " spades," is termed *ligones*, and he observes: " The resemblance of the object represented on cards of that suit to one of the forms of the agricultural spade is striking, and hence we may account for the origin of this denomination." So also Chatto, who remarks in a note at p. 230 : " It is but fair to observe here that the Dutch name for the suit which we call spades is *scop*, or shovel, or spade ; and that, as this name has been evidently given to the suit from the mark bearing some resemblance to a spade, the same suit might have been called spades by the English, for the same reason. This objection, however, does not affect the conjecture with respect to clubs." In the " Nugæ Venales," printed in Holland, 1648, we meet with the following : " Query.—Why are the four kings of cards, Diamonds, Trefoil, Hearts, and Spades—Rhombuli, Trifolii, Cordis, et Ligonis—always poor ? Answer.—Because they are always at play, and play, according to the proverb, is man's perdition. Their state is also in other respects most miserable, for when through them much money is lost, they are condemned to the flames, and burnt like wizards. The modern Dutch names for the suits of French cards are *hart*, heart ; *ruyt*, a lozenge-shaped figure, a diamond-shaped pane of glass—diamonds ; *klaver*, clover, trefoil—clubs ; *scop*, a spade, shovel, or scoop=spades."

In some systems of cartomancy the suit of diamonds is considered to offer, during the operations, the signs of bad omen ; while in others the suit of spades performs that function. On the " king of diamonds " reference may be made to vol. i. p. 162 ; and on the " nine of diamonds " or the " curse of Scotland," Chatto, Bibl. 4, p. 266, should be consulted.

PLATE VI.   LOWER PORTION.

ANIMATED MARKS OF SUITS.

N the lower part of plate 6 are very slightly reduced facsimiles of four circular cards, from the series described in vol. i. p. 209 as the " Circular Cards by Telman von Wesel" (G. 144).

These specimens are given for the purpose of illustrating a variety of the so-termed "animated suits" of early German playing-cards (vol. i. pp. 47, 207). The pieces selected are : the four and five of the suit of *parroquets*, the ace of that suit, and the ace of *hares*.

Of the engraver of these cards—" TW"—very little is known. He must have lived during the first decade of the sixteenth century, since he copied some of the earlier works of Albert Dürer; though judging from the general style of his technic he may have worked also during the latter portion of the fifteenth century. Telman von Wesel has been considered to have been a goldsmith-engraver of the lower Rhine, as his name indeed would indicate. On his copy (Heller, No. 135) of Albert Dürer's " Nativity " (Heller, No. 127) is the following inscription :—

"DJT: HUS: JS : GOT: BEKANT:
IT : HUS: TO: ....LEM: IT: GENANT:
TELLMAN : OP: DEN: DJCK: TO: WESEL."

The set of cards from which the present examples have been taken is considered to represent the engraver at his best.

It has been supposed that cards having animated marks of suits and delicately engraved on copper, produced at the end of the fifteenth century and beginning of the sixteenth, were not intended to be used in actual play.

The earliest German cards known have animated suit-marks, and are considered by Merlin as belonging probably to the end of the fourteenth or the beginning of the fifteenth century. They are preserved in the Royal collection at Stuttgart. The suits appear to have been formed in illustration of the pleasures of sporting, as one suit has for its sign the "dog," another the "falcon," a third the "stag," and a fourth the "duck." Admirable representations of four of the figure-cards may be found in Merlin's Treatise, plates 60, 61.

PLATES XIII. AND XIV.

SUIT-MARKS OF A COMPOSITE CHARACTER.

N plate 13 are represented facsimiles, the actual size, of three cardpieces from the sequence described in vol. i. p. 189, G. 120.

The suit-marks in the rare and interesting series from which these examples have been taken are of a mixed character. The signs of three of the suits are of Italian import, viz., cups, swords, and clubs, while the fourth suit has fruit or the pomegranate for its symbol.

Although the actual design of the sword—here a scimitar—and that of the club are not Italian in character, yet the interlaced manner in which the marks of the suits on the nine of swords and on the eight and nine of clubs are figured, evinces the spirit of the Italian numerals. The designs of the vessels on the different pieces of the suits of cups are of a Mediæval or Gothic character, their feeling and technic evincing the craft of both goldsmith and goldsmith-engraver.

The cardpieces selected are the sevens of cups and pomegranates and the queen of swords (vol. i. p. 191).

The remarks previously made (p. 64) in reference to *schellen*, or bells, as a suit-mark should be referred to, as the pomegranate is therein mentioned.

On plate 14 is given, in facsimile and of actual size, a full page from the series G. 161, described in vol. i. p. 221, as the " Charta Lusoria," or " Book of Cards," by Jobst Amman.

The series in question characteristically illustrates the curious and varied suit-marks occasionally employed by the German designers, for we have in the " Charta Lusoria " printers' ink-balls, books, metal wine-cups, and glass or earthenware bossed vases, as marks of the suits. It also affords an example of the amusing and grotesque auxiliary compositions with which the Teutonic artists adorned their cards. The example selected is the three of the suit of bossed vases.   The lines below the design may be freely translated as follows :—

> " Since man and wife are drunk and blind,
> Behold, my friends, the dog has mind
> To have *his* share and fill his jowl,
> So claims at once the roasted fowl ;
> Thus, in such cases, none need wonder
> Honour and riches oft sink under,
> For such example as the master
> Sets, will his servants follow after."

As to whether this series of cardpieces was intended for ordinary play or not consult vol. i. pp. 222, 224.

PLATES XV., XVI., AND XVII.

N these plates are represented facsimiles, the actual size, of three sheets from the series of German numerals described at p. 192, G. 122 of vol. i.

The sheets chosen are No. 2 (plate 15), No. 5 (plate 16), and No. 3 (plate 17).

On plate 15 may be seen a knave of *herzen,* or *roth,* a king of *schellen, grelots,* or bells, a knave of *eicheln,* or glands, and portions of five other figures.

On plate 16 are a king of *herzen,* or *roth,* a knave of *herzen,* a king of *eicheln,* and portions of cardpieces of the suits *laub* or *grün, schellen, herzen,* etc.

On plate 17 are shown the four of *herzen,* the five of *schellen,* the two of *schellen,* and portions of three other cards, the central piece being of the suit *schellen.*

On the two of *schellen,* in plate 17, is the figure, comparatively large, of a lion, below the marks of the suit. We may here recall to mind that Mr. Chatto, who first described these cardpieces (G. 122), and as not, probably, of a later date than 1440, and executed from stencils, was of opinion that they were not unlikely the production of a Venetian card-maker. This opinion was based on the circumstance that "a lion, the emblem of St. Mark, the patron saint of Venice, and a distinctive badge of the city, appears, as in the annexed cut, in the suit of bells, and a similar figure, with part of a mutilated inscription, occurs in the suit of acorns." (Bibl. 4, p. 89.)

It is a curious circumstance that the most ancient document supposed to refer to wood-engraving in Italy is an order of the Venetian Senate, of the date 1441, refusing to permit the importation of playing-cards and *figure stampide* into Venice. It has hence been assumed, and no doubt correctly, that playing-cards were then made in that city, or otherwise the Senate would not have been petitioned by the card-makers to preserve their monopoly. It has also been assumed that such cards and *figure stampide* were executed by means of wood-engravings; an assumption of very doubtful accuracy, since they may have been the product of pure hand-work and of stencils, or of a process like that known as "block-printing," or stamping. Passavant, however, maintained that from this order of the Venetian Senate, and the particular terms made use of in it, "engraving on wood was already (1441) known, and practised throughout the extent of the Republic at a rather early period; and if not any examples remain of Italian playing-cards, or other engravings on wood of this period, we are forced to conclude that the art of wood-engraving had never obtained but a very secondary rank there, and that it soon fell into desuetude."

Passavant then refers to the opinion of Chatto as to the Venetian origin of the series of cards which plates 15, 16, and 17 partly illustrate:—"Chatto gives, it is true, in his work entitled 'Origin and History of Playing-cards,' London, 1848, p. 88, facsimiles of playing-cards preserved in the British Museum, which he believes to be of Venetian origin, from the circumstance that on the two of bells may be seen a lion, which he takes for the lion of Saint Mark; but it should be observed that the lion is not winged, which it would have been were it the heraldic lion. We may remark, at the same time, that these cards, engraved on wood (as is evident from the breaks observed in them), are copies of playing-cards some of the original series of which are preserved in the library at Berlin, as before stated. The latter cards are much better drawn and engraved than are the cards in London, and if it be maintained that the latter are really of Venetian manufacture (which we cannot allow), they offer us but a sorry specimen of Venetian art at that period." (Bibl. 7, vol. i. p. 130.)

We agree with Passavant as to the character of the lion on the two of bells, but believe, on the other hand, with Chatto, that the present cardspieces were worked from stencils, and not from wood blocks. Of what process the Berlin examples are the result we cannot say, as we have not seen them.

Mr. Taylor (Bibl. 9, p. 115) observes, in reference to the date of production: "It is, after all, very possible that the estimated antiquity of these cards may be erroneous; for we have before us examples of a pack answering in every respect the description given, and corresponding exactly with the plates, save that the card-makers' arms on the deuces is wanting, and on the nine of hearts the date 1546 is legibly impressed in Arabic numerals, and, in addition to the colours before mentioned, yellow is employed for the bells and the kings' crowns."

It is true that these remarks were more immediately applied by Mr. Taylor to the German pack described by Mr. Gough in the eighth volume of the " Archæologia," and generally known as the " Stukely cards " (vol. i. pp. 27, 193, 194) ; but since he considered the present set to resemble the " Gough cards " in essential particulars, his observations as to the date of production of the former series are not inapplicable here :—

" This resemblance [between the ' Stukely cards ' and the stencilled cards of 1440 ?] is most strikingly seen in the king of bells, the design of which in both packs is nearly identical. The number of ' pips ' appears also to have been the same, with the same ' coat ' or court-cards, king, knight or superior officer, and a knave or inferior—or, as Mr. Chatto expresses it, king, Jack, and Jack's man."

In connection with what has been stated regarding the order of the Venetian Senate in respect to *figure stampide*, the author's " Introduction to the Study and Collection of Ancient Prints," 2nd edition, vol. i. pp. 43-48, may be consulted for further details.

PLATES XVIII. AND XIX.

HEREON are figured two sheets from the series of French numerals described at p. 110, vol. i. F. 42, and referred to in the table of noteworthy series (p. 341) as the "Chatto cards," or the cards from the binding of the "Sermones M. Vincenti."

On plate 18 is a facsimile, the actual size, of the sheet containing the valets of *trèfles* and *piques* repeated. The valet of *trèfles* is entitled "Lancelot," the valet of *piques*, "Hogier."

On plate 19 is represented the sheet of pip-numerals containing the four, five, eight, and ten of the suit *cœurs*.

It may not be out of place to recall here the statement of Mr. Chatto, that, "From the red rose which appears on the shield held by Valery,[1] an Englishman might be justified in supposing that these cards, if not of English manufacture, were more especially, if not exclusively, fabricated for the English market, at a period shortly after the accession of Henry VII., when the Red Rose of Lancaster had obtained the ascendency." It must be remembered, however, that at the period to which Mr. Chatto refers these cards the union of the Roses had been effected by the marriage of Henry VII. (red) with the Princess Elizabeth, daughter of Edward IV. (white), A.D. 1486. The badge of Henry VII. after this marriage was the Tudor rose—quarterly *gules* and *argent*.

In a note at p. 219 of his work, Mr. Chatto remarks: "M. Duchesne observes that of all the old cards preserved in the Bibliothèque du Roi only one displays a rose—namely, a king. There is an old coat-card, engraved on copper, in the print-room of the British Museum, which, like that alluded to by Mons. Duchesne, has a rose as the mark of the suit."

We cannot strictly identify the card here alluded to by Mr. Chatto, but under I. 142 (p. 92, vol. i.), and G. 143 (p. 207, vol. i.), suits of roses are described.

---

[1] See the sheet containing the two valets of *cœurs*, in F. 42 (vol. i. p. 110).

PLATE XX.

N this plate are represented facsimiles, the actual size, of eight pieces from the Hindustani series of circular cards described under O. H. 250, p. 331, vol. i.

"In the East," writes Boiteau d'Ambly" (*op. cit.* p. 86), "the circular form is loved, is worshipped; this form which is the symbol of Pantheism. In Europe we reject it; we prefer angles."

The examples selected are from each of the suits, red, green, and yellow, and from the series or ranks of orange-yellow, medium green, deep green, light red, deep red, and chocolate-red.

No. 1 is the three of geese of the series or rank orange-yellow.

No. 2 is the six of light-coloured birds with slate wings, of the light red rank.

No. 3 is the ten of geese of the orange-yellow rank.

No. 4 is the *schah*, or king, of the light green rank, having a red bird for its symbol.

No. 5 is the mounted (camel) *wusseer* of the medium green series or rank, which has the goose for its symbol.

No. 6 is the mounted (white horse) *wusseer* of the deep red rank, which has a black bird for its symbol.

No. 7 is the seated *schah*, or king, of the deep green rank, having the goose as its symbol.

No. 8 is the seated *schah*, or king, of the medium green series, which has the goose for its symbol.

For further details connected with the series from which these examples have been taken reference should be made to vol. i. pp. 331, 332, and in connection with the subject of Oriental cards generally, to p. 58 of the first volume.

PLATE XXI.

N this plate are represented twelve pieces, from six different sets or packs of Chinese playing-cards. Nos. 1 and 2, beginning at the left hand, are from the set O. C. 251, p. 333, vol. i. The examples given are a figure from the suit of arms or *bâtons*, and the seven of chains. Nos. 3 and 4 are from the set O. C. 255, p. 335, vol. i. The examples are taken from the suits of money and heads.

Nos. 5 and 6 are from the set O. C. p. 293 of the present volume. The examples given are from the suits of tables and heads.

Nos. 7 and 8 are from the set O. C. p. 294 of the present volume. They are from the suits of carriages and horses, which have the signs of ticks and fishes respectively in the middle of the cards.

Nos. 9 and 10 are from the suit O. C. p. 296 of the present volume. The examples given are from the suits of figures and from the "animated" suit.

Nos. 11 and 12 are from the set O. C. p. 295 of the present volume. The pieces selected are from the suit of black knights and the suit indicated by contracted characters not easily decipherable.

PLATE XXII.

 COPY of a miniature in a manuscript volume[1] preserved in the British Museum, and fully described at
p. 14, vol. i. (Singer, Bibl. 8, p. 68. " Art Journal "
for 1859, p. 87.)

---

[1] " Le Roman du Roi Meliadus de Leonnoys par Helie de Borron." Additional
MSS. vol. i. 1828-1841, No. 12,228.

PLATE XXIII.

N this plate are represented the actual and relative sizes of some of the largest and smallest playing-cards known.

No. 1. Actual size of old German figure-cards of the fifteenth century. Preserved in the Royal collection at Stuttgart. (Vol. i. p. 47. Merlin, Bibl. 6, plates 60 and 61.)

No. 2. Size of the *Carte di Baldini*, or the so-called "Tarocchi of Mantegna," of the version of 1470 in the British Museum. (Vol. i. p. 65. Bibl. 2, plates 21-70. Singer, Bibl. 8, p. 202.

No. 3. Size of the cards known as the "Gringonneur cards," or the " cards of Charles VI." Preserved in the Cabinet des Estampes de la Bibliothèque Royale de France. (Vol. i. pp. 13, 19, 24. Bibl. 2, plates 2-18. Chatto, Bibl. 4, p. 198.)

No. 4. Size of a Flemish tarot belonging to a pack in the British Museum. Fl. 103. (Vol. i. p. 179.)

No. 5. Actual size of a French numeral-card of the nineteenth century. From a pack in the British Museum. F. 63. (Vol. i. p. 122.)

No. 6. Size of a tarot-card for a *tarocchino* game from a sequence in the British Museum. I. 8. (Vol. i. p. 84.)

INDEX.

INDEX TO PROPER NAMES.

INDEX TO SUBJECTS.

CHISWICK PRESS:—C. WHITTINGHAM, TOOKS COURT, CHANCERY LANE.

LE·BATELEVR·

LA·PAPESSE·

LIMPERATRISE

LEMPEREVR·

PHOTOGRAVURE & IMP. GOUPIL & C.ᴵᴱ_ PARIS _LONDRES

PHOTOGRAVURE & IMP GOUPIL & C^{IE}_ PARIS_LONDRES

LA·ROVE·DE·FORTVNE.

⊠· LERMITE ·⊠⊠

·LE·PENDV·

·LA·FORCE·

PHOTOGRAVURE & IMP. GOUPIL & CIE_ PARIS_LONDRES

PHOTOGRAVURE & IMP GOUPIL & C^{IE}_ PARIS _LONDRES

PHOTOGRAVURE & IMP GOUPIL & Cᴵᴱ — PARIS — LONDRES

VI

MISERO

Vlll

MARTE XXXXV

PHOTOGRAVURE & IMP GOUPIL & Cᴵᴱ _ PARIS _ LONDRES

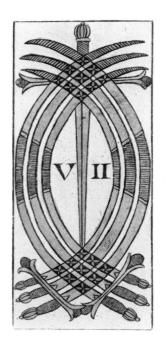

PHOTOGRAVURE & IMP GOUPIL & Cᴵᴱ _ PARIS _ LONDRES

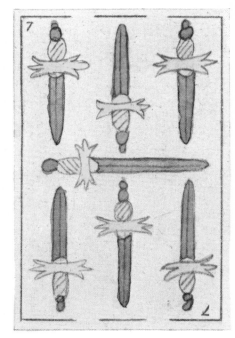
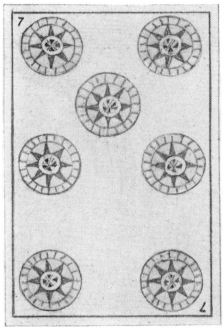
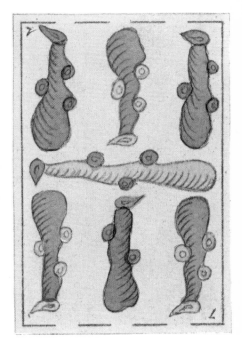

PHOTOGRAVURE &IMP GOUPIL & C^{IE}_PARIS_LONDRES

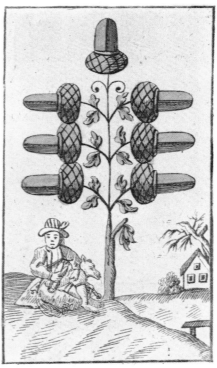

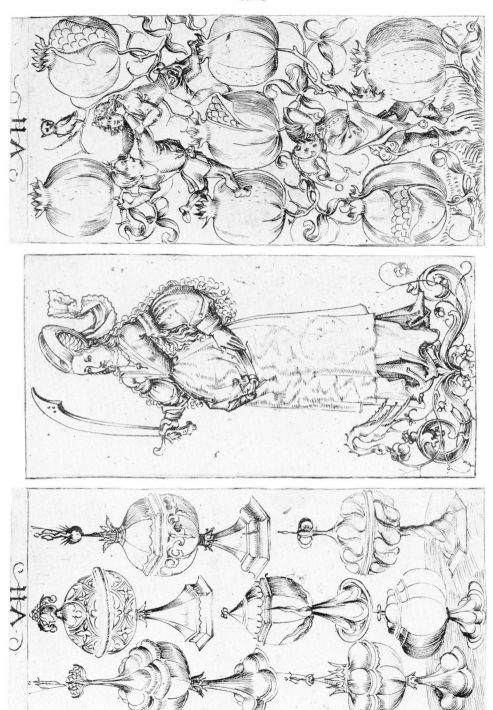

Dormit herus, potat coniunx, canis impiger escæ
Relliquias avido vendicat ore sibi:
Et miraris adhuc bona maxima dissipari
Interdum: ut Dominus, sic etiam famuli.

Weil Herr vnd Fraw sein voll vnd blind
Vom Wein: Schaw jr best Haußgesind
Der Hund/ so auch sein theil wil han/
Des braten Huns sich masset an.
Derwegen sich nur niemand wunder/
Daß groß Reichthumb offt gehet vnder:
Was jhm der Herr schetzt sein gerecht/
Dem will auch folgen nach der Knecht.   M ij

XVI

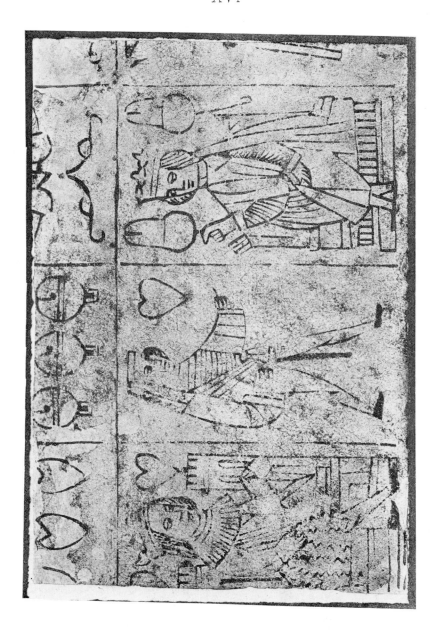

PHOTOGRAVURE & IMP GOUPIL & C.IE _ PARIS _ LONDRES

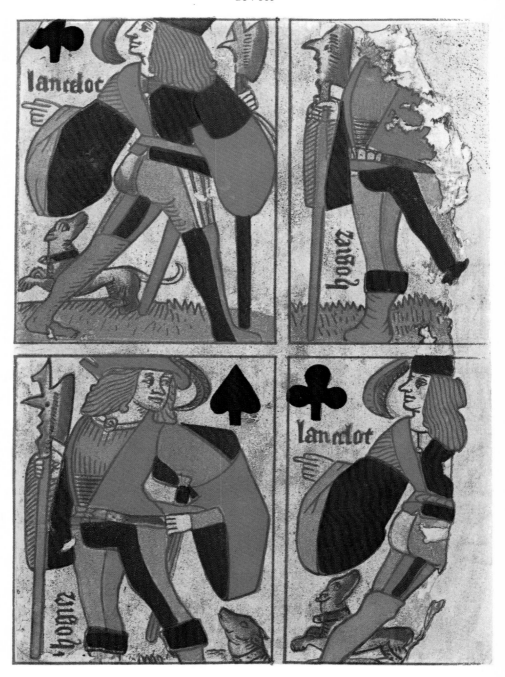

PHOTOGRAVURE &IMP COUPIL & CIE _ PARIS _ LONDRES

PHOTOGRAVURE & IMP GOUPIL & CIE _ PARIS _ LONDRES

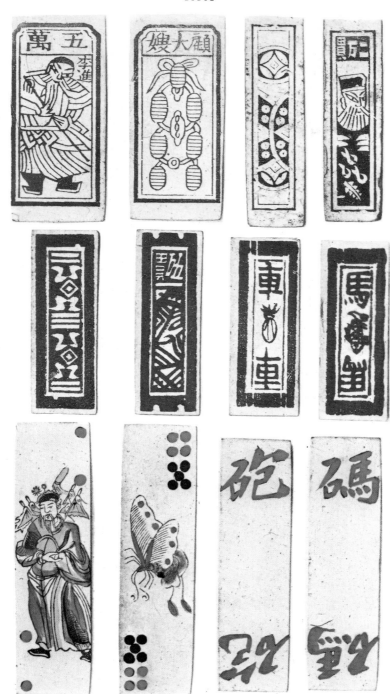

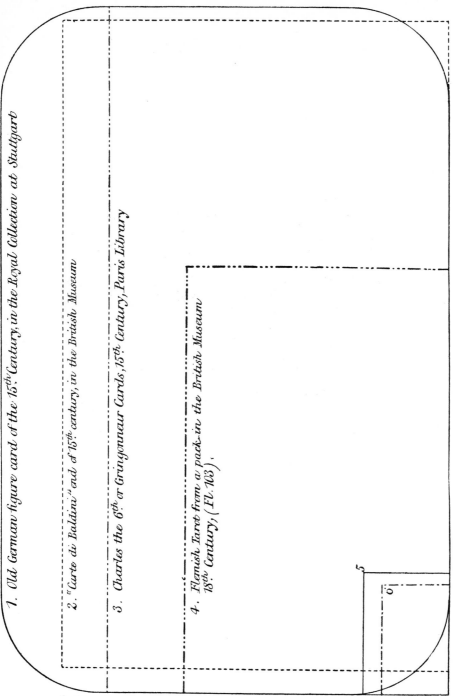

1. Old German figure card of the 15th. Century, in the Royal Collection at Stuttgart

2. "Carte di Baldini" and of 15th century, in the British Museum

3. Charles the 6th. or Gringonneur Cards, 15th. Century, Paris Library

4. Flemish Tarot from a pack in the British Museum 18th. Century, (Fl. 103).

5. French Numeral of 19th. Century, from a pack in the British Museum, (E.63.)

6. Tarocchino tarot of 17th. Century, from a series in the British Museum, (I.8.)